ILLUSTRATED INTRODUCTION TO
LATIN EPIGRAPHY

ILLUSTRATED INTRODUCTION TO

LATIN

EPIGRAPHY

ARTHUR E. GORDON

UNIVERSITY OF CALIFORNIA PRESS

BERKELEY · LOS ANGELES · LONDON

University of California Press
Berkeley and Los Angeles, California

University of California Press, Ltd.
London, England

© 1983 by
The Regents of the University of California

Printed in the United States of America

   2 3 4 5 6 7 8 9

Library of Congress Cataloging in Publication Data

Gordon, Arthur Ernest, 1902–
   Illustrated introduction to Latin epigraphy.

   Includes bibliographical references and index.
   1. Inscriptions, Latin.   I. Title.
CN510.G63   471'.7   79-63546
ISBN 0-520-05079-7   AACR2

The paper used in this publication meets the
minimum requirements of American National Standard for Information Sciences—Permanence of Paper
for Printed Library Materials, ANSI Z39.48–1984. ♾

To my wife Joyce S. Gordon

CONTENTS

List of Plates   *ix*

Preface   *xv*

Abbreviations   *xvii*

INTRODUCTION

Part One Latin Epigraphy Defined   3
    1. Latin inscriptions a meeting point   3
    2. Latin epigraphy distinguished from numismatics, etc.   3
    3. Related fields   3

Part Two The Provenience of Latin Inscriptions, Their Materials,
Numbers, Range in Time   4
    1. Provenience and present whereabouts   4
    2. Materials used   5
    3. Numbers   7
    4. Range in time   8

Part Three Sources and Collections   8
    1. The earliest extant collection   8
    2. The *Corpus Inscriptionum Latinarum (CIL)*   8
    3. Selections, yearly editions, translations   9
    4. Manuals, introductions, word indices   11

Part Four Technical Details   12
    1. The illusoriness of inscriptions in print   12
    2. The many abbreviations used   15
    3. The special interest of the earlier inscriptions 15
    4. Roman names   17
    5. Reproducing or copying inscriptions   30
    6. The work and problems of the Roman stonecutter   32

Part Five Subject Matter   33
    1. The myriad contents   33
    2. Most are probably epitaphs   34
    3. The *Laudatio Funebris*   34

Part Six Problems of Latin Inscriptions   34
    1. The main problems   34

2. Palaeography	38
3. Dating	40
Part Seven Contents of This Selection	42
1. The specially noteworthy inscriptions	42
2. Greek and Roman writers who appear here	43
Part Eight Miscellaneous Information	44
1. Roman numerals	44
2. Chronological list of Roman emperors (Augustus to Justinian)	49
3. Contents of the *CIL* volumes	50
4. Bibliography	54
5. Addenda to the Degrassi/Calabi Limentani bibliography	55

THE INSCRIPTIONS

List of Inscriptions	69
Preface to the Inscriptions	73
Inscriptions: Descriptions, Texts, and Translations	75

APPENDICES

I. Archaic and Unusual Forms of Words, with the Classical Latin Forms	189
II. Abbreviations Found in These Inscriptions	207
III. Roman Dating and the Roman Calendar	226
IV. Conventions in Printing Epigraphical Texts	234

CONCORDANCES

Concordance of Other Collections and This Volume	237
Concordance of the Other Inscriptions Cited	240

ADDENDA/CORRIGENDA — 243

SELECT INDEX

Subjects and Ancient Authors	245
Modern Authors	259

PLATES — following page 264

PLATES

Note: In presenting the photographs of the inscriptions, I have tried to have the inscriptions themselves as large as possible for legibility. This has necessitated cropping the edges of some of the stones, which is regrettable as it makes it more difficult to visualize the inscriptions *in situ*.

AEG

PLATE   INSCR. NO.

PLATE	INSCR. NO.	
1	1	Gold Fibula, formerly thought to be from Palestrina. Rome, Mus. Naz. Preistorico. Photo, Ministero della Pubbl. Istruz., Gabinetto Fotogr. Nazionale, Rome, E 35534, by courtesy of Fototeca Unione (1974) (See N.B. at end of discussion of this inscr.)
	2	Castor and Pollux Dedication, from near Pratica di Mare (or Lavinio— anc. Lavinium). Rome, Mus. Naz. Rom. Photo, Istituto di Topografia dell'Università di Roma, by courtesy of F. Castagnoli
2	3	Duenos Vase, from Rome. (West) Berlin, Staatliche Museen, Antikenab-teilung. Drawing, from CIL 1²: 2: 1, p. 371 (by permission); photos by courtesy of the Staatl. Mus., Antikenabt.
3	4	Forum-Romanum Cippus, Rome. *In situ.* Two views. Photos, Fototeca Unione, 14120 (a), 13300 (b)
4	5	Scipionic Sarcophagus with Epitaph, from the Tomb of the Scipios, Rome. Rome, Vatican. Photo, Fototeca Unione, 10560 (1963)
5	6	Dedication to Hercules by M. Minucius, from Rome. Rome, Palazzo dei Conservatori. Photo, S.P.Q.R., Mus. Capit., B 81
	7	Decree of L. Aemilius (Paulus), from Spain. Paris, the Louvre. Photo by courtesy of the Musée du Louvre
6	8	*Senatus Consultum de Bacchanalibus*, from southern Italy. Vienna, Kunsthistorisches Museum, Antikenabteilung. Photo, by courtesy of the museum
	9	Commemorative Tablet of L. Aemilius (Paulus), found at Delphi. Delphi, the museum. Photo by courtesy of the École Française d'Athènes
7	10	Honorary Inscription to M. Claudius Marcellus, from Luni, Liguria (anc. Luna, Etruria). Formerly in Florence, now at Luni. Photo by courtesy of the Museo Archeologico, Florence
	11	Dedication to Hercules by Lucius Mummius, from Rome. Rome, Vat-ican. Photo, Archivio Fotograf. Gall. Mus. Vaticani, xxii-41-27
8	12	Milestone with Acephalous Elogium, from near Polla, Lucania. Polla, in public view. Photo, Joyce S. Gordon
	13	Bilingual Dedication to Hercules. Delos, *in situ*. Photo by courtesy of the École Française d'Athènes

PLATE   INSCR. NO.

9   14   Elegiac Epigram, found at Corinth. Corinth, the museum. Photo, American School of Classical Studies, Athens, by courtesy of C. K. Williams, II

         16   Slab from Statue Base of Sulla, from Rome. Naples, Museo Nazionale. Photo, Joyce S. Gordon

         17   Record of Theater Building. Pompeii, *in situ*. Photo, Laboratorio Fotografico della Soprintendenza alle Antichità delle Prov. di Napoli e Caserta, Naples, D 4391 (1972)

10   15   Two Decrees of Gn. Pompeius (Strabo), from Rome. Rome, Capitoline Museum. Photo, Johannes Felbermeyer (1956)

11   18   Main Inscription on the Fabricius Bridge. Rome, *in situ*. Photo, Fototeca Unione, 5650 (1959)

         19   Temple Regulations, from near the anc. Vestinian *vicus* of Furfo. L'Aquila, Museo Nazionale. Photo, Deutsches Archäologisches Institut, Rome, 61.35

12   20   Epitaph of a Grain Merchant, from Rome. Rome, Palazzo Senatorio (Capitoline Hill). Photo, Joyce S. Gordon

         21   Statue (?) Base Dedicated to Julius Caesar, from Otricoli (Umbria). Rome, Vatican. Photo, Joyce S. Gordon

13   22   Trilingual Dedication by Cornelius Gallus, from Philae, in the Nile. Cairo, Egyptian Museum. Photo by courtesy of the museum

14   23   Epitaph of Caecilia Metella. Just outside Rome, *in situ*. Two photos: (a) Alinari/Editorial Photocolor Archives, (b) Simonetta Calza-Bini (1949)

15   24   Epitaphs of Octavia and Her Son Marcellus, from the Mausoleum of Augustus, Rome. In 1973 still inside the mausoleum. Photo, Fototeca Unione, 4240 (1957)

         25   Part of the Record of the Secular Games of 17 B.C. From near S. Giovanni dei Fiorentini, Rome. Rome, Mus. Naz. Rom. Photo, Fototeca Unione, 992 (1953)

16   26   Epitaph on the Pyramid of Cestius, Rome. *In situ*. Photo, Foto Studio Daisy, Via Veneto 183, Rome.

         27   Record of the Restoration of an Altar, from Rome. Rome, Palazzo dei Conservatori. Photo, S.P.Q.R., Mus. Capit., B 80

17   28   Two Fragments of the "Laudatio Turiae," one found near Rome, the other recognized in the Mus. Naz. Rom., Rome, where both were seen together in 1973. Photo, Joyce S. Gordon (1949)

18   29   Record of Repairs of Three Aqueducts in Rome. Still *in situ* on either side of the arch of the Porta Tiburtina. Photo (of the inner face) Ministero per i Beni Cult. e Amb., Ist. Centrale per il Catalogo e la Documentazione, E 26600

         30   Senatorial Inscription in Honor of Lucius Caesar. From the Forum Romanum, Rome, where it still was in 1973, in public view. Photo, Fototeca Unione, 1315 (1953)

19   31   Record of Posthumous Honors for Gaius Caesar, from Pisa. Pisa, Camposanto. Photo by courtesy of Emilio Gabba

20   32   Epitaph of Potitus Valerius Messalla. Found in Rome, probably near the original family-tomb. Rome, Mus. Naz. Rom. Photo, Joyce S. Gordon

PLATE   INSCR. NO.

33   Epitaph of Gaius Caesar (son of Germanicus), from near the Mausoleum of Augustus, Rome. Rome, Vatican. Photo, Joyce S. Gordon

35   Duplex Dedication on an Obelisk, Rome, from Egypt. Rome, Piazza S. Pietro. Two photos: (a) this inscription, Fototeca Unione, 14128 (1972), (b) superimposed on this, an earlier inscription, also duplex, naming Cornelius Gallus, *praef(ectus) fabr(um)* of Octavian, as builder of a Forum Iulium (at Alexandria?), which had been deleted and replaced by the later text but was discovered and reconstructed by Filippo Magi; photo, Stato della Città del Vaticano, Governatorato, Direzione degli Studi e Ricerche Archeologiche, neg. VT-1-5 (the duplex inscr. VT-2-4), by courtesy of F. Magi

21   36   The *Tabula Hebana*, from Magliano (near the site of anc. Heba, in Etruria). Florence, Museo Archeologico. Photo, the museum, by courtesy of Guglielmo Maetzke

22,23   34   The *Monumentum Ancyranum*, Ankara, Turkey. *In situ*. Four photos: (a) and (b) by courtesy of Prentiss S. de Jesus, (c) and (d), Deutsches Archäologisches Institut, Rome, nos. 62941 and 56169

24   37   Epitaphs of a Charioteer and His Wife, from Rome. Rome, Vatican. Photo, Archivio Fotograf. Gall. Mus. Vaticani, xxviii-21-101

38   Dedication (?) of a *Tiberieum* by Pontius Pilate, from Caesarea, Israel. Jerusalem, Israel Museum. Photo by courtesy of the Israel Department of Antiquities and Museums, neg. 3866

25   39   Epitaph of Agrippina the Elder, undoubtedly from the Mausoleum of Augustus, Rome. Rome, Palazzo dei Conservatori. Photo, S.P.Q.R., Mus. Capit., D 65

40   Dedication to the Emperor Claudius, from near the Roman theater, Verona. Verona, Museo Maffeiano. Photo, Joyce S. Gordon

26   42   Part of a Speech of the Emperor Claudius, from near Lyon. Lyon, Musée de la Civilisation Gallo-Romaine. Photo by courtesy of the museum

27   41   Ex-voto Dedication to the Emperor Claudius and His Family, from (apparently) the Forum of Augustus, Rome. Rome, Palazzo dei Conservatori. Photo, Joyce S. Gordon

43   Pomerium Boundary-Stone, found in Rome *in situ*. Rome, Mus. Naz. Rom. Photo, probably Ernest Nash (1973)

28   44   The Porta Maggiore Aqueducts, Rome. Two views (inner and outer faces). Photos, Ministero per i Beni Cult. e Amb., Ist. Centrale per il Catalogo e la Documentazione, Rome, E 26598 (exterior), 26599 (interior)

45   Epitaph of Q. Veranius and His Child, from Pratolungo, near Rome. Rome, Mus. Naz. Rom. Photo, Joyce S. Gordon

29   46   Fragment of the "Lex de Imperio Vespasiani," first reported in St. John Lateran, Rome. Rome, Capitoline Mus. Photo, Joyce S. Gordon

30   47   Dedication of a Shrine to *Fons*, from Rome. Rome, Mus. Naz. Rom. Photo, Vasari, Rome, neg. no. 14525 (by courtesy of Ernest Nash)

48   Elogium of Gaius Duilius, from the Forum Romanum, Rome. Palazzo dei Conservatori. Photo, Ernest Nash

31   49   Epitaph of a Soldier/Public Official. It stands in front of the Tomb of the Plautii near Ponte Lucano on the road from Rome to Tivoli. Photo, Ernest Nash

PLATE   INSCR. NO.

32   50   Dedication of Arch to the Deified Titus. Rome, *in situ* in the Forum Romanum. Photo (of the east face), Fototeca Unione, 7275 (1961)

51   A Military Diploma, from Egypt. Rome, Vatican Library. Photo, Alinari/Editorial Photocolor Archives

33   52   Latin Epitaph, with Greek Verses, of a Young Poet, from under the Porta Salaria, Rome. Rome, Palazzo dei Conservatori. Photo, Fototeca Unione, 3237 (1957)

34   53   *Tabula Alimentaria*, from Macchia (anc. Samnium). Rome, Mus. Naz. Rom. Photo, Archivio Fotograf. Gall. Mus. Vaticani, xxv-5-25.

35   54   Record of a Town's Request for Patronage, from Rome. Florence, Mus. Archeologico. Photo by courtesy of the museum

36   55   Commemoration of a Local Dignitary. At Ferentino (anc. Ferentinum, a town of the Hernici), cut in the living rock. Photo, Alinari/Editorial Photocolor Archives

37   56   Statue-Base Inscription in Honor of Hadrian. Athens, *in situ* in the Theater of Dionysus. Photo by courtesy of Ronald S. Stroud

57   Column-of-Trajan Inscription. Rome, *in situ*. Photo, Fototeca Unione, 10727 (1963)

38   58   Record of Building the Original Pantheon. Rome, *in situ*. Photo, Fototeca Unione, 931 (1953)

60   Verse Epitaph of a Young Boy, from a vineyard outside Rome. Rome, Vatican. Photo, Joyce S. Gordon

39   59   Commemoration of a Roman Public Official, from Aquileia. Aquileia, Mus. Archeologico Nazionale. Photo, Ministero per i Beni Cult. e Amb., Ist. Centrale per il Catalogo e la Documentazione, Rome, E 7728

40   61   Epitaph of a Freedman of Trajan's, first reported in Rome. Rome, Vatican. Photo, Archivio Fotograf. Gall. Mus. Vaticani, xxviii-11-140

62   Funerary Monument with Instructions to Heirs, from a pagan cemetery under St. Peter's (in Vaticano), Rome; seen there, *in situ*, in 1973. Photo by courtesy of Ernest Nash (1956)

41   63   Veterans' Dedication of Altar to Silvanus, from Rome. Rome, Mus. Naz. Rom. Photo, Joyce S. Gordon

64   Funerary Monument of an Imperial Freedman, from near Rome. Rome, Vatican. Photo, Archivio Fotograf. Gall. Mus. Vaticani, xxviii-35-328

42   65   Verse Epitaph of Allia Potestas, from Rome. Rome, Mus. Naz. Rom. Photo, A. Vasari e Figlio, Laboratorio Fotografico, Rome, lastra no. 14507 (by courtesy of Ernest Nash)

43   66   *Lex Collegi Aesculapi et Hygiae*, first reported in the Barberini Palace, Rome. Rome, Vatican. Photo, Archivio Fotograf. Gall. Mus. Vaticani, xxviii-3-139

44   67   Dedication of Sculptured Column to Antoninus Pius, from the Campus Martius, Rome. Rome, Vatican. Photo, Fototeca Unione, 10561 (1963)

68   Commemoration of a Local Dignitary at Ostia, where it was first reported. Rome, Vatican. Photo, Archivio Fotograf. Gall. Mus. Vaticani, xxviii-3-262

PLATE   INSCR. NO.

45   69   Three Letters (with summary) from Imperial Accountants, from Rome. Rome, Vatican. Photos, Archivio Fotograf. Gall. Mus. Vaticani, xxx-55-34/35

46   70   Pagan Epitaph from the Vatican Excavations, Rome. Still under the Vatican. Photo, Fotografia Artistica Salvatore Sansaini, Laboratorio Musei Vaticani, by courtesy of Filippo Magi

      71   Dedication to Caracalla by the *Paedagogi Puerorum a Capite Africae*, from Rome. Rome, Capitoline Mus. Photo, Oscar Savio, Rome, by courtesy of Ernest Nash

47   72   Dedication to the Imperial Family (and Others) by Members of a Cohort of Vigiles, from Rome. Rome, Capitoline Mus. Photo, Johannes Felbermeyer (1956)

48   73   Dedication of Arch to Septimius Severus and His Sons; Forum Romanum, Rome. *In situ* there. Photo, Fototeca Unione, 737 (1953)

      74   Epitaph of the Father of Elagabalus, from Velletri. Rome, Vatican. Photo Alinari/Editorial Photocolor Archives

49   75   The Arval Hymn (*Carmen Arvale*) from Rome. Rome, Vatican. Photo, Archivio Fotograf. Gall. Mus. Vaticani, xix-16-5

50   76   Request for Permission to Build a Tomb, probably from the Via Ostiensis near Rome. Rome, Mus. Naz. Rom. Photo, Joyce S. Gordon

      77   Dedication to Decius, *Nobilissimus Caesar*, from Rome. Rome, Vatican. Photo, Archivio Fotograf. Gall. Mus. Vaticani, xxviii-13-236

51   78   Record of a Meeting at Sentinum of a *Collegium Fabrum*, no doubt from Sentinum. Rome, Capitoline Mus. Photo, Johannes Felbermeyer (1956)

52   79   Epitaph of a Christian Woman, from outside Rome. Rome, Palazzo dei Conservatori. Photo, Oscar Savio, Rome, by courtesy of Ernest Nash

      80   Ex-voto Dedication to Cybele and Attis, from just outside Rome. Rome, Capitoline Mus. Photo, Joyce S. Gordon

53,54 81   Preamble to Diocletian's Edict on Prices, two fragments, one from Plataea (a), the other from Egypt (b). (a) is now in Athens in the Epigraphical Museum, (b) in Aix-en-Provence in the Musée Granet. Photos, (a) Ministry of Culture and Science, Epigraphical Collection, Athens; (b) Photos Henry Ely, Aix

      85   Epitaph of a Christian *Lector*, from outside Rome. Rome, Vatican. Photo, Joyce S. Gordon (while it was still in the Lateran in the Mus. epigr. cristiano)

55   82   Dedication of Triumphal Arch to Constantine, Rome. *In situ* there. Photo, Alinari/Editorial Photocolor Archives (view of the north side)

      83   Record of Restoration of Public Baths, Rome. Rome, Vatican. Photo, Fototeca Unione, no. 9071 (1962)

56   84   Commemoration of G. Caelius Saturninus, from Rome. Rome, Vatican (formerly in the Lateran). Photo, Alinari/Editorial Photocolor Archives

57   86   Dedication to Constantius II, from Rome. Forum Romanum, Rome. Photo, Fototeca Unione, no. 27 (1953)

      88   Dedication to Co-Emperor Valens, from Rome. Rome, Mus. Naz. Rom. Photo, Joyce S. Gordon

PLATE   INSCR. NO.

58   87   Epitaph of Iunius Bassus, from Rome. Rome, under St. Peter's. Photo, Alinari/Editorial Photocolor Archives

59   89   Commemoration of Symmachus, the Orator's Father, from Rome. Rome, Vatican. Photo, Joyce S. Gordon

        90   Dedication in Honor of Petronius Probus, from Rome. Rome, Capitoline Mus. Photos (of front and side), Joyce S. Gordon

60   91   Elogium in Verse Composed by Pope Damasus, from outside Rome. Rome, the Vatican (formerly in the Lateran). Photo (taken in the Lateran), Joyce S. Gordon

        92   Dedication of (Statue) Base to a Distinguished Pagan, from Rome. Rome, Mus. Naz. Rom. Photo, Joyce S. Gordon

        93   Dedication of (Statue) Base to Stilicho, Roman General, from Rome. Rome, Palazzo dei Conservatori. Photo, S.P.Q.R., Mus. Capit., B 99

61   94   Commemoration of Three Emperors, from Forum Romanum, Rome. Still there in 1973. Photo, Fototeca Unione, no. 46 (1953)

        95   Epitaph of a Christian Child, from outside Rome. Rome, Vatican (formerly in the Lateran, where this photo was taken). Photo, Joyce S. Gordon

62   96   Dedication of a Statue Base to a High Official, from Rome. Rome, Palazzo dei Conservatori. Photo, S.P.Q.R., Mus. Capit., C 92

63   97   Record of Erection of a Statue of a Distinguished Administrator, from Rome. Rome, Vatican (formerly in the Lateran, where this photo was taken). Photo, Joyce S. Gordon

64   98   Epitaph of Three Christians, from Rome. Rome, Mus. Naz. Rom. Photo, Joyce S. Gordon

        99   Epitaph of a Christian Boy, probably from outside Rome. Rome, Vatican (formerly in the Lateran, where this photo was taken). Photo, Joyce S. Gordon

        100   Epitaph of Maxima, "Handmaid of Christ"; from Rome, outside Porta Maggiore. Rome, Mus. Naz. Rom. Photo, Joyce S. Gordon

PREFACE

This book has a long history. It began in Ohio in 1970 (after my retirement at Berkeley) with a remark from a former student, Professor Charles L. Babcock (Ohio State University), suggesting that I should write a new introduction to Latin epigraphy, which (he assured me) I could do "off the top of my head." The remark proved insidious. Many years before, I had asked the Cambridge University Press whether they were interested in a new revision of Sir John Edwin Sandys's *Latin Epigraphy, An Introduction to the Study of Latin Inscriptions*, 2nd ed., revised by S. G. Campbell (1927); their reply, after long deliberation, was "No," but that they would consider a wholly new book. By the time I received this reply, I had cold feet, believing that after all I was not competent to do even a revision, much less a completely new book. But in 1970 I began thinking about it, making a few notes, while I was visiting professor at Ashland College (Ashland, Ohio), and I continued while in a similar position the next year at Ohio State University, to which I had been invited by Professor Mark P. O. Morford (then chairman of Classics) in order to facilitate my library research while teaching a course in Greek. While I was there, I was granted a senior fellowship by the National Endowment for the Humanities (NEH) for 1972–73, for which my sponsors were Professors Ernst Badian, Sterling Dow, and of course Charles Babcock.

While I was at Ohio State, the publication of Professor E. G. Turner's *Greek Manuscripts of the Ancient World* (Oxford University Press and Princeton University Press, jointly, 1971) gave me a model of the sort of epigraphical volume that appealed to me and that I thought I could do. Turner's book consists of a preface and introduction of twenty-seven pages, followed by forty-six plates (four of them double) on the right with facing annotation on the left, illustrating seventy-three Greek papyrus manuscripts, in all pp. v-xiv, 132 (price, only £5 or $12.50!). The feature of the book is the illustrations.

My book includes 100 Latin inscriptions dating from perhaps the sixth century B.C. (I exclude the Fibula Praenestina [below, no. **1**, *q.v.*], which once was thought to be of the seventh century) to A.D. 525, illustrated in such a way as to make them legible (with, in a few cases, the aid of a magnifying glass). In all references to the inscriptions in this book, the number will be in boldface type. So far as I am aware, this is a new feature in introductions to Latin (or Greek) epigraphy. (Diehl's *Inscriptiones Latinae*, Bonn 1912, lacks introduction and all but the barest annotation, and goes down to A.D. 1455.) My work presented difficulties that Turner had been able to avoid; his papyri had little bibliography, he usually transcribes only a part—sometimes only a few lines —of the texts, and he offers no translations; as a result, he can usually accommodate annotations at the left to the photos opposite, with sometimes room to spare. In my book, on the other hand, the bibliographies and the annotations are often extensive; this has resulted in a work of somewhat different design, with the plates put after the annotations.

In compensation for the extra labor involved for the writer, financial grants have allowed him and his wife to travel abroad —to Rome for a month in 1973, a week in 1974, to Geneva/Vandoeuvres for all of May 1975—and to visit other distant places, often to see and examine single inscriptions: Aix-en-Provence (the Preamble to Diocletian's *Edict on Prices*), Ankara (the *Res Gestae* of Augustus), Aquileia, Athens (another fragment of the Preamble), West Berlin (the Duenos Vase), East Berlin (headquarters of the *CIL*), Cairo (Cornelius Gallus's trilingual dedication), Corinth (an elegiac epigram), Florence (the Tabula Hebana), Jerusalem (the only contemporary reference to Pontius Pilate, by himself), Lyon (part of a speech of the emperor Claudius), Paris (a Roman decree from Spain), Verona (a dedication to Claudius), Vienna (twice— the *Senatus Consultum de Bacchanalibus*), and under the Vatican (twice).

Thanks are due on behalf of my wife and myself, first, to my NEH sponsors (Babcock, Badian, Dow), then to the NEH itself (not only for the 1972–73 fellowship, but also for a 1978 summer fellowship for library research in Berkeley), to the American Council of Learned Societies, the American Philosophical Society, and the California Classical Association (Northern Section) for grants for research travel in 1974, and to the Fondation Hardt for a month's residence for study in Geneva/ Vandoeuvres in 1975; to the museums that house most of these inscriptions; to the libraries of the American Academy in Rome, the American School of Classical Studies in Athens, the Fondation Hardt, the San Francisco Theological Seminary in San Anselmo, and the University of California, Berkeley; to the Academic Senate Committee on Research, Berkeley, for generous yearly grants for many years; and to the many friends and colleagues who facilitated our work: Pierre Amandry, D. A. Amyx, Amable Audin, Artur Betz, Vittorio Bracco, T. R. S. Broughton, David Brown, Frank E. Brown, Kevin Carroll, André Chastagnol, Miriam Collins, Giorgio Cracco and Lellia Cracco Ruggini, P. T. Craddock, Georg Daltrop, Georges Daux, Lawrence E. Dawson, G. De Angelis d'Ossat, Prentiss S. de Jesus, Dima Delmousou, Ivan Di Stefano Manzella, John Dorman, Werner Eck, Pierre Flobert, Emilio Gabba, Crawford H. Greenewalt, Jr., Jonas Greenfield, Pierre Grimal, Erich Gruen, Eric Hamp, H. Herzig, Mrs. Yael Israeli, Chara Karapa, Hans Krummrey, E. Larocca, Ida Calabi Limentani, Paola Lopresto, Guglielmo Maetzke, Filippo Magi, Louis Malbos, Paul G. Manolis, Lucilla Marino, Agnes Kirsopp Michels, Mark P. O. Morford, the late Ernest Nash and the Fototeca Unione in Rome, the late James H. Oliver and the two other (anonymous) Readers, Klaus Otterburig, Silvio Panciera, James W. Poultney, W. K. Pritchett, Ernst Pulgram, Joyce M. Reynolds, Robert H. Rodgers, Franco Sartori and his two associates, Albert P. Steiner, Jr., Ronald S. Stroud, Giancarlo Susini, E. G. Turner, Eugene Vanderpool, Ekkehard Weber, Michael Wigodsky, C. K. Williams, II, Fausto Zevi; to several research assistants, especially Bennett Price and Randall Colaizzi; to several typists, including Okanta Leonard and especially Patricia A. Felch (who typed the entire final copy); and especially to August Frugé for constant encouragement; and most of all, as usual, to my wife for assistance throughout the long effort of making this book.

Inverness, California   A. E. G.
May 1981

ABBREVIATIONS

ACR	*American Classical Review*
AE	*L'Année Épigraphique* (cited by year and no. of inscr.)
AJA	*American Journal of Archaeology*
AJAH	*American Journal of Ancient History*
AJP	*American Journal of Philology*
Album	*Album of Dated Latin Inscriptions, Rome and the Neighborhood*, by Arthur E. Gordon in collaboration with Joyce S. Gordon, 4 parts in 7 vols. (Berkeley/Los Angeles 1958–1965)
Ann. Inst.	*Annali dell'Instituto di Corrispondenza Archeologica*
ANRW	*Aufstieg und Niedergang der römischen Welt . . .* , ed. H. Temporini (Berlin/New York)
Ant. Class.	*L'Antiquité Classique*
APA	American Philological Association
Arch. Anz.	*Archäologischer Anzeiger*
ARS	*Ancient Roman Statutes, A Translation with Introduction, Commentary, Glossary, and Index*, by A. C. Johnson, P. R. Coleman-Norton, F. C. Bourne, Gen. Ed. Clyde Pharr (Austin, Texas, 1961) (cited by no. of text)
Athen. Mitt.	*Mitteilungen des Deutschen Archäologischen Instituts, Athenische Abteilung*
BCH	École Française d'Athènes, *Bulletin de Correspondance Hellénique*
BiblEcFr	*Bibliothèque des Écoles Françaises d'Athènes et de Rome*
Bickerman	E. J. Bickerman, *Chronology of the Ancient World*[2] (London/Ithaca 1980)
Bonn. Jahrb.	*Bonner Jahrbücher*
Broughton	T. Robert S. Broughton, *The Magistrates of the Roman Republic*, with the collaboration of Marcia L. Patterson, 2 vols. (1951, 1952 Amer. Philol. Assn., *Philol. Monogr.* 15: 1–2), and *Supplement* (1960 Amer. Philol. Assn.)
Bruns	*Fontes iuris Romani antiqui* ed. C. G. Bruns . . . , ed. 7 by Otto Gradenwitz, 2 parts in one vol. (Tübingen 1909), and *Additamentum II, Simulacra* (1912). (All reff. are to Part 1, *Leges et Negotia*; cited by page and no.)
Bull. Com.	*Bullettino della Commissione Archeologica Comunale di Roma*
Bursian	*Jahresberichte über die Fortschritte der klass.* (or *class.*) *Altertumswissenschaft*, begr. v. K. Bursian
Cagnat	René Cagnat, *Cours d'épigraphie latine*[4] (Paris 1914, repr. 1964)
CAH	*The Cambridge Ancient History.* (Cited are vols. 8 [Cambridge 1930, repr. with corrections 1954], 9 [1932, repr. similarly 1951], 10 [1934, repr. similarly 1952], 11 [1936], 12 [1939].)

Cal. Lim.	Ida Calabi Limentani, *Epigrafia latina, con un'appendice bibliografica* di Attilio Degrassi, ed. 3 (Milan 1974)
Campania	see *Guida d'Italia*
Chase	George D. Chase, "The Origin of Roman Praenomina," *HSCP* 8 (1897) 103–184
CIL	*Corpus Inscriptionum Latinarum* (unless otherwise indicated, *CIL* 1² refers to Part 2, 1918–)
CJ	*The Classical Journal*
CLE	*Carmina Latina epigraphica*, ed. by Fr. Buecheler (vols. 1–2, Leipzig 1895–1897) and E. Lommatzsch (vol. 3, 1926), the whole repr. Amsterdam 1972
Coarelli	Filippo Coarelli, con la collaborazione di Luisanna Usai per la parte cristiana, *Guida Archeologica di Roma* (Arnoldo Mondadori Editore, 1974)
Combès	Robert Combès, *Imperator . . .* (Paris 1966)
Contrib.	Joyce S. and Arthur E. Gordon, *Contributions to the Palaeography of Latin Inscriptions* (Berkeley/Los Angeles 1957 *Univ. Calif. Publ. Class. Arch.* 3: 3, repr. Milan 1977)
CP	*Classical Philology*
CQ	*The Classical Quarterly*
CR	*The Classical Review*
CRAI	*Comptes Rendus des Séances*, Académie des Inscriptions et Belles-Lettres, Paris
CSCA	*California Studies in Classical Antiquity*, University of California
CW	*The Classical World*, formerly *The Classical Weekly*
Degr. (or *ILLRP*)	Attilio Degrassi (ed.), *Inscriptiones Latinae liberae rei publicae*, 2 vols. (Florence, vol. 1 ed. 2 1965 repr. 1972, vol. 2 1963 repr. 1972) ("Add." refers to *Add. et Corr.*, vol. 1², pp. 313–334.) (Cited by no. of inscr.; vol. 2 is so indicated.)
Degrassi, *Elogia*	Idem (ed.), *Elogia* (Rome 1937 *Inscr. Ital.* 13: 3)
Degrassi, *FANI*	Idem (ed.), *Fasti anni Numani et Iuliani* (Rome 1963 same ser. 13: 2)
Degrassi, *FC*	Idem (ed.), *I fasti consolari dell'Impero Romano . . .* (Rome 1952)
Degrassi, *FCT*	Idem (ed.), *Fasti consulares et triumphales*, 2 vols. (Rome 1947 *Inscr. Ital.* 13: 1)
Degrassi, *Imag.*	Idem (ed.), *ILLRP, Imagines* (Berlin 1965 *CIL Auctarium*)
Degrassi, *Prolusione*	Idem, *L'epigrafia latina in Italia nell'ultimo ventennio . . . Prolusione al corso di epigr. lat. nell'Univ. di Roma . . .* (Padua 1957 *Scritti vari* 1.651–661)
Degrassi, *Scritti vari*	Idem, *Scritti vari di antichità*, 4 vols. (Rome, Venice/Trieste, Trieste 1962–1971)
Dennison	Walter Dennison, "Syllabification in Latin Inscriptions," *CP* 1 (1906) 47–68
De Ros.	Antonino De Rosalia (ed.), *Iscrizioni latine arcaiche* ([Palermo 1972]) (cited by no. of text)
De Rossi	G. B. De Rossi (ed.), *Inscriptiones Christianae urbis Romae sept. saec. antiquiores*, 1 (Rome 1857–1861)
De Rugg.	*Dizionario epigrafico di antichità romane*, fondato da Ettore De Ruggiero (1886–) (vols. 1–3 repr. 1961)
Dial. Arch.	*Dialoghi di Archeologia*

Diehl

Ernst Diehl (ed.), *Altlateinische Inschriften*[3] (Berlin 1930 *Kleine Texte für Vorles. u. Übungen* 38/40)

Diehl, *IL*

Idem (ed.), *Inscriptiones Latinae* (Bonn 1912 *Tabulae in usum scholarum*, 4) (15 + 50 photogr. plates of inscrs. from the Fibula Praenestina to A.D. 1455)

Diehl, *ILCV*

Idem (ed.), *Inscriptiones Latinae Christianae veteres*, 3 vols. (Berlin 1924–1931), ed. 2, 1961, by R. Grundel and J. Moreau (repr. Dublin/Zurich 1970) with vol. 4, *Supplementum* (ibid. 1967) ed. J. Moreau and H. I. Marrou

Doer

Bruno Doer, *Die römische Namengebung* . . . (Stuttgart 1937, repr. Hildesheim 1974)

Dow

Sterling Dow, *Conventions in Editing* (Duke Univ. 1969 *Greek, Roman, and Byzantine Scholarly Aids*, 2)

D/S

Ch. Daremberg and E. Saglio (eds.), *Dictionnaire des antiquités grecques et romaines*, 5 vols. in 10 parts (Paris 1877–1919)

EE

Ephemeris Epigraphica, Corporis Inscr. Latin. Supplementum, 9 vols. (Berlin 1872–1913)

E/J

V. Ehrenberg and A. H. M. Jones (eds.), *Documents Illustrating the Reigns of Augustus & Tiberius*[2] (Oxford 1955, repr. New York/London 1976 with 16 more items)

E/M

A. Ernout and A. Meillet. *Dictionnaire étymologique de la langue latine, Histoire des mots*[4], 3rd impr., with new additions and corrections by Jacques André (Paris 1979)

Ern.

Alfred Ernout (ed.), *Recueil de textes latins archaïques*, new ed., 4th impr. (Paris 1973) (cited by no. of text)

Esplor.

Esplorazioni sotto la Confessione di San Pietro in Vaticano eseguite negli anni 1940–1949, relazione a cura di B. M. Apollonj-Ghetti, A. Ferrua, E. Josi, E. Kirschbaum . . . , 2 vols., text and plates (Vatican City 1951)

FIRA

Fontes iuris Romani antejustiniani[2] (Florence). Cited are part 1, ed. S. Riccobono, 1941, and part 3, ed. V. Arangio-Ruiz, 1969. (Cited by page and no.)

Forcellini

Lexicon totius Latinitatis (ed.) Forcellini, Furlanetto, Corradini, and Perin, 4 vols., plus an *Onomasticon* in 2 vols. (Padua 1940, repr. Vatican City 1965) (ed. 5 of the *Totius latinitatis Lexicon* of Facciolati and Forcellini, 4 vols., Padua 1771)

Frank, *Econ. Survey*

Tenney Frank, *An Economic Survey of Ancient Rome* (Baltimore). Cited are vols. 1 (1933) and 5 (1940).

Frank, *RBR*

Idem, *Roman Buildings of the Republic. An Attempt to Date Them from Their Materials* (*PMAAR* 3, 1924)

G/L

B. L. Gildersleeve and Gonzalez Lodge, *Gildersleeve's Latin Grammar*[3] (Boston, etc. 1894)

Gordon, Arthur E.

see *Album* and *Contrib.*

   Epigr. I

Epigraphica, I. *On the First Appearance of the Cognomen in Latin Inscriptions of Freedmen, Univ. Calif. Publ. Class. Arch.* 1: 4 (1935)

   Epigr. II

Epigraphica, II. *On Marble as a Criterion For Dating Republican Latin Inscriptions*, same series 1: 5 (1936)

   Fib. Praen.

The Inscribed Fibula Praenestina, Problems of Authenticity, Univ. Calif. Publ., Class. Studies, 16 (1975)

   Further Remarks

"Further Remarks on the Inscribed Gold Fibula Praenestina," *Epigraphica* 40 (1978) 32–39

Letter Names	*The Letter Names of the Latin Alphabet, Univ. Calif. Publ., Class. Studies*, 9 (1973)
Notes	"Notes on the *Res Gestae* of Augustus," *CSCA* 1 (1968) 125–138
Notes/Duenos	"Notes on the Duenos-Vase Inscription in Berlin," *CSCA* 8 (1976) 53–72, plates 1–2
Origins	"On the Origins of the Latin Alphabet, Modern Views," *CSCA* 2 (1969) 157–170
Pot. Val. Mess.	*Potitus Valerius Messalla, Consul Suffect 29 B.C., Univ. Calif. Publ. Class. Arch.* 3: 2 (1954)
Rambles/More Rambles	"Rambles/More Rambles Among Latin Inscriptions," *CJ* 42 (1946–47) 151–155, 493–496
Seven Latin Inscrs.	"Seven Latin Inscriptions in Rome," *Greece & Rome* 20: 59 (1951) 75–92, pls. 105–108
Supralin. Abbrs.	*Supralineate Abbreviations in Latin Inscriptions, Univ. Calif. Publ. Class. Arch.* 2: 3 (1948, repr. Milan 1977)
Veranius	*Quintus Veranius, Consul A.D. 49* . . . , same series, 2: 5 (1952)
Grad.	Bruns, *Fontes* (see Bruns), *Additamentum: Indicem ad Fontium partem priorem* . . . , ed. O. Gradenwitz, II. *Simulacra* (Tübingen 1912) (cited by no. of document)
GRBS	*Greek, Roman, and Byzantine Studies*
Guarducci	Margherita Guarducci, *L'epigrafia greca*, 4 vols. (Rome 1967–1978)
Guida d'Italia	*Guida d'Italia del Touring Club Italiano* (Milan). Cited are *Campania*² (1940), *Lazio*³ (1964), *Roma e dintorni*⁶ (1962 and repr.), *Toscana*² (1935), and *Toscana*, 2⁴ (*Attrav. l'Italia*, 6) (1941)
Gymnas.	*Gymnasium* (Heidelberg)
Hofmann/Szantyr	J. B. Hofmann, *Lateinische Syntax und Stilistik*, rev. by Anton Szantyr (Munich 1965 *Handb. der Altertumsw.* 2: 2: 2)
H/S (or Helbig/Speier)	Deutsches Archäologisches Institut. Wolfgang Helbig, *Führer durch die öffentlichen Sammlungen klassischer Altertümer in Rom*, ed. 4 by Hermine Speier, 4 vols. (Tübingen 1963–1972) (cited usually by vol. no. and item no.)
HSCP	*Harvard Studies in Classical Philology*
Hübner	*Exempla scripturae epigraphicae Latinae a Caesaris dictatoris morte ad aetatem Iustiniani* . . . , ed. Aemilius Hübner (Berlin 1885 *CIL* Auctarium)
IG	*Inscriptiones Graecae*
IGRR	*Inscriptiones Graecae ad res Romanas pertinentes*, ed. R. Cagnat, J. Toutain, et al., vols. 1, 3, 4 (no more publ.) (Paris 1901–1927, repr. Rome 1964)
ILCV	see Diehl
ILLRP	see Degrassi
ILS	*Inscriptiones Latinae selectae*, ed. Hermannus Dessau, 3 vols. in 5 parts (Berlin 1892–1916, and repr.). Concordance with *CIL* (Berlin 1955), which had appeared also as a Fascicolo Speciale of De Rugg. (Rome 1950).
Inscr. Ital.	Unione Accademica Nazionale, *Inscriptiones Italiae* Academiae Italicae consociatae ediderunt (Rome)
Jeffery	L. H. Jeffery, *The Local Scripts of Archaic Greece* . . . (Oxford 1961, and repr.)

Jones   A. H. M. Jones, *The Later Roman Empire, 284–602 . . .* , 3 vols. (Oxford 1964)

JQR   *The Jewish Quarterly Review*

JRS   *The Journal of Roman Studies*

Kajanto   Iiro Kajanto, *The Latin Cognomina* (Helsinki/Helsingfors 1965 Soc. Scient. Fennica, *Comment. Human. Litt.*, 36: 2)

Keil   *Grammatici Latini*, edd. H. Keil et al., 7 vols. plus suppl. vol. (Leipzig 1855–1880, repr. Hildesheim 1961)

K/H   R. Kühner and Fr. Holzweissig, *Ausführliche Grammatik der lateinischen Sprache*, 1^2 (Hannover 1912, repr. 1966)

K/S   R. Kühner and C. Stegmann, op. cit. 2: $1-2^4$ (ibid. 1962, with corrections by A. Thierfelder, repr. 1966)

Larfeld   W. Larfeld, *Griechische Epigraphik*[3] (Munich 1914 *Handb. der klass. Altertumsw.* 1: 5)

Latte   K. Latte, *Römische Religionsgeschichte* (Munich 1960 *Handb. der Altertumsw.* 5: 4)

Lattimore   R. Lattimore, *Themes in Greek and Latin Epitaphs* (Urbana 1942 *Illinois Stud. in Lang. and Lit.* 28: 1–2, repr. Urbana 1962 paperback)

Laum   B. Laum, *Stiftungen in der griech. u. röm. Antike . . .* , 2 vols. (Leipzig/Berlin 1914)

Lazio   see *Guida d'Italia*

Leumann   Manu Leumann, *Lateinische Laut- und Formenlehre* (Munich 1926–1928, repr. 1963 [*Handb. der Altertumsw.* 2: 2: 1])

Lewis/Short   *Harpers' Latin Dictionary, A New Latin Dict. . . .* revised . . . by Charlton T. Lewis and Charles Short (New York, etc. 1879 and repr.; now publ. in England under the name of Lewis and Short)

Liddell/Scott[9]   *A Greek-English Lexicon*, comp. by H. G. Liddell, R. Scott, H. Stuart Jones (Oxford 1940 and repr.), plus *A Supplement*, ed. E. A. Barber (Oxford 1968) (for its origins cf. J. L. Facal, *CJ* 76: 4 [1981] 357–363)

L/R   N. Lewis and M. Reinhold, *Roman Civilization, Selected Readings*, ed. with an introduction and notes, 2 vols. (New York 1951–1955); also a later paperback ed.

Lugli   G. Lugli, *I monumenti antichi di Roma e Suburbio*, 3 vols., and *Supplemento* (Rome 1931–1940)

Lugli, *Roma ant.*   Idem, *Roma Antica, Il centro monumentale* (Rome 1946)

Lugli, *Fontes*   Idem (ed.), *Fontes ad topographiam veteris urbis Romae pertinentes*, 6 vols., incomplete (1–4, 6: 1, 8) (Rome 1952–1965)

Lugli, *Mon. Min.*   Idem, *Monumenti minori del Foro Romano* (Rome 1947)

MAAR   *Memoirs of the American Academy in Rome*

McCrum/Woodhead   M. McCrum and A. G. Woodhead (eds.), *Select Documents of the Principates of the Flavian Emperors . . . , A.D. 68–96* (Cambridge, 1961)

MélRome   École Française de Rome, *Mélanges d'archéologie et d'histoire*

MemLinc   *Atti della Accademia Nazionale dei Lincei, Memorie*, Cl. di Sc. mor., stor. e filol.

MemPontAcc   *Atti della Pontificia Accademia Romana di Archeologia, Memorie*

Meyer   Ernst Meyer, *Einführung in die lateinische Epigraphik* (Darmstadt 1973)

Momigliano — Arnaldo Momigliano, *Claudius the Emperor and His Achievement*, transl. W. D. Hogarth, with a new bibliog. (1942–1959) (Cambridge 1961)

Momigliano, *Quarto contrib.* — Idem, *Quarto contributo alla storia degli studi classici e del mondo antico* (Rome 1969)

Mon. Ant. — *Monumenti Antichi*, pubbl. per cura della (Reale) Accademia (Nazionale) dei Lincei

Mustilli — D. Mustilli, *Il Museo Mussolini* (Rome 1939)

Nash — Ernest Nash, *Pictorial Dictionary of Ancient Rome*, 2 vols., ed. 2, rev. (New York/Washington 1968)

Norden — Eduard Norden, *Aus altrömischen Priesterbüchern* (Lund/Leipzig 1939 *Skr. utg. av Kungl. Human. Vetenskaps i Lund, Acta Reg. Soc. Human. Litt. Lundensis*, 29)

NS — *Notizie degli scavi di antichità* (*Atti dell'Acc. dei Lincei*)

OCD — *The Oxford Classical Dictionary*², ed. N. G. L. Hammond and H. H. Scullard (Oxford 1970)

OGIS — *Orientis Graeci inscriptiones selectae . . .* , ed. W. Dittenberger, 2 vols. (Leipzig 1903–1905)

Olcott — George N. Olcott, *Thesaurus linguae Latinae epigraphicae: A Dictionary of the Latin Inscriptions*, vol. 1, fasc. 1–22 (Rome 1904–1912), continued by L. F. Smith, J. H. McLean, C. W. Keyes, vol. 2, fasc. 1–4 (New York 1935–1936), but only into the word "Avillinlanus (fundus)."

OLD — *Oxford Latin Dictionary*, ed. P. G. W. Glare (Oxford 1968–1982)

Oxf. Dict. Christ. Church — *The Oxford Dictionary of the Christian Church*², ed. F. L. Cross and E. A. Livingstone (London, etc. 1974)

P/A — S. B. Platner, *A Topographical Dictionary of Ancient Rome*, compl. and rev. by Thomas Ashby (London 1929, repr. Rome 1965)

Palm. — L. R. Palmer, *The Latin Language* (London 1954) ("no." refers to his Appendix of Archaic Latin Texts, A. Epigraphic, pp. 346–355)

Pape/Benseler — *W. Pape's Wörterbuch der griechischen Eigennamen,*³ by G. E. Benseler, 2 vols. (Braunschweig 1863–1870, repr. 1875, 1959)

PBSR — *Papers of the British School at Rome*

Pfister — F. Sommer, *Handbuch der lateinischen Laut- und Formenlehre . . .*⁴, Bd. I: *Einleitung u. Lautlehre*, by Raimund Pfister (Heidelberg 1977)

*PIR*¹ — *Prosopographia imperii Romani saec. I. II. III*, 3 vols., ed. E. Klebs, H. Dessau, P. von Rohden (Berlin 1897–1898)

*PIR*² — Same work, ed. 2, to date vols. 1–5: 1, ed. E. Groag, A. Stein, L. Petersen (Berlin/Leipzig vols. 1–3, Berlin vols. 4–5: 1, 1933–1970)

Pis. — Vittore Pisani (ed.), *Testi latini arcaici e volgari con commento glottologico*² (Turin 1960) (cited by no. of text)

PLRE — *The Prosopography of the Later Roman Empire*, by A. H. M. Jones, J. R. Martindale, J. Morris, vol. 1, A.D. 260–395 (Cambridge 1971), vol. 2, A.D. 395–527, by J. R. Martindale (ibid. 1980)

PMAAR — *Papers and Monographs of the American Academy in Rome*

RE — *Paulys Realencyclopädie der classischen Altertumswissenschaft*², ed. G. Wissowa et al. (Stuttgart, currently Munich, 1894–)

REA — *Revue des Études Anciennes*

REG	*Revue des Études Grecques*
REL	*Revue des Études Latines*
RendIstLomb	Istituto Lombardo, Accademia di Scienze e Lettere (Milan), *Rendiconti*, cl. di lett.
RendLinc	*Atti dell'Accademia Nazionale dei Lincei* (Rome), *Rendiconti*, cl. di sc. mor., stor. e filol.
RendPontAcc	*Atti della Pontificia Accademia Romana di Archeologia* (Rome), *Rendiconti*
RPh	*Revue de Philologie, de Littérature et d'Histoire Anciennes*
Rhein. Mus.	*Rheinisches Museum für Philologie*
Ritschl	Fr. Ritschl, *Priscae Latinitatis monumenta epigraphica ad archetyporum fidem exemplis lithographis repraesentata* (Berlin 1862, repr. 1961, 1968, with 5 supplements [1862–1864] repr. 1970 [*CIL Auctarium*])
Riv. di fil.	*Rivista di Filologia e d'Istruzione Classica*
Riv. St. Class.	*Rivista di Studi Classici*
Röm. Mitt.	*Mitteilungen des Deutschen Archäologischen Instituts, Römische Abteilung*
Roma e dintorni	see *Guida d'Italia*
Roscher	W. H. Roscher (ed.), *Ausführliches Lexikon der griechischen und römischen Mythologie*, 6 vols. in 9 parts (from vol. 5 last fasc., 1924, ed. K. Ziegler) plus 4 supplements (Leipzig 1884–1937, repr. Hildesheim 1965, 1977)
Roullet	Anne Roullet, *The Egyptian and Egyptionizing Monuments of Imperial Rome* (Leiden 1972)
Rushforth	G. McN. Rushforth (ed.), *Latin Historical Inscriptions Illustrating the History of the Early Empire*[2] (London 1930)
S/C or Sandys/Campbell	Sir John Edwin Sandys, *Latin Epigraphy . . .* , ed. 2 by S. G. Campbell (Cambridge 1927, repr. Groningen 1969)
Schanz/Hosius	Martin Schanz, *Geschichte der römischen Literatur . . .* , vol. 2, ed. 4 by Carl Hosius (Munich 1935, repr. 1967 *Handb. der Altertumsw.* 8: 2)
Schanz/Hosius/Krüger	Same work, vol. 3, ed. 3 by Hosius and G. Krüger (1922, repr. 1959, op. cit. 8: 3)
Scherer	Margaret R. Scherer, *Marvels of Ancient Rome* (New York/London 1955)
Schmalz/Hofmann	Stolz/Schmalz, *Lateinische Grammatik*, ed. 5, 2nd Lief., by J. H. Schmalz and J. B. Hofmann (Munich 1928 *Handb. der Altertumsw.* 2: 2: 2)
Schulze	Wilhelm Schulze, "Zur Geschichte lateinischer Eigennamen," *Abh. der k. Gesellschaft der Wiss. zu Göttingen*, philol.-hist. Klasse, N.F. 5: 5 (Berlin 1904)
Sherk	Robert K. Sherk (ed.), *The Municipal Decrees of the Roman West* (Buffalo 1970)
Silvagni	Angelo Silvagni (ed.), *Inscriptiones Christianae urbis Romae septimo saeculo antiquiores*, colligere coepit I. B. De Rossi, complevit ediditque Angelus Silvagni. Nova ser., vols. 1–4 (vol. 3 ed. Silvagni and A. Ferrua, vol. 4 ed. Ferrua) (Vatican City 1922–1964)
Silvagni, *Mon.*	Idem, *Monumenta epigraphica Christiana*, vol. 1 (Vatican City 1943)

Smallwood, *Gaius/Nero* — E. Mary Smallwood (ed.), *Documents Illustrating the Principates of Gaius, Claudius and Nero* (Cambridge 1967)

Smallwood, *Nerva/Hadrian* — Eadem (ed.), *Documents Illustrating the Principates of Nerva, Trajan and Hadrian* (ibid. 1966)

Sommer — Ferdinand Sommer, *Handbuch der lateinischen Laut- und Formenlehre . . .*[2-3] (Heidelberg 1914) (see also Pfister)

Stein — Arthur Stein, *Die Präfekten von Ägypten in der römischen Kaiserzeit* (Bern 1950 Diss. Bern. 1: 1)

St. Etr. — *Studi Etruschi*

St. Misc. — *Studi Miscellanei* (Rome, Seminario di Archeologia e Storia dell'Arte greca e romana dell'Univ. di Roma)

St. Rom. — *Studi Romani* (Rome, Istituto di Studi Romani, 1953–)

Strong — Eugénie Strong, *Art in Ancient Rome*, 2 vols. (London 1929)

Sturtevant — Edgar H. Sturtevant, *The Pronunciation of Greek and Latin*[2] (Philadelphia 1940, repr. Groningen 1968)

Syme, *Rom. Pap.* — (Sir) Ronald Syme, *Roman Papers*, 2 vols., ed. E. Badian (Oxford 1979)

Syme, *Rom. Rev.* — Idem, *The Roman Revolution* (Oxford 1939 and repr., paperback 1960)

Syme, *Tac.* — Idem, *Tacitus*, 2 vols. (Oxford 1958)

TAPA — *Transactions and Proceedings of the American Philological Association*

Taylor — Lily Ross Taylor, *The Voting Districts of the Roman Republic* (Rome 1960 *PMAAR* 20) (cited as *VDRR*)

Thylander, *Étude* — Hilding Thylander, *Étude sur l'épigraphie latine: date des inscriptions, noms et dénomination latine, noms et origine des personnes* (Lund 1952 *Skr. utg. av Svenska Inst. i Rom, Acta Inst. Rom. Regni Sueciae*, 8°, V)

Thylander, *Inscrs.* — Idem, *Inscriptions du Port d'Ostie*, 2 vols. (ibid. 1952 Texte, 1951 Planches, same series, 8°, IV: 1–2)

TLL — *Thesaurus linguae Latinae*

Toscana[2] — see *Guida d'Italia*

Toscana[4] (*Attrav. l'Italia*) — ibid.

Toynbee — J. M. C. Toynbee, *Death and Burial in the Roman World* (London 1971)

Toynbee/Ward Perkins — Jocelyn Toynbee and John Ward Perkins, *The Shrine of St. Peter and the Vatican Excavations* (London, etc., 1956)

Univ. Calif. Publ. Class. Arch. — *University of California Publications in Classical Archaeology*

Univ. Calif. Publ., Class. Stud. — *University of Calif. Publications: Classical Studies*

Vetter — Emil Vetter, *Handbuch der italischen Dialekte*, vol. 1 (Heidelberg 1953) (cited by no. of text)

Waltzing — J. P. Waltzing, *Étude historique sur les corporations professionnelles chez les Romains . . .*, 4 vols. (Louvain 1895–1900, repr. Hildesheim 1970)

Warm. — E. H. Warmington (ed.), *Archaic Inscriptions*, vol. 4 (1940) of his *Remains of Old Latin*, newly ed. and transl. (Cambridge, Mass./London, The Loeb Class. Libr.) (cited by page and no.)

Weaver — P. R. C. Weaver, *Familia Caesaris, A Social Study of the Emperor's Freedmen and Slaves* (Cambridge 1972)

W/H	A. Walde, *Lateinisches etymologisches Wörterbuch*, 2 vols., ed. 3 by J. B. Hofmann (Heidelberg 1938–1954), plus *Registerband* by E. Berger (1956) (repr. as ed. 4 1965)
Wingo	E. Otha Wingo, *Latin Punctuation in the Classical Age* (The Hague/Paris 1972 *Janua Linguarum*, ser. pract., 133)
Wissowa	Georg Wissowa, *Religion und Kultus der Römer*[2] (Munich 1912 *Handb. der klass. Altertums-Wiss.* 5: 4)
Woodhead, A. G.	*The Study of Greek Inscriptions*[2] (Cambridge Univ. Press 1981)
ZPE	*Zeitschrift für Papyrologie und Epigraphik*

The other abbreviations used in the annotations are self-explanatory; e.g., bibl(iography), c(irc)a, cent(ury), c(enti)m(eter), f. (and following, for one page), ff. (for more), fasc(icle), ibid., inscr(iption), loc(o) cit(ato), n(ote [or footnote]), no. (number), op(ere) cit(ato).

The capital letters used in classic Roman inscriptions are the most living element in the heritage handed down to us by antiquity. No other civilization has endowed its letters with such an unmistakable character, familiar to all those who read and write—a form which has lost none of its validity and still constitutes the means of communication in the languages of many peoples.

Giovanni Mardersteig, ed. Felice Feliciano veronese, *Alphabetum Romanum* (Verona 1960, Editiones Officinae Bodoni), Introduction p. 9 (transl. R. H. Boothroyd).

INTRODUCTION

INTRODUCTION

PART I. LATIN EPIGRAPHY DEFINED[1]

1. *Latin inscriptions a meeting point.* Latin inscriptions are the meeting point of Roman history and several arts. These are the arts of expression or composition, writing in the strictly physical sense (cutting, painting, or the like, on more or less durable material), and design or arrangement (including integration with the whole object to which the inscription pertains). The history is Roman history in its largest sense, involving men and women in many of their affairs, such as life and death, government, law, religious worship. The three arts are of minor caliber, no doubt. The products of the first—expression or composition—are hardly ever what we would call literature, though who knows what Augustus thought of his *Res Gestae* after he finally directed that it be cut as an inscription and placed in front of his great family-tomb (Suet. *Aug.* 101.4)?

2. *Latin epigraphy distinguished from numismatics, etc.* Latin epigraphy, the study of Latin inscriptions, is now commonly distinguished from numismatics, palaeography, and papyrology (which have become separate studies). Mommsen, however—undoubtedly the greatest figure in the history of our subject, *princeps studiorum nostrorum* (as Degrassi calls him, *Imag.*, praef. p. VIII, *init.*)—included Roman Republican coins in his first edition of *CIL* volume 1 (the second edition of this still contains an Appendix Nummorum), and the writing on the wax tablets found in Dacia is included in *CIL* volume 3, and on those found at Pompeii, in volume 4. This is also part of the background of Latin palaeography, being obviously a chapter in the history of handwriting.[2]

3. *Related fields.* The related fields that one finds oneself having to enter are many: besides all aspects of Roman history, such more restricted but still large fields as ancient jewelry, Etruscology, Italic and Latin philology, Greek epigraphy (one notes incidentally the paucity of archaic Latin inscriptions in comparison with archaic Greek), ancient pottery, Roman (pagan and Christian) religion and worship, comparative palaeography, Roman nomenclature (below, IV. 4), petrology (to determine kinds of stone), Latin verse, including saturnian, the Latin language, including "legalese" or "official-

---

1. For a brief introduction to Latin epigraphy (with bibl.), see Ch. L. Babcock, *CW* 52: 8 (May 1959) 237–244, or Joyce M. Reynolds, *OCD* 397–399, *s.v.* Epigraphy, Latin; cf. Gordon, *Rambles, More Rambles,* and *Seven Latin Inscrs.*; for a brief pictorial survey of the writing itself, from the earliest inscrs. (including one Greek, not Etruscan, fig. 2) to 16th-cent. printing, see James Hayes, *The Roman Letter . . .* (Chicago 1951–52); cf. S. Dow and J. P. Elder's review, *Speculum* 28 (1953) 396–399.

2. Plate 5 of Franz Steffens's *Lateinische Paläographie . . .*[2] (Trier 1909) is of "Wachstafeln aus Pompeji, A.D. 57." *CIL* 3: 2 also has some wax tablets (pp. 921–960); the Pompeian wax tablets are in *CIL* 4, Suppl. part 1.

ese,"[3] lexicography, including inconsistencies of spelling, the early lack of a standard orthography, and changing pronunciation and syntax, Roman architecture, Roman prosopography and questions of identity, and the pronunciation of Greek as revealed by the rendering of Greek words in Latin inscriptions and of Latin words in Greek.

PART II. THE PROVENIENCE OF LATIN INSCRIPTIONS, THEIR MATERIALS, NUMBERS, RANGE IN TIME

1. *Provenience and present whereabouts.* Latin inscriptions have been found, *in situ* or not, in all parts of the Roman Empire, from the middle of Scotland to southern Egypt, from Portugal to Arabia, and now are scattered, in museums or private holdings, far beyond the Empire's borders, even in Australia. Many, many more have been observed and noted, or found and reported, from antiquity to modern times, than are now extant and available. Polybius, for example (3.22.1–26.1), mentions—and implies having seen in Rome, "preserved to this date on bronze tablets"—three treaties made between Rome and Carthage. These inscriptions, so far as is known, are no longer extant (and Polybius is apparently our only source of information about them);[4] being on

bronze, they must have been particularly liable to loss because of the value of the metal, which could be melted down and reused for other purposes.[5] Perhaps no more than half of the inscriptions ever mentioned or quoted in the past are extant and accessible today; even so, some museums, at least in Rome, have more than can be exhibited, for lack of space or the personnel needed, and many inscriptions, especially fragments, have not yet been published. Those in museums are of course no longer *in situ*, and more often than not have been separated from the monuments to which they once belonged; they are now often seen attached to, or immured in, a museum wall, though the tendency nowadays seems to be to try to keep the whole monument intact despite the greater difficulty of exhibiting; in earlier times, the inscribed portion of a sarcophagus, for example, was sometimes all of it that was kept. All the more impressive, therefore, are the large inscribed monuments still *in situ*, such as—to speak only of Rome—the great Imperial arches in or near the Forum, the obelisks (one, **35**), the Tomb of Caecilia Metella 3 km. from the beginning of the old Via Appia (**23**), the Pantheon (**58**), the Columns of Trajan (**57**) and Marcus Aurelius, the Pyramid of Cestius in the Aurelian Wall near the so-called Protestant Cemetery (**26**), or the arch of the three aqueducts crossing the ancient Via Tiburtina (**29**).[6]

---

3. For "Roman Bureaucratese," esp. of the 4th cent. A.D., see Ramsay MacMullen, *Traditio* 18 (1962) 364–378.

4. "The historicity of this treaty of 508 B.C." (the earliest of the three mentioned by Polybius, which he dates to the year of "the first consuls appointed after the expulsion of the kings"—a controversial date) "is bolstered by the discovery" of four plaques, three inscribed gold ones (plus a fourth inscribed bronze sheet), one in Punic (or Phoenician), two (the bronze a third) in Etruscan, found in 1964 at Santa Severa, the ancient Pyrgi, on the coast about thirty miles north of Rome: Giovanni Colonna, "The Sanctuary at Pyrgi in Etruria," *Archaeology* 19 (1966) 22, with fig. 14; cf. Jacques Heurgon, "The Inscriptions of Pyrgi," *JRS* 56 (1966) 1–15 (with plate 1 and fig. 1). J. A. Fitzmyer considers the "Punic" inscr. to be

"Phoenician rather than Punic" and "the source of influence on its composition," "philologically and linguistically," to be Cyprus rather than Carthage: *Journ. Amer. Oriental Soc.* 86 (1966) 284–297, with full bibl.

5. See Gordon, *Notes,* 127 f. But some inscribed objects of precious metal have been preserved because of their religious character—e.g., the four of note 4, above: Colonna, op. cit. 21 col. 1, 23 *fin.* Others have become lost and later found—e.g., the *Lex de Imperio Vespasiani,* **46**.

6. The best single book in which to see photographs of the inscribed monuments that are still *in situ* in Rome is Ernest Nash's *Pictorial Dictionary of Ancient Rome* (see Abbreviations). Vol. 2, pp. 531–535, has a list of the inscriptions cited, many of them illustrated.

In situ or not, Rome has undoubtedly the largest number of Latin inscriptions still extant. Not to mention those still *in situ* in Rome itself or on one of the ancient highways leading out of it, the Museo Nazionale Romano (with about 8,000 inscrs. ten years ago: Catia Caprino, *Epigraphica*, 29 [1967] 145–172, 30 [1968] 185 f.), the Vatican (with one of the largest collections in Italy), the Musei Comunali (Capitoline and Conservatori), the Lateran (but all its inscriptions have recently been transferred to the Vatican), the American Academy in Rome, the Barberini Palace, the privately owned Museo Torlonia—all these and other buildings, mostly churches, have thousands of inscriptions, more or less accessible, more or less well displayed. Ostia, with almost 7,000 ten years ago (Fausto Zevi, *Epigraphica*, 30 [1968] 83), has perhaps the second largest number. Naples also has a large number, mostly in the Museo Nazionale, and one can expect to find collections exhibited in nearly all the other cities of Italy, in the Palazzo Comunale or a museum, a school, or a church. And inscriptions *in situ* or even worked into a modern building (as, for example, *CIL* 9.5136, apparently a twin of our **21**) may be seen anywhere in Italy or elsewhere in the Roman world. (On the preservation of this inscriptional wealth, see Augusto Campana, "Tutela dei beni epigrafici," *Epigraphica*, vol. cit. 5–19.)

2. *Materials used.* Probably most of the Latin inscriptions still extant are cut in stone of various kinds (always apparently the favorite material),[7] the rest being cut, scratched, stamped, or otherwise made on metal (bronze, lead, gold, silver, iron), bricks, tiles, earthenware, or glass, incised on wax tablets, painted on walls or pottery, formed by small stones set in mosaic, or even written on wood.[8] Different as these techniques are from one another, they all have in common the purpose of expressing and presumably communicating to the reader an intelligible text or message, long or short, formal or informal. Nowadays, for much of the information thus conveyed, paper would be used, and probably more wood than in antiquity, but for many other purposes we still use the same materials and the same techniques,[9] though sandblasting has in some places replaced handcutting (as for tombstones) and for some materials (such as bronze) the ancient technique is in question.[10]

The stones most used in and near

---

7. As with all the ancient buildings in the Graeco-Roman world, according to reports in the press, there is deterioration in the surface of the inscribed stones exposed out of doors, at least in Rome, caused not only by the perennial ravages of weather (including freezing temperatures every winter and occasional snow) but now also by air pollution. This we have noticed ourselves in repeated visits to Rome. (See below, p. 168.)

8. For a fairly comprehensive view of the materials found inscribed other than stone or wood, turn the pages of (unfinished) *CIL* 15 (there seems to be no table of contents), embracing the *instrumentum domesticum* (articles used in private life) of the city of Rome. For writing on wood, see Eric G. Turner's list in *JRS* 46 (1956) 115, and add *JRS* 50 (1960) 108–111, with pl. XI; writing in ink directly on wood was perhaps in much greater use among the Romans (and Greeks?) than is evident now, because of the deterioration and eventual loss of the wood when exposed to the air. There is a recent report in the press (Jan. 18, 1975) of the discovery at Vindolanda (mod.

Chesterholm, England) of more than 100 documents in the form of ink-written wooden tablets, some of them joined together in book form, of about A.D. 100. But E. G. Turner writes (May 5, 1976): "The rumour that an early type of codex has been unearthed in England is much exaggerated. . . . It's quite a long way from that to the codex."

9. Some modern uses of inscriptions: bricks, contractors' marks, cornerstones, manhole covers, public buildings, names of private residences, not to mention all the advertisements and slogans.

10. Pliny, *N.H.* 34.21.99, says: "The use of bronze has long been applied to securing the perpetuity of monuments by means of bronze tablets on which official enactments are incised (*inciduntur*)." Larfeld, *Handb. der griech. Epigraphik*, 1 (Leipzig 1907) 195 *init.* and *Griech. Epigr.*[3] (1914) 120, last par., and Guarducci, 1 (1967) 463 f., agree that the inscrs. on most Greek bronzes were incised. Other scholars: J. Mallon, *Paléographie romaine* (Madrid 1952) 175 *fin.*, uncertain between incising and casting; M. Hebald as quoted in *Contrib.* 218 n. 8 (incising), G. Tibiletti

Rome for inscriptional purposes are the various tufas, travertine, and marble; in least use, limestone. For a chapter on the Roman tufas (of volcanic origin) and their provenience, see Tenney Frank, *RBR*, 11–38; cf. his "Notes on the Servian Wall," Part D, *AJA* 22 (1918) 181–188, plate VII, and "On the Stele of the Forum", *CP* 14 (1919) 87 f. Tufa is the material of the earliest inscriptions of Rome; it was handy and nearby, but relatively soft and friable, and not at all suitable for inscriptions unless paint was applied to the cuttings; presumably, this was done regularly, not only for tufa but also for the other inscribed stones.[11] Some of this is still visible when the inscriptions are found. Sometimes in museums the cuttings are recolored with red paint by persons not expert in these matters, therefore the apparent writing may be incorrect. It is a question when travertine, "the stone of the Colosseum and St. Peter's as well as of several structures in New York and Philadelphia" (Frank, *RBR*, 32), came into use for inscriptions. Tenney Frank dates its discovery after ca. 150 B.C. and the earliest inscriptions using it from ca. 125 (ibid.); Lugli says (*RendLinc*. 1954, 67) that its use "is unknown before 125 B.C.," the date that he gives to *CIL* 1².31 (= 6.3692 cf. 30913, *ILS* 3794, Degr. 157, *Imag.* 77), but Coarelli dates this in the third century.[12] Degrassi in *ILLRP* gives it no date, but in *Imag.* says "saec. III." with no explanation, though previously he had implied a beginning date for travertine at about 150 B.C.[13] Lugli's dating seems to derive, uncritically, from Frank's, Coarelli's from Degrassi's "saec. III."

But apparently not noted, in this connection, is *CIL* 1².613 (= 14.2935, *ILS* 14, Degr. 321, *Imag.* 139), now in Berlin, which is on travertine and, if correctly restored (no one seems to question its attribution to L. Quinctius Flamininus), dates to 192 B.C. It is true that this comes, not from Rome, but from Palestrina, but one would think that travertine would have been in use in Rome by about the same time. Anyhow, this is the approximate date—early second century—which J. S. Gordon would tentatively assign to *CIL* 1².31 on palaeographical grounds (and the orthography—*Bicoleio* nom., *Honore* dat., *donom dedet mereto*—would seem to allow such dating). Travertine also, like the various tufas, proved to be a better material for building than for inscriptions: "though much less friable than the Italian tufas, its numerous crystal-lined cavities and fissures often cause difficulties in both cutting and reading inscriptions (the latter esp. after the inscribed side has undergone weathering), but it lies much nearer Rome than any marble,[14] was therefore cheaper and much easier to work than any of the hard Apennine limestones."[15] The lettering, as in the tufas, was undoubtedly made more legible by the addition of color. In the *Album* (of only dated or datable inscriptions

---

in De Rugg. 4: 23 (1956) 709 col. 1, 4th par. (cast, "fusa"), and 4: 24 (1957) 741, col. 2, 2nd par. (incised—of a different inscr.), E. M. Catich by letter of 5/21/70 (etching?); P. T. Craddock, Brit. Mus. Research Lab., London, by letters of 2/13 and 2/28, 1981: "It depends on the size of the letters; all the examples studied in the Brit. Mus. up to 2 cm. in height seem chased with hammer and chisel, or occasionally stippled [i.e., engraved by means of dots, not lines], not cast or incised. Etching was not used before the 15th cent. 'Incised' is not a specific metalworking term, but it would seem to mean cutting the metal with a graver rather than indenting it with a chaser." In 1929 Fabia had mentioned "le graveur" of the *Table Claudienne* of Lyon (**42**). See Jeffery, 55, for places where bronze plaques may have first become

popular in Greece, such as Olympia, and their advantages over stone.

11. Cf. Pliny, *N.H.* 33.40.122 *fin.*: *Minium* ("cinnabar, vermilion") *in voluminum quoque scriptura usurpatur clarioresque litteras vel in auro* [codd., *muro* Detlefsen, *aere* Hübner] *vel in marmore, etiam in sepulchris, facit.* For white lead found added to bronze letters, see Mommsen, *EE* 9: 1 (1903) 1 (*Ges. Schr.* 1 [Berlin 1905] 148); for Greek, L. Robert, *CRAI* (1955) 210 f.; Guarducci, 1.457 f.

12. Filippo Coarelli, *Dial. Arch.* 6 (1972) 56 n. 51.

13. *Prolusione*, 11 (*Scritti vari*, 1.658).

14. "The best quality, in fact the only reliable one in Latium, is that which is found between Bagni and the Sabine hills below Tivoli," Frank, *RBR*, 32.

15. Gordon, *Seven Latin Inscrs.* 77.

down to A.D. 525) the latest example of tufa (peperino) is of A.D. 158, 2.104, no. 222, a record of an assignment of land, etc.; of travertine, A.D. 228, 3.58, no. 282, on an altar (Henzen on *CIL* 6.13 had said it was marble). The *Album* has only one other example of tufa, of 11/4 B.C. (1.39, no. 26), but of travertine thirty-three examples from ca. 83 B.C. to A.D. 98, but only four examples from then on. The *Album* has also one example of what the petrologist Gioacchino De Angelis d'Ossat called "leucitite," "a compact lava-rock resembling the *silex* or *lapis Tuscolanus* of the Latial hills"—1.35, no. 18, of 9 B.C. Earlier editors had called it "Gabine stone," i.e., tufa. This illustrates the fact that editors sometimes disagree. A fine example is our **14**: first "limestone," then "marble," this recently confirmed. One finds also in studying marble that the early editors and commentators seem to have used Latin *marmor*, Italian *marmo*, and French *marbre* of any inscribed stone, not necessarily of marble.[16]

This brings us to marble, the latest of the kinds of stone used for Latin inscriptions. In the study cited in footnote 16, the writer found (p. 161, slightly revised) that "the date—the very end of the Republic—commonly accepted for (1) the use of marble in Italy for epigraphical purposes, and for (2) the use of Luna (modern Carrara) marble in particular, should be put considerably earlier. Unquestionably, by 155 B.C. the latter variety was being employed at least locally (i.e., in the Luna/Carrara country), and it seems that the occasional use of some kind of marble for inscriptions was established fairly well over Italy by ca. 90–80 B.C. . . . ; from Rome itself the earliest datable evidence is of ca. 64 B.C., but Lanuvium and Nemi, where the evidence goes back 10 to 20 or 25 years earlier, are so near to Rome as to offer pertinent testimony." The date 155 comes from *CIL* 1².623 (our **10**), which Luisa Banti, confirmed by Lucy T. Shoe, argued was the original inscription, not a later copy. The only other kind of stone in use to any extent for inscriptions is local limestone (*lapis calcarius*), which we find employed all over Italy wherever it was available; it is a hard stone, like marble, but less suitable for inscriptions.[17] But, *faute de mieux*, any stone might be used locally, perhaps to avoid extra expense—e.g., for milestones; one such, *CIL* 1².617 (= 11.6642, *ILS* 5803, Degr. 450, *Imag.* 189), is of "trachite of the Euganean Hills," according to the photographer of the Museo Civico, Bologna, where it was seen in May 1956.[18] Finally, not the least interesting are the inscriptions cut *in situ*, i.e., in living rock, such as our **55**, which is both honorary and legal in character, and cut in the rock along a path just outside the Porta Maggiore of Ferentino,[19] about 75 km. southeast of Rome.

3. *Numbers.* The number of Latin inscriptions now known or known about

---

16. Gordon, *Epigr.* II, 160. Correction, p. 163: *CIL* 1².632 is not on marble but on limestone; cf. Degr. 149, with ref. to Evans.

17. Limestone "had long been known but very little used because of the hardness and poor quality of the grades available within reach" of Rome: Frank, *RBR* 32 f., n. 14.

18. *CIL* 1² says nothing about the kind of stone (fasc. 4, or *CIL* 17, when they appear, should rectify this), Degrassi in *ILLRP* also nothing, but in *Imag.* he says limestone. G. Susini, *Il lapidario greco e romano di Bologna* . . . (Bologna 1960) 92, no. 94, confirms "trachite" by saying "analogo al n. 92," which is "in trachite." This stone is defined as a "roccia vulcanica, diffusa anche nei territori vulcanici italiani," of "una composizione mineralogica affine al granito" and

"utile come pietra da costruzione." A check of *CIL* 1²: 2 fasc. 1–3 might reveal many other such differences of opinion or plain lack of information available to editors, who can seldom inspect any large number of texts personally. One stone of granite proper, in this case Egyptian (Assouan, Aswan) granite, is shown in **22**, the writing of which is extremely hard to read.

19. For such inscrs., see Meyer, 19, with ref. to Keuner, *RE*, Suppl. 3 (1918) 482–491, *s.v.* Felsendenkmäler (the one at Ferentino: col. 489, 13–16). Perhaps the most famous example, seen by all travellers to Terracina, is one cut to celebrate the improvement of the Via Appia by having a limestone cliff cut to the depth of 120 Roman feet, to allow the road to skirt it and proceed at about sea level on its way to Capua: *CIL* 10.6849, which, taken together

runs to the hundreds of thousands, and every year brings hundreds more, as excavations or chance finds reveal them. The exact number, even at a given date, can never be known (a minimum of well over 200,000, quite apart from thousands of coins); this is partly because of the large number of those no longer extant (some of which might no longer be considered authentic, especially if they rest on a single witness, unless he is one of impeccable authority), partly also because any one of the many printed in *CIL* as forgeries may at any time be claimed to be genuine.[20] No one knows how many forgeries of Latin inscriptions there may be; most volumes of *CIL* contain a list of all those that the editor considered forgeries ("falsae vel alienae") in his area; these are then commonly accepted as such, but at any time someone may challenge the list, by arguing either for the deletion of an item from the list (as noted in n. 20) or for the addition of an item, as has been done for the famous Praenestine fibula.[21]

4. *Range in time.* The range in time of the Latin inscriptions thus far known is considerable—from perhaps the sixth century B.C. to the end of the Roman Empire and beyond.[22] The earliest are all of quite uncertain date and sometimes even of uncertain reading or language or interpretation,[23] partly because of the complete lack of literary material for comparison earlier than Plautus (by whose time—to judge from a comparison of Plautus with the earliest inscriptions, few and unclear though they are—the greatest changes in the Latin language had perhaps already taken place),[24] in marked contrast with the situation in Greek.

PART III. SOURCES AND COLLECTIONS

1. *The earliest extant collection.* The earliest extant collection of ancient Latin inscriptions seems to be that made by an unknown traveller to Italy (Anonymus Einsidlensis), apparently in the eighth to the ninth century, a copy of which, written about a century later by someone who did not wholly understand the traveller's notes, is now in the library of the monastery at Einsiedeln in Switzerland.[25]

2. *The Corpus Inscriptionum Latinarum (CIL).* The standard collection and edi-

---

with Dio 68.15 and *CIL* 10.6835 and 6839 (both of A.D. 110), shows that it was probably Trajan who was responsible. Cf. Degrassi, *RendPontAcc* 22 (1946–47) 179 *fin.* (*Scritti vari*, 1.578 *init.*).

20. As, for example, *CIL* 6.616* by Syme, to rescue P. Iulius Lupus as consul suffect at the end of A.D. 97 or of 98: *JRS* 43 (1953) 154, 156.

21. C. Densmore Curtis, "The Bernardini Tomb," *MAAR* 3 (1919) 21 f. See **1**, with the N.B. at the end.

22. Contrary to many references in print to the earliest Latin inscriptions, the dates of them all, both absolute and relative, are entirely conjectural and hypothetical until we get to the Scipionic epitaphs of the third century (on which see below, our **5**).

23. See **1**, the Praenestine fibula (with the N.B. at the end); **3**, the Duenos-vase inscr. from Rome (of at least uncertain word-distribution and unknown meaning, though a few words seem clear); **4**, the Roman Forum cippus (with text incomplete by apparently the Sullan age and of partly uncertain reading and so of unknown meaning, though again some words seem clear: for the latest interpretation see Robert E. A. Palmer, *The King and the Comitium, A*

Study of Rome's Oldest Public Document [Wiesbaden 1969 (*Historia, Einzelschr.* 11)] and a brief review, *ACR* 1 [1971] 51); **75**, the Arval Hymn, from Rome (whose text is uncertain at many places but, being in trilogy form, can generally be conjectured satisfactorily, though the meaning remains sometimes doubtful); and Degrassi, *ILLRP* 5 (*Imag.* 118), from Tivoli (is it in Latin? Sabine?).

24. Cf. L. R. Palmer, 62 f.

25. Cf. G. (i.e., W.) Henzen, *CIL* 6: 1 (1876) p. IX (who dates the traveller's sojourn in Rome between ca. 750 and 850); P. Gabriel Meier, *Catalogus codicum manu scriptorum qui in bibliotheca Monasterii Einsidlensis O.S.B. servantur*, vol. 1 (Einsiedeln 1899) no. 326, part IV, pp. 297 f. (he dates the MS itself "S(aec.) IX–X," as does Dessau, *ILS* 107, note). For three collections of the 16th–18th centuries, see Calabi Limentani, 425; for extensive bibliography on the history of Latin epigraphy, ibid. 131–142. Work in Greek epigraphy seems to have been much greater—deeper and broader—than in Latin, and the collecting of Greek inscriptions dates from as far back as the Alexandrian age: Larfeld, 8.

tion of Latin inscriptions, dating from the earliest (6th century B.C.?) to about the end of the sixth Christian century,[26] is the *Corpus Inscriptionum Latinarum* (Berlin). This began in 1862 with the publication of Friedrich Ritschl's *Priscae Latinitatis monumenta epigraphica* (with supplements in his *Opuscula philologica*, 4 [Leipzig 1878, repr. Hildesheim 1978], pp. 494–571, with atlas of 23 plates) and was continued by Mommsen and Henzen's edition of the earliest texts (to the death of Caesar, 44 B.C.) plus *Elogia clarorum virorum, Fasti anni Iuliani*, and *Fasti consulares ad a.u.c. DCCLXVI* (*CIL* 1, ed. 1, 1863). But *CIL* is still incomplete even after the publication of Degrassi's *Inscriptiones Latinae liberae rei publicae, Imagines* (1965), the latest fascicle of *CIL* 4 (Suppl. 3, Lief. 4, 1970), the index of cognomina (1980), and six fascicles (1974–75) of part 7 (a complete computerized index of words, including proper names) of *CIL* 6 (city of Rome), edited by E. J. Jory and D. W. Moore; the indices of *CIL* 11 (Emilia, Etruria, Umbria) are incomplete, lacking all but the first three parts.[27] Though absolutely indispensable for good libraries (and still largely available through photographic reproduction), *CIL* has some weaknesses: inevitably incomplete information about the lost inscriptions published at second hand, sometimes inadequate information about

even those published at first hand (description of material, general lack of photographs, etc.), sometimes unreliable dating based on the writing, sometimes unreliable restorations that take insufficient account of spatial requirements, a frequent failure to indicate whether the editor himself has seen and examined the inscriptions presented. *CIL* volume 1 was largely replaced by Degrassi's *Inscriptiones Latinae liberae rei publicae* (2 vols., Florence, vol. 1² 1965, 2 1963, both repr. 1972), together with his *Imagines* of 401 of its more than 1,277 texts (*CIL, Auctarium*, 1965) (but his edition of *CIL* 1²:2 fasc. 4 [forthcoming], with H. Krummrey's assistance, has restored the balance for *CIL* 1²:2), plus his *Fasti consulares et triumphales* (2 vols.), *Fasti anni Numani et Iuliani*, and *Elogia* (Rome 1947, 1963, 1937 [*Inscr. Ital.* vol. 13, fasc. 1–3, all illustrated]), and *CIL* volume 7 is being replaced by Collingwood and Wright's *The Roman Inscriptions of Britain* (Oxford, vol. 1, 1965).[28]

3. Selections, yearly editions, translations. The largest and best selection of Latin inscriptions is the *Inscriptiones Latinae selectae* of Hermann Dessau (Berlin 1892–1916, 3 vols. in 5 parts, repr. 1954–55 with tables of concordance between Dessau and *CIL*), which occupied him twenty-five years and contains about

---

26. See Mommsen's statement, *CIL* 3: 1 (1873) p. V, col. 1, 2nd par., about the range of time to be covered by *CIL*.

27. Several volumes, or parts of volumes, of *CIL* are forthcoming or in preparation: vol. 1²: 2: 4 (Addenda tertia, Indices, ed. A. Degrassi and H. Krummrey, present director of the *CIL* in Berlin, DDR) (forthcoming); vol. 2 suppl. 2 (suspended since the death of J. M.ª de Navascués); vol. 3² part 3–7; vol. 4 suppl. 3 Lief. 5; vol. 6: 7: 7 (Formae vocabulorum, Numeri inscriptionum cum additamentis); vol. 6: 8 (Supplementum, ed. S. Panciera et al.); vol. 9 suppl. 1 (ed. M. Torelli et al.); vol. 10, suppl. 1 (ed. H. Solin et al.); vol. 11, suppl. 1 (ed. W. Eck); vol. 14 suppl., Latium vetus (ed. H. G. Kolbe et al.), another suppl. for Ostia (ed. G. Barbieri—but this will probably appear in the *Inscriptiones Italiae*); vol. 16, suppl. 2 (ed. H. Nesselhauf); vol. 17 (milestones, ed. G. Walser and I. König); vol. 18 (Carmina epi-

graphica): 1: 1 (the pagan verse inscrs. of the city of Rome, ed. B. E. Thomasson); another Auctorium, H. Solin's *Die griechischen Personennamen in Rom. Ein Namenbuch*, 3 vols. (forthcoming—to be published by W. de Gruyter, Berlin/Hawthorne, New York); still another, M. Hainzmann's Computer-Index to the Roman stone-inscrs. of Noricum, 2 vols. Cf. H. Krummrey, in *Actes du VIIᵉ Congrès International d'Épigraphie Grecque et Latine . . . 1977* (Paris 1979) 399–401. For reviews of *CIL* 6: 7: 1–6, cf. H. Chantraine, *Gnomon* 49 (1977) 696–701, 51 (1979) 31–36; M. W. C. Hassall, *JRS* 67 (1977) 209–211; A. E. Gordon, *CP* 75 (1980) 269–273. The current address of the *CIL* headquarters is Akademie der Wissenschaften der DDR, Zentralinstitut für Alte Geschichte u. Archäologie, 1086 Berlin, Leipziger Strasse 3/4, (East) Germany.

28. See *CP* 63 (1968) 122–130.

9,500 texts (including about 150 in Greek, a few in both Latin and Greek—perhaps the most notable being the arrogant [and, presumably, damaging] one, no. 8995, of Cornelius Gallus, poet, general, and friend of Vergil and Augustus, our **22** [which has also Egyptian hieroglyphics above the Latin and Greek]—and at least one, no. 8757, in Latin written with Greek characters). One of Dessau's weaknesses lies in his having seen, for the most part, the extant inscriptions of only *CIL* 14 (which he had edited himself) and some of those of *CIL* 1 (ed. 2, part 2, fasc. 2, 1931), 8 (Suppl. 2–4, 1894, 1904, 1916), and 13 (Part 5, Indices, 1943), which he helped edit; another weakness, shared (apparently) by all editions of Latin (or Greek) inscriptions in bulk except *CIL* 1 and 6, is the lack of a complete index of words, though his other indices are reliable and most valuable.

For Christian Latin inscriptions the foundations were laid by G. B. De Rossi's *Inscriptiones Christianae urbis Romae septimo saeculo antiquiores*, of which he lived to publish only volume 1 (Rome 1857–1861), with 1,374 inscriptions, and volume 2, part 1 (1888), consisting mostly of essays (in rather difficult Latin) on the manuscript sources; this was continued by Iosephus (i.e., Giuseppe) Gatti (Vol. Primi *Supplementum*, fasc. 1 only [Rome 1915]) and completed by Angelo Silvagni, with a new series in four volumes (Rome 1922, 1935, 1956, 1964 [joint editor for vols. 3–4: Antonio Ferrua, who has completed the work with volumes 5–7, (Rome 1971, 1975, 1980)]) with two volumes of plates (1935, 1956), *Tabulae et indices*, 1964, and a separate *Monumenta epigraphica Christiana saeculo XIII antiquiora quae in Italiae finibus adhuc exstant*, 4 volumes in 7 parts (Vatican City, 1943—no more published?).

Ernst Diehl's *Inscriptiones Latinae Christianae veteres*, in three volumes (Berlin 1924/25–1928/31; new ed., in 4 vols., the first three [1961] corrected in some places, the fourth [1967] being a *Supplementum*,

by J. Moreau and H. I. Marrou), presents a generous selection, with 5,000 numbered texts (but with many more numbered A, B, C, etc.) and (like Dessau's) a valuable volume of indexes (though again without one of all the words). Since 1888 the French, beginning with René Cagnat and (from 1900) M. Besnier, and others, have published yearly editions (with little or no annotation) of new Latin inscriptions, edited at second hand from recent publications, together with notices of new publications in the field and new information on old inscriptions, under the title *L'année épigraphique* (Paris—until 1961, inclusively, published also as *Revue des publications épigraphiques relatives à l'antiquité romaine* in the *Revue archéologique*), now edited by several scholars (the 1978 vol., publ. 1981, by André Chastagnol, Jean Gagé, Marcel Leglay, and the late H. G. Pflaum). *Epigraphica, Rivista Italiana di Epigrafia*, founded in 1939 by Aristide Calderini, has now reached vol. 42 (1980) and is directed by Giancarlo Susini and (since 1977) Angela Donati.

Besides the books of E. H. Warmington, Richmond Lattimore, and Lewis and Reinhold (for which see Abbreviations), which all contain English versions of many Latin inscriptions, four others contain some or many in whole or in part: D. C. Munro, *A Source Book of Roman History* (Boston 1908), has seven items, including the *Laudatio Turiae* abridged (our **29**), and a few selections from the *Res Gestae* of Augustus, **34**; H. L. Rogers and T. R. Harley, *The Life of Rome . . .* (Oxford 1927), translate into verse *CLE* 1175 (= *CIL* 6.29896), a first-person epitaph, in elegiacs, of a Gallic dog named "Margarita" (*Gallia me genuit*, etc.), the *Laud. Turiae*, the *Laud. Murdiae* (*CIL* 6.10230 = *ILS* 8394), and a Republican epitaph in verse (quoted and translated below, in V.2); Wm. C. McDermott and Wallace E. Caldwell, *Readings in the History of the Ancient World* (New York 1951), have six items, including the *Senatus Consultum de Bacchana-*

libus, **8**, the *Res Gestae* of Augustus, **34**, some of the Minutes of the Secular Games of 17 B.C., **25**, most of the Charter of Salpensa, Spain (*CIL* 2.1963 = *ILS* 6088 add.), the *Lex* of the Association of Diana and Antinous, of Lanuvium (*CIL* 14.2112 = *ILS* 7212), and the preface to Diocletian's *Edict on Prices*, **81**; and *Ancient Roman Statutes* (*ARS*) has many items.²⁹

4. *Manuals, introductions, word indices.* The oldest still valuable manual of Latin inscriptions is that of René Cagnat, *Cours d'épigraphie latine* (Paris, ed. 4, revised and enlarged, 1914, repr. 1964), by one who took part in editing *CIL* 8 and *IGRR* and published much other work based on the use of Latin (and Greek) inscriptions. Still useful also, and probably irreplaceable in its comprehensiveness, though needing revision in the light of new inscriptions and recent scholarship, is Sir John Edwin Sandys's *Latin Epigraphy* . . . (Cambridge 1918, ed. 2 revised by S. G. Campbell 1927; photographically reprinted, ed. 1, Chicago 1974, ed. 2, Groningen 1969). Considering the origin of this work, as Sandys describes it, in the chapter on Latin Epigraphy that he, for lack of some "recognised expert," had written for *A Companion to Latin Studies*, which he himself edited (ed. 1 1910, ed. 2 1913), his *Latin Epigraphy*, revised by Campbell, is a good job of compilation and organization, while clearly at the same time not the work of real epigraphists. Good features are Chapter I (The Study of Latin Inscriptions [Epigraphy defined, Value of Latin inscriptions]) and seventeen pages on Latin Inscriptions in Classical Authors, which has since been replaced by Arthur

Stein's *Römische Inschriften in der antiken Literatur* [Prag 1931, pp. 86], and Appendix IV, Six Historical Inscriptions. For the earlier work in English, J. C. Egbert's *Introduction to the Study of Latin Inscriptions* (New York, etc., 1896, revised ed., with brief supplement, copyright 1906), see Cagnat⁴, p. xxiv, n. 1: "Sur les ressemblances de cet ouvrage et des précédentes éditions de nôtre *Cours d'épigraphie*, voir *Rev. Critique* [*d'histoire et de littérature*, Paris, vol. 41] 1896, p. 475 et suiv." (The pages are 475–479.)

The latest introductions to the subject are the Italian work of Ida Calabi (now Ida Calabi Limentani) and the German of the late Ernst Meyer. The former, *L'uso storiografico delle iscrizioni latine, con una appendice di avviamento bibliografico* di Attilio Degrassi (Milan and Varese 1953), appeared in a second edition under a new title, *Epigrafia latina, con un'appendice bibliografica* di Attilio Degrassi (1968), which has been reprinted in a third edition (Milan 1974), revised and corrected, bringing up to date the bibliography of the inscriptions presented as well as Degrassi's bibliography.³⁰ The latter work, *Einführung in die lateinische Epigraphik* (Darmstadt 1973), is much shorter and presents no texts and no photos of inscriptions, but, like the Italian work, is good on bibliography.³¹ Each work has its virtues: the German is compact, the Italian rich with appendices—bibliographies, two lists of abbreviations (the German has a single short one), the emperors' titles, with dates, from Augustus to Theodosius,³² and a unique list of antiquarian/epigraphical authors, editors, collectors, artists, and works, up to about 1900. The French work

---

29. Cf. A. M. Prichard, *JRS* 52 (1962) 248, who finds "some of the translation [in *ARS*] good and much at least serviceable, much also uneven, sometimes poor," but this writer realizes from doing the present work how difficult it often is to translate Latin inscrs. satisfactorily.

30. The work offers, with much else, 135 inscrs. (or groups of inscrs.) with annotation and photos, these of varying quality, but few large or clear

enough to be legible. (Note: the Praenestine fibula, our **1**, is wrongly placed in the Villa Giulia Museum, Rome, because the photo used was mislabeled.)

31. Cf. R. P. Wright's review, *JRS* 64 (1974) 243.

32. For a new, corrected dating of Augustus's 8th–21st imperial acclamations, cf. T. D. Barnes, *JRS* 64 (1974) 21–26. For example, he dates the 15th to A.D. 1, the 16th to 3, the 21st to 13 (or perhaps 12).

of Raymond Bloch, *L'épigraphie latine* (Paris 1952—an English translation is said to be under way), is necessarily much slighter (it appears in the series *Que sais-je?*) but is still useful within its limitations (112 small pages, some inscriptions, 13 figs. in the text, but no plates).

The late H. G. Pflaum was engaged in writing "un nouveau manuel d'épigraphie latine, mais . . . sur des bases assez larges et n'en avait écrit que quelques chapitres au moment de sa mort [Dec. 26, 1979]," A. Chastagnol, by letter of Nov. 1, 1980. For one appreciation of Pflaum, see G. Alföldy's obituary, *Gnomon* 52 (1980) 203–206. He considers him the greatest Latin epigraphist since Mommsen, pp. 203 f.; for another appreciation, with a photo of Pflaum and his bibliography (240 items), see M. Leglay, *Epigraphica* 42 (1980) 212–230. Emil Hübner's *Römische Epigraphik*, in the *Handbuch der (classischen) Altertumswissenschaft*, vol. 1, ed. 2 (1892), pp. 625–710, is to be replaced by a new work which Ekkehard Weber of the University of Vienna has been invited to prepare. A quite different, more basic, sort of introduction to Latin epigraphy is provided by Giancarlo Susini's important book, *Il lapicida romano* (Bologna 1966 Archivio di Stato di Bologna, *Quaderni della Scuola di Paleografia ed Archivistica*, IX–XII), translated as *The Roman Stonecutter. An Introduction to Latin Epigraphy*, by A. M. Dabrowski, and edited with an introduction by E. Badian (Oxford 1973).[33]

One of the great weaknesses of nearly all the editions of collections or large selections of Latin inscriptions is the lack of a complete index of words. Of all the volumes of *CIL*, only volumes 1 (both editions), containing less than 3,000 inscriptions of Republican or pre-Republican date, 3 (but only Diocletian's *Edict on Prices*), 4 (but only through Suppl. 2, 1909), and (since 1974–75) 6 contain an index of words. Valuable and indispensable as the other indexes are—of nomina, cognomina, emperors, etc.—none is an adequate substitute for an index of words, to show the realities, and therefore the possibilities, of the language of inscriptions. For successfully repairing damages or restoring gaps in damaged or fragmentary inscriptions, an index of epigraphical words,[34] supplemented by Gradenwitz's reverse index of Latin words in general,[35] and now for proper names by Swanson's, is indispensable. For this reason the plan, recently carried out, of publishing a computerized index of all the words in *CIL* 6 (Rome),[36] is most welcome.

PART IV. TECHNICAL DETAILS

1. *The illusoriness of inscriptions in print.* Nothing is more illusory than seeing inscriptions in print without a good photograph of the whole piece or monument (if still extant) in or on which each inscription is written, and without full informa-

33. See reviews by Joyce Reynolds, *JRS* 65 (1975) 210, and M. P. McHugh, *CW* 69 (1975–76) 282 f.

34. A complete listing of all the words (though not of all instances of them), including "geographical and mythological names but not those of living or historical persons" except "old biblical proper names," seems to have been the aim of George N. Olcott's *Thesaurus linguae Latinae epigraphicae: A Dictionary of the Latin Inscriptions*, of which he lived to publish only volume 1, fasc. 1–22 (Rome 1904–1912), continued briefly by Leslie F. Smith, John H. McLean, and Clinton W. Keyes, vol. 2, fasc. 1–4 (New York 1935–36), but only into the word "Avillinlanus (fundus)."

35. *Laterculi vocum Latinarum: Voces Latinas et a fronte et a tergo ordinandas* curavit Otto Gradenwitz

(Leipzig 1904). The reverse index is on pages 279–546; neither part includes proper names or proper adjectives, the area covered for poetry by Donald C. Swanson's *The Names in Roman Verse: A Lexicon and Reverse Index of All Proper Names of History, Mythology, and Geography Found in the Classical Roman Poets* (Madison, etc., 1967), for one review of which see Gilbert Highet, *Computers and the Humanities*, 3: 2 (Nov. 1968) 119–122.

36. This is the work of E. J. Jory and D. W. Moore, in six large fascicles (1974–75). Fasc. 5 contains vocabula T–Z, Graeca, and cognomina A–G, fasc. 6 cognomina H–Z, cognomina acephala, and vocabula acephala. Cf. H. Krummrey, *Klio*, 52 (1970) 235–239. For reviews, see above, n. 27.

tion of the place of finding, etc. Sometimes the place of finding may seem the most important aspect, along with the identity of the language in which the inscription is written; as, for example (outside of Latin), in the case of the bilingual Greek-Aramaic inscription containing an edict of the third-century (B.C.) Indian king Aśoka, which was found in 1958 in Afghanistan, cut in living rock, and which proved to be the first inscription in Greek discovered so far east and the first edict of Aśoka's found so far west and in Greek;[37] or the bilingual Punic (or Phoenician)-Etruscan plaques mentioned above (note 4), containing the first Punic (or Phoenician) inscription found on the Italian mainland.[38] Sometimes a fragmentary inscription receives light and increased importance from its place of finding, such as, for example, the Pontius Pilate fragment found in 1961 in the Roman theater at Caesarea (our **37**), which is notable in giving the hapax legomenon *Tiberieum* (with long second E indicated by an apex: É) as well as the first inscriptional, and the only contemporary, mention of Pilate and his correct title, *praefectus Iudaeae* (which confirms Hirschfeld's suspicion, in *Die kaiserlichen Verwaltungsbeamten* . . .[2] [Berlin 1905] 384 f., that Tacitus is wrong in calling Pilate a *procurator, Ann.* 15.44).[39]

What the student generally sees of an inscription is a modern printed copy, provided with punctuation and perhaps an expansion of any abbreviations that may occur in the original, perhaps also explan-

atory notes on the provenience of the inscription, its contents (including the identification of proper names), and its date (with or without the grounds for dating).

If he has before him the *original* inscription, or a photograph of it, though it now seems alive and crying to be read, its reading and meaning are likely to be less obvious. Except for a rare sentence-sign or paragraph-sign in the longer inscriptions (for these, see Wingo), the only punctuation mark will be some sort of point, variously shaped and variously placed (though in the best writing at about midheight), between most words (obviously for the purpose of separating them to facilitate reading), but generally not at line ends and often not between a preposition and its object; this interpunctuation is found in use from as early as the Castor and Pollux dedication (our **2**) and sporadically in the other earliest inscriptions, more or less regularly in the Republican ones, rather more commonly from the Augustan age on (but generally inconsistently, even in the same inscription), but then decreasing in use to the point that it may be used only before and after abbreviations (but again inconsistently), and finally, in the early-Christian inscriptions, not used at all or hardly ever (see *Contrib.* 183–185, and the *Album*, vol. 3 with its plates). Even with these interpuncts the word division is likely to be unclear, especially when the writing is small, as is often the case; the points themselves, even within the same inscription, vary consid-

---

37. Cf. *Un editto bilingue greco-aramaico di Aśoka, la prima iscrizione greca scoperta in Afghanistan: testo, traduzione e note* a cura di G. Pugliese Carratelli e di G. Levi Della Vida, con prefazione di G. Tucci e introduzione di U. Scerrato (Rome 1958 Ist. Italiano per il Medio ed Estremo Oriente [Serie Orientale Roma, XXI]), pp. V–VII, 1–35. Pp. 33 f. contain an "English translation of the Greek and Aramaic texts" "for the convenience of Asiatic readers."

38. A Phoenician inscr. in very small letters is engraved on the inside of a shallow silver bowl found in the Bernardini tomb discovered at Palestrina (anc. Praeneste) in 1876 and now in the Villa Giulia Museum, Rome; the inscr. reads *Eshmunyaad*

ben Ashto, "Eshmunyaad, son of Ashto." It is edited in the *Corpus Inscr. Semiticarum*, 1.164, pp. 214 ff. The bowl is among several silver bowls and some bronzes that are thought to be Eastern imports. Cf. Curtis, op. cit. (above, n. 21) 43–45, no. 26, with plates 22 f. (with earlier bibl.); T. Dohrn in Helbig/Speier 3.2909 (with later).

39. See Antonio Frova, "L'iscrizione di Ponzio Pilato a Cesarea," *RendIstLomb* 95 (1961) 419–434, with photo of the fragment. Cf. A. N. Sherwin-White, *Roman Society and Roman Law in the New Testament. The Sarum Lectures 1960–1961* (Oxford 1963) 6, and *JRS* 54 (1964) 259.

erably in size, position, and shape, so that one is often not sure whether there is a point between words, or even, perhaps by mistake, in the middle of a word.

Another matter of frequent uncertainty is the tall I, used as early as Lucilius (2nd cent. B.C.) to mark a metrically long I (Velius Longus, ed. Keil, 7.56, 2; cf. R. P. Oliver, *AJP* 87 [1966] 158–170). It is often a question whether a particular I is tall or not, since even within a single line there is very often considerable variation in the height of the letters; the letters F, S, and T, and any other letter when first in the line, are often taller than the rest. Naturally, when one believes a particular I to be metrically short, one will not favor the tall I when the tallness is in doubt. In a long inscription, therefore, the comparative height of many I's must remain uncertain.

Then there is sometimes a mark (called an apex, from Quintilian, 1.4.10, 1.7.2) like an acute accent, cut over a long vowel other than I (but occasionally over I also—*Contrib.* 148, nos. 5 f.), presumably to mark it as metrically long, like the tall I. But there seems to be no more consistency in its use than in that of the tall I, and sometimes the mark is not well placed—perhaps over the next letter, or, if unusually long, over both letters; and sometimes it makes no sense, not being over (or near) a long vowel, so that one wonders whether it is simply a mistake on the part of the cutter, or only an accidental cut; here a close examination of the original inscription or of a squeeze (see IV.5, below), or perhaps even a good photograph, may enable one to decide. After all, one is at the mercy of the cutter, and he was perhaps at the mercy of his copy, which he may not have been able to read well. There is also some use of doubling vowels in order to mark them as long, as in our **14**; Dessau, *ILS* 3:2, 804 f., 850, Lommatzsch in *CIL* 1²:2, 813 col. 1, 851 col. 1 (index gramm., de litteris), and Degrassi, *ILLRP* 2, 490, list their examples. This practice seems generally to have yielded to the use of the apex, though the use of double *u* in the genitive singular, nominative and accusative plural of fourth-declension masculines is still found as late as Severus Alexander (A.D. 222–235), *CIL* 6.230 (= *ILS* 2216), and double *i* as late as Constantine (A.D. 306–337), *CIL* 3.4121 (= *ILS* 704). Cf. Quintilian, 1.7.14, who says that double vowels lasted down to the time of Accius (170–90 or later, B.C.), and beyond; Sommer 29 §7 or Pfister 32 §7; Meyer 34 f.

The arrangement of an inscription may help in interpreting it.

Another fact that is generally obscure in a printed copy is that in the actual inscription there is often considerable variation in the letter heights not only within lines but also from line to line, often also a gradual decrease in letter heights from the top to the bottom of an inscription, which seems to be caused by the desire to make legible the higher, more distant writing; or there may be a heading in large, clear, well-spaced and well-punctuated letters, obviously intended to catch the eye, followed by the main text in smaller, less well spaced and less well punctuated letters, in somewhat cursive style, and then perhaps a line or two, in medium-sized letters, warning malefactors against damaging the monument.[40]

---

40. There are many references in Latin (and Greek) inscrs., and in some authors (e.g., Josephus, *Ant. Jud.*), to instructions that inscrs. of legal character be inscribed, generally in bronze, and set up in public for all to see. *ARS* contains some thirty-five such documents in Engl. translation, with intro. and notes, ranging in date from the *S. C. de Bacch.* (our **8**, 186 B.C.) to a Letter about Tariffs on Shipments to Constantinople (*OGIS* 2.521, lines 8–11, ca. A.D. 500). Most pertinent here are *ARS* nos. 45 §38 (*CIL* 1².583, pp. 450 f. [cf. pp. 723, 739, 832], §lxvi), in which the praetor is directed to have published and posted "this whole matter . . . in the Forum, where it can be read clearly from ground level" (*recte de plano*) (this thought is expressed twice), and similarly 56 §4, 113 §5, 166, and 194. The others in *ARS* that are more or less pertinent are nos. 52–54, 80, 104, 107, 111, 123, 125, 128 (i, 4), 138 (ii), 142, 143 §8, 150, 184–186, 188, 196 (§§2, 4, 7), 230 §5, 234, 266, 280, 283 f., 287 §ii, *fin.*, 298, 301 §8, 302 *fin.*, 320. (This provision is most often found at the end of the documents.)

For all these points one may observe the Allia Potestas epitaph (below, p. 34 and 65), but they hold good for many others, especially (in the last respect) the epitaphs.

2. *The many abbreviations used.* There is one special feature of Latin inscriptions that must strike anyone who tries to read them; that is, the presence of what one decides must be abbreviations. In fact, there is hardly an inscription of any length that does not contain at least one abbreviation—so different from the state of affairs in Greek inscriptions, where abbreviations occur much less often (Guarducci, 1.398–406); for example, in the long *Res Gestae* of Augustus, whereas the Latin has many abbreviations, the Greek version—so far as it is extant—contains not one.[41] The origin of this usage in Latin lies *conjecturally* in (a) the Roman family-name system (which was common also to Etruscan and Italic, and perhaps Etruscan in origin),[42] particularly in the use, for all males, of a personal, or individual, name, the praenomen, which was regularly abbreviated in writing when followed by nomen or cognomen or both; hence the regular use of C. (for "Gaius," C being the early form of G), Cn. (for "Gnaeus"), L(ucius), M(arcus), and the initials of the few other praenomina in use in the classical period; (b) the regular use of abbreviations for *filius, filia* (F), *nepos* (N), *consul*

(COS), and the other recurring words, phrases, and name-endings (such as -*us*) in lists of names and titles, such as the consular and triumphal fasti,[43] where the reason for abbreviating was probably the desire to save space on the stone or metal.[44] In fact, the abbreviation of the masculine praenomen was quite possibly due in the first place to the desire to save space—and work—in inscribing epitaphs and was facilitated by the fewness of the praenomina and by the fact that all but two of them could be indicated by a single initial letter, the exceptions being GN for "Gnaeus" and *N* for "Manius," simple C and M being already preempted for "Gaius" and "Marcus." This system of extensive abbreviation goes hand in hand with various other devices that seem to be designed, first of all, to save space, though later in some cases to be the result of fashion or whim; such things as ligatures (two or more letters written as a monogram), and small or tall letters (on all of which see above, IV.1, or *Contrib.* 148–206). (See also Appendix II for a list of the abbreviations found in these inscriptions.)

3. *The special interest of the earlier inscriptions.* In some ways the most interesting Latin inscriptions are those to be dated earlier than the Empire—the Republican and pre-Republican ones. "Pre-Republican" immediately suggests one of the

---

41. See Gordon, *Notes*, 131. For one extreme case of abbreviating, note our **66** (A.D. 153), which contains 613 words, of which 142 are abbreviated.

42. See Ernst Pulgram, "The Origin of the Roman nomen gentilicium," *HSCP* 58/59 (1948) 163–187; idem, *The Tongues of Italy, Prehistory and History* (Cambridge, Mass. 1958) 256; Massimo Pallottino, *Etruscologia*[6] (Milan 1968, rist. integr. 1973) 228 f. (= *The Etruscans*, transl. J. Cremona, ed. D. Ridgway [London and Bloomington, Indiana, 1975] 134 f.). Still basic is Schulze, 263.

43. See Degrassi, *FCT*, or his *Fasti Capitolini* (Turin, etc., 1954 *Corpus scriptor. Lat. Paravianum*). I assume that these Capitoline Fasti, of the Augustan age, reproduce in respect to praenomina and titles the earlier lists on which they were based. (But see Broughton, below, n. 54).

44. Perhaps another cause of abbreviations (it has been suggested by a Reader) was the narrowness of the monthly columns in the calendars (apparently cut in stone, generally—see below, Appendix III). E.g., the Sept. and Oct. columns of the fragmentary Arval calendar (*Fasti Fratrum Arvalium*) are each 26–27 cm. (= ca. 10¼–10⅝ in.) wide (*Album* 1.20, col. 1, cf. Degrassi, *FANI* photo pl. iv, cf. p. 29, col. 1: 89 cm. the width of the whole fragment). The Sept. column has to accommodate 7 large letters in line 1 and 2 to 6 large ones plus a maximum of 23 to 28 small ones in the remaining lines (Degrassi, *FANI* 32–35). So every word that could be abbreviated was; e.g., for Sept. 23 the line reads: *B np Merk F ex s c q e d Imp Caesar Aug pont* (several interpuncts still visible).

problems, the dates of the earliest texts. As was noted above, the dates of all the pre-Imperial inscriptions (as well as those of the Empire, of course), except those that contain matter of historical or prosopographical bearing, are conjectural, despite the fact that they are often referred to, even by epigraphists,[45] as being of a particular period or century, without the addition of question marks. Sometimes the physical surroundings of an inscribed piece suggest a date based on archaeological grounds, as in the case of the Praenestine fibula, formerly dated chiefly by its (allegedly) belonging to the Bernardini Tomb (1). Until we get to the Scipionic epitaphs (one, 5), most of which can be given a *terminus post quem* by reference to the Scipios' careers as known from other sources, no Republican—much less pre-Republican—inscriptions can be dated except conjecturally. Sometimes an acephalous text, lacking the name of the subject (which was presumably cut on another stone, now lost), can be given a name conjecturally, though with some assurance, by study of the rest of the text, that is, by identifying the man through the facts of his career as outlined; for example, the incomplete elogium of Duilius (or Duillius, 54), the details of which fit no one but the G. Duilius who, as consul in 260 B.C., defeated the Carthaginians at Mylae. His last known date is 231, when he was dictator (as noted in the Capitoline Fasti for a.u.c. 522: Degrassi, *FCT*, pp. 44 f.); but the elogium in question—there is a briefer, more fragmentary, one also (*ILS* 55 add. = *CIL* 1²:1, p. 193, no. XI = 6.31611) of probably Augustan date—cannot possibly be as old as the third century B.C. because of the character of the writing (to judge from comparable, securely datable examples) and the kind of stone used—marble, which the evidence shows

was not in use in or near Rome for inscriptional purposes till about the last century B.C. (see above, II.2); it seems to be a copy, of disputed accuracy, of the early Empire. Another acephalous text, of less certain though probably satisfactory attribution, is **12**, which is unusual in being in the first person; after the missing name and perhaps the title "consul," it goes *viam fecei ab Regio ad Capuam*, "I built a road from Regium (Rhegium) to Capua," etc. Different problems are presented by the Arval Hymn, as is noted above, n. 23: a unique text of unquestionable antiquity (though how old, no one knows), but quoted in a larger text of A.D. 218, in writing so difficult to read and in language so archaic that the correct wording is uncertain at some places.

In these pre-Imperial inscriptions, few as they are in comparison with those of the Empire (Degrassi has only about 1,282 in his *ILLRP*), the three basic questions—Is it authentic?[46] What is the reading? What does it mean?—are complicated by other problems: identity of language (is it Latin?), archaic Latin, orthography (variant or mistaken spellings vs. changing forms). One of the most fruitful inscriptions for study in this connection is the *Senatus Consultum de Bacchanalibus* in bronze (**8**), in which there is no question of authenticity (it is guaranteed by Livy, 39.8–14, cf. Cic. *De Leg.* 2.15.37) or of date (it begins with the names of the consuls of 186 B.C.) or of reading (there seem to be only a few "typographical" mistakes, such as *sacanal* for *Ba-* or *iousisent* for *-set*—mistakes arising presumably from different causes), but which abounds in forms and language that call for comment and explanation, such as—to name only a few— *Duelonae* for classical *Bellonae*, *arf-* for *adf(uerunt)*, *Claudi* for *Claudius*, *quei* for (*eis*) *qui*, *esent*, *eeis* for *ei* (nom. pl.).[47] In-

45. See E. Badian's review of Degrassi's *Imagines*, *JRS* 58 (1968) 240–249.

46. The only piece in question in the present se-

lection is **1**, for which see the N.B. at the end of the annotation.

47. The best help on the forms that require expla-

deed, a careful reading of only Dessau's Chapter I, *Monumenta historica liberae rei publicae*, containing sixty-nine inscriptions, together with his few other *antiquissima*, is an education in itself: much of the early history of Rome and much of the pre-classical Latin language are on view. It is noteworthy how the inscriptions by their spelling show us pronunciation and changes in it: for example, such Greek names as "Pampilus" (which occurs in several Republican inscriptions, as does also "Pamphilus"—see Degrassi, *ILLRP*, vol. 2, p. 433) and, in the same inscription, "[Pil]adelpus" beside Φιλάδελφος in a bilingual of (as Degrassi argued) Sullan date (*ILLRP* 180, cf. pp. 114–117; *Imagines*, 89); or "baliat" apparently for "valeat" at Pompeii (*CIL* 4.4874, not after A.D. 79—cf. Pfister, p. 129, sect. 9, and *ILS*, indices, vol. 3:2, p. 809: B *pro* V) and "triumfator" for "triumphator" by the reign of Constantine (cf. *ILS*, indices, vol. 3:1, pp. 308, 310) and regularly by about A.D.

350 (Pfister, p. 29, Bem. 2, Anm. 3, *fin.*; *Album*, 3.322, line 5, cf. vol. 4.50 *s.v.* triumphator).

4. *Roman names*. Nomenclature, the commonest element in Latin inscriptions, is one of the most fascinating aspects of Roman society.[48] Its changes and developments, its aberrations and irregularities within generally fixed patterns, are illustrated throughout these texts. The names range from the simplest type, one name (in unofficial form),[49] to multiple forms and the development of the new inherited family-name; then a gradual return to simple forms, specially typical of the early Christian and Jewish names (and perhaps due to their influence),[50] and lasting (roughly) through the Middle Ages;[51] and finally a return to the inherited family-name in modern times.

The Roman names have been much studied, especially for their sociological implications. Tenney Frank's "Race Mix-

---

nation in reading Latin inscriptions of whatever date is still Sommer (of which a rev. ed. of the first part, *Einleitung* and *Lautlehre*, by Raimund Pfister, has recently appeared: Heidelberg 1977), though the grammatical indexes of *CIL*, *ILS*, and Degrassi's *ILLRP*, as well as their annotations of the texts, are also useful. Sommer's "Wortverzeichnis" is pretty reliable, and his inscriptional examples are printed in bold type. A fine line must often separate a variant form from a wrong one, and sometimes it may be impossible to distinguish between them with certainty. (See Appendix I for a list of the archaic and unusual forms found in these inscrs.)

48. For a brief account of Greek and Italic (mostly Roman) names, see T. J. C(adoux), *OCD* 720 f., *s.v.* Names, Personal, or Sandys/Campbell, 207–221. Plutarch, *Marius*, 1 *fin.*, remarks that "in these matters [i.e., Roman onomastics] the irregularity of custom furnishes many topics for discussion." To the bibl. cited by Ernst Fraenkel, "Die lateinischen Personennamen," *RE* 16: 2 (1935) 1648, 37 ff., *s.v.* Namenwesen, add A. E. Gordon, *Epigr.* I (1935); Julius Baumgart, *Die römischen Sklavennamen* (Breslau 1936 Diss. Breslau); Doer (1937); Thylander, Ch. II–III (pp. 54–185); Johann Reichmuth, *Die lateinischen Gentilicia u. ihre Beziehungen zu den röm. Individualnamen* (Schwyz 1956 Diss. Zurich); G. Susini, "Indicazioni dell'epigrafia per la storia romana di Classe," *Studi storici, topograf. ed archeol. sul 'Portus Augusti' di Ravenna . . .* (Ravenna 1961) 39–45; Weaver, esp. Part I, "Nomenclature and Chronol-

ogy," pp. 15–92, and his earlier papers, listed p. 318. Cf. also Degrassi, *Scritti vari*, 1.530 f., 533, 600, 658 f., 3.415 (index), *s.v.* onomastica, 4.503, *s.v. eadem*; *Epigraphica* 37 (1975) 286 f., with ref. to an international conference on Latin onomastics, Paris, Oct. 13–15, 1975.

49. "Varro simplicia in Italia nomina fuisse ait existimationisque suae argumentum refert quod Romulus et Remus et Faustulus neque praenomen ullum neque cognomen habuerint," begins the late Incertus Auctor of a brief *Liber de praenominibus*, etc., usually printed at the end of editions of Valerius Maximus (cf. Schanz/Hosius, 2⁴. 592f.). But, the Inc. Auctor continues, "Qui ab eo dissentiunt aiunt matrem eorum Ream Silviam vocatam, avum Silvium Numitorem, fratrem eius Amulium Silvium, . . . In hunc modum Varronis sententia subruitur. (2) Romanos autem arbitrandum est maxime ab Albanis et Sabinis multiplicandorum nominum consuetudinem traxisse quoniam ab illis orti sunt." The great modern work on the *origins* of the Latin proper names is still Schulze's (see Abbreviations).

50. See Diehl's indices of early Christian and Jewish names, *ILCV* 3.1–183, 184–190, 4.45–47.

51. But the poet Dante (1265–1321), though generally called simply "Dante," had a family name, "Alighieri" (variously spelled), by which I am told he was regularly named until he became famous; so also Michelangelo Buonarroti (1475–1564). Cf. "Leonardo da Vinci" (1452–1519), i.e., "L. from Vinci," a town near Florence.

ture in the Roman Empire" (*Amer. Hist. Rev.* 21 [1916] 689–708), Ch. XII ("The Plebs Urbana") of his *An Economic History of Rome*[2] (Baltimore 1927), Mary L. Gordon's "The Nationality of Slaves under the Early Roman Empire," *JRS* 14 (1924) 93–111, P. R. C. Weaver's *Familia Caesaris* (see Abbreviations), and Susan Treggiari's "Family Life Among the Staff of the Volusii," *TAPA* 105 (1975) 393–401, are among the many studies based on inscriptional evidence, especially for slaves and freedmen, whose names, often Greek or oriental in character, suggest place of origin.[52] Any Roman name is likely to reveal status and, within limits, date, even if the person named is otherwise unknown. A slave's or an ex-slave's name will be quite different from that of a freeborn person, a citizen's name from a non-citizen's (if his "tribal" connection is given), a simple Christian name from an earlier multiform pagan name. Some family-names are more common at one period than at another; e.g., *Iulii, Claudii, Flavii,* and *Aurelii* tend to be more abundant during and after the reigns of emperors with such names. Some names are frequent in Rome itself, others rare; the index of nomina of *CIL* 6 will show this. The Greek, oriental, Gallic, or Germanic character of many cognomina is often clear and may indicate the bearer's origin.

Our earliest *contemporary* inscriptional record of names, of perhaps the seventh to the fifth century B.C., **3**, shows an example of a single name, *Duenos*, which (if, in fact, it is a name, not a mere adjective), in its later, classical form, "Bonus," appears rarely as a cognomen.[53] But by the beginning of the Republic, official records, as attested by the Capitoline *Fasti Consulares* (the list of yearly consuls) of Augustan date (extant in their earliest fragments from 483 B.C.—Degrassi, *FCT* 1.24, 354),[54] supplemented by Livy and other sources, show the fully developed three-part masculine name, the *tria nomina* of the freeborn Roman (Juvenal, 5.127, cf. Plut. *Marius*, 1). This includes praenomen, nomen, and cognomen (e.g., "L. Iunius Brutus," "L. Tarquinius Collatinus," for the first consuls, named by Livy, 1.60 *fin.*) and additionally, in the Capitoline *Fasti*, the praenomen of the father and of the grandfather. All three praenomina are abbreviated by one or more initials, generally only one: e.g., *Sp(urius) Postumius A(uli) f(ilius) P(ubli) n(epos) Albus Regi[llens (is)]*, a consul of 466 B.C., whose name is the earliest one (almost) completely extant in the Capitoline Fasti (Degrassi, op. cit. 1.24, 358) and already shows two cognomina in use, the second (an agnomen, according to ancient definitions) undoubtedly honorary in character, to celebrate participation in the battle of Lake Regillus.[55]

Furthermore, the Capitoline *Fasti Triumphales* (the list of those who enjoyed an official "triumph" in Rome, down to 19 B.C.) show remains of the names of five of the legendary kings, from the first, *Romulus Martis f(ilius)*, to the last, *L(ucius) Tarqui[nius Prisci f.] Dama[rati n(epos) Superb(us)]* (1.64 f., 534 f.). This apparent development from a single name to three (or four) attested by the inscriptions cited

---

52. For Greek personal names in Rome, see Heikki Solin, *Beiträge zur Kenntnis der griech. Personennamen in Rom*, I (Helsinki/Helsingfors 1971 Soc. Scientiarum Fennica [*Commentationes Humanarum Litterarum*, 48]), pp. 165; cf. H. G. Pflaum, *REL* 51 (1973) 48–54, for a review. See also above, n. 27, for Solin's new work.

53. Hey, *TLL* 2.2127 (1906) *s.v.*; *ILS* 3: 1, 176 lists three examples of *Bonus* as a cognomen; the indices of *CIL* 6 (city of Rome), part 7, fasc. 5 (1975), p. 6285, have about seven examples, including one *Bona*. For *duenos→bonus*, see Pfister 94, B.

54. Degrassi, *FCT*. On the date, see 1.19 f., Gordon, *Album*, 1.24 on no. 9, Degrassi again, *Riv. di fil.* n.s. 37 (1959) 208 (*Scritti vari*, 4.288). Broughton cautions (vol. 1, p. XII *init.*): "The numerous cognomina and the complete genealogies [in the Capitoline *Fasti*] probably betray later revision in comparison with the simpler forms of the name in Livy."

55. This was apparently inherited from Postumius's (putative) father, A. Postumius Albus Regillensis, consul in 496: Broughton, 2.608, nos. *3, *5, *Suppl.* 85. For agnomina, see Doer, 68–73.

may be deceptive, since *Romulus Martis f.* is of doubtful historicity (to say the least) and *Duenos* is unofficial in character, not necessarily complete.[56] Our Scipionic example, **5**, shows the same multiple form of the masculine name, but some men continued to eschew cognomina; G. Marius, consul seven times 107–86 B.C., is a good example, as was noted by Plutarch, *Marius*, 1.1; Mark Antony, his father (called "Creticus" unofficially), and his grandfather (in our **14**) are others. Some Republican generals in the field substitute the honorary title *Imperator* ("Commander") for their own cognomen (**7, 9, 15**).

The full masculine name customary from about 160 B.C. on (according to L. R. Taylor, *VDRR* 168—see our **15**) includes also the *tribus* (commonly anglicized as "tribe") to which the man belonged (presumably to indicate his Roman citizenship)[57] and, in at least some official lists, his place of origin, in the ablative (**73**, a list of Roman *vigiles*). To save space (and work?) in the inscriptions, the name may be abbreviated in various ways: regularly by abbreviating the praenomen when it is followed by nomen or cognomen or both,[58] sometimes by shortening the nomen by dropping the final *-us* (**6, 15** lines 4 ff., and regularly in the *Fasti Antiates Maiores*,[59] but the omission of final S alone may reflect the actual pronunciation),[60] sometimes by shortening the cog-

nomen ("Valg." in **17**) or omitting it altogether (**15**, where they are all omitted to save space, while the *tribus* always appears, in short form, and **20**, *Gn. Pompeio, cos. tert.*, without *Magno*). Sometimes, when a man's cognomen was unusual or well known or confined to a single family, it might be used alone or with the praenomen, such as *Hirrus*, **14** (here perhaps *metri causa*), *M. Agrippa*, **25, 26, 58** (apparently the regular form),[61] *Caesar*.

The multiplication of praenomina, nomina, and cognomina in a single name reaches its peak in the case of Q. Pompeius . . . Sosius Priscus, consul A.D. 169, who in an honorary inscription seen by Dessau at Tivoli (anc. Tibur) is given a total of thirty-eight names, including multiple praenomina and nomina as well as cognomina, many (but apparently not all) taken from his ancestors: *CIL* 14.3609 (= *ILS* 1104—see Dessau's notes; cf. G. Susini, in *Mélanges . . . André Piganiol* [Paris 1966] 289–299). This inscription was once thought to refer to many different men. The responsibility for the tour de force must rest with the "Senate and People of Tibur," who set it up. Our own **59** gives the name of A. Platorius A. f. Serg. Nepos Aponius Italicus Manilianus G. Licinius Pollio, on whom see *JRS* 48 (1958) 47 f., where it is conjectured that "his original name had been 'G. Licinius Pollio,' but that he was adopted by one

---

56. See above, n. 49, for Varro's secondhand testimony, which seems probably true, as it was true of Greek (and the normal Indo-European) personal names except the later romanized ones of Greeks in Roman government-service; e.g., *Ael(ius) Antipater*, a sophist and Greek secretary (*ab epistulis Graecis*) of the emperor Septimius Severus, etc. (*PIR*[2] 1.21 no. 137), and other Greeks with *multiple* cognomina. Chase, however, 161, shows that the Incertus Auctor of n. 49 is not reliable in his reff. to Varro and used mainly other authorities.

57. The *Lex Acilia* (?) *Repetundarum* of 123 or 122 B.C. provided that the panel of 450 jurymen should be listed by their *nomina*, plus *patrem, tribum cognomenque* (these three singulars seem to show that only one *nomen* was expected from each man) (*CIL* 1[2]: 2.583, p. 447, XIV); and the so-called *Lex Iulia Municipalis* of ca. 45 B.C. provided that the Roman

citizens listed by the censor should be listed by their *nomina, praenomina, patres aut patronos, tribus, cognomina* (*CIL* 1[2]: 2. 593, p. 485 [= *ILS* 6085 add.], lines 143–146; on the date, cf. G. Barbieri, in De Rugg. 4: 23 [1956] 725).

58. It has been noted how unusual the name of the emperor Septimius Severus is on his famous arch in the Roman Forum (**73**), in having "Lucio" in full at first mention; it is later "L." in the same inscr. Note also *fil.* twice, for the more usual *f.*

59. Degrassi, *FCT* 1.160–165.

60. Pfister 221 f., 5; cf. Sturtevant 161 f., §186.

61. According to Seneca the Elder, *Controv.* 2.4.13, Agrippa had been Vipsanius Agrippa, but the name "Vipsanius," as a sign of his father's humble origin, he had got rid of and was called "M. Agrippa." Cf. Syme, *Rom. Rev.* 129 with n. 3.

A. Platorius . . . Manilianus (whose name also looks like the result of adoption at some stage) and took Platorius' name, adding at the end of it his own original name for formal completeness, as normal at this period." (For the effects of adoption on names, see Doer, 74–95, and *AJP* 72 [1951] 284 f.) It has been pointed out that polyonymy, the use of many names by one person, may also be due to the desire to preserve the record of the mother's side of the family. Etruscan epitaphs sometimes record the mother's name (Pallottino, op. cit. [above, n. 42] 233. Dessau, *ILS* 3:2, p. 924, lists 14 inscrs. [actually 21] that include the mother's name, plus five in curse tablets).

The cognomen, being descriptive (like *Naso*), honorary (like *Magnus*), or family-derived (like *Agrippina* from *Agrippa*),[62] is the most personal of the names (when used) and the one by which a man or a woman (if she has one) seems generally to be called or referred to; but, being also inheritable by a descendant, it applied directly, as a description, only to the first one bearing it and often became the distinguishing mark of a whole branch of a larger *gens* or family/clan, such as the Cornelii Scipiones. Cicero's cognomen, for example, came from some ancestor who, "as it seems, had a slight dent at the end of his nose like the cleft of a chick-pea, from which he acquired his cognomen," *cicer* being the Latin for "chick-pea." Cicero could have dropped or changed the name, but chose to keep it (so Plutarch, *Cic.* 1.2 f). His brother, Quintus, had the same cognomen, and each man had a son whose name was the same as his father's (Cicero's wife and daughter, according to custom, were simply called "Terentia"

and "Tullia," resp., the feminine form of each nomen). In his letters Cicero seems generally to call and refer to his son as "Cicero," as he thus refers to Atticus, Brutus, Caesar, Varro, and other well-known men, sometimes with the praenomen in addition.[63] Only when it is necessary for identification or on first acquaintance does the nomen seem to be used; and, conjecturally, only in the case of brothers or male cousins who had no cognomina would the praenomina be used alone, in order to distinguish one from the other. If Quintus had had a daughter, how she would have been distinguished from Cicero's Tullia, if they were together, remains a question; otherwise, presumably, they would have been referred to by the addition of *Marci* or *Quinti* (*filia*), or, later, the husband's name in the genitive. The acquisition of a cognomen can sometimes be actually witnessed: e.g., Sulla's *Felix* and Pompey's *Magnus* (see note on **16**). Sometimes scholars are not agreed as to whether a particular cognomen is a regular, formal cognomen or an informal one, used perhaps to distinguish one person from another of the same name and period, as in **26** (*Augur* and *Epulo*, for example, are sometimes cognomina, sometimes titles); there are also examples of *pater* and *filius*, *senior* and *iunior*, used to distinguish father and son when added to preceding names: *f(ilius)* in our **54**, *iunior* in **100**. Sometimes a cognomen was played with, in punning fashion: the emperor Marcus Aurelius is said to have been called *Verissimus* by Hadrian, from his original cognomen *Verus* before his adoption by Antoninus Pius (*PIR*² 1.119 f.).[64]

The number of praenomina in general

---

62. The big study of cognomina is Kajanto's (see Abbreviations). See also A. E. Douglas, "Roman *Cognomina*," *Greece & Rome*, ser. 2: 5 (1958) 62–66; Weaver, 87–90.

63. For Pliny the Younger's use of Roman names, see A. N. Sherwin-White's ed. of *The Letters of Pliny* . . . (Oxford 1966) 113: a single name if it was

thought to be clear; if not, commonly nomen and cognomen, sometimes praenomen and nomen, rarely praenomen and cognomen, never the three names.

64. See V. J. Mathews, "Some Puns on Latin *Cognomina*," *Greece & Rome*, ser. 2: 20 (1973) 20–24.

use, in the classical period, was quite restricted, seventeen in all,[65] of which only about half continued to be commonly used; but many more were occasionally used, though most were given up early. The earliest such example in the Capitoline Fasti is *Agrippa* in *Agrippa M[enenius C. f.—n. Lan]atus*, who "triumphed" in 503 B.C. (Degrassi, *FCT* 1.64 f.; his full name, except his grandfather's praenomen, is known from other sources, 350 f.). There was a resurgence, in the late Republic and the Augustan age, of such unusual praenomina as *Potitus* (*Valerius Messalla*, consul suffect 29 B.C.) and *Iullus* (*Antonius*, Mark Antony's second son, consul 10 B.C.).[66]

The *special Roman contribution* to the history of personal names is the development of the inherited family-name (above, IV.2, with n. 42) and the spreading of it all over the Empire, especially the western part, where after gradual loss and centuries-long disappearance it was destined to return and become again the foundation of modern Western nomenclature.[67] The praenomen, very probably the earliest in origin, was also the earliest to disappear. The creation of *Imperator* as a new praenomen for the emperors was due to Augustus, who thus, having acquired *Caesar* from Julius Caesar by testamentary adoption and *Augustus* as an honorary cognomen from the Senate in 27 B.C. (**34**, *Res Gestae*, 34.2; Suet. *Aug.* 7.2), kept the *tria nomina* (*Imp. Caes. Aug.*, as often abbreviated) characteristic of Roman citizens.[68] These three names, or ti-

---

65. A (Aulus), AP (Appius), C (Gaius), CN (Gnaeus), D (Decimus), L (Lucius), M (Marcus), /VV (Manius), N (Numerius), P (Publius), Q (Quintus), SER (Servius or Sergius, the latter dating from the Empire, according to Cagnat, 41, n. 2), SEX (Sextus), S or SP (Spurius), T (Titus), TI or TIB (Tiberius), V (Vibius). In C and CN the C is the early form of G (from Greek gamma) before it developed its distinguishing second stroke, but in these two abbreviations it continued to be the usual form. In modern usage, however, G. and Gn. seem preferable to C. and Cn. since the sound represented is G; the spellings "Caius" and "Cnaeus," sometimes seen, are erroneous. The initial form of "Manius" is generally printed "M'." See Chase, who includes sections on the Indo-European name, Latin names, Latin cognomina, Latin *gentilicia* (family names), and women's praenomina (and cognomina), based on both literary and inscriptional sources.

66. Cagnat, 42, lists 48 praenomina that were mostly soon given up. "Potitus," originally no doubt the man's second cognomen (or agnomen), was apparently substituted for his original praenomen, "Manius," after his quaestorship (see **32**). Dessau, *ILS* 3: 2, 922 f., has a list of *Praenomina rara vel obsoleta vel peregrina* and of *Praenomina nobilium postremis liberae reipublicae et Augusti temporibus* (*vetus familiae cognomen loco praenominis adhibitum*). Cf. our own not uncommon use of earlier family-names as first ("Christian") names; e.g., "Brooks Adams" (from his mother), "Johns Hopkins" (from his great-great-grandfather), "Carey Thomas" (originally "Martha Carey Thomas," "Carey" being her father's middle name).

67. Except in Iceland, Norway (till the time of Ibsen), and Sweden (till the late 18th cent.), where the patronymic form (e.g., Norwegian "Sven Svensen," i.e., "Sven son of Sven") persisted until the development of the inherited family-name (above, IV.2, with n. 42) and the times indicated (my informant is James L. Larson, with ref. to A. Janzén, "Personnamn" and "De fornvästnordiska personnamnen," *Nordisk Kultur*, 7 [Stockholm, etc., 1947] 1–4, 22–186, and the art. "Personnamn" in *Svensk Uppslagsbok*, 22 [Malmö 1952] 838–842). It still persists in Iceland, where the telephone directory, because of its way of listing names under the first ("Christian") element, is said to be startling to those not used to it. See also Ved Mehta, *Mahatma Gandhi and His Apostles* (New York 1976) 72 f., on the origin of Hindu names under the English rule (they were needed for the records of those employed by the English), and Charles Hillinger's words about the origin of the surnames of the many Sikhs who live, mostly as farmers, in and around Yuba City, California, in the *San Francisco Sunday Examiner & Chronicle*, Sunday Punch, Feb. 6, 1977.

68. It is true that Suetonius, *Iul.* 76.1, lists among the honors accepted by Julius Caesar the *praenomen Imperatoris* (so also Dio, 43.44.2 ff., 52.41.3), but the Fasti Triumphales, sufficiently extant from 45 to 34 B.C. without a break, name Caesar's heir as the first one to use *Imp.* as a praenomen (for the year 40, *Imp. Caesar divi f.*: Degrassi *FCT* 1.86 f.), and neither the Fasti Consulares (sufficiently extant from 49 to 44: ibid. 56–59) nor the F. Triumphales give *Imp.* to Caesar. Cf. Syme, "Imperator Caesar: A Study in Nomenclature," *Historia* 7 (1958) 172–188; Combès, 123–135. For the conflict of testimony between Suetonius/Dio and the inscrs./coins with ref. to Tiberius, Claudius, and Nero, and their use of *Imperator* as a praenomen, see *PIR*[2] 2.224 f., 227 f., and 3.37. (For knowledge of this problem, thanks are due to Kevin K. Carroll, who learned of it in studying the Greek bronze-letter inscr., of A.D. 61/62, in honor of Nero, attached to the east architrave of the Parthenon [IG 2²:3:1 (1935) 92, no. 3277].) ". . . attached

tles, remained the distinctive feature of nearly all the Roman emperors for centuries, the last part to survive in ancient times being *Augustus*, *Caesar* being still given, however, by some of the later emperors, to the "heir(s) apparent," while *Imperator* came to mean "Emperor" (already in Nepos)[69] and *Caesar* eventually became both "Kaiser" and "Czar" (or "Tsar"). But in common usage the praenomen can be seen to be disappearing by late in the second Christian century—to take only our present texts. In **69**, for example, of A.D. 193, which consists of three official letters, there are five or six officials named, none with a praenomen, besides the two consuls of the date mentioned (whose names in the inscriptions are often reduced to mere cognomina), an Imperial freedman, and a servant (who also have only a cognomen). In **75**, of A.D. 218, one of the many extant Arval records, the praenomen is never present (and the nomen is more often abbreviated than not). In **78**, of A.D. 260, only one of the two consuls' names used in the date and the two officers of the *collegium* have a praenomen; the other seventeen men have none.[70]

The nomen also suffers. We begin to see such abbreviations as *Ael(ius)* (**64**, of A.D. 149), *Fl(avius)* (**66**, of 153), *Cl(audius)* (**69**, of ca. 194), and by A.D. 383 (**91**) the three Christians named have no nomen or praenomen, but only a cognomen each (one, *Proiecta*, an example of the humble or pejorative type of Christian name, like *Stercorius* or *Calumniosus*, **99**—see Kajanto, 70, 287, with ref. to his earlier paper of 1962 on "Names of Humility"), while the consuls lack praenomen and have only *Fl.* for the nomen.

Only the aristocrats manage to keep the old three-part form. From about A.D. 295, only five (two of the same person) out of thirty-six non-Imperial names that appear in **80–100** show three (once four) names: *L. Cornelius Scipio Orfitus*, a pagan senator (**80**, probably of ca. 295), *G. Caelius Saturninus*, with signum (or supernomen) *Dogmatius*, a distinguished equestrian official, and his son, *G. Fl. Caelius Urbanus*, (**84**, probably 326–337), *L. (or Lucius) Aur(elius) Avianius Symmachus*, once called *Phosphorius*, pagan father of the great orator and letter-writer Symmachus (**88** f., probably of 365/67 and 377, resp.). (Note the double-barreled nomen in -*ius*, of two of these, not uncommon since the first Christian century).[71]

---

bronze letters were themselves a late development, almost sure to be Roman. Earlier, the Greeks would have carved the letters in the marble," S. Dow, "Andrews of Cornell," *Cornell Alumni News*, Dec. 1972, p. 16. For bronze-letter inscrs., see Hans Volkmann, *Gymnasium* 74 (1967) 504, n. 17.

69. Nepos, *Att.* 19.2 (before Octavian became *Augustus* in 27 B.C.): Atticus, *contentus ordine equestri quo erat ortus, in adfinitatem pervenit imperatoris, divi filii* . . . (through Atticus's granddaughter, Vipsania Agrippina, cf. 19.4).

70. But in a bronze tablet from Banasa in Mauretania Tingitana, the names of all twelve members of the Imperial council are given in full, including praenomen, filiation, and "tribe," in an inscr. of A.D. 177 (*AE* 1971, 534, pp. 186–188). CIL 6.266 (= Bruns 406 f., no. 188 = *FIRA* 3.510–513, no. 165), *Lis fullonum de pensione non solvenda*, A.D. 244, contains three types of name plus the consuls' names at the end; e.g., P. Clodius Fortunatus, Aelius Florianus, Modestinus.

71. Presumably as a result of adoption or appropriating ancestral names. For the most convenient list of men's names in chronological order from 30 B.C. to A.D. 613, see Degrassi's list of the consuls and consuls-suffect in his *FC*. The earliest example of two nomina in these names is G. Silius A. Caecina Largus of A.D. 13, where S. Panciera, *Bull. Com.* 79 (1963–64, publ. 1966) 94–98, shows that the Gordons, though supported by R. Syme, *JRS* 56 (1966) 55–60, were wrong in arguing (*AJP* 72 [1951] 283–292) that these names belonged to two men. (*Caecina* is a nomen, like *Silius*.) Sometimes the nomina are separated by a cognomen, as in *L. Livius Ocella Sulpicius Galba*, A.D. 33. Good 2nd-cent. examples among women are found in the four daughters of the twelve children of the emperor Marcus Aurelius and Faustina the Younger: two have three nomina and one cognomen apiece, the nomina being differently arranged and the cognomen different in the two names; a third daughter has one nomen and one cognomen, the nomen different from the other two. For the fourth girl, only a cognomen is reported, different from the other three. All these nomina and cognomina are clearly ancestral in origin. See the stemma at the end of *PIR²* vol. 1. For

Twelve more, from A.D. 338 to 525, have no praenomen, but several other names, of varying types, seem strange, as of a new age; see **85, 95–97, 100.**

The last step in the later history of Roman names is the latinization of many medieval and modern names of the authors of books written or printed in Latin, down to and beyond the Renaissance, such as Nicolaus Copernicus, Polish (or Prussian) astronomer (1473–1543), founder of modern astronomy, Agricola (a translation of Georg "Bauer," 1490–1555, founder of mineralogy), Linnaeus, Swedish botanist and taxonomist (Carl von Linné, 1707–1778), Ferdinand Gregorovius, German historian (1821–1891), Jean Sibelius, Finnish composer (1865–1957), Axel Boëthius, the late Swedish classicist, and Schnell–> Snellius–>Snell.[72]

Women, slaves, and freedmen, especially Imperial slaves and freedmen, and, most striking of all, the emperors themselves, have their own name-systems. Whatever the origins, freeborn Roman women in the historical period had essentially only one name, their father's nomen in feminine form (which was not lost by marriage or exchanged for the husband's name).[73] I quote Chase, 159 f.:

"In the classical literature of Rome women are not designated by any praenomen. In republican times the commonest form of designation was the gentile name alone, as *Caesennia* (Cic. *pro Caec.* 10). . . . When this was insufficient to indicate the individual, the name of the husband or nearest male relative, or some term of relationship was added, as *Anniae C. Anni*

senatoris [filiae], Cic *Verr*. i, 153. . . . Sometimes an adjective from the place of birth was added, as *Numitoria Fregellana*, Cic. *Phil*. iii, 17. These women seem to have had no other name in either official or familiar use. Cicero always calls his daughter *Tullia*, or . . . , he makes a pet diminutive, *Tulliola*.

"Occasionally we meet with cognomina in the republican period, as *Aurelia Orestilla*, Sall. *Cat*. 15, 2. . . . Oftener such women are mentioned by their cognomina alone, as *Orestilla*, Sall. *Cat*. 35, 36. . . . In speaking of Atticus' daughter, Cicero sometimes calls her *Caecilia* . . . , sometimes *Attica* . . . , and once *Atticula*. . . . Thus we see from such cognomina as *Attica, Metella, Lepida*, etc., that an additional name might readily be made from the father's cognomen. [See below for such names as Drusilla.]

"Under the empire we find much the same state of affairs, except that there is a notable increase in the use of cognomina. . . .

"From the evidence of the use of names in literature there is little to lead us to suppose that Roman women ever had praenomina."

Chase then (160 f.) quotes and discusses Varro's remarks on women's praenomina (*L. L.* 9.60 f.) and those of the Incertus Auctor (of n. 49, above). "For further light we must turn to our collection of Roman [i.e., Latin] inscriptions."

Before turning to Degrassi's Republican evidence, let us note that scholars often differentiate one girl from another in a family by *maior* ("older") and *minor* ("younger"), as Octavia *maior* (half-sister

---

signa and supernomina, see Doer, 179–201; e.g., *Dogmatius*, 187 (where *Phosphorius*, "Light-Bringer," also should be listed).

There are also examples of the "also-known-as" type of name. *ILS* 3: 2, 927 f., lists 23 of the type *Seleucus Hermocratus qui et Diogenes* or *Iulia Cleopatra quae et Lezbia* (sic), this the name of a naval officer's wife from Syrian Antioch (several inscrs. complete the *qui* clause with *vocatur, vocitatur,* or *vocitatus est*), and nine of the type *Aemilius Epictetus sive Hedonius*

(of a Greek *grammaticus* in NE Gaul) or *Clodia Achillea sive Cyryle*. All these names belong to men or women of apparently modest circumstances.

72. This is Prof. Bruno Snell's account of his own name, from the original German "Schnell," orally in reply to the question why "Snell," not "Schnell."

73. E.g., for the commonest form, *Annius, Annia*; for the others, *Annienus, -na, Betilienus, -na, Caecina* (masc.), *Caecinia*.

of Augustus) and *minor* (his sister-german, Mark Antony's fourth wife), but how they were actually called except by the addition of their mothers' names (Ancharia and Atia, resp.—they had the same father, G. Octavius, praetor 61 B.C.) is not clear; apparently they had no cognomina; in her epitaph (our **24**) Octavia *minor* is simply called *Octavia C. f., soror Augusti Caesaris*. She herself had two daughters by the M. Claudius Marcellus lamented by Vergil and Propertius, each named (*Claudia*) *Marcella*, one called *maior* (who married Agrippa), the other *minor*. Our Caecilia Metella, **23**, also has as cognomen the feminine form of her father's cognomen. There seems to have been almost as much variation in women's names as in men's, the simplest being between cognomen and no cognomen.

For the Republican period, Degrassi's indices, *ILLRP* 2.487 f., while by no means perfectly accurate, give a good view. His *Nomina mulierum* include about a dozen types, the essential name (present all but once) being the family or gentile name (*nomen gentilicium*) in feminine form (e.g., *Claudia*). This type seems to be the most numerous, but it may be modified in various ways, which may well reflect regional features, as in the many names reported from Praeneste (*CIL* 1²: 2.64–357, Degr. 2.843–872), conjecturally from ca. 250 (Degrassi, following Vetter) to ca. 100 B.C. The nomen may be followed by some form of filiation. This may be the father's praenomen (in the genitive, plus *f(ilia)*—in full, if unusual, or, as is usual, abbreviated—e.g., *Helvia Mesi f(ilia)*, *Servia G(ai) f.*); or his cognomen—e.g., *Cornelia Africani f.* (Africanus was the famous P. Cornelius Scipio Africanus, conqueror of Hannibal, "Africanus" being an honorary second cognomen); or both praenomen and cognomen—e.g., *[Corn]elia L(uci) Scipion[is f.]*. Once, only the woman's cognomen is given, plus the father's cognomen (*Medella Dasm(i) f.*, at Canusium, mod. Canosa, 67 B.C.), and once

two cognomina, without nomen (*Lucilla Fortunata*).

There are also a few examples of a woman's praenomen plus nomen, with or without filiation—e.g., *L(ucia) Cornelia L. f.*, *M(ania) Curia*; a few more of two nomina, the second thought to be borrowed from the husband—e.g., *Agria Sueia N(umeri) f.* In twenty-four cases the woman's nomen is preceded by a cognomen, as if it were a praenomen—e.g., *Pola Livia*, *Polla Minucia Q(uinti) f.* Two of these women, both from Venetic Ateste (mod. Este), have also a cognomen at the end of their names, thought by some to be derived from their husbands' nomen: *Tertia Crumel*[written *e*]*onia Turstiaca* (from *Turstius*?), *Frema Rutilia P(ubli) f. Sociaca* (from *Socius*?). Three have names in which the husband's name is indicated by his praenomen only—e.g., *Luscia M(arci) uxor*, *Samiaria M. f. minor Q(uinti) (uxor)*.

In general, if a woman's name includes any additional element, it is much more likely to be her father's name than her husband's. It is surprising, in fact, how few examples there are, from the whole Roman period, of a woman's name that includes her husband's name in any form, as is shown by Dessau's index of names, *ILS* 3:1, pp. 1–162; this index, however, does not always include the husband's name even though it is actually given in the inscription—e.g., for Herennia M. f. Helvidia Aemiliana, whose name in Dessau's no. 1013 has at the end *L. Claudi Proculi Corneliani co(n)s(ulis) (uxor)*, and *Verania Q. Verani cos., aug(uris), f., Gemina*, whose name in his no. 240 has *Pisonis Frugi (uxor)* at the end. Note that, while the abbreviation *f(ilia)* is always, or nearly always, given when the father's name appears—for one possible exception, see the epitaph of Agrippina the Elder, **39**—the word *uxor* seems as often omitted as present when the husband's name appears.

For the whole ancient period, but mostly for the Empire, Dessau's index of nomina (3:1, pp. 1–162) and his "Nominum ratio" (3:2, pp. 921–929) are informative. A good example of the names of sisters is provided by the family of the emperor Marcus Aurelius and his wife (Annia Galeria) Faustina the Younger (see n. 71). Two earlier interesting cases are the daughters of Germanicus and of the emperor Claudius. Each had three. Those of the former and his wife Agrippina the Elder (daughter of Agrippa and Augustus's daughter Julia) were Agrippina the Younger (mother of the emperor Nero), Drusilla (whose name obviously derives from her grandfather, Drusus), and Julia Livilla (whose cognomen must be a diminutive of the name of Augustus's wife Livia).[74] (They all presumably had *Iulia* as a nomen.) Claudius's three daughters were Claudia, Antonia (so named, presumably, from his mother, Antonia *minor*, a daughter of Mark Antony), and Claudia Octavia, generally called "Octavia," from her great-grandmother, Augustus's sister-german. Apparently, "Octavia," though in form another nomen, was preferred to a derivative such as *Octaviana*, like *Agrippina* from *Agrippa*.

These names show about as much freedom as the men's names except that as a rule women used no praenomina,[75] though there seems to have been no law against it.

Slaves' names also underwent development. Our present hundred texts show only a few such: **37** *Scirtus*, a charioteer (probably a slave, ca. A.D. 25), **53** *Callistus Rutili Lupi* (*servus*), **64** *Yacinthus verna suus* (belonging to an Imperial freedman), **69** *Epaphroditus suus* (belonging to three or four men), and **71** *Anamurius ver(na)*, one of the *paedagogi puerorum* of the Imperial school for pages at the Caput Africae in Rome (A.D. 198). In the first, an epitaph, there is no mention of his status, but only a record of all his chariot races from A.D. 13 to 25 (the woman who is evidently his widow was an ex-slave herself). In the second, slave status is indicated only by the genitive of the master's name, just as the status of wife requires only the husband's name in the genitive (as in **23**). *Verna* here indicates a slave born in the household, although in some cases it means a native of a particular place.[76]

But there are traces of an earlier nomenclature: Degr.2.913 (= *CIL* 1^2.1358, *ILS* 7822), M. *Pinari(us) P(ubli) l(ibertus) Marpor*, of a freedman named *Marcus Pinarius Marpor*, former slave of *Publius* (*Pinarius*), whose slave-name had been *Marpor*. This looks like a development of *Marcipor*, which, in the plural form *Marcipores*, is joined with *Lucipores* by Pliny the Elder (33.6.26) as examples from the good old days, "when a single servant for each master, a member of his master's clan, Marcus' boy or Lucius' boy, took all his meals with the family in common."[77] As Rackham's translation suggests, these names seem derived from *Marci* and *Luci puer*. Other epigraphically attested cognomina in -*por*, which apparently have

---

74. Said to be far more productive (though much rarer in Latin) for the Romance languages (except Rumanian) than such feminine diminutives as *Domitilla, Drusilla, Livilla, Lucilla,* and *Priscilla* (all listed in *ILS* and several in Diehl, 3, index of nomina, who also has *Donatilla* and some other acephalous -*illa* names, p. 191) was the -*itta* type (of Etruscan origin?) exemplified by *Gallitta, Iulitta, Pollitta,* and *Sagitta* (all belonging to women in *ILS* except the last, which is held by three men), whence the French suffix -*et,* -*ette*. Cf. W. D. Elcock, *The Romance Languages* (London 1960) 159, n. 1. D. C. Swanson, *The Names in Roman Verse* (cited above, n. 35) lists eighteen names ending in -*illa* (p. 357, col. 1) that seem to belong to women, *Camilla* being probably the best known.

75. As was noted above, Degrassi's "Ratio Nominum" in his indices contains a section on women's names, including praenomina (*ILLRP* 2, p. 487); Dessau's corresponding section is *ILS* 3: 2, 924 f. See also Chase, 159–180.

76. Cf. Degrassi, *Latomus* 24 (1965) 352 (*Scritti vari*, 3.309), with ref. to Dessau, *ILS* 3: 2, 949, and C. G. Starr, *CP* 37 (1942) 314–317. *CIL* 6 alone has almost 400 examples of *verna* from Rome itself (part 7, fasc. 5 [1975], *s.v.*).

77. Rackham's Loeb Libr. transl. (Pliny, *Nat. Hist.* vol. 9 [1952] 23) of *Aliter apud antiquos singuli Mar-*

the same origin as *Marpor* and *Lucipor*, are *Gaipor*, *Naepor*, and *Olipor*. The first occurs in *CIL* 1².996, *P. Cornelius P. l. Gaipor* (the rest is of uncertain meaning; not in *ILS* or *ILLRP*), the second, ibid. 1342, *L.* (?) *l(iberti*[?]) *Naepori* (genitive? not in *ILS* or *ILLRP*), the last, ibid. 1263 (= *ILS* 4405, *ILLRP* 159), *A. Caecili(us) A. l. Olipor* (the I in Olipor is tall, as though to mark it long),[78] and 2046 (= *ILS* 7823), *G. Socconius G. l. Olipor*. These four men, like *Marpor* above, seem all to be freedmen, and *Gaipor*, *Naepor*, and *Olipor* their slave-names (the last, no doubt, from *Auli-por*). To these inscriptional examples, which their editors (Dessau, Leumann, Degrassi) seem to accept as derivatives of *puer* in the sense of "(young) slave" (cf. French *garçon*), Marquardt added *Quintipor* from Festus (who cites also *Marcipor* and *Gaipor*, the latter as corrected from *Gripor*)[79] and *Publipor* from Quintilian and Priscian.[80] This derivation from *puer*, attested by Priscian quoting Probus, and the development of *Marcipor* to *Marpor*, suggested by several Republican inscriptions, seem plausible and are generally accepted not only by epigraphists but by philologists as well.[81]

But it leaves us at a stage in socioeco-nomic history when a family had only one slave, so that he could be called "Marcus's boy" (or similarly) without a real name of his own to distinguish him from other slaves. At this point we note Degrassi's first three examples of slaves, Degr.2, p. 422, sect. II: *Abennaeus*, *Acastus*, and *Acerd(o?)*, which are all of non-Latin origin.[82] (In fact, nearly all of Degrassi's slaves listed under A in his index of cognomina, etc. [op. cit. 422–425], seem to have Greek names, the commonest being *Alexander*, *Antiochus*, and *Apollonius*.) But, if Mommsen was right in concluding from inscriptional evidence that the cognomina of freedmen did not begin to appear in writing before about 100 B.C., as was confirmed in a later study,[83] there must have been a stage before this (approximate) date when there was some other means of indicating the freedmen's (and slaves') names, and this we find by examining Degrassi's index of Republican "Nomina Gentilicia" (op. cit. 2, pp. 379–422). Here we find about ninety-seven freedmen without cognomen, as *T(itus) Acilius L(uci) l(ibertus)*, from which it is clear that, as a slave, he must have been called *Titus*. Furthermore, in the great majority of cases (in the proportion of about 3 to 1)

---

cipores Luciporesve dominorum gentiles omnem victum in promiscuo habebant . . .

78. Cf. G. Paci, *Epigraphica* 38 (1976) 120–125, with photos. The long I in *Olipor*, the present writer has been informed, "probably indicated word accent with enclitic *por*."

79. Joachim Marquardt, *Das Privatleben der Römer*, 1² (ed. A. Mau, Leipzig 1886, *Handb. der röm. Alterthümer* by Marquardt and Th. Mommsen, 7: 1) 19 f.

80. Festus, p. 306, lines 17–21, L: *Quintipor servile nomen frequens aput* (sic) *antiquos erat, a praenomine domini ductum, ut Marcipor, Gaipor* (corrected from *Gripor*); *quamvis sint qui a numero natorum ex ancilla quinto loco dictum putent*; Paulus's *Excerpta*, Festus (p. 307, 6 f.) read, after "Marcipor," *scilicet a Quinto et Marco*. Quintilian, 1.4.26: *In servis iam intercidit illud genus* (sc. *nominum*) *quod ducebatur a domino, unde* Marcipores Publiporesque, transl. Butler (Loeb Libr. 1.75), "Further there are obsolete slave-names such as *Marcipor* or *Publipor* (fn. 2: i.e., *Marcipuer*, *Publipuer*) derived from the names of their owners." Priscian, *Inst. Gramm.*, in Keil, 2.236.11–15. So also

Probus, ed. Keil, 4.16.16–18, quoting Sallust. (Priscian quotes both Probus and Sallust.)

81. Cf. Marquardt, loc. cit. (above, n. 79); Mommsen, *Röm. Staatsr.* 3: 1³ (Leipzig 1887, repr. Basel 1952) 201, n. 3; A. Oxé, "Zur älteren Nomenklatur der röm. Sklaven," *Rhein. Mus.* N.F. 59 (1904) 108; K/H 1. 123, 134; Sommer, 160, 365; Leumann, 114, cf. 252, 260; E. Fraenkel, op. cit. (above, n. 48) 1665, 5 ff.; W/H 2.382; E/M 543, *s.v.* puer ("peut-etre," and they think *Naepor* Etruscan; but W/H call it "ins Etrusk. . . . entlehnt," or at least "nicht echt etrusk."; it seems derived from **(G)nae(v)i-por*: cf. Felix Solmsen, *Studien zur latein. Lautgesch.* [Strassburg 1894] 103, and *Indogerm. Forsch.* 31 [1912/13] 476–478, and Schulze, 513, *init.*).

82. *Abennaeus* is derived by Kajanto, 166, from a "gent(ilicium) *Abenna*," following Otto in *TLL* 1 (1905) 49, 63–74, *s.v.* Abbius, who calls *Abenna* a *nom(en) gent. Etruscorum more fictum* and cites some inscriptional examples. *Acastus* and *Acerdo* seem to be Greek.

83. Gordon, *Epigr.* 1.

the freedman's praenomen, hence also the slave's, is different from his master's, presumably by intention.[84] There are only two freedwomen, *Plaria T(iti) l(iberta)* and *Quinctia T. l.*, but in the former case a praenomen beginning with A—the rest is lost by damage—is thought to have preceded *Plaria*. Here (Degr.93 a, *Imag.* 42 a-b = *AE* 1953, no. 195, which Degrassi dated shortly before 211 B.C. by reference to Hannibal's pillaging the temple at Lucus Feroniae in that year: Livy, 26. 11.8–10) the woman was no doubt called by her praenomen, if she had one; if not, by the name *Plaria* (as also *Quinctia* in the other example), like a daughter of the family, while any daughter or daughters might use a cognomen for distinction from the slave-girl. In the case of the seventeen freedmen with praenomen the same as that of their former masters, the sameness presumably made no difference: it would ordinarily be clear enough whether master or slave was meant when the praenomen was used, and, if necessary, the master could be called or referred to by his nomen or cognomen, or by *dominus*.

The slaves' names, which became their cognomina after manumission, when they took their masters' nomen and praenomen (such as *T. Sulpicius T. l(ibertus)* ["freedman"] *Primus*), were of diverse origins, like the cognomina of freeborn persons, but likely to be more indicative of humble status, by being foreign or descriptive of qualities desirable in servants. For example, of the 39 certain cognomina of freedmen and -women represented in the present selection (which includes 463 personal names excluding the emperors and their families) and (quite by chance) exactly the same number (39) of cog-

nomina of persons who *seem* to be ex-slaves, though their names fail to make this clear, the majority are obviously Greek (*Eutychus, Hermes, Zeno*), and the Latin ones are often favorably descriptive (*Felixs* [sic], *Fortunatus, Iustissimus, Lepidus, Velox*),[85] though some are the same as those of freeborn persons (*Felix* [Sulla's self-assumed second cognomen, or agnomen, 16], *Lepidus* [the triumvir Aemilius's cognomen], *Maximus*). One or two are specially interesting: *Valens Aug(usti) lib(ertus) Phaedimianus*, following the name of the deceased, *M. Ulpius Aug. lib. Phaedimus*, a favorite of Trajan, **67** (A.D.. 130), shows that Valens had been a slave of Phaedimus and was transferred to Trajan's ownership. (See Weaver, 217.) In another inscription, consisting of three official letters, **69** (A.D. 193), the subject's name is spelled both *Adrastus* and *Hadrastus* and is referred to, successively, as *Augg. nn.* (i.e., *Augustorum nostrorum duorum*) *lib(ertus)* (the latest reference in the covering letter), *procurator columnae divi Marci* (caretaker of the Column of Marcus Aurelius in Rome), *Aug. lib.*, and *lib. domini n(ostri)*, the change from singular to dual number for the emperor(s) being caused by Septimius Severus's having named a co-ruler, probably Clodius Albinus (A.D. 193–195 or –196). (Cf. Weaver, 58–60.) On reversed C (Ɔ), used to show that a person is (or has been) a freedman (or -woman) of some woman, see A. E. Gordon, "On Reversed C (Ɔ = *Gaiae*)," *Epigraphica* 40 (1978) 230.

The names of the emperors and their families, when written in full, officially, are the longest and most complicated of all, especially when their titles are included. (Even the women had some titles,

84. Cf. Thylander, 57 f., who confirms this usage from studying the inscrs. of *CIL* 1²: 2 (before the appearance of Degrassi's *ILLRP*).

85. Kajanto divides the Latin cognomina into fifteen categories, such as geographical, theophoric (*Apollinaris*), calendaric (*Ianuarius*), those relating to

the human body or mind (*Albus, Hilarus*), etc. His aim was to present "all Latin cognomina in so far as I have been able to find them, and to elucidate the principles of Latin cognomen-formation" (p. 11). He indexes about 6,600 "personal names [i.e., cognomina] discussed."

such as *Augusta* and *Mater Castrorum*—on this title see below.) The *Divus Iulius* of our **21**, whatever its date and meaning here, is a reminder that Julius Caesar and fifty-five of the emperors, and some of the members of their families (eleven men, sixteen women), were deified after death by decree of the Senate, and that on the other hand some of them—Caligula, Nero, and Domitian the first three—suffered *damnatio memoriae*, one result of which was that their names were erased from the monuments, though not always everywhere and though some of them were restored.[86] Our own texts include mention of the deified Julius (besides **21**, simply *divus* in **22**, **30** f., **35** [the earlier text], *divus Iulius* in **29**, **35** [the later text]), Augustus (**34**, **35** [later text, twice], **36**, **46** [5 times]), Vespasian (**50** f.), Titus (**50**, **66** [twice]), Nerva (**57**), Trajan (**61**), Antoninus Pius (**67**), Marcus Aurelius (**69**); erasure of the name of Geta after his death at the hands of his older brother, Caracalla, (**73**), of Geta, as well as of Caracalla's own wife, Fulvia Plautilla, "utpote impudica," her father, and—apparently because his cognomen was Geta—Caracalla's uncle (**72**); mention also of the deified *Faustinae mater et Pia* (Faustina the Elder and the Younger, wives of Antoninus Pius and Marcus Aurelius, resp., **76**).

The emperors' titles get longer and more fulsome with time. This is well illustrated by our **29**, in which three emperors appear, separated by over two hundred years—Augustus, Titus, and Caracalla.

Augustus's name and titles are the simplest: *Imp. Caesar divi Iuli f(ilius) Augustus / pontifex maximus, cos. XII, / tribunic(ia) potestat(e) XIX, imp(erator) XIIII*; Titus's have four more elements: *Titus Vespasianus* (to distinguish him from his father, Vespasian, who, although Titus, does not use the praenomen in his official name, but only *Vespasianus*), *cens(or)*, *cos. VII*, *(cos.) desig. IIX*, and *p(ater) p(atriae)*;[87] Caracalla, perhaps for lack of space, dispenses with all the older, run-of-the-mill titles except *pontifex maximus*, but, after *Imp. Caesar*, uses a three-part name: *M. Aurellius* (often thus spelled during his rule)[88] *Antoninus* (as against no name for Augustus except *Imp. Caesar Augustus*, which nearly all the emperors use down to A.D. 425–450,[89] and two names for Titus), plus *Pius* (assumed, at least in its Greek form Εὐσεβής, when he became co-emperor in 198, in A.D. 200 and going back through his father and Commodus to Antoninus Pius, who had himself assumed it on becoming emperor in 138), *Felix* (dating from 200, but often omitted until 211, and going back to Commodus's assumption of it in 185 after the failure of an alleged conspiracy), *Parth(icus) Max(imus)* (from 199), and *Brit(annicus) Maximus* (from 210).[90] (The dates of all these names/titles come from dated or datable inscriptions and in turn help to date other, undated inscriptions.) In addition, while Augustus takes only one line to say what he has done for "all the aqueducts," and Titus two lines for the Aqua Marcia alone, Caracalla requires three long lines, and by this time

---

86. For lists of all these, see Cagnat, 169–174; Calabi Limentani, 467–480.

87. *Pater patriae* goes back to Augustus, who tells us himself, very near the end of his *Res Gestae* (**34**, ch. 35, 1) that, while holding his 13th consulship [more precisely, Feb. 5, 2 B.C., as is known from other sources], he was given this title by "the Senate and the Equestrian Order, and the entire Roman People," and the rest of the circumstances. On Cicero called *parens patriae primus omnium*, see Pliny, *N.H.* 7.117. *(Cos.) design. IIX = VIII*, both subtraction and

addition being used by the Romans: see below, VIII, 1 (Roman numerals).

88. Cf. Degrassi, "Aurellius," *Athenaeum* 9 (1921) 292–299 (*Scritti vari*, 1.467–472); J. F. Oates, *Phoenix*, 30: 3 (1976) 284, on line 10.

89. I follow Dessau, 3: 1, 257–315 (from his list of "Imperatores et Domus Eorum").

90. I follow Cagnat, 189 f., 208 f. (from his "Liste chronologique des empereurs romains"), and A. Stein, *PIR*[2] 1.311, no. 1513; for Caracalla as *Pius* and *Felix*, see J. H. Oliver, *GRBS* 19 (1978) 375–385.

the City of Rome has become *sacram urbem suam* ("his holy [i.e., Imperial] city").[91]

One other example: the names and titles of Diocletian, his fellow-ruler Maximianus, and their *nobil(issimi) Caes(ares)* (as successors-to-be) occupy about twelve lines in *ILS* 642 (our **81**) at the beginning of the preface of Diocletian's Edict on Prices of A.D. 301 (and all the titles and some of the names are abbreviated). Besides this great increase in titles there goes a fulsomeness of wording in the titles of the later emperors, in both official and unofficial inscriptions (as well as in their official statements), which seems to begin with Trajan's being called *Optimus* unofficially before October 98, on coins from 103, and, as an agnomen in inscriptions, from July 114.[92] Then there is Antoninus as *Pius* from his accession (this name/title continues at least until Valentinian III, A.D. 424–455, and, as *Piissimus*, until Justinian, 527–565, and apparently Phocas, 602–610).[93]

For the evidence of our own texts, see **69**, **71–73**, **77**, **81**, **82**, **86**, **88**, **94**, and **97**. A few points in particular may be noted. In **71** Caracalla (with a formal name borrowed, presumably by his father and for greater respectability, from the greatly honored Marcus Aurelius, in place of "Septimius Bassianus")[94] is called *dominus indulgentissimus* (Dessau's inscriptions show *dominus n(oster)* as early as Hadrian, but Radice, op. cit. [above, n. 92] 324 f., n. 1, notes that Domitian had been addressed as *dominus et deus noster* and that *dominus*, "retained by the emperors, but without the suggestion of tyranny," "is always used by Pliny [the Younger] in addressing Trajan, except" twice). In **72** Julia Domna, wife of Septimius Severus (note the absence of *i* in her honorary title *Domna*, attested since the first century A.D.), is called *Iulia Aug., mater Augg.* [Caracalla and Geta] *et castror(um)* ("Mother of the Camp"? or, "Mother of the Imperial Household"?).[95] In **77** *Felix* in the emperor Decius's name seems to go back, through Commodus and Caracalla, eventually to Sulla's assumption of this as a second cognomen, or agnomen, **16**, and *Caesar* for the intended heir to the throne goes back to Augustus's two adopted

91. For comparison it may be noted that Queen Elizabeth II requires for all her titles about two pages in *Burke's Guide to the Royal Family* (London 1973) 119–123, beginning: "H. M. The Queen. Elizabeth the Second, By the Grace of God, of the United Kingdom of Great Britain and Northern Ireland and of Her Other Realms and Territories Queen, Head of the Commonwealth, Defender of the Faith." (Note the chiastic word order: . . . queen/head, defender. . . .)

92. Cagnat, 193, with ref. to Pliny the Younger, *Panegyricus*, 2.7 (with Betty Radice's note *ad loc.*, vol. 2, pp. 326 f. of her Loeb ed. and transl., 1969). But note that Tiberius is called *princeps optimus* in a private dedication of A.D. 15/37 (*CIL* 6.904; cf. A. E. G., *Seven Latin Inscrs.* 84, *Album* 1.80 no. 73). For the earlier use of *deus* and *dominus*, with ref. to the Flavians, see Kenneth Scott, *The Imperial Cult under the Flavians* (Stuttgart/Berlin 1936), index, p. 196, *s.vv. Deus, Dominus.*

93. I follow Dessau, loc. cit. (above, n. 89).

94. Compare our modern custom of renaming popes and sometimes prizefighters, actors, writers, and other artists; or rather, of their renaming themselves or accepting new names.

95. Apparently the first *Mater Castrorum* had been Faustina the Younger, wife of Marcus Aurelius. For her this title undoubtedly meant "Mother of the Camp" or "Camp Mother": *Quam* [i.e., Faustina] *secum et in aestivis* ["on his summer campaign," D. Magie] *habuerat* [Aurelius], *ut matrem castrorum appellaret* (*Hist. Aug., Marcus* 26.8, Loeb ed. 1.196 f., cf. Dio-Xiph. 71 [72].10.5, μήτηρ τῶν στρατοπέδων ἐπεκλήθη [Loeb ed., 9.32 *fin.*]; A. Stein, *PIR*² 1.133 *init.*, no. 716). But by this time the title may mean alternatively "Mother of the Imperial Household" (or "Imp. Residence" or "Palace"). This meaning of *castra* seems attested as early as Juvenal, 4.135, as is suggested by H. L. Wilson in his ed. (Boston, etc. 1903) and as is stated by Bannier, *TLL* 3.561, 43–50, *s.v.* castrum ("*speciatim palatium imperatoris*"). The woman most often called *mater castrorum* is Julia Domna (loc. cit.). (This meaning of *castra*, "Imperial Household," goes over also to *castrensis*, cf. Weaver, index, 327, *s.v.*) Since Julia Domna, having accompanied her husband, Septimius Severus, to the East, received the title "Mater Castrorum" from him in April 195, it seems impossible to be certain of the meaning in our **72**. Cf. *PIR*² 4: 3 (1966) 313 f., *s.v.* Iulia Domna Augusta.

sons, Gaius and Lucius, as members of the Julian family.[96] In **81**, where the names and titles of the four rulers are so long, *nobil. Caes.* twice is the only descriptive attribute. In **86**, the emperor Constantine's third son, Constantius II (sole emperor A.D. 337–361), is first called *restitutor urbis Romae adque* [sic] *orbis et extinctor pestiferae tyrannidis* (for his defeat of Magnentius, a pagan "usurper," in 351–352), then, in general terms, *d(ominus) n(oster)*, which seems to be overtaking *imp.* as the first element in the Imperial title from the reign of Septimius Severus (193–211), and *victor ac triumfator semper Augustus* (note the *f* in *triumfator* and the word *semper*, which often accompanies *Aug.* from Diocletian [284–305] on). No. **94** is an official dedication *fidei virtutique devotissimorum militum domnorum*[97] *nostrorum, Arcadi, Honori, et Theodosi perennium Augustorum* [402–406], with special reference to the *felicitas aeterni principis domni nostri Honori* as instrumental, along with the *consilia et fortitudo* of General Stilicho (whose name and titles are erased, he having been beheaded by order of Honorius), in the "ending of the Gothic War." Finally, in **97** (probably 441–445) *dd. nn. FFll.* [= *Flavii*] Theodosius and Placidus Valentinianus are called *invicti ac triumfatores principes semper Augusti* (note the new doubling of the first one or two consonants in abbreviating titles and names; sometimes they are even quadrupled, as in *dddd. nnnn. FFFFllll.* of *CIL* 8.27 [= *ILS* 787], of A.D. 383–388).

Fortunately, all the emperors, like modern long-titled books, had their short titles in the form of one or two names by which they were, and still are, commonly known;

after Augustus, the name may be a nomen (like *Claudius*), a cognomen (*Vespasianus*), or even a praenomen (*Tiberius* or *Titus*), or a praenomen plus nomen (*Marcus Aurelius*), two cognomina (*Antoninus Pius*), or even a nickname (*Caracalla*).[98]

5. *Reproducing or copying inscriptions.* There are various ways of reproducing inscriptions, each of which has its strength and its weakness. The single most useful means nowadays—apart from photography—is probably the squeeze (French "estampage [de papier]," German "[Papier]abklatsch," Italian and Spanish "calco"), which for most purposes has replaced the older rub (or rubbing). The latter requires only paper and colored chalk, crayon, or wax crayon (or, *faute de mieux*, a blunt-pointed pencil); the design or lettering is reproduced by placing the paper on the surface (of stone or metal) and rubbing it with the chalk or whatever is used; the plain portions of the design or lettering become dark, the incisions remaining white (or whatever the color of the paper); a fixative may then be applied to prevent smearing. Some of the most famous rubbings are those made of funerary brasses or stones in English churches and churchyards, wherever tombstones may be found. The weakness of such rubbings is that, being flat-surfaced, they remove all effect of incision and depth, therefore show no small details of lettering, punctuation, etc., which depend on three dimensions. They are probably the least damaging of all the methods of making impressions, and may be quite handsome, according to the design, but they are of limited value palaeographically.

---

96. For the praenomen "Lucius" (of L. Iulius Caesar) as evidence in identifying the dictator Caesar's great-grandfather, see G. V. Sumner, *CP* 71 (1976) 341–344.

97. *Sic*—no *i*, attested as early as 111 B.C., in the *Lex Agraria, CIL* 1²: 2.525, p. 459, line XXVII. (Cf. *Domna* in the name of Julia Domna, above.)

98. "Caracalla" is cited from Eutropius, Rufius Festus, Ausonius (all 4th cent.), Jerome (ca. 348–420), and Jordanes (ca. 550), "Caracallus" from Dio (cos. II, 229) and the *Hist. Aug.* (*TLL, Onomasticon*, 2 [1907–13] 178, *s.vv.*).

The squeeze requires water, a bucket or two, a piece of filter paper, and a stiff, flat brush (any size will do, even a hairbrush, but a larger one is better—Degrassi used to use one over a foot long, custom-made in Rome, with bristles of horse hair, for lack of wild boar's); one cleans the inscribed surface with a small cleaning brush, with or without water, so as to remove all dirt, incrustations of lichen, etc., and (modern) paint without damaging the surface or removing any ancient minium that may still be present, then wets it well again with clean water, dips into the water a piece of the paper (cut to about the same size as the inscribed surface, plus any borders), applies it to the surface and then beats it into all the incisions as hard as possible, proceeding from top to bottom and making sure that any bubbles are removed by further beating; if the first attempt is unsuccessful, one tries again after rewetting the surface. Our own practice, since our stones nearly always have been in vertical position, has been to tie the squeeze to the stone with string and leave it over-night to dry; and we have found that, even if the paper falls to the ground or floor and perhaps gets dirty, it hardly matters: the paper is remarkably tough and resistant. If the beating breaks the paper at any point, most likely where the incision is deep, one may either apply another thickness of paper at the broken point, beating it into the lower paper as hard as before, or (better) simply disregard the tear.[99] There is no particular kind of filter paper needed; J. and L. Robert, op. cit. (n. 99) 119, recommended a paper made specially for squeezes by the Papeteries d'Arches in Paris; G. Brusin, while director of the Museo Archeologico at Aquileia, in northeastern Italy, used a paper made by a friend who owned a nearby paper-factory (so the friend told us in 1956); we ourselves always used a paper kindly provided by the American Academy in Rome, which was made by Carter, Rice and Company, of Boston, Mass. Squeezes are very durable: J. and L. Robert, op. cit. 120, say, for example, that those of Philippe Le Bas, more than a hundred years old, "have been as useful to us as they were when new," and those of the Greek and Latin parts of the Cornelius Gallus inscription from Philae, **22**, made for the editor (presumably Mommsen) of *CIL* 3.14147[5] (publ. 1902) and now in the Berlin headquarters of *CIL*, seemed in 1973 in as good shape as ever.[100] The best way to read or photograph squeezes seems to be from the rear; in this way we have read all those that we have studied, and a competent photographer can use the same method, having the illumination come from the lower right (so as to show the letters as incised, not in relief) and printing the negative from the back (see the *Album*, where all the photos of squeezes were made in this way).

But in some situations the paper squeeze is inferior to a rub or a latex squeeze;[101] in others, perhaps, where the surface of the stone is very soft or porous or badly damaged, no sort of impression may be advisable, but only photographs or drawings. With friable tufas or very lightly inscribed marble, a rubbing is

---

99. I suppose that, if one had to squeeze and run, so to speak, one might carefully detach the squeeze at once and lay it flat, upside down, without waiting for it to dry, with no ill effects. We have not had to do this, but it is confirmed by J. and L. Robert, *REG* 66 (1953) 119 f.

100. J. and L. Robert, ibid., with ref. to Larfeld, note the occasional use of squeezes from as early as Pighius (1547–1555), and a more or less systematic use from 1833, with Champollion in Egypt. On the preservation of paper squeezes, see E. R. Caley and B. D. Meritt, "Chemical Preservation of Squeezes" (*Journ. of Documentary Reproduction*, Sept. 1940) 204 f.

101. See W. K. Pritchett, "Liquid Rubber for Greek Epigraphy," *AJA* 56 (1952) 118–120, plates 5–6; reviewed by J. and L. Robert, op. cit. 118–120. We must confess that we never learned to use latex handily. See also Pritchett, *AJA* 57 (1953) 197 f., 59 (1955) 61, col. 2, *init.*, and C. W. Beck, "Synthetic Elastomers in Epigraphy," *AJA* 67 (1963) 413–416.

probably best. We have found latex useful, in case of erasures, to confirm or correct the reading of the squeeze—e.g., *Album*, 2.260 (= *CIL* 14.4254, *ILS* 5191, add. 3:2, p. clxxxv, *Inscr. Ital.* 1:1 [ed. 2, 4:1] 254), left side. The weakness of latex, besides causing possible damage to a poor surface (as is true of paper squeezes to a somewhat lesser extent), is that it has to be carried in liquid form, and, obviously, the bigger the text to be covered, the more latex is needed. But in the case of a really large text, especially one exposed to the wind, latex seems to be the only feasible means of taking an impression; perhaps the most striking examples are the latex squeezes, including "probably the largest 'squeeze' yet made in the field," of the inscriptions found at Nemrud Dagh and Arsameia in southeastern Turkey (anc. Commagene).[102] Latex may be useful also for round surfaces—e.g., lead pipes or milestones. In general, one must use whatever means seems most practicable, or the only one available. For an inscription on stone, a good paper-squeeze (well beaten so as to show all the incisions thoroughly and sharply) or a latex squeeze or both, plus good photographs, taken with a raking light (from the side), and on-the-spot notes would seem ideal.[103]

The methods used by Ritschl and Hübner for their books of plates illustrating Latin inscriptions of the Republic and the Empire, respectively, are set forth briefly and criticized in the *Album*, 1.3 f. Their facsimiles suffer from being based on drawings. Mommsen for ed. 1 (1865 and in *CIL* 3, 1873) of his *Res Gestae Divi Augusti* relied chiefly on drawings prepared in 1861, at Ankara, by G. Perrot and

E. Guillaume, for ed. 2 (1883, repr. Aalen, Germany, 1970) on a plaster-of-Paris reproduction, in 194 pieces, made in 1882 by Carl Humann (A. E. Gordon, *Notes*, 131, n. 29).

For impressions of inscriptions in bronze, I have no special information, finding nothing pertinent in print and having only collated a few such pieces. Rubbings would seem feasible, but one should hesitate (even if allowed) to make a squeeze. The *Senatus Consultum de Bacchanalibus*, 8, has been reproduced both in plaster-of-Paris and electro-galvanically.[104] Ronald S. Stroud is leery of latex for bronze and doubts that museums would allow its use, from fear of damage. W. K. Pritchett favors plaster, and this is recommended for bronzes larger than coins by Lawrence E. Dawson, Senior Museum Anthropologist at the museum of note 104.

6. *The work and problems of the Roman stonecutter.* For an excellent treatment of the work and problems of the Roman stonecutter, one can recommend Giancarlo Susini's *Il lapicida romano* (Bologna 1966), mentioned above, III.4, with such chapters as "The Two Phases of Engraving," "Workers and Workshops," "Stones, Tools, and Their Interaction." To this it may be worth adding that the Gordons, when visiting a stonecutter's shop near the principal cemetery in Rome (the Campo Verano) in 1948–49, were told by the head workman that it took a really expert cutter to cut 300 letters a day and that 250 or more a day was considered good work. One thinks how much effort must have gone into cutting, from a scaf-

---

102. The method is described by Kermit Goell in the *Illustrated London News*, July 9, 1955, pp. 68 f., with ref. also to the issues of June 18 and July 2. See also the *New York Times*, Jan. 19, 1955, p. 4.

103. For squeezes and photos, see Woodhead's ch. VII and Guarducci, 1.17, n. 1, with ref. to E(mil) Hübner's *Ueber mechanische Copieen von Inschriften* (Berlin 1881), 28 pp. J. S. Gordon points out that, for on-the-spot checking, looking from the side before

removing dust is sometimes useful, as is also a flashlight to furnish a raking light, and feeling with one's fingertips.

104. The Robert H. Lowie Museum of Anthropology, University of California, Berkeley, has one or two plaster copies, and in 1973 there was an electrogalvanic copy in the office of Prof. Artur Betz, University of Vienna.

fold, the Latin and Greek texts of the *Res Gestae* of Augustus in Ankara, **34**, the Latin alone containing some 17,000 letters (cf. Mommsen, ed. 2, pp. xv f.).[105]

Unique as a statistical and comparative study of the palaeographical and epigraphical minutiae (especially ligatures and fancy interpuncts) of all the ancient Latin inscriptions (529 in number) of a whole country, Switzerland, is Jürg Ewald's *Paläo- und epigraphische Untersuchungen an den römischen Steininschriften der Schweiz mit besonderer Berücksichtigung der Nexus* (*Ligaturen*) (below, n. 116). The number of words, of abbreviations (including single-letter forms, separately), tall I's, words divided at line ends, and leaf-shaped interpuncts is compiled, and the results are compared chronologically and geographically, by both number and percentage, from the Augustan age to Constantine.

PART V. SUBJECT MATTER

1. *The myriad contents.* The contents are myriad, from the simplest—alphabets or the mosaic *Cave canem!*—to the long *Res Gestae* of the emperor Augustus (**34**), from the most vulgar curse-tablets or Pompeian painted wall-inscriptions to the most formal consular and triumphal fasti or legal texts. There is much verse (three volumes in Buecheler and Lommatzsch's Teubner *Carmina Latina epigraphica*, 1895–1926),[106] some obviously quoted from, or reminiscent of, well-known poets, especially Vergil and Ovid, much containing errors of meter, little deserving to be called literature.

A few inscriptions seem to combine more than one type, such as **12**, which combines an unusual kind of milestone, giving several distances plus total mileage, with another unusual kind of *elogium* glorifying the speaker, all in the first person. Change of style in similar texts cut on the same monument is well illustrated by **29**, where we have statements from three different emperors, separated by over two centuries: we go from the plain style of Augustus to the less plain style of Titus, to the new, florid style of Caracalla, who uses the fancy, brief-lived spelling *Aurellius*, the additional titles *Pius* and *Felix*, and the double-barrelled *Parth(icus) Maxim(us)* and *Brit(annicus) Maximus* (which perhaps get the *Max.* from *pontifex maximus*—where *max.* makes sense— which all the emperors, down to at least Gratian, 367–383, were *ex officio*).[107] The *bilinguals* and *trilinguals* have their own features: **13**, where the Greek uses no interpunctuation, no abbreviations for the praenomina, no word for "son" or "freedman," but simply the genitive for the father's or the ex-owner's name, and omits the consular date; **22**, where the Egyptian is reportedly not a translation at all and the Greek—the lowest of the three texts, intended no doubt for the ordinary reader—carefully bowdlerizes the presumably official Latin; and **34**, the *Monumentum Ancyranum*, where the Greek is not a close version of the Latin and the translator has once misunderstood and mistranslated it.

---

105. For Greek epigraphy, see C. G. Higgins and W. K. Pritchett, "Engraving Techniques in Attic Epigraphy," *AJA* 69 (1965) 367–371, plates 97–100, and Stephen V. Tracy, "The Lettering of an [anonymous] Athenian Mason," *Hesperia*, Suppl. 15 (Princeton 1975) 1–11, with intro., "The Study of Lettering," XIII–XXIII, by Sterling Dow.

106. For a new vol. of *CIL*, 18, planned to replace *CLE*, see above, n. 27.

107. The earliest such victory-title including *Maximus* seems to be *Parthicus Max.*, held first by Lucius

Verus (A.D. 165–) and M. Aurelius (166–), but *Maximus* as a descriptive adjective applied commonly to an emperor (with *Optimus*) goes back to Trajan, as early as 103. This usage and the *Maximus* of *Pont. Max.* may have been the sources of the later victory-titles with *Maximus*. Cf. P. Kneissl, *Die Siegestitulatur der röm. Kaiser . . .* (Göttingen 1969 *Hypomnemata* 23) 86 f., 201–203, 204 f.; for Caracalla, 225–231. Pertinent also may be the ref. to *V[i]ctori[a] [Parthica] Maxim[a] divi Seve[ri]* in the Feriale Duranum, ibid., 76, 144.

2. *Most are probably epitaphs.* Probably the largest number of inscriptions, whether lost or extant, are funerary in character, epitaphs. Here is a fine example, cut on a tablet (or large cippus?) of travertine found in Rome across the Tiber and copied in the fifteenth and sixteenth centuries but now long since lost (*CIL* 1².1211, 6.15346 [cf. p. 3517], *CLE* 52, *ILS* 8403, Lattimore, 271, Warm. 12, no. 18, Degr. 2.973, H. Häusle, *Das Denkmal als Garant des Nachruhms* . . . [*Zetemata* 75 (1980) 93 f., no. 29, with German transl. by H. Geist]), in good iambic senarii of about the Gracchan period, as Buecheler and Degrassi thought and as is consistent with the use of travertine reported by one observer:[108]

Hospes, quod deico paullum est: asta ac pellege.
Heic est sepulcrum hau pulcrum pulcrai feminae.
Nomen parentes nominarunt Claudiam.
Suom mareitum corde deilexit sovo.
Gnatos duos creavit; horum alterum
in terra linquit, alium sub terra locat.
Sermone lepido, tum autem incessu commodo.
Domum servavit, lanam fecit. Dixi. Abei.

("Stranger, what I say is little: stand near and read it through. Here is the tomb, not lovely, of a lovely woman. Her parents named her Claudia. Her husband she loved with her heart. Two sons she bore; of these, one she leaves on earth, the other she placed under the earth. She was of charming speech and of graceful movement as well. She kept the house, she worked the wool. I have spoken. Go your way.") Note the mixture of archaic and later forms: *deico* vs. *dixi*, *pulcrai* vs. *feminae*, *sovo* vs. *suom*, marks presumably of a not yet standard orthography. *Locat* seems to be a contracted perfect, as is found in poetry, though rarely; cf. Sommer, 564 *fin.*; A. Ernout, *Morphologie historique du latin*, nouv. éd. (Paris 1926 and repr.) p. 332; Cyril Bailey, ed. Lucretius

(Oxford 1947) 1. 83, 2. 611, line 70. On *tituli loquentes*, inscriptions represented as talking in the first person to the reader, see A. E. Gordon, *Fib. Praen.* 16, n. 36 *fin.*, 20 with n. 67, with references to E. Norden, M. Beeler, and M. Torelli.

For another epitaph of a Roman woman, likewise—except for the heading—in verse (not very good dactylic hexameter, pentameter, and heptameter) but otherwise quite different, being long, emotional, and not fully clear, see **65**.

3. *The Laudatio Funebris.* Epitaphs, being always personal in their reference, are among the most interesting of all Latin inscriptions, this character being shared by the *Laudatio* (*funebris*), the most famous example of which is probably the so-called *Laudatio Turiae* ("Turia" is not certain as the name of the deceased), four fragments of which are extant. Addressed to the deceased in moving words by her surviving husband, it tells the story of a young woman's fighting for her fiancé (later husband), whose life is greatly endangered in the Civil War following the death of Caesar. (See **28**.)

PART VI. PROBLEMS OF LATIN INSCRIPTIONS

1. *The main problems.* There are several main problems presented by Latin inscriptions. One is the matter of establishing the text, which is often difficult, not only for lost inscriptions, but even for those extant. Many are inadequately published, even in *CIL*, which, except for volume 1, second edition, to some extent, and volume 16, gives hardly any photographs or other illustrations. The volumes of Ritschl and Hübner and even Degrassi, which are all parts of *CIL*, are all more or less unsatisfactory (Degrassi's least so),

---

108. On travertine, see Frank, *RBR*, 32; Giuseppe Lugli, *RendLinc*, ser. 8, vol. 9 (1954) 67 f.; also above, p. 6.

because of the comparatively small number of their facsimiles, the first two also because of the character of these (lithographs and tracings—see *Album*, 1, pp. 3–4) and Degrassi's because they were dependent on the good will and expertise of museum officials and photographers (see his *Imag.*, pp. VII f., and Badian, op. cit. [above, n. 45] 241; as was noted above, museums in Italy often fill the inscribed letters with paint, not always accurately). The only way to be certain of the text is by examining the original oneself—sometimes more than once—and making notes on the spot, and by having one or more good photographs of it and, if possible, a squeeze, or at least a rub (the rub, however, will not show the fine points of the writing). Fortunately, if the whereabouts of an inscription is known, it is often possible to obtain a photograph of it; in Rome one can secure the expert services of the Fototeca Unione at the American Academy.[109] Once in a while, even when the inscription is extant, it is impossible to establish the text with certainty, either because of damage (which makes restoration uncertain, as in the *Res Gestae* of Augustus, **34**—see A. E. Gordon, *Notes*, 131) or because of illegible writing (as in the Arval Hymn, **75**).

When there is damage, this is likely to increase at the breaks with time, even in museums, where pieces are sometimes moved about. In such cases photographs are inadequate, and only on-the-spot observation plus the study of paper or latex squeezes will show the probable readings; it is the edges of breaks where the trouble is; restoration, always more or less conjectural, is often needed, but this will be facilitated if the text has been read and published by a reliable editor before later damage, or if the lost text is such as to be more easily restored, such as Roman names, as in **15**. Sometimes a letter within a word was never cut, as in **8**, line 5 *vtr a* for *verba*, 6 *senator bus*, and **36**, line 5 *int rponant*, or a considerable space within a line, where nothing seems missing, has been left uninscribed, as in **36**, line 12 [*iudi/ciorum publi*]*corum* (space for about 8 letters) *gratia*; these omissions seem to occur more often in bronze (offhand, none in stone comes to mind) and may be explicable to one who knows just how bronze inscriptions were made. In some cases the text seems to have been emended by the original cutter, as in **3**, either to correct an error caused by scribal dictation or because the cutter was unsure whether to write C or K, at a time when the use of C, K, and Q was in confusion; in such cases it may remain uncertain what the original and what the emended readings are. The text of **4** seems beyond reasonable conjecture (unlike the Sirens' song or Achilles' assumed name "when he hid himself among women," for Sir Thomas Browne, who, however, offers no suggestions); because of its poor surface and extensive damage (mostly ancient) and the difficulty of reading it now in its present protected position, the remains of the text are uncertain in too many places. In **19** the problem is increased by the text's being corrupt in several places, for whatever reason.

There is also the question of copies vs. originals. If one believes that one is looking at an ancient copy, as for example in the case of the Duilius inscription, **48**, one must face the question how accurate a copy it is; if the original is much earlier in date than the copy and its language therefore quite probably—or certainly—different from that of the later age, and if the original stone was not particularly suited

---

109. The address is Fototeca Unione presso l'Accademia Americana / Via Angelo Masina, 5 / 00153 Roma / Italy. Ernest Nash himself, the founder and longtime director of this service, died in 1974. For a report on its present program and plans, see the *Amer. Acad. in Rome News*, Winter 1975–76, p. [5] and *Amacadmy, The Newsletter of the Amer. Acad. in Rome*, 2: 1 (July 1979) p. [21].

for inscriptional purposes (as is probably true in both respects of the Duilius stone), one must realize that it is quite possible that at the time the copy was made the one responsible for it was unable to read the original correctly and fully, so perhaps made mistakes. In fact, the accuracy of the Duilius inscription is much disputed; the experts can only compare the text with the few other (original) texts of the same age (late-third century B.C.?) with respect to language and spelling, the obviously comparable group being the Scipionic epitaphs, from which it differs, however, in being much fuller. Sometimes inscriptions are suspected of being later (ancient) copies on insufficient grounds—for example, the numerous Arval fragments (see *Album*, 2.7, on no. 151).

Dating, of course, is very often a problem, probably the one most often encountered. If the contents of an inscription are not enlightening, one has to fall back on the aid of archaeology or palaeography. If the surroundings are known and datable, or if the material is known to have a *terminus post* or *ante quem*, this fact may suggest a date for the inscription, or at least a not-before or not-after date. With similar vagueness and risk, so also the writing itself. (See below, VI.2 and 3, on palaeography and dating.)

Then there is the problem of what an inscription means. The earlier inscriptions present archaic language and spelling; and some texts present special problems of interpretation: e.g., **3**, where the text of 128 (or 129) letters is almost entirely certain but the sense seems unintelligible because of the scarcity of archaic Latin for comparison; **4**, where the text is so incomplete because of ancient damage as to be unintelligible except for a few words; **19**, where several lines and a few other phrases are unintelligible without (uncertain) conjecture; **59**, where the meaning of the last clause is uncertain, partly because of damage, and **65**, where the poor verse is unclear in several places. Any inscrip-

tion may present technical matters, as of law, government, or religion, which require expert interpretation: for example, what is the meaning, in full detail, of the lateral portion of *CIL* 12.4333 (= *ILS* 112, the Narbonese Altar)? Even an epitaph in untechnical language and without questions of text or reading may contain obscurities due to poor composition (and to the lack of meaningful punctuation); the most notable example here is **65**, mentioned just above. Editors and translators seem sometimes to dodge or conceal the obscurities.

There is sometimes the problem of deciding what kind of inscription a particular one is when we lack the monument to which it once belonged; e.g., is **10** honorary, as is generally believed, despite the nominative case? (compare the clearly honorary examples, in the dative, of **16** and **21**) or simply to identify the person whose statue seems to have rested above? The problem apparently concerns only contemporary, living persons, as distinct from, e.g., the Republican worthies, such as Marius, honored with statues and inscribed bases in the Forum of Augustus in Rome, whose names and careers are all in the nominative. (A selection in *ILS* 50–60, cf. 61–64.) Likewise, there is the problem of when iteration begins in Roman titles: e.g., *consul iterum*, said of M. Claudius Marcellus, *consul iterum* in 155 B.C., **10**; if, as E. Badian says, there is no further example "noted in Roman inscriptions (official or unofficial) until well into the first century," is this perhaps a case of "a later (re-)engraving"? or does this argument rest only on negative evidence? (This is a special aspect of the problem of copies vs. originals.)

Inconsistencies in punctuation, in the use of signs to mark the long vowels, sometimes even in spelling, seem to be the rule; hardly any text of any length is consistent in these matters; these and the rather common plain mistakes make it appear that the texts were often not edited, and they are occasionally so badly cut as to be illegible (one of the worst cases is the text of the long Arval inscription of A.D. 218, which incorporates the Arval Hymn, **75**). There is also a tendency not to punctuate between a preposition and its object, as in *in ignem*, **20**, but on the other hand to punctuate within a composite word such as *duo · viri*, **17**, *stipites · que*, **19**, line 5. There are sometimes erasures caused by *damnatio memoriae*, sometimes left blank, as in **14**, line 3, sometimes replaced by a new text, as in the many references to Geta, younger brother of Caracalla (e.g., **73**, on the Arch of Septimius Severus in Rome, the dedicatory bronze **72**, and elsewhere); so also with the later General Stilicho, **94**, of A.D. 402/406.

Problems of restoration occur when something appears lost from the original text; obviously no restoration is certain—the original may have contained one or more errors—but, quite as obviously, some restorations are more probable than others; the shorter the restoration, the more likely it is, other things being equal. Perhaps the most frequent cause of failure in restoring lost text arises from the failure to observe spatial requirements; even in *CIL*, whose editors seem all to be highly expert, this carelessness can be observed, as in some of the many fragmentary Arval inscriptions (e.g., *Album*, 1. 77, no. 69). In a restored text the lines should be about equal in length unless a different design is clear; e.g., in the Roman Forum Cippus inscription, **4**, where all the lines are incomplete—and no one knows how long they were—a restoration that gives lines varying from ten to thirty-two letters seems most unlikely (A. E. Gordon, *ACR* 1 [1971] 51); here all restoration seems hopeless. Restorations in verse are clearly easier to make, but may be far from certain and vary from editor to editor, as in **14**. In faulty verse, **65**, there would of course be less certainty. Where history and prosopography are involved, experts in these fields are needed. (See in general, Cagnat

379–387, or Sandys/Campbell 198–200, or, esp. for Greek, Woodhead 67–76 or Dow 20–31.)

We find stones sometimes reused for a new text, as in **14**, where a marble block had been used for a Greek text, judged to be of the fourth century B.C., then was used for a Latin one of the late second, or **27**, where the restoration was perhaps caused by the posthumous bestowal of "Germanicus" on Drusus the Elder. Such reuse is specially common in the Latin inscriptions of late antiquity, beginning in the third Christian century (conjecturally, in order to save money), in both pagan and Christian inscriptions. Sometimes the earlier text is erased by cutting back the whole surface; at other times the other side of the stone is used for the later text, this most often (it seems) in the early-Christian epitaphs.

Some texts have received later additions, by the same hand (as apparently in **15**, to judge from its looks, but with a careless change of syntax) or by another. Inferior arrangement is often detectable, especially at line ends, when not enough space has been left for the text, this resulting in ligatures, as in **16** and **19**, letters inside others, as in **17**, line 1, smaller writing, as in **47**, final letters being cut on the side of the stone, as in **6**, or at the end of the next line, as in **12**, or continued in a perpendicular direction, as in **2**. The "monogrammatic" style of cutting *cos.*, while perhaps originating in this need to save space at line ends, seems to have become fashionable and may be used anywhere in the line. It goes without saying that it may always be possible to improve the text of a damaged or fragmentary inscription, such as so many of the Arval records (see *Album*, indices to Parts 1–3, *s.v.* Arvals), by studying them more closely, observing the cut edges (in the original stones or in good squeezes), and especially bearing in mind spatial considerations to see what is possible, what impossible, in the way of restoration; see **22**, for example. It sometimes happens to be practically impossible to obtain the exact measurements of an inscribed monument or of the inscription itself, either because of the size and, especially, the height of the monument or the inscription, or because the authorities differ in their reports; cf. **23**, **26**, **29**, **34**, **58**.

No one can be expert in all the fields opened up by the problems described and illustrated here; one must often rely on others, but at the same time should be critical in doing so and use common sense and judgment. Even so, one must sometimes remain uncertain on such crucial points as authenticity, meaning, and date. Sometimes the experts fail to agree.

2. *Palaeography*. On seeing a Latin inscription itself or well reproduced, one is immediately aware of the style of writing, its palaeography, just as when one sees any kind of writing or printing. One is seeing a piece of art and reacts at once to its character—good, bad, so-so. Apparently, like all other arts, the art of writing in any medium does not remain static, but undergoes a development, from an early amorphous, less skilled phase to a more skilled one, which in turn may deteriorate for various reasons (lack of good artists or good materials, perhaps from economic causes). So with our Latin inscriptions. The earliest ones can hardly be distinguished from contemporary Greek or Etruscan inscriptions; they all tend to look like scratches, more or less according to the kind of material inscribed, and to show considerable variation in the letters, from lack of skill or perhaps the absence of developed standards. The only superficial distinction is in the presence or absence of certain symbols that occur in one language and not in another—e.g., Greek phi and psi, or the later Etruscan symbol for F, which looks like the Arabic numeral 8. Of our **1**, for example, it was soon noted that its writing was very similar to that of a Greek inscription from Cumae, which

L. H. Jeffery (240, no. 3; pl. 47, 3) dates "*c.* 675–650?" B.C. (see A. E. Gordon, *Fib. Praen.* 17 f.). (See now the N.B. at the end of the annotation of **1**.)

The writing of Latin inscriptions, as of Latin manuscripts, is one clue to the dating of them, sometimes the only one available, but it requires caution in using it: comparison with other inscriptional writing of certain or at least probable date, as well as consideration of all internal evidence (such as the style of any names present, the use of certain formulas, punctuation, the marking of long vowels) and, when available, any external evidence (such as the archaeological milieu). Another consideration in dating is whether the inscription may be a later copy of an earlier text. Rarely is this perfectly clear, as it is in the Monumentum Ancyranum of the *Res Gestae* of Augustus, which declares itself to be an "exemplar" of the original bronze in Rome (**34**). Boundary stones, we know, had sometimes to be replaced, being specially vulnerable to theft, no doubt, because of their being valuable building material; e.g., *CIL* 1².719 (= 11.6331, *ILS* 26, Degr. 474, *Imag.* 200) reveals the setting-up of *termini* where a land commission of three men, including Gaius Gracchus, had set them up many years before. In general, the burden of proving an inscription to be a later copy rests on the claimant; our studies of the many extant Arval records, for example, make us disagree with a reviewer (*Gnomon*, 31 [1959] 138) in his contention that the Arvals are all later copies of the original archives (*Album*, 2.7, on no. 151).

There are clearly several more or less distinct periods in the palaeography of Latin inscriptions. The earliest phase includes our 2–4 and only six more in Degrassi's list of those that he dates from the seventh to the fourth/third century (Degr. 2–7, 504, 1271, 1271a, of which no. 5 may be in Sabine, not Latin—in either case it is unintelligible). These nine are all clearly archaic, primitive, but there is no agreement as to their comparative age; *CIL* 1² puts the Forum Cippus inscription, **4**, first. Between this earliest phase and the next, both the writing and the language seem to undergo the greatest changes in their whole history. By the time we reach the second phase and the Scipionic inscriptions of the third century, the writing is clearly distinctive and the language clearly Latin and, except for a few words, intelligible. (The exceptions may result from some other factor, such as poor copying, unfamiliar abbreviations, or plain ignorance on our part; e.g., **19**, line 15.) We now find the beginning of serifs (the finishing strokes, found also in Greek inscriptions by the third century B.C. [Woodhead, 64, "apices or serifs"; Guarducci, 1.372–377, with photos, "apici"]) and, toward the end of the period, shading (the gradation of depth and breadth in incised strokes, or the contrast of thick and thin strokes [*Contrib.* 80–82; for serifs, 124, 126, 128–137; for shading in Greek, Guarducci 1. 454]). The third phase extends from about Augustus to about the end of the second Christian century; it is a sort of high plateau in which we find the finest, most calligraphic examples of Latin inscriptions, such as that on the Tomb of Caecilia Metella (**23**) or that on the Column of Trajan (**57**), which were to become the objects of study and imitation, for example, in fifteenth-century Verona (see Giovanni Mardersteig, ed., *Felice Feliciano veronese, Alphabetum Romanum*, transl. R. H. Boothroyd [Verona 1960] 14–30, 54–61) and, in due course, the Column of Trajan inscription to be often shown (commonly in a photo of the plaster cast in the Victoria and Albert Museum, London) as the best example of all. The fourth and last phase, extending to the end of the Empire, is one of general decline, especially in the third century (when conditions in general seem to have greatly deteriorated), ending with early-Christian inscriptions that are often no more than scratches cut on older stones. Yet it is one of these early Christians whose work as an expert, if perhaps over-refined, stone-engraver can be identified by its appearance, its unique kind of elaborate serifs: Furius Dionysius Filocalus, composer of epitaphs and calligrapher to Pope Damasus (pope 366–384) (cf. *Contrib.* 127, with ref. to A. Ferrua's *Epigrammata Damasiana* [Vatican City 1942], and *Album*, 3.140, no. 337, with pl. 161: six illustrations of Diehl, *ILCV* 2.3446, of A.D. 389).[110] Ferrua shows (pp. 21–35) that Filocalus as an engraver had imitators also.

These four phases reveal different characteristics, one from another, but it is not always easy to distinguish between inscriptions of the late Republic and the Augustan age, nor between those of the third and fourth phases, especially when we deal with texts of different areas. The only safe procedure, in trying to date a Latin inscription of unknown date and without the benefit of historical or prosopographical evidence contained in the text itself, is to compare it carefully and in full detail with other Latin inscriptions of known date and of the same area, by means of photographs or other good reproductions. "Of the same area" means that we have some reason to believe that features of writing already in full swing in Rome itself, for example, may have taken a number of years to reach, let us say, Augusta Praetoria or Tergeste, several hundred miles north. "Full detail" means as many as possible of the points treated in the *Contributions*: Arrangement, Type of Script, Punctuation, Letter Heights, Word Division at Line Ends, Ligatures, Tall and Small Letters, Apices (on these, see

---

110. This was the pope who prompted Jerome, his secretary 382–384, to begin his work of revising the "Old Latin" translation of the Bible, which eventually became the Vulgate. Filocalus is one of only three cutters in the whole history of Latin inscrs. thus far known by name and by product, the other two being known thus far for a single product each (see below, n. 116).

above, p. 14), Numerals, Guidelines, Abbreviations, Signs and Symbols, Shading, Module (size of letters, i.e., both height and proportion of breadth to height), Serifs, Letter Forms (*Contrib*. 96–124), and Chronological Criteria such as the use of certain formulas, like *Dis Manibus*, *In Pace*, *Plus Minus*, *In Somno Pacis*, or the typically pagan sculpture of husband and wife above their epitaph.

It should be a study of many details; the dates of the stones compared should be reasonably secure and not based on palaeography alone, and this comparison should be made either by firsthand study of the stones (or other materials) themselves or through reliable reproductions (drawings alone are seldom, if ever, reliable). Even when this has been well done and all the points of resemblance or contrast have been set forth, the results must be regarded with caution. Only when all the separate conclusions reached point to a single pattern of agreement or disagreement should an opinion be ventured, and it is only an opinion, a conjecture, still wrong perhaps; there is always the possibility of individual exception, reversal, divergence, or whim. One should listen only to an expert and not believe him beyond the extent of opinion (*Album*, 1.3). It should be emphasized that within the four broad periods of writing listed above no reliable criteria have yet been established for distinguishing one century from another except for the distinctive fourth-century (A.D.) products of Filocalus and his imitators. (See also sect. 3, on dating.)

3. *Dating.* The date of an inscription is naturally of interest and, for any documentary value, essential. Assuming that the inscription is authentic (which is not always certain and sometimes difficult to establish—see above, II.3 and n. 46) and original, not a later copy (which is not always certain either—see above, p. 35),[111] one must look for either internal or external evidence, or both. Perhaps the only certain evidence is a date in the text itself, or mention of a person or an event of known date. One or the other is present in nearly all the texts here presented: a consular date, as in **13**, or a person such as Lucius Cornelius Sulla Felix, or Marcus Agrippa, both names unique. But care must be taken: there may be more than one person with the same name, and even the prosopographers may not agree as to which one he (or she) is (witness the pages of Broughton or the *PIR*, and see **23**); an epitaph may not always immediately follow the death of the deceased, but may even be a later copy or version (see the Scipionic **5** or the Duilius marble **48**). An inscription may be acephalous, and therefore, despite the historical character of what remains, the identity of the person may never be certain, as in **12**. An honorary inscription may name a single office held by a public official, but the inscription may postdate this office, as perhaps in the case of Sulla, **16**.

Apart from the text, there is also the writing, which may be conjecturally datable within a century or two (above, VI.2), or, when taken in conjunction with other factors, datable more closely. The other factors include linguistic formulas and epigraphical features. The former include such expressions as *Dis Manibus*, in full or abbreviated, which is found very rarely in inscriptions of Republican date or (reportedly) the early Empire, becomes and remains common in the second, third, and fourth centuries, and occurs occasionally in the early-Christian epitaphs. *CIL* 1².761

---

111. For the problem of original vs. later copies, see nos. **7**, **10**, **11**, **15**, **48**, **58**, in all of which except **48** and **58** I favor original, believing that the burden of proof is for the claimant of a later date (e.g., the use of marble for an inscription pertaining to the hero of the First Carthaginian War, long before the use of marble in Rome—the Duilius inscription, **48**; the size of **58** is too large for the original form of the building).

(= 14.2464, *ILS* 880, Degr. 391), of the mid-first century B.C., has perhaps the earliest extant example of *Dis Manibus* in full, and *CIL* 6.7303 (= *ILS* 7863, *Album* 1.104 f., no. 108), of A.D. 58 or 59, has perhaps the earliest such of the abbreviation *D.M.* (here followed by *S(acrum)*).[112] Epigraphical features include punctuation, tall I's, the apex to mark other long vowels, etc. (For a summary of conclusions about chronological criteria based on palaeographical and epigraphical features, see *Contrib.* 208–217.) There are also some external criteria for dating undated Latin inscriptions without the aid of historical or prosopographical evidence. One is the character of the whole monument to which the inscription belongs, if it is known or available for study—its material, art, technique, etc. Another is the precise place where the inscribed piece or monument has been found. The use of the first criterion is indicated when the monument or any one of its parts is of a sort that yields to a reliable typology, as for example ancient lamps. But otherwise one is tempted to use inadequate studies and to draw conclusions at best highly tentative and yet to state them as facts.[113] The use of the second criterion, the archaeological milieu, obviously depends on the availability of such information, whereas in fact it is seldom available, especially for monuments found in the past, i.e., most of them. Even those found currently may be no longer *in situ*—e.g., a Tiber-boundary stone found in the bed of the river. This criterion is therefore seldom of use for dating an inscribed monument with any precision. For an example of what *can* be done, see Thylander's handling of the inscriptions of Portus, the port of Ostia.[114] On such evidence depends the dating of our **2** and **3**. Worth

considering also may be the beginning and end dates of a kind of pottery, as in **3**. One would also like to have help from the surroundings in which **2** was found in 1958; the first editor (in both 1959 and 1975) used only the palaeography of the inscription in dating it, about 500 B.C., and Degrassi agreed with him.

In conjecturally dating inscriptions by epigraphical or palaeographical features or archaeological milieu, we must avoid using circular reasoning or basing conclusions on arguments *ex silentio*. For example, we must not (conjecturally) date piece A by means of some feature with only probable chronological limits and then date piece B by reference to A (which looks somewhat like B) without making it clear that the date of both is at best only probable: obviously, no dating is any more certain than the datability of the datable features. Moreover, even if present evidence shows, for example, no examples of tall long I in the fourth- or fifth-century inscriptions, this is no *proof* that any text containing such an I must be earlier than the fourth century.

Hardly any of the [epigraphical and palaeographical] criteria tentatively established above, if any of them at all, are sufficient by themselves to do more than suggest a *terminus post* or *ante quem*: they should *all*, or as many as possible, be checked, and only if they agree in the dating suggested may they give some assurance of correct chronology. Best of all is comparison in detail with one or more inscriptions of the same region and of known date, by means of good photographs of original, squeeze, or rub (or of all three) and, if possible, on-the-spot examination. Even so, the results, however positively felt, should always be designated as tentative: one must always allow for the human element, for personal variation, whim, and "error." (*Contrib.* 217, *fin.*)

---

112. See Calabi Limentani, 176; Diehl, *ILCV* 3, 653 f. (cf. F. Becker, *Die heidnische Weiheformel D.M., . . . auf altchristl. Grabsteinen. . .* , Gera [Germany] 1881); Lattimore, 90–95; Degrassi, *Riv. di fil.*, n.s. 37 (1959) 212 f. (*Scritti vari*, 4.291 f.).

113. See the review, *AJP* 76 (1955) 331–333, of an edition of a group of Latin inscrs. in Poland.

114. Thylander, *Étude* 15–38 (cf. *AJA* 58 [1954] 65 f.).

Here, finally, is an example of tentative dating of two inscriptions by photographs only, at the request of an Italian scholar (1961):

We [the Gordons] hoped that we could find elsewhere a dated example of one or more of the hands represented [he had sent us three inscriptions from the pagan cemetery under the Vatican Basilica], but we could not. Our judgment therefore is based mostly on palaeography, with consideration also of arrangement, names, etc. The dates that we give do not preclude an earlier or a later date in either case: they represent only what seems to us most probable.

We incline to consider the long inscription beginning *d.m.* / *ex codicillis* (your no. 1 [**62**]) as done probably under Hadrian, or very soon after, but we do not exclude the reign of Antoninus Pius. Not earlier, we think, partly because of the name "Ulpius" (line 8), but largely because of the lettering (particularly the shading and the module) and the arrangement of the text. Not later, we think, because of the guidelines visible (lines 3 and 4), the gradual diminution in letter height, the punctuation and its shape, the failure to bar *N(ummum)* (lines 9 and 11), and the lettering itself. (For "shading" and "module" see our *Contributions* . . . , Part One, chapters 3 and 4). . . .

No. 2, the epitaph of Matuccius [**70**], is in some ways the most challenging, because the lettering shows skill in execution and great strength, while at the same time it uses "mixed" types (e.g., the A and M are highly formalized free-hand letters, the L horizontals are the only ones unserifed, T is broad but E and L narrow, the diagonal of R and the tail of one Q are serifed). Furthermore, the punctuation is interesting, the cardinal numeral is barred (line 3), and three (out of twelve) long I's are tall. Though we have found the percentage of tall I's to have dropped by the last quarter of the second century (cf. *Contributions*, p. 216, sect. 15), the letter forms—the peculiar A, the closed P, the shape and the angles of M—, the lack of shading, the mixed alphabet, and the punctuation point to the end of the third

quarter of the second century (ca. A.D. 175), and perhaps even to a date as late as the very first years of the third century (our stone with comparable A is *CIL* 6.8420 of A.D. 183; there is also one in Thylander, *Inscrs.* B 321, datable 198–209—text, pp. 388 f.; plates, cxxi; cf. also our *Album*, 3, no. 265, probably of A.D. 202 [*CIL* 6.3768 plus 31322], for M and serifs). The use of *optimo* (line 2) instead of a fancier word such as *indulgentissimo* or *praestantissimo* inclines us to favor a date as early as is consistent with the other characteristics.

For special problems of dating, see **5**, **16**, **21**, **24**, **35**, **58**.[115]

PART VII. CONTENTS OF THIS SELECTION

1. *The specially noteworthy inscriptions.* It may be worthwhile to call attention to those of our own inscriptions that seem specially noteworthy: **5**, as typical of the Scipionic-epitaph style; **12** for its combination of contents (milestone and a first-person *elogium*); **15**, as reflecting an interesting incident in the "Social" War; **22**, for its light on the fortunes of Cornelius Gallus; **28**, for its vivid eulogy of a heroine of the late Republic; **34**, as the "Queen of Latin Inscriptions"; **35**, as unique in containing, under the duplicate dedication of the Vatican obelisk to Augustus and Tiberius on the part of (apparently) Tiberius himself, traces of an earlier duplicate inscription recording the building of a "Forum Iulium," presumably in Egypt (whence the obelisk was later brought to Rome by Caligula for his Circus), on the part of Cornelius Gallus while *praef(ectus) fabr(um) Caesaris divi f(ili)* (i.e., of the later Augustus), on the latter's instructions (it was not previously known, but only conjectured by Ronald Syme, *The Roman Revolution* 252 and n. 4, 355 and n. 2, that Gallus had held this post); **36**, as a record

115. Cf. Degrassi, *Scritti vari*, indices, 2.1100 *s.v.* epigrafia latina (datazione, paleografia), 3.407 *s.v.* datazione, 4.490 *s.v. eadem*, 504 *s.v.* paleografia; Calabi Limentani, 171–178; Meyer, 98–102.

of a rather silly honor conferred post-humously on Germanicus Caesar, un-noticed by Tacitus; **37**, as a list of the races of a short-lived charioteer; **38**, as the only contemporary mention of Pontius Pilate, by himself, which proves that he was a *praefectus* of Judaea, not (as Tacitus says) a procurator; **42**, as containing part of a speech of the emperor Claudius to the Senate (rewritten and shortened by Tac-itus), in which Claudius is quoted as addressing himself, parenthetically, as "Ti(beri) Caesar Germanice," as though some shorthand writer, present, had cop-ied down everything said by the emperor, including this amusing aside, and the edi-tor had passed it for public inspection; **43**, for its Claudian letter Ⅎ for the W-sound of consonantal V; **46**, as a beautiful bronze fragment of the so-called *Lex de Imperio Vespasiani*, rediscovered and set up in the Basilica of St. John Lateran, in Rome, in 1344, by that ardent but misguided re-former Cola di Rienzo and used by him to prove to the people there assembled the *ancient* greatness of the Roman populace and to stir them to revolt against the no-bles (for Rienzo himself, note Bulwer-Lytton's novel *Rienzi* [variant spelling], *or the Last of the Tribunes*, 1835, and Wagner's opera of 1842 based on it, with its well-known Overture); **48**, as an early-Imperial copy of an inscription celebrating the hero of the first Punic War; **49**, for quoting four lines from the emperor Vespasian's re-marks to the Senate about a notable sena-tor/soldier; **52**, as the bilingual epitaph of a young versifier who died at age eleven after having acquitted himself honorably in extemporaneous Greek verse at a po-etry contest; **53**, as documenting the Im-perial child-welfare system, devised by the emperor Nerva and implemented by Trajan; **55**, as cut in the living rock at Fer-entino; **57**, as the inscription on the Col-umn of Trajan, Rome, often considered to have lettering of perfect form; **58**, as in-dicating the emperor Hadrian's modesty in attributing the new Pantheon to Agrip-pa, as Augustus tells us he himself had done in restoring the Capitoline Temple and the Theater of Pompey (*Res Gestae*, 20.1); **60**, as a metrical epitaph, in the first person (with funerary sculpture in relief), of a boy of six or seven, to whom, he him-self tells us, "the Muses had given the gift of eloquence"; **65**, for its badly composed but touching eulogy of a female ex-slave (of whom L. Gurlitt, *Philologus*, 73 [1914] 290, n. 1, wrote, "Germanin war sie wohl zweifellos"); **74**, as a bilingual epitaph that inexplicably seems cut upside down; **75**, as containing the only extant text of the Arval Hymn, in very poor writing; **81**, as the gobbledygook preface to Diocletian's *Edict on Prices*; **82**, as the Roman Senate's dedicatory inscription on the Arch of Constantine, crediting him with being *in-stinctus divinitatis* ("divinely inspired"), as well as having *mentis magnitudo*, in aveng-ing the Res Publica; **87**, as the simple epi-taph of a distinguished Christian convert, cut on a sarcophagus remarkable for its relief sculptures of scenes from the Old and New Testaments; and **91**, as an exam-ple of the work of Filocalus, one of only three engravers of ancient Latin inscrip-tions known to us by name and product.[116]

2. *Greek and Roman writers who appear here*. Besides the other "great" figures that appear in these hundred texts, such as Duilius, a Scipio, Julius Caesar, Au-gustus, Pontius Pilate, Trajan, Septimius

---

116. Two more engravers are known by name, but thus far for only a single product: Florus (*Florus scribit*, CIL 12.2610, in Geneva) and Iul(ius) Silvester, *lapidar(ius)* (*Ber. d. Röm.-German. Kommiss.* 3.40 [1959], in Avenches); photos of both in J. Ewald, *Paläo- u. epigraphische Untersuchungen an den röm. Steininschr. der Schweiz . . .* (*Antiqua*, Bd. 3, 1974, in Kommiss. bei der Schweizer. Gesellsch. f. Ur- u. Frühgesch.) (reviewed in *Erasmus*, 29 [1977] 550–553), Taf. 1–2, cf. p. 83, Tables pp. 104 (GE 31), 131 (AV 23). Unique in the latter stone is the joining of the lower end of the R in *lapidar.* to a leaf-shaped interpunct. Neither inscription is dated.

Severus, Diocletian, there are also some well-known Greek and Roman writers who appear directly or indirectly, in their own persons, or, more often, for their testimony: Ammianus Marcellinus **38**, **87**, **88**, Appian **16**, **28**, Augustus, the emperor Claudius, Cornelius Gallus, and perhaps Ennius or Livius Andronicus (these three or four *suis ipsorum verbis* **5**, **22**, **30**, **34**, **42**), Cassius Dio **18**, **22**–**24**, **26**, **30**, **39**, **46**, **57** f., **61**, Censorinus **52**, Cicero **5**, **8**, **15** f., **20** f., **36**, **46**, **73**, **75**, Claudian **96**, the *Digest* **72**, Diodorus **12**, Dionysius of Halicarnassus **4**, Eutropius **57**, Festus **4**, Frontinus **44**, Gellius **20**, **34**, **37**, the *Historia Augusta* **58** f., **61**, **63**, Horace *in propria persona* **25** (cited also in **37**, **48**), Hydatius **82**, Livy **5**, **8** f., **16**, **19**, **34**, Lucian **52**, Macrobius **11**, Ovid **37**, **65**, Petronius **65**, Pliny the Elder **5**, **16**, **35**, **44**, **48**, **76**, Pliny the Younger **78**, Plutarch **7**, **9**, **11**, **16**, Polybius **9**, Propertius **24**, Prudentius **87**, Quintilian **41**, **43**, **48**, Seneca the Younger **24**, Servius **48**, Silius Italicus **48**, Suetonius **15**, **23**, **30**, **33** f., **39**–**41**, **44**, **46**, **48**, **50**, **52**, Tacitus **16**, **36**, **38**, **41**–**43**, **45** f., **49**, Valerius Maximus **28**, Varro **4**, **55**, **75**, Velleius Paterculus **16**, **30**, Vergil **24**, the *Vulgate* **100**.[117] In addition, there are references to these and other writers elsewhere in the Introduction.

PART VIII. MISCELLANEOUS INFORMATION

1. *Roman numerals.* In Latin inscriptions many numbers are written as words (e.g., *annos undeviginti natus*, the first phrase in Augustus's *Res Gestae*), but many others appear as numerals (e.g., D̶CCCLXXXX [= 890], ibid. 4.2);[118] sometimes we find a supralineate numeral (so marked to indicate multiplication by 1,000) followed by *milia* (e.g., HS̶ $\overline{L}$ $\overline{m}$(*ilia*) $\overline{n}$(*ummum*, gen. plu.) [= 50,000 pieces of money, i.e., sesterces], in **68**, line 7), where either the bar or the *milia* is excessive. Since to some extent we still use Roman numerals, especially in dating books and public buildings, an explanation of them seems in order.[119]

Whereas our so-called Arabic numerals are ten in number (0–9), the Roman numerals number nine: I = 1 (one), V = 5, X = 10, L = 50, C = 100, D̶ = 500 (D regularly with middle bar, the modern form being simply D), a symbol for 1,000 (see below), Q = 500,000, and a rather strange symbol for 6: Ϛ.

C is not commonly thought to be an abbreviation of *centum* (below, n. 126), as M seems to be of *mille* (below) and as Priscian says Q is of *quingenta milia: Quingenta milia (scribitur) per Q, quod est initium nomi-*

117. Cf. *ILS*, Cap. X, "Tituli virorum nonnullorum in litteris clarorum," nos. 2915–2956, including the record of an alimentary endowment set up by Pliny the Younger in his native Comum (2927 = *CIL* 5.5262, cf. *AE* 1949, 65, and his *Letters*, 7.18, with Sherwin-White's notes, op. cit. [above, n. 63] 422–424 and 732 f., "The Personal Inscriptions of Pliny"; also G. Susini, *Epigraphica*, 33 [1971] 183). For an equally fragmentary inscr. in honor of Suetonius, found in 1952 in North Africa (*AE* 1953, 73) see Wm. C. McDermott, *CW* 65 (1971–72), 92, no. 6, with bibl. (incl. Syme, *Tacitus*, 2.778), who calls it "the only Latin inscr. extant which has materially increased our knowledge of a major figure in Latin literature."

118. Of only eight numerals (out of many numbers) in the Latin (the Greek version has *all* the numbers written as words), two include D (= 500), both times medially barred, according to regular usage (Mommsen, ed. *Res Gestae*², pp. XLII 1, 27, LXVI 5, 7).

119. Bibl.: Priscian, *De figuris numerorum quos antiquissimi habent codices*, ed. Keil *Gramm. Lat.* 3.406–417, esp. 406 f.; Fr. Ritschl, *Opusc. phil.* 4 (Leipzig 1878, repr. Hildesheim 1978) 703 *fin.*–705; Hübner, pp. LXX f., Numeri; Hultsch, *RE* 2 (1896) 1110–1114 *s.v.* Arithmetica (there seems to be no article Zahlzeichen in *RE*); Mommsen, *Ges. Schr.* 7 (Berlin 1909) 765–791; Dessau, *ILS* 3: 2, 797 f., Notab. de num.; Sandys/Campbell 54–56, 311; Lommatzsch, *CIL* 1²: 2, pp. 824 f., De not. num. (not from *CIL* 1 ed. 1); Fr. Hallbauer, *De numeralibus Latinis epigraphicis*, Diss. Halle (Halle 1936); J. S. and A. E. Gordon, *Contrib.* 176–182; B. E. Thomasson, "Zu den *Notis Numeralium* in lateinischen Inschriften," *Opuscula Romana* 3 (Lund 1961 Skr. utg. av Svenska Inst. i Rom, 4°, vol. 21 / Acta Inst. Rom. Regni Sueciae, series in 4°,21) 169–178; *Album* 4.53–59 (Index of num.), 111 f. (of abbrs.) *s.vv.* M milia and M N; Meyer, 30–33. Add the index of numbers in all the *CIL* indices that have one.

nis.[120] L has an earlier form (Republican and, in some places, Imperial)[121] like an anchor or an upside-down T with a straight or curved horizontal stroke at the bottom, as in **12**, lines 4–6, three examples.

The symbol for 1,000, which nowadays is M (in English by the early-15th century),[122] seems never to have been M among the Romans,[123] except in the phrases M(*ille* or *-ilia*) N(*ummi* or *-ummum*, gen. plu.) and M. P(*assus* or *-assuum*), where it seems to be an abbreviation rather than a symbol. Instead, we find either a circle divided in half by a vertical line, like the Greek letter *phi* (φ), or a figure like an Arabic 8 on its side (which may well have developed from the *phi*-like symbol), or a recognizable variant of either one, such as (|) (which in some hands may look like a cursive M). This is clear in the photo of **48**, where we find both ∞

---

120. For Q (= 500,000) Dessau on *ILS* 5757, n. 1, cites Priscian, op. cit. 407, 24 (as emended by Mommsen, *Hermes* 10 [1876] 472 [as already in *Hermes* 7 (1873) 366, cf. 3 (1869) 467 f. and 20 (1885) 317] = *Ges. Schr.* 7.788–791), several other inscrs., including his 5799 (= *CIL* 6.3824, better 31603, thought by Huelsen to be of ca. Sullan date), and Cic. *Ad Att.* 9.9.4 (cf. 9.13.6). (According to E. J. Jory, by letters of May 6, 1980, and May 10, 1981, and in conversation with H. Krummrey [as reported in the latter's letter of Apr. 2, 1981], the symbol Q [= 500,000] occurs in *CIL* 6 only once, in the inscr. listed above, 3824 + 31603.) Pliny the Elder writes, *N.H.* 33.47.133: *Non erat apud antiquos numerus ultra centum milia; itaque et hodie multiplicantur haec, ut decies centena* [sc. *milia*] *aut saepius dicantur*; i.e., "Among the ancients there was no numeral larger than 100,000 [(((|)))], or similarly], so even today multiples of this number are used by saying ten or more times a hundred thousand" (100,000 × 10 = a million, × 20, two million, etc.). We now make some use, at least in libraries, of $\overline{\text{M}}$ (= a million), $\overline{\text{MM}}$ (= 2 million), etc., but such use of M as a numeral seems not to be ancient (Mommsen, *Ges. Schr.* 7.770; J. S. and A. E. Gordon, *Contrib.* 181 f.). The Roman symbol for a million was $\boxed{X}$ (see below). Pliny seems not to have known the Q-symbol, nor does he name the symbol for 100,000 either "apud antiquos" or in his own day, when $\overline{\text{C}}$ (100 × 1000) had apparently replaced the awkward use of Greek *phi* with two additional curves on either side of the vertical (below), and the three-sided box was used to multiply by 100,000.

121. Hübner, p. LXXI, col. 1, L—C.

122. *Oxford Engl. Dict.* 6 (Oxford 1933 and repr.) 529 *s.v.* M, ii. 4. It is uncertain when the somewhat M-like symbol of common or cursive Latin writing became interchangeable with the letter M. Documents and mss. should be examined with this in mind, since the appearance of M in modern reporting and printing of medieval documents cannot be assumed to be accurate; cf. J. Mallon, R. Marichal, C. Perrat, *L'écriture latine . . .* (Paris 1939) nos. 7–8 and pl. vi, esp. no. 7, line 9, where the MM of the numeral at the end, as printed, is unlike the M's in *Summacos* at the beginning, and no. 8, lines 6 *fin.*, 12 *fin.*, 14 *fin.*, where again the printed M's in the numerals look in the plate, lower figure, like the

old symbol for 1,000, different from M; A. Cappelli, *Lexicon Abbrev., Diz. di Abbrev. latine et italiane*⁴ (Milan 1949) 417.

123. Except perhaps (by confusion?) in *CIL* 1².590 (= *ILS* 6086, *Lex Munic. Tarent.*), line 28 *med.*, where the first publication, *Mon. Ant.* 6 (1895/96) 411, pl. 14/15 (by "eliotipia"), shows what seems to be *MD tegularum* (the M is different from most of the other M's here, but like that in *duovirum*, line 44 *fin.*; the D has no crossbar); in Degrassi's photo (*Imag.* 395) only the *D tegularum* can be seen, nothing of the M; to be certain, one should see the bronze itself, in Naples. In the Aezani copy of Diocletian's *Edict on Prices* (**81**) the M read in ch. 14, 1a, by the Naumanns, op. cit. (below, on **81**) p. 47, Giacchero, op. cit. (ibid.) 1.164, and M. Crawford and J. M. Reynolds, *ZPE* 26 (1977) 136, makes no sense, esp. in view of the Greek version, β' (= 2), and is not clearly an M in the Naumanns' photo, pl. 10 (or in Giacchero's pl. 39) col. 3, last line; presumably it should be the numeral II (and may in fact be II—if one could see the stone), as G., 1.283, and C/R, 151, suggest. In fact, Miss Reynolds, by letter of March 16, 1979, writes: "On ch. 14.1a we read [past tense] M—but the stone is bad and the lettering poor and the light often awkward; our footnote reveals our unhappiness that we felt when we sat down to the problem. Having seen the stone, I know why we saw M—I am quite sure now that we were wrong and that what stands on the stone is II (rather shaky) with a chip in the stone to the right giving \ and so the impression of M. If you want to discuss it, I shall be glad to have the error righted." The other examples of M = 1,000 listed in *CIL* 1²: 2: 2, p. 824, col. 3, are in no. 593 (= *ILS* 6085, *Lex Iulia Munic.*), where Degrassi's photos (*Imag.* 391 a-b) show no M, but either a blank space (line 50 *fin.*, *Imag.* 391 a) or a symbol (~ or a variant), including one in line 67 (*Imag.*, ibid.), where Ritschl, *PLME*, pl. 33/34, shows an M (on his facsimiles see *Album* 1, p. 3, col. 2, last par.). In the Aezani copy of D.'s *Edict*, thousands seem indicated by supralineate bars. In the Synnada copy, both places reported by Lauffer, op. cit. (below, on **81**), pp. 148 ch. 17, 2, and 150 ch. 19, 5, as reading M (= 1,000) show no M at all, but quite clearly ∞ (like an Arabic 8 on its side) in I. W. Macpherson's photo, *JRS* 42 (1952) pl. X, 1 (reproduced by Giacchero, pl. 16, no. 24), col. 1, last line

(= 1,000) and (((I))) (= 100,000). See also Cagnat 31, or *CIL* 1², pp. 824 f.; Cagnat's derivation of the *phi*-like symbol from "the phi of the Chalcidic alphabet" is confirmed by M. Guarducci, 1.220 *med.*, who notes "the numeral signs ψ = 50, ① = 1,000 (its right half D = 500)" as "belonging in origin to the Greco-Euboic alphabet and not used by the Latins with the value of letters." The Romans presumably got these symbols either directly from the Euboic colonies of southern Italy or Sicily or indirectly through the Etruscans,[124] from whom it is quite possible, if not probable, that they borrowed the Greek alphabet (A. E. Gordon, *Origins*).

The symbol Ϛ for 6 Jean Mallon considers a ligature of VI in which the V is written with a single rounded stroke and the I joined to it at the bottom; this symbol "serves indifferently, in the ancient classic-common script [cf. *Contrib.* 67], to express the figure 6 as well as the group *ui*" (J. M., *Paléographie romaine* [Madrid 1952] 126–128, §191); he quotes second-century (A.D.) examples from papyri and a first-century example from a Pompeian graffito. For a tiny barred example of A.D. 296, see the *Album* 3.107, no. 311, with pl. 148, *a* (= Diehl, *ILCV* 2.2807 A), line 3; Diehl, 3.230–263, indexes many examples from A.D. 296 to 584.[125] For the origin of the other numerals, see Sandys/Campbell 54 f., 311, with refs. to Ritschl and Mommsen.[126]

All the other Roman numerals found in Latin inscriptions are simply combinations of these basic nine, by addition, subtraction, or multiplication. The numbers 4, 8, and 9, and compounds of these, may be written by addition or subtraction, in-

differently; e.g., IIII or IV, XVIII or XIIX, XVIIII or XIX; so also XXXX or XL, LXXX or XXC, LXXXX or XC, CCCC or CD, DCCC or CCD, DCCCC or CD. (See *Contrib.* 176–181, sect. 2). The rule in forming or interpreting these combinations is that, if the symbol next to the right is larger in value than the first symbol, the first is to be subtracted from it, but if the second is of the same value as the first or of lesser value, the second is to be added to the first; e.g., XL = 40, but LX = 60 and CC = 200. The numerals, I, X, C, ① in its various forms, and presumably Q may be repeated up to a total of four times (Q presumably *ad infinitum*), but V, L, D are not repeated at all; e.g., I, II, III, IIII, likewise X, C, ①, Q, but not VV, LL, or DD; instead, X, C, and ① will be used. No use of a plural Q seems to have been found; Q in fact seems to have ceased being used by the time of Pliny the Elder (see n. 120). The use of ① in its various forms is peculiar: (I) = 1,000, whence perhaps D, the right half, for 500 (the middle bar generally added, to distinguish it from the letter D [?], or perhaps the source was a ①-type symbol with horizontal as well as vertical stroke inside the circle), I)) = 5,000, ((I)) = 10,000, I))) = 50,000, and (((I))) = 100,000. The shape of the basic ① varies considerably. To judge from the forms printed in the index of numbers in most of the *CIL* indices, the forms are often far less clear than in the marble of **48** (early Empire, not after A.D. 77), where the forms of a wide, squat *phi* for 1,000 and of an even wider *phi* with two small curves on either side of the vertical (within the left and right sides of the bottomless *phi*-form) for 100,000 are

---

(*per / passus* ∞) and col. 2, line 2 (*alba libr. XII* space X (= *denariis*) ∞DC). (Macpherson, p. 72, reads it as MDC.)

124. The Etruscans had several symbols like those of the Romans, though Mommsen thought that those for 50, 100, and 1,000 were borrowed from the Romans; cf. G. Buonamici, *Epigrafia etrusca* (Florence 1932) 243–247 (unclear), Mommsen, *Hermes* 22 (1887) 598 f. (*Ges. Schr.* 7.767 f.).

125. Larfeld, 294, *init.*, cites a similar form with

the same value, 6, in 7th- and 8th-cent. (A.D.) Greek inscrs.

126. The common view is that C (= 100) originated in Chalcidic Θ (e.g., Ritschl, *Opusc. phil.* 4.704; Mommsen *Hermes* 22 [1887] 598 f. [*Ges. Schr.* 7.767 f.]; Sandys/Campbell 84 f.), but the fact that C was the first letter of *centum* may have helped, as in the case of M for *mille/milia* in phrases with *nummi/-um* and *passus/-uum*.

striking. The vertical varies in height from text to text.

Any numeral may be multiplied by 1,000 by means of a superposed bar, such as $\overline{L}$ = 50,000; perhaps the earliest extant example is in the *Lex de Gallia Cisalpina* of 49–42 (?) B.C. (*CIL* 1².592), where it occurs three times (col. 2, lines 4, 19, 27).[127] Multiplication by 100,000 is done by writing a three-sided box around the multiplicand, such as $\boxed{X}$ = a million, as in *CIL* 10.3851 (= *ILS* 5890). Dessau, *ILS* 3: 2, 798, lists eleven more examples of this, the largest number being $\overline{|CCCLVIII|}$ $\overline{LXIII}$ CXX (= 35,863,120), if we accept Mommsen's and Dessau's plausible correction of the first unit from $\overline{CCCLVIII}$ (see D.'s note 31); the earliest of these seem to be *ILS* 5890 (above), which Groag, *PIR*² 2.274, no. 1156, dates to the early Principate, and *ILS* 2709 (= *CIL* 12.1357), which Hirschfeld dates by its "excellent lettering" to the first century (A.D.); the others seem to be of the second century.

Besides these proper, independent uses of numerals, there are a few special uses of numerals, normally barred, such as the numerical prefix of composite words like *duo-* or *duumvir(i)*—e.g., *IIvir(i)*, in which the two components are often separated from each other in inscriptions by the usual punctuation, a point at (or about) mid-height. Such words serve to indicate a member or members of an administrative Board, or the whole Board, such as the *Triumviri Capitales* in charge of capital sentences or the *Quindecimviri Sacris Faciundis* in charge of religious matters. (See H. J. Mason, "*Vir*: Member of a College," *Studies in Latin Literature and Roman History*, 2 [*Coll. Latomus*, 168, 1980] 5–20.) These barred numerals are $\overline{II}$, $\overline{III}$, $\overline{IV}$ (or $\overline{IIII}$), $\overline{VI}$ (or $\overline{IIIIII}$ or $\overline{|IIII|}$), $\overline{VII}$, $\overline{X}$, $\overline{XV}$, $\overline{XX}$, $\overline{XXX}$, $\overline{C}$ (but there may be others—in principle, there is no limit),[128] always followed by -*vir* or -*viri* (in any case desired, the gen. plu. -*um* or -*orum*) : *duo-* or *duumvir(i)*, *triumvir(i)* (hence, at least once, $\overline{III}$*viratus*, *ILS* 6858 = *CIL* 8.6948), *quattuorvir(i)*, *se-* or *sexvir(i)* (see *Contrib.* 182 for the various forms), *septemvir(i)*, *decemviri*, *quindecim-* or -*decemvir(i)*, *vigintivir(i)*, *trigintaviri* (*CIL* 14.2458 = *ILS* 3475), *centumvir(i)* (Cic. *De Lege Agrar.* 2.44, *CIL* 11.3801 = *ILS* 2592, cf. 3: 2, 675 *s.v.* conscripti). The superposed bar no doubt marks the numeral as a number. (The barred numerical prefixes in *CIL* 1²: 2 are listed in *Contrib.* 224 n. 3). The symbols ⅱS and ✕ for *sestertius* and *denarius* regularly use a medial bar (*Contrib.* 167).

Except in these numerical prefixes, cardinal numerals seem to be barred only by error. Ordinals are barred regularly when they are adverbial ("for the nth time"); the constant use of these adverbials in Imperial titles must have fostered this use of the bar. Ordinal adjectives indicating the day of the month are not, as a rule, barred, but usage for other ordinals was less clear-cut, perhaps because they were less often used. But in designating the number of a legion or a cohort the ordinal adjective seems generally barred (*Contrib.* 166–170). We find barred numerals also in inscriptions of charioteers in which their victories are listed: e.g., *CIL* 6.37834 (= *Album* 2.31–35, no. 173A), line 27, a bar over ∞ (to mean 1,000 times, though one would expect a cardinal adverb to be unbarred—*Contrib.* 168, 169, 225 n. 18); lines 23, 24 *init.*, a bar over abbreviated ordinal adjectives, *c(entesimam)* and ∞ (*millesimam*), sc. *palmam*, "victory"; and line 28, a barred ordinal adverb, $\overline{XVII}$, "for the 17th time" (this with ref. to Domitian's 17th consulship). There may be other regular uses of bars, e.g. in designating ship

---

127. For the date, cf. G. Barbieri, in De Rugg. 4: 23 (1956) 730 *s.v.* Lex.: "49–42?", B.C.

128. There are also unbarred XX and XXX in the phrases *votis XX annalib(us)*, and *votis XXX annalib(us)*, *feliciter* (*CIL* 6.428, cf. pp. 3005, 3576 = *ILS* 2219 = *Album* 3.63–65 no. 284, of A.D. 217 [?], not after 235), for *vicennalib.*, one X erased to become *decennalib.*, and *tricennalib.*, one X erased to become *vicennalib.*

types, the size of a military unit, or a civil servant's rank according to stipend (as, in fact, in our **74**, where $\overline{C}$, $\overline{CC}$, $\overline{CCC}$ = *centenario, ducenario, trecenario,* and *leg.* $\overline{III}$ = *legionis tertiae*.

For fractions of numbers, see Mommsen, *Hermes* 3 (1869) 469–475, *Hermes* 22 (1887) 605–611 (*Ges. Schr.* 7.773–780); Hultsch, *RE* 2 (1896) 1114 ff.; Cagnat 32–34; *Contrib.* 170 *fin.*–175; *Album* 4.60. In the symbol for sesterce, H̶S̶, the verticals indicate two units (*asses*), the S is the abbreviation of *semis* (½), so the symbol means 2½ (*asses,* "units"), *sestertius* being short for *semistertius,* literally "half third," as in German "halb zehn" means "9:30 (o'clock)." The fact that *sestertius* is in form an adjective explains why some form of *nummus,* "piece of money, coin" (always gen. pl., *nummum,* when thousands are indicated, generally abbreviated N or $\overline{N}$), is regularly added, as exemplified above, at the beginning of this section: H̶S̶ $\overline{L}$ $\overline{m}(ilia)$ $\overline{n}(ummum)$ (= 50,000 sesterces).

Of the present selection of a hundred inscriptions, fifty-one contain one or more numerals. A summary of their uses and peculiarities: (1) Many more inscriptions show only additive numerals than only subtractive; five show both types. (2) Up through **78** (A.D. 260), the ordinal adverbs ("for the nth time") are nearly always barred; from **79** (A.D. 279) none are. For the form of the ordinal adverb when written as a word, see the end of this section. (3) From **53** (A.D. 101) we find numerals barred to indicate multiplication by 1,000. No. **68** (A.D. 182) has four so treated along with $\overline{m}(ilia)$ $\overline{n}(ummum)$. (4) The ordinal adjective (1st, 2nd, 3rd, etc.) is always unbarred in a date whether *a(nte) d(iem)* is expressed (only once, **51**, line 16) or not (22 times); after *milliario* in **44**, it is twice unbarred (in each duplex inscr., so far as is visible in the photos), but after *milliarium* in **66**, line 4, it is twice barred; when it is the number of a legion, it is always (eight times) barred; once *hora* $\overline{II}$ (= *secunda*), sixteen times (in one inscr., **72**) *d(ie)* x (= *dec-*

imo or *-a,* unbarred). (5) A numeral to mean how many times: the rule is, no bar above; one (**37**, A.D. 25—a charioteer's career) has thirty-nine such numerals unbarred, one faintly barred (apparently by error); the other pertinent inscription is **92** (A.D. 387), where unbarred *II* (= twice) occurs (col. 2, line 13), though it seems to be out of place. (6) For the type *XV vir:* nine inscriptions show eleven examples barred, six unbarred (no. **55** shows four barred, one unbarred); the barred lead two to one. (7) Other *notabiliora:* $\overline{S}$ (= *sextariorum,* gen. plu.—a liquid measure, here of wine, **66**) five times, line 12; 6.4% interest is perhaps expressed (in **68**, lines 10 f.) by *ex usuris semissibus et* $\overset{.}{M}$ (= *minutis* ? an M with a short vertical cut just above it) *II* (= ²⁄₆₀?); if so, the interest would be ½ + ²⁄₆₀% per month x 12 (months) = 6.4% annually.

All this confirms pretty well the more general statements made above.

Tertio vs. *tertium,* and similar forms: When the ordinal adverb ("for the nth time") is written as a *word* (as a *numeral* this would regularly be written $\overline{III}$, with supralineate bar, as noted above), the inscriptions show several forms—e.g., *tertio, tertium,* and the abbreviations *ter.* and *tert.* (this last in **20**). The Republican evidence is given in *CIL* 1², pp. 765–789, 846 f. (index vocab.), to which add no. 2965 (**20**), which is to appear in fasc. 4. The pertinent forms are *primum* ("first, for the first time"), *iterum/iteru.* (on a coin) /*iter.,* *tertium/tert./ter., quinto* (no. 1911, where the ed. cites also 2 exs. of *quarto, CIL* 10.4896 and *EE* 9.348 no. 470 [= *CIL* 14 Suppl. 4710 = *ILS* 5395], the latter judged to be of the 1st cent. A.D.), and *septumo.* As is noted below, on **20**, all the examples of such ordinal adverbs in Augustus's *Res Gestae,* when not written as numerals, end in *-um,* while all the Greek forms end in the corresponding *-ov* (the Greek uses no numerical forms).

In addition, we have about two pages of discussion of the problem *-o* vs. *-um,* in

Gellius, 10.1, where he cites or quotes nine Romans, besides giving his own choice. The results: four, including Coelius (Antipater) and Q. Claudius (Quadrigarius), favored the -o form, and four, including Cato the Elder, Ennius, Varro (who says that *quarto* means, not for the fourth time, but fourth in order, as in an election), and Gellius himself, the -*um* form. Amusingly, Cicero's learned freedman Tiro is quoted as saying that Pompey, wishing to know whether to inscribe *tertium* or *tertio* to indicate his own third consulship (52 B.C.) on the temple of Victory (Venus Victrix) placed at the top of his theater, found a difference of opinion among the *doctissimi* of the state, so he asked Cicero to decide; Cicero, not wishing to offend anyone, advised Pompey to write *tert*. Many years later, Gellius adds, when the back wall of the *scaena* was restored and Pompey's inscription had to be rewritten, *tert.* was replaced by the numeral III. Then comes the famous inscription on the Pantheon, as rebuilt by Hadrian, in which Agrippa appears as *co(n)s(ul) tertium* (**58**).

So the authors, like the inscriptions, vary between -o and -*um* (as their MSS also show: see *TLL* 4.569, line 67–570, line 21, *s.v.* consul), and Pompey, we have seen, found the most learned men in the state in his own time disagreeing in their choice. Apparently, each form had its supporters, and the choice was personal. One question remains, perhaps: the form of *tertio*, *quarto*, etc. Is it ablative, as seems to be generally believed (e.g., by Lewis/Short *s.vv.*; Kühner/Holzweissig 1.630, §146, 5, Anm. 1, cf. 1006; K. E. Georges, *Ausführl. lat.-deutsches Handwörterb.*[8] 2 [1918] 3084, *s.v. tertiō*; Hallbauer, op. cit.

[above, n. 119] 127, *De iterationibus honorum*, line 5; E/M 553, col. 2, *s.v.* quattuor—three of these simply show a long *o*)? Or, as one or two scholars hold (in a letter), an old accusative "with unexpressed nasal," like *oino, optumo,* and *viro* in the Scipionic *CIL* 1².9 (= 6.1287 = *ILS* 3)? But it is incredible that, if Gellius or Varro or any of the others whom Gellius quotes or cites (loc. cit.) had believed both the -o and -*um* forms to be accusative, he or they would have failed to say so; in fact, there would have been no uncertainty or discussion, and Pompey would naturally have used -*um* as the Classical Latin of his own day. Terence, *Eun.* 530, *tertio,* and Ovid, *Fasti* 2.665 *quarto, Met.* 9.51 *quarto,* are of no help in determining the length of the -o: in Terence the word is followed by *heus,* so the -o is lost in elision or slurring, and in Ovid the -o is *syllaba anceps* at the end of the line.

2. *Chronological list of Roman emperors (bearing the title "Augustus") from Augustus to Justinian.*[129]

Augustus 31 (*trib. pot.* from June 26, 23)
  B.C.–A.D. 14
Tiberius A.D. 14–37
Caligula (Gaius) 37–41
Claudius (I) 41–54
Nero 54–68
Galba 68–69 (Jan. 15)
Vitellius 69 (early Jan.–late Dec.)
Otho 69 (Jan. 15–Apr. 25)
Vespasian 69 (July 1)–79
Titus 79–81
Domitian 81–96
Nerva 96–98
Trajan 98–117
Hadrian 117–138
Antoninus Pius 138–161
Marcus Aurelius 161–180 } jointly
Lucius Verus 161–169   } 161–169[130]

---

129. This list is compiled from several modern sources: Cagnat 177–250, Degrassi's *Fasti consulari* 275–286 (lists only the emperors who held consulships), *PLRE* vol. 1, and Calabi Limentani 479–492 (lacks a few late emperors). In case of disagreement among these, other sources have been used, but no attempt has been made to consult the ancient sources on which they depend. Excluded are em-

perors "of the Gauls" and those "in Britain," also all "Caesars" unless they became "Augusti." The division of the Empire into Western and Eastern, which took place in the course of the fourth century, seems to have occurred without any legal enactment.

130. This is the first of many examples of the joint rule of Augusti. Sometimes the association is arranged and harmonious (as in this case), sometimes

Commodus 180–192
Pertinax 193 (Jan. 1–Mar. 28)
Didius Julianus 193 (Mar. 28–early June)
Septimius Severus 193–211
Pescennius Niger 193–194
Clodius Albinus late 195 (or early 196)–197
Caracalla 198–217
Geta 211–212
Macrinus 217–218
Elagabalus (or Heliogabalus) 218–222
Severus Alexander 222–235
Maximinus 235–238
Gordian I 238
Gordian II 238
Balbinus 238
Pupienus 238
Gordian III 238–244
Philip I 244–249
Philip II 247–249
Decius 249–251
Decius, son 251
Trebonianus Gallus 251–253
Volusianus 251–253
Aemilianus 253
Valerian 253–260
Gallienus 253–268
Claudius II 268–270
Quintillus 270
Aurelian 270–275
Tacitus 275–276
Florianus 276
Probus 276–282
Carus 282–283
Carinus 283–285
Numerian 283–284
Diocletian 284–305
Maximianus 286–305
Constantius I (Chlorus) 305–306
Galerius 305–311
Flavius Severus 306–307
Maxentius 307–312
Licinius 308–324
Maximinus Daia 309–313

Constantine I ("the Great") 306–337
Constantine II 337–340
Constans 337–350
Constantius II 337–361
Magnentius 350–353
Julian ("the Apostate") 360 (or 361)–363
Jovian (Iovianus) 363–364
Valentinian I 364–375
Valens 364–378
Procopius 365–366
Gratian 367–383
Valentinian II 375–392
Theodosius I ("the Great") 379–395
Maximus 383–388
Flavius Victor 383 (?)–388
Eugenius 392–394
Arcadius (East) 383–408
Honorius (West) 393–423
Theodosius II (East) 402–450
Constantius III (West) 421
Johannes (West) 423–425
Valentinian III (West) 425–455
Petronius Maximus (West) 455
Marcianus (East) 450–457
Avitus (West) 455–456
Maiorianus (West) 457–461
Leo I (East) 457–474
Libius Severus (West) 461–465
Anthemius (West) 467–472
Olybrius (West) 472
Leo II (East) 473–474
Glycerius (West) 473–474
Nepos (West) 474–475 (or 480)[131]
Zeno (East) 474–491
Romulus Augustulus (West) 475–476[132]
Anastasius (East) 491–518
Justinus I (East) 518–527
Justinian (East) 527–565

3. *Contents of the CIL volumes*.[133] The publication of *CIL* began with a large volume illustrating the inscriptions of *CIL*

---

arranged but ending in one partner's murdering the other (as in the case of the brothers Caracalla and Geta, 211–212); sometimes there are rival claimants, usually army commanders, each hailed as "Augustus" by some body, generally his own army, e.g., in Gaul or Britain. The examples of joint or rival rule after that of M. Aurelius and L. Verus are not identified here, for simplicity's sake.

131. In 475 Nepos fled east from Italy to Dalmatia before the rebellious army-commander Orestes (who claimed the throne for his young son, Romulus Augustulus), but he was recognized by Zeno as still emperor in the West until his death in 480. Cf. *Der Kleine Pauly* 4.63, 236, 338, 1457, *s.vv.* Nepos 3,

Odoacer, Orestes 4, Romulus 4; or the corresponding articles in *RE*.

132. Romulus Augustulus, named emperor in the West, when he was only a child, by his father Orestes (above, n. 131), was never recognized in the East (Constantinople) and was removed peacefully in 476 by a German king in Italy, Odoacer, and given a *castellum* near Naples for his residence. He is commonly known as the last Roman emperor in the West. The Eastern Empire continued to exist for almost 1,000 years longer, until the capture of Constantinople by the Ottoman Turks in 1453.

133. The most complete lists are those of (1) the Verlag Walter de Gruyter & Co., Berlin 30 (now D 1,

vol. 1 the year before vol. 1 itself appeared: *Priscae Latinitatis monumenta epigraphica* (98 lithographic plates with annotation), ed. Fr. Ritschl (Berlin 1862), to which should be added his *Priscae Latinitatis epigraphicae supplementa quinque* (1862–1864), which appeared also in his *Opuscula* vol. 4 (Leipzig 1878, repr. Hildesheim 1978), with atlas of twenty-three plates. (Ritschl's work has been largely superseded by A. Degrassi's *Inscriptiones Latinae liberae rei publicae, Imagines* [*CIL Auctarium*, Berlin 1965].)

Vol. 1 (ed. 1), 1863. *Inscriptiones Latinae antiquissimae*, to the death of Caesar, 44 B.C.; also *Elogia clarorum virorum* (eulogies of the Republican leaders, notably those set up by Augustus in his new Forum in Rome [Suet. *Aug.* 31.5, *Hist. Aug., Sev. Alex.* 28.6], but also set up elsewhere), *Fasti anni Iuliani* (the Julian calendar), ed. Th. Mommsen; *Fasti consulares*, ed. G. (i.e., W.) Henzen. The indices were the work of E. Huebner.

This has been superseded by ed. 2 (though it is still profitable to have ed. 1 available, so as to make sure of having all of Mommsen's remarks): part 1 (1893) *Fasti cons.* ed. Henzen and Chr. Huelsen; *Elogia cl. vir.*, ed. Mommsen and Huelsen; *Fasti anni Iul.*, ed. Mommsen; part 2 fasc. 1–3 (1918, 1931, 1943), *Inscr. Lat. antiquiss.*, ed. E. Lommatzsch and, for fasc. 2, H. Dessau (fasc. 2 contains addenda, an appendix of coins, indices including an index of words; fasc. 3, further addenda and further indices); fasc. 4, ed. Degrassi and H. Krummrey (Director of *CIL*, Berlin), with still more addenda and corrigenda, is forthcoming. (Part 1 has been largely replaced by Degrassi's *Fasti et Elogia*, 4 vols., constituting vol. XIII of the *Inscriptiones Italiae*, Rome: fasc. 1, *Fasti*

cons. et triumphales [2 vols., 1947]; fasc. 2, *Fasti anni Numani et Iuliani*, with *Ferialia, Menologia rustica, Parapegmata* [1963]; fasc. 3 *Elogia* [1937]; part 2 largely so also by Degrassi's *Inscriptiones Latinae liberae rei publicae*, 2 vols., vol. 1 ed. 2 [Florence 1965], vol. 2 [1963], both repr. 1972.)

Vol. 2. Spain, 1869, Suppl. 1892, ed. Huebner.

Vol. 3. ⟨Egypt⟩, Asia, the Greek provinces of Europe, and Illyricum, ed. Mommsen, 1873. Part 1 (now includes Egypt in the subtitle): the first three areas plus Illyricum, parts 1–5; part 2: Illyricum, parts 6–7, plus the *Res Gestae* of Augustus (from the *Monumenta Ancyranum* and *Apolloniense*), Diocletian's *Edict on Prices*, *Privilegia militum veteranorumque* (*diplomata militaria*, like our **51**: cf. Sandys/Campbell 180–185), and *Instrumenta Dacica* (waxed tablets from Dacia: ibid. 186 f.); Suppl. (entitled *Inscriptionum Orientis et Illyrici Lat. suppl.*) ed. Mommsen, O. Hirschfeld, A. Domaszewski, parts 1–2 (both 1902); part 2 has an index of the words, Latin and Greek, in D.'s *Edict*, but pp. 1668–2038 are separately bound, entitled *Suppl.*, Fasc. Tertius, with the same three editors, dated 1893, and cover Illyricum parts 4–7, plus more on D.'s *Edict* and the *Privilegia*, now called *Constitutiones imperatorum de civitate et conubio mil. vet.que* (these 2 last parts ed. Mommsen).

Vol. 4 *Inscriptiones parietariae* (wall inscriptions or graffiti) of Pompeii, Herculaneum, Stabiae, ed. C. Zangemeister, R. Schoene, 1871; Suppl., part 1, waxed tablets from Pompeii, ed. Zangemeister, 1898; part 2, wall and vase inscriptions, ed. A. Mau, 1909; part 3, Pompeian and Herculanean wall and vase inscriptions, ed. M. Della Corte, P. Ciprotti, Lief. 1–3, 1952–1963, Lief. 4, 1970. (The other in-

---

Berlin 30, Genthiner Strasse 13, with offices also at 200 Saw Mill River Rd., Hawthorne, New York 10532) of 1970 or 1971, which lists also all the dates of reprinting, up to 1970, and the prices then in force (Ritschl's *PLME*, its 5 supplements, and most of vols.

2–15 had been reprinted by 1970), (2) Meyer 131–134, and (3) Degrassi *ap.* Calabi Limentani 425–428; S/C pp. xviii–xx has been helpful with the English explanations. All these lists are too early to have *CIL* 6, part 7 (see below).

scrs. from this area are in *CIL* 10, under Campania.)

Vol. 5. Cisalpine Gaul, ed. Mommsen: part 1, the 10th region of Italy (Venetia and Istria), 1872; part 2, the 11th and 9th regions (Liguria, Transpadane Gaul, the Cottian and Maritime Alps), 1877.

Vol. 6. City of Rome, part 1 (collected by Henzen and G. B. De Rossi, ed. E. Bormann and Henzen, 1876); part 2 (ed. Bormann, Henzen, Chr. Huelsen, 1882), part 3 (ed. the same three, 1886); part 4: 1 (coll. Henzen, De Rossi, Bormann, ed. Huelsen, 1894); part 4: 2 Additamenta (coll. et ed. Huelsen, 1902); part 4: fasc. postremus, Additamentorum auctarium (ed. M. Bang, 1933); part 5 Inscr. falsae urbi Romae attributae (ed. Bormann, Henzen, Huelsen, 1885); part 6: 1 Index nominum (ed. Bang, 1926); part 6: 2 Index cognominum (ed. L. Vidman, 1980); part 7: 1–6 Indices vocabulorum, nominibus propriis inclusis, composuerunt E. J. Jory et D. W. Moore machina computatoria usi, 1974–1975 (fasc. 1, vocabula A–C; 2, vocab. D–F; 3, vocab. G–M; 4, vocab. N–S; 5, vocab. T–Z, Graeca, cognomina A–G; 6, cognomina H–Z, cognomina acephala, vocab. acephala).

Vol. 7. Britain, ed. Huebner, 1873. (This is being replaced by R. G. Collingwood and R. P. Wright's *The Roman Inscriptions of Britain*, 2 vols.; vol. 1, *Inscriptions on Stone* [Oxford 1965—cf. *CP* 63 (1968) 122–130]; vol. 2 will include the *Instrumentum domesticum* [portable objects used in private life—cf. Sandys/Campbell 143–155].)

Vol. 8. Africa, part 1, Africa proconsularis and Numidia, coll. G. Wilmanns, ed. Mommsen (1881); part 2, Mauretania; suppl. in 4 parts, ed. R. Cagnat, J. Schmidt, Dessau, 1891, 1894, 1904, 1916; suppl. part 5, fasc. 1–3, indices, 1942, 1955, 1959 (no editors' names on title pages, but prefaces signed by H. Stroux, fasc. 1, and C. Schubring, fasc. 2–3, who name several collaborators).

Vol. 9. Calabria, Apulia, Samnium, the Sabines, Picenum, ed. Mommsen, 1883.

Vol. 10, in 2 parts, ed. Mommsen, 1883: 1, the Bruttii, Lucania, Campania; 2, Sicily and Sardinia.

Vol. 11, in 2 parts: 1, Aemilia, Etruria, ed. Bormann, 1888; 2: 1, Umbria and public roads, ed. Bormann, *Instrum. domest.*, ed. M. Ihm, 1901; 2: 2, Addenda and 3 sections of indices (nomina, cognomina, emperors), 1926.

Vol. 12. Narbonese Gaul, ed. O. Hirschfeld, 1888.

Vol. 13. Three Gauls (other than Cisalpine and Narbonese) and Two Germanies, in 6 parts: 1: 1, Aquitania and Gallia Lugudunensis (1899), 1: 2 (Gallia) Belgica (1904), both ed. Hirschfeld; 2: 1, Upper (southern) Germany, ed. Zangemeister (1905), 2: 2 Lower (northern) Germany, plus the milestones of the Gauls and the Germanies, ed. Mommsen, Hirschfeld, Domaszewski (1907); 3: 1, *Instrum. domest.* 1, ed. O. Bohn (1901), 3: 2, *Instrum. domest.* 2, ed. Bohn, plus *Signacula medicorum oculariorum* (oculists' seals and stamps: cf. Sandys/Campbell 150 f.) ed. E. Espérandieu (1906); 4, Addenda to parts 1 and 2, ed. Hirschfeld and H. Fink (1916); 5, Indices, comp. I. Szlatolawek and Dessau (1943); 6, *Signacula publice laterculis impressa* (brick stamps from public works), coll. P. Steiner, ed. E. Stein and H. Volkmann; plus the same from private sources, ed. Volkmann (1933).

Vol. 14. Latium vetus ("Old" Latium as distinguished from *Latium adiectum*: see map at end), ed. Dessau, 1887; Suppl. Ostiense (devoted to Ostia), ed. L. Wickert, 1930; Suppl. Ost. fasc. 2, with topographical indices and annotation, ed. Wickert, 1933.

Vol. 15. City of Rome *Instr. domesticum*, ed. H. Dressel: part 1 (1891), part 2 fasc. 1 (1899) (completed by Herbert Bloch, "The Roman Brick-stamps Not Published in *CIL* 15," *HSCP* 56–57 [1947], pp. 228). Nos. 8017–8622, Signacula aenea *CIL* 15: 2: 2 destinata, appeared in 1975.

Vol. 16. *Diplomata militaria* (records of

the privileges of Roman citizenship and marriage granted to veteran soldiers—cf. Sandys/Campbell 180–185), ed. H. Nesselhauf (after Mommsen), 1936. Supplementum, ed. Nesselhauf (1955).

(For the several additions to *CIL* that are in progress, see above, n. 27.)

There are also four supplementary volumes, each called Auctarium of *CIL*, including Ritschl's *PLME* (listed above, first), Huebner's *Exempla scripturae epigraphicae Latinae* from Caesar's death to the age of Justinian (1885), Degrassi's *Inscr. Latinae liberae rei publicae, Imagines* (1965), and R. Gruendel's *Addenda bibliographica praecipue ad CIL . . .* (1965). Other supplements include Bloch's completion of *CIL* 15 (cited above) and the *Ephemeris Epigraphica, CIL supplementum*, ed. the Roman Archaeological Institute, in 9 vols., 1872–1913; this includes not only new inscriptions supplementary to vols. 2, 7, 9, 10, 14, but also articles and dissertations on Latin epigraphy, such as C. Zangemeister's *Glandes plumbeae Latine inscriptae* (inscribed sling-bolts of lead [cf. Sandys/Campbell 148] from, e.g., the "Social" War of 90–88 B.C.), illustrated with 13 plates (vol. 6, 1899, pp. 225–309), and E. Ziebarth's *De antiquissimis inscriptionum syllogis* (vol. 9, 1913, pp. 187–332). Note also E. Pais's additions to *CIL* 5, fasc. 1, in *MemLinc* 4: 5 (1888).

Other supplements to *CIL* as well as other collections of Latin inscriptions are listed by Meyer 134 f., and Degrassi, *ap.* Calabi Limentani, 429–434, followed by a list of pertinent journals and journal articles, 434 f., including *L'Année épigraphique* and *Epigraphica*. Very useful also, for the listing of new books, articles, and re-

views in this field, is the section on Latin inscriptions in the yearly *L'Année Philologique* (e.g., vol. 45 [Paris 1976] pp. 552–564). Valuable also the volumes recording the proceedings of the quinquennial International Congress of Greek and Latin Epigraphy.[134]

The planner and, after years of frustration, the founder of *CIL*, as well as its most productive editor, was Mommsen. He had already edited a large volume of the *Inscriptiones Regni Neapolitani Latinae* (Leipzig 1852—superseded by *CIL* 9 and 10), at a time when there was still a (French, Bourbon) kingdom of Naples; two years later, a similar work for Switzerland, *Inscriptiones Confoederationis Helveticae* (*Mitteilungen der Antiquarischen Gesellschaft in Zürich*, vol. 10, 1854). It was in Switzerland that he had found an asylum in 1852 and had become in 1853 a (full) professor of Roman Law at Zurich, after having been dismissed from his (assistant-)professorship of Jurisprudence at Leipzig in 1851, because of his political views and activity in connection with the revolutionary movements of 1848–1849 (cf. L. M. Hartmann, *Theodor Mommsen. Eine biographische Skizze* [Gotha 1908] 22–24, 38 f., 47, 50).

His study of Latin inscriptions had begun as a result of an extended visit to Italy in 1844–1847 (including a few months in France on the way), made possible by a grant, first from the Danish government (Danish, since his Alma Mater had been the University of Kiel, which was a part of Denmark from 1773 to 1866, when it passed to Prussia), then from the Prussian government. (It was the Prussian Academy in Berlin by whose *consilium et auc-*

---

134. There have been seven such International Congresses, the proceedings of six of which have been published to date: of the first Congress, Amsterdam 1938, no proceedings were published (no doubt because of the coming of World War II); *Actes du deuxième Congrès Internat.*, etc., *Paris 1952* (publ. Paris 1953); *Atti del Terzo Congresso Internazionale di Epigrafia Greca e Latina* (*Roma 4–8 settembre 1957*) (Rome 1959); *Akte des IV. Internationalen Kongresses für* *Griechische und Lateinische Epigraphik* (*Wien, 17. bis 22. September 1962*) (Vienna 1964); *Acta of the Fifth International Congress of Greek and Latin Epigraphy, Cambridge 1967* (Oxford 1971); *Akten des VI. Internationalen Kongresses für Griechische und Lateinische Epigraphik, München 1972* (Munich 1973); *Actes du VIIᵉ Congrès Internat. d'Épigraphie Grecque et Latine, Constantza, 9–15 septembre 1977* (Bucureşti/Paris 1979); the eighth was scheduled for Athens, 1982.

toritas the volumes of *CIL* were published until the 1950s, when it became the German Academy of Sciences, Berlin [briefly, ca. 1955, the German Acad. of Letters].) Mommsen's early fellow-workers included Henzen, De Rossi, Ritschl, and, most notably, Bartolomeo Borghesi (1781–1860), Mommsen's senior by thirty-six years, whom Mommsen addresses as "magister, patronus, amicus" in dedicating his Inscriptions of the Kingdom of Naples.[135]

There have been only two publishers of *CIL* in its long history: Georg Reimer, Berlin, and (since 1933) his successor, Walter de Gruyter & Co., Berlin (and now Hawthorne, New York).[136]

4. *Bibliography.* The best unified bibliography in topical or categorical form is A. Degrassi's as printed and supplemented by Calabi Limentani[3], 423–466, with a new section (XVIII, p. 457) on slaves and freedmen, and new items up to 1973; there are twenty-six sections on

practically all aspects of the subject except a listing of the International Congresses of Greek and Latin Epigraphy and their publications (above, n. 134). For later additions to Degrassi/Calabi Limentani, see the next section below. See also Calabi Limentani, 131–142, for bibliography on the history of Latin epigraphy. Meyer also has an excellent bibliography, pp. 126–147, and shorter lists scattered throughout.

The most important general aids to the student are *Paulys Realencyclopädie der classischen Altertumswissenschaft*[2] (commonly called "Pauly-Wissowa" or "*RE*"), now complete except for a forthcoming index volume (useful meantime is J. P. Murphy's *Index to the Supplements and Suppl. Volumes of Pauly-Wissowa's R.E.*, with an appendix containing an index to Suppl. Vol. XV, Chicago 1980), *Der Kleine Pauly*, 5 vols. (Stuttgart 1962/64–1975), the *OCD*[2], and other dictionaries and encyclopedias such as Fr. Lübker's *Reallexikon des klassischen Altertums*[8], ed.

---

135. This long dedication is repeated in full, and now entitled "Epistula praemissa Inscriptionibus Regni Neapolitani Latinis editis Lipsiae a. MDCCCLII," at the beginning of *CIL* vols. 9 and 10. To Borghesi is dedicated also Henzen's *Supplementa et Indices* (Zurich 1856) forming vol. 3 of J. C. Orelli's *Amplissima Collectio* of Latin inscrs., 2 vols. (Zurich 1828). Borghesi's works, in 10 vols., were published, as his *Oeuvres complètes*, by order of Napoleon III (Paris 1862–1897). Borghesi spent his last thirty-nine years as a prominent citizen of the tiny hill-town Republic of San Marino, an enclave within Italy, 24 km. SW of Rimini above state highway no. 72 and strikingly visible, by its altitude, to one going down the coast from Ravenna. (On Borghesi, see A. Campana, *Diz. biograf. degli Italiani* 12 [1970] 624–643; for a brief account, *Encycl. Brit.*[11] *s.v.*). For those interested in Mommsen: he was awarded the Nobel Prize for literature in 1902; when the codicil to his will (dated Sept. 2, 1899) was published in 1948, forty-five years after his death in 1903, it revealed him as having wanted no detailed biographies of himself written and as being disappointed in the course of his life despite its outer success: "Ich habe in meinem Leben trotz äusseren Erfolge nicht das Rechte erreicht." The German text is given in *Die Wandlung* 3 (Heidelberg 1948) 69 f.; cf. G. Pasquali, *Riv. stor. ital.* 61 (1949) 337–350 (with Ital. transl.); *Past and Present* 1 (1952) 71 (Engl. transl.); J. Moreau, *Scripta minora*, ed. W. Schmitt-

henner (Heidelberg 1964) 299–305 (French transl.). One of Mommsen's grandsons, Theodor Ernst Mommsen, became a professor of medieval history in the U.S.A. and taught at Princeton, then at Cornell; by his own account, everywhere he went in Europe, his great name was recognized, often embarrassingly so; he died in 1958. (See F. G. Marcham's Introduction, pp. vii–xii, to Theodor E. Mommsen's *Medieval and Renaissance Studies*, ed. E. F. Rice, Jr. [Ithaca, N.Y. 1959].) The detailed biography of the elder Theodor is Lothar Wickert's *Theodor Mommsen, Eine Biographie*, 4 vols. (Frankfurt a/M. 1959, 1964, 1969, 1980); it quotes many letters and has many illustrations and many long notes; one chapter of vol. 4 is devoted to Mommsen's long years at the University of Berlin, 1858–1903; for Mommsen and the *CIL*, see vol. 2 pp. 2 ff., 105 ff., 160 ff., 185 ff., vol. 3, 255 ff., with the corresponding notes.

136. For more of the background of *CIL* and the history of Latin epigraphy, cf. S/C pp. xviii, 20–33, Meyer 7–16, Calabi Limentani 131–142. The French Academy of Inscriptions and Belles-Lettres (1839) and later the Minister of Public Instruction (1843) had decided to prepare a corpus of Latin inscrs., but gave up in favor of the Prussian Academy of Berlin, which had already put out 2 vols. (1828, 1843) of a corpus of Greek inscrs. under the direction of August Boeckh. Cf. Cagnat pp. XX f., n. 2, Larfeld 34–38, Woodhead 97 f., Guarducci 1.35, Meyer 13 f.

J. Geffcken and E. Ziebarth (Leipzig/ Berlin 1914), and the *Lexikon der alten Welt* (Artemis Verlag, Zürich/Stuttgart 1965). (The older Daremberg/Saglio *Dictionnaire des antiquités grecques et romaines* . . . , 5 vols. and index in 10 parts [Paris 1877–1919, repr. 1962–63], while still useful, suffers from having obsolete reff. to modern editions and secondary sources.)

Philological aids, besides the general Latin dictionaries (the new *OLD* cites inscrs., with reff. to *CIL*, and is very well organized, but it goes down to only ca. A.D. 200, so Lewis and Short or others are still needed for the later period), are the *Thesaurus linguae Latinae*, still incomplete (which also cites many inscrs. and has an *Onomasticon*, which goes to the end of the letter D) and Forcellini (see Abbreviations).

Specifically epigraphical are E. De Ruggiero's *Dizionario epigrafico di antichità romane* (1886–), since 1924 ed. G. Cardinali and others and now arrived at the entry Luperci, vol. 4, fasc. 69 (Rome 1980) (a special fasc. of 1950 gives tables of concordance between *CIL* and *ILS*), and G. N. Olcott's *Thesaurus linguae Latinae epigraphicae* (see Abbreviations), which has reached only to *Avillinlanus* (see above, n. 34) and will probably remain unfinished. (For an appreciation of Olcott as a "pacesetter of Romance linguistics," see Y. Malkiel, *Romance Philology* 31: 3 [Feb. 1978] 583.)

The most useful journals are *L'Année Épigraphique* (*AE*), *Epigraphica*, and *Zeitschrift für Papyrologie und Epigraphik* (*ZPE*). Useful for bibliography (books, articles, reviews) is *L'Année Philologique*, section Épigraphie latine, with reference also to other sections such as Calendaria, Carmina epigraphica. Other journals for articles, reviews, and listings of new books, including those epigraphical or of epigraphical interest, include *Gnomon* (Bibliogr. Beilage, Sect. 8), *Historia*, *The Classical Review* (*CR*), *The Journal of Roman Studies* (*JRS*), *Classical Philology* (*CP*), *Greek, Roman, and Byzantine Studies*

(*GRBS*). (For a good list of journals and standard works in the whole field of classical antiquity, see *Lexikon der alten Welt* [cited above], cols. 3463–3486.)

Still worth consulting is the 11th edition of the *Encyclopaedia Britannica* (1910–11—for an appreciation of this ed., see Hans Koning in *The New Yorker*, March 2, 1981, pp. 67–83), as well as the *Enciclopedia italiana di scienze, lettere ed arti* (Milan/Rome 1929–).

For prosopography—*Who's Who*—we have the *Prosopographia imperii Romani saec. I. II. III*, ed. 1. (*PIR*[1]), 3 vols. (Berlin 1897–98), ed. 2 (Berlin 1933–), 4 vols. plus vol. 5 fasc. 1 (1970) to date (through the letter L), and *The Prosopography of the Later Roman Empire* (*PLRE*), vol. 1 (A.D. 260–395), vol. 2 (A.D. 395–527) (Cambridge 1971, 1980). (Cf. J. R. Martindale, *Historia* 23 [1974] 246–252, for addenda and corrigenda to vol. 1.) For Christian archaeology, there is the large *Dictionnaire d'archéologie chrétienne et de liturgie*, ed. F. Cabrol and H. Leclercq (Paris 1903–1950), which has many articles on Christian inscriptions.

5. *Addenda to the Degrassi/Calabi Limentani bibliography* (see also Abbreviations). (Some of these items are listed in Calabi Limentani, 131–142, bibliographical note to ch. III.)

SECT. I (COLLECTIONS OF INSCRIPTIONS)

2, *a* (*CIL*)

CIL 15: 2: 2.8017–8622, collegit H. Dressel (Berlin 1975)

2, *b–c* (Supplements to *CIL*, and other collections)

H. H. Armstrong (ed.), "Inscriptions from Privernum," *AJA* ser. 2, 14 (1910) 318–323; cf. 15 (1911) 170–194, 386–402

L. R. Taylor and A. B. West, "Latin Elegiacs from Corinth," *AJA* ser. 2, 32 (1928) 9–22

Pompeiana. Raccolta di studi per il se-

condo centenario degli scavi di Pompei (Naples 1950)

S. Dow, "Corinthiaca," *HSCP* 60 (1951) 81–100

J. Reynolds, "Inscriptions of Roman Tripolitania: A Supplement," *PBSR* 23, n.s. 10 (1955) 124–147, pls. 33–38

M. Della Corte, "Le iscrizioni di Ercolano," *Rend. Acc. di Arch., Lett. e Belle Arti di Napoli* 33 (1958) 239–308

C. Pietrangeli, *Scavi e scoperte di antichità sotto il pontificato di Pio VI* [1775–80], ed. 2 (Rome 1958)

G. Susini, "Genesi e cultura di una comunità Romana nell'Italia superiore: Forum Corneli," *Imola nell'antichità* (Rome 1958) 91–255, pls. VI–XVII

———, *Fonti per la storia greca e romana del Salento* (Bologna 1962 Acc. delle Scienze, Ist. di Bologna, cl. di sc. mor.)

S. Panciera, "Corpus inscriptionum Latinarum vol. VI, Suppl.," *Helikon, Riv. di Tradizione e Cultura Class., Univ. di Messina,* 4 (1964) 376–381

A. R. Burn, *The Romans in Britain, An Anthology of Inscriptions, with translations and a running commentary*[2] (Oxford/Columbia, S.C., 1969)

R. J. Smutny (ed.), "Inscriptiones Latinae quinque nuper repertae," *Mnemosyne,* ser. 4, vol. 22[2] (1969) 191–194

London Association of Classical Teachers, Original Records No. 4: *Some Inscriptions from Roman Britain* (London [?], no date [not before 1969])

J. M. Reynolds and S. Fabbricotti, "A Group of Inscriptions from Stabiae," *PBSR* 40 (1973) 127–134, pls. 22–25

Le iscrizioni della necropoli dell'autoparco vaticano, edited, under the direction of V. Väänänen, by P. Castrén et al. (Rome 1973 *Acta Inst. Romani Finlandiae,* 6) (cf. *Erasmus* 27 [1975] 299–302)

J. Ewald, *Paläo- und epigraphische Untersuchungen an den römischen Steininschriften der Schweiz . . .* ([Basel] 1974, *Antiqua* vol. 3) (cf. *Erasmus* 29 [1977] 550–553)

Serge Ducroux (ed.), *Catalogue analytique des inscriptions latines sur pierre conservées au Musée du Louvre* (Paris 1975 Musée du Louvre, Départ. des Antiquités Grecques et Romaines)

E. Weber, "Inschriften aus Niederösterreich," *Jahresschrift der österreich. Ges. f. Archäologie* 5/6 (1977/1978) 247–254, pls. 14–25

C. Marangio, "Nuovi contributi al supplemento del *CIL* IX, *Municipium Brundisinum,*" *Studi storicolinguist. in onore di Francesco Ribezzo* (Mesagne 1978 *Testi e Monumenti,* 2) 49–103, pls. I–VIII

M. Steinby, "Appendice a CIL XV, 1," *Bull. Com.* 86 (1978–79, publ. 1980) 55–88

H. G. Pflaum (ed.), *Inscriptions latines de l'Algérie,* 2: 2 (Algiers 1976) (cf. R. P. Duncan-Jones, *JRS* 70 [1980] 221 f.)

E. Weber, "Neue Inschriftenfunde aus Carnuntum," *Jahresschrift der österreich. Ges. f. Archäologie,* 7 (1979) 141–153, pls. 9–11

SECT. I, 2, *d* (COLLECTIONS OF CHRISTIAN AND JEWISH INSCRIPTIONS)

R. Monceaux, *Enquête sur l'épigraphie chrétienne d'Afrique* (Paris 1907 *Mémoires prés. par divers savants à l'Acad. des Inscrs. et Belles-Lettres,* 12:1)

E. Diehl (ed.), *Lateinische altchristliche Inschriften mit einem Anhang jüdischer Inschr.,* ed. 2 (Bonn 1913 *Kleine Texte . . . ,* 26/28)

A. Ferrua (ed.), *Inscriptiones Christianae urbis Romae septimo saeculo antiquiores.* Nova ser., vols. 5–7 (Rome 1971, 1975, 1980) (for vols. 1–4, see Abbreviations *s.v.* Silvagni)

J. P. Frey (ed.), *Corpus inscriptionum Iudaicarum, Recueil des inscriptions juives qui vont du IIIe siècle avant Jésus-Christ au VIIe siècle de nôtre ère*, 2 vols. (Vatican City 1936, 1952) (cf. H. J. Leon, *Jewish Quarterly Rev.* 28: 4 [Apr. 1938] 357–361)

H. J. Leon, "An Unpublished Jewish Inscription at Villa Torlonia in Rome," *JQR* n.s. 42: 4 (1952) 413–418, 3 pls.

———, "The Jewish Community of Ancient Porto," *Harv. Theol. Rev.* 45 (1952) 165–175

———, "The Daughters of Gadias," *TAPA* 84 (1953) 67–72, 2 pls.

———, "Two Jewish Inscriptions of Rome Rediscovered," *Riv. di archeol. cristiana* 29 (1953) 101–105

S. L. Agnello (ed.), *Silloge di iscrizioni paleocristiane della Sicilia* (Rome 1953) (mostly Greek)

H. J. Leon, "The Jews of Venusia," *JQR* 44 (1954) 267–284

M. Guarducci, *I graffiti sotto la Confessione di San Pietro in Vaticano*, 3 vols. (Vatican City 1958) (cf. P. M. Fraser, *JRS* 52 [1962] 214–219)

H. J. Leon, "The Greek Inscriptions of the Jews of Rome," *GRBS* 2 (1959) 47–49

Sodales Inst. Romani Finlandiae (edd.), curante H. Zilliacus, *Sylloge inscr. Christianarum veterum Musei Vaticani*, 2 vols. (Helsinki/Helsingfors 1963 *Acta Inst. Rom. Finlandiae* 1: 1–2) (cf. D. Fishwick, *Phoenix* 19: 4 [1965] 332–336, or A. G. Woodhead, *JRS* 55 [1965] 283)

H. Petersen, "The Earliest Christian Inscriptions of Egypt," *CP* 59 (1964) 154–174

A. Ferrua, "Corona di osservazioni alle iscrizioni cristiane di Roma incertae originis," *MemPontAcc*, ser. 3: 3, 1979, 128 pp.

SECT. I, 2, *e* (SELECTIONS, METRICAL INSCRIPTIONS)

Fr. Buecheler (ed.), *Carmina Latina epigraphica*, 2 vols. (Leipzig 1895, 1897), *Supplementum*, ed. E. Lommatzsch (1926): all 3 vols. repr. Amsterdam 1972)

G. McN. Rushforth, *Latin Historical Inscriptions Illustrating the History of the Early Empire*[2] (London 1930)

R. H. Barrow (ed.), *A Selection of Latin Inscriptions* (Oxford 1934, repr. 1950)

S. Mariné Bigorra, *Inscripciones hispanas en verso* (Barcelona/Madrid 1952 *Publ. de la Escuela de Filología de Barcelona, Filol. Clasica*, 11)

A. De Rosalia (ed.), *Iscrizioni latine arcaiche* (Palermo 1972) (texts, translations, notes)

SECT. I, 3 (REPORTS, REVIEWS)

A. Merlin, "Vingt ans d'études sur l'épigraphie latine (1923–1943)," *Mémorial des Études Latines publ. à l'occasion du 20e anniversaire de la Soc. et de la Revue des Études Latines offert par la Soc. à son fondateur J. Marouzeau* (Paris 1943) 481–499

J. Reynolds, "Inscriptions and Roman Studies," *JRS* 50 (1960) 204–209

———, "Roman Epigraphy, 1961–65," *JRS* 56 (1966) 116–121

———, "Roman Inscriptions 1966–1970," *JRS* 61 (1971) 136–152, pl. X

E. Weber, "Zur lateinischen Epigraphik in Österreich 1902–1975," *Römisches Österreich, Jahresschrift der österreich. Ges. für Archäologie* 3 (1975) 237–293, pls. 20–22

SECT. II (MANUALS)

W. M. Lindsay, *Handbook of Latin Inscriptions Illustrating the History of the Language* (Boston/Chicago 1897)

C. M. Kaufmann, *Handbuch der altchristlichen Epigraphik* (Freiburg i/B 1917)

Ernst Meyer, *Einführung in die lateinische Epigraphik* (Darmstadt 1973) (see above, Introduction, III.4) (cf. R. B. Wright, *JRS* 64 [1974] 243)

SECT. III (DICTIONARIES)

Forcellini, Furlanetto, Corradini, Perin, *Lexicon totius Latinitatis*, 6 vols. including 2 vols. of *Onomasti-*

con (Padua 1940, repr. Vatican City 1965) (see Abbreviations)

J. R. Martindale, "PLRE: addenda et corrigenda to Volume I," *Historia* 23 (1974) 246–252

Der kleine Pauly is now complete: 5 vols. (vol. 5, 1975)

SECT. IV (WRITING, ABBREVIATIONS, MATERIALS INSCRIBED)

A. E. Gordon, *Supralineate Abbreviations in Latin Inscriptions* (1948), repr. Milan 1977

N. Gray, "The Paleography of Latin Inscriptions in the Eighth, Ninth and Tenth Centuries in Italy," *PBSR* 16, n.s. 3 (1948) 38–167

Alec Miller, *Stone and Marble Carving: A Manual for the Student Sculptor* (Berkeley/Los Angeles) 1948 (Ch. 4, An Inscription in Incised Roman Letters)

Oscar Ogg, *The 26 Letters* (New York 1948, repr. 1950) (Ch. 4 The Greeks, Ch. 5 The Romans)

R. Marichal, "L'écriture latine et l'écriture grecque du Ier au VIe siècle," *L'Antiquité Classique* 19 (1950) 113–144, 6 pls.

James Hayes, *The Roman Letter* (catalogue for an exhibition held by R. R. Donnelley & Sons Co., Chicago 1951–52) (fig. 2 shows a Greek, not an Etruscan, inscr. of Syracuse)

J. S. and A. E. Gordon, *Contributions to the Palaeography of Latin Inscriptions* (1957), repr. Milan 1977

G. Mardersteig, "Leon Battista Alberti e la rinascita del carattere lapidario romano nel quattrocento," *Italia medioevale e umanistica*, 2 (Padua 1959) 285–307 (on Mardersteig, see Winthrop Sargeant's Profile of him in *The New Yorker*, July 11, 1970, 32–47)

Felice Feliciano veronese, *Alphabetum Romanum*, ed. G. Mardersteig, transl. R. H. Boothroyd (Verona 1960) (Ch. 1, The Revival of Roman Inscription Letters)

E. M. Catich, *Letters Redrawn from the Trajan Inscription in Rome*, with 93 plates (Davenport, Iowa, 1961) (see below, on **57**)

A. Donati, *Tecnica e cultura dell'officina epigrafica brundisina* (Faenza 1969)

S. V. Tracy, "Identifying Epigraphical Hands," *GRBS* 11 (1970) 321–333 (refers to Greek, but enlightening for Latin)

Stanley Morison, *Politics and Script: Aspects of Authority and Freedom in the Development of Graeco-Latin Script from the Sixth Century B.C. to the Twentieth Century A.D.*, ed. and compl. Nicolas Barker (Oxford 1972 *The Lyell Lectures* 1957)

E. O. Wingo, *Latin Punctuation in the Classical Age* (The Hague/Paris 1972 *Janua Linguarum*, ser. practica, vol. 133)

G. Susini, *The Roman Stonecutter. An Introduction to Latin Epigraphy*, ed. with an intro. by E. Badian, transl. A. M. Dabrowsky (Oxford 1973)

T. F. C. Blagg, "Tools and Techniques of the Roman Stonemason in Britain," *Britannia* 7 (1976) 152–172, pls. xvii–xxi

A. E. Gordon, "On Reversed C (Ɔ = Gaiae)," *Epigraphica* 40 (1978) 230

N. Herz and D. B. Wenner, "Tracing the Origins of Marble," *Archaeology* 34: 5 (Sept./Oct. 1981) 14–21 (with bibliog.)

SECT. V (LANGUAGE)

J. E. Church, Jr., *Beiträge zur Sprache der Lateinischen Grabinschriften*, Erster Theil (Diss., Munich 1901)

R. G. Kent, *The Textual Criticism of Inscriptions* (Philadelphia 1926 *Language Monographs* publ. by the Linguistic Soc. of America, 2) (Ch. 6 Lex Julia Municipalis, Ch. 7 Edict of Diocletian)

M. G. Bertinelli Angeli, "Termini romani, pubblici e sacri, in epigrafi 'latino-libiche,'" *Studi di storia antica in memoria di Luca De Regibus* (Genoa 1969) 217–224

H. Solin, *Beiträge zur Kenntnis der griechischen Personennamen in Rom*, I (Helsinki/Helsingfors 1971 [Diss. Helsinki] Societas Scientiarum Fen-

nica, *Comment. Human. Litt.* 48) (cf.
H. G. Pflaum, *REL* 51 [1973] 48–54)
H. J. Mason, *Greek Terms for Roman
Institutions: A Lexicon and Analysis*
(Toronto 1974 *Amer. Stud. in Pa-
pyrology* 13) (cf. Th. Drew-Bear, *CP*
71 [1976] 349–355)
M. Leumann, *Lateinische Laut- und
Formenlehre* (Munich 1977 *Handb.
der Altertumsw.* 2: 2: 1, Neuausgabe
of ed. 5, 1926–28) (pp. 6–8, §5, Die
ältesten latein. Sprachdenkmäler)
F. Sommer, *Handbuch der lateinischen
Laut- und Formenlehre* . . . ,[4] Band I:
Einleitung und Lautlehre, von
R. Pfister (Heidelberg 1977)
J. L. Barbarino, *The Evolution of the
Latin /b/–/u̯ Merger: A Quantitative
and Comparative Analysis of the B-V
Alternation in Latin Inscriptions*
(Chapel Hill 1978 *North Carolina
Studies in the Romance Languages and
Literatures*, 203)
G. Perl, "Doppelte Negation in pom-
pejanischen Inschriften," *Philologus*
122 (1978) 111–119

SECT. VI (ONOMASTICS)

A. E. and J. S. Gordon, "Roman
Names and the Consuls of A.D.
13," *AJP* 72 (1951) 283–292, 1 pl.
———, "More on the Consuls of
A.D. 13," *AJP* 74 (1953) 421 f. (cf.
R. Syme, *JRS* 56 [1966] 55–60, and
S. Panciera, *Bull. Com.* 79 [1963–64,
publ. 1966] 94–98; see above n. 71)
G. Forni, "Il tramonto di un'istitu-
zione. Pseudo-tribù romane deri-
vate da soprannomi imperiali,"
*Studi giuridici in memoria di Alfredo
Passerini* (Milan 1955 *Studia Ghisle-
riana* 1: 2) 89–124
E. Badian, review of L. R. Taylor's
*The Voting Districts of the Roman
Republic* (1960), *JRS* 52 (1962)
200–210
I. Kajanto, *Onomastic Studies in the
Early Christian Inscriptions of Rome
and Carthage* (Helsinki/Helsingfors
1963 *Acta Inst. Romani Finlandiae*,
2: 1)
H. Chantraine, *Freigelassene und
Sklaven im Dienst der römischen Kai-*

ser. Studien zu ihrer Nomenklatur
(Wiesbaden 1967) (cf. *CW* 64: 3
[Nov. 1970] 95 f.)
*L'onomastique latine, Paris 13–15 oc-
tobre 1975* (Paris 1977 *Colloques In-
ternationaux du Centre National de la
Recherche Scientifique*, 564)
D. R. Shackleton Bailey, *Two Studies
in Roman Nomenclature* (New York
1976 APA, *Amer. Class. Studies*, 3)
(cf. T. P. Wiseman, *CR* n.s. 29
[1979] 180 f.)
R. F. Thomas, "L. Lucullus' Triumphal Agnomen," *AJAH* 2: 2
(1977) 172

SECT. VII (FASTI CONSULARES/
TRIUMPHALES, CONSULAR DATINGS,
ERAS)

A. Degrassi, "Sui Fasti consolari
dell'Impero," *Athenaeum* n.s. 33
(1955) 112–117 (= *Scritti vari*
1.639–644)
G. B. Townend, "The Consuls of
A.D. 69/70," *AJP* 83 (1962) 113–129

SECT. IX (ELOGIA)

Max Niedermann, "L'inscription de
la colonne rostrale de Duilius," *REL*
14 (1936) 276–287 (= *Recueil M.
Niedermann* [Neuchâtel 1954, Univ.
de N., *Rec. de travaux publ. par la
fac. des lettres*, 25] 209–220)
M. Durry, "Du nouveau sur l'inscription de Turia," *REL* 28 (1950)
81 f.
L. Koenen, "Die 'Laudatio Funebris'
des Augustus für Agrippa auf
einem neuen Papyrus (P. Colon.
inv. nr. 4701)," *ZPE* 5 (1970)
217–283, pl. VIII a; "Summum
Fastigium. Zu der Laudatio
funebris des Augustus . . . ," *ZPE*
6 (1970) 239–243; "Korrektur . . . ,"
ZPE 7 (1971) 186
M. Torelli, *Elogia Tarquiniensia* (Florence 1975 *Studi e Materiali di
Etruscologia e Antichità Italiche*, 15)
(cf. T. J. Cornell, *JRS* 68 [1978]
167–173)
M. W. Haslam, "Augustus' Funeral
Oration for Agrippa," *CJ* 75: 3
(1980) 193–199

E. Badian, "Notes on the *Laudatio* of Agrippa," *CJ* 76 (1980–81) 97–109

SECT. X (ACTA PUBLICA)

A. C. Johnson, P. R. Coleman-Norton, F. C. Bourne (eds.), Clyde Pharr (gen. ed.), *Ancient Roman Statutes*, a transl. with introduction, commentary, glossary, and index (Austin, Texas, 1961)

M. Giacchero, *Note sull'Editto-Calmiere di Diocleziano*, Ist. di Storia Antica dell'Univ. di Genova, 4 (Genoa 1962) (cf. L. Cracco Ruggini, *Riv. di fil.* 92, ser. 3 [1964] 364–368)

S. Lauffer (ed.), *Diokletians Preisedikt* (Berlin 1971 *Texte u. Komm.* 5)

J. Reynolds, review of R. Sherk, *Roman Documents from the Greek East* . . . (1969), *JRS* 61 (1971) 284–286

M. Giacchero (ed.), *Edictum Diocletiani et Collegarum de pretiis rerum venalium in integrum fere restitutum e Latinis Graecisque fragmentis*, 2 vols. (Genoa 1974 *Pubbl. Ist. di Storia Ant. e Sc. Ausil.*, 8) (for new fragments, new readings, and reviews, see below, on **81**)

SECT. XI (RELIGIOUS INSCRIPTIONS)

A. E. Gordon, *The Cults of Aricia* (Berkeley 1934 *Univ. Calif. Publ. Class. Arch.* 2: 1)

C. M. Stibbe, G. Colonna, C. de Simone, H. S. Versnel, *Lapis Satricanus. Archaeological, Epigraphical, Linguistic and Historical Aspects of the New* [Latin] *Inscription from Satricum* ('s-Gravenhage 1980 *Arch. Stud. Nederlands Inst. te Rome, Scripta Minora*, 5)

S. Panciera, "Nuovi luoghi di culto a Roma dalle testimonianze epigrafiche," *Quaderni del centro di studio per l'archeologia etrusco-italica*, 4, 1980, "Archeologia Laziale III. Terzo incontro di studio del Comitato per l'archeologia laziale" ([Rome] Consiglio Nazionale delle Ricerche) 202–213, pls. XLVII–L

SECT. XII (INSCRIPTIONS OF THE SENATORIAL CLASS, GOVERNORS OF PROVINCES, STATE ADMINISTRATION)

S. E. Stout, *The Governors of Moesia* (Diss. Princeton 1910) (Princeton 1911) (superseded by A. Stein's *Die Legaten von Moesien* [Budapest 1940 *Diss. Pannonicae*, ser. 1, fasc. 2])

G. Barbieri, *Addendum* to his *L'albo senatorio da Settimio Severo a Carino (193–295)* (Rome 1952), in reply to J. Morris's review (*JRS* 43 [1953] 167 f.), with J. M.'s comment: *JRS* 44 (1954) 164 f. (For another review, see H. G. Pflaum, *Rev. de Phil., de Litt. et d'Hist. Anciennes*, ser. 3 vol. 30 [1956] 68–82.)

R. Syme, review of T. R. S. Broughton's *The Magistrates of the Roman Republic* (2 vols. 1951, 1952), *CP* 50 (1955) 127–138

E. Badian, review of T. R. S. Broughton's *Supplement to the Magistrates of the Roman Republic* (1960), *Gnomon* 33 (1961) 492–498

G. Susini, "La dedica a Caio Mario nel foro di Rimini," *Studi Romagnoli* 13 (1962) 1–16

E. Badian, "Notes on Roman Senators of the Republic," *Historia* 12 (1963) 128–143

R. Syme, "Governors of Pannonia Inferior," *Historia* 14 (1965) 342–361

G. Susini, "Q. Pompeius Senecio, console nel 169 d. C.: alcune note," *Mélanges d'arch. et d'hist. offerts à André Piganiol*, ed. R. Chevallier (Paris 1966) 289–299

J. Šašel, "Pro legato," *Chiron* 4 (1974) 467–477

H. G. Pflaum, *Les Fastes de la province de Narbonnaise, XXXᵉ supplément à "Gallia"* (Paris 1978)

R. K. Sherk, "A Chronology of the Governors of Galatia: A.D. 112–285," *AJP* 100 (1979) 166–175

R. J. A. Talbert, "Pliny the Younger as Governor of Bithynia-Pontus," *Studies in Latin Literature and Roman History* 2 (*Coll. Latomus* 168, 1980) 412–435

A. R. Birley, *The Fasti of Roman Britain* (Oxford 1981)

R. C. Knapp, "L. Axius and *Pro Legato*," *Phoenix* 35 (1981) 134–141

SECT. XIII (INSCRIPTIONS OF THE EQUESTRIAN CLASS)

R. Syme, review of A. Stein's *Die Präfekten von Ägypten in röm. Zeit* (1950), *JRS* 44 (1954) 116–119

N. Lewis, "The Prefects of Egypt in A.D. 119," *AJP* 76 (1955) 63–69

H. G. Pflaum, *Abrégé des Procurateurs Équestres*, adaptation française de Serge Ducroux et Noël Duval, revu et augmenté par l'auteur (Paris 1974)

SECT. XIV (IMPERIAL INSCRIPTIONS, IMPERIAL CULT, RES GESTAE)

Mommsen's ed. 2 (Berlin 1883) of the *Res Gestae* of Augustus, reprinted Aalen (Germany) 1970

H. C. Newton, *The Epigraphical Evidence for the Reigns of Vespasian and Titus* (Ithaca, New York, 1901 Cornell Studies in Class. Philol. 16)

D. M. Robinson, *The Deeds of Augustus As Recorded on the Monum. Antiochenum*, repr. from *AJP* 47: 1 (1926) 1–54, 7 pls.

E. Kornemann, "Monumentum Ancyranum," *RE* 16: 1 (1933) 211–231

Hans Volkmann (ed.), *Res gestae divi Augusti*. Teil 1: *Kritische Textausgabe*, Bursian, Supplbd. Bd. 276 (1942), Teil 2: *Besprechung des Schrifttums der Jahre 1914–1942*, Supplbd. Bd. 279 (1942, publ. 1943)

G. Barbieri, "Aspetti della politica di Settimio Severo," *Epigraphica* 14 (1952) 3–48

V. Ehrenberg and A. H. M. Jones (eds.), *Documents Illustrating the Reigns of Augustus and Tiberius*, ed. 2 (Oxford 1955) and repr. 1976 (New York/London) with 16 additional items

Ch. L. Babcock, "An Inscription of Trajan Decius from Cosa," *AJP* 83 (1962) 147–158

L. J. Swift and J. H. Oliver (eds.),

"Constantius II on Flavius Philippus," *AJP* 83 (1962) 247–264 (text of letter, with transl. and notes)

Maria Bollini, "Massimino il trace e il figlio in una iscrizione di Claterna," *Studi Romagnoli* 14 (1963) 305–318

Gertrude J. Donnelly, "Columna Disputata" [the Col. of Trajan], *CJ* 61: 1 (Oct. 1965) 19–21

G. Forni and D. Manini, "La base eretta a Nicopoli in onore di Antonino Pio dai veterani della legione II Traiana," *Studi di Storia Antica in memoria di Luca De Regibus* (Genoa 1969 *Pubbl. Ist. di Storia Ant. e Sc. Ausil. dell'Univ. di Genova*) 177–210, pls. 4–7

K. Erim, J. Reynolds, M. Crawford, "Diocletian's Currency Reform: A New Inscription," *JRS* 61 (1971) 171–177, pls. XII–XIII

J. Gagé (ed.), *Res Gestae divi Augusti ex monumentis Ancyrano et Antiocheno Latinis, Ancyrano et Apolloniensi Graecis*, nouvelle (3rd) éd. revue et augmentée (Paris 1977 Coll. Budé)

SECT. XV (MILESTONES, POMERIUM MARKERS, BOUNDARY MARKERS, CATASTA INSCRIPTIONS)

S. Ribaille-Rogier, "The Land-Register of a Roman Town" [Orange, in Provence], *Archaeology* 11: 3 (1958) 172–174

SECT. XVI (INSCRIPTIONS CONCERNING THE ARMY AND NAVY)

N. Criniti, *L'epigrafe di Asculum di Gn. Pompeo Strabone* (Milan 1970 Pubbl. Univ. Cattolica del S. Cuore, Saggi e Ricerche, ser. 3, sc. stor. 3) 266 pp.

M. Šašel Kos, "A Latin Epitaph of a Roman Legionary from Corinth," *JRS* 68 (1978) 22–25, pl. I

Valerie A. Maxfield, *The Military Decorations of the Roman Army* (Berkeley and Los Angeles 1981)

SECT. XVII (INSCRIPTIONS
CONCERNING *COLLEGIA, FASTI* AND
ACTA OF *COLLEGIA*)

Acta Fratrum Arvalium edidit quae post annum 1974 reperta sunt (et) commentario instruxit Aelius Pasoli (Bologna 1950 Univ. degli Studi di Bologna, Fac. di lett. e filos., *Studi e Ricerche*, 7)

R. G. Tanner, "The Arval Hymn and Early Latin Verse," *CQ* 55 (n.s. 11) (1961) 209–238

L. Cracco Ruggini, *Le associazioni professionali nel mondo romano-bizantino* (Spoleto 1971 Settimane di studio del Centro italiano di studi sull'alto Medioevo, 18: *Artigianato e tecnica nella società dell'alto Medioevo occidentale, Spoleto, 2–8 aprile 1970*) 59–227

———, "Stato e associazioni professionali nell'età imperiale romana," *Akten des VI. Internat. Kongr. f. Griech. u. Latein. Epigraphik München 1972* (Munich 1973 *Vestigia* 17) 271–311

———, "*Collegium* e *corpus*: la politica economica nella legislazione e nella prassi," *Istituzioni giuridiche e realtà politiche nel tardo impero (III–V sec. d. C.), Atti di un incontro tra storici e giuristi Firenze, 2–4 maggio 1974,* a cura di G. G. Archi (Milan 1976 Circolo Toscano di Diritto Romano e Storia del Diritto) 63–94

H. J. Mason, "*Vir*: Member of a College," *Studies in Latin Literature and Roman History* 2 (*Coll. Latomus* 168, 1980) 5–20

Sir Ronald Syme, *Some Arval Brethren* (Oxford/New York 1980)

SECT. XVIII (SLAVES AND FREEDMEN)

P. R. C. Weaver, "Dated Inscriptions of Imperial Freedmen and Slaves," *Epigr. Studien* 11 (1976) 215–227

Marleen B. Flory, "Family in *Familia*," *AJAH* 3: 1 (1978) 78–95

SECT. XIX (ARTS AND CRAFTS)

G. Susini, *Officine epigrafiche e ceti sociali, contributo alla storia del Sa-lento romano* (Urbania, no date—1959 or soon after)

———, "L'officina lapidaria di Urbino," *Studi in onore di Luisa Banti* (Rome 1965) 309–318, 2 pls.

———, "Le officine lapidarie romane di Ravenna," *Corsi di cultura sull'arte ravennate e bizantina, Ravenna, 1965* (Faenza) 547–575

T. E. Kinsey, "A Poor Schoolmaster?" *Mnemosyne* ser. 4: 32 (1978) 381 (on *CIL* 10.3969 = *ILS* 7763)

SECT. XX (GAMES, *LUDI SAECULARES*)

M. A. Cavallaro, "Economia e *religio* nei ludi secolari: Per una nuova interpretazione di *CIL* VI 32324; 32323, 59," *Rhein. Mus.* N.F. 122 (1979) 49–87

SECT. XXII (CITY ADMINISTRATION. MAGISTRATES, AUGUSTALES, POPULATION)

M. W. Frederiksen, "The Republican Municipal Laws: Errors and Drafts," *JRS* 55 (1965) 183–198

R. Duthoy, "Recherches sur la répartition géographique et chronologique des termes *sevir Augustalis, Augustalis* et *sevir* dans l'Empire romain," *Epigr. Studien* 11 (1976) 143–214 (résumé in *AE* 1976 [publ. 1980] p. 7)

SECT. XXIII (SEPULCHRAL INSCRIPTIONS)

F. Becker, *Die heidnische Weiheformel D·M (diis manibus sc. sacrum) auf altchristlichen Grabsteinen. Ein Beitrag zur Kenntniss des christlichen Alterthums* (Gera 1881)

The date of Fr. Vollmer's *Laudationum funebrium historia et reliquiarum editio* is 1891.

Harry Armini, *Sepulcralia Latina* (Gothenburg 1916 Diss. Goth.)

A. E. Gordon, "A New Fragment of the *Laudatio Turiae*," *AJA* 54 (1950) 223–226, pls. 26 f. (see **28**)

———, "The Epitaph of Marcianus" (text and transl.), *Archaeology* 4: 1 (spring 1951) 48 f. (see **60**)

On the *ascia* ("adze") often found carved on tombstones and the formula *sub ascia dedicavit*, there is a large literature: cf. Sandys/Campbell 78–82, J. Carcopino, *Le mystère d'un symbole chrétien, l'ascia* (Paris 1955), Toynbee/Ward Perkins 97 n. 6, and F. De Visscher, *Le droit des tombeaux romains* (Milan 1963) 277–294 (cf. Degrassi's review, *Bull. Ist. Diritto romano V. Scialoja*, ser. 3, vol. 6 [1964] 269 [= *Scritti vari* 4.315: "great progress, but not the last word"])

G. Highet, "Love Among the Romans," *Horizon* (New York) 1: 2 (Nov. 1958) 108–111 (about the *Laud. Turiae*, **28**)

H. Geist (ed.), *Römische Grabinschriften* (with German transl.), betreut v. G. Pfohl (Munich 1969 Tusculum-Bücherei) (cf. *CW* 1969, 97)

E. Wistrand, *The So-Called Laudatio Turiae: Introduction, Text, Translation, Commentary* (Gothenburg 1976 *Studia Graeca et Latina Gothoburgensia* 34) (**28**)

A. E. Gordon, "Who's Who in the Laudatio Turiae," *Epigraphica* 39 (1977) 7–12

H. Häusle, *Das Denkmal als Garant der Nachruhms. Eine Studie zu einem Motiv in lateinischen Inschriften* (*Zetemata*, 75 [1980])

SECT. XXV (INSTRUMENTUM, "PORTABLE OBJECTS USED IN PUBLIC OR PRIVATE LIFE": CF. SANDYS/CAMPBELL 143–155)

a) (Roof Tiles, Brick Stamps)

H. Bloch, "Consules Suffecti on Roman Brick Stamps," *CP* 39 (1944) 254 f.

———. "I bolli laterizi nella storia ediliz. di Ostia," *Scavi di Ostia*, 1 (Rome 1953) 215–227

———, "The Serapeum of Ostia and the Brick-Stamps of 123 A.D., A New Landmark in the History of Roman Architecture," *AJA* 63 (1959) 225–240, pls. 49 f.

———, *I bolli laterizi e la storia edilizia romana*[2] (Rome 1967)

P. Setälä, *Private Domini in Roman Brick Stamps of the Empire. A Historical and Prosopographical Study of Landowners in the District of Rome* (Helsinki 1977 *Annales Acad. Scient. Fennicae, Diss. Hum. Litt.* 10)

M. Steinby, "Ziegelstempel von Rom und Umgebung," *RE* Suppl. 15 (1978) 1489–1531

Lateres signati Ostienses, schede a cura di T. Helen et al., sotto la direzione di J. Suolahti. Part 1: testo di M. Steinby in collab. con T. Helen, appendix di H. Solin; part 2, tavole a cura di M. Steinby (Rome/Helsinki 1977, 1978, *Acta Inst. Romani Finlandiae*, 7: 1–2)

f) (Curse Tablets)

Wm. S. Fox, *The Johns Hopkins Tabellae Defixionum* (Baltimore 1912 Suppl. to *AJP* 33: 1)

E. G. Turner, "A Curse Tablet from Nottinghamshire," *JRS* 53 (1963) 122–124, pl. IX

p) (Jewels)

A. E. Gordon, *The Inscribed Fibula Praenestina: Problems of Authenticity* (Berkeley, etc. 1975 *Univ. Calif. Publ. Class. Studies*, 16)

———, "Further Remarks on the Inscribed Gold Fibula Praenestina," *Epigraphica* 40 (1978) 32–39 (see also below, on **1**, esp. the N.B. at the end)

M. Guarducci, "La cosiddetta Fibula Prenestina. Antiquari, eruditi e falsari nella Roma dell'ottocento (con un Appendice di esami e di analisi a cura di Pico Cellini, Guido Devoto, ed altri)," *MemLinc* 8: 24: 4 (1980) 413–574, pls. I–XI

s) (*Glandes*, missiles discharged from a sling)

Judith P. Hallett. "Perusinae Glandes and the Changing Image of Augustus," *AJAH* 2: 2 (1977) 151–171

t) (additional category: Vases other than Arretine and Amphoras)

A. E. Gordon, "Notes on the Duenos-Vase Inscription in Berlin," *CSCA* 8 (1976) 53–72, pls. 1–2

E. Tiffou, "Remarques sur le Vase de Duenos," *Mélanges d'Études Anciennes offerts à Maurice Lebel* (St-Jean-Chrysostome, P. Qué., Canada 1980) 223–230

SECT. XXVI, 3 (HISTORY OF EPIGRAPHY: COLLECTIONS AND MUSEUMS)

Guida speciale della Galleria Lapidaria del Museo Vaticano . . . (Rome 1912) (the Avvertenza is signed by O. Marucchi) (to be superseded by a new edition of all the pagan inscriptions of the Vatican by Ivan Di Stefano Manzella)

G. Susini, *Il lapidario greco e romano di Bologna e Supplementum Bononiense ad C.I.L., XI* (Bologna 1960) (the same as Cal. Limentani's second item, p. 465, sect. 3?)

K. Herbert, "Greek and Latin Inscriptions at Bowdoin," *AJA* 60 (1962) 381–387, pls. 104 f.

Nicholson Museum (Univ. of Sydney, New South Wales, Australia), New Gallery, *Inscriptions* (1978), pp. 68–88 a catalogue, preface signed by Alexander Cambitoglou (17 sepulchral inscrs.—16 Latin, 1 Greek—mostly from Misenum/Pozzuoli [the Roman fleet], all but one previously publ., mostly in *CIL* 10)

Martha W. Baldwin and Mario Torelli (eds.), *Latin Inscriptions in the Kelsey Museum, the Dennison Collection* (Ann Arbor 1979)

I. Di Stefano Manzella, "Il riordinamento del Lapidario Profano ex Lateranense . . . ," *Epigraphica* 41 (1979) 131–135

ADDITIONAL CATEGORIES

1. Collected Works and Bibliographies

Th. Mommsen, *Gesammelte Schriften*, 8 vols. (Berlin 1905–1913) (vol. 8 is entirely epigraphical; at least another vol. was planned but no more were published)

A. Degrassi, *Scritti vari*, 4 vols. (1962–1971) (see Abbreviations)

V. Arangio-Ruiz, *Studi epigrafici e papirologici* [1920–1964], a cura di L. Bove (Naples 1974 Società di Scienze, Lettere e Arti in Napoli, Acc. di Sc. Morali e Politiche)

Sir Ronald Syme, *Roman Papers*, 2 vols., ed. E. Badian (Oxford 1978)

M. José Fontana et al., edd. Φιλίας χάριν: *Miscellanea di studi classici in onore di Eugenio Manni*, 6 vols. (Rome 1980) (contains epigraphical articles by M. Lejeune, S. Panciera, G. Susini, et al.)

J. H. Oliver, "Bibliography," *AJP* 100 (1979), 8 unnumbered pages following an Introduction; many items concern Latin, or Greco/Latin, epigraphy

Mélanges de littérature et d'épigraphie latines, d'histoire ancienne et d'archéologie. Hommages à la mémoire de Pierre Wuilleumier (Paris 1980 Coll. d'Études Latines, sér. scientif., fasc. XXXV) (contains a bibliography of P. W. and several epigraphical articles)

2. Journals

Epigraphica, Rivista Italiana di Epigrafia, 1939– (see above, Introduction, III.3)

Epigrafia e Antichità, Collana diretta da Giancarlo Susini (Faenza, 5 vols. to date, 1969–1979)

Tituli, Pubblicazioni di Epigrafia e Antichità Greche e Romane dell'Università di Roma, a cura di Silvio Panciera (Rome, 2 vols. to date, 1980)

3. Miscellaneous

L. Ruggini, "Ebrei e orientali nell'Italia settentrionale fra il IV e il VI secolo d. Cr.," *Studia et Documenta Historiae et Iuris* 25 (Rome 1959) 186–308

H. Nordberg, *Biometrical Notes. The Information on Ancient Christian Inscriptions from Rome Concerning the Duration of Life and the Dates of Birth and Death* (Helsinki/Helsingfors 1963 Acta Inst. Romani Finlandiae 2: 2)

J. M. Flamm, "Experiments with Rubber Silicone Compounds," *AJA* 69 (1965) 62 f.

M. Avi-Yonah, "The Latin Inscription [*sic*] from the Excavations in Jerusalem," pp. 22–24 (pl. XII, no. 6) of B. Mazar's *The Excavations in the Old City of Jerusalem, Prelim. Report of the First Season*, 1968 (Jerusalem 1969)

H. Hofmann, "Satorquadrat," *RE* Suppl. 15 (1978) 477–565

G. J. Szemler, "Pontifex," ibid. 331–396

R. T. Ridley, "In Collaboration with Theodor Mommsen: Ettore Pais and the Corpus Inscriptionum Latinarum," *Klio* 61 (1979) 497–506

Hans Krummrey and Silvio Panciera, "Criteri di edizione e segni diacritici," *Tituli*, 2 (Rome 1980) 205–215 (on the new rules for editing, in minuscule, inscriptions to be published in future volumes of *CIL*)

(See also Abbreviations.)

These Addenda to the Degrassi/Calabi Limentani bibliography, numerous though they are, are only some of the many hundreds that could be found by consulting, e.g., *L'Année Philologique, Epigraphica, Gnomon*, or the reports of the International Congress of Greek and Latin Epigraphy.

THE INSCRIPTIONS

LIST OF INSCRIPTIONS

(An asterisk before the date means "probably.")

1. Gold Fibula, Rome, formerly thought to be from Palestrina (*CIL* 1².3) (see N.B. at end of annotation of this inscr.) — (a forgery)

2. Castor and Pollux Dedication, Rome, from near Pratica di Mare (*CIL* 1²:4.2833) — VI(?) B.C.

3. Duenos Vase, Berlin, from Rome (*CIL* 1².4) — VII/V(?) B.C.

4. Forum Romanum Cippus, Rome (*CIL* 1².1) — late VI(?)

5. Scipionic Sarcophagus with Epitaph, Rome (*CIL* 1².6–7) — *III B.C.

6. Dedication to Hercules by M. Minucius, Rome (*CIL* 1².607) — 217 B.C.

7. Decree of L. Aemilius (Paulus), Paris, from Spain (*CIL* 1².614) — *ca. 190 B.C.

8. *Senatus Consultum de Bacchanalibus*, Vienna, from southern Italy (*CIL* 1².581) — 186 B.C.

9. Commemorative Tablet of L. Aemilius (Paulus), Delphi (*CIL* 1².622) — *167 B.C.

10. Honorary Inscription to M. Claudius Marcellus, Luni (*CIL* 1².623) — *155 B.C.

11. Dedication to Hercules by Lucius Mummius, Rome (*CIL* 1².626) — *144 B.C.

12. Milestone with Acephalous Elogium, Polla (*CIL* 1².638) — 143(?) B.C.

13. Bilingual Dedication to Hercules, Delos (*CIL* 1².2504) — 113 B.C.

14. Elegiac Epigram, Corinth (*CIL* 1².2662) — ca. 101 B.C.

15. Two Decrees of Gn. Pompeius (Strabo), Rome (*CIL* 1².709) — *90 or 89 B.C.

16. Slab from Statue Base of Sulla, Naples, from Rome (*CIL* 1².721) — 82/78 B.C.

17. Record of Theater Building, Pompeii (*CIL* 1².1633) — *ca. 75 B.C.

18. Main Inscription on the Fabricius Bridge, Rome (*CIL* 1².751) — 62 B.C.

19. Temple Regulations, L'Aquila, from Furfo (*CIL* 1².756) — 58 B.C.

20. Epitaph of a Grain Merchant, Rome (*CIL* 1².2965) — 52 B.C.

21. Statue (?) Base Dedicated to Julius Caesar, Rome, from Otricoli (*CIL* 1².797) — ca. 44 B.C.

22. Trilingual Dedication by Cornelius Gallus, Cairo, from Philae (*CIL* 3.14147⁵) — 29 B.C.

23. Epitaph of Caecilia Metella, outside Rome (*CIL* 6.1274) — *Augustan

24. Epitaphs of Octavia and Her Son Marcellus, Rome (*AE* 1928, 88) — *23 B.C.

25. Part of the Record of the Secular Games, Rome (*CIL* 6.32323) — 17 B.C.

26. Epitaph on the Pyramid of Cestius, Rome (*CIL* 6.1374) — *not after 12 B.C.

27. Record of the Restoration of an Altar, Rome (*CIL* 6.37063) — 9 B.C.

28. Two Fragments of the "Laudatio Turiae," Rome (*AJA* 54 [1950] 223) — Augustan

29. Record of Repairs of Three Aqueducts, Rome (*CIL* 6.1244–1246) — 5/4 B.C. and later

30. Senatorial Inscription in Honor of Lucius Caesar, Rome (*CIL* 6.36908) — 2 B.C.

31. Record of Posthumous Honors for Gaius Caesar, Pisa (*CIL* 11.1421) — A.D. 4

32. Epitaph of Potitus Valerius Messalla, Rome (*CIL* 6.37075) — Augustan

33. Epitaph of Gaius Caesar (son of Germanicus), Rome (*CIL* 6.889) — A.D. 12

34. The *Monumentum Ancyranum*, Ankara, Turkey (*CIL* 3:2, pp. 769 ff.) — *early-Tiberian

35. Duplex Dedication on an Obelisk, Rome (*CIL* 6.882) — *early-Tiberian

36. The *Tabula Hebana*, Florence, from Magliano (*AJP* 75 [1954] 225 — A.D. 19/20

37. Epitaphs of a Charioteer and His Wife, Rome (*CIL* 6.10051) — A.D. 25–

38. Dedication (?) of a *Tiberieum* by Pontius Pilate, Jerusalem, from Caesarea Maritima (*AE* 1971, 477) — A.D. 26/36

39. Epitaph of Agrippina the Elder, Rome (*CIL* 6.886) — A.D. 37

40. Ex-voto Dedication to the Emperor Claudius, Verona (*CIL* 5.3326) — A.D. 44/45

41. Dedication to the Emperor Claudius and His Family, Rome (*CIL* 6.918) — A.D. 47/48

42. Part of a Speech of the Emperor Claudius, Lyon, from nearby (*CIL* 13.1668) — *A.D. 48

43. Pomerium Boundary-Stone, Rome (apparently *NS* 1913, 68) — A.D. 49

44. The Porta Maggiore Aqueducts (earliest inscr.), Rome (*CIL* 6.1256) — A.D. 52

45. Epitaph of Quintus Veranius and His Child, Rome, from nearby (*AE* 1953, 251) — A.D. 58/59

46. Fragment of the "Lex de Imperio Vespasiani," Rome (*CIL* 6.930) — A.D. 69/70

47. Dedication of a Shrine to *Fons*, Rome (*CIL* 6.39416) — A.D. 70

48. Elogium of Gaius Duilius, Rome (*CIL* 1^2.25, 6.1300) — not after A.D. 77

49. Epitaph of a Soldier/Public Official, below Tivoli (*CIL* 14.3608) — *A.D. 74/79

50. Dedication of Arch to the Deified Titus, Rome (*CIL* 6.945) — A.D. 81–

51. A Military Diploma, Rome, from Egypt (*CIL* 16.32) — A.D. 86

52. Latin Epitaph, with Greek Verses, of a Young Poet, Rome (*CIL* 6.33976)   *A.D. 94–

53. *Tabula Alimentaria*, Rome, from Ancient Samnium (*CIL* 9.1455)   A.D. 101

54. Record of a Town's Request for Patronage, Florence, from Rome (*CIL* 6.1492)   A.D. 101 or 102

55. Commemoration of a Local Dignitary, Ferentino (*CIL* 10.5853)   Trajanic?

56. Statue-Base Inscription in Honor of Hadrian, Athens (*CIL* 3.550)   A.D. 112

57. Column-of-Trajan Inscription, Rome (*CIL* 6.960)   A.D. 113

58. Record of Building the Original Pantheon, Rome (*CIL* 6.896)   *Hadrianic

59. Commemoration of a Roman Public Official, Aquileia (*CIL* 5.877)   *A.D. 122/124

60. Verse Epitaph of a Young Boy, Rome (*CIL* 6.7578)   A.D. 126 or 127

61. Epitaph of a Freedman of Trajan's, Rome (*CIL* 6.1884)   A.D. 130

62. Funerary Monument with Instructions to Heirs, Rome (*AE* 1945, 136)   Hadrianic?

63. Veterans' Dedication of Altar to Silvanus, Rome (*CIL* 6.31152)   A.D. 145

64. Funerary Monument of an Imperial Freedman, Rome, from nearby (*CIL* 6.10235)   A.D. 149

65. Verse Epitaph of Allia Potestas, Rome (*CIL* 6.37965)   ca. A.D. 150–175?

66. *Lex Collegi Aesculapi et Hygiae*, Rome (*CIL* 6.10234)   A.D. 153

67. Dedication of Sculptured Column to Antoninus Pius, Rome (*CIL* 6.1004, 31223)   A.D. 161/169

68. Commemoration of a Local Dignitary, Rome, from Ostia (*CIL* 14.367)   A.D. 182

69. Three Letters (with summary) from Imperial Accountants, Rome (*CIL* 6.1585, *b*)   *A.D. 193/195

70. Pagan Epitaph from the Vatican Excavations, Rome (*Esplor.* 1.43–53)   late-Hadrianic/ca. A.D. 200?

71. Dedication to Caracalla by the *Paedagogi Puerorum a Capite Africae*, Rome (*CIL* 6.1052)   A.D. 198

72. Dedication to the Imperial Family (and Others) by Members of a Cohort of Vigiles, Rome (*CIL* 6.220)   A.D. 203

73. Dedication of Arch to Septimius Severus and His Sons, Rome (*CIL* 6.1033)   A.D. 202/203

74. Epitaph of the Father of Elagabalus, Rome, from Velletri (*CIL* 10.6569)   A.D. 217/218

75. The Arval Hymn (*Carmen Arvale*), Rome (*CIL* 6.2104, *a*)   A.D. 218

76. Request for Permission to Build a Tomb, Rome, from Via Ostiensis (*CIL* 6.33840)   A.D. 227

77. Dedication to Decius, *Nobilissimus Caesar*, Rome (*CIL* 6.1101)   A.D. 251

78. Record of a Meeting at Sentinum of a *Collegium Fabrum*, Rome, no doubt from Sentinum (*CIL* 11.5748)   A.D. 260

79. Epitaph of a Christian Woman, Rome (*ILCV* 1.645)   A.D. 279

80. Ex-voto Dedication to Cybele and Attis, Rome, from nearby (*CIL* 6.506) — *ca. A.D. 295

81. Preamble to Diocletian's Edict on Prices, Athens, from Plataea (*CIL* 3 suppl. 1, p. 1913) — A.D. 301

82. Dedication of Triumphal Arch to Constantine, Rome (*CIL* 6.1139, 31425) — *A.D. 315

83. Record of Restoration of Public Baths, Rome (*CIL* 6.1136) — before ca. A.D. 325?

84. Commemoration of G. Caelius Saturninus, Rome (*CIL* 6.1704) — *A.D. 326/333

85. Epitaph of a Christian *Lector*, Rome (*ILCV* 1.1266) — A.D. 338

86. Dedication to Constantius II, Rome (*CIL* 6.1158) — A.D. 352/353

87. Epitaph of Iunius Bassus, Rome (*CIL* 6.32004) — A.D. 359

88. Dedication to Co-Emperor Valens, Rome (*CIL* 6.31402) — *A.D. 365/367

89. Commemoration of Symmachus, the Orator's Father, Rome (*CIL* 6.1698) — A.D. 377

90. Dedication in Honor of Petronius Probus, Rome (*CIL* 6.1751) — A.D. 378

91. Elogium in Verse Composed by Pope Damasus, Rome (*ILCV* 2.3446) — A.D. 383

92. Dedication of (Statue) Base to a Distinguished Pagan, Rome (*CIL* 6.1778) — A.D. 387

93. Dedication of (Statue) Base to Stilicho, Roman General (*AE* 1926, 124) — A.D. 400/404

94. Commemoration of Three Emperors, Rome (*CIL* 6.31987) — A.D. 402/406

95. Epitaph of a Christian Child, Rome (*ILCV* 2.2921) — A.D. 408

96. Dedication of a Statue Base to a High Official, Rome (*AE* 1928, 80) — A.D. 421–

97. Record of Erection of Statue of a Distinguished Administrator, Rome (*CIL* 6.1725) — *A.D. 441/445

98. Epitaph of Three Christians, Rome (*ILCV* 2.3058A) — *A.D. 454

99. Epitaph of a Christian Boy, Rome (*ILCV* 2.2650) — A.D. 471

100. Epitaph of Maxima, "Handmaid of Christ," Rome (*ILCV* 1.1469) — A.D. 525

PREFACE TO THE INSCRIPTIONS

My wife and I have seen all these one hundred inscriptions and, wherever physically possible, have collated them with some printed text such as *CIL* or *ILS*. The only exceptions are **9** (seen, no doubt), **13** (perhaps seen on Delos), **34** (seen and studied in Ankara), and **35** (seen many times).

The inscriptions were planned to be legible in the photographs, but a few will probably require the use of a magnifying glass; even so, photos are sometimes deceptive (see occasional notes in the annotation). When (as generally) two (or three) inscriptions appear on the same plate, their relative size there does not necessarily indicate their *actual* relative size.

In the descriptions of the inscribed objects the order of dimensions is: height, width, thickness or depth. In many cases two figures are given, a smaller and a larger; e.g., in **2** "5.0–5.3 × 24.1 × 0.10–0.15 cm." means that the height varies from 5.0 to 5.3 cm., the thickness from 0.10 to 0.15 cm. Such variation is very common, perhaps because of inexact cutting of the material used, more often probably because of damage to the edges.

In dates, A.D. 85/96 means "at some point between 85 and 96," 85–96 means "lasting from 85 to 96."

For pre-classical, post-classical, and otherwise strange word-forms, see Appendix I.

In the Texts words in capitals are those that make no sense as they stand, uncorrected; e.g., in **19** and **64**. Hooked brackets indicate superfluous letters or words that

should be deleted; angular brackets add letters or words that should be supplied to make sense of the Latin or to make the correct form in Classical Latin. Square brackets are used to restore letters or words lost by damage. Parentheses are used to fill out abbreviations, to indicate incorrect forms, to add words that seem required by the Latin (mostly *est* or *sunt*, as in **14**), and in other ways that are self-explanatory.

All the texts are given in full, and so translated, except nos. **3**, **14** f., **19**, **25**, **28**, **31**, **34**, **36**, **42**, **45**, **48**, **53**, **60**, **63**, **66**, **71** f., **75**, **78**, and **81**. The exceptions arise from various causes; e.g., **34**, the *Monumentum Ancyranum* of Augustus's *Res Gestae*, in which the Latin alone covers some twenty-eight pages in a standard text; **81**, the Preamble to Diocletian's *Edict on Prices*, which is very long and almost nauseating because of its verbiage. In most such cases a summary of the meaning is given.

References to *CIL* 1² are all to Part 2 unless otherwise indicated.

In transcribing the praenomina *Gaius* and *Gnaeus* abbreviated C and CN (as regularly when followed by nomen or cognomen or both), I have written G. and *Gn*. In these words the symbol C represents the sound of G, C being the early form of G before this symbol was invented by adding a tail-like stroke to C. (See Intro., n. 65.)

In the transcripts of texts, vocalic V is modernized as *u*.

The translations are intended to be, not elegant, but plain and as close to the Latin word-order as is consistent with intelligible English. Some texts are very challenging in this respect because of the difficulty of composing—and therefore of translating—the long periodic-style Latin sentence (as in **8**, **22**, **31** [which contains only one sentence, of 59 lines, with one main verb], **36**, and others), or because they are poorly cut, such as **19** and **75**. One text, **65**, is unique in being long, metrical, and so badly composed as to be incomprehensible at several points. Some of the later inscriptions include titles of office that would perhaps be better left untranslated, like such familiar titles as "consul" and "praetor"; nevertheless I have tried to translate them. Some of the late texts suffer also from exuberance of style, the worst being **81**, mentioned above.

In translating texts containing the names and titles of the emperors, I often simplify the names; e.g., in **57**, for "Imp. Caesari divi Nervae f(ilio) Nervae Traiano Aug(usto) Germ(anico) Dacico" I simply write "to (the emperor Trajan)." Some-

times also this is done with the names of consuls.

Within the translations parentheses are used as just noted but also to enclose supplements to the translation, which might have been expressed in the Latin; e.g., of Castor and Pollux called "sons (of Zeus)," in **2**. Square brackets are used for explanations, often historical (e.g., in **11**, the date 146 B.C. after "Corinth destroyed"); also to indicate parts lost in the Latin but conjecturally restored (e.g., in **12**, line 1). But I fear that in the choice of parentheses and square brackets I have not been perfectly consistent.

Most of the inscriptions are approximately datable by internal evidence, such as a consular date or the name of a well-known person. In the List of Inscriptions it appears that the dates of ten (excluding **1**) are questioned, those of twenty-three are marked as "probable." The dating of **48** depends on the kind of material used and on the date of the Preface to Pliny the Elder's *Natural History*.

INSCRIPTIONS: DESCRIPTIONS, TEXTS, AND TRANSLATIONS

1. Gold Fibula, Rome, formerly thought to be from Palestrina. 7th (?) cent. B.C. A gold brooch, reportedly found in 1871 at Palestrina (anc. Praeneste); now in Rome, in the Mus. Naz. Preistorico "Luigi Pigorini" (not on public display). Total length 11 cm., the sheath alone 8 cm. (C. D. Curtis, *MAAR* 3 [1919] 22 no. 2 B), the inscr. 7.8 cm.; the letters ca. 2–4 mm. tall. (See N.B. at the end of this annotation.)

CIL 14.4123, *ILS* 8561, *CIL* 1².3 (with pp. 717, 831, and fasc. 4 [ed. A. Degrassi, H. Krummrey]), Diehl 719 and *IL* p. VII, Warm. 196 f., Degr. 1, *Imag.* 365, Ern. 1, Vett. 365, Palm. no. 1 with p. 60, Pis. A 3, Cal. Lim. 317 no. 102. For details of its history, bibliography, problems of authenticity, etc., see Gordon, *Fib. Praen.* (1975) (quotes a letter from Adolf Greifenhagen of Berlin, who examined both the fibula and, for comparison, the 19th-cent. Castellani collection of imitations of ancient gold jewelry in the Villa Giulia Mus., Rome, and found no reason to doubt the fibula's genuineness); G. Colonna, in *Civiltà del Lazio primitivo, Palazzo delle Esposizioni, Roma 1976* ([Rome 1976]) 372 f., no. 126 with pl. C (also accepts the fibula as genuine and from the Bernardini Tomb, Palestrina); D. Ridgway, "Manios Faked?" *Bull. Inst. Class. Stud. Univ. London* 24 (1977) 17–30 (suspicious of its authenticity); Gordon, *Further Remarks* (1978); E. Pulgram, *Italic, Latin, Italian . . .* (Heidelberg 1978) 161 f. (thinks it genuine); G. Colonna, "Ancora sulla fibula prenestina," *Epigraphica* 41 (1979) 119–130; E. P. Hamp, "Is the Fibula a Fake?" *AJP* 102 (1981) 151–153; for a re-view of Gordon, *Fib. Praen.* (1975), see J. Heurgon, *JRS* 70 (1980) 219–221; for an account of a method of detecting forgeries of ancient gold objects, with only slight damage to the object tested, cf. A. Hartmann, *Arch. Anz.* 1975, 300–304.

Text:
MANIOS:MED:FHE:FHAKED:NVMASIOI

i.e., *Manios med fhefhaked Numasioi*, Class. Latin *Manius me fecit Numasio* (or, as generally interpreted, *Numerio*). It is usually taken to mean "Manios (has) made me for Numasios," but perhaps better: "M. has had me made for N." The lettering is like that of early Greek and Etruscan writing, esp. like that of the 7th(?)-cent. Tataie aryballus from Cumae (Jeffery 240 no. 3, pl. 47 no. 3). Colonna (1976), 373, was apparently the first to note that *vhaked* (as he writes *fha-*) was first written *vhe-*, then corrected.

The inscription is unique, or nearly so, in several respects: its retrograde lettering, its use of the digram FH for Latin F (the symbol F, alone, in Greek having the value of English *w*), the perfect *fhefhaked* for Class. Latin *fecit* (remarkable in several respects), the name "Numasios," and its naming both the maker (or the donor) and the recipient. (For details, see *Fib. Praen.* 17–21.) *Manios* and *med* are normal archaic Latin; the case-ending of *Numasioi* is attested centuries later by a Roman grammarian. In form, the inscription is a *titulus loquens*, or "redende Inschrift," in which the object inscribed, as here, or, more often, the deceased is represented as speaking in the first person.

The 7th-cent. dating comes from (a) the now generally accepted date of the ancient tombs excavated at Palestrina (from one of which the fibula probably came) and (b) comparison with the lettering of the Greek inscrs. of Cumae and now the Caeretan inscriptions of 670–630 B.C. (Colonna, 1976). R. Bloch, in *Acta of the 5th International Congress of Greek and Latin Epigraphy, Cambridge 1967* (Oxford 1971), 177, dates the fibula, on the basis of its form, "in the second half, and even at the very end, of the 7th cent."

N.B. Presentation of this fibula now seems moot. M. Guarducci, "La cosiddetta Fibula Prenestina. Antiquari, eruditi e falsari nella Roma dell'ottocento (con un'Appendice di esami e di analisi a cura di Pico Cellino, Guido Devoto ed altri)," *MemLinc* ser. 8: 24: 4 (1980) 413–574, pls. I–XI, has, I believe, proved that the fibula is a 19th-cent. forgery, master-minded by F. Martinetti, unscrupulous Roman antiquarian and art dealer, and the inscription concocted by W. Helbig in order to further the latter's career and, in particular, his ambition to succeed Henzen as head of the German Archaeological Institute in Rome; G. Pinza is now the hero of the story. But the fibula is left here as a salutary exemplum. See D. Ridgway's review of Guarducci, (London) *Times Literary Supplement*, June 19, 1981, p. 691.

2. Castor and Pollux Dedication, Rome, from near Pratica di Mare. Mid- or late-6th (?) cent. B.C. A thin bronze lamina (broken in two pieces, found separately, but complete), found in 1958 in excavating an archaic sanctuary outside Pratica di Mare (or Lavinio—anc. Lavinium), about 30 km. from Rome, by road (*Roma e dintorni* 687 f., map between pp. 568 f.), near three of thirteen altars, but not *in situ*; now kept "in cassaforte," visible on request, in the Mus. Naz. Rom., Rome. 5.0–5.3 × 29.1 × 0.10–0.15 cm. (Castagnoli, 1975). Five holes indicate that it was attached to something else, no doubt a religious offering, perhaps a tufa base like one found nearby.

F. Castagnoli, *Studi e Materiali di Storia delle Religioni* 30 (1959) 109–117 (with photo and drawing); Degr. 2.1271 a, *Imag.* 30 (C.'s photo and bibl.); *CIL* 1²: 2: 4.2833; Pis. A 6 *ter*; cf. G. Radke, *Glotta* 42 (1964) 214–219; M. Cristofani, in *ANRW* 1: 2.476; N. E. Collinge, *Journ. Indo-Europ. Studies*, 1 (1973) 264–270, with drawing (but the interpunct should be single, not double; the lower point is a nail hole); Castagnoli again in *Lavinium*, vol. 2, by him et al. (Rome 1975) 441–443, no. LI, fig. 507 (with bibl.).

The text is retrograde, i.e., cut, and to be read, from right to left, but the last two letters of -*que*, instead of beginning line 2, are cut under each other (boustrophedon style), as though unwilling to be separated (for other similar examples, see **12** line 8, **66** line 7, **78** line 2). In the following Text no attempt is made to reproduce the archaic, Greek-looking letters, all of which except T (which looks like a North Semitic shape, but cf. Guarducci's pl. I at end of vol. 1, the first example of T) can be found in Jeffery's Table of (Archaic Greek) Letters at the end of her book. Noteworthy: the character for C (see her Table, under Gamma), that for D (see her Delta), that for L (see her Lambda), the small O (see her p. 32 *fin.*), the character for P (see her Pi; in our photo [Castagnoli's later one] it is clearer than in his earlier one and seems almost closed), that for Q (see J.'s Koppa), that for R (see her Rho), that for S (see her Sigma and note that the two S's in our inscr., as in **3**, are properly reversed— cf. **4**), and that for V (like several of Jeffery's examples of Upsilon).

Text:

```
ϘΙƎVϘVϘＪᗡOꟼ·IƎЯOTƧAϽ
Λ                      ƧΙOЯVϘ
Ǝ
```

i.e., *Castorei Podlouqueique qurois*, Class. Lat./Greek *Castori Pollucique* κούροις. (One interpunct: after *Castorei*.)

"To Castor and Pollux, sons (of Zeus)."

Noteworthy (besides the letter shapes): the high-placed interpunct, and esp. the spelling of Pollux and the use of *qurois*. *Castorei* (with the older diphthongal dat. sing. ending) and *-que* are Latin, but *Podlouquei* is a strange hodgepodge and *qurois* is simply a transliteration of the Greek, with Q for K (because of the following *u*) and *-ois*, otherwise unattested as the earliest Latin dat.-abl. masc. pl. ending. *Podl.* remains a puzzle; perhaps the λ-δ of Πολυδεύκης has been erroneously transposed into *dl* and *-quei* written for *-kei* (or *-cei*) in anticipation of the following *-que*.

Castagnoli (1975) dates the inscr. palaeographically as probably of the end of the 6th cent., by comparison esp. with the Forum Cippus inscr. (4), but he quotes J. Heurgon (1969) as allowing an earlier (mid-6th cent.) date, also on palaeographical grounds (by comparison with Etruscan inscrs. of the late-7th and mid-6th cents.). Degrassi in *ILLRP* had dated it "inter saec. VI et V," i.e., ca. 500 B.C., Pisani "forse VI–V sec. (?)." Some strictly archaeological evidence from the rest of the sanctuary would be helpful.

3. Duenos Vase, Berlin, from Rome. 7th–5th (?) cent. B.C. It consists of three small, brownish-black clay vessels joined together with clay, found in Rome in 1880; now in the Staatliche Museen, Antikenabteilung, Berlin (inv. no. 30894, 3). 3.4–3.6 cm. high, 10.3–10.5 cm. each side of the triangle, 32.3 cm. max. circumference (these figures from Berlin).

CIL 1².4 (cf. pp. 717, 739, 831, fasc. 4), *ILS* 8743, Diehl 720 and *IL* p. VII, Warm. 54–57, Degr. 2, *Imag.* 366 a–f, Ern. 3, Palm. no. 2 with p. 62, Pis. A 4, R. E. A. Palmer *Riv. Stor. dell'Ant.* 4 (1974) 129–133, Gordon *CSCA* 8 (1976) 53–72 with 3 plates, E. Tiffou in *Mélanges d'études latines offerts à Maurice Lebel* (St-Jean-Chrysostome, P. Québec, Canada 1980) 223–230.

The vase, soon acquired and published by Enrico (Heinrich) Dressel (1880), has since received an enormous bibliography and over fifty interpretations, no two in full agreement. Two claims of forgery are frivolous or superficial.

The dating ranges from 7th cent. to ca. 200 B.C., the arguments being archaeological, linguistic, metrical, or palaeographical. Of these, only the first and last deserve serious consideration, the metrical being worthless and the linguistic having so little comparable material. The type of pottery used led Degrassi, following three Italian archaeologists, to favor the 7th cent., but posthumously, in *CIL* 1² fasc. 4, he leaves the date uncertain; while seeming to favor ca. 550/500, he notes that the inscr. was thought to be a little earlier than our **4**, but that the palaeographer Giorgio Cencetti favored the 5th cent. because of the letter shapes. (For details, see Gordon op. cit. 56–58.)

Four letters appear to be corrected, one added, by the cutter; one is damaged; these six, plus another stroke, remain uncertain, but only four matter.

Text (as read from right to left, with the vase upside down; the order of units is that generally agreed upon):

unit 1 ᴑƎISOϽЯIVƨIMƨOƆOᗡᴎƎᗡƎTIᴎTATIMᗡƎMIOꝙƨOVIƎᗡTAƨ\ƎVOI

unit 2 ƨIOVIЯAꝲAᗡAIAIƨƎTIOTƎꝙOIƨIOᴎᗡƎTƨA

unit 3 ᗡOTATƨOꞱAMᗡƎMƎᴎIOᴎƎᗡUᴑMOᴎIƎᴎOMMAMᴎƎᗡƎꝲᗡƎMƨOᴎƎᴑᗡ

i.e.,

iove satdeivosqoimedmitatneitedendocosmisvircosied (49 letters)
astednoisiopetoitesiaipac(?)arivois (32)
due(?)nosmedfec(?)edenmanomeinomdu(?)enoinemedmal(?)ostatod. (47)

Unit 1: The thin vertical after IOVE seems to be a separator, not the letter I or accidental. The first A seems to be corrected from an E. Unit 2 (the most baffling to interpret): The C in PACARI, like that in FECED (unit 3), seems to result from uncertainty whether to write C or K. Unit 3: The third letter is damaged, J. F. K. Dirichs (1934) reading DVFNOS as the potter's Sabine name. Farther on, personal inspection convinces me of the correctness of the reading DVENOI, dat. sing. of *Duenos*. The last uncertain letter seems intended as L rather than N, and first cut as A, perhaps by dittography.

Scholars are not agreed as to the purpose of the vase or the meaning of the inscription. The only intelligible phrase seems to be *Duenos med feced*, "Duenos (or, "A good man") (has) made me," the vase (or "had me made").

4. Forum Romanum Cippus, Rome. Truncated obeliskoid cippus of Grotta Oscura (Veientine) tufa, *in situ* (its original site: Lugli, *Mon. min.* 24, 26), in the Forum Romanum, Rome; unearthed in 1899 near the Rostra, under a black-marble pavement commonly since called the Lapis Niger. Late-6th (?) cent. B.C. Height 45.5 to 61 cm. (it is very unevenly broken at the top, by "a violent and deliberate work of destruction," Boni; similarly also Lugli, 23: at the time of the Gallic capture of Rome?), width at base 47 to 51.9 cm., the sides being of unequal width (G. Boni, *NS* for May 1899, pp. 151, 153, with five photos of a plaster copy [so D. Comparetti, *Iscrizione arcaica del Foro Romano* (Florence, Rome 1900) 1]).

CIL 1².1, with one of Boni's photos (cf. pp. 717, 739, 831; fasc. 4, with further bibl.), *CIL* 6.36840 (5 photos—of the stone?), *ILS* 4913 (add.), Bruns 14 f., no. VII add., Diehl 254 and *IL* tab. 1 (4 photos), Warm. 242–245, *FIRA* 1, 19 f., Ern. 2, Palm. no. 3 with p. 62, Pis. A 1, Degr. 3 (add. pp. 315 f.), *Imag.* 378 a–d (all with bibl., which is large). Add P/A 482–484

s.v. Sepulcrum Romuli (1); P. MacKendrick, *The Mute Stones Speak* . . . (New York 1960) 74–78 (photo); Nash 2.21–23 *s.v.* Lapis Niger (5 photos); R. E. A. Palmer, *Historia, Einzelschr.* 11 (Wiesbaden 1969) (4 photos, including the best available to date for line 16, and drawing); T. N. Gantz, "Lapis Niger: the Tomb of Romulus," *La Parola del Passato* 158–159 (1974) 350–361.

The black pavement, dated by Lugli, *Mon. min.* 24, 26, as Caesarian and preceded, he thought, by an earlier pavement also of black stone, of Sullan date or even perhaps as early as 210 B.C., is generally identified with Festus's *Niger lapis in Comitio*, which he says (p. 184, 19–25, L) *locum funestum significat, ut ali, Romuli morti destinatum, sed non usu ob in . . .* ; the rest is fragmentary and of quite uncertain restoration, but presumably the *ali* (i.e., *alii*) was followed by another *ali* and a verb such as *dicunt*, to indicate different opinions. There are also passages in Dion. Hal. and remarks by ancient commentators on Horace, *Ep.* 16.13, from all of which Lommatzsch in *CIL* 1², p. 368 *init.*, concluded that the area uncovered in 1899 was the one which Varro, the supposed source of Festus, etc., had claimed as the tomb of Faustulus (who, in legend, had found Romulus and Remus) or Hostus Hostilius (legendary grandfather of Rome's third king) or Romulus himself, that the black-marble pavement is the Niger Lapis of Festus, and that the present cippus is the inscribed stele of Hostilius mentioned by Dion. Hal. 3.1. (But our Cippus inscr. does not appear to testify to Hostilius's ἀρετή.)

The dating depends on such historical considerations, the kind of tufa used, and the palaeography of the inscr. Lommatzsch, *CIL* 1² p. 369, conjectured ca. 500 B.C. (Bang, in *CIL* 6, p. 3771 *fin.*, merely quotes him); Degrassi (*ILLRP*) reports most scholars as agreeing on the second half of the 6th cent., but he notes that some believe that the *rex* who seems to be mentioned in the inscr. is the post-regal *rex sacrorum*. Frank, *RBR* 61 f., dates the use of this Veientine tufa to the 6th cent., when the Etruscans controlled both Veii and Rome. F. Castagnoli, *St. Rom.* 22 (1974) 426, with reference to Frank E. Brown, dates to the end of the 6th cent. all the monuments under the Lapis Niger, including the inscribed cippus.

The writing, while it must be read vertically, was no doubt cut horizontally. It reads boustrophedon, up line 1, down line 2, etc., except that line 12, beginning the south face, reads up (i.e., right to left) like line 11; lines 8–9, the first two on the east face, and line 16, cut along the southwest edge, which was sliced back to a width of 5.3 cm. (Boni, op. cit. 153), while boustrophedon, appear to be upside down if considered from the same point of view as the other thirteen lines, presumably because the cutter forgetfully changed his position vis-à-vis the cippus. Actually, line 8 must have been cut from right to left, like line 7, line 9 from l. to r., like line 10, and line 16 from l. to r., like line 15: it is more credible that the cutter changed his position than that he cut anything upside down. Letter heights: from ca. 6 (first O, line 1) to ca. 14 cm. (R, line 2), according to Comparetti's drawing, which is scaled 1:6 (cf. p. 8, col. 1).

Text, based on personal examination of the cippus itself and the plaster copy in the Forum Antiquario, on all the photos available, and on a comparison of *CIL* vols. 1 and 6, Comparetti, P. G. Goidanich (cited by Degrassi), Degrassi, and R. E. A. Palmer (no attempt is made to reproduce the Greek-like letters—see below):

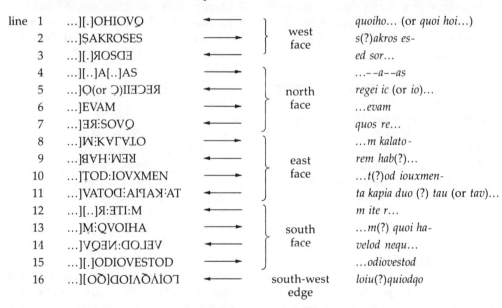

line	1	...][.]OHIOVϘ	←	}	west face	quoiho... (or *quoi hoi...*)
	2	...]ṢAKROSES	→			s(?)akros es-
	3	...][.]ЯOSꟼƎ	←			ed sor...
	4	...][..]A[..]AS	→	}	north face	...--a--as
	5	...]Ọ(or Ɔ)IIƎƆƎЯ	←			*regei ic* (or *io*)...
	6	...]EVAM	→			...evam
	7	...]ƎЯ:SOVϘ	←			quos re...
	8	...]ꟽ:KⱯꓑⱯꓕO	→	}	east face	...m kalato-
	9	...]ꓭVH:ꟽƎЯ	←			rem hab(?)...
	10	...]ṬOD:IOVXMEN	→			...t(?)od iouxmen-
	11	...]VATOꓷ:AIꓑⱯꓘ:AT	←			ta kapia duo (?) tau (or *tav*)...
	12	...][..]Я:ƎTI:M	←	}	south face	m ite r...
	13	...]Ṃ:ϘVOIHA	→			...m(?) quoi ha-
	14	...]VϘƎꟽ:ꓷOꓶƎV	←			velod nequ...
	15	...][.]ODIOVESTOD	→			...odiovestod
	16	...][OꝹ]ꓷOIⱯꝹⱭ̇IOꓶ	←		south-west edge	loiu(?)quiodqo

In the composite photo line 16 appears at the right, followed by lines 1–15, right to left.

Because of the quality of the tufa and the present condition of the inscribed surfaces, both text and punctuation are often uncertain. The photo sometimes fails to show what inspection of the stone itself or of the plaster copy reveals; sometimes there has been further damage along the edges (e.g., the B in line 9, where the plaster copy shows something like J). Line 11, the O seems to have a tiny Y cut inside of it, hence the conjectural reading *duo*. Greek-like letter shapes: besides those mentioned on **2**, above, note the open C-shaped G (line 5, right to left), the H closed at top and bottom, lines 1, 9, 13 (cf. Jeffery, Table of Letters, *Heta*, and p. 28), K for the later C, the two shapes of 5-stroke M, lines 6, 9, 10, 12 (Jeffery, Table, *Mu*, and p. 31), the unreversed S in lines 3, 7 (just like those in lines 2, 4, 15: cf. Larfeld 135, 2nd par., *fin.*: ". . . S and Ƨ werden häufig verwechselt . . ."), T like the usual Tau (Jeffery, Table, *Tau*), but the Y-shaped V, clear in lines 7, 10, 13 (not quite like any of Jeffery's Table, *Upsilon*, or the V's in **2**) and the almost cross-like X, line 10 (unlike any of Jeffery's Table, *Chi*). The only words generally agreed on are *sakros* (Class. Latin *sacer*), *recei* (*regi*, "king"), *kalatorem* (*cal--*), and *iovxmenta* (*iumenta*), with less agreement on *quoi* (*qui?*) and *iovestod* (*iusto?*). There have been many interpretations, based on the impossible task of restoring the whole text (see Palmer, op. cit., for the latest), but beyond judging, from the references cited above and the little that seems clear of the present text, that it is of religious or funerary significance, I find it baffling and incomprehensible.

5. Scipionic Sarcophagus with Epitaph, Rome. Probably 3rd cent. B.C. In the Atrio del Torso Belvedere, Vatican (inv. no. 1191). Of peperino tufa (*lapis Albanus*), *pace* Helbig/Speier (cf. Frank, *RBR* 22 f., G. De Angelis d'Ossat *Bull. Com.* 64 [1936] 47–49, G. Lugli *La tecnica edilizia romana . . .* 1 [Rome 1957] 302). Found in 1782 in excavating the tomb of the Scipios, who seem to have continued to bury their dead, in their own cemetery on the Via Appia, outside Porta Capena, long after most Romans had turned to cremation (Cic. *De Leg.* 2.22.56, Plin. *N.H.* 7.54.187; cf. Toynbee, 103 f., 113); the tomb (*sepulcrum, monumentum*) is mentioned by several ancient authors, e.g., Cic. *Tusc.* 1.7.13, *Pro Arch.* 9.22, Livy 38.56.4. (For the systemization of the cemetery carried out by the city of Rome in 1926, see *CIL* 1².2:1, p. 373; A. M. Colini, *Capitolium*, 3 [1927] 27–32, 5 [1929] 182–195.)

Length 2.77 m. at base, width ca. 1.10 m. at base, height 1.42 m. (Degrassi *ILLRP*

and Helbig/Speier). Restored: the left half of the cover and the upper-left corner of the base (Helbig/Speier).

Dates: the original inscription painted on the cover, not visible in this photo, as well as the earlier one cut on the front, no doubt followed Barbatus's death (ca. 270 B.C.? he was consul in 298, censor in 280 [?], *pont. max.* till perhaps later: Broughton, 2.556), but the present elogium, which obviously replaced an earlier, no doubt simpler, epitaph in plain prose, merely listing S.'s full name (including "Barbatos," for which evidently there was no room on the cover) and his titles in the usual Roman style, without embellishment, is generally dated later (see below).

CIL 1².6–7 (cf. pp. 373–377, 718, 739, 831, fasc. 4), *CIL* 6.1284 f. (add. pp. 3135, nos. 31587 f., 3799 no. 37039), *ILS* 1, *CLE* 7, Diehl 539, Warm. 2 f., Degr. 309 (add. p. 325), *Imag.* 132 (but the bust shown is extraneous, and "Cornelius" on the cover is restored incorrectly), Ern. 13, Palm. no. 12, Pis. A 7, E. Meinhardt and E. Simon in H/S 1.266, Nash 2.352–356 *s.v.* Sep. Scipionum (plan and 5 photos), De Ros. 6. Add U. Scamuzzi, *Riv. St. Class.* 5 (1957) 248–268; Lucy T. Shoe, *MAAR* 28 (1965) 79; A. La Regina, *Dial. Arch.* 2 (1968) 173–190, V. Saladino, *Der Sarkophag des L. Corn. Scip. Barb.* (Würzburg 1970); F. Zevi, *St. Misc.* 15 (1969–70) 63–73; R. Till, in *Festschrift Karl Vretska* (Heidelberg 1970) 276–289; F. Coarelli, *Il sepolcro degli Scipioni* (Rome 1972) and in *Dial. Arch.* 6 (1972) 36–106.

Text of inscr. painted on cover ("litteris adhuc miniatis," *CIL* 1².6), as read by the first editor, 1782: [*L. Corneli*]*o Gn. f. Scipio,* Class. Lat. *L*(*ucius*) *Cornelius Gn*(*aei*) *f*(*ilius*) *Scipio.* "L. Cornelius Scipio, son of Gnaeus."

In line 2 of the earlier, erased, inscr. cut on the front, Huelsen on *CIL* 6.31588 (1902) was sure of having read traces of *ESO*, above the *FOR* of *fortis* in the present elogium, which he took to be the remains of *ce*(*n*)*sor.* The earlier inscription was eventually deleted and replaced by the present elogium, judged since the time of an early editor to be in saturnians, the line divisions clearly marked on the stone by a dash except after line 1 (regularly thought by editors to end with *Barbatus*); perhaps the cutter found the available space not adequate for six saturnian lines after erasing the earlier inscription, which, if complete, had been poorly arranged.

Text of the elogium: *Cornelius Lucius Scipio Barbatus, [—] Gnaivod patre / prognatus, fortis vir sapiensque, — quoius forma virtutei parisuma / fuit, — consol, censor, aidilis quei fuit apud vos; — Taurasia⟨m⟩, Cisauna⟨m⟩ / Samnio capit, — subigit omne⟨m⟩ Loucanam (terram?) opsidesque abdoucit.* Class. Lat. forms: *Gnaeo, cuius, virtuti, parissima, consul, aedilis, qui, (in or ex?) Samnio (or Samnium, acc.?), Lucanam, obsides, abducit.*

"Lucius Cornelius Scipio Barbatus ('Long-beard,' Warm.), son of Gnaeus, a brave man and prudent, whose looks were fully equal to his valor; he was aedile, consul, (and) censor among you; he took Taurasia (and) Cisauna in (or, from) Samnium (or: "he took T., C., (and all) Samnium"? cf. *hec cepit Corsica(m) Aleria(m)que urbe(m)*, of Barbatus's son, *CIL* 1².9); he subdues all Lucania and takes away hostages."

The order of words seems caused at times (e.g., lines 1 and 3) by metrical needs. Most editors seem to prefer *Samnio*, abl., with prep. omitted (*metri causa?*). Some letters are worn. The M of *Loucanam* is damaged but fairly certain. Ritschl's two drawings, pl. XXXVII, B and b, disagree: b shows no M at all except perhaps the first stroke, concealed in the break. Scamuzzi argues in favor of *Loucana*, 256 f.; his own examination of the inscr. itself, in the Vatican, was inconclusive; but there are remains of what seems to be an M and space left for it. *Terram* is supplied by Wölfflin, *Rev. de phil., de litt. et d'hist. anc.* n.s. 14 (1890) 122, *init.*: "nullum enim illo tem-

pore exstitit nomen Lucaniae." Note the change, so common in the Latin historians, from the perfect tense to the historical present; "a sequence like *subegit omne Loucanam* is less metrical than *subigit . . .*," Thomas Cole, "The Saturnian Verse," *Yale Class. Stud.* 21 (1969) 25.

A likely date for these verses would be soon after Livius Andronicus's adaptation of the *Odyssey* to Latin saturnians (ca. 240 B.C.?), a generation after Scipio's death. Others have dated them ca. 200, connecting them with the newly acquired fame of Scipio Africanus the Elder and even considering the versifier to have been Ennius (cf. H/S 1, p. 214 *fin.*), said by Cicero (*Pro Arch.* 9.22) to have been "carus Africano superiori" and to be thought represented by a marble effigy in the tomb of the Scipios, where Livy also says (38.56.4) there were three statues, one of Africanus, one of his brother Lucius, and one of Ennius. But I find no evidence that Ennius ever wrote saturnians. Palaeographically and otherwise, Barbatus's son's two inscrs. from his sarcophagus (*CIL* 1².8 f., *ILS* 2 f., Degr. 310, *Imag.* 133, with his father's) seem *earlier* than his father's, for whatever reason; the son died perhaps ca. 240–230 (cos. 259, censor 258). It is hard to see how the son's sarcophagus could have waited till the end of the century to receive his identifying epitaph and elogium. (Barbatus's had had its two inscrs. presumably from the time of his burial, until the frontal one was replaced by the saturnians.) I therefore incline to date the son's two inscriptions about the time of his burial, and Barbatus's saturnians some years later, but still within the 3rd cent. (Degrassi, *Imag.*, dates B.'s inscrs. about 250, but in *ILLRP*, p. 182, on no. 210, in discussing Wölfflin's dating of both elogia ca. 200, he says, "Mihi vero res parum liquet.") The reason why the son's inscriptions are, as it seems, earlier than Barbatus's may simply be that he, or perhaps one of his sons, was personally known to some versifier of the period, such as

Livius Andronicus, who may have suggested a new fashion—an elogium in saturnians—for B.'s son, which later was applied to B. himself as the earliest Scipio buried in the family cemetery, his handsome sarcophagus being the most prominent one there.

6. Dedication to Hercules by M. Minucius, Rome.

217 B.C. Of peperino tufa (cf. Frank, *RBR* 22 f.). Found in 1862 in the Campo Verano, near San Lorenzo fuori le Mura, Rome; now in Sala I of the Braccio Nuovo, Palazzo dei Conservatori, Rome (inv. no. 6979). Called both an altar and a base, it seems in fact to have been a statue base—there are two foot-holes cut in the top—intended to hold a statue of Hercules. 94 × 70–71 × ca. 68 cm. Letter heights: lines 1, 3, 4, 8.5–9.0 cm., 2, 9.0–9.5 cm.; left side 7.5 cm., right side 8+ cm.

CIL 1².607 (add. fasc. 4), 6.284, *ILS* 11, Diehl 87, Warm. 76 f., Degr. 118, *Imag.* 59, Pis. A 18 *bis*, E. Meinhardt in H/S 2.1596, De Ros. 18 (some of whom call the stone travertine, on whose authority is not indicated).

Text (left and right sides not shown in photo): left side, L·I·XXVI; center, *Hercolei / sacrom: / M(arcus) Minuci(us), G(ai) f(ilius), / dictator, voṿit* right side.

"To Hercules, sacred. Marcus Minucius, son of Gaius, dictator, vowed (it)." The left-side inscr. is apparently a stonecutter's note (Degr.).

Minucius, after being *Magister Equitum* (Master of Horse) under the dictator Q. Fabius Maximus Verrucosus in 217, was elected co-dictator with him the same year (Broughton, 1.243); Degrassi points out that the compiler of the Fasti Consulares failed to name Minucius as co-dictator (*FCT* 44 f., 118, 444 f.).

Minuci is simply an abbreviation, not a variant form. Note the wide C, narrow D, angled L, wide M, slanted N, round O, all characteristic of the period. The punctuation is round, there is no shading (distinction between thick and thin strokes: *Contrib.* 79–82), and only primitive serifs on C and S (a kind of thickening, except at the top of the first C) and at the ends of some E bars.

7. Decree of L. Aemilius (Paulus), Paris, from Spain.

Probably ca. 190 B.C. Bronze copy of a decree of L. Aemilius (Paulus or Paullus), *Imperator*, while praetor (191) or proconsul (190–189, or –188) in Farther Spain; doubtfully a later copy. Found in 1866 (d'Ors) east of Cádiz (anc. Gades), southern Spain. Now in the Louvre, Paris. 14.0–14.3 × 22.2–22.5 cm. × ca. 2–3 mm. The attached handle—the larger part 4 cm. long—has a hole (not visible in the photo) through its shorter part, presumably for hanging up. Letter heights: mostly ca. 1 cm., the O's down to 75 mm.

CIL 1².614 (with photo or drawing of same size as the bronze; cf. fasc. 4), 2.5041 (cf. p. 843), *ILS* 15, Bruns 240 no. 70 (with photo, Grad. 2), Diehl 263, *FIRA* 1.305 no. 51, Warm. 254 f., Ern. 125, L/R 1.311 no. 121 (transl.), Alvaro d'Ors, *Epigrafía jurídica de la España rom.* (Madrid 1953) 349–352 no. 12 (cf. *Emerita*, 32 [1964] 327 f.), Palm. 9, Pis. A 30, Degr. 2.514, *Imag.* 396 (Grad. 2), De Ros. 25 (all with bibl.), *ARS* 22 (transl., with change from past to present tenses and a slight mistake in the date). The earliest Roman inscription from Spain (A. Schulten, *CAH* 8.313).

Text: *L(ucius) Aimilius L(uci) f(ilius) Inpeirator decreivit / utei quei Hastensium servei / in Turri Lascutana habitarent / leiberei essent; agrum oppidumqu(e) /⁵ quod ea tempestate posedisent / item possidere habereque / iousit dum poplus senatusque / Romanus vellet. Act(um) in castreis / a(nte) d(iem) XII K(alendas) Febr(uarias).* Class. Latin forms: *Aemilius, Imperator decrevit ut* (or *uti*) *qui, servi, liberi, possedissent, iussit, populus, castris.* (Orthography not yet stable with respect to double consonants.)

"L. Aemilius, son of Lucius, *Imperator,*

(has) decreed that what slaves of the Hastenses [the inhabitants of Hasta Regia, near Gades] were living in the Tower of Lascuta [identified with Alcalá de los Gazules] should be free; the land and the town which at that time they had possessed, he ordered (them) likewise to possess and hold so long as [or, provided that] the Roman people and senate were willing. Done in camp on the 12th day before February 1 [i.e., Jan. 19]."

The dating involves two debatable questions, so is uncertain, though probably ca. 190. (1) Is this a contemporary copy of the original decree, or a later one? *Pace* d'Ors, *Epigr. jur.*, and E. Badian, *JRS* 58 (1968) 243, Degrassi seems right in thinking it, for palaeographical reasons, contemporary. (2) What does *Imperator* mean here? "acclaimed *Imp.*" (by P.'s soldiers for his victory over the Lusitani, Livy 37.57.5 f.)? perhaps the common view, but cf. Alb. Deman, *Latomus* 35 (1976) 805–807, and R. Develin, *Latomus* 36 (1977) 110 f.; see also A. Momigliano, *Bull. Com.* 58 (1930) 44 (= *Quarto contrib.* 285), Broughton 1.353 (with ref. to Plut. *Aem.* 4.1), 362, *Suppl.* 3, and Combès 28, 61, 68–72, 98, 452 *fin.* In any case we are in the period of P.'s incumbency in Spain (191 to 189 or 188). The position of *Imp.* here (as later in **9** and **15**), in place of the missing cognomen and in the absence of P.'s proper title, makes it look like a cognomen (above, p. 19), as Augustus later initiated its use as a praenomen (cf. R. Syme, *Historia* 7 [1958] 172–188 [= *Rom. Papers* 1.361–377]).

8. *Senatus Consultum de Bacchanalibus*, in Vienna. 186 B.C. Bronze tablet inscribed with a copy of the consuls' letter to the Teurani (?) embodying a decree of the Roman senate of 186. Found in 1640 in southern Italy; since 1727 in Vienna, now in the Kunsthistorisches Museum, Antikenabteilung (inv. no. III 168). 27.3 × 28.7 × 0.6–0.7 cm. Letter heights: 4–6, the last phrase 5–7, mm.

CIL 1².581 (cf. pp. 723, 832, fasc. 4), 10.104, *ILS* 18, Bruns 36 (with photo, Grad. 3), Diehl 262, Warm. 254–259, *FIRA* 1.240 f., no. 30, Ern. 126, Palm. no. 8, Degr. 2.511, *Imag.* 392 (Grad. 3), Pis. A 29, De Ros. 26. Cf. Ed. Fraenkel, *Hermes* 67 (1932) 369–396, L/R 1.472 f., no. 176 (transl.), F. C. Grant, ed., *Ancient Roman Religion* (New York 1957) 54–56 (bibl., transl.), *ARS* 28 (transl., with notes), A. Dihle, *Hermes* 90 (1962) 376–379, R. Noll, *Griech. u. latein. Inschriften der Wiener Antikensammlung* (Vienna 1962) 126 no. 420 (with history, description, bibl., photo, but no text or annotation). Apparently the oldest extant Roman *Senatus Consultum* and the earliest extant piece of non-literary ("legalese") Latin of any length. For the subject, see Cic. *De Leg.* 2.15.37, Livy 39.14; for a brief account, with bibl., M. P. Nilsson, *OCD* 157 f., *s.v.* Bacchanalia, to which add T. Frank, *CQ* 21 (1927) 128–132.

The interpuncts are often tiny and faint, some uncertain. Some damage, some since *CIL* 1²; in a few places the text seems to have been restored by cutting the undersurface. For the spacing, cf. Wingo 70–72 (but no "heading" or "long space at the end of line 2").

Text (only the first example of each abbr. is expanded):

[*Q(uintus)*] *Marcius L(uci) f(ilius), S(purius) Postumius L. f., co(n)s(ules), senatum consoluerunt N(onis) Octob(ribus) apud aedem* / *Duelonai. Sc(ribendo) arf(uerunt)* [i.e., *adf-*] *M(arcus) Claudi(us) M(arci) f., L(ucius) Valeri(us) P(ubli) f., Q. Minuci(us) G(ai) f. De Bacanalibus, (sc. eis) quei foideratei* / *esent, ita exdeicundum censuere: neiquis eorum Sacanal* [sic] *habuise velet* [i.e., *vellet*]; *sei ques* / *esent quei sibei deicerent necesus ese Bacanal habere, eeis* [sic] *utei ad pr(aetorem) urbanum* /⁵ *Romam venirent deque eeis rebus, ubei eorum utr a* [sic, for *verba*] *audita esent, utei senatus* / *noster decerneret, dum ne minus senator⟨i⟩bus C(entum) adesent* [*quom e*]*a res cosoleretur.* / *Bacas vir nequis adiese velet ceivis Romanus neve nominus Latini neve socium / quisquam nisei pr. urbanum adiesent isque de senatuos sententiad dum ne / minus senatoribus C adesent quom ea res cosoleretur iousisent* (for *-set*). *Censuere.*

/[10] *Sacerdos nequis vir eset; magister neque vir neque mulier quisquam eset / neve pecuniam quisquam eorum comoinem [h]abuise velet neve magistratum / neve pro magistratuo neque virum [neque mul]ierem quiquam fecise velet; / neve posthac inter sed cnioura[se nev]e comvovise neve conspondise / neve conprome sise* [sic] *velet neve quisquam fidem inter sed dedise velet.* /[15] *Sacra in dquoltod* [sic] *ne quisquam fecise velet; neve in poplicod neve in / preivatod neve exstrad urbem sacra quisquam fecise velet nisei / pr. urbanum adieset isque de senatuos sententiad dum ne minus / senatoribus C adesent quom ea res cosoleretur iousisent* (read *-set*). *Censuere. /*

Homines plous V oinvorsei virei atque mulieres sacra ne quisquam /[20] fecise velet neve inter ibei virei plous duobus mulieribus (for *mulieres*) *plous tribus / arfuise velent nisei de pr(aetoris) urbani senatuosque sententiad utei suprad scriptum est.*

Haice utei in coventionid exdeicatis ne minus trinum / noundinum senatuosque sententiam utei scientes esetis, eorum / sententia ita fuit. Sei ques esent quei arvorsum ead fecisent quam suprad /[25] scriptum est, eeis rem caputalem faciendam censuere; atque utei / hoce in tabolam ahenam inceideretis, ita senatus aequom censuit, / uteique eam figier ioubeatis ubei facilumed gnoscier potisit; atque / utei ea Bacanalia sei qua sunt exstrad quam sei quid ibei sacri est, / ita utei suprad scriptum est, in diebus X quibus vobeis tabelai datai /[30] erunt faciatis utei dismota sient. In agro Teurano.

"(The two consuls) consulted the Senate on October 7 [186 B.C.] in the Temple of Bellona. Present at the writing (of the decree) were (three senators). With reference to the Bacchic cult they passed a decree that the following proclamation should be issued to those allied (with the Romans) by treaty: 'Let none of them be minded to maintain a place of Bacchic worship. Should there be any who say that they must maintain a place of Bacchic worship, they must come to Rome to the urban praetor, and about these matters, when their words have been heard, our Senate shall make a decision, provided that no less than 100 senators be present when this matter is deliberated. Let no man, (whether) Roman citizen or anyone of the Latin name [i.e., those enjoying *ius Latii*, a restricted form of citizenship: *OLD* 1186 *s.v.* nomen, 19] or of the allies, be minded to attend a meeting of Bacchic women unless they go to the urban praetor and he gives permission with the approval of the Senate, provided that no less than 100 senators be present when this matter is deliberated.' They so voted.

" 'Let no man be a priest. Let not anyone, neither man nor woman, be a master; nor let any of them be minded to keep a common fund; nor let anyone be minded to make either man or woman a master or a vice-master, nor be minded henceforth to exchange oaths or vows or pledges or promises with one another; nor be minded to plight faith with one another. Let no one be minded to perform ceremonies in secret, nor let anyone be minded to perform ceremonies, either in public or in private or outside the city, unless he goes to the urban praetor and he gives permission in accordance with the will of the Senate, provided no less than 100 senators be present when this matter is deliberated.' They so voted.

" 'Let no one be minded to hold services in a group larger than five persons, men and women together, and let no more than two men and three women be minded to be present there among (them), except by authorization of the urban praetor and the senate, as is written above.'

"That you proclaim this at a public meeting for a period of not less than three market days and be cognizant of the Senate's decree, such was their decree. If there were any who acted contrary to what is written above, they decreed that a capital charge should be made against them. And that you have this engraved on a bronze tablet, the Senate considered proper, and that you order it to be fastened up where it can most easily become known; and that those places of Bacchic worship, if there are any, except if there is anything sacred (there), just as is written above, should be dismantled within ten days of the delivery of this letter. In the Ager Teuranus." (This last phrase probably by a different, perhaps later, hand.)

Note *volo* (*velet*, i.e., *vellet*) with perf. infin. (cf. K/S 2: 1.133 f., §10; Pharr, *ARS* p. 27, n. 1a, with ref. to D. Daube, *Forms of Roman Legislation* [Oxford 1956, repr. Westport, Conn. 1979] 37–49, to which add *The Class. Tradition . . . Studies in Honor of H. Caplan* [Ithaca 1966] 222–231); note also the mixture of primary and secondary sequence (e.g., last par., *exdeicatis, esetis; inceideretis, ioubeatis, dismota sient*) and *interibi* (line 20) with local meaning, "among (them) there." Lines 22 f., *trinum noundinum*, "3 market days" = 25 days, cf. App. III, §10, with n. 25. Line 25, *eeis rem caputalem faciendam*, the dative apparently not one of "agent" (as perhaps suggested by the gerundive), but of "indirect object"—"for them," i.e., "against them"; cf. *TLL* 3.344, 56–58, *s.v.* capitalis, 6.96.10 *s.v.* facio; *OLD* 271 *s.v.* capitalis, 1 c (no other examples are cited of *rem capitalem facere*).

9. Commemorative Tablet of L. Aemilius (Paulus), Delphi.

167 B.C. or very soon after. Found in 1893 at Delphi in the area of the Temple of Apollo; now in the museum there. 0.91 × 1.70 × 0.30 m. (Th. Homolle, *BCH* 21 [1887] 621 f.). Letter heights ca. 7.3 cm. (G. Colin, *Fouilles de Delphes*, 3: 4 [Paris 1930] 32). The tablet is generally thought to have formed part of the marble base of one side of a pillar set up as a monument to celebrate Aemilius's defeat of Perseus, the last Macedonian king, in 168, which was pictured in four

scenes carved, one on each side, near the top of the pillar. The monument is mentioned by Polybius (30.10.2), Livy (45.27.6 f., for 167 B.C.), and Plutarch (*Aem.* 28.4), of whom the first two mention pillars in the plural (κίονας, *columnas*), Plutarch only one (κίονα μέγαν τετράγωνον ἐκ λίθων λευκῶν συνηρμοσμένον—these details sound as though he had actually seen it); all three agree that the pillar(s) had been prepared by Perseus for "statues" (Livy) or a "gilded statue" (Plutarch) of himself, but appropriated by Aemilius for his own statue(s). According to Colin, op. cit. 33, "En réalité, les fouilles ont confirmé l'existence de deux piédestaux, de dimensions assez voisines, le nôtre et un autre, plus mutilé. . . . Peut-être Paul-Émile s'était-il contenté d'en adopter un seul, celui sur lequel il a orgueilleusement gravé 'qu'il l'avait pris au roi Persée et aux Macédoniens'; il y avait fait ajouter une frise représentant sa victoire, et, par-dessus, une statue, probablement dorée, comme devait l'être celle de Persée, où on le voyait montant un cheval cabré sur ses pattes de derrière (attitude classique, confirmée par les trous de scellement de la plinthe). L'autre monument étant demeuré anonyme, on en aura peu à peu oublié l'origine, et Plutarque n'aura plus attaché d'importance qu'à celui dont nous nous occupons ici."

Our tablet seems, from its inscription and especially from the verb *cepet*, to belong to a monument supporting, not a statue or statues of Paulus, but some trophy or spoils of war taken from the Macedonians. So perhaps it belonged to Colin's second monument. For Guarducci's tentative solution of the question of one statue or two, see *RendPontAcc* 3: 13 (1937) 49–53, 55.

CIL 1².622 (with photo—cf. pp. 725, 739, 835, fasc. 4), 3.14203²², *ILS* 8884, Diehl 344 and *IL* tab. 6, a, Warm. 78 f., Degr. 323, *Imag.* 142 (all with bibl.). Our plate shows a later, Greek, inscr. cut below the Latin: it is one of many such

(Colin, op. cit. 32, lists 37) cut on the monument as far up as the fifth course (Homolle, op. cit. 623).

Text: *L(ucius) Aimilius L(uci) f(ilius) Inperator de rege Perse / Macedonibusque cepet.*

"Lucius Aemilius, son of Lucius, *Imperator*, took (this trophy, *or* these spoils of war?) from King Perseus and the Macedonians." Note again the absence of Paulus's cognomen and regular title, Proconsul, in favor of *Imperator* (on which see above, on **7**).

Colin, loc. cit., describes the punctuation as "most often in the form of a little dash (or hyphen: *tiret*)." He also calls this inscription a "dédicace," Warmington agrees in listing it among his "Tituli Sacri, Dedicatory Inscrs.," but Degrassi has it among his "Magistratus Romani."

10. Honorary Inscription to M. Claudius Marcellus, Luni.

Probably 155 B.C. The plinth of a Luna-marble capital, found in 1857 in ruins of the forum of anc. Luna, in Etruria (mod. Luni in Liguria, near Carrara); formerly in the Mus. Arch., Florence, but sent back to Luni ca. 1962 or 1963 (as reported in Florence in 1973). The oldest monument of Luna marble (Luisa Banti, *Luni* [Florence 1937] 114). Writing surface: ca. 14.7–15 × 92 cm., overall height ca. 42, depth 91.5 cm. Letter heights: 3.2–4.5 cm., average ca. 4 cm.

CIL 1².623 (cf. fasc. 4), 11.1339, Diehl 345, Warm. 130 f., Degr. 325, *Imag.* 144, Cal. Lim. 252 no. 52 (with photo).

Text: *M(arcus) Claudius M(arci) f(ilius) Marcelus / consol iterum.* Class. Latin forms: Marcellus, consul.

"Marcus Claudius Marcellus, son of Marcus, consul for the second time," 155 B.C.

In this year Marcellus celebrated a triumph over the [———] and the Apua-[nei], the Apuan Ligurians (cf. Broughton, 1.448, with ref. to Degrassi), and very probably the column with the plinth (and a statue above) was set up to Marcellus at Luna (Henzen in *CIL* 1², Banti loc. cit.,

Degrassi *ILLRP ad loc.*). So, being on an honorary monument, this is judged to be an honorary inscription, though the use of the nominative case might seem simply to identify the man presumably sculptured above rather than to honor him by the use of the dative (or, under Greek influence, the accusative). Cf. Cal. Lim. 249–254, where this example and the quite different Duillius inscr. (**48**) are in the nomin. case, as against the dative of the column of Trajan, **57**; cf. p. 239 for another example involving the same Marcellus (cos. III, 152 B.C.), his own statue (and those of his father and grandfather), and the nomin. case.

Because of the iteration of the consulship here, of which there is no further example "noted in Roman inscrs. (official or unofficial) until well into the first century," E. Badian (*JRS* 58 [1968] 244 f.) thought it was perhaps a case "of a later (re-)engraving." But Banti had considered this not "probable, because its molding is not that of the other Luna bases of Imperial date, but has a character clearly archaic and . . . recalls many Etruscan monuments . . ." (*St. Etr.* 5 [1931] 488), and Lucy T. Shoe, *Etruscan and Republican Roman Mouldings* (*MAAR* 28 [1965] 14, 97, 107 no. XXVII, 8), obviously accepts the 155 B.C. date.

11. Dedication to Hercules by L. Mummius, Rome.

Probably 144 B.C. A travertine tablet originally, no doubt, attached to a shrine of Hercules Victor in Rome, though neither of his two shrines in Rome mentioned by Macrobius, *Sat.* 3.6.10, was on the Celian Hill, where this inscription was found and where there is other evidence for a cult of Hercules (A. M. Colini, *MemPontAcc* 3: 7 [1944] 41; cf. P/A 256 f., s.v. Herc. Vict.; Lugli, *Roma ant.* 588 f., 609).

Found in 1786, not *in situ*; now in the Vatican, attached to the wall of the Sala (or Gabinetto) dell'Apoxyomenos (inv. no. 1158). Ca. 56 × 60 cm.; it protrudes 4–4.5 cm. from the wall. According to information received from G. De Angelis d'Ossat, the material is travertine, not (as some report) peperino (*lapis Albanus*). Letter heights: from 5.0–8.5 cm. (line 1) down to 4–5 cm. (lines 2–7).

CIL 1².626 (cf. fasc. 4), 6.331, *ILS* 20, *CLE* 3, Diehl 91, Warm. 84 f., Ern. 129, Palm. no. 35, Degr. 122 (add. pp. 319 f.), *Imag.* 61, Cal. Lim. 271 f., E. Meinhardt in H/S 1.257 (with German transl.), De Ros. 36. Cf. Develin, loc. cit. (above, on **7**).

Probably 144 B.C., or as soon after late 145 (the apparent date of M.'s "triumph" for his victories in Greece: Broughton 1.470) as the *aedes* could be built and the *signum* made that are mentioned in the inscription. If the date were 142, while M. was censor (with Scipio Africanus Aemilianus), as some scholars maintain, surely the word "censor" would appear here. Plutarch, *Praec. rei p. ger.* 20 (816 C), is not pertinent; he calls M. a fellow-consul (συνάρχοντα), not a fellow-censor, of Scipio (cos. 147, the year before M.), and though he mentions the dedication of "the temple of Hercules" (in a year not specified), there were a fair number of Hercules temples or shrines in Rome besides the Ara Maxima (see P/A 251–258).

The argument that this is a later, poorer copy of the original inscription initiated by Buecheler on *CLE* 3 and accepted, or considered possible, by some later editors (notably Diehl, Warm., Ern., and Meinhardt), seems to fail on epigraphical, palaeographical, and other grounds.

Text: *L(ucius) Mummi(us) L(uci) f(ilius) co(n)s(ul). Duct(u), / auspicio imperioque / eius Achaia capt(a est). Corint⟨h⟩o / deleto Romam redieit /⁵ triumphans. Ob hasce / res bene gestas, quod / in bello voverat, / hanc aedem et signu⟨m⟩ / Herculis Victoris / imperator dedicat.*

"Lucius Mummius, son of Lucius, consul. Under his leadership, auspices, and *imperium*, Achaia (was) seized. Corinth destroyed [146 B.C.], he returned to Rome in triumph. For these successful exploits, as he had vowed in the course of the war,

this temple and statue of Hercules Victor he dedicates as *Imperator.*"

The general meaning is clear enough, but the syntax not fully so, the crucial word being *eius*. If *ductu . . . imperioque* belong together, *eius* must go with it; *Mummi* therefore is an abbreviated nominative, but out of syntax, absolute. If so, *Achaia capt.* also is nomin., *est* understood (no room for it in the verse?). Is *quod* a relative, used proleptically with ref. to *hanc aed. ded.*? or a causal conjunction? *Cos.* is perhaps the earliest extant example of this sort of monogrammatic style of writing (*Contrib.* 156 f.). *Corinto*: generally feminine in Latin as in Greek. From *ductu* on, most scholars have followed Marini (1795) in seeing saturnians here, but disagree on the division of the verses.

12. Milestone with Acephalous Elogium, Polla. 143 (?) B.C. A slab of local limestone (Vittorio Bracco of Polla, by letter of Mar. 7, 1956) now immured in a monument standing on state highway no. 19, in front of the former Osteria del Passo, just beyond the turn into Polla, in Lucania (probably near anc. Forum Popillii), as one comes from Salerno or Eboli; reported in this vicinity from the 15th cent. on. 71 × 74.6 × 10 (original?) cm., max. Letter heights: 3.0–3.5 cm.

CIL 1².638 (cf. pp. 725, 833, fasc. 4), 10.6950, *ILS* 23, Cagnat pl. II, 2, S/C 132, Diehl 430, Warm. 150 f., Ern. 131, L/R 1.246 (transl.), Palm. no. 49, Degr. 454 (add. pp. 330–332), *Imag.* 192 a-b, Cal. Lim. 288–290 no. 80, De Ros. 38 (Ital. transl.); V. Bracco, *Inscr. Ital.* 3: 1 (1974) 153–157 no. 272; cf. G. P. Verbrugghe, *CP* 68 (1973) 25–35, whose interpretation is favored here and by H. Krummrey, *CIL* 1²: 2: 4, in his additions to Degrassi. On the run-over of XXI from the end of line 8 to the end of line 9, cf. Suet. *Aug.* 87, 3: (Augustus) in his writing does not "carry superfluous [i.e., run-over, *abundantis*] letters from the end of one line to the beginning of the next, but writes them just below the rest of the word and draws a loop around them" (Rolfe's Loeb transl.), as here. See also **2**, *-que*, **66** line 7, **78** line 2.

A unique sort of inscription, combining a kind of milestone with an elogium type of self-glorification of the road-maker. Ironically, his name and probably his title *cos.* are missing, having presumably been cut on a separate stone, now lost, which rested on top of this slab and on which, in turn, rested perhaps a statue of him, like the one mentioned in the inscr. as being "at the Strait" (of Messina). (Though not properly a milestone, it will appear in the corpus of Roman milestones being edited by G. Walser for *CIL* vol. 17.)

Text: [(?) *Ap(pius) Claudius Pulcher, G(ai) f(ilius), co(n)s(ul).(?)*] (no doubt on a separate stone, now lost) / *Viam fecei ab Regio ad Capuam et* / *in ea via ponteis omneis, miliarios* / *tabelariosque poseivei. Hince sunt* / *Nouceriam meilia LI, Capuam XXCIIII,* /⁵ *Muranum LXXIIII, Cosentiam CXXIII,* / *Valentiam CLXXX, ad fretum ad* / *Statuam CCXXXI, Regium CCXXXVII:* / *suma af Capua Regium meilia CCCXXI.* / *Et eidem praetor in* /¹⁰ *Sicilia fugiteivos Italicorum* / *conquaeisivei redideique,* / *homines DCCCCXVII eidemque* / *primus fecei ut de agro poplico* / *aratoribus cederent paastores.* /¹⁵ *Forum aedisque poplicas heic fece[i].*

[" (?) Appius Claudius Pulcher, son of Gaius, consul (143 B.C.) (?)]

"I (have) built a road from Rhegium to Capua, and on this road I (have) placed the bridges—all (of them)—, the milestones, and the stade-markers [?]. From here (Forum Popillii) it is 51 miles [north] to Nuceria, 84 to Capua, 74 [south] to Muranum, 123 to Cosentia, 180 to Valentia, 231 to the Statue at the Strait, 237 to Rhegium: total, from Capua to Rhegium, 321 miles. And likewise, as praetor in Sicily [by 146 B.C.?], I rounded up the runaway slaves of the Italici and handed back (to their owners) 917 persons; and likewise I was the first one to make sheepherders withdraw from public land in favor of plowmen. A market and public buildings I (have) built here."

Note the arrangement, line 1 protruding, lines 8 and 15 indented. The ends of several lines are now slightly eroded, so that the last letter (or numeral) is lost or partly lost. In lines 6, 7, and 9 (run-over from 8, the cutter clearly wishing to begin a new line with *Et*) an unwanted numeral, I or perhaps II, has been erased in order to correct the three figures, the cumulative error having begun in line 6 in giving the distance "from here" (Forum Pop.) to Valentia. (Apparently the correct distance from Cosentia to Valentia was 57 miles.) The arithmetic is correct. (See a map showing the ancient names.) For the Class. Latin forms, see Appendix I. The position of *omneis* shows that it modifies only *pont.* For the meaning of *tabelarios*, see Degrassi, *ILLRP*, 1.454, note 3. *Miliarios* and *tabel.* must modify *lapides* understood. On the doubled A in *paastores*, line 13, see above, p. 14.

Who is the subject of the inscription and who are the *Italici*? Mommsen's identification of the subject as P. Popil(l)ius C.f. Laenas, cos. 132 B.C. (on *CIL* 1¹.551, repeated in *CIL* 1²), has been followed by all the editors cited above (for Degrassi, add his three articles in *Scritti vari*, 2.1027–1040, 3.206 f.), also by Broughton, 1.489, 490 n. 3, and Volkmann, *RE* 22: 1 (1953) 63 *s.v.* Popillius 28, but not by E. T. Salmon, *Samnium and the Samnites* (Cambridge, Eng., 1967) 323 n. 3, or G. P. Verbrugghe, op. cit., who is followed by H. Krummrey and favored here. For the date of the praetorship, see Broughton, 1.466.

It is uncertain whether the Italici are Sicilian landowners or south-Italians. Mommsen, loc. cit. (quoted in *CIL* 1²: 2, p. 510, col. 1), favored the former, so also Warm. and apparently L/R; but H. Last, *CAH* 9.14, n. 3, the latter. V. Ilari has a long note on *Italicus* and its lack of "a constant meaning in our sources" in his *Gli*

Italici nelle strutture militari romane (Milan 1974 *Pubbl. dell'Ist. di Diritto Romano,* Univ. di Roma, 49) 3 f., n. 9. Our Italici resemble the Ἰταλικοί landowners of Diodorus 34.2, 27, 32, 34 (cf. T. Frank, *Econ. Survey,* 1.279) rather than the businessmen of the inscrs. (cf. *CIL* 1²: 2, pp. 811, 851, under Nomina Geogr., and Degr. 2, p. 470, *s.v.* Italicei).

It is generally thought that the action of lines 13 f. was a result of the Lex Sempronia Agraria, of 133, of Tiberius Gracchus (cf. Last, op. cit. 3 f., 36), but Degrassi, *Scritti vari,* 2.1028 n. 4, 1038, agreed with P. Fraccaro and G. Tibiletti that it refers only to the small distribution of lands to the peasants living along the new road. The *forum* of line 15 must be the "foro popili" of the *Tabula Peutingeriana* (see the table, *CIL* 1²: 2 p. 510, or E. Weber's new ed. [Graz, Austria 1976] Segments V, 5 /VI, 1).

13. Bilingual Dedication to Hercules, Delos. 113 B.C. Found there *in situ,* on its base, in 1907 and still there (inv. no. 1753 [?], formerly 477). Description (from the first editors): a block of white marble, 0.59 × 1.16 × 1.01 m.; letter heights, Latin, 2.2 cm., lines 13–16 1.8–2.0 cm. The Greek letters are smaller. Varied and interesting interpuncts in the Latin; as usual, the Greek has none. Serifs (fully developed finishing strokes: *Contrib.* 128) in both the Latin and the Greek letters (called in French "apices," in Italian "apici": Guarducci, 1.372–377). (This has nothing to do with apices in Latin inscrs., for which see the Index below, *s.v.* apices.)

First publ. by P. Roussel and J. Hatzfeld, *BCH* 33 (1909) 493–496 no. 15; then by F. Durrbach, *Choix d'inscriptions de Délos* . . . , 1: 1 (Paris 1921) 192 f., no. 116, *CIL* 1².2504 (cf. fasc. 4), *ILS* 9417, Diehl 101 and *IL* tab. 7, b, Warm. 118 f., no. 141 (no Greek nor all the Latin names), Degr. 2.759.

A Latin/Greek dedication to Her-cules/Herakles on the part of a *collegium* (private club or association: cf. *OCD s.vv.* Clubs, Roman, and Collegium), whose twelve officers call themselves Masters of Mercury, Apollo, and Neptune (in Greek: Hermes, Apollo, and Poseidon). Dated by the names of the Roman consuls of 113.

Text of the Latin: *P(ublius) Sexteilius L(uci) f(ilius) Pilo, / G(aius) Crassicius P. f., / M(arcus) Audius M. f., / M. Cottius N(umeri) f., /⁵ Gn(aeus) Tutorius Gn. f., / N. Stenius M. f., / P. Arellius Q(uinti) l(ibertus), / Ti(berius) Seius M. l., / N. Tutorius Gn. l., /¹⁰ Q. Nummius Q. l., / D(ecimus) Maicius L. l., / P. Castricius P. l., / magistreis Mirquri, Apollini (all sic), / Neptuni, Hercolei coeraverunt, /¹⁵ eisde (sic) dedicaverunt Gn(aeo) Papeirio, / G(aio) Caecilio co(n)s(ulibus).* (ILS is the first ed. to present the text correctly.)

Six freeborn men and six freedmen, "Masters (in the service) of Mercury, Apollo, (and) Neptune [in the Greek, called "the Hermaistai, Apolloniastai, and Poseidoniastai"], attended (to this offering) to Hercules/Herakles and likewise made the dedication, in the consulship of Gnaeus Papirius (Carbo) and Gaius Caecilius (Metellus Caprarius)."

Note in the Greek the lack of date, of all cognomina, and of the words for "son" and "freedman" with the genitive of the father's or the ex-owner's praenomen. *Mirq.* and *Apol.* seem to be mistakes on the part of the writer, or the cutter, whereas *Sextei-, Pilo, magistreis, Herc., eisde,* and *Pap.* are archaic forms. *Pilo* (for *Philo*) is one of many words taken from Greek that show that the sound of Φ was not yet F (Pfister 29 Anm. 3); *eisde,* nom. plu., is doubly archaic (Sommer 301, 346 *fin.*). Between lines 12 and 13 the name ΑΧΙΛΛΙΩΝ is roughly cut in a quite different, no doubt later, hand, perhaps by some passerby, as though to say, "Achillion has been here." In line 13, for the hook-shaped rough breathing apparent over οι, apparently not previously noted, see A. Wilhelm, *Beiträge zur griech.*

Inschriftenkunde . . . (Vienna 1909 *Son-derschr. des österr. arch. Inst. in Wien, 7*) 160–162, 312 no. 139; Larfeld, 301, "Lese-zeichen." Specially interesting are the Greek renderings of the Latin names; cf. Pape/Benseler *s.vv.*

14. Elegiac Epigram, Corinth. Ca. 101 B.C. A block of marble found at Corinth in seven pieces in 1925; now in the museum there. 0.786 × 1.175–1.20 × 0.22 m. Let-ters mostly ca. 3.2 cm. tall, some a little taller. "The earliest and on the whole the most important published Latin inscr. of Corinth," Dow. It apparently contained no more than the present 10 lines; most of it is on one piece. The block had been pre-viously used for an inscr. in Greek.

CIL 1².2662 (cf. pp. 739 f., fasc. 4), Diehl 306, Warm. 132–135, Degr. 342 (add. p. 327), *Imag.* 151 a-b (cf. E. Badian, *JRS* 58 [1968] 242). Add L. R. Taylor and A. B. West, *AJA* ser. 2, 32 (1928) 9–22 (first publ., with photos and transl.); West alone, *Corinth, Results of Excavations* 8: 2 *Latin Inscrs. 1896–1926* (Cambridge, Mass., 1931) 1–4 (photo and drawing);

S. Dow, *HSCP* 60 (1951) 81–96, 97–100 (with photos of squeezes); A. Ernout, *Studii Clasice,* 2 (1960) 73–76 (text, app. crit., notes, French transl.). For the date, Broughton, *TAPA* 77 (1946) 35–40 and *MRR* 1.568.

An epigram in elegiac couplets cele-brating the feat of hauling a Roman fleet across the Isthmus of Corinth in 102 (De-grassi) or 101 or (less probably) 100 (Broughton) B.C., under the auspices of a proconsul, who must be Mark Antony's grandfather, M. Antonius (cos. 99), and with the aid of a propraetor named Hir-rus. The former's name has been erased, either because of mistaken identity or as part of the *damnatio memoriae* suffered by his grandson after the fall of Alexandria in 30 B.C. (W. W. Tarn, *CAH* 10.108, 112), but enough remains to make the name cer-tain. The unknown poet probably served in the Roman fleet, and his verses are "perhaps the first record found for the ac-tivity of such a poet on the scene of ac-tion," Taylor/West, 22.

Text of lines 1–8 (based on Dow's text):

Quod neque conatus quisquanst neque [– – – – – – –¹⁹ ᶜᵐ·]av[it (?)]
    noscite rem, ut famaa facta feramus virei.
Auspicio [Ant]oni [M]arci pro consule classis
    Isthmum traductast missaque per pelagus.
Ipse iter eire profectus (est) Sidam; classem Hirrus Atheneis
    pro praetore anni e tempore constituit.
Lucibus haec pauc[ei]s parvo perfecta (sunt) tumultu
    magna[a quo]om ratione atque salut[e– – – – –¹¹·⁸(?) ᶜᵐ·]

(plus remains of 2 more lines, for which several conjectural restorations have been suggested).

"What no one has (ever before) at-tempted or carried out [? reading Ernout's spondaic ending *consummavit*] learn, so that we may celebrate a man's deeds. Un-der the auspices of Marcus Antonius, pro-consul [101–100 B.C.], a fleet was taken across the Isthmus (of Corinth) and sent over the sea. He himself (the proconsul) set out for Side [a coastal city in Pam-phylia]; Hirrus, propraetor, because of the

season of the year, stationed the fleet at Athens. Within a few days this was ac-complished, with little confusion (and) with great skill and good [? or "simul-taneous," reading *bona* or *simul*? at the end of line 8] success. . . ."

Quisquanst is doubly unusual: the N for M and (as also in *traductast*) the elision of the E of *est* indicated in writing—to save space? The use of an *(id) quod* clause picked up by *rem* enables the poet to fill the line and avoid the succession *noscite ut,* impossible without hiatus. The *-aa's* are for long A (but only twice). Line 3: the order nomen, praenomen, is obviously *metri causa*; also *metri causa*, to make a dactyl, the S of *profectus* must be omitted, as in Catullus 116, 8. Line 7, for *lucibus,* "days," cf. *OLD* 1054 *s.v.* lux, 5. Hirrus, *(legatus) pro praetore*, is thought to be a G. Lucilius Hirrus, otherwise unknown but probably a relative of both the satirist and the *trib. pleb.* of 53 B.C. (West 4, Broughton 1.569, 570 n. 7, *Suppl.* 37). Lommatzsch in *CIL* makes Hirrus the boastful hero of this epigram, but this seems wrong: the poet celebrates them both, but first Antonius, superior in command, then the lower-ranking Hirrus. For a more detailed treatment, see Gordon in *Corinthiaca. Studies in Honor of D. A. Amyx* (forthcoming?).

15. Two Decrees of Gn. Pompeius (Strabo), Rome. Probably 90 or 89 B.C. (or a Vespasianic copy?). A bronze tablet (29 × 51–52 cm.—G. Gatti, 1908) originally attached to something by nails (3 holes still appear); in two pieces, found by 1910, in Rome, in private hands, by G. Gatti, who first published them (reff. in *CIL*); somewhat damaged, with one gap, but apparently complete all around. Now in a glass-covered case in the Capitoline Mus., Rome, in the Sala delle Colombe (Apr. 1973); inv. no. 7337. The bronze seems to be cast, but this is quite uncertain (see above, Intro., n. 10). Letter heights: 0.5– 2.0 cm., as estimated through the glass.

CIL 1².709 (cf. pp. 714, 726, fasc. 4), 6.37045, *ILS* 8888, Diehl 267, Warm. 272–275, L/R 1.266 (transl.), Degr. 2.515, *Imag.* 397, *ARS* 60 (transl.), Cal. Lim. 356–360, E. Meinhardt in H/S 2.1275 (all with bibl., but in several not all the names in the inscr. appear). The chief publ. is by N. Criniti, *L'epigrafe di Asculum di Gn. Pompeo Strabone* (Milan 1970) 266 pp., with enlarged photo); since then, H. B. Mattingly, *Athenaeum* 53 (1975) 262–266.

Copy of two decrees issued by Pompey's father (while either *legatus* of a con-

sul, 90, or consul himself, 89 B.C.), by which he presented Roman citizenship, while encamped at Asculum (in Picenum), to a troop of thirty Spanish cavalry, "for valor." The date is Nov. 17 of a year much disputed and uncertain: 90 or 89 B.C. (if a contemporary copy, as seems probable, with Criniti, 12–14) or Vespasianic (if it is one of the "3,000 bronze tablets" restored by Vespasian after the burning of the Capitoline Temple in Rome, A.D. 69 [Suet. *Vesp.* 8.5]); for the choice 90 or 89 B.C., see Criniti 47–61; in support of the 90/89 date are the uncorrected errors in writing, including the wrong case in the last phrase, and the fact that the lettering definitely fits the earlier date better than the later (Criniti 13, n. 11, misunderstands L. R. Taylor, *VDRR* 20, in believing her to favor the later date; cf. Taylor 177).

A document of the "Social" War, important in several respects; e.g., the enfranchisement, in the field, of thirty Spaniards (with interesting Iberian names) and the naming of all fifty-nine members of the general's *Consilium,* among them some young men later to become famous (or infamous), including his seventeen-year-old son Pompey (*Gn. Pompei(us) Gn. f. Clu(stumina tribu)*, line 8) and Catiline (*L. Sergi. L. f. Tro(mentina tribu)*, line 11). (To save space, all but the first seven of these nomina are abbreviated in the inscr., and all lack cognomina; a few also are lost or damaged; hence some uncertainties in identification.) Cicero was also a *tiro* in this army at about this time (*Phil.* 12.11.27) but is not listed here, perhaps because he had left Asculum to join Sulla in Campania.

Text of lines 1–3: *[G]n(aeus) Pompeius, Se[x(ti) f(ilius), Imperator,] virtutis caussa, / equites Hispanos ceives [Romanos fecit in cas- tr]eis apud Asculum a(nte) d(iem) XIV K(alendas) Dec(embres) / ex lege Iulia. In consili[o fuerunt] / . . . (59 Roman and 30 Iberian names, these in 3 cols. headed by Turma Salluitana).* Col. 4: *Gn. Pompeius, Sex. f., Imperator, / virtutis caussa Turmam / Sal-*

luitanam donavit in / castreis apud Asculum /[5]
cornuculo et patella, torque, / armilla, palereis
et frumentum / duplex.

"Gn. Pompeius Strabo, son of Sextus, *Imperator*, in reward for valor, made the Spanish cavalrymen Roman citizens in camp at Asculum on Nov. 17, in accord with the Julian Law [of 90 B.C.]. In the (general's) council were . . ." Col. 4: ". . . presented the Salluitan Troop . . . with a helmet-horn [an ornament] and a plate, a necklace, a bracelet, breast-pieces, and a double ration of grain."

The last phrase—*et frum. dupl.*—because of its change of syntax, from abl. to acc. (as though *donavit* were *dedit*), seems a later addition, but by the same hand; *frum.* is written *fau—ium.* Note again, as in nos. **7** and **9**, the omission of the cognomen before *Imperator.* On the *Lex Julia de civitate Latinis et sociis danda*, see G. Tibiletti in De Rugg. 4.23 (1956) 719 *s.v.*

16. A Slab from a Statue Base of Sulla, Naples, from Rome. 82/78 B.C. All that remains of a travertine statue-base found on the Quirinal, in Rome, in the 16th cent.; now in the Mus. Nazionale, Naples (no. 2640). 40.7–8 × 60–60.8 × 7 cm. Datable in Sulla's dictatorship (late 82 or early 81/79), or perhaps between then and his death in 78 (hardly after).

CIL 1².721 (cf. fasc. 4), 6.1297, *ILS* 872, Diehl 301, Warm. 136 f., no. 13, Degr. 352, *Imag.* 154, Cal. Lim. 243 no. 45 (who notes, above, "the passion for statues" that "was one of the most typical manifestations of the importance given to social rank").

Dedication to Sulla of what, no doubt, was a statue of him (perhaps equestrian and gilded, like the one mentioned by Cic. *Phil.* 9.6.13 and others) set up in his honor by a *vicus* of Rome.

Text: *L(ucio) Cornelio, L(uci) f(ilio), / Sullae Felici, / dictatori, / Vicus Laci Fund(ani).*

"To L. Cornelius Sulla Felix, son of Lucius, Dictator: the Vicus Laci Fundani."

This *Vicus* was "a street that probably corresponded in general with the Via del Quirinale from the Piazza del Qu. southwards" and that took its name from "a spring [better "tank," "cistern," or "reservoir"?] on the western slope of the Quirinal" (where the base was found), P/A 311 *s.v.* Lacus Fundani. (Warm. translates, "the quarter of the Reservoir of Fundanius," *Fundani* being probably the gen. of *Fundanius*: Mommsen, *CIL* 1¹, p. 168, on this inscr., 584 [ed. 2, p. 531, no. 721]; *CIL* 6: 7: 2 lists about 34 examples of *Fundanius*, only 8 of the cognomen *Fundanus*). Tacitus has the *Lacus Fundani*, in Rome (*Hist.* 3.69), *CIL* 6.9854 a *redemptor* ("contractor") *a Laco* [sic] *Fundani*, and in no. 311 a *Hercules Fundanius* (where *F.* is clearly adjectival). *Laci*, genitive, is one of the 2nd-decl. forms occasionally found in 4th-decl. nouns, no doubt as a result of confusion (Sommer 403–405). Note the ligature of ND in line 4, typically at a line end, where the cutter has failed to allow enough space.

Sulla's second cognomen, or agnomen, *Felix*, Livy says (30.45.6), "began with the flattery of his friends" (*ab adsentatione familiari*), as later (he says) did Pompey's *Magnus*; Velleius (2.27.5) has him take the name after the slaying of Marius's son (in 82); Pliny the Elder (*N.H.* 7.43.137) calls Sulla "the only person to date (*ad hoc aevi*)" who "has assumed the cognomen 'Felix'" (*superbum cognomen*, 22.5.12), *civili nempe sanguine ac patriae oppugnatione adoptatus* (*-tum*, Hardouin). Cf. Plutarch, *Sulla*, 34.3, Appian, *BC* 1.97, and Frölich, *RE* 4 (1901) 1558, 2–30, *s.v.* Cornelius 392; J. P. V. D. Balsdon, "Sulla Felix," *JRS* 41 (1951) 1–10, H. Erkell, *Augustus, Felicitas, Fortuna, Lateinische Wortstudien* (Diss. Göteborg 1952) 71–107, and B. Wosnik, *Untersuchungen zur Gesch. Sullas* (Diss. Würzburg 1963) 25–31.

17. Record of Theater Building, Pompeii. Probably ca. 75 B.C. One of two identically worded inscriptions found, resp., in 1769 and 1794, attached to the entrances of the so-called Little Theater (Odeum), the building of which, and its approval, they document; still *in situ*. *CIL* 1² calls the material travertine, Degrassi *Imag.* limestone; the latter is confirmed by the director of the Pompeii excavations, by letter of May, 1975.

CIL 1².1633 (add. fasc. 4), 10.844, *ILS* 5636, Diehl 390, Warm. 188 f., no. 56, Degr. 2.646, *Imag.* 252. The duplicate stone has no vertical hole cut at the lower left, which must be modern. (On the date, see below.)

Text: *G(aius) Quinctius G(ai) f(ilius) Valg(us), / M(arcus) Porcius M(arci) f(ilius), / duovir(i), dec(urionum) decr(eto) / theatrum tectum /⁵ fac(iendum* or *-iundum) locar(unt) eidemq(ue) prob(arunt).*

"G. Quinctius Valgus, son of Gaius, (and) M. Porcius, son of Marcus, Board of Two, by decree of the decurions [local town-councillors] contracted for the building of a roofed theater and likewise approved (it)."

The LG in somewhat monogrammatic style (line 1) and the smaller writing of the last word indicate imperfect planning. *Valgus*, of apparently the same man, is written in full in *CIL* 1².1547, 1632 (= Degr. 2.565, 645). Note the interpunctuation of the composite *duo·vir(i)* (cf. *Contrib.* 184: "some tendency to add an interpunct after a numerical prefix of a noun, and—more frequently—after the prepositional prefixes of nouns and verbs"). For the possible gerundive ending *-undum*, see **18**, and Sommer 616–618; for *eidem*, cf. Pfister 65 (*ei = ī*).

The latest study of Pompeian government and society is that of Paavo Castrén, *Ordo Populusque Pompeianus, Polity and Society in Roman Pompeii* (Rome 1975 *Acta Inst. Romani Finlandiae*, 8), in which (p. 90, *init.*) he dates the duovirate of Quinctius and Porcius as "probably in the mid-seventies." (For reviews, cf. R. P. Duncan-Jones, *JRS* 67 [1977] 195–198, and T. P. Wiseman, *CR* n.s. 27 [1977] 230 f.) Earlier scholars—A. Maiuri, Degrassi, H. Gun-

del—had dated it soon after 80, or in 80/75. Palaeographically, a later date within this period would seem preferable to an earlier one. Castrén notes that "this was Pompeii's second stone theatre, whereas Rome had not yet acquired its first" (which was to be Pompey's theater of 55 B.C.).

18. Main Inscription on the Fabricius Bridge, Rome. Of travertine and—the intrados (interior curve)—peperino (*Rome e dintorni* 436). East side of the arch adjoining the left bank of the Tiber (our view looks upstream), with inscrs. of L. Fabricius, *curator viarum* (perhaps while also *tribunus plebis*: Broughton, 2.174), who had the bridge built in 62 B.C. (Dio 37.45.3), and of the consuls of 21 B.C., who approved something unspecified, very possibly repairs or restoration after damage done by the inundation of the Tiber in 23 (Dio 53.33.5). The three inscrs., one over each of three arches, are repeated on the other side of the bridge, the main inscr.—of Fabricius—appearing four times, on both sides of the two larger arches, the smaller, central arch carrying the inscriptions *idemque probavit* (north side) and *eidemque probaveit* (south).

CIL 1².751 (cf. fasc. 4), 6.1305 (cf. 31594 and p. 3799), *ILS* 5892, S/C 119 f., Diehl 411, Degr. 379, *Imag.* 167. Add Nash 2.189 f., *s.v.* Pons Fabricius (3 photos). Sandys/Campbell note that the smaller, central arch is at a higher level than the two larger arches, in order to carry "off the water when the river was in full flood." Platner/Ashby 400 *s.v.* Pons Fabricius call it "the best preserved bridge in Rome, being practically the original structure."

Text of the main inscr. of 62 B.C., cut on the east side of the arch adjoining the left bank of the river: *L(ucius) Fabricius G(ai) f(ilius), cur(ator) viar(um), / faciundum coeravit.*

"L. Fabricius, son of Gaius, Superintendent of Roads, had (the bridge) made."

The variance in spelling the two words of the central inscription is perhaps best explained by the theory of two cutters at work, one old-fashioned, using forms with *ei*, the other using the later forms; the results are different forms cut presumably at about the same time, whence it follows that one must be careful not to dogmatize from mere spelling: it is evidence, but not proof.

19. Temple Regulations, L'Aquila, from Furfo. 58 B.C. A large limestone slab (1.02–1.03 × 1.91–1.915 × 0.09–0.21 m.), found in the 16th cent. near the anc. Vestinian *vicus* of Furfo; now in two pieces joined together, attached to the wall of Sala III of the Mus. Naz. at L'Aquila (1956). The Temple Regulations of Jupiter Liber at Furfo. Letter heights (from a squeeze): from 1.5–1.8 (2 small O's) to ca. 5.7–6.5 (line 1), mostly ca. 3.2–3.3 cm. Consular date.

CIL 1².756 (cf. pp. 727, 839, fasc. 4), 9.3513, ILS 4906, H. Jordan, *Kritische Beiträge zur Gesch. der latein. Sprache* (Berlin 1879) 250–263, Bruns 283 f., no. 105, Diehl 260, Degr. 2.508, *Imag.* 382 (photo of a plaster cast, whose letters look painted). Add Fr. Richter (ed.), *Latein. Sacralinschriften* (Bonn 1911) 3 f., no. 3; *FIRA* 3.225–227 no. 72; Norden 44 n. 1, 54 f., 55 n. 3; P. Grimal, *REL* 20 (1942), 10 f.; U. Laffi, in *La cultura italica. Atti del Convegno della Soc. Ital. di Glottologia, Pisa 19 e 20 dic. 1977* (Pisa 1978) 121–144 (text and notes).

Text: *L(ucius) Aienus L(uci) f(ilius), Q(uintus) Baebatius Ṣẹx(ti) f. aedem dedicaruṇṭ / Iovis Liberi Furfone a(nte) d(iem) III Idus Quinctileis L(ucio) (Calpurnio) Pisone (Caesonino), A(ulo) Gabinio co(n)s(ulibus), mense flusare, /* COMVLA·TEIS *olleis legibus illeis regionibus, utei* EXTREMAE VNDAE OVAE *lapide / facta hoiusque aedis ergo uteique ad eam aede(m) scalasque lapide* STRVCTVENDO /⁵ *columnae stant citra scalas ad aedem versus stipitesque aedis* HVMVS *tabula/mentaque: utei tangere sarcire tegere devehere defigere* MANDARE *ferro oeti / promovere referre ⟨liceat⟩ fasque esto. Sei quod ad eam aedem donum datum donatum dedicatum/que erit, utei liceat oeti venum dare; ubei venum datum erit, id profanum esto. Venditio / locatio aedilis esto, quemquomque Veicus Furfens(is) fecerit, quod se sentiunt eam rem /¹⁰ sine scelere sine piaculo ⟨vendere locare⟩; alis ne potesto. Quae pequnia recepta erit, es pequnia emere / conducere locare dare, quo id templum melius honestius seit, liceto. Quae pequnia ad eas / res data erit, profana esto, quod d(olo) m(alo) non erit factum. Quod emptum erit aere aut argento / ea pequnia quae pequnia ad id* TEMPLVM *(for emendum?) data erit quod emptum erit, eis rebus eadem / lex esto quasei sei dedicatum sit. Sei qui heic sacrum surupuerit, aedilis multatio esto /¹⁵ quanti volet idque Veicus Furf(ensis)* MAI(or) *(?) pars* FIFELTARES, *sei apsolvere volent sive condemnare, / liceto. Sei quei ad huc templum rem deivinam fecerit Iovi Libero aut Iovis Genio, pelleis / coria fanei sunto.*

(For words in capital letters, see the annotation below.)

Translation of lines 1–2, 6 (*utei*)–11 (*liceto*), 16 (*sei*)–end: "Lucius Aienus, son of Lucius, (and) Quintus Baebatius, son of Sextus, dedicated the Temple of Jupiter Liber at Furfo, on July 13, in the consulship of Lucius Piso (and) Aulus Gabinius, in the month of flowers . . . (6) . . . (with these regulations, *olleis legibus*, line 3), that it shall be permitted to touch, repair, cover, carry away, affix, MANDARE, use iron (tools), move forward, (and) take away, and it shall be proper; if any gift for this temple is given, donated, and dedicated, that it shall be permitted to use (or) sell (it); when it has been sold, it shall be profane. The sale or leasing (of any gift?) shall be up to whatever aedile the village of Furfo has chosen, so far as they feel (?) that they are selling (or) leasing this without impiety (and) without guilt; no one else shall be able to. With what money is received it shall be allowed to buy, hire, lease, (or) make a gift in order that this temple-precinct may be better (and) more beautiful. . . . (16) If anyone performs sacrifice at this temple to Jupiter Liber or to Jupiter's Genius, the skins (and) the hides shall belong to the holy property."

Note the ten ligatures (line 1 RV, NT, 9 NT [2], 12 VT, 15 NT [2] and MA, 16 AM, 17 NT—some occur where there is plenty of space), and the inconsistency in punctuating between *ad* and its object (3 times with, 3 times without); the corruption of text in lines 3, *init.* and *fin.*, 4 *fin.*, *humus* presumably for *huius* in 5, *mandare* for what? in 6, the apparent omission of *liceat* in 7 and of *vendere* and *locare* in 10, *templum* undoubtedly for *emendum* in 13, the strange MAI(?) in 15.

Line 1, *Aienus* a non-Latin name, probably Umbrian in origin (Cagnat 51). Cf. the nomen of Q. Salvidienus Rufus, an associate of Octavian's in 44, later one of his chief generals, who perhaps came from this Vestinian country (*OCD* 948 *s.v.*). Line 2. G. Radke, *Rhein. Mus.* N.F. 106 (1963) 313–315, shows that July 13, of the pre-Julian calendar, by corrected dating would be 89 days earlier, i.e., April 13 (a better month for "flowers" than hot July); *flusare* is dialectical ("Sabine or Vestinian") for *florali* (Vetter 160 on no. 227, 404 *s.v.* *flusare*). Line 3. Grimal (op. cit. 10) interpreted *comulateis* as one word equivalent to *collatis* ("having been proposed"?) and compared Livy 4.4.9 (unemended), *confertis* (sc. *legem*), but by letter of Oct. 27, 1976, he wrote that he had long been less certain of understanding this passage than formerly, so had never published his 1942 communication to the Société des Études Latines. From *extremae* through line 5, *humus*, the text is corrupt in several places, the meaning uncertain; but it is clear that the *utei* . . . *tabula/mentaque* clause (lines 3–6) defines the limits of the dedication, as in *CIL* 3.1933 (= *ILS* 4907), *ollis legib. ollisque regionibus dabo dedica-*

boque quas hic hodie palam dixero, similarly *CIL* 12.4333 (= *ILS* 112 add.); cf. Jordan, op. cit.

Line 9. In *sentiunt* the I is short in height, confined by the crossbar of T in the ligature NT. *CIL* emends it to *sentiat*, subjunctive because the "rule" seems to require it (cf. *quod sciam*), singular to suit *aedilis.* Norden, 55 with n. 1, accepts the subj., but defends the plural as also in **8**, *iousisent*, lines 9, 18, following the subject *is. Quod sciam* but *quantum scio*, according to the rule; but Quintilian, 3.1.19, has *quantum ego quidem sciam*; confusion seems inevitable; cf. K/S 2.307, 9 and 308 2nd par. Line 15. MAI(*or*)(?) *pars Fifeltares* seems to add a restriction to *Veicus Furf.*, not the whole *veicus* but only the more important part, called *Fifeltares*, on whom see Mommsen in *CIL* 9 or as quoted in *CIL* 1²: 2. Line 16. For Jupiter's Genius see Wissowa, 180. 16 f. For *pelleis* (nom., Class. Lat. *pelles*) and *coria*, see De Rugg. 2: 2 (1910) 1211 *s.v. corium*. Note *aedes*, *templum, fanum*, not synonymous but apparently referring to different aspects of the same concept: *aedes* the most restrictive, meaning only the temple itself as the god's dwelling; *templum* next larger, meaning the sacred precinct (with or without an *aedes*); *fanum* perhaps the whole (including the personnel of the *templum* with the *aedes*). Cf. Varro, *De L. L.* 7.9.10, 8.41.83, Livy 10.37.15, Gellius 14.7.7 (quoting another work of Varro's); Mommsen (ed.), *Res Gestae divi Aug.²* 78 f.; J. Marquardt, *Römische Staatsverwaltung* 3, ed. 2 by G. Wissowa (Leipzig 1885) 154–158; Wissowa *RKR²* 467 ff., 527 f.

20. Epitaph of a Grain Merchant, Rome. 52 B.C. A slab found in Rome in 1955; seen in 1973 in the rear basement of the Palazzo Senatorio (inv. no. 6763), which had been built in the 12th cent. over the Tabularium on the south-east slope of the Capitoline (*Roma e dintorni*, 116). Dimensions: 59.2

max. × 90 max. × 10.9–13 cm.; writing field: 43.1–.2 × 67.8–68.1 cm. Of Luna marble (Degrassi).

CIL 1²: 4.2965. Apparently first published by B. Andreae, *Arch. Anz.* 72 (1957) (Berlin 1958) 235, no. 19; then by A. Merlin, *AE* 1959, 146 (adding an interpunct after *Non.*, line 5); Degr. 2.786 a, *Imag.* 400; A. E. and J. S. Gordon, in *Calligraphy and Palaeography, Essays presented to Alfred Fairbank . . .* , ed. A. S. Osley (London 1965) 35–37, plate 7a.

Text: *Sex(tus) Aemilius, Sex(ti) l(ibertus), / Baro, / frumentar(ius), / in ignem inlatus est / prid(ie) Non(as) Quinct(iles), / Gn(aeo) Pompeio co(n)s(ule) tert(ium or -io).*

"Sextus Aemilius Baro, freedman of Sextus, a grain merchant, was cremated the day before the Nones of July, while Gnaeus Pompey was consul for the third time." (July 6, 52; this year Pompey was sole consul in Rome until August: Broughton 2.234.)

Note the omission of punctuation and space between *in* and its object (*Contrib.* 184), as well as after *Non.*, this a much less orthodox type (sheer carelessness?).

Baro is like *Brutus* in being a pejorative cognomen (Kajanto 264), but was originally a common noun ("blockhead, lout, simpleton") rather than adjectival, and is rarely found used, though several times in Cicero. *In ignem inferri* seems an uncommon, though picturesque, way of saying *(igni) cremari*. For *tertium* vs. *tertio*, etc., "for the third time," etc., see *Album*, 3.167, on no. 355, line 11, *quarto* (the *locus classicus* is Gellius, 10.1); all examples of such ordinal adverbs in Augustus's *Res Gestae* (**34**) end in *-um* (when not written as numerals), while all the Greek end in the corresponding *-ov*. (See above, p. 48.)

There may be a question of what case *tertio, quarto*, etc., are in when used adverbially to mean "for the nth time." It would seem logical for it to be an old accusative form, with *-m* omitted (as in the Scipionic *CIL* 1².9, where both *Luciom* and *optumo*

viro, acc., are found), though confirmation by philologists seems lacking and it is clear from Gellius 10.1 that neither he nor Varro nor Cicero understood the form in *-o*. Ovid, *Fasti* 2.665 *fin.*, proves nil, *quarto* being at the end of the line.

21. Statue (?) Base Dedicated to Julius Caesar, Rome, from Otricoli. Ca. 44 B.C. Found at Otricoli (Umbria) (ca. 69 km. from Rome, on the Via Flaminia) before 1781 (C. Pietrangeli, *Epigraphica* 3 [1941] 155); now in the Vestibolo Rotondo of the Vatican (E. Meinhardt in H/S 1.251 gives the dimensions as 49.5 × 60 × 44.5 cm.; inv. no. 1140). Presumably intended as a base to support a statue of Caesar. Just before or just after Caesar's death in 44. White marble. Letter heights: line 1, 3.75–5 cm., line 2, 3.25–3.5 cm., lines 3–4, ca. 3.5 cm.

CIL 1².797 (cf. fasc. 4), 6.872 (cf. 31188), *ILS* 73, Diehl 314, Degr. 409, *Imag.* 173 (photo of a plaster copy). Add L. R. Taylor, *The Divinity of the Roman Emperor* (Middletown, Conn., 1931 *Philol. Monogr.* publ. by the APA, 1) 268 f., cf. 69; *Album*, 1.17 no. 4, with ref. to Pietrangeli, loc. cit. and *RendPontAcc* 3:19 (1942–43) 79 no. 60, and Degrassi, *Doxa*, 2 (1949) 77; E. Meinhardt, loc. cit.

Mommsen, on *CIL* 1¹.626, followed by Henzen on *CIL* 6.872 (implicitly), Münzer *RE* 1A (1914) 1200 f., *s.v.* Rufrenus 1, Lommatzsch on *CIL* 1².797, Broughton 2.360, *init.*, with ref. to G. Niccolini, *I fasti dei tribuni della plebe* (Milan 1934) 444 ("probably 42 B.C."), Degrassi, and Meinhardt dated it after Caesar's death (Mommsen "u.c. 711 [= 43 B.C.]?," the others in 42), but Taylor, with ref. to Dessau, *Gesch. d. röm. Kaiserzeit*, 1 (Berlin 1924) 354, with n. 2, inclined to put it *before* his death; so also Elizabeth Rawson, *JRS* 65 (1975) 149, with n. 14 and ref. to Cic. *Phil.* 2.110, and J. A. North, same vol., 175, reviewing S. Weinstock's *Divus Julius* (Oxford 1971). A near mate of this inscr.,

CIL 1².798 (= 9.5136, *ILS* 73ᵃ), could be seen in May 1956 at Campovalano in the church of San Pietro, a short distance left of the highway from Ascoli Piceno to Teramo; it was being used, face-up, on the floor of the central altar, under a wooden platform that left visible only the left side of the inscr., which has only three lines, reads *deivo* and *p. R.* (abbreviated), and, according to Mommsen, is incomplete. For a third example, found by Degrassi at Minturno (anc. Minturnae) in 1965, also with *deivo*, no *statutum*, but with *e* before *lege*, see his "Epigraphica III," *Mem. Acc. Naz. Lincei*, Cl. di Sc. mor., stor. e fil., ser. 8, vol. 13 (1967) 12–15 (= *Scritti vari*, 3.102–106), with discussion of the date.

Text: *Divo Iulio iussu / populi Romani / statutum est lege / Rufrena.*

"To the deified [or, the divine?] Julius by order of the Roman people, (this monument) has been erected in accordance with the *Lex Rufrena*."

Note the typical inconsistency: one of three long I's tall, one of ten (or eleven) other long vowels marked by an apex, here hook-shaped—perhaps to emphasize the first two words. The translation of *divo* will depend on the date of the inscr.; if *divo* here is simply equivalent to *deo*, as Taylor is inclined to think, then "the divine" or "the god" seems best. For the *lex Rufrena* cf. G. Barbieri, in De Rugg. 4:23 (1956) 730 f., *s.v.* Lex, who dates it "712/42?"; for Rufrenus, "probably a Tribune of the Plebs," Broughton 2.354, 360.

22. Trilingual Dedication by Cornelius Gallus, Cairo, from Philae. Mid-April, 29 B.C. A stele of Aswan (anc. Syene) granite, found in 1896, already cut vertically into two pieces and damaged, in the ruins of the Temple of Augustus on the island of Philae, in the Nile; by 1903 in the Egyptian Museum, Cairo (inv. no. 9295), in April 1974 seen in room 34. An unsightly monument, pink and dark-gray or black in color, very hard to read because of its rough, worn, and, in places, patched surface; the photo is hardly worse to read than the original. Minium was apparent (in 1974) in the Egyptian and the Greek. Dimensions: left half, ca. 1.36 × 0.52 m., right half 1.54 × 0.56, the whole originally ca. 1.65 × 1.16 m. (est.); aver. thickness, ca. 35 cm.; the loss down the middle estimated in 1896 as ca. 8 cm., in 1974 as ca. 8.5–9.0 cm., with some extra loss elsewhere because of damage. (The loss down the middle is imperfectly suggested by the photo.) Height of the Latin, ca. 31.5–32 cm. Letters: line 1, first O, ca. 3.8 cm., at right end ca. 4 cm.; lines 2–8 ca. 2.5–3.0 (second O, line 6, ca. 2.3) cm., line 9, *patrieis*, ca. 1.5 cm. (the Greek is smaller). Line 1 apparently protruded slightly, while line 9 was perhaps intended to be centered (it is indented ca. 29 cm.).

A dedication to the *dei patriei* and the Nile on the part of G. Cornelius Gallus, Augustus's first prefect of Egypt, who boastfully describes the great achievements of his first eight months in office (Aug., 30–Apr., 29 B.C.). The ten lines of Egyptian-hieroglyphic text, which, without the two scenes depicted at the top, occupies as much space as the Latin and Greek combined, is of uncertain reference, but the opinion that it refers to Gallus rather than to Caesar (Augustus) seems preferable, though Gallus is not specifically mentioned so far as the damaged text can be read; it is said to be not a transl. of the Latin or the Greek. The date given by the Egyptian is said to correspond to mid-April, 29 B.C. (For a somewhat earlier inscr. of Gallus in Egypt, see **35**.)

CIL 3.14147⁵ (1902, ed. Mommsen ?), whence *IGRR* 1.1293 and *ILS* 8995, both with bibl., to which add *OGIS* 2.360–365 no. 654; J.-P. Boucher, *Caius* (sic) *Cornelius Gallus* (Paris 1966 Bibl. de la Fac. des Lettres de Lyon, 11) 33–57, esp. 38 ff.; cf. M. Treu, *Chiron* 3 (1973) 223–226, P. A.

Brunt, *JRS* 65 (1975) 125, 128, 142, App., no. 1 (but the *AE* 1964 ref. should be to no. 255); a good photo (from a cast?) in R. Paribeni, *L'Italia imperiale* . . . (Milan 1938) 94 fig. 50, cf. 92; E. A. Judge, *Vestigia* 17 (1973) 571–573; G. Bastianini, *ZPE* 17 (1975) 267, 38 (1980) 75. Engl. transl. by J. P. Mahaffy, *The Athenaeum*, no. 3568 (London, March 14, 1896) 352, and by Lewis and Reinhold, 2.45. The *CIL* headquarters in Berlin has squeezes of the Latin and the Greek, which may well have been Mommsen's; by courtesy of Dr. H. Krummrey, Director, we have had the use of these.

The tone of this inscription, perhaps unique in being set up by such a man during his lifetime (cf. the Scipionics—see 5), may have resulted from Gallus's emotional reaction to the many magnificent buildings and sculptures of the Pharaohs and the Ptolemies visible all over Egypt. Its boastfulness is hardly mitigated by its dedicatory form, which becomes clear only at the end. It was perhaps one item among the reasons for Augustus's (apparent) recall of Gallus (poet, general, and friend of Vergil and Augustus himself) as prefect of Egypt (perhaps the emperor's chief appointment, because of its wealth) and his subsequent suicide in 26 B.C. Cf. Dio, 53.23.5–24.1; J. G. C. Anderson, *CAH* 10.240 f., A. Stein, *PIR*² 2.326–328, no. 1369, and *Präf.* 14–16; F. Magi, *Studi Romani*, 11 (1963) 55, who shows that the "pyramids" of Dio 53.23.5 may rather be "obelisks"; Boucher and Treu, locc. citt.

Text of the Latin: *G(aius) Cornelius Gn(aei) f(ilius) Gallu[s, eq]ues Romanus, post rege[s] / a Caesare, deivi f(ilio), devictos praefect[us Ale]xandreae et Aegypti primus, defectioni[s] / Thebaidis intra dies XV quibus hostem v[icit Π̄] acie victor, V urbium expugnator—Bore[se]/os, Copti, Ceramices, Diospoleos meg[ales, Op]hieu—ducibus earum defectionum inter[ce?]/⁵[p]tis, exercitu ultra Nili catarhacte[n trad]ucto, in quem locum neque populo / [R]omano neque regibus Aegypte[i arma ante s]unt prolata, Thebaide, communi omn[i]/um regum formidine, subacta, leg[atisq(ue) re]gis Aethiopum ad Philas auditis eoq(ue) / rege in tutelam recepto, tyran[n]o Tri[acontas]choenunḍi Aethiopiae constituto, die[is] / patrieis et Nil[o adiut]ori ḍ(ono or -onum) ḍ(edit)* (or, *dedit dedicavit?* —the Greek has simply χαριστήρια, "thank-offerings," and no verb). (The text is now not entirely certain even with study of the squeeze and on-the-spot inspection.)

"Gaius Cornelius Gallus, son of Gnaeus, a Roman knight, after the thorough defeat of the Kings (of Egypt) by Caesar, son of the deified (Julius), first Prefect (Governor) of Alexandria and Egypt, twice victor in battle within 15 days in a revolt in the Thebais, taker-by-storm of five cities—Boresis, Coptos, Ceramice, Diospolis Megale (Magna), (and) Ophieum—, seizing the leaders of these revolts; having taken his army beyond the (first) cataract of the Nile, to which place no military expedition either by the Roman people or by the kings of Egypt was ever made before; having subdued Thebes, a common threat of all the kings, and given audience at Philae to the envoys of the king of the Aethiopians and taken the king under his protection, (and) having set up a ruler of the Triacontaschoenon of Aethiopia, gave (or dedicated) (this monument) to the native gods and to the Nile, his helpmate."

Note the emphatic postponed position of *primus*, the phrase *defect. . . . victor* (like *belli* or *bellorum victor*, which is specially noted by Lewis and Short), *populo Rom.* and *regibus* as datives of agent (?—influenced perhaps by two such datives in the Greek), and the fact that the Greek seems to be a somewhat bowdlerized version of the Latin. It looks as though it were the Greek, at the lowest level, that was intended to be commonly read (apart from the Egyptian, for the few who could read it) rather than the Latin, which can hardly have been known yet in Egypt, Greek having been for centuries the official language and, in Alexandria, the common one.

Except in line 1, there is no complete agreement among the editors as to the readings and the restorations at the middle break and the right edge; the Greek, not being a close version, is of little help. Some interpuncts are uncertain. Line 2. Alexandria and Egypt are often thus mentioned as though A. were considered separate: cf. Olcott, 1.152 f., 236 f., *s.vv.* Aegyptus, Alexandria; Dessau, *ILS* 3: 2, 603 *s.v.* Alexandrea. Line 3. *CIL* restores [*icit bis a*] at the break, but eight letters here seem too many. Lines 4/5. Some editors read *interfe/ctis.* Line 5. *CIL* restores [*n transd*]. Line 6. *CIL* reports several readings for *Aegypt-*; *-te[i*, with *ei* for long I as elsewhere here, seems best to fit the space and the remains. Line 7. *CIL's leg[atisque re]gis* and *eoq[ue]* seem too long; better [*atisq(ue) re*] and *eoq[(ue)]*? Line 8, *tyranno*: either only one N is left or else NN is in ligature.

The Latin of *defectionis . . . victor* (lines 2 f.) seems awkward; the Greek says, clearly and smoothly, "having forcefully conquered the revolting Thebais in 15 days, in battle array." The boast of having been the first to lead an army beyond the (first) cataract of the Nile rests on an untruth, both Pharaohs and Ptolemies having done this at times. The meaning of *dieis patrieis* (9) is uncertain, but "the native gods (of Egypt)" seems, in the circumstances, preferable to "his ancestral gods." The Greek reads like a softened, less offensive version of the Latin: it says nothing of "the kings defeated by Caesar," nothing of Alexandria, or of the Roman people, or of Thebes as a common terror, and for "this king taken into (Roman) protection" it has "receiving official friendship (προξενία) from the king."

For an account, with photos, text, translation, and notes, of a Latin papyrus with fragments of the elegiac poetry of Gallus, "very probably of the reign of Augustus, quite possibly of the lifetime of Gallus himself," and, "with *PHerc* 817 (*Carmen de bello Aegyptiaco*), by far our oldest MS of Latin poetry," see R. D. Anderson, P. J. Parsons, R. G. M. Nisbet, "Elegiacs by Gallus from Qaṣr Ibrîm," *JRS* 69 (1979) 125–155.

23. Epitaph of Caecilia Metella, outside Rome. Undoubtedly Augustan. A marble slab *in situ* inserted in the side (toward the road) of her massive round tomb (diam. 20 m.), 3 km. from Rome on the ancient Via Appia. Probably early- or mid-Augustan, later than the Mausoleum of Augustus in Rome (built in 28 B.C.: Suet. *Aug.* 100.4), which would seem to have inspired it architecturally, but perhaps (as T. Frank thought from a study of its building materials) as late as 10 B.C. To judge from plate CCXVIII, fig. 2, of Luigi Canina, *L'architettura romana*, 3 (Rome 1842) [vol. 9. of his *L'archit. antica*]), the slab is ca. 1.63 m. wide.

CIL 6.1274, *ILS* 881, *Album* 1.30–32, no. 13 (with further bibl.). Cf. Frank, *RBR* 144 f., E. Nash, *Roman Towns* (New York 1944) 41, pl. 137, *Roma e dintorni* 398, R. Ross Holloway *AJA* 70 (1966) 171–173. The inscription, one of the most beautiful in Latin and fully equal in this respect to the often-pictured inscription of the Column of Trajan, is centered. Letter heights: Hübner, on his no. 61, gives 9, 8, and 6 cm., from Canina (which seems approximately correct, to judge from C.'s *Gli edifizj di Roma antica . . .* , 4 [Rome 1851] pl. 272 fig. 7).

Text: *Caeciliae, / Q(uinti) Cretici f(iliae), / Metellae, Crassi (uxori).*

"To Caecilia Metella, daughter of Quintus (Caecilius Metellus) Creticus [probably the consul of 69 B.C.], (and wife) of (Marcus [?] Licinius) Crassus."

From looking at many other epitaphs in print (e.g., in Dessau, *ILS*) I would judge this one to be in the dative case rather than the genitive, but obviously, without "wife" included in the text (this seems more often omitted than included in such epitaphs), one cannot be certain: cf. Cal. Lim. 200, 3, a, first paragraph.

On the identity of Crassus and the dating, see *Album* 1.31 f., Frank 145, Holloway loc. cit.; Crassus would be one of the triumvir's two sons, probably Marcus. (On these, see now T. P. Wiseman, *JRS* 65 [1975] 198, with ref. to G. V. Sumner, *The Orators in Cicero's Brutus* . . . [Toronto 1973 *Phoenix*, suppl. vol. 11] 149 f.; W. would have Marcus born in 87/86 and quaestor in 54, Publius born in 86/85 and quaestor in 55, not "perhaps 55," as in Broughton, 2.580, line 1.)

Piranesi (*Le antichità romane* [Rome 1756] 3, pl. L) called this tomb a "nobilissimo sepolcrale monumento." Perhaps the genesis of such large Roman tombs was not single, but multiple: the tumuli/tombs of the princes of Troy (of the *Iliad* and *Aeneid*), the archaic Etruscan tumuli not far north of Rome, and the tomb of Alexander the Great at Alexandria, which Coarelli thinks "almost certainly circular" and which Octavian is said to have visited after occupying the city in 30 B.C. (Suet. *Aug.* 18.1, Dio 51.16.5): cf. Holloway, loc. cit., A. Boëthius in his and J. B. Ward-Perkins's *Etr. and Rom. Archit.* (*Pelican History of Art*, 1970) 563 n. 96, and Coarelli 275, *init.*

24. Epitaphs of Octavia and Her Son Marcellus, Rome. Probably 23 B.C. A single, damaged block of marble, found in 1927 in excavating the crypt of the Mausoleum of Augustus. Dimensions: m. 0.73 (max. at front) × 1.45 max. (inscr. surface 1.42) × ca. 0.33 (at left side); letters, line 1 ca. 7.5 cm., line 2 ca. 7.2–7.5 cm. In April 1973 seen still inside the Mausoleum. Marcellus (M. Claudius Marcellus, nephew of Augustus) died in the latter half of 23 B.C. (cf. A. Stein, *PIR*[2] 2.214 no. 925) and was the first to be cremated, and his ashes preserved, in the Mausoleum (built in 28—

see above, on **23**); his mother died in 11 B.C. (Dio 54.35.4). The same hand apparently cut both inscrs., so it seems likely, in view of Seneca's account of Octavia's bereavement (*Dial.* 6.2.3 f.), that on her instructions the cutter chose a stone large enough for both epitaphs and cut first Marcellus's, then Octavia's, without waiting for her death, there being nothing in her epitaph that would require bringing it up to date later.

Publ. by Franz Cumont, *CRAI* 1927, 313, whence *AE* 1928, 88; cf. Lugli, 3.194–212, Nash 2.38–43 *s.v.* Mausoleum Augusti.

Text: *Marcellus G(ai) f(ilius),* / *gener* / *[A]ugusti Caesaris*; and *Octavia G(ai) f(ilia),* / *soror* / *Augusti Caesaris]*. (Cumont, followed by *AE*, has an interpunct after each F in line 1.)

"(Marcus Claudius) Marcellus, son of Gaius (Claudius Marcellus [cos. 50 B.C.]), son-in-law of Augustus Caesar [by his marriage to A.'s daughter, Julia]." "Octavia, daughter of Gaius (Octavius [praetor in 61, proconsul of Macedonia 60–59 B.C.]), sister of Augustus Caesar." Marcellus's death is lamented by Vergil, *Aen.* 6.860–886, and Propertius, 3.18.

25. Part of the Record of the Secular Games, Rome. 17 B.C. Several fragments of white-marble blocks (the lower-right one reportedly 16–20 cm. thick) that formed one side, presumably the front, of a large monument (somewhat more than 3.02 × 1.12 m.), all the fragments of which except one in the Vatican are set up, in restored form, near the NW corner of the Chiostro of the Mus. Naz. Rom., Rome (inv. no. 1023), where they were seen in 1948 and 1973. The Vatican fragment was found in the 15th or 16th cent. in Rome, apparently near where the other fragments, plus many others belonging to a Severan monument of the same character for the games of A.D. 204, were found in 1890—on the left bank of the Tiber near S. Giovanni dei Fiorentini. Letter heights:

1.0–1.35, mostly 1.1–1.2, cm.; tall letters ca. 1.5 or 1.6 to 2 cm.

CIL 6.32323 (our photo shows lines 137–168, lacking 5 line-ends), cf. p. 3824 (further bibl.), *ILS* 5050 (lines 90–168), Diehl *IL* tab. 9 f. (lines 85–168), *Album* 1.27–30 no. 12 (the Vat. fragm. plus lines 147–155 of the Mus. Naz. Rom. fragms., further bibl.), E/J 60 f., nos. 30–32 (4 selections). Cf. P/A 152 *s.v.* Dis Pater et Proserpina, Ara, Nash 1.57–59 *s.v.* Ara Ditis Patris et Proserp. L/R, 2.57–61, translate most of the text. On the Secular Games, cf. L. R. Taylor, *OCD* 969 f., *s.v.* Sec. Games.

Text of lines 147–154: . . . / *sacrificioque perfecto pueri [x]xvii quibus denuntiatum erat, patrimi et matrimi, et puellae totidem / carmen cecinerunt; eo[dem]que modo in Capitolio. / Carmen composuit Q(uintus) Hor[at]ius Flaccus. /*[150] *XVvir(i) adfuerunt Imp(erator) Ca[e]sar, M(arcus) Agrippa* [plus 17 more names].[153] *Ludis scaenicis dimissis, h(ora)* [1–3 letters], *iuxta eum locum ubi sacrificium erat factum superioribus noctibus et / theatrum positum et sca[le]na, metae positae quadrigaeq(ue) sunt missae et desultores misit Potitus Messalla.* / (plus 14 more lines)

". . . and the sacrifice having been completed, 27 previously designated boys, who had both parents still alive, and as many girls, sang a hymn, and in the same way on the Capitol. Quintus Horatius Flaccus composed the hymn [Horace's *Carmen Saeculare*]. The College of Fifteen were present: the Emperor Caesar (Augustus), Marcus (Vipsanius) Agrippa [plus 17 more names]. The theatrical performances having come to an end, at the – –[?] hour (of the day) near the place where the sacrifice had been carried out on the preceding nights and the theater and stage set up, turnposts were set up and chariot races started, and (Marcus Valerius) Potitus Messalla started [i.e., gave the signal to] the circus riders [who jumped from one horse to another]. . . ."

The ends of lines 147, 150 f., 153 f. extend beyond our photo. Line 152, the

mark to the right of the point after *Rebilus*, apparently not previously noted, looks like a major punctuation-mark, presumably to show, in the absence of Messalla's praenomen and nomen, that Rebilus and Messalla were not the same man; Wingo agrees, p. 117. Line 153, the number of the *hora* could be III, VI, or XI, or (second choice) II, V, or X.

This is apparently the only extant contemporary reference to the poet Horace, who is given a whole line in the inscription. Clearly, the College of Fifteen at this time consisted of more than 15: 19 present at these games, and Martha W. Hoffman Lewis, *PMAAR* 16 (1955) 48–51, lists two more. (For the College, cf. H. J. Rose, *OCD* 906 f., *s.v.* Quindecimviri.)

26. Epitaph on the Pyramid of Cestius, Rome. Probably not after 12 B.C. "The most notable pyramidal tomb in Italy," Neuerburg. Just outside, and (to one leaving Rome) to the right of, the Porta San Paolo (anc. Porta Ostiensis), incorporated in the Aurelian Wall (late-3rd cent. A.D.), it is the sepulchral monument of G. Cestius Epulo, who died probably not after 12 B.C. An example of Egyptian art in Rome, which was "less an influence than a fashion" (Strong 1.148), it rests on a travertine base and is built of brick-faced *opus caementicium*, sheathed in white-marble blocks; but its dimensions as reported vary greatly, from 27 to 36.40 m. high × 22 to 29.50 m. square; cf. Lugli, 3.613, P/A 478 *s.v.* Sepulcrum C. Cestii, Bayard Taylor (1847) as quoted by Scherer on pl. 199; *Roma e dintorni* 418, Toynbee 127. (G. Bunsen, 1837, cited by *CIL* 6 on no. 1374, gave the height as 164 palms [about the same as can be estimated from Piranesi's drawing, with scale in "Roman palms," of 1756: op. cit. (above, on **23**) 3, pl. XLIV], the base as 130 palms square.) As the longer inscription on the opposite (east) side says, it took 330 days to finish the pyramid.

CIL 6.1374 (cf. 31639 and p. 3805), *ILS* 917, Cal. Lim. 221–223 no. 32. Cf.

E. Groag, *PIR*² 2.151 f., no. 686 (who, following Klebs in *PIR*¹ 1, C 569, calls the deceased only "C. Cestius," "Epulo" being added like a cognomen to distinguish him from others of the same nomen and period; but others consider "Epulo" a regular cognomen), Lugli 3.612–615, Scherer 122–124 pls. 196–199 (cf. index, 425, *s.v.* Pyramid of Cestius), *Album*, 1.34 f., nos. 16 f. (nearly identical inscrs. on the twin marble statue-bases, now in the Atrio of the Capitoline Mus., Rome, found in 1660 in front of the west side of the Pyramid), *Roma e dintorni* 418, Nash 2.321–323 *s.v.* Sep. C. Cestii (3 photos, bibl.), Norman Neuerburg, "Greek and Roman Pyramids," *Archaeology*, 22 (1969) 113 f. (photo), Toynbee 127 f., pl. 33 (photo), Roullet 42, 84 no. 94. Besides Shelley's lines in *Adonais*, XLIX–L, see Thomas Hardy's poem "Rome. At the Pyramid of Cestius near the Graves of Shelley and Keats," 1887.

Text of the inscription on the west side, facing the beautiful and fascinating non-Catholic ("Protestant") Cemetery: *G(aius) Cestius L(uci) f(ilius) Pob(lilia tribu) Epulo, pr(aetor), tr(ibunus) pl(ebis), / VIIvir epulonum.*

"Gaius Cestius Epulo, son of Lucius, of the Publilia 'tribe,' praetor, tribune of the plebs, *septemvir epulonum* [a priesthood]."

Cestius was a praetor in the late Republic or the early-Augustan period (Broughton 2.463), and, because Agrippa, who died in 12 B.C. (Dio 54.28.2–3), is mentioned, and seems to be alive, in the inscription on the two statue-bases, Cestius probably died before Agrippa. (The lower inscr. refers to a restoration of the pyramid in 1663 by Pope Alexander VII.) The inscr. on the east side adds to Cestius's name and titles the statement: *Opus apsolutum (est) ex testamento diebus CCCXXX / arbitratu / [L.] Ponti P.f. Cla(udia tribu) Melae heredis et Pothi l(iberti).* Pontius's praenomen is known from the two statue-bases mentioned above: *CIL* 6.1375, *ILS* 917ᵃ, *Album*, loc. cit.

27. Record of the Restoration of an Altar, Rome. 9 B.C. Found in Rome in 1897, near S. Francesco di Paola; seen in June 1949 and April 1973 in Sala I of the Braccio Nuovo of the Palazzo dei Conservatori (formerly the Sala Repubblicana), Rome (inv. no. 6980).

Not of Gabine Stone, as H/S 2.1598 repeats from *CIL* and earlier editions, but of "a compact lava rock resembling the *silex* or *lapis Tuscolanus* of the Latial hills, the scientific name of which is leucitite," G. De Angelis d'Ossat, as quoted in the *Album* 1.35 no. 18 and by Shoe.

Dimensions: *NS* 1897, 104, gave m. 0.75 square (at bottom) × 0.60 high, but Mustilli, Shoe, and H/S, while agreeing approximately on the first dimension (Shoe adds m. 0.745 square at the top), give m. 1.075–1.15 for the height (which seems more likely); *NS* calls it an "ara antichissima," while Shoe, 108, and H/S speak of its Etruscan form; the inscribed surface, within the molded border, is 14.8 × 61.5 cm. Letters: 2.5–4.0 cm. high. The whole inscription is reportedly cut over an erasure, no doubt on the occasion of the restoration, the successive borders, being cut as moldings, concealing this except to close examination.

The consuls named are those of 9 B.C.; the death of the first named, Drusus the Elder (son of Livia and younger brother of the emperor Tiberius) in summer camp, in Germany, while in office, prompted the Senate to bestow on him and his descendants, for the first time, the honorary cognomen "Germanicus," which may have caused the restoration of this altar by re-cutting the inscr. in order to include "Germanicus."

CIL 6.37063, Mustilli 7 no. 12, *Album* loc. cit., Lucy T. Shoe *MAAR* 28 (1965) 109, E. Meinhardt in H/S 2.1598 (all with bibl.).

Text: *Nero Claudius Drusus Germanic(us), / T(itus) Quinctius Crispinus, co(n)s(ules), / ex s(enatus) c(onsulto) restituer(unt).*

"Nero Claudius Drusus Germanicus (and) Titus Quinctius Crispinus (Sulpicianus), consuls, restored (this altar [of what god?]) by decree of the Senate."

A similarly shaped ("hour-glass") altar, in the same room as this—*CIL* 1².804, cf. pp. 727, 839 = 6.3732, 31057, cf. p. 3758 = *ILS* 4019, Degr. 281 add., *Imag.* 115—is dedicated to Verminus: cf. Nash, 2.500 *s.v.* Verminus, Ara, with bibl. and photo.

28. Two Fragments of the "Laudatio Turiae," Rome. Of Augustan date; generally thought to be of ca. 8–2 B.C. Two of the four extant marble fragments (besides three others not extant) of probably the most famous *Laudatio* (funerary eulogy) preserved in Latin, the only Latin inscription independently edited in the Budé Collection des Univ. de France. The larger fragment (39 × 59 × 9 cm.) was found in or shortly before 1898, ca. 4 km. from Rome, near the Via Portuense, the smaller (24–27.5 × 24–25 × 3–7.5 cm.) recognized in 1949 in the Antiquario of the Mus. Naz. Rom., Rome, both seen together there in April 1973 (inv. nos. 30515, 115582). Both fragments adjoin the right edge of the inscr., the larger at the top, the other lower down; two other fragments, *d* and *e*, originally one piece, are now in the Villa Albani, Rome. For more details, see *Album* 1.40–42 no. 28; Bruns 321–326 no. 126, Marcel Durry, ed., *Éloge funèbre d'une matrone romaine* (Paris 1950 Coll. Budé), cf. *REL* 28 (1950) 81 f.; *FIRA* 3.209–218, no. 69; *The So-Called Laudatio Turiae*, ed. with intro., transl., and comm. (all in English) by Erik Wistrand (Gothenburg 1976 *Studia Graeca et Latina Gothoburgensia*, 34), with the only available photos of fragments *d* and *e*. The larger fragment: *CIL* 6.37053 (cf. 1527, 31670), *ILS* 8393 (add.); both together, first in *AJA* 54 (1950) 223–226, pls. 26 f. Cf. F. Della Corte, "L'autore della cosiddetta *Laudatio Turiae*," *Giorn. Ital. di Filol.* 3 (1950) 146–149 (= *Opuscula* 2 [Genoa 1972 Ist. di Filol. Class. e Medioe-

vale] 287–290) and "Il nuovo frammento F della [Laudatio . . . Uxoris]," journ. cited, 4 (1951) 226–230 (= op. cit. 291–295); V. Arangio-Ruiz, "Il caso giuridico della cosiddetta 'Laudatio Turiae,'" *Studi epigrafici e papirologici*, a cura di L. Bove (Naples 1974) 166–171.

Text of heading and lines 1–4 of larger fragm. (with Durry's restorations [*Éloge*, 13 f.] in lines 1, 3, 4, and De Sanctis's [cf. *Album* 1.40, col. 1 *fin.*] in line 2): (heading) [*Dis Manibus . . . U*]*xoris* / (remains of col. 1) / col. 2, line 1 [*Amplissima* (?) *subsi*]*dia fugae meae praestitisti; ornamentis* / [*tuis iuvisti me* (?)], *cum omne aurum margaritaque corpori* / [*tuo detracta trad(?)*]*idisti mihi et subinde familia, nummis, fructibus,* / [*callide deceptis* (?) *a*]*dversariorum custodibus, apsentiam meam locupletasti.* / (plus remains of 6 more lines, then perhaps ca. 12 lines, lost, before the smaller fragm.). Letter heights: heading, 5.2–5.4 cm., lines 1–9 progressively shorter from 1.9–2.3 down to 1.5–1.7 cm., tall I's 2.5 down to 1.8.

"To the sacred memory of Turia (?), wife of Q. Lucretius Vespillo (?)." (Col. 1, *CIL*'s lost, but reported, fragments *a–c*.) Col. 2: "You furnished most ample means (?) for my escape; with your (?) jewels you aided me (?) when you took off all the gold and pearls from your person and handed them (?) over to me; and promptly [or, "over and over again"? cf. Wistrand, p. 42, on line II 4a] with slaves, money, (and) provisions, having cleverly deceived (?) the enemies' guards, you enriched my absence. . . ."

Noteworthy the spaces left for paragraph- and sentence-breaks, the rare use of "apexed" I (*Contrib.* 148 nos. 5 f.) twice, the interpunct within *ad·versariorum* (op. cit. 184 *init.*, 227 ch. 8, n. 8), and the tense of *polliceretur*, smaller fragm., 3, instead of the pluperfect.

For the smaller fragment (with shorter line-endings), see *AJA* or *Album*, locc. citt.

In answer to Durry's contention (*Éloge*, pp. LIV–LXIV, esp. LXI f.) that the deceased cannot be Turia nor the *laudator* her husband, Q. Lucretius Vespillo, cos. 19 B.C. (Val. Max. 6.7.2, App. *B.C.* 4.44), which had been the hitherto prevailing view (of Mommsen, W. Warde Fowler, *Soc. Life at Rome* . . . [London 1908 and repr.] 158–167, et al.), see "Who's Who in the *Laudatio Turiae*," *Epigraphica*, 39 (1977) 7–12: while Turia and Vespillo are certainly not *proved* to be the chief characters here, so many others having been tragically involved in the civil war and the proscriptions of 43 B.C., they still *may* be the hero and heroine and they best fit the story given by Appian.

29. Record of Repairs of Three Aqueducts, Rome.

The Porta Tiburtina has a monumental arch carrying three aqueducts, the Marcia, the Tepula, and the Julia. The inscriptions (which are cut on each face of the arch) refer to restorations of the conduits, general repairs, completed by Augustus in 5/4 B.C. (the top one, *a*) and restorations A.D. 79 by Titus (bottom, *b*), and in 212/213 by Caracalla (middle, *c*). The arch is of travertine, but its dimensions are lacking.

CIL 6.1244 (*a*), 1246 (*b*), 1245 (cf. p. 3125) (*c*); *ILS* 98. Cf. P/A 23–28, 601 f., *s.vv.* Aqua Iulia, Marcia, Tepula, 417 f., *s.v.* Porta Tiburtina; Thomas Ashby, *The Aqueducts of Ancient Rome* (Oxford 1935) 88–166, esp. 145 f.; Nash 1.47–51 (esp. photo no. 44), 2.232 f. (esp. photo no. 980) *s.vv.* Aqua Iulia, A. Marcia, Porta Tib. Our photo is of the inner face of the arch.

Text of *a*: *Imp(erator) Caesar divi Iuli f(ilius) Augustus, / pontifex maximus, co(n)s(ul) XII, / tribunic(ia) potestat(e) XIX, imp(erator) XIIII, / rivos aquarum omnium refecit.*

"Emperor Caesar Augustus, son of the deified Julius, *pontifex maximus*, consul for the 12th time, with tribunician power for the 19th time, (acclaimed) Imperator for the 14th time, rebuilt the channels of all the waters (i.e., the aqueducts)."

Omnium is an important word, as is suggested by its position: Augustus "repaired the aqueducts as a whole," Ashby op. cit. 13 *init.*, cf. 89, and P/A 24 f., *s.v.* Aqua Marcia. The date is determined by Augustus's 19th trib. power, July 1, 5– June 30, 4 B.C. (cf. *PIR*² 4.162, *fin.*, *s.v.* Iulius 215).

The text of *b* and *c* is as follows: (*b*) *Imp(erator) Titus Caesar divi f. Vespasianus Augustus, pontif(ex) max(imus), / tribuniciae potestat(is) IX, imp(erator) XV, cens(or), co(n)s(ul) VII, desig(natus) IIX, p(ater) p(atriae), / rivom aquae Marciae vetustate dilapsum refecit / et aquam, quae in usu esse desierat, reduxit.* Note the genitive *trib. pot.*: either abl. or gen. or, more often, an abbreviation, seems to be in use from Augustus on; the barred ordinal adverbs, not barred in *a* (cf. *Contrib.* 166–168); and IIX rather than VIII (ibid. 176–181). (*c*) *Imp(erator) Caes(ar) M(arcus) Aurellius Antoninus Pius Felix Aug(ustus), Parth(icus) Maxim(us), / Brit(annicus) Maximus, pontifex maximus, / aquam Marciam variis kasibus impeditam, purgato fonte, excisis et perforatis / montibus, restituta forma, adquisito etiam fonte novo Antoniniano, / in sacram urbem suam perducendam curavit.* "Aurell-" is often found in this new name created by Septimius Severus for his son Septimius Bassianus, nicknamed "Caracalla" —cf. Dessau, 3: 1, 289, line 5, n. 2, and above, Intro., n. 88; *Brit.* might also be completed "Britt—," Dessau, *pag. cit.*, *fin.*; for the archaistic *kasibus*—the *k* caused no doubt by the following *a*—cf. Pfister 31, 6th par.; the tall first *I* in *impeditam*, clear even in the photo, caused by over-correction? by its frequent use in *Imp(erator)*? by its being the first letter in the word?

According to inscr. *b*, Titus "rebuilt the channel of the Aqua Marcia, disintegrated with age, and brought back the water, which had ceased to be available." In *c*, Caracalla "arranged to have the Aqua Marcia, blocked up by various mishaps, brought into his holy (Imperial) city, after having cleaned out its source, cut down and dug through hills, restored the channel, and also acquired a new source, 'Antoninianus'."

30. Senatorial Inscription in Honor of Lucius Caesar, Rome.

2 B.C. (He was Augustus's second grandson, by Julia and Agrippa.) Found in 1899 in the Roman Forum (where it still was when seen in 1973), in three pieces (now joined together), much damaged and incomplete, the marble block is thought to have belonged to the Portico of Gaius and Lucius (Suet. *Aug.* 29.4, Dio 56.27.5) and to have lain on an arch over the "new branch" of the Sacra Via (Nash, 2.244–246, photos 993 f., 996 f., *s.v.* Porticus Gai et Luci, with special ref. to Lugli and Degrassi; cf. 2.288, photo 1048, *s.v.* Sacra Via, and 1.93, photo 94, *s.v.* Arcus Augusti). Dimensions: 1.50 × 4.75 × 0.60 m. (Lugli, *Mon. min.* 84; found to be approximately correct in April 1973); letters: line 1, 24.5–25.5, lines 2–3, 16.5, line 4, 15 cm. tall. For the date, see below.

CIL 6.36908 (ed. Bang) with drawing and some bibl.; add Nash's bibl., 2.244. Cf. S. Panciera, *Epigraphica* 31 (1969) 104–112; our inscr. is noted p. 109 n. 12.

Text: *L(ucio) Caesari, Aug[u]sti f(ilio), divi n(epoti), / principi iuventu[ti]s, co(n)s(uli) desig(nato) / ¢um [e]sset ann(os) n[a]t(us) XIIII, aug(uri), / senatus.*

"To Lucius Caesar, son of Augustus, grandson of the deified (Julius Caesar), Prince of the Youth, designated consul when he was 14 years of age, augur: the Senate."

The inconsistency of punctuation is noteworthy in so official an inscr.; line 3, most of *cum* is restored, but the VM is certain: cf. Nash's photos 993, 996 f. Note the subjunctive with *cum*. Line 3, *aug.* is not completed or explained by Bang, but the honor is mentioned in at least 12 inscrs. (*PIR²* 4.186 *s.v.* Iulius no. 222), e.g., *CIL* 11.1421 = *ILS* 140 [31], line 15, where the word is written in full. Lucius is

called "son of Aug." (as Aug. himself calls him), having been adopted by Aug., immediately after his birth, along with his older brother, Gaius (Dio 54.18.1).

The dating depends on Lucius's birth in 17 B.C. (Dio, loc. cit.), his being 14 in this inscr. (confirmed by Augustus himself, *Res Gestae*, 14.1), and Augustus's having asked for a 13th consulship so as to be holding the highest office when he introduced Lucius (as he previously had his older brother—Suet. *Aug.* 26.2) to public life on his coming of age (Aug. was cos. XIII in 2 B.C.). The day of L.'s birth is not known, but Dio's mentioning it as his first item of the year suggests that it was early. Jan. 29, mentioned by *PIR²*, loc. cit., as "perhaps" the birthday, rests on false evidence: the reading "[natalis?] Luc(i) Caesar(is)" seen by G. Mancini in a calendar fragment found in Rome in 1928 is incorrect, the correct reading being *Fęri[ae] Imp(eratoris) Caesar(is)* (cf. Degrassi, *Bull. Com.* 63 [1935] 174 and pl. 1, correcting Mancini, vol. cit. 49; idem, *FCT* 280, Jan. 29, and pl. 88; *Album*, 1.44, Jan. 29, and pl. 19). Augustus was still consul on Aug. 1, 2 B.C., when he dedicated the new Temple of Mars Ultor (Vell. Pat. 2.100.2, Dio 60.5.3, cf. *Res Gestae* 21.6, and Degrassi *FANI* 490), but no longer by Sept. 18 (*CIL* 6.36809 = *ILS* 9250). Lucius therefore was 14 in the year 3/2 B.C., but Augustus's 13th consulship narrows the date of our inscr. to the year 2, possibly as late as Sept. 17, but probably earlier, perhaps quite early.

31. Record of Posthumous Honors for Gaius Caesar, Pisa.

A.D. 4. White-marble ("of Luna," *CIL*) tablet, now in two pieces (combined width m. 0.875, lacking the right edge; height m. 1.55 [*CIL*], found to be approximately correct in April 1974); found with a similar tablet honoring Gaius's younger brother, Lucius (*CIL* 11.1420 = *ILS* 139—see 30), in Pisa in the early-17th cent.; still there, set in a frame attached to the wall, next to the other tablet, near the south-east corner of the south corridor of the Camposanto. (The two pieces of this inscr. have been placed a little too near each other for the restorations required; and the painted-plaster restorations shown in our photo, received in 1965, are unreliable, sometimes clearly wrong.) A record of honors bestowed on Gaius, as previously on Lucius, by the decurions, the colonists, and the local senate of the (undoubtedly) Augustan colony of Pisa (Colonia Obsequens Iulia Pisana), following his death in Lycia Feb. 21, A.D. 4. (Gaius and Lucius were sons of Julia and Agrippa.)

CIL 11.1421, cf. p. 1263; ILS 140; A. Neppi Modona, Inscr. Ital. 7: 1 (1953) 4–7 no. 7; E/J 70–72 no. 69 (text without notes); Sherk 44 f. (text), 63–65 (transl. of lines 51–60, with commentary); transl. L/R 2.75 f.; cf. Toscana², 115, col. 2, init.; Toscana⁴ (Attrav. l'Italia, 6) 2.59, photos 108, 110. The tablet has a border along the left side and the bottom, at a slightly lower level than the inscr.; at the left it is 4–5 cm. wide, at the bottom 3.4–3.7 cm. high.

Lines 1–6 (originally preceded by another line, now lost, containing the date and meeting-place of the local senate: cf. CIL 11.1420, line 1) give the names of the twelve men who participated in writing the following decree and the fact that this was passed "when there were no magistrates in our colony on account of an election campaign." Lines 7–17 med. contain a long cum ("whereas") clause explaining the background: a report received April 2 (A.D. 4) of the death of Gaius Caesar of wounds received in his country's service (in Armenia), when Pisa had not yet recovered from grief at the death of Gaius's brother Lucius (see 30), A.D. 2.

Text of lines 17 med.–24 fin. (as checked in 1974): . . . ob eas res universi decu/ri[one]s colonique, quando eo casu in Colonia neque IIvir(i) neque praefecti / er[ant] neque quisquam iure dicundo prae⟨e⟩rat, inter sese consenserunt pro /²⁰ m[ag]nitudine tantae ac tam

inprovisae calamitatis oportere ex ea die / qu[a ei]us deces⟨s⟩us nuntiatus esset usqui [sic] ad eam diem qua ossa relata atque / co[nd]ita iustaque eius Manibus perfecta essent cunctos veste mutata templis/qu[e d]eorum immortalium balneisque publicis et tabernis omnibus clausis, / co[nvi]ctibus sese apstinere matronas quae in colonia nostra sunt sublugere / . . . (plus 35 more lines, which, except for the last word, Censuere, "They (so) voted," complete one long sentence of 59 lines with one main verb, consenserunt, line 19).

". . . for these reasons all the decurions [members of the town council] as a body and the colonists, since at this crisis there were in the Colony neither Duoviri [Board of Two] nor Prefects nor anyone in charge of the administration of justice, agreed with one another that, in view of the magnitude of so great and so unexpected a disaster, it was proper, from the day when his decease was reported until the day when (his) remains should be brought back and buried, and the proprieties performed for his Manes [Spirit], for everyone, with clothing changed and all the temples of the immortal gods and the public baths and the shops closed, to refrain from social intercourse, for the matrons who are in our colony to lament, . . ."

In the remaining lines the decurions and the colonists agree on the ceremonies to be performed for Gaius and the honors to be paid him, and to inform Augustus of all these.

32. Epitaph of Potitus Valerius Messalla, Rome. Of Augustan date. A marble block found in Rome in 1908, probably near the original family-tomb; seen in 1948 and 1973 in the garden of the Mus. Naz. Rom., Rome (inv. no. 39507). The tabula ansata (handle-like) design is not infrequently a feature of epitaphs, D(is) M(anibus) being sometimes written within the ansae, as in CIL 12.1824 (S/C 70 fig. 22). (Tab. ansata seems not to be an ancient term).

Ca. 0.89–0.90 × 0.74–1.17 (originally ca. 2.33? revised est.) × 0.22–0.32 m. Letter heights: line 1, 5.8–6.1 (initial P, 6.4), lines 2–4, ca. 4.75–5.0 cm.

Augustan, not before May/June, 17 B.C., more probably late-Augustan, perhaps by A.D. 10/12 (*Album* 1.33 col. 1 *fin.*).

CIL 6.37075, ILS 8964, Gordon *Pot. Val. Mess.* (1954), *Album* 1.32 f., no. 14 (all with bibl.). Add Broughton 2.631, line 1, *Suppl.* 66; H. G. Pflaum, *REL* 32 (1954) 435–437; R. Syme, *JRS* 45 (1955) 155–160 (= *Rom. Papers* 1.260–270); J. and L. Robert, *REG* 69 (1956) 160 no. 252.

Text: *Potitus Valę[rius, M(arci) f(ilius), M(ani) (?) n(epos), Messalla], / XVvir sac(ris) fa[c(iundis), IIIvir a(ere) a(rgento) a(uro) f(lando) f(eriundo), trib(unus) milit(um) (?)], / q(uaestor), pr(aetor) urb(anus), ç[o(n)s(ul), proco(n)s(ul* or *pro consule) provinc(iae) (or provinciae) (?)] / Asiae bis, leg(atus) [Imp(eratoris) Caesaris Augusti in Syria (?)].* (The restorations, all conjectural, have been revised in the light of Pflaum's and Syme's criticisms of the 1954 monograph; some restorations are less certain than others.)

"Potitus Valerius Messalla, son of Marcus, grandson of Manius (?), member of the College of Fifteen [before 31, and still attested in 17, B.C.], member of the Board of Three Masters of the Mint (?), military tribune (?), quaestor [in Greece, 38–35 B.C.? L. Robert's conjectured date], urban praetor [32 B.C.], consul [suffect 29 B.C.], proconsul of the province of Asia twice [i.e., for 2 years, ca. 23 B.C.? see Syme 158 f. (= 266 f.)], legate of the Emperor Augustus in Syria (?)."

For "Potitus" as a fashionable praenomen, originally no doubt his second cognomen (agnomen), which he changed to praenomen, dropping "Manius," apparently after his quaestorship—if L. Robert's Greek inscr. from Claros refers to him, as it seems to (it names a Μάνιος Οὐαλέριος Μεσσάλα Ποτῖτος ταμίας)—see Syme 156 (= 261 f.). For the dates of his priestly office, see Broughton *Suppl.* 66

and CIL 6.32323 (= ILS 5050) (25), lines 150, 154: "Potitus Messalla"; the date of his suffect consulship comes from the *Fasti Magistrorum Vici* (Degr. *FCT* 283: "Suf(fectus) Potit(us) Valeri(us)"; for the question whether *bis* looks forward or, as Dessau and Syme believe, backward, see *Pot. Val. Mess.* 39 f.; for P.'s province, op. cit. 40–43, Syme 158 f. (= 266 f.).

P.'s father's praenomen is certain (Capitoline *Fasti Cons.*, A.D. 5, ref. to P.'s son Volesus: Degr. *FCT* 60 f., 528), but the grandfather's is not: it is "Manius" if P. is the son of M. Valerius Messalla Rufus, cos. 53 B.C. ("a fair assumption," Syme 157 [= 264]) and if the latter was "M'. f. M'. n.," as Syme, 157 f. (= 263 f.), thinks "presumably" true. In line 2 the restoration *trib. milit.* better fits the space allowed by a revised reconstruction of the text (which depends on the correctness of line 1, as restored) than *trib. mil.* (which Syme disapproved) or Syme's own *tr. mil.* (which Dessau says, 3: 1, 503, was the form used *plerumque*); *trib. milit.* is attested ca. A.D. 60 (*ILS* 981).

33. Epitaph of Gaius Caesar (son of Germanicus), Rome. A.D. 12. He was one of the three short-lived children of Germanicus Caesar (15 B.C.–A.D. 19) and Agrippina the Elder (ca. 14 B.C.–A.D. 33). A travertine cippus, found in 1777 along with five other large rectangular cippi—all containing epitaphs of members of the Augustan house—near the Mausoleum of Augustus, from the crematory of which (*Ustrinum domus Augustae* or *Bustum Caesarum*) they are believed to have come; seen in 1949 and 1973 in the Braccio Nuovo of the Vatican (inv. no. 2307, but marked no. 6). Inscribed surface: ca. 20.8 × 58.8 cm. Letter heights: line 1, 4.7–5.05, line 2, 3.45–4.0 (tall I 4.15), line 3, 3.2–3.9 (I 4.0) cm. The inscr. is centered.

Gaius was born "about a year before" the birth of the later emperor Caligula (Aug. 31, A.D. 12) and died *iam puerascens* (Suet. *Calig.* 7, 8.1–2), undoubtedly before the birth of the brother who received the same praenomen.

CIL 6.889, ILS 181, Album 1.56 no. 41, E. Meinhardt in H/S 1.420 (all with bibl., including Mommsen, Hirschfeld, Dessau in PIR¹, Gardhausen, P/A, Lugli; add L. Petersen, PIR² 4.173 no. 218).

Text: G(aius) Caesar, / Germanici Caesaris f(ilius), / hic crematus est. (Here both long I's are consistently tall.)

"Gaius Caesar, son of Germanicus Caesar, was here cremated."

34. The *Monumentum Ancyranum*, Ankara, Turkey. It comprises the *Res Gestae* of Augustus, inscribed on both interior walls (from ca. 15 ft. above the pronaos floor-level down to almost 7.5 ft. above it) of the white-marble antae of the pronaos of the Temple of Rome and Augustus in Ankara (anc. Ancyra, capital of Roman Galatia). The Greek version occupies fully 50 ft., or most of the exterior length (from ca. 11 ft. 4 in. above floor-level down to about the same level as the Latin, but on 3, instead of 6, courses of stone) of the right (south) side of the pronaos and the naos (cella). (These figures are estimated from photos and from the measurements and drawings pp. 13–17, plates 5–6, of D. Krencker and M. Schede's *Der Tempel in Ankara* [Berlin/Leipzig 1936]). Access to the inscriptions is restricted, subject to entering a locked gate in the fence around the Temple precinct, which requires permission of the authorities of the mosque to which it belongs. The ruined Temple and the inscriptions were seen in May 1973. The Latin is a copy, no doubt fairly accurate (with a few slips), of the inscription ordered by Augustus to be cut on bronze tablets after his death (Aug. 19, A.D. 14) to be set up in front of his Mausoleum in Rome (Suet. *Aug.* 101.1 and 4). There exist also another copy of the Latin (*Mon. Antiochenum*) and another of the Greek (*Mon. Apolloniense*), both very fragmentary and incomplete, and

both found, not *in situ*, elsewhere in Roman Galatia. (The original bronze no longer exists, having no doubt been melted down in antiquity.) At the end of both the Latin and the Greek at Ankara is a summary of the contents, in the third person and no doubt of local origin.

This inscription, which Mommsen called the "titulus inter Latinos primarius" and "die Königen" of all Latin inscriptions (*Res Gestae*, ed. 2, p. XXXVIII; *Historische Zeitschr.* 57 [N. F. 21, 1887] 385), though the present writer finds the Latin flat, without style, and too self-centered (*Notes* 127, 132 f., 137), is probably, along with Diocletian's *Edict on Prices*, **81**, the longest extant Latin inscription. Though neither the Latin *Res Gestae* nor its Greek version is quite complete, because of damage, each supplements the other, so that at only one small place—a single word—is it impossible, for lack of other evidence, to know the approximately correct reading: in chapter 32, at the end of sect. 1, in the name of a German king, the Latin is entirely missing in both the Ankara and the Antioch texts, and the Ankara Greek has only the last three letters, -ρος (cf. Gagé 55 *init.* [ch. 32, not 33], 140 f.).

CIL 3: 2 (1873), pp. 769–799 (ed. Mommsen, who also edited it separately, Berlin 1865, ed. 2 1883, repr. Aalen 1970, *Res Gestae Divi Augusti ex monumentis Ancyrano et Apolloniensi*, neither of which monuments Mommsen saw personally). The Antioch (Latin) fragments, not found until 1914 and 1924, were seen in 1973 lying on the ground in front of, or leaning against, the inner right-hand (south) wall of the naos of the Temple at Ankara, embedded in plaster and encased in wooden frames, though Akurga', 284, had located them in 1970 in the Ankara Museum. Though Mommsen's ed. 2 is still indispensable, the most useful edition now available is Jean Gagé's *Res Gestae Divi Augusti ex mon. Ancyr. et Antiocheno Latinis,*

Ancyr. et Apollon. Graecis, ed. 3 (Paris 1977). This is ed. 2 (1950) plus an "Avertissement," pp. I f., and "Compléments," pp. 211–232, of ed. 3. But no editor of the *Res Gestae* seems to have examined personally, and collated, all the remains of the *Mon. Anc., Ant.,* and *Apoll.*; it would be almost impossible for a single person to do so.

To Gagé's long bibl. (pp. I f., 61–69) add U. v. Wilamowitz-Moellendorff, *Hermes* 21 (1886) 623–627 (= *Kleine Schriften* 5: 1 [Berlin 1937, repr. Amsterdam 1971] 267–271, with an add. by W.-M.); *Res gestae divi Augusti, Krit. Textausgabe* von Hans Volkmann (Leipzig 1942 *Bursian*, Suppbd., Bd. 276); E/J 1–31 (Latin and Greek); P. Grenade, *Essai sur les origines du principat . . .* (Paris 1961 *Bibl. Écoles Franç.* 197) ("in effect, an *expl. de texte* of *Res Gestae* 34," S. I. Oost, *CP* 58 [1963] 55 col. 1, in his review); P. A. Brunt and J. M. Moore (edd.), *Res Gestae Divi Augusti . . . , with an intro. and comm.* (Oxford 1967) (includes the Latin text and a facing Engl. transl.); Gordon, *Notes* (p. 125, n. 4: correct χαλκὰς to -κᾶς); Guarducci, 2.315–327 (esp. for the Greek version); Ekrem Akurgal, *Ancient Civilizations and Ruins of Turkey . . .* (Istanbul 1970) 284–287, with plan and photo; Wingo, 29–49, on the "fairly large number of signs . . . obviously inserted for . . . making the meaning more perspicuous and thereby facilitating the reading of the inscribed text." Engl. translations since the first (1914) discoveries of the Antioch fragments: F. W. Shipley's in the *Loeb Class. Libr.*, with the Latin and the Greek (and Vell. Pat.) (1924), and Lewis and Reinhold's, 2.9–19.

The letters of both the Latin and the Greek texts at Ankara are surprisingly small (except in the headings) in comparison with the size of the building, the reason being, no doubt, the great length of the texts; the Latin alone has, besides the long heading, 285 lines of ca. 49–56 letters each (so, e.g., ch. 19). In the last line of col. 2 of the Latin, the average letter-height is ca. 2.5 cm. (excluding the tall letters); in the last line of the Greek, about the same.

Text of the Latin heading (over cols. 1–3, north anta) and col. 4, ch. 19 (beginning of south anta), based on Mommsen's ed. 2, Gagé's ed. 3, and photos:

(heading) *Rerum gestarum divi Augusti, quibus orbem terrarum imperio populi Rom(ani)* / *subiecit et inpensarum quas in rem publicam populumque Romanum fecit, incisarum* / *in duabus aheneis pilis, quae sunt Romae positae, exemplar subiectum.* (The beginning of this, through *fecit*, may well be a copy of the original in Rome.)

(col. 4, ch. 19) *Curiam et continens ei Chalcidicum templumque Apollinis in* / *Palatio cum porticibus, aedem divi Iuli, Lupercal, porticum ad cir/cum Flaminium, quam sum appellari passus ex nomine eius qui pri/orem eodem in solo fecerat Octaviam, pulvinar ad circum maximum,* / *aedes in Capitolio Iovis Feretri et Iovis Tonantis, aedem Quirini,* / *aedes Minervae et Iunonis Reginae et Iovis Libertatis in Aventino,* / *aedem Larum in summa Sacra Via, aedem Deum Penatium in Velia,* / *aedem Iuventatis, aedem Matris Magnae in Palatio feci.*

(heading) "Of the achievements of the deified Augustus, by which he brought the whole world under the power of the Roman people, and of the expenditures that he made for the state and the Roman people, (as) inscribed on the two bronze pillars that are set up in Rome, a copy (is) subjoined."

(col. 4, ch. 19) "The Senate House and, adjacent to it, the Chalcidicum, and the Temple Precinct of Apollo on the Palatine, with (its) porticoes, the Temple of the deified Julius, the Lupercal, the portico at the Circus Flaminius, which I allowed to be called 'Octavia,' from the name of the man who had built an earlier one on the same site, the state box at the Circus Maximus, the temples on the Capitoline of Jupiter Feretrius and Jupiter Tonans, the Temple of Quirinus, the temples of Minerva and Juno Regina and Jupiter Libertas on the Aventine, the Temple of the Lares at the head of the Sacra Via, the Temple of the Di Penates on the Velia, the Temple of Iuventas, the Temple of the Mater Magna on the Palatine, I built." (For *templum* vs. *aedes*, see above, on **19**.)

There has clearly been some further damage to the text since the drawings and plaster casts were made on which Mommsen based his two editions. The lettering seems quite like that of such long, roughly contemporary texts in Rome as the Capitoline Fasti, the *Laudatio Turiae* (**28**), and the *Ludi Saeculares* (**25**); the heading, as one might expect, is "monumental" (*Contrib.* 66 ff., 229 n. 13). J. Marcillet-Jaubert notes (*Gnomon* 31 [1959] 140) that the apices over long vowels are of "quelque huit formes plus ou moins diverses."

Philologically, the most interesting word in the whole inscr. is *profligata* (ch. 20 §3, or col. 4, line 13), which apparently means "prope absoluta adfectaque" (which Gellius, 15.5, calls an incorrect use of the word, though it obviously bears this meaning in such respectable authors as Cicero, Livy, and Tacitus; e.g., *bellum . . . commissum ac profligatum conficere*, Liv. 21.40.11—cf. *OLD* 1477 *s.v.* profligo, 2, a) and which the Greek translator apparently understood in its literal meaning ("cast down") and mistranslated by προκαταβεβλημένα (of which προκατα- is preserved by only the *Mon. Apoll.*).

35. Duplex Dedication on an Obelisk, Rome. Probably early-Tiberian (A.D. 14–).

Brought to Rome from Egypt, with four blocks of the same red granite to serve as a base for it, by order of the emperor Caligula and set up *in Vaticano circo* (Pliny, *N.H.* 16.76.201, cf. 36.15.74 as emended by P. Künzle *ap.* F. Castagnoli, *RendPontAcc* 32 [1960] 99 f.); since 1586 standing in the center of Piazza San Pietro; height 25.36 m. (*P/A* 371 *s.v.* Obel. Vat.). The duplex inscr. is cut on opposite sides (east/west) of the shaft, low down, but because of the obelisk's tall base it remains more than 10 m. above ground (F. Magi, *Rend.* 50, *Capitolium*, 489, cited below). Conjecturally, the inscr. was cut in Egypt (where it would have been legible from the ground, the obelisk having no base then), but later (probably after the obelisk came to Rome, and by order of Caligula) the shaft was cut back on both sides to a depth of 1.5 cm. in order (presumably) to erase the inscr., but the erasure was never completed, perhaps because C.'s reign was too short; the space cut back measures, east side 0.80 × 2.33 m., west side 0.80 × 2.46 m. (Magi, *St. Rom.* 51). Letter heights: lines 1–2, ca. 11.6 cm., line 3, ca. 10.9 cm., as estimated from Magi, op. cit. pl. 8. (The figures 12.5 max., ca. 8 min., "unciae Romanae," quoted by Hübner, on his no. 78, from G. Zoega, *De origine et usu obeliscorum* [Rome 1797] 52, n. 1, col. 2, actually refer to *Augustus*'s two obelisks, elsewhere in Rome, *CIL* 6.701 f. = *ILS* 91.)

A dedication in honor of the deified Augustus and of Tiberius, on the part of someone unnamed but very likely a prefect of Egypt in the reign of Tiberius. On the obelisk, see *P/A* 370 f., or Nash 2.161 f., *s.v.* Obel. Vat. (bibl., but nothing on the inscr.); Erik Iversen, *Obelisks in Exile*, 1 (Copenhagen 1968) 19–46, plus 2 pp. of photos between pp. 16–17; Roullet 14, 43 f., 67–69 no. 68; the duplex inscr., *CIL* 6.882 (cf. 31191), *ILS* 115 (both editors identify the dedicator as Caligula, despite Mommsen's warning note quoted by Henzen in *CIL*, and show no erasures, these being invisible to Henzen from the ground). Iversen was the first to argue— convincingly, *pace* Volkmann—that the dedicator was not Caligula: *Journ. Egypt. Arch.* 51 (1965) 149–154, with figs. showing both erasures; H. Volkmann, *Gymnas.* 74 (1967) 501–508.

The picture is complicated by the fact

that under the duplex inscr. there are traces of an earlier inscr., also duplex, of which there remain only the holes—or rather the bottoms of the holes, because of the erasures—for attaching the letters (of bronze, no doubt); this was discovered, deciphered, and, in Dec. 1962, first reported by Filippo Magi, *RendPontAcc* ser. 3, vol. 35 (1963) 4 f., then publ. by him in *St. Rom.* 11 (1963) 50–56, plates 7–12 (whence *AE* 1964, 255, cf. 1968, 531), *Capitolium* 10 (Oct. 1963) 488–494, and *L'Osservatore Romano* (Vatican City) May 15, 1966, p. 5 (where he accepts Iversen's dating of the later duplex inscr.). The earlier duplex inscr. celebrates Cornelius Gallus's building a *Forum Iulium* (the later Forum Augusti at Alexandria? cf. P. M. Fraser, *Ptolemaic Alexandria* [Oxford 1972] 1.30, 2.96 f., n. 218) by order of *Imp. Caesar divi f(ilius)*, who must be Octavian, while Gallus was his aide-de-camp (*Praef(ectus) fabr(um)*); it must date shortly before Gallus became prefect of Egypt (**22**). For other photos of the earlier and the later inscr., superimposed one on the other, see Magi, *St. Rom.* plates 11–12, or (for the two on the east side) Iversen, *Obelisks*, top figure of plate following p. 16. (The earlier inscrs. are reconstructed by Magi from the holes for attaching the letters.)

Text of the later duplex inscription (from *CIL* 6.882 without regard to the erasures at the left side of the east inscr. and the right side of the west one): *Divo Caesari divi Iulii f(ilio) Augusto, / Ti(berio) Caesari divi Augusti f(ilio) Augusto, / sacrum.*

"To the deified Caesar Augustus, son of the deified Iulius, (and) to Tiberius Caesar Augustus, son of the deified Augustus, sacred."

The inscriptions are so high up that one cannot read them well without binoculars, quite apart from the erasures. All the long I's seem to be tall, as well as the T in *Ti(berio)* and in *Augusto*, but not in *Augusti*, where a tall I follows (*CIL* here has the T, but not the I, tall: cf. Magi, *St. Rom.* pls. 7–8, 11–12).

36. The *Tabula Hebana*, Florence, from Magliano. A.D. 19/20. A bronze tablet (perhaps the second of at least three, originally) found at Magliano (province of Grosseto), in the Tiber valley near the site of anc. Heba (in Etruria); damaged and in three pieces found separately (in 1947 and 1951), but now joined together in the Mus. Arch., Florence (inv. no. 90187), where it was studied in April 1973. Three of the borders are mostly extant. Writing surface: 83.3 × 58.1 cm., max.; thickness 4–6 mm.; letters ca. 6–8 mm. high. The letters are said to be incised, not cast: G. Tibiletti, in De Rugg. 4:24 (1957) 741, col. 2, 2nd par. (see above, Intro., n. 10).

Part of the text of a *rogatio* of A.D. 19 or 20, conferring honors on the dead Germanicus Caesar (d. Oct. 10, A.D. 19); not mentioned by Tacitus, *Ann.* 2.83. (For a brief summary, see E. S. Staveley, *OCD* 1032 *s.v.* Tab. Heb.) The date is no doubt shortly after G.'s death became known in Rome, not after Dec. 8, A.D. 19 (*Fasti Ostienses*: Degrassi, *FCT* 184 f., 216, cf. G. Tibiletti, op. cit. 740, col. 2).

First publ. by P. Raveggi, A. Minto, U. Coli, *NS* 72 (1947) 49–68 (main fragm., ed. Coli); Coli, *La Parola del Passato*, 21 (1951) 433–438 (the other two); *AE* 1949, 215; 1952, 164; the first complete text publ. by J. H. Oliver and R. E. A. Palmer, *AJP* 75 (1954) 225–248 (with photo, bibl., notes, but apparently not from autopsy of the bronze), whence Cal. Lim. 336–343 no. 113; E/J 76–79 no. 94a; *ARS* 158 (intro., Engl. transl., notes). Cf. G. Tibiletti, *Principe e magistrati repubbl. . . .* (Rome 1953) passim; idem, in De Rugg. vol. cit. 740–748 *s.v.* Lex, Rogatio Iunia Petronia . . . , with long bibl., to which add Syme, *Tac.* 2, pp. 756–760; Wingo 75 no. 8; Jean Béranger, *Principatus . . .* (Geneva 1973 Univ. de Lausanne, Publ. Fac. Lettres, 20) 209–242 (on *destinatio*); M. Pani, *Comitia e senato . . .* (Bari 1974) ch. 1 and app.; E. S. Staveley, *JRS* 65 (1975) 201; J. Gagé, op. cit. (above, on **34**) 212–215.

Corrected text of lines 1–5 (of 62),

based on collating the bronze itself with Oliver and Palmer's text (at least one other tablet precedes):

[. . . *senatui placuit uti* (as below, **46** ?) . . .] *utique in Palatio in porticu quae est ad Apollinis (templum), in eo templo in quo senatus haberi solet,* [*inter ima*]/*gines virorum inlustris ingeni, Germanici Caesaris et Drusi Germanici, patris eius naturali*[*s fratrisq(ue)*] / *Ti(beri) Caesaris Aug(usti), qui ipse quoq(ue) fecundi ingeni fuit, imagines ponantur supra capita columna*[*rum eius fas*]/*tigi quo simulacrum Apollinis tegitur;* (extra space) *utiq(ue) Sali⟨i⟩ carminibus suis nomen Germaniçi Caesạ*[*ris pro ho*]/[5]*norifica memoria inte⟨r⟩ponant, qui honos G(aio) quoq(ue) et L(ucio) Caesarib(us), fratr(ibus) Ti(beri) Caesaris Aug(usti), habitus est;* / . . . (plus 57 more lines)

". . . (it pleased the Senate (?) that) . . . and that on the Palatine in the portico that is by the Temple of Apollo, in the precinct in which the Senate is customarily convened, among the images of men of distinguished character those of Germanicus Caesar and Drusus Germanicus, his natural father [as distinguished from his uncle Tiberius, who had adopted him] and the brother of Tiberius Caesar Augustus, who himself [i.e., Drusus] was also of productive genius, be placed above the capitals of the columns of the pediment by which the image of Apollo is protected; and that the Salii place the name of Germanicus in their hymns in honorary memory, which honor was given also to Gaius and Lucius Caesar, brothers of Tiberius Caesar Augustus [all three had been adopted by the emperor Augustus, G. and L. in 17 B.C., Ti. in A.D. 4, so could be said to be brothers]; . . ."

The interpunctuation is haphazard. The consistent barring of the cardinal numerals (in the text beyond) is foreign to the practice in Rome and the vicinity except by error or when they served as numerical prefixes, as in *IIIviri* (*Contrib.* 166 *fin.*). Line 2, the bronze reads INIVSIRIS;

5, INT RP- (E never cut), HABIIVS (no crossbar to the T). Lines 5/6. No *utique ad X* should be restored at the end of 5, it being clearly at 6, *init.* Line 7. The reading is *appellentur*, not *adp-*. Line 9, read șeṇ[*at*]*u*. Lines 11/12. E/J's restoration [*rum quae / iudiciorum publ*] seems best suited to the spatial requirements / possibilities. Line 12. The eight-letter gap in the first phrase is mysterious, without any parallel that comes to mind, but cf. the strange failure to cut the E in *interponant* in line 5; Oliver and Palmer's suggested explanation and their seeing no need to supply a word here seem satisfactory. At the end, several restorations suggested are too long for the space, but could be reduced by abbreviations to ten or eleven, or even eight, letters; there are many abbreviations here, common in such "legalese."

Line 1, (*templum*). Cf. our "St. Paul's." The omission of *aedes* or *templum* in such phrases with *ad* is not uncommon (e.g., Cic. *Pro Quinct.* 4.17, *ad Castoris*), with *in*, *ante*, or *ab* less common (cf. K/S 1.232 Anm. 6, G/L 231 f., §362 Rem. 3). The phrase "of productive genius" is borrowed from *ARS*.

37. Epitaphs of a Charioteer and His Wife, Rome.

A.D. 25–. A marble *tabula ansata* (above, **32**), with 4 holes for attaching; found in Rome, on the Via Latina, before 1855, in a tomb; now in the Vatican, Gall. lap. (inv. no. 14938), embedded in the wall (seen in 1973). Writing field, within borders: 19 × 26.2 cm.; max. height of the "pediment," 5.5. cm.; letter heights 1.6–2.1 (line 1) down to 0.55–0.7 cm. (line 17).

The epitaph of Scirtus (perhaps a freedman of M. Livius ——, if he is the same as the Scirtus of *CIL* 6.2288, *a* [cf. 32457], 21414, cf. 32471, *a*), a charioteer of the Whites, and of Carisia Nesis, some woman's freedwoman and undoubtedly Scirtus's wife, with a list of all his races from

A.D. 13 to 25. *CIL* 6.10051, 1²: 1, p. 73, *ILS* 5283, *Album* 1.67 f., no. 60, with further bibl.

Transcript of lines 1–6, 16 f.: *Carisia Nesis Ɔ. (= Gaiae) l(iberta). / Scirtus, agitator faction(is) albae, / L. Munatio et G. Silio co(n)s(ulibus) quadr(igis) vic(it) I (= semel), sec(undas) I, ter(tias) I; / Sex. Pompeio, Sex. Appuleio cos., vic. I, sec. I, ter. II (= bis); /⁵ Druso Caesar(e), G. Norbano cos., vic. I, sec. II, ter. V (= quinquies); / Sisenna Statiil(io) (sic), L. Scribonio cos., vic. II, r(evocatus) I, s(ecundas) V, t(ertias) V; / . . . /¹⁶ sum(ma) sum(marum): quadr. vic. VII (= septies), revoc(atus) IIII (= quater), sec. XXXIX (= novies tricies), ter. / LX (= sexagies) et iustitiale I, seiuges II.*

"Carisia Nesis, a woman's freedwoman. Scirtus, charioteer of the Whites, in the consulship of L. Munatius and G. Silius, in a 4-horse chariot won once, took second place once, third once; . . . (6) won twice, (was) called back once [apparently, to repeat the race], took second five times, third five times; . . . (16) grand total: in a 4-horse chariot, he won 7 times, (was) called back 4 times, took second 39 times, third 60 times, and (raced) once in a contest held during a *iustitium* (?), twice (raced with) a 6-horse chariot."

Noteworthy: the fancy praenomina of two consuls, *Sisenna* (line 6) and *Cossus* (15) (besides the imperial *Drusus* and *Germanicus*), the nomen *Norbanus* (9), the misspelling—or rather miswriting—of Statilius's name (6), the accidental (?) cut before *Nesis* (1); the inconsistencies in naming the consuls, with or without *et*, and in abbreviating (e.g., *s.* or *sec.*). *Quadr(igā,* as *CIL* and Dessau have it) or *quadr(igis)*: either seems possible (cf. Gell. 19.8.3 f., who quotes Fronto as saying that Julius Caesar in his *De Analogia* preferred the plural). For the ordinal adverbs ("for the nth time") *iterum* vs. *secundo, tertium* vs. *tertio, quartum* vs. *quarto* (lines 8, 11), see above, on **20**; these numerals, which avoid the choice of ending, are all marked with a line above, as usual, at least through the second cent. A.D. (*Contrib.* 166, 168 f.). *Sec(undas), ter(tias):* sc. *partes tulit,* "took 2nd, 3rd place" (cf. Hor. *Sat.* 1.9.46, *posset qui ferre secundas,* "who could play second fiddle"; *CIL* 6.10050 [= *ILS* 5285] line 18: *secund(as) tulit CXXX*). Evidently only the first three places in the race counted. Lines 6, 7, 9, 13: the abbreviation R is largely explained by *revoc.* in 16.

Scirtus is evidently the Greek Σκίρτος, "Leaper." For *revocatus,* "called back (to repeat a race)," with apparently the same meaning as *remissus* in other charioteer-inscriptions, cf. F. Drexel in L. Friedlaender's *Darstellungen aus der Sittengeschichte Roms . . . ,* ed. 9–10 by G. Wissowa, vol. 4 (Leipzig 1921) 182 f., who compares Ovid, *Am.* 3.2.73 ff. The translation of *iustitiale* (17) comes from *OLD* 986 s.v., where it is added, "prob(ably) one (contest) marking the funeral of one of the imperial household"; if this is true, the funeral here might well be that of Augustus, in August, A.D. 14. The grand-total figures are correct; in 106 races in 13 years Scirtus took 7 firsts, 39 seconds, 60 thirds, and was called back to repeat the race four times. On the general subject of chariot racing, see Friedlaender, op. cit. 2¹⁰ (1922) 21–50, vol. 4, 179–196 (Drexel); J. P. V. D. Balsdon, *Life and Leisure in Ancient Rome* (London, etc., 1969) 314–324; Alan Cameron, *Circus Factions . . .* (Oxford 1976) passim, esp. 202 n. 4: S.'s 7 first prizes are called "a wretched total."

38. Dedication (?) of a *Tiberieum* by Pontius Pilate, Jerusalem, from Caesarea. A.D. 26/36. A block of local limestone, excavated in 1961 in the Roman theater at Caesarea, capital of Roman Judaea; now in the Israel Mus., Jerusalem (inv. no. 61–529), where it was seen in May 1973. Found no longer *in situ,* it must originally have had some connection with the *Tiberieum* named in line 1 of the inscription, perhaps set in a wall, but later got separated and reused as a stepping-stone in the theater; hence presumably the damage to the left side and line 4 of the inscription.

Dimensions: 81.5 max. × 67.7 max. (original width, Frova *ap.* Degrassi) × 19–20 cm. Letter heights: line 1, ca. 6 cm., 2, ca. 5.5 cm., 3, ca. 5 cm.

A statement to the effect that Pontius Pilate, while prefect of Judaea, dedicated (?) a *Tiberieum.* The date is within his governorship, 26–36 (PIR[1] 3.84 no. 607). The inscription is unique in being thus far the only contemporary reference to Pilate (the governor under whom the execution of Jesus Christ took place) and in containing the hapax legomenon *Tiberieum;* because of the damage to line 2, it still leaves P.'s praenomen unknown, but proves Tacitus wrong ("probably proleptic," in anticipation of the Claudian title) in calling him a procurator (*Ann.* 15.44); the Greek sources are inconsistent or nontechnical, cf. A. N. Sherwin-White, *PBSR* 15 (1939) 12 n. 7, with ref. to Hirschfeld; both had favored P. as a *praefectus* despite Tacitus; cf. also A. H. M. Jones, *Studies in Roman Government and Law* (Oxford 1960) 117, 119, 125 (he seems not to know this inscr.). (Similarly, in a later mistake, Amm. Marc. 17.4.5 calls Cornelius Gallus, **22,** *procurator* of Egypt.)

First publ. by A. Frova, *RendIstLomb* 95 (Milan 1961) 419–434, hence *AE* 1971, 477 (cf. 1963, 104; 1964, 39); cf. J. Vardaman, *Journ. Bibl. Lit.* 81 (1962) 70 f., B. Lifshitz, *Latomus* 22 (1963) 783; A. Degrassi, *RendLinc* 8: 19 (1964) 59–65 (= *Scritti vari,* 3.269–275); *idem, Athenaeum,* n.s. 42 (1964) 302 (= op. cit. 3.280) n. 15; C. Brusa Gerra, in *Scavi di Caesarea Maritima* (Rome 1966) 217–220; H. Volkmann, *Gymnas.* 75 (1960) 124–135; A. Frova, *Ist. Studi Romani,* Sez. Lombarda, Rome (Pavia 1970) 216–227 (p. 227, line 2: correct "se non" to "che non"); E. Weber, *Bonn. Jahrb.* 171 (1971) 194–200.

Text: [ca. 7–9 letters?]s *Tiberieum* / [1 or 2 letters? Po]*ntius Pilatus,* / [*Praef]ectus Iuda[ea]e,* / [*dedicávit* (?)] (only the apex remains).

"[On the Kalends of July (?)] a *Tiberieum* [Lucius? Marcus? Gaius?] Pontius Pilate, Prefect of Judaea, [dedicated (?)]."

Line 1. A maximum of ca. 22 cm. is estimated left of S, space for 7–9 letters including one or two protruding left of lines 2–3, as seems likely; of the various restorations suggested, only Weber's [*Kal(endis) Iulii]*s (the first day of Tiberius's first *trib. pot.*) fits the conjectured space and makes good sense. Note the apex over long E. Line 2. Tall I and T in *Pilatus.* Lines 2–3. Ca. 16 cm. is estimated for P.'s praenomen (e.g., *M.* easily, but hardly *Sex.*) plus *Po-,* and *Praef-,* resp.

The *Tiberieum* was evidently some structure, presumably of religious bearing, such as a temple (cf. Αὐγουστεῖον, Καισαρεῖον, Σεβαστεῖον), built in Tiberius's honor and perhaps near the theater; or, alternatively, a nonreligious site set aside in his honor. The scholars named above have various views.

39. Epitaph of Agrippina the Elder, Rome. A.D. 37 (soon after Mar. 18, when Caligula became emperor). Undoubtedly from the Mausoleum of Augustus, Rome, where her ashes were brought by Caligula from the island of Pandateria (mod. Ventotene, Tyrrhenian Sea, ca. 34 km. west of Ischia), where she had persisted in starving to death (apparently in 33: Dio 58.22.4–5) while in exile (Suet. *Tib.* 53.2, *Calig.* 15.1, Dio 59.3.5); on the Capitoline for several centuries; now in the Passaggio del Muro Romano (Mus. Nuovo) of the Pal. dei Conservatori (inv. no. 6968). A large marble block, with a cavity in the top obviously intended to hold an urn, but enlarged in the Middle Ages to serve as a grain measure. Dimensions: m. 1.14 × 0.89 × 0.89 (from Meinhardt); letter heights: from 8.8–9.0 (line 1) down to

5.1–5.3 (line 6) cm.; tall I's, line 3, 6.6 cm.

The epitaph of Agrippina the Elder (daughter of Agrippa and Augustus's daughter Julia), wife of Germanicus, mother of Caligula, and grandmother of Nero.

CIL 6.886 (cf. 31192 and p. 3777 no. 886), ILS 180, Album 1.83 f., no. 79, E. Meinhardt in H/S 2.1678 (all with bibl.); cf. Roma e dintorni 113, P/A 334 or Nash 2.43 s.v. Mausol. Aug.

Text: Ossa / Agrippinae, M(arci) Agrippaẹ [f(iliae)?], / divi Aug(usti) neptis, uxoris / Germanici Caesaris, /⁵ matris G(ai) Caesaris Aug(usti) / Germanici principis. (Line 2, fin. It is questionable whether f(iliae) was ever cut; for the arguments, see Album 1.84, col. 1, 2.5 f., on no. 79.)

"The bones (or ashes: Suetonius, Calig. 15.1, calls them cineres; Dio, 59.3.5, ὀστᾶ, "bones") of Agrippina, (daughter) of Marcus Agrippa, granddaughter of the deified Augustus, wife of Germanicus Caesar, mother of Gaius Caesar Augustus Germanicus, emperor." Note the chiastic order: "of Agrippa (daughter), of Aug. granddaughter," but then "wife of Germanicus, mother of Gaius," as in the title of Queen Elizabeth II (above, Intro., n. 91).

40. Dedication to the Emperor Claudius, Verona. A.D. 44/45. Part of the marble architrave of a building, presumably honorary, found in 1851 at Verona, near the Roman theater; apparently not from the theater itself, originally, but from some nearby structure (Mommsen, in CIL); now in the Museo Maffeiano, Verona (Catalogo Cipolla, no. 737). Record of an official dedication to Claudius, jointly with at least two others (Dessau conjectures C.'s wife and son, or some of his ancestors), remains of whose names (and of their dedication) appear to the left and right, on the part of the town councillors of Verona. Dimensions: 0.54 × 1.51 × 0.50 m. (from the director of the museum).

CIL 5.3326, whence ILS 204.

Text: Ti(berio) Claudio Drusi f(ilio) / Caesari Aug(usto) Germanico, / pontif(ici) max(imo), trib(unicia) potest(ate) / IIII, co(n)s(uli) III, (cos.) designato IIII, /⁵ imp(eratori), publice d(ecreto) d(ecurionum).

"To Tiberius Claudius Caesar Augustus Germanicus, son of Drusus [the Elder, Livia's second son, born in 38 B.C., about the time of her marriage to Octavian], pontifex maximus, with tribunician power for the 4th time [Jan. 25, A.D. 44–45], consul for the 3rd time [43], (consul) designate for the 4th [not until 47], acclaimed Imperator: officially, by decree of the town councillors."

Line 4: for the solution of the three numerical adverbs (e.g., quartum? quarto?) see above, on 20. Line 5: Imp., presumably no. VIII; perhaps the Veronese were uncertain what no. it should be; he had received nos. IV–VII in 43, and received no. VIII sometime in 43–45, cf. PIR² 2.228; the second abbreviation shows that it is not always certain what a particular abbr. in a Latin inscr. means; sometimes the original local readers must have wondered. Three circumstances here support Mommsen's solution, as above: Verona's having decurions, as one would expect (on these, cf. A. N. Sherwin-White, OCD 318 s.v. decuriones), the fact that Dessau's six examples of d d = dedicatum (ILS 3: 2, 763 col. 2) are followed in the text by a date, and the interpunct between the D's (though this is not proof—cf. Contrib. 184, init.).

Claudius had inherited the honorary cognomen "Germanicus" from his father, to whom it had been decreed posthumously ("for himself and his descendants," Suet. Claud. 1.3, and others—see above, 27) by the Senate by virtue of his military services and his death in Germany, 9 B.C. (For Claudius's family-relations, see the Stemma Iuliorum Claudiorum at the end of PIR² 4; for his own life, vol. 2.225–229, no. 942; his father's, 194–199, no. 857.) Claudius's name here lacks Imp(erator) as its first element, in accordance with his own preference: *prae-nomine Imperatoris abstinuit* (Suet. *Claud.* 12.1), though it is found "in some Greek inscrs. and coins" (*PIR²* 2.227 f.), no doubt through ignorance. The additive form of the numeral 4 (i.e., IIII) seems to have been used more often than the subtractive form (IV) (*Contrib.* 176–181, and above, pp. 46, 48).

41. Ex-voto Dedication to the Emperor Claudius and His Family, Rome. A.D. 47/48. Corniced front of a long, narrow, thick piece of marble (m. 1.26 × 0.28 × 0.27: R. Lanciani, *Bull. Com.* 1872/73, 93, *d*), reported by ca. 1550 as being in Rome, apparently in the ruins of the Forum of Augustus; seen in 1949 and 1973 in the garden of the Mus. Nuovo of the Pal. dei Conservatori, Rome, in whose possession it was reported by 1872; inv. no. 6944. A record of an ex-voto dedication of some object, made of 16 lb. of gold, to Claudius, his wife Messallina, and their children, by G. Iulius Postumus, prefect of Egypt. Stein, 30, calls the object dedicated a golden statuette, probably correctly; the marble's size and shape suggest that the object was given special prominence by being placed alone in a large niche. (In our photo the capital resting on the inscribed marble is extraneous.) The date is determined by C.'s *trib. pot.* number (no. 7 was from Jan. 25, 47, to Jan. 24, 48), with which the *cos.* and *imp.* nos. agree (seen most easily in Cagnat, 185; cf. Cal. Lim. 480, in substantial agreement).

CIL 6.918, cf. 31202; *ILS* 210, *Album* 1.94 f., no. 94. For Iul. Postumus, see Stein 30, *PIR²* 4.253 no. 483, G. Bastianini, "Lista dei prefetti d'Egitto . . . ," *ZPE* 17 (1975) 272.

Text: *Pro salute / Ti(beri) Claudi Caesaris Aug(usti) Germanici, pont(ificis) max(imi), trib(unicia) pot(estate)* $\overline{VII}$, *co(n)s(ulis)* $\overline{IIII}$, / *imp(eratoris)* $\overline{XV}$, *p(atris) p(atriae), censoris, et Valeriae Messallinae Aug(ustae)* [these 4 words erased] *liberorumque eorum* [this

word erased], / *ex voto suscepto: G(aius) Iulius Sex(ti) f(ilius) (tribu) Cor(nelia) Postumus, praef(ectus) Aegypti /⁵ Ti. Claudi Caesaris Aug. Germanici, ex auri p(ondo) XVI.*

"To the good health of" the emperor Claudius, "*pontifex maximus*, with tribunician power for the 7th time, consul for the 4th, (acclaimed) *Imperator* for the 15th, Father of His Country, censor, and of Valeria Messallina Augusta and their children: in accordance with a vow undertaken, Gaius Iulius Postumus, son of Sextus, of the Cornelia 'tribe'," the emperor Claudius's "prefect of Egypt (has dedicated a statuette [?]) of 16 lb. of gold."

The name of Messallina (second cousin of C., married to him at age fourteen, and by him the mother of Octavia and Britannicus) must have been erased after she was put to death in 48 (Tac. *Ann.* 11. 26–38; cf. J. P. B., *OCD* 675 *s.v.* Messal(l)ina (1)). The erasure at the end of line 4 is strange; perhaps *Ti.* was first cut, then erased in order to have it begin a new line. The addition of Claudius's name to the title "Prefect of Egypt," together with the 16 lb. of gold given *ex voto*, makes one wonder at the story behind it. Momigliano, 117 n. 70, places the inscr. among "the large number of inscriptions of gratitude to Claudius."

The character Ⅎ in *Aegypti* obviously represents Greek upsilon (probably short). It is one of three new letters added to the Latin alphabet by Claudius himself, "as greatly needed" (Suet.), which, however, fell out of use after his reign (Tac.). This particular character is found in Latin inscriptions only in words of Greek origin; it always represents Greek *ŭ*, but since Y was already in use for this purpose, its exact function is uncertain; perhaps, as R. P. Oliver thought probable, it was intended to represent a sound between *ē* and *ī*. For its form and for the other two Claudian characters, only one of which has thus far been found in Latin inscriptions (see **43**), see Quint. 1.7.26, cf.

1.4.8, Tac. *Ann.* 11.13 f., Suet. *Claud.* 41.3, and R. P. Oliver, "The Claudian Letter Ⱶ," *AJA* 53 (1949) 248–257.

42. Part of a Speech of the Emperor Claudius, Lyon, from nearby. Probably A.D. 48 (or 54?). A large, beautiful bronze tablet (m. 1.36–37 × 1.91 at center × 0.008–0.014 or 15; its weight more than 200 kg. [440 lb.], Fabia, 1929, p. 9), already, when found in 1528, broken into two pieces, each one apparently intact at the bottom but broken off at the top; the text is therefore incomplete at the beginning and in the middle, but the missing parts seem not extensive. Seen in May 1975 as one of ca. 300 Latin inscrs. in the new Musée de la Civilisation Gallo-Romaine, Lyon. Letter heights: 1.8–2.0 cm. (Fabia, 1929, p. 56, still saw traces of the letters' being gilded.) No signs of guidelines, though the lines of writing are straight; the apices sometimes badly placed, the interpuncts irregular, often placed within the preceding letter. The inscription seemed to J. S. Gordon to be incised. (see Intro., n. 10.)

The date *post quem* is the date of Claudius's speech in the Senate at Rome in 48, as is known from Tac. *Ann.* 11.23 f.; a date soon after the speech, despite the absence of all three Claudian letters (**41**), seems more plausible than one after C.'s death in 54; the Claudian letters may be absent because (as Fabia, loc. cit., plausibly argues) the tablet was prepared and inscribed in Gaul, not in Rome. The document was presumably copied from the *Acta Senatus* in Rome (cf. J. P. B., *OCD* 7 s.v. Acta, with ref. to Tac. *Ann.* 5.4, *init.*) and displayed near Lugdunum, as the capital of Gallia Lugdunensis, at the Ara Romae et Augusti, near which the pieces were found. It is unique in being a verbatim report of a speech made by Claudius and later reshaped by Tacitus.

CIL 13.1668, *ILS* 212, Bruns 195–198 no. 52, *FIRA* 1.43, Smallwood, *Gaius/Nero* 369. See K. Wellesley, "Can You Trust Tacitus?" [his answer, in brief, No!] *Greece & Rome* 1954, 13–35, with chief bibl. to 1949; Syme, *Tac.* 1.317–321, 2.703–708; Momigliano 10–19 (with Engl. transl. of col. 1). Other translations: Ph. Fabia, *La Table Claudienne de Lyon* (Lyon 1929—the basic modern ed., to which add his suppl. art. in *REA* 33 [1931] 117–138, 225–260) 63, 65; E. G. Hardy, *Three Spanish Charters* . . . (Oxford 1912) 147–154; L/R 2.133 f.; *ARS* 175.

Text of col. 1, lines 2–7: . . . / *Equidem primam omnium illam cogitationem hominum, quam / maxime primam occursuram mihi provideo, deprecor, ne / quasi novam istam rem introduci exhorrescatis, sed illa /⁵ potius cogitetis, quam multa in hac civitate novata sint et / quidem statim ab origine urbis nostrae in quod* [sic, for *quot*] *formas / statusque res p(ublica) nostra diducta sit. /* . . . Col. 2, lines 20–22: *Tempus est iam, Ti(beri) Caesar Germanice, detegere te patribus conscriptis, / quo tendat oratio tua; iam enim ad extremos fines Galliae Nar/bonensis venisti.*

"As for me, that first thought on everyone's part which I foresee will meet me the very first, I deprecate, lest you shudder at the introduction of that matter as if new, but (I beg you) rather reflect how many new things have been introduced in this state, and indeed, from the very beginning of our city, how many forms and phases our community has been brought into. . . . It's high time, Tiberius Caesar Germanicus, to reveal yourself to the members of the Senate—what the point of your speech is; for you've already reached the farthest limits of Narbonese Gaul."

The syntax and style are strikingly conversational, as though it were not a prepared speech but spoken *ex tempore*; e.g., line 2, *illam cogitationem* is not explained as a "thought" (with following indirect statement or question), but is replaced by a *ne*-clause, which seems to be a second object of *deprecor*, then by (*ut*) *cogitetis*, which seems to be the object of the *precor* in *deprecor*. But the most striking such feature is the aside addressed to C. himself in lines 60–62 (col. 2, 20–22), translated above, which the editor responsible for the copy has allowed to stand. (For note-takers and stenographers, cf. *OCD* 1033 f., *s.v.* Tachygraphy.)

43. Pomerium Boundary-Stone, Rome.

A.D. 49. Travertine cippus (m. 1.90 × 0.70 × 0.47, if this is the cippus of *NS* 1913, 68, as seems certain from the no. CXXXIX cut on the side); seen in 1948 and 1973 in the garden of the Mus. Naz. Rom., Rome (inv. no. 61132). Found in 1913 in Rome, *in situ* near the Via Flaminia. One of at least eight or nine examples thus far discovered of the emperor Claudius's pomerium boundary-stones, set up by him by virtue of his censorship in 47–48. Letter heights: from 7–8 cm., line 1, gradually decreasing to 3.3–5.0 cm. Line 9 has two examples of the second of the Claudian letters found in inscrs. of his reign: a reversed, upside-down F (Ⅎ), to indicate the sound of consonantal V (English W), and obviously based on the Greek vau or digamma (F) but differentiated so as not to be confused with Latin F (see Quint. 1.7.26., cf. 1.4.8, and **41**).

Album 1.95 f., no. 96, with bibl.

Text: *Ti(berius) Claudius / Drusi f(ilius) Caisar* [sic] / *Aug(ustus) Germanicus, / pont(ifex) max(imus), trib(unicia) pot(estate) / V̅I̅I̅I̅I̅, imp(erator) XVI, co(n)s(ul) I̅I̅I̅I̅, / censor, p(ater) p(atriae), auctis populi Romani / finibus pomerium / ampliaⅎit terminaⅎitq(ue).* On top is inscribed *pomerium*, on the left side *CXXXIX*.

"Tiberius Claudius Caesar Augustus Germanicus, son of Drusus, *pontifex maximus*, with tribunician power for the 9th time, (acclaimed) *Imperator* for the 16th time, consul for the 4th, censor, Father of His Country, having extended the boundaries of the Roman people [by the conquest of Britain, A.D. 43–48], enlarged the pomerium and marked it with boundary stones."

The spelling of *Caisar* in inscriptions of the Empire appears most often in official inscrs. of the age of Claudius (to judge from Dessau *ILS* 3: 2, 808, "AI *pro* AE *in ipsis vocabulis*"); in *CIL* 6.921 (= *ILS* 222, *Album* 1.101 f., no. 103) of A.D. 51/52, consisting of 5 inscrs. of Claudius's family thought to have accompanied portrait statues adorning the monumental arch built in Rome by Claudius to commemorate his victories in Britain (Nash 1.102 f., *s.v.* Arcus Claudii), all 13 examples of *ae* are written *ai*, not only in *Caesar* but elsewhere. Rather than an archaizing feature, as has been thought, it seems a practical measure, initiated most likely by Claudius himself, to preserve the proper sound of the diphthong at a time of confusion in sound between *ae* and open *ĕ* (Sturtevant 129 §134). There are horizontal bars over *V̅I̅I̅I̅I̅* and *I̅I̅I̅I̅*, but apparently not over *XVI* (but in travertine this could easily become illegible) to mark them as ordinal adverbs ("for the nth time"), which, at least from Augustus to Nerva, seem to be barred much oftener than not (*Contrib.* 166–169).

For the pomerium, see *P/A* 392–396 *s.v.* Claudius was censor in 47–48, but "censor" appears in his titles thereafter. The date 49 for this inscr. is fixed by Tacitus, *Ann.* 12.23 (cf. 12.5 and 22, both *init.*, reff. to consuls), and by the *trib. pot.* number, the most reliable of all the items in imperial titles, since it increased by one every year (no. 9 ran from Jan. 25, 49, to Jan. 24, 50).

44. The Porta Maggiore Aqueducts, Rome.

A.D. 52. The earliest (and highest) of three inscriptions cut in travertine in duplicate (i.e., one inside the gate, the other outside) in the attic of the double arch carrying the Aqua Claudia and the Aqua Anio Nova over the Via Labicana and the Via Praenestina, where they leave Rome together (Porta Praenestina, now Porta Maggiore). (The two later inscrs. belong to Vespasian and Titus, resp.) Commemoration of the emperor Claudius's having brought into Rome the two waters mentioned, "at his own expense" (though Frontinus, *De Aquis*, 1.13, Pliny *N.H.* 36.122, and Suetonius, *Claud.* 20.1, credit Caligula with having begun the work, Front. indicating A.D. 38). The date is given by Frontinus, loc. cit., by naming the consuls of 52, a little less closely by Claudius's *trib. pot.* number, XII (Jan. 25, 52–Jan. 24, 53).

CIL 6.1256 (cf. pp. 3129, 3798), *ILS* 218 (first inscr.), Smallwood *Gaius/Nero* 309. Cf. Nash 1.37, 39, esp. 39, *s.vv.* Aqua Claudia, A. Iulia, A. Marcia (with bibl., to which add E. Albertini, "L'inscription de Claude sur la Porte Majeure et deux passages de Frontin," *MélRome* 26 [1906] 305–318, and P/A 22 f., 412 f., *s.vv.* Aqua Claudia, Porta Praenestina).

Text of the duplex inscription: *Ti(berius) Claudius Drusi f(ilius) Caisar* [sic] *Augustus Germanicus, pontif(ex) maxim(us), / tribunicia potestate* $\overline{XII}$, *co(n)s(ul)* $\overline{V}$, *imperator* $\overline{XXVII}$, *pater patriae, / aquas Claudiam ex fontibus, qui vocabantur Caeruleus et Curtius, a milliario XXXXV, item Anienem Novam, a milliario LXII* [corrected from *LIX*?], *sua impensa, in urbem perducendas curavit.*

"(The emperor Claudius) had the Claudian Water brought into the City from its springs, which were called 'Sky-Blue' and 'Curtian,' at the 45th milestone [from Rome], at his own expense, likewise the New Anio Water, from the 62nd [originally 59th?] milestone."

Both inscriptions are a little damaged, but each supplements the other. Note *Caisar*, with *ai*, but *patriae*, with *ae*, as though the imperial name were more important than the title (above, on **43**). The adverbial numerals in the title are barred, as regularly, but not the following ordinal adjectives, in respect to which the use of the bar is less clear-cut (*Contrib.* 166 f.). In order to explain the discrepancy between *mill. LXII* (line 4) and Frontinus's "58,700 paces" (1.15) Albertini, 305–307, 311–318, argues plausibly, against the note in

CIL 6: 1, p. 272, that the original figure in line 4 was LVIII or, more probably, LIX, and that this was changed to LXII by Trajan after the publication of the *De Aquis* of Frontinus (appointed *Curator Aquarum*, "Water Commissioner," by Nerva in 97) so as to conform to the increase in mileage caused by Trajan's moving the source of the Anio Novus (masc. in Front., to agree with *Anio*) a few miles *above* Subiaco, the correction being made (Albertini suggests) by replacing the proper travertine-block on each face of the gate with one bearing the correct number LXII, there being no room available to add the inscr. formulated by Frontinus, 2.93, *fin.*: . . . *novum auctorem imperatorem Caesarem Nervam Traianum Augustum praescribente titulo* ("and the inscr. will proclaim" Trajan "as its new founder" [C. E. Bennett, Loeb ed./transl. 423]). Ashby, op. cit. (above, on **29**), 253, accepts Albertini's argument.

45. Epitaph of Quintus Veranius and His Child, Rome, from nearby. A.D. 58/59. A large but incomplete marble tablet (m. 1.825 max. × 1.02 max. × 0.15), found in 1926 at Pratolungo, off the Via Tiburtina, ca. 10 km. from Rome; now in two pieces, joined together and attached to a wall on the south side of the garden of the Mus. Naz. Rom., Rome (inv. no. 108746); seen in 1948 and 1973. The date must be soon after Veranius's death; he had succeeded A. Didius Gallus as governor of Britain, the evidence shows in 58, but he died *intra annum* (Tac. *Agr.* 14.2), so in 58 or perhaps 59. (R. M. Ogilvie and Ian Richmond, in their 1967 Oxford ed. of the *Agr.*, p. 192, and E. Birley, *Roman Britain* . . . [Kendal 1953, repr. 1961] 8, date V.'s appointment in 57, without explanation or ref. to D. Atkinson, *JRS* 12 [1922, publ. 1924] 62; A. R. Birley, "The Roman Governors of Britain," *Epigraphische Studien*, 4 [*Beihefte der Bonn. Jahrb.* 25 (Köln/Graz 1967)] 65, dates his incumbency "57/58–58/59.") Letter heights: from cm. 6.9–7.5, tall I's 7.9–8.2 (last line), down to 3.2–3.7 (lines 8, 10).

Epitaph of Q. Veranius, cos. A.D. 49, and of a child (daughter?); undoubtedly from the family tomb. (For a decree of Veranius found recently at Myra, in anc. Lycia, see Joyce Reynolds, *JRS* 66 [1976] 185, with ref. to M. Wörrle, *ap.* J. Borchardt, *Myra . . .* [Berlin 1975] 254.)

Album 1.105 f., no. 109 (with bibl., esp. J. H. Oliver's critical rev., *AJP* 75 [1954] 206–210, of its first publ; Gordon, *Veranius*, 1952); *AE* 1953, 251, cf. 1954, 4; Smallwood, *Gaius/Nero* 231 (c); H. Zosel in H/S 3.101–104 no. 2180 (with German transl.). Cf. Anthony R. Birley, *The Fasti of Roman Britain* (Oxford 1981) 50–54.

Text: (several lines missing) / (ca. 41 letters) *quinq[ue]nnio pr[a]ęfui[t], / [(ca. 36–37) in pot]est[a]tem Ti(berii) Claudii Caesaris Aug(usti) / [Germanici (ca. 26–27) Tr]ącheotarum expugnatum delevit / [(ca. 40–41) Ti.] Claudii Caesaris Augusti Germanici, /⁵ [(35–36) dir]utionem moenium remissam et interceptam / [ca. 41]b̨[1 or 2] pacavit, propter quae auctore / [Ti(berio) Claudio Caesare Augusto Germanico (?)] consul designatus, in consulatu nominatione / [(ca. 32)]ni augur creatus, in numerum patriciorum adlectus est; / [iussu (?) Ti. Claudii Caesaris Aug. Germ(?)]anici aedium sacrarum et operum locorumque /¹⁰ [publicorum curam ei dedit (?) equester o]rdo et populus Romanus consentiente senatu; ludis / [(?) praefectus est, in quibus ipse praemium (?) p]etierit, ab Augusto principe, cuius liberalitatis erat minister; / [praepositus est (?)tempore motus bell]ici provinciae Britanniae, in qua decessit. / [Verania, filia (?) Q(uinti) Ve]rani vixit annis VI et mensibus X.*

(Lines 6 *med.*–13) ". . . Wherefore, at the suggestion [of the emp. Claudius], (he was) selected as consul; in the course of his consulship, having been named as an augur on the nomination of —— nus (or -nius), he was elected to the class of patricians; [at the behest of the emp. Claudius] the equestrian order and the

Roman people, with the approval of the senate, gave him the management of Sacred Buildings and [Public] Works and Areas; by the presently ruling emperor (Nero), of whose generosity he was the dispenser, [he was placed in charge of] games, [in which (the emperor) himself] sought [a prize; at the time of an uprising (?), he was appointed governor] of the province of Britain, where he died. [Verania, daughter (?) of Quintus Ve]ranius, lived 6 years and 10 months."

For a clearer picture of the text and the 1952 reconstruction, see *Veranius* 234, 270, where much more restoration, highly tentative, is attempted. In the five prepositional phrases in the extant text, there is no interpunctuation and no spacing between prep. and object (cf. *Veranius* 233, *Contrib.* 184). Lines 1–6, however fragmentary, confirm other evidence that V. was a provincial governor (now seen to be for 5 years) before going to Britain to his last post, and show that he was involved in military operations. (See *Veranius* 240 f., 246–253, 272.) Lines 1, 13. Three ablatives of Duration of Time: perfectly proper and, in the inscriptions at least, quite as common as the accus., if not more so. Lines 11 f. The restoration and translation are due to J. H. Oliver (by letter of Oct. 30, 1978), who explains "the perf. subj. *petierit* as part of a clause of characteristic and thinks that no specific ref. occurred to the games as those of A.D. 51 (so K. R. Bradley, *GRBS* 16 [1975] 308) or as the ludi maximi (so Gordon originally [*Veranius* 262–264]), because V. was probably dead by the latter occasion and Nero was not yet entering competitions on the former and because there is really no space or need to identify or date the occasion." Oliver "still thinks that line 12 contained a ref. to the appointment of V. as governor of Britain in a serious situation, but that the exact wording of the difficulty, e.g. 'at the first sign of war' or 'at the time of an uprising,' eludes us. Leaning rather to the latter phrase, he now hesitantly restores" as shown above.

Proof of Veranius's identity lies in the -*rani* of line 13 and in the fragmentary details of his career as given in the lines above (cf. *Veranius* 231, 1st par.); for the reasons for preferring a daughter in line 13, op. cit. 266–269.

46. Fragment of the "Lex de Imperio Vespasiani," Rome. A.D. 69/70. A large, handsome bronze tablet, which from the floor looks like black marble (m. 1.64 × 1.13 × ca. 0.043); found (where?) and set up in 1344 by Cola di Rienzo in the Basilica of St. John Lateran, Rome, moved in 1576 to the Capitoline, later to the Capit. Mus., where it is attached to the east wall of the Sala del Fauno (Hawthorne's "Marble Faun") (inv. no. 7180); seen in 1948–49 and 1973. To J. S. Gordon the letters seemed cut, not cast (*contra*, G. Tibiletti: cf. Intro., n. 10); tallest letters, in *Sanctio* (line 33), ca. 6.0–6.2 cm., those in the last lines 1.9–2.0 cm.; E, F, T go higher, Q lower.

The end—probably the second of two tablets—of an inscription (the rest is lost; it is a question whether Cola di R. ever saw more: cf. Barbieri 757 f.) recording an enactment conferring imperial powers on Vespasian early in his reign (Dec. 69/Jan. 70); he is named in lines 25, 28, 30; the document is first called a *lex rogata* (29), then simply a *lex* (34, 36), but except for the *Sanctio* with its future imperatives (as in a *lex*), it is in the form of a *senatus consultum* (Mommsen, *Röm. Staatsr.* 2: 2³ [1887] 878). It is the only extant example "of the single legislative act by which the Princeps was constitutionally invested with the various powers which made up the Principate" (Rushforth 83 f.).

CIL 6.930 (cf. 31207 and p. 3777), *ILS* 244 (add.), Bruns 202 f., no. 56, S/C 280–282, Rushforth 82–87 no. 70 (add. p. xxvi, fin.), *FIRA* 1.154–156 no. 15, McCrum/

Woodhead 1 (text only). Cf. Grad. 18 (good photo), H. Last, *CAH* 11.404–406, Gordon, *Seven Latin Inscrs.* 80–82, pl. II, G. Barbieri in De Rugg. 4: 24 (1957) 750–758 *s.v.* Lex de imp. Vesp. (mod. views, bibl.), E. Meinhardt in H/S 2.1413, H. H. Scullard *OCD* 602 *s.v.* Lex, P. A. Brunt, *JRS* 67 (1977) 95–116; transl., with intro. and notes, by L/R 2.89 f., and in *ARS* 183.

Text: (preceding tablet, probably no. 1: . . . *senatui placuit* [Mommsen, loc. cit., n. 2] [?] *uti . . . de ea re ita censent uti . . .) foedusve cum quibus volet facere liceat, ita uti licuit divo Aug(usto),* / *Ti(berio) Iulio Caesari Aug(usto), Tiberioque Claudio Caesari Aug(usto) Germanico;* /

utique ei senatum habere, relationem facere, remittere, senatus / *consulta per relationem discessionemque facere liceat,* /⁵ *ita uti licuit divo Aug., Ti. Iulio Caesari Aug., Ti. Claudio Caesari* / *Augusto Germanico;* /

utique, cum ex voluntate auctoritateve, iussu mandatuve eius, / *praesenteve eo senatus habebitur, omnium rerum ius perinde* / *habeatur, servetur, ac si e lege senatus edictus esset habereturque;* /

¹⁰*utique quos magistratum, potestatem, imperium curationemve* / *cuius rei petentes senatui populoque Romano commendaverit,* / *quibusve suffragationem suam dederit, promiserit, eorum* / *comit⟨i⟩is quibusque extra ordinem ratio habeatur;* /

utique ei fines pomerii proferre, promovere, cum ex republica /¹⁵ *censebit esse, liceat, ita uti licuit Ti. Claudio Caesari Aug.* / *Germanico;* /

utique quaecunque ex usu reipublicae, maiestate divinarum, / *hum⟨an⟩arum, publicarum privatarumque rerum esse {e}* / *censebit, ei agere facere ius potestasque sit, ita uti divo Aug.,* /²⁰ *Tiberioque Iulio Caesari Aug., Tiberioque Claudio Caesari* / *Aug. Germanico fuit;* /

utique quibus legibus plebeive scitis scriptum fuit ne divus Aug(ustus) / *Tiberiusve Iulius Caesar Aug., Tiberiusque Claudius Caesar Aug.* / *Germanicus tenerentur, iis legibus plebisque scitis imp(erator) Caesar* /²⁵ *Vespasianus solutus sit, quaeque ex quaque lege, rogatione / divum Aug. Tiberiumve Iulium Caesarem Aug., Tiberiumve / Claudium Caesarem Aug. Germanicum facere oportuit / ea omnia imp(eratori) Caesari Vespasiano Aug. facere liceat; /*

utique quae ante hanc legem rogatam acta, gesta, /³⁰ decreta, imperata ab imperatore Caesare Vespasiano Aug., / iussu mandatuve eius a quoque sunt, ea perinde iusta rataq(ue) / sint ac si populi plebisve iussu acta essent. /

Sanctio

Si quis ⟨quid⟩ huiusce legis ergo adversus leges, rogationes plebisve scita /³⁵ senatusve consulta fecit, fecerit, sive, quod eum ex lege, rogatione / plebisve scito s(enatus)ve c(onsulto) facere oportebit, non fecerit huius legis / ergo, id ei ne fraudi esto neve quit (for quid) ob eam rem populo dare debeto, / neve cui de ea re actio neve iudicatio esto, neve quid de ea re apud / [s]ẹ ạgi sinito.

"(. . . it pleased the senate that . . .) he (Vespasian) be allowed to make ⟨friendship? an alliance?⟩ or a treaty with whom he wishes, just as was allowed to the deified Augustus, (the emperor Tiberius), and (the emp. Claudius);

"and that he be allowed to convene the senate, make a motion (in it), remit (any matter to it), (and) effect decrees of the senate by motion and division [i.e., by calling for a vote by division of the house], just as was allowed to (the same three emperors);

"and that, when the senate is convened according to his will or authority, order or charge, or in his presence, the legality of all matters (carried out) shall be maintained and preserved just as if the senate had been called, and were being held, by law;

"and that those whom, seeking a magistracy, a public office, or the management of anything, he has recommended to the senate and people of Rome, and those to whom he has given (or) promised his support shall at each election be considered separately;

"and that he shall be allowed to advance (and/or) move forward the boundaries of the pomerium when he thinks it useful for the State, just as was allowed to (the emperor Claudius);

"and that whatever he judges to be of benefit to the State (or) in accord with the dignity of matters divine, human, public and private, he shall have the right and the power to carry out (or) do, just as was allowed to (the emperors Augustus, Tiberius, and Claudius);

"and that by what laws or plebiscites it was written that (the same three emperors) should not be held (i.e., should be exempt from them), from these laws and plebiscites (the emperor) Vespasian is exempt, and what things it was proper for (the same three emperors) to do by virtue of each (i.e., any) law (or) bill, all these things (the emperor) Vespasian shall be allowed to do;

"and that what things, before this law was introduced, were done, performed, decreed (or) ordered by (the emperor) Vespasian, (or) by each person (i.e., anyone) at his order or behest, these things shall be just as lawful and valid as if they had been done by order of the people or the commons.

"Exemption from Penalty

"If anyone because of this law has done (or) will have done ⟨anything⟩ contrary to laws, bills, or plebiscites or decrees of the Senate, or if, because of this law, he will not have done what it will be proper to do in accordance with a law, a bill, or a plebiscite or a decree of the Senate, he shall not be held responsible, nor on this account shall he have to give anything (i.e., pay damages) to the people, nor shall anyone have the power to bring suit nor to render legal judgment against him, nor shall anyone (i.e., a judge) allow a case to be pleaded before him concerning this matter."

Note the paragraphing by extension left while enlarging the first letter of *utique* at the beginning of several paragraphs; the centering of *Sanctio*; the consistent use of *uti* instead of *ut*; *quibusve* line 12, *init.*

(not, as commonly read, *quibusque*, as in line 13); *republica* and *reipublicae* written as one word (lines 14 *fin.*, 17); the inconsistency in the names of the four emperors named, only Augustus having one form, *divus Aug.*; the omission of the names of Caligula and Nero, the former as a result of a virtual, though not formal, *damnatio memoriae* (Dio 60.4.5 f.), the latter from a *damn. mem.* inferred from his having been declared a *hostis* ("public enemy") by the Senate (Suet. *Nero* 49.2) and from the erasure of his name from some inscrs. (cf. *ILS* 3: 1, 268), including most extant examples of his name in Athens (Kevin K. Carroll, by letter of Aug. 17, 1977, who also cites Tac. *Hist.* 1.16.2, Suet. *Otho* 7.1, and Joann. Antioch. as quoted in the Loeb Dio, vol. 8. 190 f.); inconsistencies in the spelling of *-iis* words (lines 13, 14, 24), in the use or absence of "and" or "or" between elements of a group (e.g., in naming the emperors), and in the spelling of the genitive of *plebs/plebes* (22, 24, 32, 34, 36); *quaecunque* for the usual *-cumque* (17) and *quit* for *quid* (37); *quoque* for the expected *quo*, "anyone" (31); *quid* apparently omitted once (34). These inconsistencies and irregularities are specially noteworthy in this official document, whose syntax, however, compares favorably with that of other legal documents (e.g., the *S. C. de Bacch.*, **8**, whose sequence varies between primary and secondary, cf. Cic. *Ad Fam.* 8.8.5–8); it is clear that the Latin periodic style was difficult to achieve satisfactorily, esp. in long sentences (cf. Cornelius Gallus's long, involved sentence, **22**).

47. Dedication of a Shrine to *Fons*, Rome. A.D. 70. Marble tablet (40 × 63 cm., *NS*), found in Rome in, or shortly before, 1914, *in situ* ca. 5 m. below ground, in the work of building the Ministry of Public Instruction in the Viale del Re (now V. di Trastevere); seen in 1949 and 1973 in the Antiquario of the Mus. Naz. Rom., Rome (inv. no. 106505). Letter heights: from ca. 3.4– 3.9 (line 1) down to 1.5–2.3 (line 6) cm.; tall I (line 5) 2.8 cm. Consular date.

Record of the dedication, May 24, A.D. 70, of a shrine to Fons (as representative of all springs: Wissowa, 221) by the two chief officials of the shrine and their wives. All four seem, from their cognomina and lack of filiation, to be freedmen or -women, like the *magistri/ministri* of Fons/Fons Scaurianus of *CIL* 6.154, 164 (= *ILS* 3888 f.). Publ. by G. Mancini, *NS* 1914, 362 f., whence *AE* 1915, 100 (both read *Tutilla*, line 6); *CIL* 6.39416 (not yet publ.—cf. index of nomina, 6: 6: 1, *s.vv.* Pontius, etc.); *Album* 1.122 no. 128, add. p. 10, col. 2 no. 128; cf. *Contrib.* 87, 91, 97, 98 (twice), 132, 136, 140, 141, 148 (4 times), 149 (twice), 166 (all under no. 128), for details of the lettering.

Text: *Imp(eratore) Vespasiano Caesare Aug(usto) II, / Caesare Aug(usti) f(ilio) Vespasiano, co(n)s(ulibus), / dedicatum VIIII K(alendas) Iunias: / P(ublius) Pontius Eros, G(aius) Veratius Fortunatus, /⁵ mag(istri) II̅ quinquennales lustri primi, / cum Tutilia Helice et Popillia Pnoe, coniugib(us) suis, / aedem a fundamentis, sua pecun(ia), Fonti d(ono) d(ederunt).*

"In the consulship of" the emperor Vespasian, "for the second time," (and) his son Titus, "dedicated May 24: Publius Pontius Eros (and) Gaius Veratius Fortunatus, 5th-year Masters, for the second time, of the first 5-year period, together with Tutilia Helice and Popillia Pnoë, their wives, have given a shrine, from its foundations, at their own expense, to Fons."

The use of tall letters and of apices is rather irregular (*Contrib.* 148 f., 186–206). Some guidelines are visible. E and F throughout are much alike, easily confused (except the F in line 4, with its lower-left serif); also I, L, T in 3–7. No bar is visible over *II* in line 1, *fin.* (as one would expect with an ordinal adverb, *Contrib.* 166 *fin.*), perhaps for lack of space (cf. the fancy bar in line 5), perhaps because of the discoloration in lines 1 f., due presumably to vegetation. The lettering is striking, but not uniform or well designed (some letters hardly distinguishable, two cut in the right margin, line 6 particularly bad), and, if the date were not expressed, the inscription might easily be dated later (but there is no evidence or likelihood of its being a later copy).

It seems most unusual for the praenomen *Titus* not to appear here in the name of Vespasian's older son (cf. *ILS* 3: 1, 270, and *PIR*² 3.184 f., no. 399, add. p. XIV). The omission of "and" between the names of members of groups, as twice here, is common, esp. with officials' names. Line 7, *fin.*, or *d(ederunt) d(edicaverunt)*. Note that *dedicatum* does not agree in gender with *aedem* (fem.), perhaps through carelessness—they are four lines apart.

48. Elogium of Gaius Duilius, Rome. Probably early-Imperial (Claudian?); not after A.D. 77. A large, fragmentary, damaged block of "Luna marble, not Parian," (Degrassi, *Elogia*), found in 1565 near the Arch of Septimius Severus in the Roman Forum, and recently (1973) seen in the Passaggio del Muro Romano, Pal. dei Conservatori, Rome (inv. no. 6970). The block measures m. 1.015 × 1.325 × 0.78 (Degrassi, *ILLRP*), the inscr. cm. 75 × 87 max. (Meinhardt). Undoubtedly most of the inscribed base of a *columna rostrata* (a column adorned with ships' beaks or rams) set up in the Roman Forum in honor of Duilius (cos. 260 B.C., a hero of the First Punic War) and reported as seen there by Pliny the Elder (34.11.20) and Quintilian (1.7.12). Both obviously accept the monument without reservation, Quintilian noting particularly as archaic the words in the inscription ending in -*d*, which in fact are one of its conspicuous features. Silius Italicus also (6.663–666) describes a commemorative column set up to celebrate D.'s naval victory and D. himself dedicating the spoils of war to Mars, as seen by Hannibal (in the poet's imagination) in a temple wall-painting in Italy. If such a column was set up in D.'s time (as no doubt

happened), with its base inscribed with a text in the third person, that base was probably the original model of the present base. The 4th-cent. grammarian Servius, in a note on *Georgics* 3.29 (edd. Thilo and Hagen, 3: 1 [Leipzig 1887] 277), confuses the picture by having D. set up two *rostratae (columnae)* in Rome, "one of which we see on the Rostra, the other in front of the Circus (Maximus) on the entrance side"; the former would presumably be the column that rested on our present base, but the latter is inexplicable.

The material of our base (marble) and the lettering of the inscription preclude this from being the original inscribed base of any column set up by Duilius or in his honor in his own lifetime; such a monument would certainly have been of tufa, like our **4**. The question arises whether our inscr. is a copy of an original of D.'s own time (as accurate as possible, but quite possibly with some errors caused by the difficulty of reading an old inscr. cut in tufa and by imperfect knowledge of 3rd-cent. Latin on the part of the one[s] responsible for the text) or, on the other hand, an entirely new inscr. somewhat like the *elogia* of Republican leaders inscribed on the bases of statues set up by Augustus in his new forum in Rome (Suet. *Aug.* 31.5, cf. Horace, *Odes*, 4.8.13– 15, *CIL* 1²: 1, pp. 186–197, and Degrassi, *Elogia* 1–8). The fragments of these *Elogia*, incidentally, include one that must belong to Duilius though his name is lost (*CIL* 1²: 1, p. 193 no. *XI*, 6.31611, *ILS* 55 add., Degrassi, op. cit. 20 f., no. 13).

This question scholars have answered differently. Mommsen, Ritschl, and Lommatzsch, for example, favored the latter view, Wölfflin, Niedermann, and Degrassi the former. These last seem to have the stronger case: Quintilian obviously accepted the inscription, and why would a Roman scholar (except possibly the eccentric antiquarian emperor Claudius) concoct an archaic text? is there any analogy? the Augustan *elogia* show no signs of archaic forms (see *ILS* 50–60, most easily), and the only strange forms in the present inscr. (besides *magistr[a]tos*, line 3)— *[opsidione]d, praesente[d Hanibaled], [d]ictatored, navaled* (lines 2, 9, 10, 17)—seem to have a parallel in *[c]osoled*, read on a fragmentary tufa base, *CIL* 1².19 (= *ILLRP* 318, "saec. III"), first published in 1900, too late for Mommsen and Ritschl. (Lommatzsch, on *CIL* 1².19 and 25, makes no connection; Sommer, 375 Anm. 1, who calls our *-ed* forms "archaizing products of a later age," of no value as testimony, accepts *[c]osoled* as "incontestable" though "too isolated for certain judgment.")

For the date, the *terminus ante quem* is the date of Pliny the Elder's Preface, with dedication of the completed *Natural History* to "his (friend) Vespasian," "six times consul," who it is clear from this and a reference to a father and brother (sects. 1, 3, 5) must be Titus, holding his 6th consulship (A.D. 77). Palaeographically, the early Empire, generally favored, seems satisfactory; "Claudian or perhaps somewhat earlier," J. S. Gordon. (For an argument that the present text was copied in turn from a copy of ca. 150 B.C., see T. Frank, *CP* 14 [1919] 74–82, who explains the expansive style of the inscr. by reference to the Greeks of 3rd-cent. [B.C.] Sicily; cf. E. W. Fay, *CP* 15 [1920] 176–183).

CIL 1².25 (ed. Lommatzsch—cf. pp. 718, 739, 831), 6.1300 (cf. 31591, 37040), *ILS* 65, S/C 95 f., Diehl 271, Degrassi, *Elogia* 44–49 no. 69, idem in Mustilli, 19 f., pl. XVII 59, Warm. 128–131, L/R 1.152 (transl.), Palm. no. 11, Ern. 109–111, no. 147, Pis. A 33, *ILLRP* 319 (add. p. 325), E. Meinhardt in H/S 2.1680 (with German transl.), De Ros. 31 f., 71–74, no. 7 (with Ital. transl.), Cal. Lim. 250–252 no. 51. Cf. also P/A 134 *s.v.* Col. Rostr. C. Duilii (2 entries), Lugli 106 f., M. Niedermann, *REL* 14 (1936) 276–287 (= *Recueil M. Niedermann* [Neuchâtel 1954] 209–220), Nash 1.282 *s.v.* Col. rostr. C. Duilii.

The restorations proposed by scholars, while of course conjectural, are based on the testimony of Polybius and later historians, as well as on spatial requirements. Most of those accepted since Ritschl (1862) and Mommsen (1863, on *CIL* 1¹.195) go back to a much earlier Spanish editor, P. Chacon (Rome 1586). The differences between Mommsen and Degrassi (3 texts, 1937–1965) are few and unimportant (except in line 1, which D. restores as the first line of the original text), and result from D.'s close attention to spatial needs. D. seems plausible in restoring line 1 and in holding that Duilius's name, with perhaps no more than his title as consul, was inscribed separately on the capital of the column that once stood on the base, and that only one or two lines are lost at the end, perhaps no more than the line of which the tops of a few letters are visible at the right. (Space must be provided for surrounding margins.) D.'s *[triump]oque navaled*, line 17, was suggested by F. Buecheler on *CIL* 1².25, p. 385, col. 1, 1st par., fin., following Chacon; its merit is that Duilius in fact did have a *(triumphum) navalem* in 260 (Degrassi, *FCT* 76 f., 548), but it would leave *triumpo* as the only abl. sing. here not ending in *d*.

Text (as prepared by J. S. Gordon on the basis of Ritschl, *CIL* 1² and 6, Degrassi, and photos, and with D.'s restorations except in line 2, where, following Mommsen [*CIL* 1¹.195] and Henzen [*CIL* 6], he has the last two words end in *-is*, i.e., *-īs* [as nomin. plurals], for which no justification appears, esp. if the second *e* of *legiones* was correctly read by earlier observers, including Ritschl and Henzen—Mommsen seems not to have seen the stone itself, but to rely on Ritschl):

[Consol Segest]ano[s, socios p(opli) R(omani), Cartaginiensiom] / *[opsidione]d exemet legion[esque Cartaginienses omnes]* / *[ma]ximosque magistr[a]tos l[uci palam post dies]* / *[n]ovem castreis exfogiont Macel[amque opidom]* /⁵ *[p]ugnandod cepet. Enque eodem mag[istratud bene]* / *[r]em navebos* (the O corrected from V) *marid consol primos g[eset copiasque]* / *[c]lasesque navales primos ornavet*

pa[ravetque] / *çumque eis navebos claseis Poenicas om[nis, item ma]/[x]umas copias Cartaginiensis praesente[d Hanibaled]* /[10] *ḍictatored oḷ[or]om in altod marid pug[nad vicet]* / *ṿique naṿe̩[is cepe]t cum socieis septer[esmom I, quin]/[queresmo]ṣque triresmosque naveis X[XX, merset XIII.]* / *[Auro]m captom numei* ⊕⊕⊕ ⅭC(?). (space) / *[Argen]tom captom praeda numei* (a symbol for 100,000 [space for 4 or 5 more symbols]. /[15] *[Omne] captom aes* (8 symbols for 100,000) [space for 5 or 6 more] / [2 symbols for 100,000] (13 more such) [space for 5 more]. / *[Triump[oque navaled ṕraedad poploṃ [donavet]* / *[multosque] Cartaginịe̩[nsis inge]nuos ḍ[uxit ante]* / *[curum* (space for ca. 24 letters)*] capt——.*

"As consul [260 B.C.] he (i.e., Duilius) freed the people of Segesta (in NW Sicily), allies of the Roman people, from the Carthaginians' siege, and all the Carthaginian army and highest official (Hamilcar, son of Barca), by daylight, openly, after nine days flee from camp; and he (Duilius) captured in battle the town of Macella (also in Sicily, probably near Segesta)," etc. In the sequel, D. is described as the first consul to wage war at sea (and successfully) and to equip and prepare naval forces and warships, with which he defeated on the high seas all the Punic fleets and the mighty Carthaginian forces in the presence of Hannibal (son of Gisgo); "and he captured, with their crews, one septireme and 30 quinqueremes and triremes, (and) sank 13" (cf. L. Casson, *The Ancient Mariners* . . . [New York 1959] 162 f. and index, 285 col. 2, *s.v.* warships, types). There follow the amount of gold and silver seized and the value of the total in Roman bronze money (between 2,800,000 and 3,400,000 *asses* [depending on how far right the inscr. is restored in lines 15 f., each symbol indicating 100,000 *asses*—for denarii, divide probably by 10: cf. T. Frank, *Econ. Survey* 1.74 f.]); then "at his naval [triumph] he (Duilius) presented the (Roman) people with the booty and led [many] free-born Carthaginians [ahead of his chariot]——."

Some damage at the edges is evident since the earlier editions and first photos. Lines 1 and 13 may have been indented for "paragraphing." Line 13, *fin.* Some editors read (in Roman numerals) 3,700; Lommatzsch's 3,500 plus CⅠƆ seems out of the question. Editors generally print C for G following the evidence of the stone, where C is cut for both C and G; but about a third of these C's have the phonetic value of G's (as in C. for *Gaius*), C having been the earlier form of G, in imitation of the Greek gamma, until a second stroke was added to C to make a new letter G and differentiate it from C; the date of this new G is apparently ca. 250 B.C. (Gordon, *Letter Names* 58 and n. 76). The three tall I's (in *marid*, *primos* twice) appear anachronistic (cf. *Contrib.* 186 f.); none of the 3rd-cent. Scipionics show any.

Noteworthy also the abl. sing. ending -*ed* of *[opsidione]d*, line 2, restored by Mommsen, *CIL* 1[1], accepted by Lommatzsch, *CIL* 1[2] (but both, like Ritschl, believed the text to be a concoction of the early Empire: cf. Lommatzsch, op. cit. 386, col. 1 *fin.*), rejected by Sommer 373 Anm. 1 and by Leumann 274 §191 d, defended by Wölfflin, *Sber. k. bayer. Akad. Wiss.* (Munich), phil.-phil. Cl., 1890, vol. 1, 312, Niedermann op. cit. above, 279 (= 211) (by implication), and, in a general way, Degrassi *ILLRP* 1[2] pp. 189 f., fn.; the nom. sing. ending -*os* in *magistratos*, line 3 (also accepted by some, rejected by others, but passed over in silence by most editors); the *en* (line 5) vs. *in* (10); the anomalous combination *triresmos* (masc.) *naveis* (fem.) (12) (commented on by Buecheler, loc. cit., col. 2, and Niedermann, op. cit. 281–284 [= 213–216]); *ae* for early *ai* (*praeda*, 14); the use of seven -*que*'s and the absence of *et*, *ac*, and *atque* (noted by Wölfflin, op. cit. 298, who compares the *Sen. Cons. de Bacch.* [our **8**] and other examples of "Curialsprache" which avoid *et*), and what is probably the largest Roman numeral extant in Latin inscrs., which shows no use of M̄ (only modern?)

for "a million" but only 10 symbols for 100,000 each.

49. Epitaph of a Soldier and Public Official, below Tivoli.
Probably A.D. 74/79. Large marble tablet (m. 3.60 × 2.20: Mancini) standing in front of the great circular tomb of the Plautii, near Ponte Lucano on the road from Rome to Tivoli (anc. Tibur), 25.9 km. from Rome, 5.6 km. from Tivoli (*Roma e dintorni* 611 f.); this tomb, like that of Caecilia Metella (**23**), became a fortress in the Middle Ages because of its strategic position and strong walls (*Lazio*, 28 pl. 19; Nash, *Roman Towns* [New York 1944] 41 pl. 37). The marble is somewhat damaged along the edges, and its surface somewhat worn; a few letters are now lost, others and the interpuncts not always clear. The epitaphs of four other family members, including the builder of the tomb, are still *in situ*, that of the builder cut on the tomb itself and repeated, with an addition, on a larger, more handsome marble tablet; another epitaph is now lost.

The long epitaph (37 lines) of Ti. Plautius Silvanus Aelianus, recording his senatorial career (cf. S/C 110 f.) and military achievements and including four lines quoted from Vespasian's remarks about him to the senate when it granted him triumphal honors during his last post. (He was consul A.D. 45 and 74.) It is one of the inscriptions that greatly supplement the rather meager evidence from literary sources in giving a view of the Roman provincial system. Plautius is mentioned by Tacitus, *Hist.* 4.53, as taking part, as a *pontifex*, in the dedication of the restored Capitoline Temple in Rome in June 70.

CIL 14.3608 (cf. pp. 390 f.; add Dessau, EE 9: 3 [1910] p. 470), *ILS* 986, Rushforth 117–120 no. 93, *Inscr. Ital.* 4: 1² (ed. Mancini, 1952) 62–65 no. 125 (add. p. 210), McCrum/Woodhead 261; cf. L. Halkin, *Ant. Class.* 3 (1934) 121–161; *CAH* 10, index p. 1025, *s.v.* Plautius Silv. Ael.; A. Stein, *Die Legaten von Moesien* (Budapest 1940) 29–31; M. Hofmann, *RE* 41.

Halbbd. (1951) 35–40 *s.v.* Plautius 47; Degrassi, *FC* 12 f., on A.D. 45; L. R. Taylor, *MAAR* 24 (1956) 9–30, esp. 28–30, with stemma of the Plautii Silvani, 24; E. Condurachi, *Epigraphica* 19 (1957) 49–65; R. Syme, *OCD* 843 *s.v.* Plautius 5.

Text: *Ti(berio) Plautio M(arci) [f(ilio) (tribu) Ani(ensi)]* / *Silvano Aelian[o]*, / *pontif(ici), sodali Aug(ustali)*, / *IIIvir(o) a(ere) a(rgento) a(uro) f(lando) f(eriundo), q(uaes-tori) Ti(berii) Caesaris*, /⁵ *legat(o) leg(ionis) V̄ in Germania*, / *pr(aetori) urb(ano), legat(o) et comiti Claud(ii)* / *Caesaris in Brittannia, consuli*, / *pro co(n)s(ule) Asiae, legat(o) pro praet(ore) Moesiae*, / *in qua plura quam centum mill(ia)* /¹⁰ *ex numero Transdanuviano-rum* / *ad praestanda tributa cum coniugib(us)* / *ac liberis et principibus aut regibus suis* / *transduxit; motum orientem Sarmartar(um)* / *compressit quamvis parte⟨m⟩ magna⟨m⟩ exercitus* /¹⁵ *ad expeditionem in Armeniam misisset;* / *ignotos ante aut infensos p(opulo) R(omano) reges signa* / *Romana adoraturos in ripam quam tuebatur* / *perduxit; regibus Bastarna-rum et* / *Rhoxolanorum filios et regi (or regibus) Dacorum fratrem (or fratres, instead of fratrum)* /²⁰ *captos aut hostibus ereptos remisit; ab* / *aliquis eorum opsides accepit; per quae (instead of quem) pacem* / *provinciae et confirmavit et protulit*, / *Scytharum quoque rege{m} a Cherronensi*, / *quae est ultra Borus-tenen, opsidione summoto.* /

²⁵ *Primus ex ea provincia magno tritici modo* / *annonam p(opuli) R(omani) adlevavit. Hunc, legatum in* / *{in} Hispaniam, ad praefectur(am) urbis remissum* / *senatus in praefectura tri-umphalibus* / *ornamentis honoravit, auctore Imp(eratore)* /³⁰ *Caesare Augusto Vespasiano, verbis ex* / *oratione eius q(uae) i(nfra) s(cripta) s(unt):* / *Moesiae ita praefuit ut non debuerit in* / *me differri honor triumphalium eius* / *orna-mentorum—nisi quod latior ei* /³⁵ *contigit mora titulus praefecto urbis.* / *Hunc in eadem praefectura urbis Imp(erator) Caesar* / *Aug(ust-us) Vespasianus iterum co(n)s(ulem) fecit.*

"To Ti. Plautius Silvanus Aelianus, son of Marcus, of the Aniensis 'tribe,' a *ponti-fex, sodalis Augustalis* [member of a minor priesthood charged with the cult of Caesar and Augustus], member of the Board of Three in charge of coinage, quaestor of [i.e., chosen by the emperor] Tiberius Caesar, commander of the 5th legion in Germany, urban [city of Rome] praetor, deputy and companion of Claudius Caesar in Britain, consul (suffect, A.D. 45), proconsul of (the province of) Asia, governor of Moesia, in which he led across (the Danube) more than 100,000 from the multitude of Transdanubians, with their wives and children and leaders or kings, to pay tribute; a growing movement of the Sarmatae he quelled, though he had sent a large part of the army on an expedition into Armenia; kings previously unknown or hostile to the Roman people he led to the bank (of the Danube) that he was guarding, for them to pay homage to the Roman standards; to the kings of the Bastarnae and the Rhoxolani their sons, and to the king [or, kings] of the Dacians his [or their] brother [or brothers], captured or rescued from the enemy, he sent back; from some of them he took hostages; by these measures he both established and extended the peaceful condition of the province (Moesia); a (or, the) king of the Scythians also he dislodged by siege from (Tauric) Chersonese (a town in SW Crimea), which is beyond the Borysthenes (mod. Dnieper).

"He was the first man to alleviate (the problem of) the grain supply of the people of Rome with a large amount of wheat from this province (Moesia). This man, recalled (to Rome) while governor of Spain (Tarraconensis) to become Prefect of the City, the Senate honored with the ornaments of a triumph, at the suggestion of the emperor Vespasian, from whose speech comes the following quotation: 'He (Plautius) so governed Moesia that the granting of triumphal honors ought not to have waited for me—except that because of the delay a broader title of rank has come to him as Prefect of the City." This man during the same Prefecture of the City the emperor Vespasian made consul for the second time."

The barring of the cardinal numeral in $\overline{III}viro$ and of the ordinal in *leg. $\overline{V}$* (lines 4, 5) is normal (*Contrib.* 166 f.); the former word and *procos.* (8) are interpunctuated as if two words each; this is regular in such composite words as *IIIviro* and common in such forms as *procos.* (see Appendix II *s.v.* *pro-* and at the end, *s.v. IIvir*, etc., and *Contrib* 184 *init.*); other examples occur in these inscrs.—e.g. **56**, lines 2, 7. The long title for "moneyer" in 4 is generally thus abbreviated. For the spellings *Britt.* (7) and *aliquis* (abl., 21: note the tall long *i*) see Appendix I *s.vv. Line 31, q. i. s. s.,* a legal phrase, commonly thus written.

50. Dedication of Arch to the Deified Titus, Rome. A.D. 81/early Trajanic? The marble Arch of Titus at the upper (east) end of the Roman Forum. It was so badly damaged in the Middle Ages while forming part of a family fortress that, when isolated by G. Valadier in 1821 (*Dissertazioni dell'Accademia Romana di Archeologia* 1: 2 [Rome 1823] 275–286, 3 plates), it had to be taken down and reerected, the missing parts being added in travertine. It had been dedicated by the Senate and People of Rome to the deified Titus in commemoration (as the sculptures show) of the siege, capture, and destruction of Jerusalem (A.D. 70), in which he had played the chief rôle.

The inscribed panel on the east face of the arch (facing the Colosseum) measures m. 2.03 × 6.82 (Magi, 105), the letters (once filled with bronze, no doubt—the holes for attaching the bronze are visible in a good photo, most easily in the O's, at the left and right center) from 45 cm. (line 1) down to 36 cm., average (Magi, 106, 112 n. 43). The *terminus post quem* of this inscr. is the death of Titus, Sept. 13, 81 (Suet. *Titus,* 11), soon followed, no doubt, by his deification by the Senate. On the other face of the arch (facing the Forum) is a papal inscr. recording the restoration of the arch by Pius VII "in the 24th year of his office" (1823). If there was an ancient inscription on this side and if it was *CIL* 6.946—found fragmentary and incomplete in demolishing the old basilica of St. Peter (in Vaticano), long since lost but copied, in from five to eight lines (in four different mss.), not later than 1623 (Magi, 100: Grimaldi)—this would date the arch to the time of Trajan, after his acquisition of the title "Dacicus" (late in 102). In the latest (and rather convincing) demonstration of this "hypothesis," F. Magi (*Röm. Mitt.* 82 [1975] 99–116, 2 figs., and pls. 4–15) rearranges in five lines (pp. 101, 103), as in the later Arch of Trajan at Beneventum (*CIL* 9.1558 = *ILS* 296), the 5–8 lines of the earliest copy (p. 101) and the 3 lines of *CIL* 6.946. Here, as in the other inscr. (*CIL* 6.945), the cuttings contained holes to be filled with (bronze) letters.

CIL 6.945 (cf. 31211 and p. 3777), *ILS* 265, Diehl *I.L.* tab. 26, a, S/C 125; cf. P/A 45–47 *s.v.* Arcus Titi; Lugli, *Rom. Ant.* 231–233; *Roma e dintorni* 134 f.; Nash 1.133–135 *s.v.* Arcus Titi (with 3 photos of the archway—coffered ceiling and sculptures representing Titus's triumphal car and procession, spoils from the Temple of Jerusalem including a 7-branch candlestick); Coarelli, 98 (colored photo of the east side).

Text: *Senatus / Populusque Romanus / Divo Tito Divi Vespasiani f(ilio) / Vespasiano Augusto.*

"The Senate and People of Rome to the Deified Titus Vespasianus Augustus, son of the Deified Vespasian." It has been noted that neither this inscription nor, apparently, the incomplete *CIL* 6.946 contains any motivation for the dedication.

Magi's reconstruction of *CIL* 6.946 (p. 103, as designed by G. Gatti): *Divo Tito Divi [Vespasiani f(ilio)] / [Vespa]siano Augusto / Imp(erator) Caesar Divi Nervae f(ilius) Nerva / [Traianus Aug(ustus) Germa]nicus Dac(icus), [pont(ifex)] /[5] max(imus), trib(uni-*
cia) po[t(estate)——, imp(erator)——, co(n)-s(ul)——,] p(ater) p(atriae) fecit. If Magi is correct in identifying this inscription as the one originally cut on the west side of the Arch, the explanation of its Trajanic date may be that, though the "Senate and People" had voted to dedicate an arch to Titus, Domitian, perhaps embittered by his lack of "real power" under, first, his father, then his elder (and popular) brother, failed to build the arch, that Nerva in his brief rule lacked time and money to do it, that therefore the arch had to wait for Trajan. Cf. *OCD* 360, 730 f., *s.vv.* Domitian, Nerva (1).

51. A Military Diploma, Rome, from Egypt. A.D. 86. Two bronze tablets cm. 19.5 × 15.5 × 0.2–0.3 (*CIL* 16), originally fastened together by some sort of thong passing through the holes visible. Bought in Egypt in 1735 (*CIL* 16); examined in 1973 in the Museo Profano of the Vatican Library, while it was being restored by the Vatican Laboratory by immersion in a bath in order to remove (or decrease) the corrosion, especially present on the exterior of the tablets. A diploma (so called because it was composed of two tablets folded together like a diptych) recording the privileges of Roman citizenship and marriage granted by the emperor Domitian to the marines/sailors serving in the Roman fleet stationed at Alexandria, who had received an honorable discharge after 26 or more years of service, and in particular to Gaius Gemellus of Coptus. The date Feb. 17, A.D. 86 (the year determined by the consuls' names), is given in the text. The letters seem cut, not cast (as is stated also of the Tabula Hebana, **36**, *q.v.*). The outside of both tablets is corroded and hard to read, as is also, to some extent, the inside of tablet 2.

CIL 3, p. 856 no. XIII (cf. pp. 1064 no. XIII, 1964 no. XVIII), whence *CIL* 16.32 (with photo). For such diplomata, see Cagnat 302–307, pl. IX, S/C 180–185, or

OCD 355 *s.v.* diploma; L/R 2.522–524 translate 3 other diplomata.

The consecutive inner text of both tablets: (tablet 1) *Imp(erator) Caesar divi Vespasiani f(ilius) Domitianus / Augustus Germanicus, pontifex ma/ximus, tribunic(ia) potestat(e) $\overline{V}$, imp(erator) $\overline{XI}$, censor / perpetuus, co(n)s(ul) $\overline{XII}$, p(ater) p(atriae), /⁵ classicis qui militant in Aegypto sub / G(aio) Septimio Veceto* (sic) *et Claudio Clemente / praefecto classis, item dimissis hones/ta missione ex eadem classe senis et / vicenis pluribusve stipendiis emeri/¹⁰tis, quorum nomina subscripta sunt, / itsis* (read *ipsis*), *liberis posterisque eorum civi- / (tablet 2) [ta]tem dedit et conubium cum uxo/[ri]bus quas tunc habuissent cum / [e]st civitas iis data aut siqui caelibes /¹⁵ [e]ṣsent cum iis quas postea duxissent / [du]mtaxat singuli singulas; / a(nte) d(iem) XIII K(alendas) Mart(ias) / G(aio) (space) Secio (space) Campano, / Sex(to) Cornelio Dolabella Petroniano co(n)s(ulibus)* (*cos* written at the right, between lines 18 and 19): /²⁰ *G(aio) Gemello Croni e(ilio)* (read *f-*) *Coptit(ae). / Descriptum et recognitum ex tabula / aenea quae fixa est Romae in Capitolio.* (Other F's are cut like E's.)

"(The emperor Domitian, with titles that point to early A.D. 86), to the marines/sailors who are serving in Egypt under G. Septimius Vegetus (prefect of Egypt) and Claudius Clemens, prefect of the fleet (stationed at Alexandria), likewise to those honorably discharged from the same fleet after having served 26 or more years, whose names are written below: to themselves, their children and descendants, (the emperor) has given (Roman) citizenship and (the right of) marriage with the wives whom they had at the time when they were granted citizenship, or, if any were single, with those whom they might later take (in marriage), with the proviso of (only) one wife for each man; Feb. 17, in the consulship of Gaius Secius Campanus (and) Sextus Cornelius Dolabella Petronianus [A.D. 86]: (in particular) to Gaius Gemellus, son of Cronius, of Coptus (in Egypt). Copied and checked from the bronze tablet that is posted at Rome on the Capitoline (hill)."

On the outside of tablet 2 are the names (in the genitive, dependent on an implied noun such as *testimonium?*) of seven Roman citizens who certify the authenticity of the diploma, i.e., that it is a true copy of the original in Rome.

52. Latin Epitaph, with Greek Verses, of a Young Poet, Rome.

Probably A.D. 94 or soon after. A large marble gravestone (m. 1.61 × 1.06 × 0.70, inscribed surface 1.15 × 0.87) having a gabled top adorned with a laurel wreath in the center, fillets left and right, and palmette acroteria at the corners, all in relief; inside a deep niche, a sculptured figure, in high relief, of a boy dressed in a toga and holding in his left hand a scroll inscribed in Greek, surrounded on three sides (left, right, below) by further inscriptions, all in Greek verse except for the Latin epitaph. Found in Rome in 1871 under the east tower of the Porta Salaria, which had been built over it; seen in 1949 and 1973 in Sala VI (Museo Nuovo) of the Pal. dei Conservatori, Rome (inv. no. 7015).

Epitaph of Q. Sulpicius Maximus, who died at age 11, after having "departed with honor" from a competition in Greek verse at the third celebration of a poetry contest identified as part of the *quinquennale certamen* established by Domitian in honor of Jupiter Capitolinus (Suet. *Dom.* 4.4: the poetry must be part of the *certamen musicum*); this is dated with respect to its inception by Censorinus (*De Die Nat.* 18.15, who calls it the *Capitolini agones*) in the year 86; the *tertium lustrum*, it is generally agreed, indicates the year 94 (86–90–94, counting both first and last years of each *lustrum*, in Roman style). How long the boy survived the rigors of the contest is not stated, but since he died at only eleven (or twelve, as he is made to say in the first Greek epigram, perhaps only *metri causa*) it can hardly have been very long. The Latin *cum honore disces-*

sit, together with the sculptured laurel wreath above the boy's head, is taken by some to mean that he won first prize; others disagree and consider his verses (here inscribed) not good enough; still others (including the present writer) merely note that he acquitted himself honorably (perhaps a second or third place). Cf. Henzen's arguments against the boy's award of first prize, pp. 103 f., and *CIL* 9.2860 (= *ILS* 5178), where a boy of thirteen, in the same *certamen* (A.D. 106), *claritate ingenii coronatus est inter poetas Latinos omnibus sententis* (sic) *iudicum*.

CIL 6.33976 (cf. p. 3906), *ILS* 5177 (the Latin and 7 lines of the Greek: cf. *PIR*[1] 3 [1898] 287 no. 727[a]), Henzen *Bull. Inst. Corr. Arch.* 1871, 98–113, G. Kaibel (ed.) *Epigrammata Graeca ex lapidibus conlecta* (Berlin 1878, repr. Hildesheim 1965) 250–253 no. 618 and *Inscr. Graecae Siciliae et Italiae . . .* (Berlin 1890 *IG* 14) 494–496 no. 2012, Friedlaender op. cit. (above, on **37**) vol. 4[9-10], 276 (only the Latin—cf. 2[10].150 f., 231), Mustilli 97, pl. 56 no. 224, *Album* 1.144 f., no. 153 (only the Latin—cf. 2.7 f., further bibl.). Cf. also Christ/Schmid/Stählin *Gesch. d. griech. Lit.*[6] 2: 2 (Munich 1924) 671 fn. 14, *P/A* 486 f. *s.v.* Sep. Q. Sulp. Max., Strong 2.65, Fluss *RE* 4A: 1 (1931) 816 *s.v.* Sulpicius 79, Schanz/Hosius[4] 2.434, 811, H. I. Marrou Μουσικὸς ἀνήρ . . . (Grenoble 1938) 205 f., W. Peek (ed.) *Griech. Vers-Inschriften* 1 (Berlin 1955) 591–594 no. 1924, E. Simon in H/S 2.1734, Nash 2.371–373 *s.v.* Sep. Q. Sulp. Max. (3 photos).

The Greek contains the boy's "extempore" (καίριον) 43 verses (in 101 short lines, as cut) of dactylic hexameter (which end in the scroll held in his hand) on the subject of "what words Zeus might use in reproving Helios for trusting his chariot to Phaëthon" (cf. Lucian, *Dial. Deor.* 25), plus two 10-line Epigrammata in elegiacs, one put in the boy's mouth ("illness and exhaustion destroyed me"), the other addressed to him admiringly.

Text of the Latin: *Deis Manibus Sacrum. /*

Q(uinto) Sulpicio Q(uinti) f(ilio) Cla(udia tribu) Maximo, domo Roma; vix(it) ann(is) XI, m(ensibus) V, d(iebus) XII. / Hic, tertio certaminis lustro inter Graecos poetas duos et L / professus, favorem quem ob teneram aetatem excitaverat /⁵ in admirationem ingenio suo perduxit et cum honore discessit. Versus / extemporales eo subiecti sunt ne parent(es) adfectib(us) suis indulsisse videant(ur). / Q(uintus) Sulpicius Eugramus et Licinia Ianuaria parent(es) infelicissim(i) f(ilio) piissim(o) fec(erunt) et sib(i) p(osterisque) s(uis).

"Sacred to the Spirits of the Dead. Quintus Sulpicius Maximus, son of Quintus, of the Claudian 'tribe,' his home Rome, lived 11 years, 5 months, 12 days. This (boy), having enrolled among 52 Greek poets in the third lustrum (5-year period) of the (Capitoline) contest, by his talent brought to admiration the sympathy that he had roused because of his tender age, and he came away with honor. The extemporaneous verses are subjoined so that the parents may not seem to have indulged their affections. Quintus Sulpicius Eugramus and Licinia Ianuaria, most miserable parents, have had (this monument) built for their most dutiful son and for themselves and their descendants."

Line 1. This is the complete form of a masculine name, including filiation, voting district (or "tribe"), place of origin. The parents' cognomina and lack of filiation point to their being ex-slaves (prosperous enough to afford this monument), but their son was a full citizen. Line 6, *eo* is perhaps best taken as an adverb introducing the *ne* purpose (final) clause that follows; cf. *OLD* 611 *s.v.* eō³, 1 c. Lines 6 f. have interesting abbreviations, some unusual, apparently required by lack of space. Line 7, *Eugramus* for *Eugrammus*? Not listed by Kajanto. Cf. Εὔγραμμος.

53. *Tabula Alimentaria*, Rome, from Ancient Samnium. A.D. 101. An incomplete and damaged bronze tablet (m. 1.23 × 0.72–0.738 × ca. 0.006), found in 1831 at Macchia, ca. 40 km. north of Benevento, in Campania (*Campania*, 214, map between pp. 16 and 17); seen in 1973 in the Mus. Naz. Rom., Rome (inv. no. 449), where it was "in ristauro" for cleaning. Part of the local record of mortgages on farms belonging to the Ligures Baebiani (whose administrative center was apparently in or near Macchia), in connection with the Imperial system of child welfare established by the emperors Nerva and Trajan, whereby the mortgage interest of 5 percent was given locally for the support of poor children. (*OCD* 45 *s.v.* Alimenta, with bibl.; add P. Veyne, *MélRome* 69 [1957] 81–135, 70 [1958] 177–241, who compares, p. 196, a similar enterprise on the part of Catherine the Great of Russia, 1786.) The date is given by the consuls' names in lines 1 f.

G. (i.e., W.) Henzen, *Ann. Inst.* 16 (n.s. 1) (1844, publ. 1845) 5–111, esp. 57 ff., *CIL* 9.1455 (ed. Mommsen, but with no minuscule text except of the heading, p. 127 *fin.*), *ILS* 6509, Bruns 348 f., no. 145 b, Diehl *IL* tab. 27, *FIRA* 3.380–382 no. 117, Veyne op. cit. 84–90, Smallwood *Nerva/Hadrian* 139–142 no. 435 (only Henzen, *CIL*, and Veyne give the full text); L/R 2.344–347 translate part of this and of the similar bronze from Veleia (*CIL* 11.1147 = *ILS* 6675). Cf. R. Duncan-Jones, *PBSR* 32 (1964) 123–146; P. Garnsey, *Historia* 17 (1968) 367–381. For the Ligures Baebiani—Ligurians defeated by the Romans and transplanted, 181–180 B.C., from northern Italy to Samnium, and named Ligures Baebiani from the name of M. Baebius Tamphilus, consul in 181, responsible, with his colleague, P. Cornelius Cethegus, for the transfer— cf. E. T. Salmon, *Samnium and the Samnites* (Cambridge 1967) 310 f.

Part of the heading and two full columns of the text survive, plus the right half of a third column to the left, which the remains of Trajan's title and of the other consul's name in the heading show must have been the first column. (Veyne, 83, thinks that this col. was the second,

but Duncan-Jones seems right in following Henzen, 67, and *CIL*.) Lines 1–4 form the heading; the columns below contain eight, sometimes nine, items concerning sixty-six mortgages (incl. the fragmentary ones of col. 1), including the names of the owners (extended left, for "paragraphing"), the names and locations of the mortgaged properties, names of the neighbors, evaluations of the properties, the amount of each mortgage (these two items in thousands of sesterces), and to the right, separately, the amount of interest owed, at what was undoubtedly 5 percent. (In the Veleia bronze this is clearly specified, line 3: the sign for *quincunx*, Cagnat 33f.) Mommsen's commentary is still indispensable, Duncan-Jones's (145 f.) and Smallwood's tabulations useful, Veyne's study the most comprehensive.

Text of heading, lines 1–4 (with Mommsen's readings in 1 f., Dessau's restorations in 3 f., where M.'s are too long for the space available, which can be determined pretty well by ref. to the heading itself and to the width of col. 1 as compared with that of cols. 2–3): *[Imp(eratore) Caes(are) Nerva T]ŗaiano Aug(usto) [Germanic]o ĪĪĪĪ, / [Q(uinto) Articu]leio* (space) *Paeto* (space) *[co(n)s(ulibus)]*, / *[ex praecepto* (?) *optimi maxi]miq(ue) principis obligarunt pra[edia* (5 or 6 letters)] . . . *o Ligures Baebiani (-ani* in ligature) / [(ca. 6–17 letters, according to whether the line was centered or went left as far as line 3) *u]ţ* (?) *ex indulgentia eius pueri puaellaeq(ue)* (sic) *a[limenta a]ccipiant.*

Col. 2, lines 14–16: *(debentur a?) Neratio Corellio fund(i) Pacciani et casae /*[15] *Aureliani, adf(ine) Iulio Saturtino* (read *-nino*)*, aest(imatorum) ḤṢ (= sestertium*, gen. pl.*) / X̄X̄ĪĪ, in ḤṢ (= sestertium) ĪĪ; ñ(umerat?) Neratius Marcellus;* at the end of line 14, *ḤṢ (= sestertii) L.*

"In the consulship of (the emperor Trajan), 4th time, (and) Quintus Articuleius Paetus (A.D. 101), at the bidding of the Best and Greatest Ruler the (following)

Ligures Baebiani have mortgaged properties of theirs in order that . . . by his indulgence boys and girls may receive support.

"By Neratius Corellius, the Paccian farm and Aurelianus's cottage, his neighbor being Iulius Saturninus, valued at 22,000 sesterces, (mortgaged) for 2,000 sesterces; the administrator is (?) Neratius Marcellus [no doubt a relative of N. Corellius]; 50 sesterces [apparently the semiannual interest, 2½ %]."

Heading. Henzen, p. 93, and Mommsen saw more at the left than is now extant: ¹*Nerva T-* / ²*Articu-* / ³*-i maxi-* / ⁴ the top of a letter which Henzen interpreted as *[und]e*, Mommsen as *[e]t*. Col. 2, line 14, *debentur a*, suggested by Henzen, pp. 68, 94, was accepted by Mommsen, p. 128 col. 1 item no. 1; *fund.* and *casae* seem to be genitive (so Henzen, p. 68, and M., loc. cit. item no. 2: dependent on *obligatio* ["mortgage"], implied by *obligarunt* ?) rather than nom. pl.; one might expect the acc., objects of *obligarunt*. All the *fundi* have adjectival names derived not from the owners' names but presumably from those of previous owners and still used for identification.

Col. 2, lines 15 f. The case of $\overline{XXII}$ may be gen. or abl. (Price or Value) preceded by the partitive gen. *sestertium*; the case of $\overline{II}$, following *in*, is probably acc., as Mommsen, loc. cit. col. 2 item no. 7, shows, though his comparison with a formula of the Veleian bronze, *ille* ("so-and-so") *fundum professus est* ("listed" or "registered") *sestertiorum tot in sestertios tot*, as in items nos. XVI f. of the *ILS* text, 6675, is weakened by the fact that, as in the present inscr., the case of neither *sestert-* form is clear, since the word seems never written out but always symbolized by ~~HS~~. But it shows us M.'s opinion of the two cases (though, in item no. 6, he writes "Summa qua quisque fundus *aestimatus est*," not "summa cuius." *Numerat* is M.'s solution (p. 129, col. 2 item no. 9), previously accepted by Henzen, 69 (see also

below, **62**, line 10). Dessau notes (*ad loc.* n. 10) that here, as at Veleia, the mortgage rarely comes to a tenth of the valuation of the property listed. (Duncan-Jones, 145, App. II, gives 7.46% as the average here, ca. 8% at Veleia); the interest rate paid on the mortgage is easily figured, 50 being one 40th of 2,000, or 2½ percent, hence 5 percent yearly.

It would be too long to elucidate the many problems presented by the rest of the text (which seems less well written, and less well cut, than the Veleia bronze). One point, however: col. 2, line 12, *cum circeis*: abl. plu. of what word? *circeis*, not explained in *CIL*, is tentatively explained by Henzen, 97, n. 12, as from *circei* or *circea* (plurals), not found even in medieval writers, connected apparently with *circa*, *circum*, and perhaps meaning *muri* or *saepes*, "walls" or "hedges," by which the *fundi* were surrounded. *TLL* s.v. *circus*, col. 1184, line 1, lists *circeis* as an abl. pl. of *circus*, but it appears nowhere in the following discussion of *circus* and in fact seems impossible as a form of it (there are no other *ei*'s for long I here, and at this date one would expect a tall I instead, if anything); the only dictionary or similar work that records *circeis* seems to be Forcellini, 1.619, col. 1, *init.*, which follows Henzen (and Garrucci). Veyne, 115 f., who does not mention Henzen's conjecture, suggests that the word means "oak-groves" (chênaies): "a form *cĕrcea* for oak still has a representative in the Hirpinian dialect," with ref. to W. Meyer-Lübke, *Romanisches etymologisches Wörterbuch*, s.v. Quercea no. 6949. Another possible meaning might be "threshing floors," circular hard-dirt areas where oxen or other animals trample out the new grain (still in use in the Mediterranean), the usual word for which is *area*; our word might be local.

54. Record of a Town's Request for Patronage, Florence, from Rome. A.D. 101 or 102. A bronze tablet (cm. 43.3 × 35.8 overall, 39.0 × 31.3 writing surface) found in Rome in 1558, but long since in Florence, where it is in a frame attached to a wall of room XIV in the Museo Archeologico (inv. no. 1651); here the white in the letters is said to be "undoubtedly modern." It would seem to have been set up originally in the house of the senator named (cf. P/A 188 *s.v.* Domus:Pomponii).

A decree of the senate of the municipium of Ferentinum (mod. Ferentino, ca. 75 km. by road, SE of Rome, in the country of the anc. Hernici) that a committee of two men be sent to call upon the Roman senator T. Pomponius Bassus (no doubt in Rome) to request him respectfully to receive their town into his patronage; this action follows his success in a task assigned to him by the emperor Trajan, which must be that of *curator rei alimentariae* (on which see **53**). The date is that of the consuls of lines 1 f., A.D. 101 or 102 (the year is still uncertain: *PIR*[2] 1.227 f., no. 1151, 4.235 no. 408, Degrassi, *FC* 30, *fin.*).

CIL 6.1492 (cf. p. 3142), *ILS* 6106, A. Bartoli, *RendPontAcc* 25–26 (1949–50, 1950–51, publ. 1951) 89–93; idem, *RendLinc* ser. 8, vol. 9 (1954) 473–475; Smallwood, *Nerva/Hadrian* 437, Sherk 23 no. 9 (text, bibl.).

Text: *L(ucio) Arruntio Stella, / L. Iulio Marino co(n)s(ulibus) / XIIII K(alendas) Nov(embres), / M(anius) Acilius Placidus (et) L. Petronius Fronto, /* [5] *IIIIvir(i) i(ure) d(icundo), s(enatum) c(onsuluerunt) Ferentini in curia aedis Mer/curi. Scribundo adfuerunt Q(uintus) Segiarnus Mae/cianus (et) T(itus) Munnius Nomantinus.*

Quod universi v(erba) f(ecerunt) T(itum) Pomponium Bassum, claris/simum virum, demandatam sibi curam ab / [10] *indulgentissimo imp(eratore) Caesare Nerva Traiano / Augusto Germanico, qua aeternitati Italiae / suae prospexit, secundum liberalitatem eius / ita ordinare ut omnis aetas curae eius merito / gratias agere debeat futurumque ut tantae /* [15] *virtutis vir auxilio sit futurus municipio /*

nostro, q(uid) d(e) e(a) r(e) f(ieri) p(laceret), d(e) e(a) r(e) i(ta) c(ensuere): /

placere conscriptis legatos ex hoc ordine / mitti ad T. Pomponium Bassum, clarissi-/mum virum, qui ab eo impetrent in clien-/[20] *telam amplissimae domus suae muni/cipium nostrum recipere dignetur / patronumque se cooptari, tabula / hospitali incisa hoc decreto in domo / sua posita, permittat. Censuere. /*[25] *Egerunt legati / A(ulus) Caecilius A(uli) f(ilius) Quirinalis et / Quirinalis f(ilius).*

"In the (suffect) consulship of L. Arruntius Stella and L. Iulius Marinus, on October 19, M'. Acilius Placidus and L. Petronius Fronto, Board of Four for applying the law, consulted the senate of Ferentinum in the meeting-hall of the Temple of Mercury. Present as witnesses to the record were Quintus Segiarnus Maecianus and Titus Munnius Nomantinus.

"Whereas they all as one man declared (1) that the illustrious Titus Pomponius Bassus, in accord with the policy of the most indulgent emperor Trajan, was organizing the task assigned to him by him (the emperor), whereby he (Trajan) has provided for the endless duration of his Italy, in such a way that each generation should properly give thanks for his (Bassus's) administration, and (2) that a man of so much merit is bound to be of assistance to our town; as to what it was pleasing should be done about this matter, they thus voted:

"'that it pleased the senators that representatives from this body be sent to the illustrious T. Pomponius Bassus to persuade him to deign to receive our town into the patronage of his great house and to allow himself to be chosen as patron and a tablet engraved with this decree to be set up in his house.'

"They (so) voted. The envoys who carried this out were Aulus Caecilius Quirinalis, son of Aulus, and Quirinalis junior."

Interesting writing and arrangement—paragraphing (by extension left), centering (lines 3, 25, 27), and spacing (1–3, 16, 26 f.). Except for the omission of *ut* after *impetrent* (19), the long periodic sentence (8–24, *permittat*) seems to be in unexceptionable Latin (note the primary sequence after *v(erba) f(ecerunt)* [8] and *c(ensuere)* [16]), but the *qua-* clause used of Trajan (11 f.) and the repetition of *clar. virum* with Bassus (8 f., 18 f.) suggest the florid prose of post–Silver Age Latin; *futurum (esse) ut . . . sit futurus* means no more than *futurum (esse) virum*, no *ut*-clause being needed, but the periphrasis adds bulk and weight. Noteworthy the number of words—six—divided at line ends.

Lines 4 f. Only two men, but called *IIIIviri*; of the four members, these were the two *iure dicundo* (the other two being *aedilicia potestate*), so more logically called *IIviri iure dicundo*; cf. *ILS* 3: 2.687, 696 f. (several other examples of this title applied to two men, 697 lines 7 f.).

Segiarnus (6) presumably a Hernican nomen (Latinian? Oscan? cf. E. T. Salmon, *OCD* 505 *s.v.* Hernici). *Nomantinus* (7) appears in the photo as *-linus*, an error no doubt in applying the white coloring to the letters in the museum. With *placere* (17) either the accus. with infin., as here, or *ut* / *ne* with subjunct. is found; cf. *OLD* 6.1385 col. 3 §5 b. The abbreviations of lines 8 and 16 are regular in legal Latin.

A *tabula hospitalis* was a tablet attesting to the relation of *hospitium* ("guest friendship," "family friendship") between two families or similar groups, as here between a town and a person (or perhaps his family as well); cf. A. D'Ors, op. cit. (above, on 7) 367–380, Tables de hospitalidad y patronato.

55. Commemoration of a Local Dignitary, Ferentino. Trajanic?

An inscription cut in the living rock (apparently limestone) on the SE side of the hill of Ferentino (see on 54), outside Porta S. Maria (or Porta Maggiore); the inscription is cut within a sculptured framework like the front of a small temple. (See *Lazio* 432, "Testamento di Aulo Quintilio," and the little map of Ferentino, on the back of the map of Frosinone, 432/433.) The surface was rather worn, the lettering not always certain, when it was examined in 1973.

Commemorated is A. Quinctilius Priscus, a local dignitary and patron, whose inscribed statue base (no doubt of the statue mentioned in this inscr.) is also extant. The inscription lists his local offices, his one military post, his honor in having a statue of himself set up by the local senate in the forum of Ferentinum (the expense of which he then paid for, himself), and his arrangements with the local government whereby he provided in perpetuity for a yearly distribution, on his birthday, of pastry, a honey-and-wine drink, and a little money, a special distribution of nuts and wine to boys of the plebeian class, and the adornment/upkeep of his statue and other likenesses of himself.

CIL 10.5853 (add. p. 1013 and cf. 5852, the statue-base inscr.), *ILS* 6271, Laum 2.171 no. 23 (has lines 8–19); cf. A. Bartoli, *RendLinc* (loc. cit., above, on **54**) 487. Neither Mommsen (*CIL*) nor Dessau conjectures the date, but Bartoli dates the inscr. in the first half of the second cent. (A.D.) and, more closely, as Trajanic by palaeographical comparison with *CIL* 10.6887, a milestone of A.D. 115 (not 118, and *tr. pot.* XVIIII, not XVIII); he is followed by *Lazio*, loc. cit., and "Trajanic" seems satisfactory palaeographically.

Text: *A(ulo) Quinctilio A(uli) f(ilio)* / *(tribu) Pal(atina) Prisco,* / *IIIIvir(o) aed(ilicia) potest(ate),* *IIIIvir(o) iure* / *dic(undo),* *IIIIvir(o) quinq(uennali) adlecto ex s(enatus) c(onsulto),* /⁵ *pontif(ici); praef(ecto) fabr(um).* / *[Hu]ius ob eximiam munificent(iam) quam in munic(ipes)* / *suos contulit, senat(us) statuam publice ponend(am) in foro, ubi ipse* / *vellet, censuere. H(onore) a(ccepto) i(mpensam) r(emisit). Hic ex s(enatus) c(onsulto) fundos Ceponian(um)* / *et Roianum et Mamian(um) et pratum Exosco ab r(e) p(ublica) redem(it) /*[10] *H̶S̶ (= sestertium,* gen. pl.) *L̅X̅X̅ m(ilibus) n(ummum) et in avit(um) r(ei) p(ublicae) reddid(it), ex quor(um) reditu de H̶S̶ (= sestertium) I̅V̅ m(ilibus) (et) CC (= ducentis) / quod annis* (i.e., *quotannis) VI Id(us) Mai(as), die natal(i) suo, perpet(uo* or *-um) daretur praesent(ibus) / municipib(us) et incol(is) et mulierib(us) nuptis crustul(i) p(ondo) I, mulsi hemin(a); / et circa triclin(ia) decurionib(us) mulsum et crust(ulum) et sportul(a) H̶S̶ (= sestertii) X (= deni) n(ummi), / item puer(is), curiae increment(is); et VIvir(is) Aug(ustalibus) quibusq(ue) u(na?) v(escendum?) e(st?) crust(ulum), /*[15] *mulsum, et H̶S̶ (= sestertii) VIII (= octoni) n(ummi); et in triclin(io) meo ampl(ius) in sing(ulos) h(omines) H̶S̶ I (= sestertii singuli) n(ummi); et in orn(atum) / statuae et imag(inis* or *-inum) mear(um) res p(ublica) perpet(uo* or *-um) H̶S̶ (= sestertios) XXX n(ummos) impend(at) arbitr(atu) I̅I̅I̅I̅vir(um), / aedilium cura. Favorabil(e) est si puer(is) plebeis sine distinctione liber/tatis nucum sparsion(em) mod(iorum) XXX et ex vini urnis VI potionum / eministration(em) digne incrementis praestiterint.*

"To Aulus Quinctilius Priscus, son of Aulus, of the Palatine 'tribe,' member of the Board of Four with the power of aediles, of the Board of Four for applying the law, of the Board of Four with the power of censors, elected in accordance with a decree of the (local) senate, priest; *praefectus fabrum.*

"Because of this man's extraordinary generosity toward his fellow-townsmen the (local) senate ordered a statue (of him) to be set up officially in the forum where he himself might wish. On receipt of this honor he remitted the expense.

"This man, by arrangement with the senate, purchased for 70,000 sesterces the Ceponius, Roianus, and Mamianus farms and the Exosco meadow from the community and gave them back to the community for its perpetual possession, and from their yearly revenue of 4,200 sesterces, on May 10, his birthday, there should be given in perpetuity to the (town's) citizens and (other) residents and married women, who are present, one pound of confectionery and a half sextarius of honey wine (each); and, around table-couches, to the town councillors honey wine and confectionery and a gift of ten sesterces (each), likewise to (the councillors') sons, (future) additions to the (local) senate,

"and to the *seviri Augustales* and to those (?) who are to eat with them (?), confectionery, honey wine, and eight sesterces (each); and, at my (own) table-couch, furthermore, to each person one sesterce; and for the adornment/upkeep of my statue and (other) likenesses (painted portraits?), let the community, in perpetuity, expend thirty sesterces at the discretion of the Board of Four, with the aediles in charge. It is agreeable (to me, the testator) if they (the town councillors?) provide the plebeian boys, whether of free birth or slave, a scattering of nuts—thirty measures—and the serving of drinks from six urns of wine, in a manner worthy of the next generation of senators."

In all four examples of I̅I̅I̅I̅vir(—) and perhaps in *VIvir(is),* the two elements are interpunctuated (*Contrib.* 184); there are two tall I's (one not long, *iure* line 3), three tall T's (ibid., 205), six 2-letter ligatures, and the first vertical in the sign for sesterces is always taller; several lines protrude left, two or three as if for paragraphing (1, 6 [?], 14); some letters are imperfect (e.g., E in *et,* line 10, has no middle bar).

Priscus's last-named post, of aide-de-camp to some general, was in the Roman army and probably brief (cf. Kornemann, *RE* 6.1922, 5 ff., 34 ff., *OCD* 428, both *s.v.* Fabri). Priscus's "tribe," Palatina, though of city-of-Rome origin (Varro, *L. L.* 5.45), came to include members in many communities all over Italy, including Ferentinum (Dessau, *ILS* 3: 1, 595); anyhow, by the time of Trajan, "the tribe had no political meaning, and the connection of tribe and land had largely disappeared" (Taylor, *VDRR* 323 *fin.*). Priscus seems to have belonged to the municipal equestrian aristocracy, to have briefly held the post of *praef. fabrum*, and then returned to F. and there held these high civil and religious posts, and become a wealthy landowner and philanthropist. (See Addenda/Corrigenda.)

Note the change from third person to first at line 15 *med.* (*meo*) and with it the change of syntax and sequence from *daretur* (11) to *impend(at)* (16); *senatus . . . censuere* (7 f.), as in English "The Cabinet are agreed." Lines 8 ff.: *h. a. i. r.*, clearly a regular formula; *Exosco*, an interesting indeclinable name for a meadow; *in avit. r. p.*, "to become its property in perpetuity" (Mommsen and Dessau, *ad loc.*, *TLL* 2.1442, 27 ff.); the first renter of the four properties was probably Priscus himself, as Mommsen suggests; the yearly rent of 4,200 sest. is 6 percent; for *municipes* vs. *incolae*, cf. F. F. Abbott and A. C. Johnson, *Municipal Administration in the Roman Empire* (Princeton 1926) 57 f.; though the numerals for 70 and 4 are both barred, so as to indicate thousands, they are followed, as often, by *m(ilibus)*.

56. Statue-Base Inscription in Honor of Hadrian, Athens. A.D. 112. A marble base (cm. ca. 55.5 × 83 × 83, at the top surface), found in 1862 *in situ*, in the excavations of the theater of Dionysus, at the foot of the central section of the auditorium, "in the best place of all" (Graindor), just behind the throne of the priest of Dionysus Eleuthereus (partly visible in plate 684, p. 547, of John Travlos's *Pictorial Dictionary of Ancient Athens*, London 1971). On top of the base are a circular cut and places for two feet, for the statue that must have once stood there. The writing field, indented slightly, cm. ca. 40 × 76; letter heights of the Latin, line 1, 4.1–4.3 cm., 2–3, ca. 3.2 cm., the rest, ca. 3.0–3.2 cm., excluding the lower extensions of G, L, and Q; of the Greek, ca. 1.6–1.8 cm. Ivy-leaf interpuncts generally in the Latin, none in the

Greek; one tall long I (*Traiani*, line 2, *fin.*); bars over all the numerals in the Latin, as was normal (numerical prefixes and ordinal adjectives: *Co,.rib.* 166 f.).

A dedication to Hadrian as archon of Athens, before he became emperor; the Latin describes most of his career to date, the Greek briefly honors him as archon. The date of H.'s archonship is given, by naming the Roman consuls of A.D. 112, by Phlegon of Tralles, a freedman of H. (F. Jacoby, *FGrH* 2 B [Berlin 1929] 1184, no. XXV), but W. Kolbe, *Athen. Mitt.* 46 (1921) 106 f., shows that the Athenian year 112/3 is more likely than 111/2; *IG* 2² also says 112/3.

CIL 3.550, *ILS* 308, *IG* 3.464 (superseded by *IG* 2²: 3 [Berlin 1935, repr. Chicago 1974] 3286); photo and brief commentary in P. Graindor, *Athènes de Tibère à Trajan* (Cairo 1931 Univ. Égyptienne, *Rec. de Travaux publ. par la Fac. des Lettres*, fasc. 8) 26 f., fig. 3. Cf. *PIR*² 1.28 f., no. 184.

Text of the Latin: *P(ublio) Aelio P(ubli) f(ilio) (tribu) Serg(ia) Hadriano, / co(n)s(uli), VIIviro epulonum, sodali Augustali, leg(ato) pro pr(aetore) Imp(eratoris) Nervae Traiani / Caesaris Aug(usti) Germanici Dacici Pannoniae Inferioris, praetori eodemque / tempore leg(ato) leg(ionis) I Minerviae P(iae) F(idelis) bello Dacico, item trib(uno) pleb(is), quaestori Imperatoris /⁵ Traiani et comiti expeditionis Dacicae donis militaribus ab eo donato bis, trib(uno) leg(ionis) II / Adiutricis P. F., item legionis V Macedonicae, item legionis XXII Primigeniae P. F., seviro / turmae eq(uitum) R(omanorum), praef(ecto) feriarum Latinarum, Xviro s(tlitibus) i(udicandis).*

"To P. Aelius Hadrianus, son of P., of the Sergia 'tribe,' consul, *septemvir epulonum* (a major priesthood), *sodalis Augustalis* (a minor), the emperor Trajan's legate for Lower Pannonia, praetor and at the same time commander of the 1st Minervia legion (*p., f.*) in the Dacian War, likewise tribune of the plebs, quaestor of the emperor Trajan and his companion in the Dacian expedition, twice presented with military prizes by him, tribune of the second Adiutrix Legion (*p.*, *f.*), likewise of the 5th Macedonian legion, likewise of the 22nd Primigenia legion (*p.*, *f.*), president of a division of Roman knights, prefect of the Latin Festival, member of the Board of Ten for judging law-suits."

Some of these titles are hardly translatable. *Pia* ("dutiful") and *fidelis* ("loyal") are titles of honor granted by the emperor, *Minervia*, *Adiutrix*, *Primigenia* determinatives for distinguishing one legion from another bearing the same number, with of course their own connotations. The posts listed are in descending (i.e., reversed chronological) order except for the two priesthoods, which as often are listed immediately after the highest civil office held without respect to when H. entered them (for life). H. was a consul suffect in 108. The *item*s ("likewise") do not mean "at the same time."

57. Column-of-Trajan Inscription, Rome.
A.D. 113. A marble slab, somewhat damaged (4 ft. 5¾ in. × 10 ft., the lower edge 10½ ft. above the pavement: Catich 5 f.), set in the SE side of the square marble base of the Column of Trajan and inscribed with an inscription (often considered the finest example of Roman lettering, with letters from ca. 11.5 down to ca. 9.7 cm. tall, as measured on Catich's drawings) dedicated to the emperor Trajan by the "Senate and People of Rome, in order to make clear how high a *mons et locus* were removed *tantis operibus*."

This plan, which required only a plain column of proper height, must have been soon modified to allow for (1) a column sculptured with scenes from Trajan's earlier Dacian campaigns and surmounted by a statue of him (replaced under Sixtus V by one of St. Peter) and (2) an inner spiral staircase leading to the top of the column and a tomb chamber cut in the base (with entrance below the inscr.) to receive T.'s ashes, which in due course were placed there in a golden urn (Dio

Epit. 69.2.3, Eutrop. 8.5.2, [Aur. Vict.] *Epit. de Caes.* 13.11). The date of the inscr. is given by T.'s *trib. pot.* number, 17 (Dec. 10, 112/113), narrowed rather securely to 113 by a fragment of the *Fasti Ostienses*, *NS* 1932, 201.

CIL 6.960 (cf. p. 3777), *ILS* 294, S/C 127, Smallwood, *Nerva/Trajan* 378 (*a*). Cf. P/A 238 *s.v.* Forum Traiani, Strong 2.75–81, J. Weiss in *RE* 6A: 2 (1937) 2079, 26 ff., *s.v.* Traiani forum 1, Lugli, *Roma ant.* 286–295, L. Rocchetti in *Encicl. dell'arte antica . . . ,* 2 (Rome 1959) 756–760 *s.v.* Colonna (large bibl.), Edward M. Catich, *Letters Redrawn from the Trajan Inscription in Rome* (Davenport, Iowa, 1961) (portfolio with book and 93 plates, including the best photo available of the inscr., pl. 70; cf. the anon. review in the *Times Literary Supplement* [London] May 4, 1962, p. 328), G. J. Donnelly, "Columna Disputata," *CJ* 61: 1 (1965) 19–21, Nash 1.283–286 *s.v.* Col. Traiani, G. A. Mansuelli, *Epigraphica* 31 (1969) 124–138, Calabi Limentani 252–254 no. 53, Coarelli 116–127.

Text (from Catich's pl. 70): *Senatus Populusque Romanus* / *Imp(eratori) Caesari divi Nervae f(ilio) Nervae* / *Traiano Aug(usto) Germ(anico) Dacico, pontif(ici)* / *maximo, trib(unicia) pot(estate)* $\overline{XVII}$*, imp(eratori)* $\overline{VI}$*, co(n)s(uli)* $\overline{VI}$*, p(atri) p(atriae),* /⁵ *ad declarandum quantae altitudinis* / *mons et locus tanti[s ope]ṛibus sit egestus.*

"The Senate and People of Rome, to (the emperor Trajan), in order to make clear how high a hill and area [or, hilly area, by hendiadys] were (was) removed for (or, by?) such great works [i.e., public works, monuments? Mansuelli, 125]."

Line 1, *fin*. S is present but slightly damaged. Line 6 was damaged, probably in 975, but the full text had been reported by Anonymus Einsidlensis of the 8th/9th cent. (above, Intro., III.1). The top of the tall I of *tantis*, or at least the serif, seems visible in Catich's photo. Apart from the problem of the case of *operibus* (either dat. or abl. makes sense, the abl. seems favored by most scholars, but I incline to favor the dative, with Mansuelli), Dio (*Epit.* 68.16.3) confirms the sense of the *ad decl.* clause: "(Trajan) set up in the Forum (of T.) an enormous column both for his own burial-place and as an indication of the work (done) throughout the Forum. For, that whole area being hilly, he cut it down to a depth equal to the height of the column [100 Roman feet, m. 29.78: Lugli, 293] and thus made the Forum level." It seems best to agree with those who believe that the hill was the spur of the Quirinal in the direction of the Capitoline; the discovery of earlier dwellings and a paved road under the foundations of the column is not pertinent.

58. Record of Building the Original Pantheon, Rome. Probably copied from the original inscription by order of Hadrian while he was emperor; the letter grooves are now filled with 19th-cent. "orichalcum." The original building was begun by Agrippa, while he was consul for the third time, in 27, finished by him in 25 B.C. (Dio 53.27.2), restored by Domitian after a fire A.D. 80, and after another fire entirely rebuilt by Hadrian, again repaired by Septimius Severus and Caracalla in 202 (their inscr. is in small letters under Agrippa's, in order to accommodate all their titles). Hadrian, as always but once in building public buildings (*Hist. Aug.*, *Hadrian* 19.9), has not inscribed his own name. It is generally agreed, and seems almost certain, that the present inscr., cut in the white-marble (Licht, 40 col. 2) architrave, is not the original one of Agrippa's Pantheon, but belongs to Hadrian's architecturally revolutionary rebuilding: so, except for Strong, 1.132 ("transferred presumably from the original building"), all those consulted, including R. Vighi, *The Pantheon*, transl. J. B. Ward Perkins (Rome 1962) 9, Kjeld de Fine Licht, *The Rotunda in Rome . . .* (Copenhagen 1968 Jutland Archaeol. Soc., *Publ.* 8) 189, 287 n. 38 (im-

plied), and Frank E. Brown by letter of Sept. 17, 1975 (the inscr. "is perfectly centered on the indubitably Hadrianic frieze and scaled to its height. What is reported about the Agrippan bldg. and deducible from the remains of its foundations suggests a much smaller member, and from what we know of Augustan moldings and carving one would expect something quite different").

The grooves were no doubt once filled with bronze, this replaced after loss with "litteris ex orichalco inscite factis" (Huelsen, *CIL* 6.31196) by "the Minister (of Public Instr., Guido) Baccelli" (sometime in 1881/1900: M. Crespi, *Diz. biogr. degli Italiani* 5 [Rome 1963] 13–15), Lugli, 3.125. Scherer, pl. 192, gives a view of the Pantheon before 1881, which "shows the empty matrices of the inscr." (see on pl. 190). One sees nothing in the lettering to interfere with a Hadrianic date, but Huelsen's phrase about Baccelli's "clumsily made" new letters gives no confidence that the new metal fills the ancient grooves perfectly.

If the pronaos is m. 34 wide (P/A 384), the Agrippa inscr. would seem to be ca. m. 21.6 long. K. Ziegler, *RE* 18: 3 (1949) 736, 29 f., *s.v.* Pantheion, gives the width as m. 39, but his plan, 735 f., shows a pronaos much less wide, and *Roma e dintorni*, ed. 5 (1940 and repr.) 159 and ed. 6 (1962 and repr.) 196, gives m. 33.40 and 33.10, resp., as the width. Vighi, op. cit. 22, gives this as m. 33.10.

CIL 6.896 (cf. 31196 and p. 3777), *ILS* 129, Cal. Lim. 275 f., no. 65. Add Nash, 2.170–175 *s.v.* Pantheon (7 photos and large bibl. to 1965); J. B. Ward-Perkins, in his and A. Boëthius's *Etruscan and Roman Architecture* (1970) index 618 *s.v.* Pantheon.

Text: *M(arcus) Agrippa L(uci) f(ilius) co(n)s(ul) tertium fecit.*

"Marcus (Vipsanius) Agrippa, son of Lucius, consul for the third time, had (this building) built."

For *tertium*, etc., "for the third time," see above, on **20**.

59. Commemoration of a Roman Public Official, Aquileia. A.D. 122/124, or perhaps a little later.

A statue base of white marble (m. 1.0 × cm. 65 × 23) found in Aquileia in 1805 (or 1815), taken to Vienna in 1816, but eventually back in Aquileia in the Mus. Archeologico Nazionale (in 1978, in the lapidario in the garden). Base of a statue set up by decree of the local decurions in honor of a patron (of Aquileia, no doubt), A. Platorius Nepos Aponius Italicus Manilianus G. Licinius Pollio, consul suffect A.D. 119. He seems to have been originally G. Licinius Pollio, then adopted by A. Platorius . . . Manilianus (Gordon, *JRS* 48 [1958] 47). His latest post here listed seems to be the governorship of Britain (attested A.D. 122–124; perhaps as late as 126 or 127: A. R. Birley, op. cit. [above, on **45**] 69 f., no. 19), so this inscr. would seem to date from that period. He is not known to have held any post after Britain, probably because he fell out of favor with Hadrian (*Hist. Aug., Hadrian* 4.2, 15.2, 23.4).

CIL 5.877 (ed. Mommsen), *ILS* 1052, Artur Betz *RE* 20: 2 (1950) 2545–2548 *s.v.* Platorius 2. Cf. *PIR*[1] 3.43 f., no. 337; G. Brusin, *Aquileia, guida storica e artistica* (Udine 1929) 106 no. 42; A. Calderini, *Aquileia romana* . . . (Milan preface 1930, Pubbl. Univ. Cattol. del Sacro Cuore, ser. 5, sc. stor., vol. 10) 281 f. ("una statua per decreto decurionale"); cf. L. Harmand, *Le patronat sur les collectivités publiques* . . . (Paris 1957 Univ. de Paris, Fac. des Lettres, *Thèse*) 224.

Text: *A(ulo) Platorio A(uli) f(ilio) / (tribu) Serg(ia) Nepoti / Aponio Italico / Maniliano /*[5] *G(aio) Licinio Pollioni, / co(n)s(uli), auguri, legat(o) Aug(usti) / pro praet(ore) provinc(iae) Bri/tanniae; leg(ato) pro pr(aetore) pro/vinc(iae) German(iae) Inferior(is), /*[10] *leg. pro pr. provinc. Thrac(iae), / leg(ato) legion(is) Ī Adiutricis, / quaest(ori) provinc. Maced(o/niae), / curat(ori) viarum Cassiae, / Clodiae,* *Ciminiae, Novae /*[15] *Traianae, candidato divi / Traiani, trib(uno) mil(itum) leg(ionis) XXII / Primigen(iae) P(iae) F(idelis), praet(ori), tri/b(uno) / pleb(is), IIIvir(o) capitali; / patrono: /*[20] *d(ecurionum) d(ecreto).* (Mommsen moves the phrase *quaest. provinc. Maced.*, line 12, to before *candidato*, line 15; so *quaest. provinc. Maced. cand. divi Tr.* forms one unit.)

"To Aulus Platorius Nepos Aponius Italicus Manilianus Gaius Licinius Pollio, son of Aulus, of the 'tribe' Sergia, consul, augur, Imperial governor of the province of Britain, governor of the province of Lower Germany, governor of the province of Thrace, commander of the 1st Adiutrix legion, quaestor of the province of Macedonia on the recommendation of the deified Trajan [following Mommsen's transposition], supervisor of the Via Cassia, the Via Clodia, the Via Ciminia, (and) the Via Nova Traiana; military tribune of the 22nd Primigenia legion (*p., f.*), praetor, tribune of the plebs, *triumvir capitalis* (Board of Three in charge of capital sentences); patron (of Aquileia): by decree of the town councillors."

Of some sixteen inscriptions that name Platorius, this is the only one that gives his name complete. As often in such career-inscrs., his consulship (A.D. 119) is listed first, then his religious title (the augurate was one of the four highest such *collegia*); the remaining titles seem to be in descending order (the governorship of Britain certainly later than the consulship, and probably later also that of Lower Germany, the others before 119), but there are questions about the proper order of lines 12 ff. and about what *cand. divi Tr.* goes with (probably with *quaest. prov. Mac.*, as Mommsen thought); the latest (and, very likely, last) title is that of "patron" (of Aquileia).

60. Verse Epitaph of a Young Boy, Rome.

A.D. 126 or 127. Marble tablet (cm. ca. 37 × ca. 53–54 overall, 27.8 × 41.7–ca. 42.3 writing field within borders and including sculpture, thickness ca. 11.5 cm. (but not uniform), found in 1817 with an urn (presumably the boy's) in a vineyard on the Via Appia, outside Rome; in the Vatican collection by 1820, in the Galleria lapidaria by 1882, where it still is, sect. XVII (inv. no. 9387). To the right of the inscription is a figure in low relief representing no doubt the deceased: a boy dressed in tunic and toga, with a *bulla* (amulet) around his neck and a book bag at his feet; his right arm points to the inscr., and his face looks in the same direction as though he were speaking the epitaph (which is appropriately in the first person).

Epitaph in dactylic hexameters (with some faults) of a boy named Marcianus, who was born A.D. 120 and died (apparently) early in his 7th year. The consuls of 120 are named in lines 3 f. Letter heights: gradually decreasing from 10 to 8 mm. from top to bottom. The run-over seems intended to be centered.

CIL 6.7578, whence Buecheler, *CLE* 1.422; Gordon, *Archaeology* 4 (1951) 48 f. (photo, notes, transl.), *Album* 2.47 f., no. 183.

Text:

> Hoc ego sum tumulo Marcianus redditus
>   aevo.
> Nondum Persephones sperabam visere regna.
> Consulibus tunc natus eram iteroque Severo
> et Fulvo pariter, quo coepi dulcis haberi.
> 5   Sextus ut excessit, coepi languescere in
>   annum.
> Apstulit o saeva lux nona parentibus orta
> planctibus heu miserae matris patrisque
>   simitu.
> Spes mihi quam magna fuerat, si me mea /
>   fata tulissent!
> 10   Musae mihi dederant puero facundus ut
>   essem.
> Invidit Lachesis, Clotho me saeva necavit,
> tertia nec passa est pietate rependere matri.
> Quam pie, quam crebre venit Sacra Via tota,
> flevit et inmensa turba funusque secuta!
> 15   Dixerunt ferale⟨m⟩ diem stationibus atris,
> quod tenerae aetati spes fallax apstulit annos.
> Nec non omnigena passim vicinia venit,
> ut mecum florem fato moriente⟨m⟩ viderent.
> Tu reddas, Aeterne, piis solacia semper
> 20   et vitam serves cunctis generisque piorum.

For a translation, see *Archaeology* 4.49.

Line 1. Apparent traces of earlier writing under *hoc ego. Hoc tumulo*: no room for *in*, nor is it needed with a noun having a local sense. *Redd. aevo*: cf. [(?)*ossa somno hic* (?) *a*]*eterno reddita co*[. . .], *CIL* 6.35516; cf. B. Lier, "Topica carminum sepulcralia Latinorum," *Phil.* 62 (1903) 581, with reff. to *CLE*, but *redditus aevo* seems unparalleled. Lines 3 f. A rather labored way of naming the consuls of A.D. 120— -*que, et*, the excessive *pariter*—no doubt *metri causa*. They were L. Catilius Severus, for the second time, and T. Aurelius Fulvus (the later emperor Antoninus Pius). Instead of *itero*, a rare variant of *iterum* (cf. *primo, secundo*, etc), the regular form would have suited the meter quite as well. Line 4. If Buecheler's punctuation *pariter, quo* is correct, then *quo = ubi* ("when"), as occasionally elsewhere ("late Latin," Schmalz/Hofmann, 2.767, cf. Hofmann/Szantyr 652 f.). Lines 8 f. For the indic. *fuerat* in the apodosis of an Unreal Condition ("when the conclusion is confidently anticipated," or, perhaps here, *metri causa*), cf. G/L 386 §597 Rem. 2. Line 12, *tertia*: sc. Parca, "Fate," i.e., Atropos. Line 13, *Sacra Via tota*: nominative, though *Sacra* is apparently spondaic here. Line 14, *inmensa turba*, also nomin. despite the metrically long *a*'s. Line 19, *Aeterne*: sc. *deus*, cf. Cumont, *RE* 1 (1894) 696 *s.v.* Aeternus, or Wissowa 364 f. Line 20, *generisque*: parallel with *cunctis*, so in error for *generique*? or in error for *generesque*, so parallel with *serves*? see Buecheler's note *ad loc.*, 1.197 *init.*

61. Epitaph of a Freedman of Trajan's, Rome. A.D. 130. One inscribed side (front or back), now apparently in two pieces joined together, of a marble base inscribed in front and back with the same inscription and now cut into two tablets; first reported in a private house in Rome before 1489; by 1876, both tablets in the Vatican, the present one in the Gall. lap. (inv. no. 5633), sect. VI, when last seen (1973).

Writing field (framed by a double molding) cm. 61.3–62.0 × ca. 52.5, overall 79.2 × 70.3; letter heights, from cm. 3.3–3.7 (line 1) down to 2.2–2.6 (13).

Epitaph (originally under a portrait statue?) of an Imperial freedman, M. Ulpius Phaedimus, formerly Trajan's personal servant, who died at age 28 at Selinus (far-west coast of Cilicia, southern Asia Minor), Aug. 12, 117 (shortly after T.'s own death there, news of which reached Hadrian while he was governor of Syria, Aug. 11: cf. *Hist. Aug., Hadrian* 4.7, Dio, *Epit.* 68.33.3), and whose remains were transferred (presumably to Rome) in 130; set up by another Imperial freedman, whose agnomen "Phaedimianus" shows that he had been a slave of Phaedimus before passing into the ownership of the emperor, probably Trajan himself (cf. Weaver, 217).

CIL 6.1884 (cf. p. 3229), *ILS* 1792, *Album* 2.52 f., no. 187. For Trajan's and Phaedimus's deaths and Hadrian's succession, see Dessau, in *Beiträge z. alten Gesch. u. Geogr., Festschrift f. H. Kiepert* (Berlin 1898) 88–91, R. Paribeni, *Optimus Princeps . . .* , 2 (Messina 1927) 310 n. 16, W. Weber, *CAH* 11.300.

Text: *M(arco) Ulpio Aug(usti) lib(erto) Phaedimo, / divi Traiani Aug. a potione, / item a laguna et tricliniarch(ae), / lictori proximo et a comment(ariis) /⁵ beneficiorum; vixit ann(is) XXVIII; / abscessit Selinunte pri(die) Idus Augus(tas), / Nigro et Apro[nia]no co(n)s(ulibus); / reliquiae treiectae (sic, for tra-) eius / III Nonas Febr(uarias) ex permissu /¹⁰ collegii pontific(um), piaculo facto, / Catullino et Apro cos.: / dulcissimae memoriae eius, / Valens Aug(usti) lib(ertus) Phaedimianus, / a veste, ben(e) mer(enti) fecit.*

"To M. Ulpius Phaedimus, Imperial freedman, personal servant of the deified Trajan (chief table- and wine-servant, closest attendant, and secretary for the emperor's patronage); he lived 28 years, (and) departed (this life) at Selinus (on the coast of Cilicia Tracheia), Aug. 12, in the consulship of (Q. Aquilius) Niger and (M. Rebilus) Apronianus; his remains (were) transferred (to Rome?) Feb. 3, in the consulship of (Q. Fabius) Catullinus and (M. Flavius) Aper, by permission of the college of pontiffs, a propitiatory sacrifice having been performed: to his very dear memory, Valens Phaedimianus, Imperial freedman (and) valet, had (this) monument made—he well deserved it."

For *a, ab* used to indicate "the posts or duties of slaves, and other servants," see *OLD* 2 f., *s.v.* ab, 24, c; for many more inscriptional examples, Olcott, 1.29 col. 1–33 col. 2, *s.v.* a, sect. g. Note the smaller O in *cos.* twice (*Contrib.* 156 f.). Line 3, *laguna*: see *OLD* 997 *s.v.* lagona (*a lagona*, "cellarer"). Lines 8–11: on the transfer of corpses, see E. Gabba and G. Tibiletti, *Athenaeum* n.s. 38 (1960) 255–258.

62. Funerary Monument with Instructions to Heirs, Rome. Hadrianic? Marble slab (size?) found in 1944 *in situ*, immured above the door of a tomb (called "Tomb A," the easternmost in the northern row) in a pagan cemetery discovered under St. Peter's (in Vaticano), Rome; seen there in 1973.

It contains a request from G. Popilius Heracla to his heirs to build him a tomb on the Vatican Hill by the Circus of Gaius and Nero (this shows that the Circus was near the cemetery).

AE 1945, 136 (from a photo in *Il Vaticano nel 1944* [Vatican City 1944] 207 [cf. 206 and 190], but *AE*, like all the other editions seen, missed line 1 of the inscr., cut in the upper border, which marks the monument as funerary, and in line 11 [*AE's* 10] has *coheredes* for *coheres*); F. De Visscher, *Ant. Class.* 15 (1946) 117–126 and *Le droit des tombeaux romains* (Milan 1963) 295–309 (both with text and legal comm.); Toynbee/Ward Perkins 9 f., 19 n. 28 (text and transl., cf. index, 290, *s.v.* Tombs, A); cf. Degrassi, *Doxa* 2 (1949) 115 f.; G. Townend, *AJA* 62 (1958) 216; M. Guarducci, *The Tomb of St. Peter . . .* , transl. J. McLellan (New York 1960) 48 f.; Nash, 1.234 *s.v.*

Circus Gai et Neronis (with bibl.—the photo cuts off line 1); Toynbee, *Death and Burial* 87–91, fig. 4, tomb A.

The dating is conjectural, but De Visscher, 120 and 298 resp., Guarducci 49, Toynbee 88, and J. S. Gordon (above, p. 42) agree that it is probably Hadrianic or at least of the first half of the 2nd cent.

Text (from photo): *D(is) M(anibus)* (upper margin). / *Ex codicillis triplicibus Popili / Heraclae, / G(aius) Popilius Heracla heredib(us) salut(em) (dicit).* /[5] *Vos, heredes mei, rogo iubeoque / fideique vestrae committo uti / monumentum mihi faciatis in (monte) Vatic(ano) / ad Circum, iuxta monumentum Ulpi / Narcissi, ex ꟾꟾ (= sestertium,* gen. pl.) *V̅I̅ n(ummum), in quam rem /[10] numerabit Novia Trophime ꟾꟾ I̅I̅I̅ n(ummum) / et coheres eius ꟾꟾ I̅I̅I̅ n(ummum); ibique reliquias / meas et Fadiae Maximae uxoris meae, / si quid ei humanitus acciderit, poni volo; / cuius monumenti ius lego libertis liberta- /[15] busq(ue) meis et (eis) quos testamento manumisero, / sive quem in statu libertatis reliqui, et hoc amplius / Noviae Trophime, libertis libertabusq(ue) eius / posterisque suprascriptorum; et itum, aditum, am/bitum ⟨habere?⟩ sacrificique faciendi causa* [read *sacrificiumque facere?*] *ad id monu- /[20] ⟨men⟩tum uti ei⟨s?⟩ liceat.*

"To the Spirits of the Dead. From the codicil (i.e., supplement to the testament), in triptych, of Popilius Heracla. Gaius Popilius Heracla, to his heirs, greetings. You, my heirs, I ask and bid, and trust to your good faith, to build me a tomb on the Vatican (Hill) near the Circus (of Gaius and Nero), beside the monument of Ulpius Narcissus, at the cost of 6,000 sesterces, for which purpose Novia Trophime will pay out the sum of 3,000 sesterces and her coheir 3,000; and there I wish placed my remains and those of Fadia Maxima, my wife, if anything happens to her in the manner of human beings; of which monument I bequeath the legal control to my freedmen and freedwomen and to those whom I shall have freed by will, or to anyone (else) whom I have left in the status of freedom, and fur-

thermore to Novia Trophime, her freedmen and freedwomen, and to the descendants of those named above; and let it be allowed to her (or, them?) to have the right to go to, enter, go around, and perform sacrifices at, this monument."

The naming of Novia Trophime as coheiress, without identifying her further, and the fact that the testator's wife is still living (note the euphemism of *si quid ei humanitus acciderit*, for "when she dies") suggest a *ménage à trois*.

Line 1. *Dis Manibus:* cf. Lattimore 90–95 §17, E/M 383 *s.v.* Manes. Lines 9–11. The symbol for sesterces should have two verticals, since it represents 2½ (*asses*): IIS(*emis*). The bar over the numerals multiplies by 1,000. *N(ummum)*, gen. pl. (Sommer 349, 1): x thousands of *nummi*, "coins." Line 10. The bar over the VI of *Novia* carelessly repeats the bar just above? Line 17. *Trophime:* for the dative ending -*ē* in such Greek names, see *ILS* 3: 2.853 f. Lines 18–20. Note the change of syntax from *et itum* on, with difficulties in the Latin; *itum aditum ambitum*, a common formula on tombs, cf. Olcott 1.87 and 276, *s.vv.* aditus, ambitus. Line 19, *sacrificique faciendi:* the F in both words shows badly in the photo or else was badly cut in the first place, the first F showing only the vertical, the second looking like an L. For the awkward phrase *itum . . . causa*, cf. *CIL* 3.9315 (= *ILS* 8358), *iter ambitum actum aditum sacrificique causa.* Line 20. De Visscher (1946), 121 n. 1, would correct *ei* to *eis*; *ei* would mean that only Novia Trophime was to be allowed access to the tomb. The plural seems better.

63. Veterans' Dedication of Altar to Silvanus, Rome. A.D. 145. A marble altar (writing field 41.3–41.7 × 41.5 cm.; overall, ca. cm. 85 in front × ca. 55.5 at base × 26.2–31), now in two pieces joined together, on the east side of the garden of the Mus. Naz. Rom., Rome (inv. no. 72454); seen there in 1948, 1955, 1973. Letter heights: from 2.1–2.3 cm. (line 1) down to ca. 1.2–1.3 cm. (lines 7–9, 12 f.). The smaller, upper-left piece was found in 1885 in Rome in the ruins of the barracks of the Equites Singulares, near the Lateran Palace (P/A 105 *s.v.* Castra Equ. Sing.), the larger piece seen by G. Gatti in private possession near the same site and recognized by him as belonging with the smaller piece. (For a plan and views of the ruins of the Castra Nova Equ. Sing. of Severan date, which Platner/Ashby say was probably adjacent to the older barracks, or even a part of the same building, see Nash, 1.214–218 *s.v.* Castra Nova Equ. Sing.)

An ex-voto dedication (Jan. 4, 145) of an altar to Silvanus (sculptured with various attributes, in a central niche) by the veterans of the Equites Singulares (a select cavalry-corps that served as the emperor's bodyguard) who were honorably discharged at that time and whose twenty names, including eight with rank given, appear on the left and right sides. (For Silvanus among the deities worshipped by the Equ. Sing., cf. R. Peter in Roscher, 64th Lief. [1911] 864, 29 ff., *s.v.* Silvanus, with ref. to v. Domaszewski—cf. col. 824.)

CIL 6.31152 (cf. p. 3758), *ILS* 2183 (add.), *Album* 2.78 f., no. 207. The consuls of lines 1–6 are those of A.D. 145.

Text of frontal inscription: *Imp(eratore) Caes(are)* (space) *T(ito) Aelio* / *Hadri-*(space)*ano* / *Anto*(space)*nino* / *Aug(usto)* Pio (space) p(atre) p(atriae) ĪĪĪĪ, /⁵ M(arco) Aelio (space) Aurelio* / *Caesare* (space) ĪĪ co(n)s(ulibus),* / *pr(idie) Non(as)* (space) *Ianuar(ias),* / *vetera*(space)*ni ex* / *numero* (space) *eq(uitum) s(i)ng(ularium)* /¹⁰ *imp(eratoris) ñ(ostri),* (space) *missi* / *honesta* (space) *missione,* / *quibus* (space) *praefuit* / *Tattius* (space) *Maximus, tribu*(space)*nus,* /¹⁵ *Silvan(o)* (space) *aram* / *votum* (space) *animo* / *libentes posuer(unt).*

"In the consulship of Antoninus Pius, 4th time, and Marcus Aurelius, 2nd time, on Jan. 4, the veterans from the corps of our emperor's bodyguard, honorably discharged, who were under the command of Tattius Maximus, *tribunus*, gladly set up an altar to Silvanus as a votive offering."

Line 2. After HA an I was apparently cut, then erased. Line 6, tall C and S, small O, in *cos.*, as often. Line 7, right. Apparently AI was cut first, then corrected to IA. Line 10. *Noster* is found thus barred and abbreviated, esp. in Imperial titles (for any case, sing., plu., or dual) from ca. A.D. 40/60; cf. Gordon, *Supralin. Abbrs.* 85, *s.v.* noster, with ref., p. 132, to two works of L. Traube, and below, Appendix II. Line 13. For (G.) Tattius Maximus, see Stein, *RE* 4A: 2 (1932) 2477 f., *s.v.* Tattius; he rose to become *praefectus praetorii* (Prefect of the Guard) under Antoninus Pius (*Hist. Aug., Ant. Pius* 8.7). Line 16, *votum* is strange: "as a votive offering"? One would expect either *ex voto* ("in accordance with a vow") or *votam* ("vowed") modifying *aram*. Editors do not comment.

64. Funerary Monument of an Imperial Freedman, Rome, from nearby. A.D. 149.

A marble tablet (42 × 44.6 cm., max.), first reported (ca. 1741/42) near Rome; now set in the wall of the Gall. lap. of the Vatican (inv. no. 6932). Epitaph of an Imperial freedman, P. Aelius Iobacchus (his "P. Ael." indicates a freedman of Hadrian), with instructions about the *ius* of the monument. Letter heights: cm. 1.9–2.2 (line 1) down to 1.2–1.7 (line 11). A consular date, line 14.

CIL 6.10235 (cf. pp. 3502, 3908), *ILS* 8364, Bruns 383 no. 46, *FIRA* 3.271 no. 84 *b* (these two have only the legal part of the inscr.), *Album* 2.85 f., no. 213. The writing shows much variation and irregularity, as is normal in freehand capitals rather markedly influenced by common ("cursive"), i.e., non-lapidary, script (cf. *Contrib.* 74, 75–79).

Text: *D(is) M(anibus).* / *P(ublius) Ael(ius) Aug(usti) lib(ertus) Iobacchus fecit et* / *pedaturam dedit ante titul(um) p(edes) XXX,* / *ante fronte* (for *in fronte*?) *p(edes) XXX et in agro quoq(uoversus)* /⁵ *p(edes) centenos,* ⟨H⟩*yacin-*

tho, verna⟨e⟩ suo, / et sibi, liber(is), lib(ertis), libertabus suis pos/terisque eorum. Excipit ⟨ius?⟩ itus, actus, / aditus, ambitus, item aquae, AERAM / FVNEM pistrini, furni, virgar(um), ligni / [10] *sacrificiis faciundis et cetera (iura?) quae / in lege publica continentur. Hoc mo/numentum heredem non 'sequitur. / H(uic) m(onumento) d(olus) m(alus) a(besto). B(ene) m(erenti) m(emoriae) c(ausa)* (this phrase?). / *Orfito et Prisco co(n)s(ulibus).*

"To the Spirits of the Dead. P. Aelius Iobacchus, Imperial freedman, has built (this monument) and provided space in front of the inscr. for 30 ft., with frontage (?) of 30 ft., and in depth, in every direction, 100 ft., for Hyacinthus, his homeborn slave, and for himself, his children, freedmen, freedwomen, and their descendants. He specially reserves (for his heirs) the right of access by foot, approach (with beast of burden and vehicles), entry, walking around (the tomb), likewise the right to bring in water, (?) the right of carrying out funeral arrangements of the burial society (?)—mill/bakery, oven, kindling, firewood for performing sacrifices—and the other rights included in the public law.

"This monument does not follow the heir (i.e., is inalienable, cannot be disposed of by the heir). This monument shall be free from intentional desecration. (?) In memory of an estimable person.(?) In the consulship of Orfitus and Priscus." (A.D. 149)

The editions cited above, including the *Album*, are of practically no help to a translator. Not clear are lines 3–5, 7–9, 13 (second phrase). Line 2. *Ael.* Such abbreviations of *Aelius, Aurelius, Flavius, Ulpius* (AEL, AVR, FL, VLP) are attested in the inscrs. by A.D. 102 (FL, probably), certainly by 133 (FL), 135 (AEL, VLP), 158 (AVR): cf. *Album* 2.21 f., no. 166 with note on line 8, 56 no. 190, 100 no. 220, and vol. 4, 122 ff. (names of persons); these nomina, derived no doubt from emperors' names, seem to have become so common, as a result of manumission, as not to need

to be written in full. *Iobacchus*: Greek Ἰόβακχος. Line 4, *ante fronte* for the usual *in fronte*, the frontage of the burial plot, *ante* repeating the first *ante*? *quoq(uoversus)* seems unwanted, *in agro* being enough to show the depth of the plot. This seems to be large, 30 ft. in front, 100 ft. deep, with the inscribed face of the tomb 30 ft. from the road. Line 4, *fin.*, an interpunct, as at the end of 8 other lines; what else appears in the photo is extraneous. Line 5, *centenos* for *centum* presumably because of the distributive nature of *quoq*.

Line 7. All the editions cited read *excipit(ur)*, passive; this takes care of *itus . . . ambitus* (which can be nominative), but not of *pistrini . . . ligni*, whereas all the nouns following *excipit* except the puzzling AERAM FVNEM can be genitive, hence the suggestion of *ius* ("the right of, the right to use") as the first object of *excipit*, omitted perhaps by oversight because of the likeness of IVS and ITVS. Lines 8 f. J. H. Oliver (by letters of 1978–79) suggests capitalizing AERAM FVNEM and explains AERAM as *erani* (from eranus [Greek ἔρανος], "a kind of mutual benefit society") spelled *aerani* (the stonecutter having cut M by mistake for NI) and FVNEM as *fune⟨ru⟩m*. His translation of lines 7–11 is embodied in the version above. Line 9, "mill/bakery" is from *OLD* 1383 *s.v.* pistrinum; some sort of grinding apparatus plus an oven for cooking? Line 13, *h. m. d. m. a.*, a regular tomb-formula; *h. m.* can be either dat. or abl., but when written in full in the inscrs. it seems to be always dat.; cf. Olcott 43 f., *s.v.* absum, *ILS* 3: 2, 722 *s.v.* H M D M A, *OLD* 13 f. *s.v.* absum; the solution of *b. m. m. c.* is Orelli's (*Inscr. Lat. selectarum amplissima collectio . . .* , ed. Io. Casp. Orellius, 2 [Zurich 1828] 281 no. 4379), quoted but questioned by Dessau, *ILS*.

65. Verse Epitaph of Allia Potestas, Rome. Ca. A.D. 150–175? A large marble tablet with five holes for attaching it (67 max. × 59 × 2.5 cm.), found in 1912 in Via Pinciana, Rome, in two pieces, now connected; in 1948 and 1973 seen attached to the wall of Aula XI of the Mus. Naz. Rom., Rome (inv. no. 58694). Apart from the heading, the epitaph is in verse, another *Laudatio*, mostly in the third person, but partly in the first and second: 50 lines, in two columns of 25 lines each, of dactylic hexameters mixed with pentameters and heptameters (some metrically faulty), followed by an elegiac distich (the first line marked by diastole in *poterit*: ⌣⌣–) warning against damaging the stone. (This is probably the only Latin inscription that has been the cause of a lawsuit, brought by one editor/commentator against another, N. Terzaghi vs. M. Lenchantin de Gubernatis, 1914: cf. *Atene e Roma* 17 [1914] 258.)

The date is entirely conjectural and is generally put late, following the first editor, G. Mancini (*NS* 1912, p. 157), who dated it, on stylistic and palaeographical grounds, in the late-third or early-fourth cent. A.D.; but A. F. Liljeholm (*Eranos* 21 [1923] 97 f.) dated it not later than A.D. 200 (in consideration of the apices, tall I's, and metrical, palaeographical, and linguistic criteria), and Carlo Pascal (*Atene e Roma* 16 [1913] 258 col. 1) favored a date earlier than the end of the third cent. (on palaeographical grounds), but (272 *fin.*) not earlier than the first cent. (on literary grounds—echoes of Augustan poetry, esp. Ovid). J. S. Gordon, studying the inscr. in 1971, inclined, on epigraphical and palaeographical grounds, to favor "the unorthodox date of late-Augustan or early-Tiberian, though" she could "not rule out a later date, even the second cent., down to ca. 175." On linguistic grounds, P. Flobert favors the second half of the 2nd cent. (see below).

CIL 6.37965, *CLE* 3.1988; col. 1, lines 8–15, 17–23 transl. Lattimore 298 f.; all these with bibl., to which add the list of 13 items in J. Tolkiehn, in Bursian 171 (1915) 2 Abt., 92, or in Schanz/Hosius/Krüger 48 §15. The meaning is obscure at several points; Allius should have written plain prose. L. Gurlitt, *Philol.* 73 (1914) 291 f., has a German verse-translation. H. Häusle, *Das Denkmal als Garant des Nachruhms . . .* (*Zetemata*, 75 [1980] 94–97, no. 30) has text with another German translation.

Text: (heading) *Dis Manib(us) / Alliae, A(uli) l(ibertae), Potestatis.* Col. 1 (only one of several possible interpretations):

> *Hic Perusina sita est, qua non pretiosior ulla*
> *femina (est); de multis vix una aut altera*
> *visa (est)*
> *sedula. Seriola parva tam magna teneris!*
> *"Crudelis fati rector duraque Persiphone,*
> 5 *quid bona diripitis ex(s)uperantque mala?"*
> *quaeritur a cunctis; iam respondere fatigor.*
> *Dant lachrimas, animi signa benigna sui.*
> *Fortis, sancta, tenax, insons, fidissima*
> *custos,*
> *munda domi, sat munda foras, notissima*
> *volgo;*
> 10 *sola erat, ut posset factis occurrere cunctis.*
> *Exiguo sermone, inreprehensa manebat.*
> *Prima toro delapsa fuit, eadem ultima lecto*
> *se tulit ad quietem positis ex ordine rebus;*
> *lana cui e manibus nuncquam sine caussa*
> *recessit*
> 15 *opsequioque prior nulla moresque salubres.*
> *Haec sibi non placuit, numquam sibi libera*
> *visa.*
> *Candida luminibus pulchris aurata capillis*
> *et nitor in facie permansit eburneus illae,*
> *qualem mortalem nullam habuisse ferunt,*
> 20 *pectore et in nivę[o] brevis illi forma papillae.*
> *Quid crura Aṭalaṇtes? Status illi comicus ipse.*
> *Anxia non mansit sed corpore pulchra benigno.*
> *Levia membra tulit, pilus illi quaesitus ubique.*
> *Quod manibus duris fuerit culpabere forsan.*
> 25 *Nil illi placuit nisi quod peṛ se sibi fecerat*
> *ipsa.*

Col. 2 (with the same reservation):

> *Nosse fuit nullum studium, sibi se satis esse*
> *putabat;*
> *mansit et infamis quia nil admiserat umquam.*
> *Haec duo dum vixit iuvenes ita rexit*
> *amantes*
> *exemplo ut fierent similes Pyladisque et*
> *Orestae.*
> 5 *Una domus capiebat eos unusque et spiritus*
> *illis.*
> *Post hanc nunc idem diversi sibi quisq(ue)*
> *senescunt.*

Femina quod struxit talis nunc puncta
lacessunt.
Aspicite ad Troiam quid femina fecerit olim:
sit, precor, hoc iustum exemplis in parvo
grandibus uti.
10   *Hos tibi dat versus lachrimans sine fine*
patronus,
muneris amissae cui nuncquam es pectore
adempta
quae putat amissis munera grata dari,
nulla cui post te femina visa proba est.
Qui sine te vivit cernit sua funera vivos.
15   *Auro tuum nomen fert ille refertque lacerto*
qua retinere potest auro conlata POTESTAS.
Quantumcumq(ue) tamen praeconia nostra
valebunt
versiculis vives quandiucumque meis.
Effigiem pro te teneo solacia nostri
20   *quam colimus sancte sertaque multa datur,*
cumque at [read ad] te veniam mecum
comitata sequetur.
Sed tamen infelix cui tam sollemnia mandem.
Si tamen extiterit cui tantum credere possim,
hoc unum felix amissa te mihi forsan ero.
25   *Ei mihi, vicisti! Sors mea facta tua est.*

Postscript:

   Laedere qui hoc poterit ausus ⟨erit?⟩ quoque
   laedere divos.
   Haec titulo insignis, credite, numen habet.

"To the Blessed Memory of Allia Potestas, freedwoman of Aulus (Allius).

"Here lies a woman of Perugia, than whom there (is) no woman more precious; of many, scarcely one or a second has seemed industrious (by comparison). In a little jar, you, so big (in life), are contained (i.e., your ashes). 'O cruel ruler of fate, and harsh Persephone, why do you snatch the good things, and (why do) the bad prevail?' is asked by many; already I am tired of answering (? or, importuned to answer?). They weep tears, gracious marks of their feeling.

"Brave, pure, tenacious, guiltless, most faithful guardian, neat at home, elegant away from home, well known to everyone; she was alone [i.e., without a servant? or a 'loner'?] so that she was able to cope with all contingencies ["the only person who could rise to all occasions," Lattimore]; a woman of few words, she re-

mained beyond reproach. She was the first to leave bed (in the morning), the last to take herself to bed (at night), after having put things in order. She was never without wool in her hands (for working) without (good) reason, and no woman was ahead of her in (wifely) obedience, and her habits were healthful. This (woman) failed to please herself, never seeming free (?) to herself.

"(She was) fair, with beautiful eyes, golden-haired, and her complexion was always the color of ivory, such as they say no (other) mortal woman has ever had, and on her snow-white bosom small breasts. What of Atalanta's legs (in comparison)? Her (Atalanta's) very posture belongs to the comic stage! She (Potestas) was never fretful for long, but beautiful with generous body (generous with her beautiful body?). She kept her limbs smooth, (and) every hair was looked for (and removed) (Lattimore). For having rough hands you will perhaps blame her.

"Nothing pleased her save what she had done by herself for herself. To get acquainted (with others) she had no desire; she thought herself sufficient to herself. And she was never the subject of gossip, because she had never committed a wrong.

"This woman, while she lived, so guided her two young men, loving (her as they did), that they were a model (of brotherly love), like Pylades and Orestes. One household held them both, and one spirit. Now, after her (death), they go each his own way and are losing their youth. What a woman built the moments (i.e., the march) of time are weakening. See what a woman did once at Troy—let this be proper, I beg, to use great examples in a small matter (i.e., to compare small things with great). These verses to you, as a last service (*muneris*) to one lost, the master gives, weeping without cease, from whose breast you were never (before) taken—(verses) which he thinks given as welcome gifts to those lost—he, to whom no woman after you has seemed virtuous—living without you, he sees his own funeral rites while alive. Your name in gold he carries back and forth on his arm (on a bracelet?), (?) where (the name) POTESTAS, carried (i.e., written?) in gold (?) can be a constant reminder (of you) [with *te* understood as object of *retinere*?]. But, whatever power our praises will have, in my verses you will live, however long it may be. In place of you I keep a likeness, as a comfort to us [himself and the *iuvenes*], which we piously cherish, and many a garland is offered (it). And when I shall come to you, along with me will follow your likeness (a drawing? painting?). But yet, unhappy the one to whom I commit so solemn a matter(?). If, however, there appears someone to whom I can entrust so much, in this one respect perhaps I shall be happy though having lost you. Alas for me, you have won: your fate has become mine!

"He who is able to damage this (memorial) will have (?) dared to injure also the gods. This woman, made memorable by an inscription, believe me, has divine power."

Problems: how to punctuate col. 1, lines 2 f.? the meaning of *seriola*, 3? of line 10? who are the *duo iuvenes amantes* of col. 2, line 3? (sons or stepsons, hardly "young lovers" in the context); the meaning of line 7? 11 f.? the syntax of *muneris*? (cf. Catullus 101); the meaning of 15 f.? 21–27? the plurals *nostra* 17, *nostri* 19, *colimus* 20 may be *metri causa*. Postscript: how to punctuate and interpret? Some take it as a single sentence, but fail to explain or translate it; it seems impossible to construe it as such satisfactorily.

Philologically, one of the most interesting of Latin inscriptions. Note the mixture of grammatical persons, the name "Potestas" (about 15 examples in *CIL* 6; cf. the Greek fem. name Δύναμις, of which it seems to be a transl.), the spellings *Persiphone*, *lachrimas* / *-ans*, *nuncquam* / *numquam*, *caussa* (not uncommon in the inscrs.), *opsequio*, *atte* (for *ad te*), *illae* / *illi* (fem. dat. sing.), *vivos* (nom. sing., not uncommon), the unique deponent *culpabere* ("you will blame"—see below), *foras* (colloquial for *foris*, as in Petron. 30.3, *foras cenat?*), *infamis* ("not the subject of gossip"); also the paragraph sign at col. 2, line 3, the lack of punctuation after all the prepositions except *post* (col. 2, line 6).

Culpabere is not cited by Pierre Flobert, *Les verbes déponents latins des origines à Charlemagne* (Paris 1975), but the author writes (in English), by letter of April 22, 1977, that this example "seems unquestionable," and he justifies "this deponent variant" by comparison "with *queror* and overall [he means "especially"? *surtout*?] *criminor*; this semanticism affords many late deponents: *accusor, incusor, increpor, insimulor*. . . ." "The 'vulgarisms' *de multis* (col. 1, line 2), *foras* (9), *delapsa fuit* (12), *illae* (18), *per se sibi* (25), *ad Troiam* (2, 8), as well as *forsan* with future (24) and *quandiucumque* (18, which is elsewhere late)," lead him to favor "the second half of the second century (A.D.)."

66. Lex Collegi Aesculapi et Hygiae,

Rome. A.D. 153. A thick marble tablet (cm. 70.0–70.6 × m. 1.187 at line 1), first reported (17th cent.) as being in the Barberini palace in Rome; since 1910 in the Vatican, now in two pieces joined together and attached to the wall of the Sala dell'Apoxyomenos (inv. no. 1172); seen there in 1948, 1956, 1973. Letter heights: line 1, 2.65–2.9 (tall I 3.0) cm., line 2, ca. 2.1–2.3 (tall I 2.4, small I ca. 0.9) cm., the rest ca. 1.0–1.5 (tall letters up to 1.9, small down to 0.8–1.2) cm.

Text of what the heading calls the Regulations of the Society of Aesculapius and Hygia (obviously a benevolent and funeral society), as voted at a meeting held in Rome March 11, 153, in the Templum Divorum (in the Campus Martius), but which consists rather of (1) a record of the benefactions to the society on the part of the widow and the brother of an Imperial freedman, M. Ulpius Capito, assistant to the Imperial procurator in charge of the Palace's picture galleries, in memory of him and (on her part) also of the procurator himself, Flavius Apollonius, and (2), not clearly separated syntactically from (1), a calendar of the meetings of the society for various purposes. The date must be soon after the meeting of the whole society in March (lines 9, 23 f.).

CIL 6.10234 (ed. Bormann, with bibl. and 3 notes by Mommsen), cf. pp. 3502, 3908; ILS 7213; Waltzing, 3.268–271 (cf. 2, index p. 515, s.v. Aesc. et Hygiae coll., 4.180 f., 316, etc.—see Table des matières 717 ff.), Bruns 391–393 no. 176; FIRA 3.105–109 no. 36; Album, 2.90–94 no. 217 (with a few corrections of earlier editions).

Text of lines 1–7 init., 17 fin.–19 init., 23 f.: *Lex collegi Aesculapi et Hygiae. / Salvia G(ai) f(ilia) Marcellina ob memoriam Fl(avi) Apolloni, proc(uratoris) Aug(usti), qui fuit a pinacothecis, et Capitonis Aug(usti) l(iberti), adiutoris /³ eius, mariti sui optimi piissimi, donum dedit collegio Aesculapi et Hygiae locum aediculae cum pergula et signum marmoreum Aesculapi et solarium tectum iunctum, in /⁴ quo populus collegi s(upra) s(cripti) epuletur, quod est via Appia ad Martis (aedem) intra milliarium Ī et ĪĪ ab urbe euntibus, parte laeva, inter adfines Vibium Calocaerum et populum; item /⁵ eadem Marcellina collegio s(upra) s(cripto) dedit donavitque H̶S̶ (= sestertium, gen. pl.) Ī m(ilia) ñ(ummum) hominibus ñ(umero) LX sub hac condicione, ut ne plures adlegantur quam numerus s(upra) s(criptus) et ut in locum /⁶ defunctorum loca veniant (read veneant) et liberi adlegantur, vel siquis locum suum legare volet filio vel liberto, dumtaxat ut inferat arkae ñ(ostrae) partem /⁷ dimidiam funeratici . . . ¹⁷ . . . Item P(ublius) Aelius Aug(usti) lib(ertus) Zenon /¹⁸ eidem collegio s(upra) s(cripto) ob memoriam M(arci) Ulpi Aug(usti) lib(erti) Capitonis, fratris sui piissimi, dedit donavitque H̶S̶ X̄ m(ilia) ñ(ummum), uti ex reditu eius summae in contri- /¹⁹ butione sportularum dividerentur . . . ²³ Hoc decretum ordini ñ(ostro) placuit in conventu pleno, quod gestum est in* Templo Divorum in Aede D̲ivi Titi V Id(us) Mart(ias) G(aio) Bruttio Prae- /²⁴ sente, A(ulo) Iunio Rufino co(n)s(ulibus), q̄(uin)-q̄(uennali) G(aio) Ofilio Hermete, curatorib(us) P(ublio) Aelio Aug(usti) lib(erto) Onesimo et G(aio) Salv̲io Seleuco.

"Regulations of the Society of Aesculpaius and Hygia. Salvia Marcellina, daughter of Gaius (Salvius), in memory of Flavius Apollonius, Imperial procurator who is in charge of (the Palace's) picture galleries, and of (Marcus Ulpius—line 18) Capito, Imperial freedman, his assistant (and) her excellent (and) most faithful husband, has given as a gift to the Society of A. and H. land for a chapel with a pergola, and a marble image of Aesculapius, and a covered solarium attached (to the chapel) for the membership of the above-named society to dine in, which is on the Via Appia by the Temple of Mars, between the first and second milestones, on the left to those leaving the City, between the property of Vibius Calocaerus and public land; likewise the same Marcellina handed over and gave to the above-named Society 50,000 sesterces, to the 60 persons [the membership], on these terms, that in place of the deceased (their) places be sold and (their) children be chosen (for membership), or if anyone wishes to bequeath his place to a son or a brother or a freedman, provided that he [any one of these three?] contribute to our treasury one half of the funeral expenses (of the deceased, the other half being paid by the society); . . . (line 17) . . . Likewise Publius Aelius Zenon, Imperial freedman, to the same above-named society, in memory of Marcus Ulpius Capito, Imperial freedman, his very devoted brother, handed over and gave 10,000 sesterces, so that from the income from this sum distributions of gifts might be made. . . .

(Line 23). "This decree was approved by our membership at a full meeting held in the Temple of the Divi, in the shrine of the Deified Titus, on March 11, in the consulship of G. Bruttius Praesens (and)

A. Iunius Rufinus (A.D. 153), the president being G. Ofilius Hermes, the curators P. Aelius Onesimus, Imperial freedman, and G. Salvius Seleucus."

The Latin suffers from the difficulties of writing long periodic sentences, esp. those of a legal character; the writing also is rather poor, many letters being imperfect, incomplete, or not clear, indistinguishable from one another; I for E in *veneant* (line 6); some erasures and corrections; in line 7 *fin.* the last two letters, NT, are cut under the preceding RE (for Augustus's manner of writing such run-overs, see **12**, the quotation from Suetonius); in line 19 a large space (enough for ca. 26 letters) is left vacant; in two passages (7–9, 19–22), as Mommsen noted (on *CIL* 6.10234), the language is badly mixed up. Note the many barred letters: N often as an abbreviation for *natali*, forms of *noster*, *numero*, *nummum*; Q Q for any form of *quinquennalis*; two ordinal adjectives (line 4) and three cardinals (5, 18, 22), these latter to indicate thousands, though in each case *m(ilia)* follows; medially barred are two symbols for coins (X for *denarios*, lines 10–12, IIS the regular symbol for sesterces, 5, 18, 22), and S for *sextariorum*, "pints of wine" (12, 5 times); very many abbreviations (142 in 613 words: see Appendix 11, *init.*).

For the full text, with many textual notes, see *Album*, loc. cit. Addenda: lines 1, 3 *Hygiae*: Hygīa, also written *Hygeia*, is the Greek ὑγίειᾰ, sometimes ὑγιείᾱ, and "from ca. the 2nd cent. B.C. written ὑγεία (pronounced ὑγῖα)" (Liddell/Scott⁹), hence the Latin *Hygia*; 4, *populus collegi*, elsewhere only *populo*, 11, 12, once *ordo collegi*, 20, the membership of the society, presumably the sixty called *hominibus* in 5; in 4, no *in* needed with *via Appia* or *parte laeva*; *ad Martis*, sc. *aedem* (see above, **36**, note on line 1—for this temple, cf. P/A 327 f., *s.v.* Mars, aedes); 5, 18, *dedit donavitque*, legalese; 6, 22, *arkae*, a fancy spelling of *arcae*, like *kar(a)e* for *carae*, 13 (see Appendix I *s.vv.*); 8, *si quod comparaverint*, "if they

make any (money)," *quod* apparently in error for *quid* or *quem (reditum)*; 8, *sportulas*, "gifts," repeated in 9, perhaps for clarity; 8, 10, 23, *templo* ("temple precinct") *Divorum*, really a large portico in the Campus Martius, with the *aedes Divi Vespasiani* and the *aed. D. Titi* flanking the entrance, a monumental triple arch (cf. Nash 1.304 fig. 361 *s.v.* Divorum Templum); 9, for *qui dies* read *die qui*; the two consuls have their praenomina in 23 f.; here Ofilius is *q(uin)q(uennalis) p(er)p(etuus)* ("permanent president"), in 14 and 24 only *q.q.* (he is the chief official, presumably elected every 5 yrs., but apparently he might be called *p.p.*, perhaps as an honor: cf. Waltzing 1.356); 10–12, note *pater* and *mater collegi*, "honorary Father/ Mother of the Society" (Waltzing 2, index 535, 539 *s.vv.*); 10, 12, *imm(unibus)*, "dues-exempt members" (ibid. 530, *s.v.* immunis); 12, 13, 15, *pane⟨m⟩*, *vinu⟨m⟩*; 13, for *strenuas* read *strenas*; *die kar(a)e cognationis*, "on the day of the family- or love-feast" (cf. Wissowa 233 line 2 or *OLD* 344 f., 277, *s.vv.* cognatio, caristia); 14, here Ofilius has no praenomen (*G.* in 10, 24); 15, *die violari*, *die rosae*, "on the day of violets, of the rose," when the graves were decorated with these flowers, as on our Memorial Day, traditionally May 30 (cf. Wissowa 434 n. 3); 17, *vēnirent*, "should be sold," from *veneo*; read *detinentur*; *Zenon* here, *Zeno* in 12 (both forms were in use: *ILS* 3: 1, 255) has no praenomen in 10; 18, Capito is only "Capitonis Aug. l(ib.)" in 2; 18 f., read *contributio sportularum divideretur*, with no *in*; 20, read only *quam eos*; 21, read *ut ita fiant dividanturque* (or *-aturque*, "distribution be made").

67. Dedication of a Sculptured Column to Antoninus Pius, Rome. A.D. 161/169.

Inscribed monolithic base, of white marble (m. 2.47 × 3.38 width of each side: Simon) of the Column of Antoninus Pius erected in his memory by his two adopted sons, Marcus Aurelius and Lucius Verus. The column with its base originally stood in the Campus Martius, in front of one of the Ustrina (Crematoria) of the Antonini; in 1703 the base was excavated, in 1764 the column was badly damaged by fire and not reerected; the base, decorated on three sides with reliefs, was later moved to the Vatican and set up in the Cortile della Pigna (inv. no. 5115); when seen there in 1973, it was covered by a tarpaulin for protection against the weather, having been found too heavy for the place intended for it inside the Museo Nuovo. Cf. P/A 131 *s.v.* Columna Ant. Pii, Nash 1.270–275 *s.v. eadem*, 2.487 *s.v.* Ustrina Antoninorum.

CIL 6.1004, 31223 (cf. pp. 842, 3777), *ILS* 347, E. Simon in H/S 1.480 (cf. 4, p. 388), who confirms (as does our photo) Hübner, 99 on no. 294, that only the cuttings for the (originally no doubt bronze) letters are ancient, the present letters themselves being modern. The date is that of the joint rule of M. Aurelius and L. Verus, 161–169.

Text: *Divo Antonino Aug(usto) Pio / Antoninus Augustus et / Verus Augustus, filii.*

"To the Deified Antoninus Augustus Pius: Antoninus Augustus and Verus Augustus, (his adopted) sons."

68. Commemoration of a Local Dignitary, Rome, from Ostia. A.D. 182.

Large marble base (cm. 83.5–84.3 × 66.3 writing field × 71.5 right side) of a statue set up in honor of P. Horatius Chryseros by the Seviri Augustales of Ostia. Reported found there in 1801/04, but long since in Rome, in the Museo Chiaramonti of the Vatican (inv. no. 1247). The date, now barely legible, is inscribed on the right side: Oct. 18 (not Dec. 17), A.D. 182.

The Seviri Augustales (a special freedmen's priesthood for the Imperial cult, important at Ostia, as elsewhere) decreed the erection of a statue to Chryseros for his having given them 50,000 sesterces; 10,000 of this outright because they had appointed Sex. Horatius Chryserotianus (probably a son of his) as *curator* (of that

body); the interest on the balance (at 6.4%?) was to be distributed each year, on Chryseros's birthday, among all the members present at a meeting, after certain deductions. If those conditions were not met, the balance of 40,000 sest. was to be given to the town of Ostia under the same conditions. For the honor of the commemoration Chryseros gave 5 denarii (apiece, no doubt) to the decurions (of the town) and to the Augustales, and he remitted to the latter the cost of the statue.

CIL 14.367 (ed. Dessau), *ILS* 6164, Bruns 400 no. 182, 2 (only lines 10–17), Laum 2.168 no. 15 (lines 1–17), *FIRA* 3.119 f., no. 44, *Album* 2.139–142 no. 240. Cf. R. Meiggs, *Roman Ostia*[2] (Oxford 1973) 221, 379, index 619 *s.v. Seviri Aug.*

Text: *P(ublio) Horatio / Chryseroti, / seviro Augustal(i), ⟨e⟩idem / quinq(uennali) et immuni (collegi) Larum Aug(usti) /*[5] *ex s(enatus) c(onsulto): seviri Augustales statuam / ei ponendam decreverunt quod / is arcae eorum* H̶S̶ *(= sestertium, gen. plu.)* L̄ *m̄(ilia) n̄(ummum, gen. pl.) dederit, ex qua summa* H̶S̶ *(= sestertium)* X̄ *m̄(ilia) n̄(ummum) ob honorem curae / Sex(ti) Horati Chryserotiani et reliquorum* (read *reliqua*) /[10] H̶S̶ *(= sestertium)* X̄L̄ *m̄(ilia) n̄(ummum) excepta stipulatione ⟨ut⟩ ex usuris / semissibus et* Ṁ *II s(ummae) s(upra) s(criptae) quodannis* (read *quot-*) *Idib(us) Mart⟨i⟩is / natali suo, inter praesentes hora II usque / ad asse⟨m⟩ dividiatur* (read *dividantur*) *deducta ornatione statu⟨a⟩e / et familiae Augustal(ium)* H̶S̶ *(= sestertiis) c(entum) n̄(ummis); quot* (read *quod*) *si ita /*[15] *factum non erit, tum ea* H̶S̶ *(= sestertium)* X̄L̄ *m̄(ilia) n̄(ummum / dari rei p(ublicae) Ost(iensi)* or *-sium) sub eadem condicione / qua⟨e⟩ s(upra) s(cripta) est. Ob cuius dedicatione⟨m⟩ dedit / decurionib(us)* X̄ *(= denarios) V et Augustalibus* X̄ *V; / isque honore sibi habito sumptum sta- /*[20] *tuae ordini Augustalium remisịt [-it in ligature].*

Right side: *dedic(ata)* (or *dedicat-?*) *XV Kal(endas) Nov(embres) / Mamertino et Rufo / co(n)s(ulibus).*

"To Publius Horatius Chryseros, *sevir*

Augustalis, likewise dues-exempt president of the (local body of the) *Lares Augusti*, (a body) authorized by the (Roman) senate: the Seviri Augustales have decreed that a statue be set up to him because of his having given their treasury 50,000 sesterces, of which sum 10,000 (outright) because of the honor of the curatorship given to Sextus Horatius Chryserotianus, and the remaining 40,000 with the stipulation that the interest, 6.4 percent (?), be distributed, to the last copper, every year on March 15, his birthday, among those (Augustales) present at the second hour (of the day) after deducting the (cost of) decorating his statue and giving the servants of the Augustales 100 sesterces; and, if it is not done in this way, then this 40,000 sesterces (is) to be given to the community of Ostia with the same condition as is written above.

"Because of this dedication he has given the town councillors five denarii (apiece?) and to the Augustales five denarii (apiece?), and, the honor (of the statue) having been paid him, he has remitted the cost of the statue to the body of the Augustales.

"Dedicated October 18 in the consulship of Mamertinus and Rufus." (A.D. 182)

Line 2. *CIL*'s Y crossbar, shown also in the modern rubrication, is apparently "merely an old scratch, not an intended incision or part of the letter" (*Contrib.* 121 no. 4). 4 f., *collegi* (or *cultorum*) seems needed after *immuni* and *ex s.c.* seems short for *cui* (or *quibus*) *ex s. c. coire licet*; cf. Wissowa in Roscher 2: 2 (1894–97) 1881, 39–47, and Rel. u. Kultus 172 f., G. Vitucci in De Rugg. 4: 13 (1946) 402 f., *s.v.* Lares. 7, note *dederit*, perf. subj., as quoting their reason. 11. The text after *semissibus et* and its meaning are uncertain; for arguments that it reads M with a short vertical cut just above it (as appears in our photo), that this vertical may represent the letter I, that MI stands for *minutis*, that this means 60ths, and that therefore the

total amount of interest indicated is (½% plus ²⁄₆₀% × 12 = 6.4%) see *Album* 2.141. 13, *deducto sumptu ornationis statuae* would perhaps be clearer (as in 19 f., *sumptum statuae*); here *statue*, below *statuae*; the other misspellings are noted in the text; 14, the bar over *C(entum)*, visible in our photo, is not on the stone, but only museum paint and in error; 16, *dari* has no syntax, nothing to depend on; *quod si factum non sit, ut tum . . . dentur* would be better. 17, read *qua s(upra) s(criptum)* (with Dessau) or *qua⟨e⟩ s. scripta*. 20, *fin.* The photo shows no ligature and no special damage—museum paint, no doubt.

69. Three Letters (with summary) from Imperial Accountants, Rome. Probably A.D. 193/195 (or /196). Marble cippus (m. 1.10 × ca. 0.34 × ca. 0.22–.26), reported found in 1777 in excavating in Piazza di Monte Citorio near the Column of Marcus Aurelius, Rome; in the Vatican by 1783 or 1784, where it is now in the Gall. lap. (inv. no. 9304).

Summary and text of three letters of Aug. and Sept., 193, from Aelius Achilles, Cl(audius) Perpetuus, Flavianus, and Eutychus (as Pflaum interprets the names). Imperial accountants and—the last two—freedmen office-heads; the first letter to Epaphroditus (apparently overseer of Imperial bldgs. in Rome), the second to Aquilius Felix (apparently procurator of public works), the third to Seius Superstes and Fabius Magnus (apparently commissioners of public works), giving permission to Adrastus (once "Hadr-"), caretaker of the Column of M. Aurelius, to build, in place of the existing hut, a separate lodge as his own property, at his own expense, but subject to the usual ground-rent. The dates of the original letters appear in lines 24–26, 38 f., 55 f.; that of the heading is probably 193/195 (or /196). On the evidence for the posts held by the four addressees, see *Album* 2.164 f.

CIL 6.1585, *b* (cf. pp. 3163, 3811), *ILS*

5920 (add.), Mommsen, *Ges. Schr.* 3 (Berlin 1907) 102–106, Bruns 345 no. 144 *b*, *FIRA* 3.360 f., no. 110 *b*, *Album* 2.164–170, no. 255 (piece *b*), E. Meinhardt in H/S 1.395 (with German transl.), and 4, p. 386. Cf. Grad. 28, Lugli 3.240–248, and H. G. Pflaum, *REL* 43 (1965) 142 f., with reff.

Text:

"Exemplaria litte/rarum rationali/um do-minorum nn̄. (= nostrorum duorum) / scrip-tarum pertinen/⁵ tes ad Adrastum, / Augg., nn̄. (= Augustorum nostrorum duorum) lib(er-tum), quibus aei (read ei) / permissum sit aedifi/care loco cannabae, / a solo, iuris sui, pecunia /¹⁰ sua, pr⟨a⟩estaturus solari/um sicut caeteri (read cet-). /

Aelius Achilles, Cl(audius) Perpetu/us, Flavianus, Eutychus / Epaphrodito suo sa-lutem. /¹⁵ Tegulas omnes et inpensa⟨m⟩ / de casulis, item cannabis / et aedificiis idoneis ad-signa / Adrasto procuratori / Columnae divi Marci, ut /²⁰ ad voluptatem suam hospi/tium sibi exstruat, quod ut / habeat sui iuris et ad he/redes transmittat. / Litterae datae VIII Idus /²⁵ Aug(ustas) Romae Falcone et / Claro co(n)s(ulibus). /

Aelius Achilles, Cl(audius) Perpetu/us, Flavianus, Eutychus Aqui/lio Felici. {H}ad-rasto Aug(usti) lib(erto) /³⁰ ad aedificium quod custodi/ae causa Columnae Cente/nariae pecunia sua exstruc̣/turus est tignorum ve-hes / decem quanti fisco consti/³⁵terunt cum pontem neces/se fuit compingi petimus / daṛi iubeas. Litterae datae / XIIII Kal(endas) Sep-t(embres) Romae / Falcone et Claro cos. /

⁴⁰Rationales Seio Superstịti / et Fabio Mag-no. Procura/tor Columna⟨e⟩ Centenaṛị[a]ẹ / divi Marci, exstruere haḅ[i]/tationem in con-termini[s] /⁴⁵ locis iussus, opus adgredi/etur si auctoritatem ves/tram acceperit. Petimus / igitur aream quam demo/nstraverit Adrastus lib(ertus) /⁵⁰ domini ñ(ostri) adsignari ei iuḅea/tis, praestaturo secundum / exemplum ceterorum so/larium. Litterae datae / VII Idus Sept(embres) Romae, red/⁵⁵ditae IIII Idus Sept. Romaẹ / isdem cos.

"Copies of letters written by the accountants of our (two) Lords [apparently

Septimius Severus and Albinus] concerning Adrastus, freedman of our (two) emperors, by which he has been allowed to build (a building) in place of the (present) hut, at ground level, subject to his own control, at his own expense, on which he is to pay ground-rent like everyone else.

"Aelius Achilles, Claudius Perpetuus, Flavianus, and Eutychus to Epaphroditus, their (servant), greetings. All the tiles and the building material from suitable cottages, likewise shacks and (other) buildings allocate to Adrastus, caretaker of the Column of the deified Marcus (Aurelius), so that he may build to his satisfaction a lodging for himself which he may have for his own and bequeath to his heirs. Letter dispatched August 6 in Rome in the consulship of Falco and Clarus. (A.D. 193)

"Aelius Achilles, Claudius Perpetuus, Flavianus, (and) Eutychus to Aquilius Felix. We request that you order given to Adrastus, Imperial freedman, for the building that he is to build, at his own expense, for the purpose of taking care of the Hundred-Foot Column, ten loads of lumber at the price that they have cost the treasury when a bridge has had to be constructed. Letter dispatched Aug. 19 in Rome in the consulship of Falco and Clarus.

"The accountants (Ael. Ach. and Cl. Perp.) to Seius Superstes and Fabius Magnus. The caretaker of the Hundred-Foot Column of the deified Marcus, having been invited to build a dwelling on land adjacent (to the Column), will begin the work if he receives your authority. We therefore request that the area that Adrastus, freedman of our Lord, has indicated you order allocated to him, with the understanding that he will pay ground-rent in the manner of everyone else. Letter dispatched Sept. 7, in Rome, (and) returned Sept. 10 in Rome, in the consulship of Falco and Clarus."

Conjecturally, the summary was composed by Adrastus himself, hence perhaps its several errors and awkwardness. Lines 3–5 are clumsy; perhaps *pert.* should agree with *litt.* 7, *sit*, why subjunctive? apparently quoting the accountants (Implied Indirect Discourse)—or by overcorrection? 8, *cannabae*, cf. *TLL s.v.* canaba, with reff. to De Rugg. and *RE*; Mommsen, strangely (p. 103), took *cannabae* as the object of *aedificare*. 10, *praest.* (*est*) as in 32 f., *exstructurus est*, or else *praest.* and *ceteri* should be dative (like *praest.* in 51) to agree with *ei*. 12 f., 27 f. According to Pflaum, loc. cit., these are four men, the first two being the *rationales* (i.e., the (*procurator*) *a rationibus*, Ael. Ach., and his associate, the *procurator summarum rationum*, Cl. Perp.), the other two, Flav. and Eut., being freedmen in charge of the offices *a rationibus* and *summae rationes*, resp. 15, *inpensa*, i.e., *imp-*.

Line 19, here *Columnae divi Marci*, in 31 f. *Col. Centenariae*, in 42 f. *Col. Cent. divi Marci*, but in *CIL* 6.1585, *a, Col.* [---] *Marci et Faustina[e]*: the Column of Marcus Aurelius in Piazza Colonna, Rome (so named, no doubt, from the Column), 100 ft. high (cf. Nash 1.276–279 *s.v.* Columna Marci Aurel. Ant.; Coarelli 268 f. ["the height of the shaft is 29.601 m., ca. 100 ft."]). 20 f., *hospitium*, 30 *aedificium*, 43 f. *habitationem*, all of the same bldg. (Adrastus himself—note his Greek name—in his summary has no word for the new structure, either by a slip or intentionally.) 35 f., *cum . . . compingi*, a particular bridge? or any bridge? Meinhardt, 301, translates: "als die Brücke renoviert werden musste." 48 f., *demo/nstraverit* (badly divided, better *demon-*: cf. Dennison 60 f. [but he lacks this example], 62, 67 f.), another fut. perf. 54 f., *redditae*: the letter was dispatched Sept. 7 and sent back by the recipients (with their approval) Sept. 10, to be referred to the emperor(s) for final approval (*FIRA* 3.361 n. 5).

70. Pagan Epitaph from the Vatican Excavations, Rome. Late-Hadrianic/ca. A.D.

200? Marble tablet (55 × 92 cm.) found *in situ* set in the wall above the door of Tomb O, situated (like Tomb A—**62**) along the northern row of tombs in the pagan cemetery excavated in 1940–1949 under St. Peter's. It documents the tomb as made for T. Matuccius Pallas (whose name indicates a freedman) by two freedmen of his, as well as for themselves, etc. The letters are reported to be 3.5–4.0 cm. tall.

Esplor. vol. 1.43–53, vol. 2 pl. IX *b*; Toynbee/Ward Perkins 119 no. XVII (cf. index, 291, *s.v.* Tombs, O); cf. H. Torp, *Acta Archaeologica*, 24 (Copenhagen 1953) 28–37. The date is conjectural: *Esplor.* 1.43, n. 1, says "about the middle of the second cent." (where it is also noted that against the right half of the inscr. there later rested a Christian tomb, hence the different color of this half, visible in the photo); Torp, 32, conjectures ca. 180–190 (cf. 30 f.); Toynbee/Ward Perkins give several datings: 32 f., "the later years of the Emp. Hadrian," 64, "either Hadrianic or later," 79, "possibly Hadrianic" (of the original decoration of Tomb O); J. S. Gordon in 1961 (from only a photo of the inscr.) conjectured ca. 175 or perhaps even as late as ca. 200 (above, Intro., VI.3).

Text: *T(ito) Matuccio Pallanti, patrono* / *optimo, fecerunt* / *Matucc⟨i⟩i* $\overline{II}$, *Entimus et* *Zmara/gdus, lintear⟨i⟩i, et sibi liberis/⁵que* *posterisque eorum* / *et libertis libertabusque* / *suis.*

"For T. Matuccius Pallas, excellent patron, two Matuccii, Entimus and Zmaragdus, sellers (or weavers) of linen, have made (this monument), and for themselves and their children and their (the children's) descendants and their own freedmen and freedwomen."

The spacing of line 2 seems to be caused by the desire to begin the makers' names with a new line. Zmaragdus (the Greek is σμα——, "name of several green stones, including the *emerald*," Liddell/Scott⁹ *s.v.*; Σμάραγδος is also used as a name, cf. Pape/Benseler *s.v.*) is poorly divided; the cutter had no room for the G at the end. All three cognomina are Greek; Entimus ("honored"). *Matucci* and *linteari* are contracted forms.

71. Dedication to Caracalla by the *Paedagogi Puerorum a Capite Africae*, Rome.

A.D. 198. Marble tablet (writ. field ca. m. 1.01 × 0.62–0.622), which may be only the front of a statue base (so described by Gatti, 194, 212 f., but this is unconfirmed; Fabretti [1702] 296, no. 257, gives no description), reported (by Fabretti) as found in Rome in 1663 under the convent attached to the Church of Ss. Giovanni e Paolo on the Caelian; seen in 1949, 1956, 1973, attached to the north wall of the second Stanza terrena a destra of the Capitoline Mus., Rome, where it was by ca. 1775 (inv. no. 7147). (Our photo shows modern rubrication; pl. 121 of the *Album*, photo of a squeeze, shows the letters more faithfully.) Letter heights: cm. 4.25–4.7 (line 6) down to 1.3–2.2 (lines 10–21), tall I's up to cm. 5.3, tall L 5.7 (both in line 4). (For Fabretti's long title cf. Calabi Limentani, 528.)

A dedication to the emperor Caracalla on the part of 24 *paedagogi* of the boys from the *Caput Africae*, generally thought to have been a school for the training of Imperial pages and apparently connected somehow with the so-called Paedagogium Palatini. The *paedagogi* are all freedmen, no doubt Imperial.

CIL 6.1052 (cf. p. 3701), G. Gatti *Ann. Inst.* 54 (1882) 191–220, *Album* 2.174 f., no. 259, E. Meinhardt in H/S 2.1221 (with German transl. and bibl.). Cf. De Rugg. 1 (1895) 350 *s.v.* Africae (caput), Hülsen, *RE* 3 (1899) 1564 *s.v.* Caput Afr., Olcott 1.195 *s.v.* Africa, sect. IV (only a *vicus* "Caput Afr."), P/A 98 f., *s.v.* Caput Afr., Lugli *Roma ant.* 521–523 and *Fontes* 3 (1955) 82, 100 f., *s.vv.* Caput Afr., Paedag. Puer. a Cap. Afr., Nash 1.316 f., 335–337, *s.v.* Domus Augustiana (bibl. on the Paedag. Palatini, 317), Weaver 121.

Text of lines 1–9, 22–24: *Imperatori Caesari / M(arco) Aurelio Antonino / Aug(usto), /* *L(uci) Septimi Severi Pii /⁵ Pertinacis Aug(usti) filio, / domino indulgentissimo, / paedagogi puerorum a Capite / Africae, quorum nomina infra / scripta sunt: . . . , /²² procurantibus Saturnino et Eumeniano, / dedic(ata ?) Idib(us) Oct(obribus), Saturnino et Gallo / co(n)s(ulibus).*

"To the emperor (Caracalla), son of L. Septimius Severus Pius Pertinax Augustus, most indulgent ruler, the teachers (?) of the boys from the *Caput Africae* whose [i.e., the teachers'] names are written below": (24 names of freedmen, in 2 cols., six marked by *ver(na)* as being names of home-born slaves); "dedicated, with the special attention of Saturninus and Eumenianus, Oct. 15, in the consulship of (P. Martius Sergius) Saturninus and (L. Aurelius) Gallus."

"Caracalla" or "Caracallus" was a nickname given to this emperor (see Intro., n. 98, and cf. *TLL* 3 [1907] 427 f., *s.v.* caracalla). His official name, from when he was named "Caesar" in 196—"M. Aurelius (or -ell-) Antoninus (Pius)"—was simply taken, presumably for greater respectability, from the last of the "good" emperors of the 2nd cent., Marcus Aurelius, whose grandson (*nepos*) he is named in listing his (pseudo-) ancestors back to Nerva. Line 5, *filio* unabbreviated is unusual in such filiations. The self-adoption into the Antonine and pre-Antonine families (back to Nerva) had begun in fact with Severus himself, as early as 196: cf. *ILS* 3: 1, 286 *s.v. maiores*.

The *paedagogi* seem to have been teachers, preceptors (so Gatti 212, 214, 215, and Meinhardt 72) rather than those who merely took the boys to and from school. The *pueri* are generally thought to have been slaves. "Caput Africae" seems to be the actual name of the school (why so named? Cf. P/A), and except in this inscr. *Caput* is undeclined; e.g., an Imperial freedman called *paedagog(us) puerorum a Caput Africas* (sic), *CIL* 6.8983 (cf. p. 3891) (= *ILS* 1832), cf. Lugli, *Fontes*, for other examples.

72. Dedication to the Imperial Family (and Others) by Members of a Cohort of Vigiles, Rome. A.D. 203. Bronze tablet (writ. field cm. ca. 48 × 40 × 0.5 or 0.6), first reported in 1662 in a modern house at the foot of the Quirinal (*CIL* 6 p. LIX no. LXXX, ref. to Gudius, MS 106), but conjecturally found on the Aventine on the site of the station of the 4th cohort of Vigiles (G. B. De Rossi, *Ann. Inst.* 1858, p. 289); later in the Capitoline Mus., where, when seen in 1973, it was in the Sala delle Colombe, under glass (inv. no. 7341). The letters seemed to be incised, not cast (cf. *Contrib.* 69, 218 n. 8—but see above, Intro., n. 10). Letter heights (estimated): line 1, tall I 2 cm., the rest 1.7+ cm., the other lines 0.7–1.2 cm. Above the inscr. are busts, in relief, of (conjecturally) Julia Domna (left) and Caracalla (right); the third, in the center, appears to be lost, presumably (if removed in antiquity) as part of the *damnatio memoriae* suffered by Geta. (Strangely, *CIL* shows all three busts as extant and assigns them to Severus, Geta, and Caracalla, but D. A. Amyx identifies the one on the left as certainly that of a woman.)

A dedication to the joint emperors Septimius and Caracalla, and (originally) to Geta as Caesar (C.'s younger brother, murdered by his order in 212 after their father's death), to Julia Domna (wife of Sept. Sev.), and (originally) to Fulvia Plautilla (wife of Caracalla, but rejected by him and the object of *damn. mem.*, like Geta), as well as to the Genius of a *centuria* (of the 4th Cohort of Vigiles), and finally to five junior officers, on the part of sixteen "soldiers" of the *centuria* who became Roman citizens in 203, whose names are inscribed below. (Fourteen had enlisted in 199, lines 7–22, two in Feb., 200, lines 23–25.) That this *cent.* was part of the 4th cohort of *Vigiles*—neither item is mentioned in the inscr., presumably because it was set up in their own station—is proved by (1) *CIL* 6.1055, which names Iunius Rufinus as *praef(ectus) vig(ilum)* in 205,

clearly identical with our G. Iunius Rufinus, *pr(aefectus)*, line 4, and (2) the *Digest*, 1.15.4 (from Ulpian), where "Iunius Rufinus, praefectus vigilum," appears as the recipient of a rescript from the emperors Severus and Antoninus, i.e., Caracalla. Note that it required only three or four years of service to attain citizenship, but this does not mean that they obtained their discharge at that time.

CIL 6.220 (cf. p. 3004), *ILS* 2163, E. Meinhardt in H/S 2.1267 (lines 1–9, with German transl., notes, bibl.); cf. P. K. Baillie Reynolds, *The Vigiles of Imperial Rome* (London 1926), passim, but esp. pp. 67 f., 70, 74–76, 79 f., 81 f., 91, 124 (but *ii* in line 6 of our inscription is not a Roman numeral, but the demonstrative pronoun, = *ei*); P/A 128 f., *s.v.* Cohortium Vigilum Stationes; Nash, 1.264–267 *s.v. eadem.*

Text of lines 1–8, 26–end: *Impp. (= Imperatoribus duobus) Severo et Antonino Augg. (= Augustis duobus) / Brittanicis, p(atribus?) p(atriae?), et Iuliae Aug(ustae), matri Augg. (= Augustorum duorum) et castror(um), / et Fulviae Plautillae Aug(ustae), G(aio) Fulvio Plautiano p̄r(aefecto) p̄r(aetorio)* (this whole line erased, but still legible), / *c(larissimo) v(iro), IĪ (= iterum), P(ublio) Septimio Geta, IĪ (= iterum)* (this name erased but still legible), *co(n)s(ulibus), G(aio) Iunio Rufino p̄r(aefecto),* i.e., *vigilum), G(aio) Iunio Balbo s̶(ub) p̄r(aefecto vig.), /*[5] *M(arco) Ulpio Constantino t̄r(ibuno vig.), G(aio) Atticio Sperato (centurione vig.), / (et) Genio (centuriae), ii qui frument(o) publ(ico) incisi sunt Kal(endis) Mart⟨i⟩is / de suo posuerunt, quorum nomina infra scripta sunt, milites fact(i) / Anullino IĪ (= iterum) et Frontone co(n)s(ulibus):* . . .

Lines 26 to end: *item principalibus quibus honorem habuerunt, / P(ublio) Tuticanio Hermeti b̶(eneficiario) pr(aefecti), P. Aelio Stefano libr(ario) i(nstrumentorum?) d(epositorum?), / L(ucio) Cornelio Honorato vex(illario) (centuriae), L. Cornelio Herculano opt(ioni) (centurionis), / M(arco) Sentio Vitali tess(erario) (centuriae), cura⟨m⟩ agente /*[30] *L. Cornelio L(uci) f(ilio) Honorato vexil(lario) (centuriae) /*

et L. Cornelio L. f. Herculano opt(ione) (centurionis).

"To the emperors, Severus and Antoninus, Augusti, Brittanici, Patres Patriae (?), and to Julia (Domna), mother of (two) Augusti [more correctly, of one Augustus, Caracalla, and one Caesar, Geta] and of Camp [this title first appears in 195 (*CIL* 8.26498, part 9), apparently from her accompanying Severus on his military expedition to the East], and to Fulvia Plautilla Aug., in the consulship of G. Fulvius Plautianus, praetorian prefect, *clarissimus vir*, (and) P. Septimius Geta (both consuls for the second time, A.D. 203), while G. Iunius Rufinus is prefect, G. Iunius Balbus sub-prefect, M. Ulpius Constantinus tribune, (and) G. Atticius Speratus centurion [these 4, officers of the Vigiles], (and) to the Genius of the *centuria* (a group of 100-plus men, perhaps "battalion"): those who were enrolled (in the list of citizens eligible) for public (i.e., free) grain on March 1 set up (this tablet) at their own expense, whose names are written below, having become soldiers (i.e., members of the Vigiles) in the consulship of (P. Cornelius) Anullinus (for the second time) and (M. Aufidius) Fronto (A.D. 199); . . .

"likewise to the junior officers whom they have honored: Publius Tuticanius Hermes *beneficiarius* of the prefect (G. Iunius Rufinus, line 4), P. Aelius Stefanus storeroom clerk (?), Lucius Cornelius Honoratus ensign (or standard-bearer) of the *centuria*, L. Cornelius Herculanus assistant to the centurion (G. Atticius Speratus, line 5), Marcus Sentius Vitalis *tesserarius* of the *centuria* (charged with receiving the password from the commander and passing it on), those in charge (of making this inscr.) being L. Cornelius Honoratus, son of Lucius, ensign of the *centuria*, and L. Cornelius Herculanus, son of Lucius, assistant to the centurion."

Line 2. The original writing under *Britt. pp.* was *et Getae Caes.*; *PP*: or perhaps *Piis (duobus)*? *Britt.* seems to be written in full

(*tt, n* for the regular *t, nn*) to fill up the space, so also perhaps the enigmatic *PP.* Line 3, *G. Fulv. Plaut. pr. pr.* erased because he was Fulvia's father. Line 4. *P. Sept. Geta* erased apparently by error because of the cognomen *Geta*: this man was a brother of Severus. 4, *fin.* Note the S, with bar through it, for *sub-*; similarly B with transverse line, for *beneficiarius*, in line 27. Line 5, *fin.* Note the symbol for *centurio.* Line 6, and a similar one for *centuria.* Lines 6–7, *ii (ei) . . . posuerunt*, main subject and verb; this whole inscr. is only one sentence.

Lines 9–22, 24 f. consist of two parts: the new complete, official names of the sixteen *milites* who set up this tablet, then a statement about their enlistment and new citizenship. The names include seven items each: praenomen, nomen, filiation or freedman status (2 items), "tribe" (abl.), cognomen, place of origin (abl.). But the fifth item in six of the names is exceptional. Instead of tribe—Fab(ia), Maec(ia), Arn(iensi), sc. *tribu*, or some other—which these six men may not have known yet, there appears *Iul.* (lines 12, 14, 24), or *Thars.* (13), *Ulp.* (18), or *Agor.* (22), and in one case no word at all (19). *Thars(o)* goes with *Cilic(iae)* to show place of origin, Tharsus in Cilicia. *Iul(ia)* goes first with *Utin(a)* for Colonia Iulia Uthina, Africa (cf. *CIL* 6.36917 f., and 8, p. 112), then with *Karth(agine)* for Col. Iulia Karthago (Carthage), then with *Regio* for Iulium Regium (Rhegium, Strait of Messina), and *Ulp(ia)* with *Hadr.* for Col. Ulpia Hadrumetina (Hadrumetum, African coast). (For *Iul., Ulp.*, and a few other such abbreviations, derived from Imperial *supernomina*, used as pseudo-tribal names, cf. G. Forni, "Il tramonto di un'istituzione. Pseudo-tribù romane derivate da soprannomi imperiali," in *Studi giuridici in memoria di Alfredo Passerini* [Milan 1955, *Studia Ghisleriana* ser. 1 vol. 2] 89–124, esp. 104 f. [type III, Iulia III, Ulpia III], where our examples are listed.)

Line 22, *Agor.* and *Lepidus* are perhaps

transposed for the intended *Lepido Agor. Regio*, to indicate Lepidum Regium (or Reg. Lep., northern Italy), *Agor.* being perhaps an abbreviated cognomen such as *Agorianus*. Line 25, *init.* Instead of SD the bronze seems to read LIB Ɔ (or D?), which, like *CIL*'s SD, is unintelligible.

To the right of these names is a much abbreviated formula, which varies only for the date: e.g., line 9 (Scutrius): *m(iles) f(actus) pr(idie) K(alendas) Iun(ias), (T. Flavio) Magno p̄r(aefecto vigilum), f(rumentum) p(ublicum) a(ccepit) d(ie) X (decimo)* (10th day of what?), and (conjecturally) *t(abula) CXLIV, k(apite) c(entesimo)* (Mommsen's interpretation, in *CIL* 6), presumably with ref. to tablet and chapter of the public records of Roman citizens. Line 25, *fin.* Before C, the vertical of *K(apite)* was read in 1973.

Line 22, *adiut(or)*, "assistant" (of a centurion? [so conjectures Dessau, *ILS* n. 16] of a *cornicularius*, "adjutant"? [so conjectures Henzen in *CIL* 6]). Lines 27–31, the junior officers: *b(eneficiarius)* (B with long transverse cut through it), "a soldier granted special privileges by his commander [here the prefect], such as exemption from camp fatigues, usually to serve on bodyguards, etc." (*OLD* 230 s.v.), *libr. i. d.* (the tentative expansion in the text above is Mommsen's), *optio* (cf. *OLD* 1260, s.v. optio, 2, a), *tesserarius (centuriae)*, and *vexillarius (cent.)*. In respect to its size, *centuria* seems about equivalent to our "battalion." Cf. Baillie Reynolds, index, 131–133, or the relevant articles (including *vigiles*) in *RE* or *D/S*. Note that only five of these *milites*, and none of the junior or senior officers, appear from their names to have been freedmen.

73. Dedication of Arch to Septimius Severus and His Sons, Rome. A.D. 202/203.

A triple arch, richly decorated with relief sculpture, erected in the Roman Forum by the Senate and People of Rome in honor of the emperors Sept. Severus, Caracalla, and (originally) Geta in the year Dec. 10, 202/Dec. 9, 203, probably in 203. The arch is m. 23 × 25 × 11.85, the attic m. 5.60 high (Platner/Ashby); the marble panel of each façade is inscribed with the same inscription, of which only the cuttings are left, the (no doubt bronze) letters long since removed and lost.

CIL 6.1033 (cf. 31230, 36881), *ILS* 425, Diehl *IL* tab. 26, c, Richard Brilliant, *The Arch of Septimius Severus in the Roman Forum (MAAR* 29, 1967) 91–95, plates 2, 4, 14; cf. *P/A* 43 f., 602, *s.v.* Arcus Sept. Sev.; Nash 1.126–130 *s.v. eadem*; Anthony Birley, *Septimius Severus, The African Emperor* (London 1971) 222 f.

Text (from *CIL* and photos of the inscription as seen from the Forum [east side]): *Imp(eratori) Caes(ari) Lucio Septimio M(arci) fil(io) Severo Pio Pertinaci Aug(usto), patri patriae, Parthico Arabico et / Parthico Adiabenico, pontific(i) maximo, tribunic(ia) potest(ate) X̄I, imp(eratori) X̄I, co(n)s(uli) ĪĪĪ, proco(n)s(uli), et / Imp. Caes. M(arco) Aurelio L(uci) fil. Antonino Aug. Pio Felici, tribunic. potest. V̄I, cos., procos., p(atri) p(atriae), / optimis fortissimisque principibus, /⁵ ob rem publicam restitutam imperiumque populi Romani propagatum / insignibus virtutibus eorum domi forisque, S(enatus) P(opulus)q(ue) R(omanus).*

"To (the emperors Septimius Severus, with all his titles, and Caracalla, with all his), and [originally] Geta, son of Lucius, most noble Caesar [erased to say: Father of his Country, most excellent and brave rulers], in recognition of the restoration of the State [against Pescennius Niger and the Parthian vassals who had helped him while a claimant to power] and the extension of the Empire of the Roman People by their (military) talents ["outstanding virtues," Birley 223] at home and abroad: the Senate and People of Rome (dedicate this arch)."

The inscription on the west side, facing the Capitoline, is damaged in lines 3–6 by an entrance cut into the attic, probably in the time of Innocent III (1198–1216), when this half of the arch became "a feudal stronghold" (Brilliant 256 col. 2, with pl. 14, cf. pl. 2). The inscr. is unusual or noteworthy in several respects: line 1, *Lucio* written in full, *fil.* instead of *f.*; *M(arci)*, the praenomen not of Septimius Severus's real father (*Publius*), but of his self-adopted one, Marcus Aurelius; lines 1–2, "the old-style titulature," *Parth. Arab. et Parth. Adiab.*, which "maintains the convention of 195 A.D." (Brilliant 92 col. 2 with reff.) and reflects S. S.'s campaigns against Parthian vassals, including Adiabene, which had aided Pescennius Niger; line 3, *fil.*, as in line 1; lines 3 *fin.*–4: *p.p. . . . princ.* is all written over an erasure, the best restoration of the original seeming to be Antonio Nibby's *et / P(ublio) Septimio L(uci) fil. Getae nobiliss(imo) Caesari* (*Roma nell'anno MDCCCXXXVIII*, 1 [Rome 1838] 478 f.), approved by Dessau, *ILS* 425, n. 3, and M. Bang, *CIL* 6.4: 3 (1933) 36881 (35 letters, including 6 I's, vs. 34, with 8 I's—cf. Bormann's restoration, *CIL* 6.31230); Geta is *nobiliss. Caesar* in eleven other inscrs. in *ILS* (3: 2, 291). *Rem (publicam) restituere* must be a hallowed phrase, or perhaps by now only a cliché, going back to Ennius's famous phrase about Q. Fabius Maximus Verrucosus (Cunctator) *Unus homo nobis cunctando restituit rem (publicam)*, *Ann.* 370, ed. Vahlen[2] (Leipzig 1928, repr. Amsterdam 1967), quoted first by Cicero, *De Off.* 1.24.84 and *De Sen.* 4.10. The dating comes from the tribunician powers mentioned.

74. Epitaph of the Father of Elagabalus, Rome, from Velletri. A.D. 217/218.

A bilingual (Latin-Greek) text cut on the smooth side of a white-marble sarcophagus (m. 0.51 × 1.985 × 0.595, Meinhardt), found in 1764 at Velletri (anc. Velitrae, ca. 40 km. S.E. of Rome, where A. Passerini, *Le coorti pretorie* [Rome 1939] 350, thought it probable the deceased had died and where Klass, *RE* 8A: 1 [1955] 410, 7–10, believes his widow had his remains placed, "perhaps for political reasons"); seen in 1949, 1956, 1973 in the Cortile del Belvedere of the Vatican (inv. no. 983), where it was by 1772/73. The epitaph shows the *cursus honorum*—first equestrian, then senatorial—of Sex. Varius Marcellus (father of the later emperor Elagabalus), set up by his wife, Julia Soaemias Bassiana (niece of Severus's wife Julia Domna), and their children. For the dating, see *Album*, 3.38 *fin.*

As the sarcophagus is now placed, with the inscrs. legible in normal fashion, the opening is underneath; originally, if the opening was on top, the inscrs. must have been upside down. (A mistake by the planner? the sarcophagus later discarded?) Letter heights of the Latin: cm. 5.6–6.0 (line 1) down to 3.1–3.3 (line 6).

CIL 10.6569 (copied by Henzen for Mommsen), *ILS* 478, *Album* 3.37 f., no. 274, E. Meinhardt in H/S 1.233, 4 p. 383 (both these with bibl., including reff. to editions of the Greek only; Meinhardt has also a German transl. and notes). Cf. H. G. Pflaum, "La carrière de C. Iulius Avitus Alexianus, grand'père de deux empereurs," *REL* 57 (1979) 298–314.

Text: *Sex(to) Vario Marcello, / proc(uratori) aquar(um) $\overline{C}$ (= centenario), proc. prov(inciae) Brit(anniae) $\overline{CC}$ (= ducenario), proc. rationis / privat(ae) $\overline{CCC}$ (= trecenario), vice praeff. (= praefectorum) pr(aetorio) et urbi functo, / c(larissimo) v(iro), praef(ecto) aerari militaris, leg(ato) leg(ionis) $\overline{III}$ (= tertiae) Aug(ustae), /⁵ praesidi provinc(iae) Numidiae: / Iulia Soaemias Bassiana, c(larissima) f(emina), cum fil⟨i⟩is, / marito et patri amantissimo.*

"To Sex. Varius Marcellus, procurator of the aqueducts (salary 100,000 sesterces), procurator of the province of Britain (sal. 200,000 sest.), procurator of the Imperial private property (sal. 300,000 sest.), vice-praetorian prefect and vice-urban prefect, *clarissimus vir* [i.e., now of senatorial rank], prefect of the military exchequer, commander of the Third Augustan legion [stationed at Lambaesis, Numidia], governor of the province of Numidia [these last two posts held probably at the same time]: Julia Soaemias Bassiana, *clarissima femina* [i.e., as wife of a *clariss. vir*], together with her children, to a most affectionate husband and father."

There are two ligatures in line 2: RI and TI, I being obviously the easiest letter to form a ligature. The Greek omits the $\bar{C}$, $\overline{CC}$, and $\overline{CCC}$ (lines 2–3), has no abbreviations, and partly translates, partly transliterates, the Latin terminology.

75. The Arval Hymn (*Carmen Arvale*), Rome. A.D. 218. Part of the frontal inscription of a damaged marble tablet (cm. 77.3 × 63.1, max.), found in 1778 when the foundations were laid for the Sagrestia of St. Peter's built by order of Pius VI; the tablet was seen in 1949, 1956, 1973, attached to the wall of the Sala a croce greca in the Vatican (inv. no. 215); beside it is the rear half of the tablet (whose text apparently continues that of the front), which has been sawed off from the frontal half.

Part of the records of the Arval Brethren for the year 218, which contains the only extant copy of the ancient Arval Hymn (lines 32 *fin.*–38 *init.*). (For the Arvals, see H. Bloch, *OCD* 447, *s.v.* Fratres Arv.) A consular date for A.D. 218 appears on the rear half of the tablet, line 30, and one for A.D. 219, line 38. Letter heights: average ca. 8 or 9 mm., some down to 5 mm., others up to 1.3 cm., excluding the flourishes above or below the line of writing.

CIL 6.2104, *a, ILS* 5039 (add.); the Hymn alone, ed. Mommsen, *CIL* 1¹.25, ed. 2 by Lommatzch, 1: 2: 1, no. 2, pp. 369 f. (cf. pp. 717, 831, all with bibl.), Buecheler *CLE* 1.1, Diehl 138, Norden 107–224, 286–290 (the text itself, 114 f.); Warm. 250–253, Pis. A 2, Ern. 146, Gordon, *Seven Latin Inscrs.* 85–88, Degr. 4, *Album* 3.41–46 no. 276. Cf. Latte 1 n. 1, 65 n. 2, E. Meinhardt in H/S 1.26, 4 p. 378 (notes, bibl., and J. Marquardt's German transl.). One of the worst written, least legible, Latin inscrs., esp. in the *Carmen*, not even the text of which is entirely cer-

tain, much less the meaning (see *Album*, 3.42, Lettering). It seems generally agreed that it is in saturnians (most recently Cole, "The Saturnian Verse" [1969] 48 f., 70 f.), though Mommsen (*CIL* 1 p. 10 *fin.*) washed his hands of the matter, leaving it to the experts.

Text (many letters uncertain) of lines 32 *med.*–38 *init.*: ... *carmen descendentes tripodaverunt in verba haec: E nos, Lases, iuvate, / [E] nos, Lases, iuvate, E nos, Lases, iuvate; neve luae rue, Marma⟨r⟩, sins incurrere in pleores, neve lue rue, Marmar, / [s]ins incurrere in pleoris, neve lue rue, Marmar, sers [or serp] incurrere in pleoris; satur fu, rere [for fere] Mars, limen /³⁵ [sa]le sta berber, satur fu, fere Mars, limen sall [for sali] sta berber, satur fu, fere Mars, limen sni [for sali] sta berber; / [Sem]unis alternei advocapit conctos, Semunis alternei advocapit conctos, Simunis alternei advocapit / [conct]os; e nos, Marmor, iuvato, e nos, Marmor, iuvato, e nos, Ma⟨r⟩mor, iuvato; triumpe, triumpe, triumpe trium/[pe tri]umpe,* etc.

"Then the priests [to go back to line 31, *fin.*,] the doors being closed, girded up their robes, took their little books and, *descindentes* the hymn [the meaning of *desc.*, a *hapax legomenon*, is unknown: cf. English "descant" and *TLL s.v.* descindo], danced to these words."

The hymn that follows is an appeal first to the Lares for help (pre-rhotacism form *Lases*), then to Mars (addressed apparently by a duplicated form of his name) not to allow (*sins* for *sinas? sers* or *serp*, line 34, a sheer mistake?) pestilence or affliction to attack more people (?); again to fierce Mars to be sated (*fu* an old imperative of *sum?*), to leap the threshold (?) and stand there (? Norden 142–145); then something more incomprehensible about the Semunes (Semones: cf. Wissowa 130 n. 2, or Latte 51, 65 f.); another appeal to Mars for help (*iuvato* fut., or 2nd, imper.); lastly a cry of "Triumph!" (apparently an exclamation/interjection: cf. Varro, *L.L.* 6.68, Cic. *Orator* 48.160, *OLD s.v.* triumpe.

Many letters and some word-divisions

are uncertain; despite the poor text and the archaic Latin (no one knows how old), the repetitions make most of the text probable, though the meaning is only partly clear. The intended text seems to be: *E nos* (or *Enos*), *Lases, iuvate* (3 times); *neve lue(m?) rue(m?), Marmar, sins incurrere in pleores* (or *-is*) (3 times); *satur fu, fere Mars, limen sale* (or *sali*), *sta berber* (3 times); *Semunis alternei advocapit conctos* (3 times); *e nos* (or *enos*), *Marmor, iuvate* (3 times); *triumpe* (5 times). Some read *e nos* (*e* an interjection, "Oh"?), others *enos* (i.e., *nos*, cf. Greek ἐμοῦ, etc.); some separate *lue, rue* (i.e., *luem, ruem*), CIL 6 reads *luerve*.

76. Request for Permission to Build a Tomb, Rome, from Via Ostiensis.

A.D. 227. Marble tablet (overall, cm. ca. 58.0–58.5 × 86 × ca. 4.9 at lower right) found in (or shortly before) 1887, probably on the Via Ostiensis, not far from Rome; seen in 1949, 1955, 1973, in the Antiquario of the Mus. Naz. Rom., Rome (inv. no. 444), where it has been since sometime after 1887. Letter heights: ca. 2 cm. aver. (line 1) down to ca. 1.7 cm. aver. (lines 5–7); some single letters 2.2–2.5 cm., others go down below the line.

Copy of (1) a request from Geminius Eutychetes, who raised vegetables on a piece of land on the Via Ostiensis which he rented from the Collegium Magnum Arkarum Divarum Faustinarum Matris et Piae, at a yearly rent of 26,000-plus sesterces (which he says he has paid punctually for several years), to Salvius, one of two heads of the Collegium, to join his colleague Euphrata in allowing the petitioner to build a funerary monument on a plot 20 ft. square, to be granted in perpetuity, with the usual right of access to, and movement about, the tomb, and (2) a note from Euphrata and Salvius to the four quaestors and the two clerks (of the Collegium), mentioning G. E.'s request as attached to their own letter and directing them, since the request involved (possi-

ble) permission to other farmers also [reading *adliget* as unemended, line 11], to make sure that G. E. did not build a larger place for the tomb than he had set forth in his petition. Dated by the consuls of A.D. 227.

CIL 6.33840, Bruns 373 no. 168, FIRA 3.458–460 no. 147, Album 3.55–58 no. 281 (all with bibl.).

Text: *Cum sim colonus hortorum ⟨h⟩olitoriorum qui sunt via Ostiensi, iuris / Collegi Magni Arkarum Divarum Faustinarum Matris et Piae, colens in / asse annuis SS (= sestertium, gen. plu.) XXVI et quod excurrit per aliquod (read -quot) annos in ho/diernum pariator, deprecor tuam quoq(ue) iustitiam, domine Salvi, sic- /⁵ ut Euphrata, v(ir) o(ptimus), collega tuus, q(uin)q(uennalis) Faustinae matris, aditus a me, permis(it) / (ut) consentias extruere me sub monte m[e]moriolam per ped(es) XX in quadra/to; acturus ginio (read ge-) vestro gratias si memoria mea in perpetuo const(abit?), / habitus (for habitura?) itum ambitum. Dat(us?) a Geminio Eu/tychete, colono. /*

Euphrata et Salvius Chrysopedi Pudentiano, ⟨H⟩yacintho Sophroni, q(uaestoribus) /¹⁰ et Basilio et Hypurgo, scrib(is), salutem: eximplum (read exem-) libelli dati nobis a Geminio / Eutychete, colono, litteris nostris adplicuimus et cum adliget aliis quoq(ue) / colonis permissum curabitis obsirvare (read -ser-) ne ampliorem locum memoriae / extruat quam quod libello suo professus est. Dat(ae?) VIII Kal(endas) Aug(ustas), / Albino et Maximo co(n)s(ulibus).

"Being a farmer of vegetable gardens on the Via Ostiensis which belong to the Great Board-of-Directors of the Trusts of the Deified Faustinae, Mother and (Daughter) Pia, (and) paying an annual rent of 26,000-plus sesterces, paid regularly for several years to date, I pray for justice on your part also, Salvius, sir, just as your most excellent colleague Euphrata, head officer of the senior Faustina (Trust Fund), when approached by me, allowed you to agree to my building a monument 20 ft. square under the hill; (I am) going to give thanks to your Genius if my monument stands in perpetuity, with access to and around it. (Petition) sent by Geminius Eutychetes, farmer.

"Euphrata and Salvius to Chrysopes, Pudentianus, Hyacinthus, (and) Sophron, financial officers, and to Basilius and Hypurgus, clerks, greetings: a copy of the petition submitted to us by Geminius Eutychetes, farmer, we have attached to our letter, and since it involves (possible) permission to other farmers also, you will take care to see that he does not arrange a bigger place for the monument than what he has set forth in his petition. Sent July 25, in the consulship of Albinus and Maximus." (A.D. 227)

Lines 1–4, 7 f., 11. Clearly, G. E. is not a sharecropper, but one who rents the land and thus gets the whole produce. Line 1, *fin.*, no *in* is needed before *via*. Line 2, *k* for *c* before *a* in *arkarum*, a holdover from the distant past when *k* was used before *a*, as regularly in *Kalendae* (Pfister 30–32, §9, 5). Lines 2–11. For *collegium magnum . . . Piae, colens in asse, et (id) quod excurrit* ("what runs over," i.e., "plus"), *pariator* ("one who pays his bills properly"), *const. / habitus*, and *adliget*, see *Album* 57 f., with ref. to Mommsen, Scialoja, et al.; add Waltzing 1.394 n. 4 (but he seems to give no help on *magnum*). Line 3, S̶S̶ is a mistake for H̶S̶, the latter being needed to show 2½, IIS(emis). Lines 3 f. For *in hodiernum* (sc. *diem*), "to date," cf. Pliny, *N. H.* 33.7.30. Lines 8, 13. On *datus* and *datae*, see *Album* 3.58 no. 281 *ad loc.* Line 9 is indented for paragraphing.

77. Dedication to Decius, *Nobilissimus Caesar*, Rome. A.D. 251. Marble tablet, now in some nine or more pieces joined together (ca. 79.4 cm., max. × ca. 63.3 cm., max.) seen in 1949, 1956, 1973, set in the wall of the Gall. lap. of the Vatican (inv. no. 6905); found in Rome in 1611 in the building of the foundations of the new choir of St. Peter's. A dedication to Q. Herennius Etruscus Messius Decius,

while *nobilissimus Caesar*, by three groups jointly (*collegia?*), which very likely had shops or offices near one another, perhaps in the forum Vinarium (at least four inscrs. mention *argentarii de foro vinario*, *CIL* 6.9181 *a, b, c,* 9182: P/A 245 *s.v.*).

CIL 6.1101 (cf. pp. 3071, 3778), *ILS* 519, Waltzing 3.201 no. 742 (cf. 296 f., 4.8 no. 10, 17 no. 41, 34 no. 103); Diehl, *IL* tab. 16, A 5–6, *Album* 3.90 f., no. 297. Letter heights: from cm. 5.5–6.15 (line 8) down to 3.1–4.0 (line 11), tall I's 7.5 down to 3.8 cm. (lines 5, 11).

Text: *Q(uinto) Herennio Etrusco / Messio Decio, nobilis/simo Caes(ari), principi / iuventutis, / co(n)s(uli), filio /⁵ Imp(eratoris) Caes(aris) G(ai) Messi Quinti / Traiani Dec(i)i Pii Felicis / Invicti Aug(usti): / Argentarii et Exceptores / ịtemq(ue) Negotiantes vini /¹⁰ Supernat(is) et Arimin(ensis), devoti / numini maiestatique eius.*

"To Q. Herennius Etruscus Messius Decius, Most Noble Caesar, Prince of the Youth, consul, son of the Emperor Caesar G. Messius Quintus Traianus Decius Pius Felix Invictus Augustus: the bankers, the shorthand writers, and likewise the retailers of Adriatic and Ariminum wine, in devotion to his divine nature and majesty."

Interesting names, of Decius and his son. "Herennius Etruscus" is from his mother, Herennia Cupressenia Etruscilla; "Messius Decius" shows two family-names, of which "Decius" comes from Lower Pannonia, where the father was born; "Traianus" is thought to have been added soon after D.'s arrival in Rome; cf. Wittig, *RE* 15: 1 (1931) 1246–1250, 1284 f., *s.v.* Messius 9 and 10.

Lines 2 f., *Nobil. Caes.*: "Nobilissimus, as a title of rank, became a regular attribute of the Caesares and from Constantine the Great an independent designation of rank for members of the Imperial House," W. Ensslin, *RE* 17: 1 (1936) 791, 8–11, *s.v.* Nobilissimus. Lines 3–4, *princ. iuven.*: from Septim. Severus on, this title was given an increased significance for the emperors' sons: W. Beringer, *RE* 22: 2 (1954) 2305, 20 ff., *s.v.* Princeps iuvent. Line 4 *fin.*, noteworthy the position and lack of abbreviation of *filio.* Line 8, for *argentarii*, cf. *OLD* 167 *s.v.* -*ius*; *exceptores*, De Rugg. 2: 3 (1922) 2180 *s.v.*; the meaning of neither term is perhaps quite certain, but all three groups (not necessarily *collegia*, *pace* Waltzing) may well have been connected with the wine trade. Lines 10–11: *devoti . . . eius* has become a formula, datable from the early-3rd cent.; *TLL* 5.883 *s.v.* devoveo, cites inscrs. from A.D. 212.

78. Record of a Meeting at Sentinum of a *Collegium Fabrum*, Rome.

No doubt from Sentinum (in anc. Umbria; mod. Sassoferrato, in the Marche, ca. 175 km. N.N.E./N.E. of Rome). A.D. 260. Bronze tablet (ca. 57 [est.] × 40 cm., overall; *CIL* gives 60 cm. as max. height) brought to Rome ca. 1728, in the Capitoline Mus. by ca. 1750, where in 1973 it was seen in the Sala delle Colombe under glass (inv. no. 7342). Letter heights (est.): line 1, 1.5–2+ cm., small O's 0.5–1.0 cm.; line 19, 1.7–2.0 cm.; the rest generally 0.7–ca. 1.0 cm.; many guide-lines visible, ca. 1 cm. apart. There are traces of earlier writing, e.g., line 19, *fin.* On whether the inscr. was incised or cast, see above, on **72**, and Intro, n. 10.

Record of a meeting July 1, A.D. 260, at Sentinum of the local Collegium Fabrum (Fire Dept. and/or Building Workers' Club), which voted to offer an inscribed bronze tablet (no doubt the present one) to Coretius Fuscus, a patron, in honor of his (late?) mother, Memmia Victoria, called the "mother of our company." The writer of the inscription found it beyond his powers to compose a clear, correct Latin sentence of 32 lines (or else the cutter misread his copy and was also a poor speller); hence some mistakes on his or their part, uncertainty on ours. Bormann gave up trying to correct all the *plurima vitia.*

CIL 11.5748 (ed. Bormann, who checked Henzen's reading), *ILS* 7220, Waltzing 3.505 f., no. 1898, cf. 1.429, 2.190, 4.17 f., 71 no. 64.

Text: *P̄(ublio) Cornelio Saeculare IĪ et Iunio Donato IĪ, / Kal(endis) Iul⟨i⟩is, co(n)s(ulibus)* [*cos.* should be at the *beginning* of line 2], */ Sentini cum in sc(h)ola sua freque⟨n⟩s numerus Coll(egi) Fabr(um) / Sentinatium convenissent, numerum ⟨h⟩abentibus /⁵ G(aio) Iulio Martiale et G(aio) Casidio Rufino, q(uin)q(uennalibus), et referentib(us) / ipsis: semper it* (read *et*) *in praeteritum ita splendidissimum n̄(umerum) n̄(ostrum) / conisum esse ut adfectione⟨m⟩ splendoris sui in singulos / quosquae* (read *-que*) *condignos merentes exibeant* (read *exh-*), *vel maxime / in honore adque* (read *at-*) *dignitate Memmiae Victoriae quon/¹⁰dam indoles* (read *indolis? inlustris?*) *mamoriae* (read *me-*) *femin⟨a⟩e, matris numeri nostri, / proorsus* (read *pror-*) *usquaeque* (read *-quaque*) *esse provectum nomen domus / eius, ut per ordinfm* (read *-em*) *generis sui omnes in numerum n̄(ostrum) / patroni in collegium nostrum appellarentur, optan-/daove* (read *-que*) *erant ut omnes universisquae* (read *-sique*) *incolumes in /¹⁵ numerum nostrum viderentur, et quoniam vir splen-/didus Coretius Fuscus patronus numeri debeat ex/emplo pietatis parentium et matris honorificientia* (read *-centia*), */ itaque si omnibus videretur tabula⟨m⟩ aeream ei offer/ri, q(uid) f(ieri) p(laceret), d(e) e(a) r(e) i(ta) c(uncti) c(ensuerunt): /²⁰ gloriosam esse relationem b.b. v.v. (= bonorum virorum duorum) q(uin)q(uennalium) collegi n̄(ostri) / et ideo cum sit Coretius Fuscus splendide natus ut / potius honorificientiae* (read *-centiae*) *nostrae modum intel/legat necessaque* (read *-eque*) *sit ei tabulam aeream titulis / ornatam scriptam offeri* (read *-erri*) *petique ab eo ⟨ut⟩ hanc /²⁵ oblationem nostram libenti animo suscipe/re dignetur legatosque in eam rem fieri qui / {qui} digne prosequantur Titratium* (the *m* corrected?) *Ampliatum, Orfium Veri/tatem, Aemilium Victorem, Bebidium Iustum, Casidium Mart⟨i⟩a/lem, Iulium Martialem, Casidium Rufinum, Bebidium Ienua/³⁰ rivium* (read *Ianuarium*), *Aetrium Romanum, Casidium Clementinum, Aetrium* (-*um* in ligature) / *Vernam, Vassidenum Favorem, Ca-sidium Iustissimum, Sa/trium Verecundum, Statium Velocem, Veturi⟨um⟩ Celerinu⟨m⟩.*

"In the consulship of P. Cornelius Saecularis and (G.) Iunius Donatus, both for the second time [A.D. 260], on July 1, at Sentinum: whereas the full membership of the *Collegium Fabrum* of Sentinum had met in their clubhouse, G. Iulius Martialis and G. Casidius Rufinus, chief officers, being in charge of the company and themselves stating that [to summarize lines 6–19 *init.*: it has always been our practise to show our esteem for worthy individuals and in particular for Memmia Victoria, 'Mother' of the Club, she and her whole family being called our patrons, and since her son Coretius Fuscus ought (to be moved?) by his parents' example (to show similar kindnesses?), therefore, if it pleased everyone that a bronze tablet be offered him], on the question what their pleasure was, they all voted as follows: that the statement of our two worthy officers was a matter for pride and therefore, since Coretius Fuscus is of distinguished birth, in order that he may better appreciate our manner of bestowing honor, it is our decision [reading, with Bormann, *placere* for *necessaque sit*] that a deluxe inscribed bronze tablet be offered him and that he be asked to deign to accept our offering with good will and that delegates be chosen for this purpose who should pursue the matter properly" (the names of 16 delegates follow, lines 27 *med.*–end).

Some A's lack crossbars, other horizontals are quite short, the lettering generally poor, the E's often very narrow, etc. Note the supralineate abbreviation of *noster* and *numerus*, N̄, the dual-number abbreviations BB VV, line 20. Line 19, a regular formula, commonly abbreviated. Such forms as *Iulis, scola, freques, abentibus, it* for *et, adfectione* and *femine* may well reflect actual pronunciation; other incorrect forms, e.g., *proorsus, quosquae, honorificientia/ae,* seem due to ignorance. Note the

position of *cos.* at the end of line 2; compare, above, **2** *-que,* **12** line 8, **66** line 7, for similar run-overs.

Coretius Fuscus was a local decurion and a patron of all three *collegia principalia* at Sentinum, *CIL* 11.5749 (= *ILS* 7221), lines 10 f. (A.D. 261). For *collegia fabrum,* which, whether originally only building-workers' clubs, certainly came to be associated with fire-fighting, see Pliny, *Ep.* 10.33, who, after a big fire at Nicomedia, the capital of Bithynia, asks Trajan to consider whether a *coll. fabrorum* should be established to fight fires there; cf. W. Liebenam, in De Rugg. 3: 1 (1895) 4–14, esp. 4 col. 2, *s.v.* fabri, Waltzing 2.193, 194 f., Kornemann, *RE* 4 (1901) 393, 50–395, 16, *s.v.* collegium, 6 (1909) 1893 ff., 1905 ff., *s.v.* fabri. Some phrases are hopeless for a translator: e.g., line 7, *adfectione(m) splendoris sui* ("their feeling of distinction"?), 9/10, *quon/dam indoles* (for *indolis? inlustris?* see Dessau's n. 6) *mamoriae* (for *me-; CIL* reads *mu-*); 14/15, *incolumes in numerum nostrum;* others difficult, e.g., line 9; 12, *per ordinem generis sui omnes* ("all of her family in succession"?); 17, *honorificientia* ("graciousness"?). In lines 12/13 *in numerum n.* is repeated as *in collegium nostrum.* Note that except for the first consul (line 1) and the two *quinquennales* the first time mentioned (5), not a single name includes a praenomen; clearly, it is passing out of use, or at least ceasing to be written.

79. Epitaph of a Christian Woman, Rome.

A.D. 279. Marble tablet, now in three pieces joined together (cm. 30 × 73, Bovini); reported in 1655–1667 as found in a Christian cemetery outside Rome (a catacomb); seen in 1949, 1956, 1973, in the second Sala dei Monumenti Cristiani in the Pal. dei Conservatori (inv. no. 6858); formerly in the Capitoline Mus. Letter heights: cm. 2.5–4.3 (line 1) down to 1.6–2.3 (line 6), tall L's up to 4.0–5.1. Poor spacing between lines.

The epitaph seems to say that Severa

Seleuciane lived seventeen years with Aurelius Sabutius, to A.D. 279, having lived thirty-two years and two months as a pagan to A.D. 269 (plus 10 yrs. as a Christian). She must have died at age forty-two. At the right are engraved what De Rossi describes as wool-working instruments and Bovini as a loom; left of the loom there seems to be a shuttle; the couple may have been weavers. Two consular dates.

De Rossi 21 f., no. 14, cf. G. Gatti's *Suppl.* fasc. 1 (Rome 1915) 7 f., no. 1387; *ILCV* 1.645 (bibl.), with 4 p. 6, O. Marucchi *Bull. Com.* 57 (1929) 312 f., no. 14 (text, photo, notes), G. Bovini (ed.), *Musei Capitolini, I monumenti cristiani* (Rome 1952) 51 no. 34, pl. VII, *a. Album* 3.96 f., no. 302.

Text (as interpreted by J. H. Oliver): *cum{cum}vixit Severa Seleuci/ane cum Aurelio Sabutio annis / dece⟨m⟩ et septe⟨m⟩, Imp(eratore) Probo Aug(usto) III et Nonio / Paterno bis cons(ulibus)* [A.D. 279]. *Quot (sc. annis) vixit in s⟨a⟩eculo? /⁵ Annis tricinta* [for *trig-*] *et duo et menses duo, Imp. / Claudio Aug. et Patern(o) con{e}s(ulibus)* [A.D. 269]. Two ligatures: *no* (line 4), *ne* (line 6).

De Rossi, 21, col. 1, found the meaning of this "most obscure"; he added that *cumcumvixit = convixit* (which makes sense—dittography), and he approved an earlier conjecture that Aur. Sab. had predeceased his wife (which seems an open question), but his solution of the obscurities is unsatisfactory, as is Diehl's also ("either the numbers of the years or the names of the consuls are confused"); no other ed. has anything of value apropos. J. H. Oliver's version (presented here with permission) follows:

"Severa Seleuciane lived for 17 years with Aur. Sabutius by the ⟨time of⟩ the consulship of Imp. Probus Aug. for the 3rd time and Nonius Paternus for the second. How many (years) did she live in worldliness? Thirty-two years and two months (until her conversion) in the consulship of Claudius Aug. and Paternus."

He adds: "She died at the age of 42. She lived 32 yrs. a pagan and 10 yrs. a Christian. The simple inscr. carries the spirit of early Christianity."

The inscription is typically early-Christian in other respects (apart from coming from a Christian cemetery): its poor, in fact unclear, Latin, its poor writing, the phrase *vixit in seculo*, usually "in the (wicked) world." (cf. Diehl 3.401 *s.v.* saeculum), and probably the two-element names (later to decrease to a single element—e.g., Euticius, Leopardus, Proiecta, Bonifatius, Adeodata). Note both ablative and accusative for duration of time, line 5.

One wishes that the writer of the inscr. had written better, less obscure, Latin; the dittography in the first word sets the tone. For Oliver's version one would like an explanation, with parallels, of the simple abl. in the two consular dates (for which one would expect something like *(usque) ad* with the accus.), and at least one parallel to the meaning "in the (pagan) world" for *in seculo*, and to the *Quot* question. Few direct questions in Latin inscriptions come to mind; there are a few in the epitaphs, mostly rhetorical (e.g., *ILCV* 2487–91, *si deus pro nobis, quis contra* (or *adversus*) *nos? CLE* 801, *Quid sumus aut loquimur, vita est quid deniq[ue nostra*?]). (A study of all the direct questions in Greek/Latin inscrs. might be worthwhile.)

80. Ex-voto Dedication to Cybele and Attis, Rome. Probably ca. A.D. 295. Marble altar (overall, cm. ca. 80 × 54.0–54.7 (at base ca. 63.5) × apparently 46–47 (at base perhaps 49) (much restoration following damage), found just outside Rome in 1745 in a vineyard on the Appian Way; now in three pieces (plus 2 more apparently not original) joined together, seen in 1949, 1956, 1973, on the floor in front of the south wall of the Galleria (primo piano) of the Capitoline Mus. (no. 4629), where it was by 1775/78. Letter heights: 4.0–4.5 cm.

An ex-voto dedication to Cybele and Attis by L. Cornelius Scipio Orfitus, senator and augur, after the ritual of *taurobolium/criobolium*. The same man "made" another *taur. sive criob.* in late February, A.D. 295 (*CIL* 6.505 = *ILS* 4143), hence the approximate dating of our inscr.

CIL 6.506 (cf. 30782), *ILS* 4144, *Album* 3.103 f., no. 308 (wrong in having Orfitus himself perform the ritual: he must have been the recipient). The altar is described and illustrated by H. Stuart Jones (ed.), *A Catalogue of the Ancient Sculptures . . . of Rome: the Sculptures of the Museo Capitolino* (Oxford 1912), text p. 114 no. 40 a, pl. 34A nos. 40A 1–3; below the inscr. are incised "the priestly Phrygian cap and a *pedum* [shepherd's crook]." On Orfitus, cf. E. Groag, *PIR*² 2.357 no. 1443; *PLRE* 1.651 Orfitus 1 ("his family ancient and aristocratic"); on the cult, Wissowa 322–326 or Latte 353–356 (see also below).

Text: *M(atri) D(eum) M(agnae) [I(daeae)?] et Atti[di] / L(ucius) Corne[l]ius Scipio / Orfitus, v(ir) c(larissimus), / augur, ex voto /⁵ taurobolio sive / criobolio facto.*

"To the Great Mother of the Gods (of Mt. Ida?) and to Attis, L. Cornelius Scipio Orfitus, of senatorial rank (and) augur, in accordance with a vow (dedicated this altar), a *taurobolium* or *criobolium* having been performed."

CIL (1876) and Hübner (1885) mention no damage to the stone. Line 1. Previous editors have read only *M. D. M.*, without *I(daeae)*, but a squeeze shows apparently the remains of an interpunct close to the second M, and even perhaps the suggestion of an I close to the point. *I(daeae)* appears in the companion piece, *CIL* 6.505 (= *ILS* 4143, where, line 1 *fin.*, *Attinis* should apparently be *Attini* [dat.] *s(acrum)*), and is part of Cybele's full name; in the inscrs. of *ILS*, if *magna* is added to *mater deum*, *Idaea* also is added much more often than not (3: 1, 541 f.). In *CIL* 6.505, apparently a dedication to the same pair by Orfitus, the reading is *taurobolium sive criobolium fecit* (Feb. 26, 295).

Here, as *PLRE* notes (O. "received the *taurobolium*"), *fecit* seems clearly used of the recipient of the ritual (there is no reason for believing Orfitus to be a priest of Cybele/Attis), though the commoner words seem to be *accipere, percipere, suscipere*, whereas *facere, conficere, perficere* are said of the priest officiating. But the word *sive*, used of the same man in both inscrs., is perhaps unique; the regular connective, if both terms are used, is *et* or *-que*. The taurobolium, sacrifice of a bull or a steer, is in honor of Cybele, the criobolium, sacrifice of a ram, in honor of Attis. Unless *sive* here = *et*, it looks as if Orfitus had not known (or cared?) which blood he was getting bathed in. Cf. F. Cumont, *RE* 4 (1901) 1718 f., *s.v.* Criobolium, *TLL* 4.1206 (1908) 26 ff., *s.v. eadem*, L. Cesano in De Rugg. 2: 2 (1910) 1275–78 *s.v. eadem*, Schwenn, *RE* 11: 2 (1922) 2274–79 *s.v.* Kybele, H. Oppermann, *RE* 5A: 1 (1934) 16–21 *s.v.* Taurobolia.

81. Preamble to Diocletian's Edict on Prices, Athens, from Plataea.

A.D. 301. Mommsen/Blümner's Fragment no. 29. White, fine-textured marble stele (m. 1.35 × 0.80–0.835 × 0.18), found in 1889 at Plataea, not *in situ*; now in Athens in the Epigraphical Museum (no. 10064), where it was seen in 1974. (For comparison we show also Fragment no. 1, in Aix-en-Provence, from Egypt, *CIL* 3, pp. 802 f., 1910; its writing is much harder to read, but it contains most of the Imperial names and titles, plus the operative verb *dicunt*, "declare," line 3, *med.*)

Two of the nineteen extant, or lost but reported, fragments of the Preamble, which thus far has been found only in Latin (the fragments, besides these two, come from ten other places in Crete, the Greek mainland, Libya, Turkey); many fragments of the text of the prices/wages list have been found in either Latin (Crete, Libya, Turkey) or Greek (only on the Greek mainland except one small piece found in Italy but of questioned origin). The Preamble, with its many fragments, seems complete except for some words, or parts of words, in the Imperial titles and a few letters or words elsewhere, all easily restorable.

The Edict of Diocletian and his three colleagues (1 Augustus, 2 Caesars) in 301 (the year is fixed by D.'s *trib. pot. no.*, 18) fixed maximum prices and wages, in order to try to stop their rapid rise (inflation). (Cf. W. Ensslin, *CAH* 12.404 f.; *OCD* 347 *s.v.* Diocletian.) The early-Christian apologist Lactantius reports the Edict's failure (*De Mort. Pers.* [A.D. 318?] 7.6 f.: goods disappeared from the market, until finally, "by sheer necessity the law was abrogated" after "much bloodshed" and the "ruin of many people"; L.'s word for high prices/inflation is *caritas*, both this and *licentia pretiorum* being used in the long, grandiloquent, verbose Preamble (cf. J. C. Rolfe, *AJA* ser. 2, 6 [1902] 50 f.; R. MacMullen, "Roman Bureaucratese" [cited above, n. 3], esp. 370; R. G. Kent, *Univ. Penn. Law Review* 69 [1920–21] 40 f.; idem, *The Textual Criticism of Inscrs.* [Philadelphia 1926 *Lang. Mon.*, Ling. Soc. Amer., 2] 57–76).

First publ. by J. C. Rolfe and F. G. Tarbell, *Pap. Amer. Sch. Class. Stud. Athens*, 5 (1886/90, publ. 1892) 233–244 (= *AJA* ser. 1: 5 [1889] 428–439), with transl. of almost all the Preamble, whence Mommsen, *CIL* 3 Suppl. [1:] 3 (1893) p. 1913 (the whole Preamble, pp. 1928–1930), *ILS* 642 (parts of the Preamble).

The whole edict: *CIL* 3, pp. 801–841, 1055–1058, 1909–1953, 2208–2211, 2328[57-63]; Mommsen's 3rd ed. (*CIL* 3, Suppl, 1: 3), with H. Blümner's commentary, publ. separately as *Der Maximaltarif des Diocletian*, Berlin 1893, repr. 1958; Kent op. cit. (1920–21) 35–47 (intro., transl. of Preamble, some notes on the rest); Elsa R. Graser, in T. Frank's *Econ. Survey*, 5.305–317 (text and transl., repr. Paterson, N.J., 1959), L/R 2.464–472 (partial transl.), *ARS* 235–237 (transl. of Pream.), Siegfried Lauffer (ed.), *Diokletians Preisedikt* (Berlin

1971), Marta Giacchero (ed.), *Edictum Diocletiani et Collegarum de pretiis rerum venalium . . .* , 2 vols. (Genoa 1974 *Pubbl. Ist. Storia Ant. e Sc. Ausil., Univ. di Genova*, 8), with Ital. transl. New fragments and readings: K. T. Erim and J. Reynolds, *JRS* 60 (1970) 120–141, Erim and Reynolds and M. Crawford, *JRS* 61 (1971) 171–177, Erim and Reynolds, *JRS* 63 (1973) 99–110, R. and F. Naumann, *Der Rundbau in Aezani . . .* (Tübingen 1973 Deutsches Arch. Inst., *Istanbuler Mitt.*, Beih. 10), chs. I and II, E. J. Doyle, *Hesperia* 45 (1976) 77–97, M. Crawford and J. Reynolds, *ZPE* 26 (1977) 125–151. Cf. Crawford and Reynolds, *JRS* 65 (1975) 160–163, J. Reynolds, *JRS* 66 (1976) 183 and (with H. Plommer, review of Naumann) 251 f., A. Chastagnol, *REL* 53 (1975) 475–477 (rev. of Giacchero), M. H. Crawford, *CR* n.s. 27 (1977) 316 (rev. of G.), A. M. Rossi, *Epigraphica* 37 (1975) 305–307 (rev. of G.). Lauffer's ed. seems the most useful of all to date, though G.'s, particularly vol. 2, with 95 plates, is valuable.

Text of Preamble, lines 1–6 (text of line 1 and of missing parts of lines 2–6 are in parentheses, taken from Lauffer): [1](*Fortunam rei publicae nostrae, cui iuxta inmortales deo*⟨*s*⟩ *bellorum memoria quae feliciter gessi-*)[2]*mus gratulari licet tranquillo* [*o*]*rbis statu* (*et in gremio altissima*[*e*] *quietis l*)*oca*(*to, etiam pacis bonis, pro-*)[3]*pter quam sudore largo laboratum est,* (*disponi fideliter adque* (*for at-*) *ornari decen*)*te*(*r honestum publicum*) [4]*et Romana dignitas maiestasque de*[*si*]*de-ra*⟨*n*⟩*t ut nus* (for *nos*), (*qui benigno favore numinum aestuantes de*) [5]*praete*ṛ[*ito*] *rapinas gentrum* (for *-tium*) *barba*[*rarum*] *ips*[*a*]*ru*[*m nationum*] *clad*(*e conpressimus, in aeternum*) [6]*fundat*[*am qu*]*ietem dibitum* (for *debitis*) *iusticiae* (for *iustit-*) *munime*[*ntis*] *saepiamus.*

"Public rectitude (? The public sense of right ?) and the dignity and majesty of Rome require the fortune of our state— which, along with the immortal gods, in memory of the wars that we have successfully waged, we may thank for the (present) state of the world, quiet (as it is) and resting in the bosom of the deepest tranquility, (thank) also for the blessings of peace, for which exertions have been made with much sweat—to be faithfully set in order and properly arranged, so that we, who by the kind favor of the divine powers have crushed the long-rampant plunderings on the part of barbarian peoples, with great damage to the nations themselves, may surround peace, established for eternity, with the appropriate bulwarks of justice." Rolfe and Tarbell (followed by Kent, 1920–21) translate *honestum publicum* (end of line 3) as "the national honor," L/R as "the law-abiding public," Graser and *ARS* as "public opinion."

There are traces of -*rarum* in line 4, perhaps of -*si*- in line 3; line 4, *clad*- cannot be identified in the squeeze. Line 6, *iusticiae*: the squeeze shows *i*, then what seems to be a tall *i*, then *usticiae*. "The lettering of the Plataea stone, like that of most, if not all, of the copies of the Edict, is mixed, combining capital forms, some quite ordinary (A [though bar-less], C, I, L [though the 'horizontal' slants down], N, O, P, R, and X), some rounded (E, M, V, bottom of T), with 'common' script or 'cursive' forms (B, D, F, G, H, Q, and S, which is easily the most prominent letter of all)," J. S. Gordon. Robert Marichal uses the Preamble of the Plataea copy and its errors to postulate the nature of the "copy" sent out by the emperors: see pp. 342–344 of his article "L'écriture de la chancellerie impériale," *Aegyptus* 32 (1952) 326–350.

82. Dedication of Triumphal Arch to Constantine, Rome. Probably A.D. 315, possibly 316. Standing between the Colosseum and the Palatine, it is the latest, and said to be the largest, of the three triumphal arches extant in Rome. A triple arch, of white-marble exterior, m. 21 high × 25.70 wide × 7.40 deep (Platner/Ashby; Coarelli, 162, says "almost 25 m. high," Lugli

"21 m."). The dedicatory inscription is duplicate, cut in the center of each face of the attic; only the large cuttings remain, the (bronze) letters lost (De Rossi, *Bull. Arch. Crist.* 1 [1863] 58; Hübner, 240, on no. 702). The surface of the arch is suffering from corrosion, presumably from the great flow of automotive traffic rushing by it. (For a description of the bacterial infections devouring the marble monuments, see James Hansen, "Ailing Treasures," *Science 80* [Washington, D.C., American Assn. for the Advancement of Science] Sept./Oct. 1980, pp. 58–61.)

The arch was dedicated by the Senate and People of Rome to celebrate Constantine's victory over his rival Maxentius in 312 at the Mulvian Bridge just north of Rome; typically, Maxentius is not named in the inscr. but only referred to as the "tyrant." Cf. Benjamin, *RE* 4 (1901) 1014–1018 *s.v.* Constantinus 2; *CAH* 12.343 f. (H. Mattingly), 678–684 (N. H. Baynes).

The implied mention of *decennalia* in the inscr. ("a festival held on the 10th anniversary of an emperor's accession")—*votis X* and *votis XX* (i.e., *decennalibus, vicennalibus*), on the north face, one phrase to the left, the other to the right, above the smaller arches and the circular panels, and *sic X, sic XX*, correspondingly on the south face—indicates ten years of rule, since C. was proclaimed "Augustus" by the army in Britain immediately after the death of his father, Constantius, at York, July 25, 306 (Hydatius, on this year, in his continuation of Jerome's *Chronicle: Levatus est Constantinus VIII K(alendas) Aug(ustas)*, quoted by Mommsen, *CIL* 1²: 1, p. 302, col. 1, sect. 3); according to the Romans' usual inclusive counting, at both ends (cf. Bickerman, 43), ten years should date the arch to 315 (Henzen in *CIL* 6 considered 315 certain, Dessau probable; Lugli, p. 313, favored 316).

CIL 6.1139, 31245, *ILS* 694, S/C 127 (cf. 92). Cf. P/A 36–38 *s.v.* Arcus Const., Lugli, *Roma ant.* 313–317, P. Veyne, *REL*

38 (1960) 306–322, esp. 319 f., Nash, 1.104–112 *s.v.* Arcus Const. (pp. 104 f. show both faces; some of the cuttings, with holes for attaching the letters, can be seen p. 108), *PLRE* 1.223 f., *s.v.* Fl. Val. Constantinus 4, Coarelli 162–166 (photo of south face, in color). We show the north (strictly speaking, N.N.E.) face.

Text of each face: *Imp(eratori) Caes(ari) Fl(avio) Constantino Maximo / P(io) F(elici) Augusto, S(enatus) P(opulus)q(ue) R(omanus), / quod instinctu divinitatis, mentis / magnitudine, cum exercitu suo /⁵ tam de tyranno quam de omni eius / factione, uno tempore, iustis / rem publicam ultus est armis, / arcum triumphis insignem dicavit.* (No interpuncts evident except in lines 1 [first 3 only] and 2; the letter cuttings somewhat damaged.)

"To the emperor Constantine the Great, *Pius, Felix,* Augustus, the Senate and the People of Rome, because by divine inspiration (and) greatness of mind, with his army he avenged the State against both the tyrant and his whole army, at one (and the same) time, with righteous arms, have dedicated (this) arch, conspicuous with (scenes of his) triumphs."

This seems to be the first use of *Maximus* in an emperor's titles, apart from its frequent use with such military titles as *Parthicus* (these from Marcus Aurelius?) (cf. *ILS* 3: 1, 257–307). The much-discussed phrase of line 3, *inst. divin.,* as S/C 92 point out, "may be interpreted either in a pagan or in a Christian sense." (Cf. J. H. W. G. Liebeschuetz, *Continuity and Change in Roman Religion* [Oxford 1979] 285, 288 with n. 4, on the "neutrality of the sculpture" and the "neutral monotheistic style" of the inscr.) The minor inscrs.: *votis X (solutis)* and *XX (susceptis),* "the 10-yr. vows (for the emperor's welfare) (having been fulfilled)," "the 20-yr. vows (having been undertaken)," abl. abs. with the participle omitted, as in a formula? cf. Veyne, op. cit. 319 f., n.

3; *sic X, sic XX,* "as he has reigned ten yrs., so may he reign twenty" (S/C 127; similarly Veyne, loc. cit.); *liberatori urbis* and *fundatori quietis* (inside the central arch, west and east sides, resp., the latter visible in Nash, 107), "(to Constantine,) liberator of the City" and "founder of Peace." The *quod*-clause is stated as a fact, not as an opinion on the part of the dedicators; hence the indic. The text has some style: chiastic order and lack of connective, line 3, the use of *tam . . . quam,* the order of words in *iustis . . . armis.*

83. Record of Restoration of Public Baths, Rome. Before ca. A.D. 325? Fragments of a large marble slab (m. ca. 1.20 × 7.10) joined together, much restored, and set up in the Sala a croce greca of the Vatican (inv. no. 209), where it was seen in 1973; fragments reported seen in Rome by the 17th century. The inscription is restored much as is indicated in *CIL* 6, but of some of the ancient letters only a part is extant—e.g., line 3, only the bottom of STR in *destructas.*

Record of the restoration of some public baths, destroyed by fire, by Helena, mother of Constantine the Great. If she was given the title "Augusta" in ca. 325 (*PLRE*), her lack of it here (*pace PLRE*) should date the inscr. accordingly. P/A 530 *s.v.* Thermae Helenae and Nash 2.454 f., *s.v. eadem,* identify these baths as those situated on the eastern part of the Caelian, inside Porta Maggiore, of which there were considerable remains still visible in the 16th cent. (Nash shows plans.)

CIL 6.1136, cf. 31244 (apparently not in *ILS* or *ILCV*). Cf. *PIR*² 3, p. XIV, no. 426a, *s.v.* Flavia Iulia Helena Augusta; A. M. Colini, *MemPontAcc* 8: 3 (1955) 177; *PLRE* 1.410 *s.v.* Fl. Iulia Helena 3.

Text: *D(omina) N(ostra) Helena venerabilis, domini n(ostri) Constantini Aug(usti) mater et / avia beatissimor(um) et florentissimor(um) Caesarum nostrorum, / thermas incendio destructas restituit.*

"Our Lady the venerable Helen, mother of Our Lord the Emperor Constantine and grandmother of our most blessed and illustrious Caesars, restored the baths destroyed by fire."

PLRE takes *Aug.*, line 1, to go with *Helena* (loc. cit. 3rd par., line 3); this seems wrong. The chiastic order in lines 1 f.— genitive/*mater, avia*/gen.—we have seen before—e.g., in **82** and in the epitaph of Agrippina the Elder, above, **39**; it may arise from the desire to state the *great* name as soon as possible. Of Constantine's four sons (*PLRE* 1.223 f., *s.v.* Fl. Val. Constantinus 4), the "Caesars" here could be any two or all three of the oldest—Crispus (not after 326), Constantinus junior (317–), Constantine II (323 or 324—cf. *ILS* 712, note). Cf. *PLRE* 1.233, 223, 226, resp., *s.vv.* Fl. Iulius Crispus 4, Fl. Claudius Constantinus 3, Fl. Iul. Constantius 8.

84. Commemoration of G. Caelius Saturninus, Rome. Constantinian, probably A.D. 326/333. A previously used marble statue-base (cm. 90.75 without plinth above × 75.5 max. × 54.0–54.5 as restored; extant original thickness, left side 31.5, right side 40), found in Rome in 1856 near Piazza della Pilotta (between the Fontana di Trevi and Ss. Apostoli), perhaps near its original location, which Mommsen surmised (p. 300) had been the "paternal home" of the man honored in this inscription and in a later one. As it stood formerly in the Lateran Mus. (by 1867) and now stands in the new Mus. Gregoriano ex Lateranense in the Vatican (inv. nos. 10493–94), the base is surmounted by an inscribed plinth (17.1 cm. high), on which rests a portrait statue (m. 2.02 high). All this was reported found together (apparently in one piece) by the first editor, R. Garrucci (*Rev. Arch.* ser. 2: 5–6 [1862] 384–393, 31–42), and although he gives no details of the finding, it became generally accepted that the statue (with plinth) and the base belong together, though experts in Roman sculp-

ture soon saw that the 4th-cent. head rests on an earlier togate statue, which presumably were joined originally. Cf. the dating of the sculptures and reliefs of the Arch of Constantine, mostly from Trajan to M. Aurelius, Nash 1.104. For the epigraphist it matters little whether *Dogmatii* (genitive: "(statue) of D.") belongs to the man named two lines below and was his nickname, or somebody else's. But the base seems to be a statue base; if so, it seems more likely than not that the present statue and base belong together. Perhaps the son found for sale in a marble-worker's shop a used statue-base with plinth and an old togate headless statue, had a sculptor make a portrait-head of his father and new inscriptions cut for the plinth and the base, and then had the whole thing set up at home.

Commemoration of G. Caelius Saturninus, *v.c.*, whose long civil-service career (17 posts) was capped by his being named a *comes* of Constantine and, "by request of the Senate," an honorary ex-consul (and later a praetorian prefect: *CIL* 6.1705 = *ILS* 1215); by his son, G. Fl. Caelius Urbanus, *v.c.* The dating comes from Constantine's title "Victor" (probably not before 324: C. T. H. R. Ehrhardt, *ZPE* 38 [1980] 180 f.) and the offices held by Saturninus: not yet praet. prefect (ca. 333–336?), but already deputy prefect of the city-of-Rome (after 326?) (cf. Meinhardt p. 816, *PLRE* 806).

CIL 6.1704 (cf. pp. 3173, 3813), *ILS* 1214, *Album* 3.111–113 no. 315, E. Meinhardt in H/S 1.1134, with German transl. (cf. H. von Heintze, vol. cit., no. 1133, and 4, p. 393) (all these with bibl. and all including "Dogmatius" as part of S.'s name). Cf. John Crook, *Consilium Principis . . .* (Cambridge 1955) 98–101, *PLRE* 1.806 *s.v.* Saturninus 9; these also assign *Dogm.* to S.

Text: *Dogmatii* (plinth). *Honori / G(aio) Caelio Saturnino, v(iro) c(larissimo), / allecto petitu senatus inter /⁵ consulares, comiti d(o-mini) n(ostri) Constantini / Victoris Aug-*

(usti), vicario praefecturae / urbis, iudici sacra-rum cog(nitionum), vicario / praeff. (= prae-fectorum duorum) praetorio bis, in urbe Roma / et per Mysias, examinatori per Ita- /[10] iiam (for -liam), praefecto annon⟨a⟩e urbis, ratio-/nali (rei) privat⟨a⟩e, vicario summae rei / ra-tionum, rationali vicario per / Gallias, magis-tro cens⟨u⟩um, vicario / a consiliis sacris, magistro stu- /[15] diorum, magistro libellorum, duce/nario a consiliis / ⟨sacris⟩, sexag(enario) a consiliis / sacris, sexag(enario) studiorum adiutori, / fisci advocato per Italiam: / G(aius) Fl(avius) Caelius Urbanus, v(ir) c(larissi-mus), /[20] consularis: patri.

"To the honor of G. Caelius Satur-ninus, of senatorial rank, named as ex-consul at the Senate's request, member of Our Lord Constantine's travelling suite, deputy-prefect of the City with the duty of hearing Imperial appeals, deputy praetorian-prefect twice, in the city of Rome and for the Moesias (Upper and Lower), *examinator* for Italy, prefect of the City's grain supply, administrator of the Emperor's private property, sub-director in the ministry of finance, deputy finance-minister for the Gallic provinces, master of the census rolls (?), deputy-head of the Imperial judicial council (?), master of legal research and questions of cult (?), master of private appeals to the Emperor, 200,000-sesterce official at-tached to the Imperial council, 60,000-sest. similar official, 60,000-sest. assistant for legal research, etc. [see the 4th post above], legal representative of the Impe-rial treasury for Italy: G. Flavius Caelius Urbanus, *v.c.*, of consular family, to his father."

The orthography seems transitional, reflecting changes of pronunciation: *prae-fecturae* v. *annone*, etc., *censum* (gen. plu.) vs. *consiliis*. Note the dots over *d(omini) n(ostri)*, presumably to mark the abbre-viations. The use of *per* here seems to foreshadow its coming to mean "for" in Italian. *Sacer* means "Imperial," as al-ready in **29**, the middle inscr., of Cara-calla. *Honori . . . Saturnino*, a "double da-

tive": cf. Dessau, *ILS* 1214 n. 2, G/L 227 §356. "Moesia" is variously spelled, often "Mys-", as here: *ILS* 3: 2, 630. For the meaning of the titles (sometimes uncer-tain), cf. the bibl. cited in the *Album* and by Meinhardt, to which add O. Seeck, *RE* 6 (1909) 1551 *s.v.* Examinator, *TLL s.v.* eadem, W. Ensslin *CAH* 12.382; Momm-sen, "De C. Caelii Saturnini Titulo," in *Memorie Inst. Corr. Archeol.* 2 (1865) 298–332 (not in his *Ges. Schr.*, never com-pleted); E. Cuq, *Mémoire sur le Consilium Principis . . .* (Paris 1884 *Mém. prés. par di-vers savants à l'Acad. des Inscrs. et Belles-Lettres*, ser. 1, vol. 9) 466–479, 497 f.; Jones, index, 3.416 *s.v.* Caelius Saturni-nus; W. G. Sinnigen, *The Officium of the Urban Prefecture during the later Roman Em-pire* (Rome 1957 *PMAAR*, 17) 76–80, for the *mag. censuum*; *RE* is of little help here, though the index, said to be forthcom-ing, may prove different.

85. Epitaph of a Christian *Lector*, Rome. A.D. 338. Marble tablet (cm. 44.5 max. × 89.5 writ. field, m. 1.06 overall; Silvagni gives cm. 45 × 106), formerly the front of a sarcophagus (De Rossi, Silvagni), from which the first inscription (which had ap-parently occupied only the left half of the tablet, within borders and *ansae*) and all the sculpture had been deleted (but most of the borders and part of one *ansa* are still visible). First reported in 1720 in Rome in a Christian cemetery (catacomb); formerly in the Mus. epigr. cristiano of the Lateran, now in the Vatican in the Lapidario Cristiano ex Lateranense. Let-ter heights: cm. 4.3–5.3 (line 5) down to 1.1–2.1 (line 8).

Epitaph of Eq(uitius?) Heraclius, *lector* of (Rome's) second region; set up pre-sumably by his parents.

De Rossi 1.42 f., no. 48; Gatti, op. cit. (above, **79**) 23 no. 1432; Diehl *ILCV* 1.1266, 4 p. 10; Silvagni, 3.8719; *Album* 3.113 f., no. 316.

Text: *Eq(uitius?) Heraclius, / qui fuit in saeculum / an(nis) XVIIII, m(ensibus) VII,*

d(iebus) XX, / lector r(egionis) sec(undae).
⟨*Parentes?*⟩ *fecerun*⟨*t*⟩ *sibi /*[5] *et filio suo bene-
merenti. In p(ace) / deces*⟨*s*⟩*it VII Irus (for
Idus) Feb(ruarias) / Urso e (for et, or ET in
ligature?) Polemio / conss (= consulibus).*

"Eq. Heraclius, who was on earth [or,
in the (wicked) world] 19 yrs., 7 mos., 20
days, a *lector* of the second region (of
Rome). (His parents?) have made (this
tomb) for themselves and their estimable
son. He died in peace Feb. 7, in the consulship of Ursus and Polemius." (A.D.
338)

The writing and lettering are typical of
the early-Christian inscrs.; noteworthy
the great differences in letter sizes within
lines, the ivy leaves (which continue the
pagan use but are now symbolic of fidel-
ity or eternal life), the strokes through D
and R (lines 3, 4—as marks of abbreviation?), the wrong case in *in saeculum*, the
Christian symbolism (ivy leaves, palm
branches for victory, the chi-rho monogram for the first two letters of "Christus,"
the dove as symbol of peace or a pious
soul: cf. Oscar Doering, *Christliche Symbole . . .* [Freiburg i/B 1933] 118 Palme, 120
Taube), the Christian formulas *in saeculum*
(for *-o*), *in p(ace) decesit* (for *-ssit*). The editors all agree on *Equitius*; it and *Equitia*
are the only *Eq.* names in Diehl's list of
Christian names. For lectors (readers) in
the Christian community, see H. Leclercq
in *Dict. d'arch. chrét. et de lit.*, ed.
F. Cabrol and H. Leclercq, 8: 2 (Paris
1928) 2241 ff., esp. 2251 no. 11, 2253 no.
16, *s.v.* lecteur, or the *Oxf. Dict. Christ.
Church* 808 *s.v.* lector (an art. on Leclercq
himself is on pp. 807 f.). The "second region" in Rome is probably an ecclesiasti-
cal region, as Leclercq thought (op. cit.
1826 *fin.*, *s.v.* Latran), which "corresponded to the 2nd, 8th, 10th, and 11th
civic regions."

86. Dedication to Constantius II, Rome.

A.D. 352/353. A large marble base, on a
brick pedestal, of an equestrian statue
(no doubt of Constantius, but not extant),

excavated in 1547 at the foot of the Capitoline; later removed to the Farnese Gardens on the Palatine; in 1875 returned to
its original site (all this from *CIL* and
Nash) and in 1973 seen near the NE corner of the Arch of Septimius Severus
in the Roman Forum (marked "Base di
statua equestre" on map between pp. 128
f. in *Roma e dintorni*). Writing surface:
m. 1.16 × 2.30; thickness of base m. 1+
(est.); letter heights 13.0–13.5 (line 1)
down to 10.0–10.5 cm. (lines 5–6).

A dedication to the emperor Constantius II on the part of Neratius Cerealis,
prefect of the city of Rome, whose tenure
is dated by the Chronographer of A.D.
354 as from late Sept. 352, to early Dec.
353; this agrees with the dates 352 and
353 for the expulsion from Italy, and
death, of the "tyrant" (Magnentius, a pagan rival of the emperor) in line 2 (*OCD*
640 *s.v.* Magnentius).

CIL 6.1158 (cf. pp. 3071, 3778), *ILS* 731.
Cf. *P/A* 201 and Nash 1.387 *s.v.* Equus
Constantii (with bibl.), *PLRE* 1.197–199
s.v. Naeratius Cerealis 2 ("presumably
descended from senatorial Neratii of the
principate"). (The name is found spelled
both *Nae-* and *Ne-*.)

Text: *Restitutori urbis Romae adque* (sic)
*orb[is] / et extinctori pestiferae tyrannidis, /
d(omino) n(ostro) Fl(avio) Iul(io) Constantio,
victori ac triumfatori, / semper Augusto: /*[5]
*Neratius Cereạlis, v(ir) c(larissimus), praefec-
tus urbi / vice sacra iud[i]cans, d(evotus)
n(umini) m(aiestati)que eius.*

"To the restorer of the city of Rome
and of the world, and the destroyer of
a pernicious tyranny, our Lord Flavius
Iulius Constantius, victor and conqueror,
ever Augustus: Neratius Cerealis, of senatorial rank, prefect of the city (of Rome)
and deputy-judge of Imperial appeals,
in devotion to his divine nature and
majesty."

Adque for *at-*, as often. The spelling of
triumfatori shows clearly that the sound
of *ph* has become *f*, in a long development of the aspirate to the spirant, the

earliest indication of which is found "in a few carelessly written Latin inscrs. of the first cent. A.D. at Pompeii"—*Dafne, Fileto, fisica* (cf. Sturtevant 84 §92 a). For *Nae/ Neratius*, cf. *ILS* 3: 2, 807 f., *AE pro* E; Sturtevant 127 f., §132 f. Again, as in **82**, the "tyrant" goes unnamed. *Semper Aug.*, to judge from Dessau's list of emperors, begins with Diocletian (*ILS* 3: 1, 303). In *ILS* 1245 (= *CIL* 6.1745) the same man as here (named *Nae-*) is called simply *praef. urb.* without *vice sacra iudicans*. The latter phrase is interesting; *vice* seems to be one of those ablatives of manner without *cum* or an attribute, such as *ratione, moribus, silentio*, which are found with adverbial force from early Latin on (cf. G/L 256 f., §399 Note 1; Hofmann/Szantyr 116 f., §77); cf. the contemporary use of *vicarius* (adjective/noun, "deputy"), as in **84**, and our "vicariously." The "devoted" formula, as in **77**.

87. Epitaph of Iunius Bassus, Rome. A.D.

359. A large sumptuous marble sarcophagus (m. 1.17 high × 2.41 long, Hanfmann), sculptured on one side with ten scenes from the Old and New Testaments; found in 1595 in (or near) the Confessio of the Basilica of St. Peter's before this was finished and consecrated (in 1626); now preserved among early-Christian sarcophagi in room VIII of the Grotte Vecchie under St. Peter's (map facing p. 513 of *Roma e dintorni*); seen there in 1973 (by special permission), as well as a plaster copy in the Galleria dei sarcofaghi in the new Mus. Gregoriano ex Lateranense of the Vatican.

Epitaph of Iunius Bassus, *v.c.*, who died soon after being promoted to be prefect of the city of Rome (Amm. Marc. 17.11.15, on A.D. 358)—the highest position in Rome after the emperor— baptized as a Christian, very likely on his deathbed. His father was "possibly Christian," *PLRE* 1.155 *s.v.* Iunius Bassus 14; cf. Prudentius, *Contra Symm.* 1.558 ff. (which is perhaps pertinent).

CIL 6.32004, *ILS* 1286 (add.), *ILCV* 90 (add. vol. 4, p. 1, text of 8 fragmentary elegiac distichs in praise of Bassus, discovered on the cover of the sarcophagus: *AE* 1953, 239); Silvagni 2.4164; first publ. by De Rossi, 1.80 no. 141. Cf. Jones, index, 3.430 *s.v.* Iunius Bassus; *Roma e dintorni* 505; *PLRE* 1.155 *s.v.* Iunius Bassus 15. On the sarcophagus, "a milestone in the history of early Christian art," see George M. A. Hanfmann, *Roman Art . . .* (London 1964) 122 f., no. 139 (one scene, p. 219), with translation and bibl.; "although, like Constantine, he was baptized only on his deathbed, the elaborate, essentially Christian sarcophagus shows that he had prepared himself to die a Christian."

Text: *Iun(ius) Bassus, v(ir) c(larissimus), qui vixit annis XLII, men(sibus) II; in ipsa praefectura urbi, neofitus, iit ad deum VIII Kal(endas) Sept(embres), Eusebio et ⟨H⟩ypatio coss (= consulibus).*

"Iunius Bassus, of senatorial rank, who lived 42 yrs., 2 mos.; during his very prefecture of the City (Rome), a new convert, he went to God, Aug. 25, in the consulship of (Flavius) Eusebius and (Flavius) Hypatius." (A.D. 359)

Note the clear abl. of *annis*. *Praefectura*, like *praefectus*, may be followed by either gen. or dat. *Neofitus* = νεόφυτος, "newly planted"; metaphorically, "new convert, neophyte." *Ypatio*: H seems well on its way to disappearing from Latin, in writing as in speech (see **64**, **69**, **76**, **78**, from A.D. 149 on). "In popular Latin *h* seems to have been completely lost in Pompeii in the 1st cent. A.D., and not much later everywhere in the empire. The Romance languages contain no trace of it except in the scholastic orthography just mentioned," Sturtevant 156 f., §180 b.

88. Dedication to Co-Emperor Valens,

Rome. Probably A.D. 365/367, possibly 373. A large marble base (writ. field, cm. 88.5–89 × m. 1.03 at top; overall, m. 1.468 × ca. 1.32 × 1.165–1.627 including projection at rear) found in Rome in 1878 in the Tiber under an arch of the Ponte Sisto; seen in 1948, 1955, 1973, standing at the center of the south side of the garden of the Chiostro grande, Mus. Naz. Rom., Rome (inv. no. 714), where it was by 1902.

A dedication to the co-emperor Valens by the "Senate and People of Rome," in connection with the Valentinian Bridge. R. Lanciani in 1878 showed (ref. in *Album*) that this base had supported the left-hand column of a memorial arch standing at one entrance to the bridge; it was probably matched on the right side of the arch by a column-supporting base inscribed with a dedication to V.'s older brother and co-emperor, Valentinian I. On the bridge, which apparently was not new but a restoration of an existing one, which probably went back to Caracalla, cf. P/A 398 f., *s.v.* Pons Aurelius, Nash 2.185 f., *s.v. eadem*, Lugli 2.315–318. Date: probably 365/367, certainly before the death of Valentinian, Nov. 17, 375 (*Album* 3.129); *PLRE* 1.865 says "possibly 373" because of another inscr. found nearby which mentions Valentinian's *decennalia* (he was emperor from Feb. 364).

CIL 6.31402 (cf. p. 3778), *ILS* 769, *Album* 3.127–129 no. 327 (with bibl.); cf. Jones, index, 3.443 *s.v.* Symmachus; *PLRE* 1.863–865 *s.v.* L. Aurelius Avianius Symmachus signo Phosphorius no. 3, 930 f., *s.v.* Flavius Valens no. 8, 933 f., *s.v.* Flavius Valentinianus no. 7.

Text: *Imp(eratori) Caesari d(omino) n(ostro) / Fl(avio) Valenti, max(imo), p(io), f(elici), victori ac / triumfatori, semper Aug(usto), / S(enatus) P(opulus)q(ue) R(omanus), /⁵ ob providentiam quae illi semper / cum inclyto fratre communis est / instituti ex utilitate urbis aeternae / Valentiniani pontis atq(ue) perfecti, / dedicandi operis honore delato, iudicio princip(um) maximor(um), /¹⁰ L(ucio) Aur(elio) Aviano Symmacho, v(iro) c(larissimo), ex praefectis urbi.*

"To the Emperor, our Lord Flavius Valens, *maximus, pius, felix*, victor and con-

queror, ever Augustus, the Senate and the People of Rome, because of his foresight (which he has in common with his illustrious brother [Valentinian I, 364–375]) in planning and completing the Valentinian Bridge to serve the needs of the eternal city, the honor of dedicating the work being conferred, by decision of the emperors, upon L. Aurelius Avianius Symmachus, of senatorial rank, former Prefect of the City (Rome)."

Lines 7 f. *Instituti . . . pontis atque perfecti*: perhaps the perf. pass. participles, on the model of *ab urbe condita*, were used instead of the alternative gerund/gerundive (*instituendi pontis*—or *pontem*—*atq. perficiendi*) because of the desire to use a gerundive in the next phrase (*dedic. operis honore*). Lines 2, 10, *Fl., Aur.*: note the continuing tendency (see **64**, note on line 2) to abbreviate these (apparently) increasingly insignificant nomina, in favor of cognomina or second nomina. Line 10, *ex praefectis*, the earliest example that comes to mind of *ex* to indicate a *former* official, as in "ex-president" (but still in syntax, keeping the abl. plu.: "from among").

Symmachus may well have begun construction of the bridge while prefect, in 364–365, as *PLRE* 1.865 thinks probable (Amm. Marc. 27.3.3 rather suggests this), though it seems a long time, from 364/365 to "possibly 373," for what was apparently only a restoration of an older bridge. This Symmachus was the father (see also **89**) of the orator Symmachus, "the greatest orator of his day" and "the most prominent opponent of Christianity in his time" (*OCD* 1027 f., *s.v.* Symmachus 2).

89. Commemoration of Symmachus, the Orator's Father, Rome. A.D. 377. A large marble base (ca. m. 1.24 at rear × 67–68 cm. [at cornice 75.5 cm. max.] × 38–39 cm. [at cornice ca. 44 cm.], but originally 10–20 cm. thicker—the rear must have

been cut off), which no doubt once supported the gilded statue mentioned in the inscr.; reported ca. 1550 as found "under the Capitol," Rome; seen in 1956 and 1973 standing on a modern base on the west side of the Cortile della Pigna of the Vatican (inv. no. 5173), where it was (in the Gall. lap.) by 1876. Letter heights: from 3.7–3.9 cm. (line 1, cornice) down to 1.7–2.3 cm. (lines 2–24), tall letters 2.4–2.9 cm.

Commemoration of L. Aurelius Avianius Symmachus, *v.c.*, called Phosphorius ("Light-Bringer"), by the emperors at the repeated request of the Roman Senate. Dated by an inscription on the left side of the base, by year and day. He is the Symmachus of **88**.

CIL 6.1698 (cf. pp. 3173, 3813, further bibl.), *ILS* 1257, *Album* 3.134 f., no. 332. Cf. *PLRE* 1.863–865 *s.v.* Symmachus 3.

Text: *Phosphorii* (on cornice). / *Lucio Aur-(elio) Avianio Symmacho v(iro) c(larissimo), / praefecto urbi, consuli, pro praefectis / praetorio in urbe Roma finitimisque /⁵ provinciis, praefecto annonae ur/bis Romae, pontifici maiori, quinde/cemviro s(acris) f(aciundis), multis legat[io]nibus / pro amplissimi ordinis desideriis / apud divos principes functo, qui, /¹⁰ primus in senatu sententiam roga/ri solitus, auctoritate, prudentia, atq(ue) / eloquentia pro dignitate tanti ordi/nis magnitudinem loci eius inpleve/rit, auro inlustrem statuam, quam /¹⁵ a dominis Augustisq(ue) nostris sena-tus / amplissimus decretis frequentib(us) in-/petrabit* (read *-vit*), *idem triumfatores prin-cipes / nostri constitui adposita oratione ius-/serunt / quae meritorum eius ordinem /²⁰ ac seriem contineret; quorum perenne / iudicium tanto muneri hoc quoque ad/didit, ut alteram statuam pari splen/dore etiam apud Constan-tinopolim / conlocaret.* (Left side) *[dedi]cata III Kal(endas) Maias / [d(omino) n(ostro)] Gratiano IIII et Merobaude / [co(n)s(ulibus)].*

"(Statue) of Phosphorius. In honor of L. Aurelius Avianius Symmachus, of senatorial rank, prefect of the city (Rome), consul, deputy of the praetorian prefects in the city of Rome and the neighboring provinces, prefect of the grain supply of the city of Rome, major priest, member of the College of 15, who has carried out many embassies on behalf of the Senate to former emperors, and who, being usually the first to be asked his opinion in the senate, has given to this great place a full measure of dignity, sagacity, and eloquence to match the grandeur of so great a body, our victorious rulers have ordered a (bronze) statue lustrous with gold, which the distinguished senate by repeated decrees succeeded in obtaining from our Lords/Augusti, to be set up and an inscription added which should contain a full list of his services in proper order; and to this great tribute their unfailing judgment has added this too, that a second statue of equal splendor (the senate) should set up also at Constantinople." On the side: "Dedicated April 29, in the consulship of our Lord Gratian (for the 4th time) and Merobaudes." (A.D. 379)

Noteworthy: the praenomen written in full, the (first) nomen abbreviated; the number of words divided at line ends (perhaps a feature of the later inscrs.), *quindecemviro* (lines 6 f.) for the more usual *-decimviro*, *inple-* and *inpe-* (lines 13 f., 16 f.) preferred to *im-* (both spellings attested in inscrs. from 111 B.C. on: Pfister 192 ff., §151); *inpetrabit*, for *-vit*, as evidence for the changing pronunciation of consonantal *u* (confused with *b* and so written, by the first cent. A.D., but destined to become *v* in most Romance languages: Sturtevant 143 §155); *apud Const.* (line 23), an uncommon substitute for the loc. abl. (Olcott 1.379 f., sect. I, B; *OLD* 156 *s.v.* apud, 3).

The addition of an *agnomen*, *signum*, or *supernomen* such as "Phosphorius" is a feature of these late (4th-cent.) epitaphs of distinguished civil servants (several examples in the *Album*, from "Dogmatius" on—no. 315, here **84**), but sometimes the name that appears above, in the genitive, is identical with one of the man's regular names listed below; see *ILS* 3: 2, 927–929, lists of *agnomina* introduced by *qui et* (rarely with *vocatur* or similar) or by *sive*, and of *signa* such as *Dogmatii, Hymetii, Phosphorii*, some of which, like these three, seem to be created from Greek to indicate some particular virtue in the bearer; cf. I. Kajanto, *Onomastic Studies in the Early Christian Inscriptions of Rome and Carthage* (Helsinki/Helsingfors 1963 *Acta Inst. Romani Finlandiae*, 2: 1) ch. VII, and *Cal. Lim.* 159 f.

90. Dedication in Honor of Petronius Probus, *v.c.*, Rome. A.D. 378. A large marble (statue-)base (overall, cm. ca. 79 × 64.3 × ca. 38–42 so far as ancient—there is modern restoration), found in Rome in 1742 in a garden on the Pincio; seen in 1949, 1956, 1973, standing on a modern base on the east side of the Sala del Gladiatore, Capitoline Museum, Rome (inv. no. 7179). Letter heights: lines 1–14, 2.2–3.5 cm. (excluding the Q tail), line 15, 2.9–3.6 cm.

Inscription in honor of (Sextus Claudius) Petronius Probus, *v.c.* (whose statue no doubt stood on top of the base), set up by the Veneti and Histri (northern Italy), whose patron he was; for his outstanding relief-measures in their behalf; dedicated Aug. 8, 378.

CIL 6.1751 (cf. pp. 3174, 3813, further bibl.), *ILS* 1265, Gordon *Seven Latin Inscrs.* 88–90 (case for the prosecution), *Album* 3.135–137 no. 333. On Probus, perhaps a native of Verona, "the doyen of Roman society" (P. R. L. Brown, *JRS* 51 [1961] 5, also 9, 11), who became a Christian (or perhaps was never a pagan), see also Jones, index, 3.439 *s.v.* Probus, and *PLRE* 1.736–740 *s.v.* Probus 5.

Text (frontal inscr.): *Nobilitatis culmini, / litterarum et eloquentiae lumini, / auctoritatis exemplo, / provisionum ac dispositionum magistro, /⁵ humanitatis auctori, / moderationis patrono, / devotionis antistiti, / Petronio / Probo, v(iro) c(larissimo), proconsuli*

Africae, /¹⁰ praefecto praetorio / per Illyricum, Italiam, et Africam, / consuli ordinario, / ob insignia erga se remediorum cenera (read *ge-*) / *Veneti adque* (sic) *Histri, peculiares eius, /¹⁵ patrono praestantissimo.*

(lateral inscr.): *dedicata / VI Idus Aug(ustas) / dd. nn.* (= *dominis nostris duobus*) / *Valente VI* (= *sextum*) *et /⁵ Valentiniano II* (= *iterum*) / *Augg.* (= *Augustis duobus*) *cons(ulibus).*

"Doyen of the aristocracy, glory of letters and eloquence, model of leadership, master of the arts of foresight and management, champion of humanity, patron of restraint, high-priest of devotion (to the emperors?): (to this man), Petronius Probus, of senatorial rank, proconsul of Africa (A.D. 358), praetorian prefect for Illyricum, Italy, and Africa (368–375), consul ordinary (371), for his notable relief-measures in their behalf the Veneti and Histri, his own people, (have erected a statue) in honor of a most outstanding patron." Lateral inscr.: "dedicated Aug. 8, in the consulship of our Lords Valens (6th time) and Valentinian (2nd time), Augusti" (378).

Not a very handsome inscription for a man so illustrious, but unusual for the postponement of his name and interesting for the order of words in lines 1–7.

(The modern inscr. on the plinth above the anc. inscr. refers to Benedict XIV, who in 1753, the 14th yr. of his pontificate, had the base taken to the Capitoline Mus. Such papal inscrs. are not uncommon, esp. in Rome, on ancient objects that have belonged to the Roman Catholic Church.)

91. Elogium in Verse Composed by Pope Damasus, Rome. A.D. 383. Marble tablet (cm. 57.7–58 × m. 1.961) first reported in Rome in 1592; no doubt from one of the suburban Christian cemeteries (catacombs); now in six pieces joined together (including one restored at the bottom left), seen in 1949 and 1956 in the Lateran, but now in the Vatican in the Lapidario

Cristiano ex Lateranense. Letter heights: lines 1–9, 3.2–3.65 cm., line 10, 2.2–2.5, tall F 2.8, cm.

Epitaph (metrical except line 10) of Proiecta, daughter of Florus and wife of Primus, who died at age 16 and was buried Dec. 30, 383; lines 1–9 composed by Pope Damasus (366–384—the pope who about this time, 382/385, prompted Jerome, his secretary, to prepare what became the Vulgate version of the Bible: *Oxf. Dict. Christ. Church* 374, 731 f., *s.vv.* Damasus, Jerome), the whole undoubtedly cut by his official engraver, Filocalus (on whose work see Max. Ihm [ed.], *Damasi Epigrammata*, Leipzig 1895, A. Ferrua [ed.], *Epigr. Damasiana*, Vat. City/Rome 1942, Nicolette Gray, "The Filocalian Letter," *PBSR* 24 [1956] 5–13, pl. i–iv, and above, p. 43).

De Rossi 1.145 f., no. 329; Buecheler *CLE* 1.670; Ihm 55 f., no. 53; Silvagni 1.1440; Diehl *ILCV* 2.3446; Ferrua 201–205 no. 51 (has the best annotation); *Album* 3.140–142 no. 337. Silvagni, *Monum. epigraphica Christiana*, 1 (Vat. City 1943) pl. v, no. 3, has a good photo, which, however, like ours, suffers from paint applied to the cuttings, which greatly magnifies all the fine lines of Filocalus's curly serifs; these, his precise use of them, and his manner of shading are his specialty.

Text:

> Quid? loquar aut sileam? Prohibet dolor ipse
>   fateri.
> Hic tumulus lacrimas retinet, cognosce,
>   parentū(m)
> Proiectae, fuerat Primo quae iuncta marito,
> pulcra decore suo, solo contenta pudore,
> 5 heu dilecta satis miserae genetricis amore.
> Accipe—quid multis?—thalami post foedera
>   prima
> erepta ex oculis Flori genitoris abiit,
> aetheriam cupiens caeli conscendere lucem.
> Haec Damasus pr⟨a⟩estat cunctis solacia
>   fletus.
>
> 10 Vixit [an]n(os) XVI, m(enses) IX, dies XXV;
>   dep(osita est) III Kal(endas) Ian(uarias),
>   Fl(avio) Merobaude et Fl(avio)
>   Saturnin(o) conss. (= consulibus).

"What? should I speak, or be silent? Grief itself prevents speaking out. This tomb holds the tears (learn, [reader,]) of the parents of Proiecta, who had been the wife of Primus, beautiful in her elegance, content with modesty alone; cherished (ah!) by the love of her [now] most wretched mother. Understand, [reader,]—in few words—(that) soon after the marriage, snatched from the sight of Florus, her father, she departed, seeking to rise to the ethereal light of heaven. These (lines) Damasus offers to all as a relief for tears.

"She lived 16 yrs., 9 mos., 25 days, (and) was buried Dec. 30, in the consulship of Flavius Merobaudes and Flavius Saturninus." (A.D. 383)

The meter of lines 1–9 is dactylic hexameter; if we read *abivit* at the end of line 7 (as *CLE* suggests), the scansion is correct. Line 1, *init.* Ferrua's punctuation (p. 204), followed here, seems better than the alternative, *Quid loquar aut sileam?* Line 2, *fin.* This supralineate abbrev. is missing from Gordon's *Supralineate Abbrs.*, which is based on *CIL* (which lacks this inscr.). Line 9. *Prestat* no doubt shows how *ae* was then being pronounced; cf. *ILS* 3: 2, 812 f., E *pro* AE, Sturtevant 128 §133. Lines 9 f., *init.* The restoration affects a little of *Damasus* and part of *vixit* and of *annos*, where the type of serif is quite different. Ferrua notes that the number of months was first written X, then the I crowded in.

Cf. *PLRE* 1.750, *s.v.* Proiecta, where it is conjectured that Proiecta may have been the wife of the Christian Turcius Secundus (p. 817 *s.v.* Secundus 4), but this is impossible if her husband was Primus (as seems certain); two possible Primuses for husband are listed in *PLRE*, Flavius (Rhodinus) P., proconsul of Africa ca. 392, and his son, Fl. Rhodinus P. iunior, legatus of Numidia ca. 392, neither one known to be a Christian. Her father, Florus, might be the *praef. praetorio* of Constantinople, 381–383, and her brother Numerius Proiectus, *praef. annonae* 393/394. Cf. *PLRE* 1.367 *s.v.* Florus 1, 725 *s.v.* Primus 2–3, 750 *s.v.* Proiectus.

92. Dedication of (Statue) Base to a Distinguished Pagan, Rome. A.D. 387. A large marble (statue-)base (overall m. 1.41 × 0.795 × ca. 0.65) first reported (late-16th cent.) in private gardens in Rome; seen in 1948, 1955, 1973 standing on the south (left) side of Aula VII of the Mus. Naz. Rom., Rome (inv. no. 80733). Letter heights: line 1 (cornice) ca. 2.5 cm., line 14, 2.1–5.5 cm., the rest 3.6–4.8 (VR ligature, line 12, 5.2) cm.

Dedication (no doubt of a statue) to Vettius Agorius Praetextatus (called "Agorius" for short), *v.c.*, who had risen from *quaestor candidatus* to consul designate (and died in late 384, 2-plus years before this dedication). His many priestly offices are all pagan; he "now stands for the culmination of the most vital tendencies in late Roman Paganism," P. R. L. Brown, op. cit. (on **90**) 1 (with n. 5), 4, 6.

CIL 6.1778 (cf. p. 3174), *Album* 3.144–146 no. 339. Cf. *CIL* 6.1777, 1779, 1780 (= *ILS* 1258–60); H. Bloch, *Harv. Theol. Rev.* 38 (1945) 203–209; W. Ensslin, *RE* 22: 2 (1954) 1575–79 *s.v.* Praetextatus 1 (extensive bibl.); Jones, index, 3.438, *s.v.* Praet.; *PLRE* 1.722–724 *s.v.* Praet. 1 (anc. sources).

Text: *Agorii* (cornice). / *Vettio Agorio Praetextato, v(iro) c(larissimo),* / (col. 1) *pontifici Vestae,* / *pontifici Soli(s),* /⁵ *quindecemviro,* / *auguri,* / *tauroboliato,* / *curiali,* / *neocoro,* /¹⁰ *hierofantae,* / *patri sacrorum;* (col. 2) *quaestori* / *candidato,* /⁵ *praetori urbano,* / *correctori Tus/ciae et Umbriae,* / *consulari* / *Lusitaniae,* /¹⁰ *proconsuli* / *Achaiae,* / *praeeecto* (for *-fecto*) *urbi,* / *praee(ecto)* (for *praef-*) *praet(orio)* {*II* (= *bis*)} / *Italiae ei* (for *et*) *Yllyrici* (for *Ill-*), /¹⁵ *consuli* / *designato.*

"(Statue) of Agorius. To Vettius Agorius Praetextatus, of senatorial rank, priest of Vesta, priest of the Sun, member of the College of Fifteen (presumably *sacris faciundis*), augur, initiated as priest of

Cybele, *curialis* (of Hercules: *CIL* 6.1779 = *ILS* 1259), temple warden, hierophant [of Hecate?], *pater sacrorum* [on this mass of priestly offices held by one of the last defenders of paganism, cf. Wissowa 98 f. and the various titles in his index]; quaestor (nominee [of an emperor?]), city-of-Rome praetor, governor of (the provinces of) Tuscia and Umbria, governor of Lusitania, proconsul of Achaia, praefect of the city (Rome), praetorian praefect of Italy and Illyricum (A.D. 384), consul designate (also 384)."

Noteworthy: the separation, by columns, of priestly and civil posts; the large number of the former; so also of ligatures (VR twice, VM) and small letters (A twice, C, R) needed apparently because of space wasted by the arrangement in columns; the mistakes in cutting; *quindecemviro* (as in **89**); for *Yll-*, cf. K/H 25 f., De Rugg. 4: 1 (repr. 1942) 20 *s.v.* Illyricum (this example not listed in either place).

The inscr. on the right side dates the dedication to Feb. 1, 387. On the late-Empire offices listed—*corrector, consularis, praef. praet.*—see Jones 3, index. The number II after *praef. praet.*, right col., line 12, though repeated in *CIL* 6.1779 (= *ILS* 1259), does not appear in *CIL* 6.1777 (= *ILS* 1258) and is considered an error in *PLRE* 1.723 (h). Praetextatus must have been a remarkable man: see *PLRE* or *OCD* 873 *s.v.*

93. Dedication of (Statue) Base to Stilicho, Roman General, Rome. A.D. 400/404, probably 400. Incomplete and damaged marble base (overall ca. m. 1.36–1.37 × 60.5 cm., at cornice 72 cm. × 61–75 cm.: it had a molded base also, and the back too was finished for a writing surface and has a molding all round, as though the base had been meant to be seen from all sides), found in Rome in 1925 at a depth of m. 2.50 near the Corso and Piazza Colonna; seen in 1948, 1956, 1973, standing against the wall of the Passaggio del Muro Romano (Museo Nuovo), Pal. dei Conservatori, Rome (inv. no. 6963). Letter heights: line 1 (cornice) ca. 3 (up to 3.3) cm., lines 2–4, 3.85–ca. 4.1 (tall L's up to 4.6) cm., lines 5–11, 3.2–3.9 (tall letters up to 4.3) cm. The whole surface is perhaps reused.

A (statue) base set up in honor of Flavius Stilicho, *v.c.*, apparently while Master of Both Services (Horse and Foot) and consul, to celebrate the defeat of the rebel Gildo and the restoration of Rome's grain supply; by the boatmen and fishermen engaged in carrying food supplies up river to the City. (On Stilicho, his father a Vandal, and Gildo, his father a Moorish king, cf. Jones, index, 3.443 and 426, resp., *PLRE* 1.853–858, 395 f., resp., with all the anc. sources; on the rivermen, J. Le Gall, *Le Tibre flume de Rome . . .* [Paris 1953] 319, 325, Meiggs, op. cit. [above, 68], index, *s.v.* codicarii.) Stilicho was cos. I in 400, II in 405, hence the inclusive dating 400/404; *PLRE*, 855, gives "? a. 400," perhaps best, since, in a non-obituary inscr. of this sort, the consulship would probably be listed only during his tenure.

G. Mancini, *NS* 1925, 226–228; *AE* 1926, 124 (both of these inadequate or inaccurate); Mustilli 23 no. 16; *Album* 3.153–155 no. 346.

Text: (cornice) *[Fl(avi) St]ịlichoṇiṣ ṿ(iri) c(larissimi).* / *Fl(avio) Stilichoni, v.c. et inlustri,* / *magistro utriusque militiae* / *et consuli ordinario,* /⁵ *pro virtutum veneratione inter ceteṛ[a]* / *ḅeneficia quae per eum urbi Romae delatạ s[unt?]* / *[ca]udicarii seu piscatorẹs corporat[i]* / *[urbi]ṣ Romae per quọs amnicis na[vigiis?]* / *[alime]ṇta urḅi devehuntur, hoc m[onument(um) ?]* /¹⁰ *[aureum (?) qu]od Gildone hoṣṭ[e] p[ublico de]victo (?) ali]ṃoniis Rom[am refecerit ?]* / *[———] . . au (?) ———* / *——— (?).*

"(Statue of) Flavius Stilicho, of senatorial rank. In honor of Fl. Stilicho, *v.c.* and *inlustris*, Master of Both Services (Horse and Foot), and consul ordinary (A.D. 400), out of high regard for great deeds, among the other benefits which have been conferred through him upon the city of Rome, the river-boatmen or [i.e., "and"?] the associated fishermen of the city of Rome through whom food supplies are conveyed to the City in river boats, have set up (?) this gilded (?) memorial (?) because of his having replenished (?) Rome with food supplies by subduing (?) Gildo, public (?) enemy, . . ."

The Greekish spelling of Stilicho is notable; a variant is *Stel-*, *ILS* 800 (twice), on a gold amulet. Line 2, *v.c. et inlustri: v.c.* apparently by now a mere title of honor, *inlustris* indicating a higher grade of the senatorial aristocracy; cf. *ILS* 3: 1, 364 *s.v.* v.c. et inlustris, the earliest example apparently our Agorius (**92**) in an inscr. of A.D. 384 or a little later (*ILS* 1258 = *CIL* 6.1777), Jones 3, index, 418, 428, *s.vv.* clarissimus, illustris. Line 5, *pro veneratione* is perhaps to be noted; cf. *OLD* 1463, sects. 16 f., *s.v.* pro¹. Line 7, *seu,* "and"? see above, on **80**, line 5, *sive.*

94. Commemoration of Three Emperors, Rome. A.D. 402/406. A marble block (m. 2.30 [*CIL*] × ca. 1.5 × ca. 1.0), which originally stood with its present left side uppermost so as to hold an equestrian statue, as is shown by the cuttings for the horse's hooves visible at the left in the photo; the inscription obviously does not belong to the original use of the block. Found (*in situ?*) in 1880 in the Roman Forum between the Column of Phocas and the Arch of Sept. Severus (*Roma e dintorni* 127); seen there in 1973, resting on a base (apparently ancient); much damaged (*CIL* 6 says nil about damage). Letter heights: 5 cm. (*CIL*).

Dedication by the Senate and People of Rome to the *Fides* and *Virtus* of the emperors Arcadius, Honorius, and Theodosius (II), to celebrate Honorius's ending a Gothic war with the assistance of Stilicho, **93** (whose name and titles were erased after his execution in 408). The date depends on which Gothic war is meant: in

402 and 403 Stilicho defeated the Visigoth Alaric, in 406 the "Scythian" (Crimean Goth?) Radagaisus and his horde of "Gotti" or "Gothi" (both names and date in *Chronica Minora* . . . , ed. Mommsen [*Mon. Germ. Hist., Auct. Ant.* 9 (Berlin 1892)] 299); Theod. II, born in 401, was named "Augustus," with his father Arcadius, in 402. Cf. J. B. Bury, *History of the Later Roman Empire* . . . , 2 vols. (London 1923, paperback repr. New York 1958) 1, 160–168, *PLRE* 1. 99, 771 f., 856, *s.vv.* Arcadius 5, Romulus 5, Stilicho.

CIL 6.31987, *ILS* 799. Cf. Nash 2.401 *s.v.* Statua Stilichonis.

Text: *Fidei virtutiq(ue) devotissimorum / militum domnorum nostrorum, / Arcadi, Honori, et Theodosi, / perennium Augustorum, /⁵ post confectum Gothicum / bellum felicitate aeterni / principis domni noṣtri Honori, / consiliis et fortitudine / inlustris viri, comitis et /¹⁰ [erased] / [erased], / S(enatus) P(opulus)q(ue) R(omanus), / curante Pisidio Romulo, v(iro) c(larissimo), / praef(ecto) urbi vice sacra /¹⁵ iterum iudicante.*

"To the honor and virtue of the most devoted soldiers, Our Lords Arcadius, Honorius, and Theodosius, perpetual Augusti, after the ending of the Gothic War through the good fortune of the lifelong ruler, Our Lord Honorius, (and) the policy and bravery of the illustrious Comes ("Privy Councillor"? its derivative "Count"?) and [Master of Horse and Foot, in immediate attendance on the emperor (?), Fl. Stilicho]: the Senate and People of Rome, the preparation of this monument being in the hands of Pisidius Romulus, *v.c.*, prefect of the City (Rome) (and) deputy (for the second time) in charge of judging Imperial appeals."

This translation, like those of all the inscriptions of these late-Empire officials, may serve chiefly to rouse discussion and bring about improvement. The abstract nouns, the adjectives, and the titles are all a challenge.

The spelling of *domnus* is attested as

early as the Lex Agraria of 111 B.C., *domna* by the 1st cent. A.D., at Pompeii/Herculaneum (cf. *TLL* 5: 9 [1930] 1935, 27 ff., *s.v.* dom(i)na; E/M 183, col. 1, 3rd par., *s.v.* domus; Pfister 109, *fin.*). Line 10 presumably read *magistri utriusque militiae* (25 letters as against 22 in line 9, but with 6 *i*'s), but S.'s name, *Fl.* (or *Flavii*) *Stilichonis* is not long enough for line 11; perhaps *praesentalis* (abbreviated?) "in immediate attendance on the emp." (Bury, 1.36), followed *mag. utr. mil.* (cf. *PLRE* 1.855, *init.*); *praes.* in full, plus S.'s name (written *Fl. Stilichonis*) would again give 25 letters. If one could make a squeeze of these lines with the help of a ladder or a platform, it would probably be possible to restore them; Henzen made no attempt for *EE* 4 or *CIL* 6.

95. Epitaph of a Christian Child, Rome.

A.D. 408. A marble slab (ca. 19 × 58 cm., thickness? [studied in 1949, in the Lateran, inserted in a wall]), from the cemetery (catacomb) of Commodilla (outskirts of Rome); formerly in the Lateran, but now in the Vatican in the Lapidario Cristiano ex Lateranense.

Epitaph of Siddus (or Siddius), who died in 408. The slab is incised with a design of the monogrammatic cross, with the letters omega and alpha suspended from the crossbar as though from a pair of scales, the whole within a wreath of palm branches flanked by a dove and an olive branch on either side; and, perhaps subordinate to all this, an inscription broken in two by the central design. All the details of the symbolism are common in early-Christian inscrs.: the monogr. cross (one of the post-4th-cent. forms of the Constantinian monogram—**85**) formed of the first two letters of Χριστός, the alpha and omega signifying Christ the Lord (Rev. 1.8), the wreath of palm branches expressing perhaps victory, the doves and olive branches symbolizing peace. The date is A.D. 408, when Flavius Anicius

Auchenius Bassus was consul in the West (in 431 the consul was Flavius Anicius Bassus).

De Rossi, 1.288 no. 666, *ILCV* 2.2921, cf. 4, p. 26, Gordon *Seven Latin Inscrs.* 90–92.

Text: *Innocus puer, nomine S*[wreath]-*iddi, hic bixit meses / quator, dies biginti qua*[wreath]*tor, petitus in pace III Id(us) / Aprilis, Anicio Auchenio* [wreath] *Baso, consule.*

"An innocent boy by the name of Siddus (or, Siddius) lived here (i.e., in this world? or in Rome?) four months, 24 days; summoned in (or, to?) (Christian) peace, April 11, in the consulship of Anicius Auchenius Bassus."

The correct Classical Latin would have *innocuus, vixit, menses, quattuor, viginti, Basso*; the *b*'s for *v*'s reflect the changing, or changed, pronunciation of consonantal *v* (above, **89**, note on *inpetrabit*); for "vulgar" *quator*, see Sommer 466. *Innocuus* and its relatives are favorite words of approval in the Christian inscrs. (Diehl, *ILCV* 3.539 f.); the spelling with one *u* occurs a number of times (V for VV is found also in the pagan inscrs.—cf. *ILS*, 3: 2, 835, V *simplex pro* V *gemina*). Note the two uncial H's. *Nomine* with the genitive, though apparently much rarer than with the nominative in early-Christian inscriptions, is found occasionally (*ILCV* 3.559 s.v. nomen, d); it seems not to be Classical. *Pace* may be for *pacem* (final M is often not written, because not pronounced, throughout the history of Latin: Sturtevant, 151–153 §174), and the phrase may be equivalent to *arcessitus in pace(m)* (as in *ILCV* 1230). For the single *t* and *s* in *quator* and *Baso*, see Pfister 157 §119.

96. Dedication of a Statue Base to a High Official, Rome. A.D. 421 or later. A large marble statue-base (m. 1.22 × 61 cm., max., × 60.5 cm. at cornice and base, 56 cm. at center), found in Rome in 1926 on the Aventine, ca. 20 m. east of the Via di S. Sabina, near the monastery of S. Anselmo and near remains of what seemed to be the house in which it had originally stood; seen in 1949, 1956, 1973, standing on the west side of the Giardino Caffarelli (inv. no. 7056) of the Mus. Nuovo of the Pal. dei Conservatori, Rome. It is finished on three sides, as if to stand against a wall; still visible are the holes into which to fit a statue. Letter heights: line 1 (cornice), 3.9–4.3 (L's 4.5) cm., the rest 2.6–3.5 cm.

Base of a statue (line 12) set up in honor of Iunius Quartus Palladius, *v.c.*, by his (hitherto unknown and here unnamed) brother, who considered it proper for it to be placed "among himself and his family" as a token of his affection and as an ornament of his house. Date: Palladius was *praef. praet.* for six years (lines 8–9), from 415 or 416 (each year has its supporters) to 421 (the latest rescript to him from the emperor—*Cod. Theod.* 2.27.1—is dated July 28, 421). He had been consul in 416. The inscr. does not show whether he had died before the base was set up. (For details, see *Album* 3.168; but for *quarto*, see below.)

Publ. by L. Cantarelli, *Bull. Com.* 54 (1926) 35–41; *AE* 1928, 80 (from *Bull. Com.*, but with *kadidato*, line 7); A. Degrassi, *Riv. di fil.* 56 (n.s. 6) (1928) 516–522, with text and commentary (= *Scritti vari*, 1.483–489); *Album* 3. 166–168 no. 355; *PLRE* 2.822–824 s.v. Palladius 19.

Text: *Iunii Quarti Palladii, v(iri) c(larissimi)* (on cornice). / *Amplissimorum honorum magnitu/dine et nobilitate conspicuo, / Iunio Quarto Palladio, clarissimo /⁵ et inl(ustri) viro, avorum honores super/gresso et diu in rep(ublica) perseveranti, / praet(ori) et quaest(ori) kandidato, not(ario) et trib̦(uno), / com(iti) sacrar(um) larg(itionum), praef(ecto) / praetorii / per annos sex Illyrici, Italiae, et /¹⁰ Africae, consuli ordinario, legato̦ / senatus amplissimi quarto: eius / statuam, ob egregiam propinqui/tatis affectionem, ad decorem / domus, germanus eius inter se /¹⁵ ac suos locari constituique / ius habuit.*

"(Statue of) Iunius Quartus Palladius, *v.c.* To one notable for the greatness and renown of his magnificent public offices, Iunius Quartus Palladius, *c.v.* and *inlustris*, who (has) surpassed his ancestors in respect to public career and was (has been) untiring in civic affairs (or, the State), praetor and quaestor as a nominee (of the emperor), notary and tribune, head of the Imperial treasury (?), praetorian prefect, for six years, of Illyricum, Italy, and Africa, consul ordinary, envoy of the most distinguished senate four times (?): a statue of him, because of strong affection arising from kinship (and) for the adornment of the house, his brother has considered it proper to be placed and set up among himself and his family."

Note the tall letters: F and L always, T generally, Y; words divided properly at line ends (according to Dennison's rules); bars over six of the twelve abbreviations, that over *rep(ublica)*, line 6, together with the lack of interpunct, marking it as a single word; the archaistic spelling of *kandidato*, as also before *a* in *kasibus*, **29**, and *Karthagine*, **72**, not to mention the almost universal *Kalendae* (Pfister, 31) and the truly archaic *k*'s in **4**; the uncommon (*frater*) *germanus*, line 14, to mean "full brother" (cited from Ennius on).

Lines 4 f., *clar. et inl. viro* varies the usual form, *v.c. et inl.*, of **93**, line 2 (on which see the note). Line 7. *Quaest.* should precede *praet.* in an ascending list such as this. The proper order seems to be *trib. et not.*, as in Claudian, *Carm. min.* 25, heading (his *Epithalamium* in honor of Palladius and his wife Celerina, *Mon. Germ. Hist., Auct. Ant.* 10 [Berlin 1892] pp. xliv f., ed. Birt). For the duties involved, cf. Jones, index, 3.435, 419, *s.vv.* notaries, imperial, and *comes sacr. larg.*, resp.; the above transl. of the second title is not satisfactory (Jones seems to translate no titles, perhaps wisely). Line 11. The view implied in the *Album* 3.167 f.

that *quarto* here = "for the 4th time" now seems wrong; it seems rather = *quater* (as implied also in *PLRE* vol. cit. 823, (f)); cf. Hofmann/Szantyr 214 *med.* Lines 14 f. Degrassi, op. cit. 518 (= 485), agreed with Cantarelli that *inter . . . suos* means "among his own and his relatives' statues" (tra la propria statua e quelle dei suoi congiunti); either version seems satisfactory.

97. Record of Erection of Statue of a Distinguished Administrator, Rome. Probably A.D. 441/445. A large marble statue-base (overall, ca. m. 1.62, so far as seems original × 0.77–ca. 1.0 × 0.72–ca. 0.93) unearthed in Rome in 1852 in the foundations of Palazzo Savorelli, near Ss. Apostoli; seen in 1949, 1956, in the courtyard of the Lateran; now in the Cortile della Pigna of the Vatican.

Inscription in honor of Fl. Olbius Auxentius Draucus, *v.c. et inl.*, cut on the base of a gilded statue by order of the emperors Theodosius II and Valentinian III, at the request of the Senate, because of his distinction as an administrator. If (as seems generally agreed) he is the same as the "Auxentius, Urban Prefect," to whom are addressed two Novels of Valentinian III (*Leges novellae ad Theodosianum pertinentes*, ed. P. M. Meyer [Berlin 1905, repr. 1954, vol. 2 of Mommsen's ed. of the Theodosian Code], titles 8.2 and 20), the date must be between 440/441 (Jan. 27) and Apr. 14, 445, by which time Auxentius is addressed as urban pref. for the second time. (A different man was pref. in June 440.)

CIL 6.1725 (cf. pp. 3173, 3813), *ILS* 1284, E. Meinhardt in H/S 1.1159 (with German transl.), cf. 4 p. 393, *Album* 3.172–174 no. 360. Cf. Diehl *IL*, tab. 29, a; O. Seeck, *RE* 2 (1896) 2616 *s.v.* Auxentius 6; E. Sachers, *RE* 22:2 (1954) 2524–2532 *s.v.* Praefectus urbi; *PLRE* 2.380 *s.v.* Fl. Olb. Aux. Draucus.

Text: Ḟḷ(*avi*) *Olbi Auxenti Drauç[i]* (cornice). / *Fl(avio) Olbio Auxentio Drauco, v̄(iro) c̄(larissimo) et inl(ustri), patriciae familiae / viro, senatus mun⟨i⟩is prompta devotione perfuncto, / comiti ordinis primi et vicario urbis Romae, comiti /⁵ sacri consistorii, praefecto urbis Romae, ob egregia / eius administrationum merita, quae integritate, / censura, et moderatione ita viguerunt ut sublimissi/mae potestatis reverentiam honorifica eius aucto-/ritas custodiret et humanitatem amabilis censura /¹⁰ servaret, petitu senatus amplissimi, qui est iustus / arbiter dignitatum, excellentibus et magnificis / viris legatione mandata ut inpetratorum digni/tas cresceret, quae paribus studiis amore iustitiae / et providentiae desiderabantur, d̄d̄. n̄n̄. Ffll. (= domini nostri Flavii duo) /¹⁵ Theodosius et Placidus Valentinianus, invicti / ac triumfatores principes semper Augusti, / ad remunerationem titulosque virtutum quib(us) / circa rem publicam eximia semper probitas / invitatur, statuam auro fulgentem erigi /²⁰ conlocarique iusserunt.*

"(Statue of) Fl. Olbius Auxentius Draucus. In honor of [the same], *v.c. et inl.*, a man of patrician family, who has performed his senatorial duties with prompt devotion, *comes* of the first class and vicar of the city of Rome, member of the Imperial consistory, prefect of the city of Rome (A.D. 441): because of the outstanding merits of his administrative services, which have been so strong in probity, judgment, and moderation that his honorific authority kept alive the respect for exalted power and his refreshing judgment preserved human kindness, at the request of the most distinguished Senate (which is the proper judge of high offices), which sent (to the emperors) an embassy of distinguished and high-ranking men so as to enhance the worth of the benefaction (which was desired, with equal zeal, by the love of justice and of prudence), Our Lords Fl. Theodosius and Fl. Placidus Valentinian, unconquered and conquering rulers, ever Augusti, have ordered a statue gleaming with gold to be erected and set up, to recompense and record the virtues for which, around the State, outstanding probity is constantly invited."

Lines 2, 14, *v.c.* and *dd. nn.* are supralineate; no interpunct between *v* and *c*, as though one word. With *munis* (3), cf. *consistorii* (5) and *studiis* (13). Line 12, *ILS* has *imperatorum* for *inpetratorum* (i.e., *imp-*), needed as the antecedent of *quae* (13). The translation suffers from an imperfect understanding of the exuberant Latin, esp. the *quibus* clause, lines 17–19. For *v.c. et inl.*, see on **93**, note on line 2. For *comes ord. pr.*, *vicar. urb. Romae* (apparently deputy of the prefect), *comes sacri consist.*, see Jones, index, 3.419, 447, 420, *s.vv.* comes pr. ord., vicar, consistory, resp.; for consistory, also *OCD s.v.* consistorium. For *sacri*, see above, **84**, note on *sacer*.

98. Epitaph of Three Christians, Rome.

Probably A.D. 454. A marble tablet (ca. 29.5 cm., max. × 57 × 2.5–3.0 cm.) unearthed in Rome in (presumably) 1913 in building the foundations of the new palace of the Ministry of the Interior, on the Viminal; seen in two pieces patched together in 1949 and 1955, resting on a narrow shelf, or wide molding, of Galleria XXXVIII in the Mus. Naz. Rom., Rome (inv. no. 60994).

Epitaph of Saturnina and her sons Valentinus and Eusebius, buried June 1 in (probably) 454. The inscr. begins and ends with a Latin cross. Letter heights: line 1, 2.5 (the cross)–3.2 cm., lines 2–5, 2.1–3.15 cm., line 6, 2.0–2.8 (the cross 3.0) cm.

AE 1914, 142 (from G. Mancini, *NS* 1913, 171 no. 2), Silvagni 1.1946, Diehl *ILCV* 2.3058A, *Album* 3.174 f., no. 361 (the last three with bibl.).

Text: ✝ *Hic iacet Saturnina cum / filiis, qui filii Valentinus / vixit ann(is) V, m(ensibus) II, et Eusebius / vixit ann(is) VIIII; depositus /⁵ die Kal(endarum) Iuniarum, post / cons(ulatum) Opilionis.* ✝

"Here lies Saturnina with her sons, of whom Valentinus lived 5 years., 2 mos., and Eusebius lived 9 yrs.; buried on the day of the Kalends of June, (in the year) after the consulship of Opilio."

Line 2, for *qui filii* one would expect simply *quorum* (or *ex quibus*). Line 4, *depositus* must be an error, presumably for *depositi*, to refer to all three persons; perhaps they died on the same day, from a common illness, or an accident.

Fl. Venantius Rufius Opilio was consul in the West (Rome) in 453, so "(the year) after Opilio" would be 454, named thus because in this year there was no consul in the West but both were in the East (Constantinople). In Degrassi's list of consuls from 30 B.C. to A.D. 613 (*FC*) we find a consul in both West and East, or two consuls in only West or East, sporadically from 307 (even before the transformation of Byzantium into Constantinople, 324–330). It seems clear that the one responsible for dating our inscr. did not yet know the names of the two (Eastern) consuls (though Degrassi says, p. 91, on 454, that they were made known at Rome in mid-May), so dates the year as "(the year) after the consulship of Opilio."

99. Epitaph of a Christian Boy, Rome. A.D. 471. A marble tablet (38.1 or 38.2 cm., max. × 52.5 cm., max.; thickness?), of irregular shape (and very possibly reused) when inscribed; probably from one of the many suburban Christian cemeteries (catacombs), but first reported (by De Rossi) as in the storerooms of the Vatican Library; seen in 1949, 1956, set in the wall in the Mus. epigr. crist. (sect. VII, 12) of the Lateran; but now in the Vatican in the Lapidario Cristiano ex Lateranense.

Epitaph of Calumniosus, who died at the age of six and was buried on Sept. 2 in the year when Probianus was consul in the West (A.D. 471). Letter heights: line 1, 6.2–7.8 (L 10.2) cm., line 2, 4.2–6.2 cm., line 3, 5.3–7.0 cm., line 4, 4.7–5.8 cm.

De Rossi 1.368 no. 833; Silvagni 1.1471;

Diehl *ILCV* 2.2650, *Album* 3.176 f., no. 363.

Text: *Calumnios/us in pace; vixit ann(is) VI, / m(ensibus) VIII, d(iebus) XXII; dep(ositus) IIII N(onas) / Sep(tembres), Probiano cons(ule).*

"Calumniosus in peace; he lived 6 yrs., 8 mos., 22 days; buried Sept. 2, in the consulship of Probianus."

The abbreviations are all supralineate; there are two ligatures, DE (line 3) and AN (4). The earlier pagan dating used except when the day in question is the Kalends, Nones, or Ides, or the day before one of these fixed days—e.g., *a(nte) d(iem) tertium Kalendas Ianuarias*—seems seldom, if ever, used in the early-Christian inscrs., the *a. d.* being dropped and many varieties of the rest of the formula used instead (cf. *ILCV* 3.302–310). (See below, Appendix III. 8.)

With the first phrase, a verb such as *est, requiescit,* or *abiit* may be supplied, but the bare phrase, as here, seems most common (cf. *ILCV* 2.2501 ff. and 3.379 f., *ad f–h*). *Calumniosus* ("one who makes groundless accusations") is one of the new descriptive names typical (among other types) of the early Christians, pejorative names of humility, "unknown or rare in pagan documents," though (Kajanto adds) "completely in the ancient tradition of 'uncomplimentary nicknames'" (I. Kajanto, op. cit. [above, p. 176] 66 f., cf. his *Latin Cognomina*, 267). (Caelius Aconius) Probianus is the consul's full name (Degrassi, *FC* 93).

100. Epitaph of Maxima, "Handmaid of Christ," Rome. A.D. 525. A tablet of Luna marble (ca. 47.3 cm. × 48 cm., max. × 1.9–2.5 cm.) found in (presumably) 1909 in Rome outside Porta Maggiore; seen in 1949, 1955, attached to the wall and standing on a narrow shelf or wide molding, in Galleria XXXVIII of the Mus. Naz. Rom., Rome (inv. no. 40744). Letter heights: line 1, the cross, 5 cm., the letters 2.9–5.0 cm., lines 2–4, 1.4–4.7 cm. (L's up to 5 cm.), line 5, 2.2–4.0 cm., line 6, 1.2–3.9 (second L, 5.0) cm., line 7, 2.15–3.8 cm.

Epitaph of Maxima, "handmaid of Christ," who lived ca. 25 yrs. and was buried June 23 in the consulship of Flavius Probus Iunior (A.D. 525).

Publ. by A. Pasqui, *NS* 1909, 15, *g*; G. Gatti, *Bull. Com.* 1909, 316; Silvagni 1.3252 (further bibl.), *Mon.* 1 pl. xi no. 4; Diehl *ILCV* 1469; *Album* 3.178 f., no. 365.

Text: † *Hic requiescit in pa/ce ancilla C⟨h⟩risti, Maxima, / qu⟨a⟩e vixit ann(is) pl(us) m(inus) XXV; d(e)p(osita) VIIII Kal(endas) / Iulias, Fl(avio) Probo Iuniore, v(iro) c(larissimo), cons(ule); /⁵ qu⟨a⟩e fecit cum maritum suum* (sic) / *ann(is) VII, m(ensibus) VI, amicabilis, fidelis / in omnibus, bona, prudens.* (palm branch)

"Here lies in peace a handmaid of Christ, Maxima, who lived about 25 yrs.; buried June 23 in the consulship of Flavius Probus Iunior, *v.c.*; she lived with her husband 7 yrs., 6 mos., friendly, loyal in all respects, good, prudent."

The lettering, to say the least, is interesting: all the lines and nearly all the words uneven in height, many small letters, the three Q's (cf. *Contrib.* 111), erasure and correction in line 3 (XXX changed to XXV), possible correction at end of line 5 (VM in ligature, perhaps corrected from A), the supralineate abbreviations except *Fl.* (here instead a curly mark to the right), the cutting of *ann.* (6) so as to avoid the damage after A, and the addition of *-lis* between lines 5 and 6, *plus minus* and *viro clarissimo* each treated as a single word (*plus minus* probably also pronounced so, with accent on *plus*) by the use of the single horizontal line above;

interesting also the "vulgar" spellings, *Cristi* and *que*, the use of the second *que* ("connective use of the relative"?), and the accus. in *maritum suum* (5), which may be the result of over-correction, final M being so often omitted because unpronounced; the Latin cross, as in **98**; the palm branch, as in **85**.

Ancilla Christi: Diehl has 6 or 7 examples in *ILCV* (3.320 *s.v.* ancilla), and *TLL* on *ancilla*, 2.28, 3 f., says, "*saepissime apud ecclesiasticos scriptores dei vel Christi ancillae dicuntur feminae fideles*," and quotes the Vulgate (1 Kings, 1.11), Augustine, etc., but no inscrs. Line 3. *Plus minus*, often and variously abbreviated, is a very common and typically Christian phrase (see *ILCV* 3.566 *s.v.* plus), due perhaps to the belief that the exact amount of time that a Christian has lived in this world matters little; no word for "or," as in our "more or less," ever seems to appear. Line 4. Fl. Probus Iun. was consul in the West in 525. Line 5. *Facere cum*, "to live with," while anticipated in pagan Latin in the sense of "pass a total of, spend (time)" (*OLD* 668 *s.v.* facio, 10), seems to be more typically Christian (cf. *ILCV* 3.525 *s.v.* facio, F, b; 3.549, col. 1, *s.v.* maritus, fecit cum marito). Line 6. *Amicabilis* was perhaps a second thought for *amica* ("friendly," not "a friend"), hence the recourse taken with *-bilis*. Line 7. *In omnibus* may go with *fidelis* and/or *bona*; Diehl, on his 1469, takes it with *fidelis*, citing the Vulgate, 1 Tim. 3.11, (*Oportet esse) mulieres similiter pudicas, non detrahentes, sobrias, fideles in omnibus* ("faithful in all things," King James version).

APPENDICES

APPENDIX I

ARCHAIC AND UNUSUAL FORMS OF WORDS, WITH THE CLASSICAL LATIN FORMS

This list may contain more forms than are necessary. "Unusual" ones include all those that may give trouble in looking them up in Lewis/Short or the *OLD*. References in col. 4 are to Quintilian (twice) and to such modern authors, collections, and journals as Sommer, *ILS*, and *AJA*, all of which are listed in Abbreviations. (To save space, Barbarino, Ernout/Meillet, Kühner/Holzweissig, Leumann, Lommatzsch, Pfister, Sommer, and Sturtevant are sometimes or always cited briefly as Barb., E/M, K/H, Leum., Lomm., Pf., Somm., St. or Sturt. For Barb., see p. 59).

The longer inscriptions are cited not only by their number but also by line number, or by chapter and section (Augustus's *Res Gestae*, **34**, cited from J. Gagé's text, ed. 3, 1977), or by column and line (*Laudatio Turiae*, **28**, cited from E. Wistrand's ed., 1976; Claudius's Speech, **42**; the verse epitaph of Allia Potestas, **65**). Inscriptions are separated from one another by a semicolon; the line number is separated from the number of the inscription by a comma, or by a colon if more than one line is involved; the numbers of examples appear in parentheses followed by an x, which means "times" (as in a medical prescription); column and line numbers or chapter and section numbers appear in parentheses. A suprascript 1, 2, or 3 refers to sections of chapters of the *Res Gestae*; sometimes a line or a section has more than one example, such as "**34** (21³, 2x)"; such a figure as "1/2x" means one example, or two, where it is uncertain because of loss of text.

Examples:

7; **9** = inscrs. **7** and **9** (one example in each)

8: 12, 15 f., 20 (4x) = **8**, lines 12, 15, 16, 20 (four examples in all)

28 (2, 54) = **28**, col. 2, line 54

28 (2: 12 [?], 23) = **28**, col. 2, lines 12 (?) and 23

34, H = **34**, Heading

34 (13) = **34**, ch. 13

34 (14¹) = **34**, ch. 14 sect. 1

34 (15³, 21³ [2x], App. 4) = **34**, ch. 15 sect. 3, ch. 21 sect. 3 (two examples here), and Appendix sect. 4

36: 39, 44 = **36**, lines 39 and 44

42 (2, 37) = **42**, col. 2, line 37

48 (1/2x) = **48** (one example or two examples)

75 (3x) = **75** (three examples)

78, 4 = **78**, line 4.

Included in this list are the pertinent examples in the full text—whether this is presented here or not—of all 100 inscriptions except nos. **19** (the last third of line 4 is excluded as corrupt), **25** (all of what shows in the photo—itself only part of the total extant inscription—is excluded except lines 147–154, the rest being generally too fragmentary), and **81** (all excluded except the lines presented in the text). The abbreviations used in cols. 3 and 4 include, besides common and obvious ones, affirm(ative) part(icle), altern(a-tive) form or spell(ing), app(arently), arch(aic) doubl(et), cop(ie)s, f(oot)n(ote), fr(om), indef(inite), infl(uence), in lig(a-ture), sing(ular), or only s., pl(ural), var-(iant) spell(ing), and the names of the cases (n. or nom., gen., etc.).

FORM	INSCRIPTION NUMBERS	CLASSICAL LATIN	REFERENCE OR EXPLANATION
abdoucit	5	abducit	Pfister 42 §28; 87, 2
abentibus	78, 4	habentibus	St. 155–160 §180 ff., Pf. 147–149 §113
adcensus	42 (2, 37)	a census (gen.)	carelessness
adesent	8: 6, 8, 18	adessent	Pfister 32 §8
adfectione	78	affectionem	St. 151 §174 a, Pf. 219–221, 3
[ad]fu[e]re	31, 1	adfuerunt	alternative form
adiese	8, 7	adiisse	Sommer 588 §368
adie sent (*sic*)	8, 8	adiissent	ibid.
adieset	8, 17	adiisset	ibid.
adit	34 (26^4, 30^1)	adiit	ibid.
adque	34 (21^3); **78**, 9; **81**; **86**; **90**	atque	Pfister 203 *init.*
advocapit	75 (3x)	advocabit?	Norden 178–182
aede	**19**, 4; **34** (21^1)	aedem	see *adfectione*
aei	69, 6	ei (dat.)	carelessness? ignorance?
aeram	64	erani?	see note *ad loc.*
af	12	a, ab	Pfister 219 §170, 2, a *fin.*
agentis	34 (14^1)	agentes (acc.)	alternative form
ahenam	8, 26	aenam	St. 156 §180, Pf. 147 §113
aheneis	34, H	aenis	ibid., and Sommer 350
aidilis	5	aedilis	Pfister 63 §61 *init.*
Aimilius	7; 9	Aemilius	ibid.
aiquom	8, 26	aequum	ibid. and Sommer 345 §198
ali	31, 55	alii	Sommer 347 *med.*
aliquīs	49	aliquibus	altern. form; *OLD* 100 *s.v.* aliquis[1]
aliquod	34 (10^2); 76	aliquot	see *adque*
alis	19, 10	alius	Somm. 442 §283 (dialectical?)
alternei	75 (3x)	alterni (loc.)?	Norden 180, 182 f.
altissima	81	altissimae (gen.)	carelessness? ignorance?
altod	48	alto (abl.)	Pf. 202 *med.*, Somm. 344 f., §197
annone	84	annonae	Somm. 326 *fin.*, Sturt. 123–129
ante	64	in?	carelessness
Apollini	13	Apollinis	ditto (done in Greece)
aput	28 (2, 46)	apud	Pfister 203 *init.*
arf(uerunt)	8, 2	adfuerunt	Pfister 195, ad-
arfuisse	8, 21	adfuisse	ibid.

FORM	INSCRIPTION NUMBERS	CLASSICAL LATIN	REFERENCE OR EXPLANATION
argen[tom]	48	argentum	Pf. 116, 4; Somm. 342 §195
arkae	66: 6, 22	arcae	Pf. 31 Anm. 6, cf. Quintil. 1.7.10
Arkarum	76	Arcarum	ibid.
arvorsum	8, 24	adversum	Pfister 195, ad-
asse	68, 13	assem	see *adfectione*
Atalantes	65 (1, 21)	Atalantae (gen.)	altern. form, cf. *OLD* 195 *s.v.* Atalanta
Atheneis	14	Athenis	Pf. 64 f., §62; Sommer 350
atte	65 (2, 21)	ad te	see *adque*
Aurellius	29, c	Aurelius	see note *ad loc.*
auro[m]	48	aurum	see *argentom*
auspicis	34 (4², 30²)	auspiciis	Somm. 331 §188, St. 113 f., §118 a
[av]onc[ulus]	42 (2, 1)	avunculus	Leum. 61, 7; *OLD* 221 *s.v.* auunculus
Bacanal	8, 4	Bacchanal	Sturt. 80 §90 k; Pf. 32, 8
Bacanalia	8, 28	Bacchanalia	ibid.
Bacanalibus	8, 2	Bacchanalibus	ibid.
Bacas	8, 7	Bacchas	ibid.
Baso	95	Basso	ignorance?
berber	75 (3x)	?	see note *ad loc.*, cf. E/M *s.v.*
biginti	95	viginti	St. 142 f., §154 f.; Pf. 129 *med.*; Barb. 146, 4.2
bixit	95	vixit	ibid.
Bore[se]/os	22		Greek gen. of *Boresis*
Borustenen	49, 24	Borysthenem	altern. spell., cf. Pf. 29 Anm. 3
Brittanicis	72, 2	Britannicis	altern. spell., cf. *OLD* 242 *s.v.* Brita-
Brittannia	49, 7	Britannia	ibid.
caeteri	69	ceteri	Sturt. 123–129, esp. §131 b, 134
Caisar	43; 44	Caesar	Pf. 63 *med.*; see note on **43**
cannabae	69, 8	canabae	altern. spell.; see note *ad loc.*
cannabis	69, 16	canabis	ditto
captom	48 (3x)	captum	see *argentom*
caputalem	8, 25	capitalem	Sturt. 119 f., §126, 126 a
[Cartaginienses]	48	Carthaginienses	Pfister 29 Anm. 3
[Cartaginiensiom]	48	Carthaginiensium	ibid. and Somm. 382 §217
Cartaginiensis	48 (2x)	Carthaginiensis (acc. pl.)	ibid.
Castorei	2	Castori	Sommer 373 §211
castreis	7; 15 (1/2x); 48	castris	Sommer 350 *med.*

FORM	INSCRIPTION NUMBERS	CLASSICAL LATIN	REFERENCE OR EXPLANATION
catarhacte[n]	22	cataractan	Greek spell., cf. *OLD* 284 *s.v.* catara-
caussa	**15** (1/2x); **34** (14[1], 34[2]); **65** (1, 14)	causa	Pfister 159, 4
caussam	**28** (1, 18)	causam	ibid.
ceives	**15**	cives (acc.)	Pfister 64 f., §62
ceivis	**8**, 7	civis (nom.)	ibid.
Celerinu	**78**, 32	Celerinus	lack of space: see photo
cenera	**90**	genera	careless, cf. *ILS* 3: 2, 810, C *et* G
censum	**84**	censuum	Somm. 393 *init.*, *ILS* 3: 2, 850, 4th decl.
centuris	**36**: 39, 44	centuriis	see *auspicis*
cepet	**9**; **48** (1/2x)	cepit	Sommer 577 *med.*
Ceramices	**22**		Greek form of gen. of *Ceramice*
circeis	**53**	circe-?	see note *ad loc.*
circienses	**31**, 30	circenses	carelessness
Cisauna	**5**	Cisaunam	see *adfectione*
claseis	**48**	classis (acc.)	Pf. 32, 8; 64 f., §62; Somm. 385 §219
[c]lases	**48**	classes	Pfister 32, 8
[cl]aussum	**34** (13)	clausum	Pfister 159, 4
clupei	**34** (34[2])	clipei	altern. spell., cf. *OLD* 337 *s.v.* cli-
[clu]peus	**34** (34[2])	clipeus	ditto
coeraverunt	**13**	curaverunt	Pfister 66 §63
coeravit	**18**	curavit	ibid.
colleci	**78**, 19	collegi	carelessness
colonis	**34** (15[3], 21[3] [2x], App. 4)	coloniis	see *auspicis*
columna	**69**, 42	columnae	carelessness
comitis	**46**, 13	comitiis	see *auspicis*
comoine[m]	**8**, 11	communem	Pfister 66 §63
comvovise	**8**, 13	convovisse	Pfister 32, 8
conctos	**75** (3x)	cunctos	app. early form, cf. *OLD* 471 *s.v.* cu-
conerequentare/ nt	**66**, 7	confrequentarent	carelessness
cones(ulibus)	**79**	consulibus	ignorance?
conioura[se]	**8**, 13	coniura(vi)sse	Somm. 563 *med.*, Pf. 32, 8
conquaeisivei	**12**	conquaesivi	Pfister 64 Anm. 1
consol	**10**; **48** (1/2x)	consul	Pfister 183 *med.*
consoluerunt	**8**, 1	consuluerunt	Pfister 84 *fin.*
conspondise	**8**, 13	conspondisse	see *adesent*
Corinto	**11**	Corintho	Pfister 29 Anm. 3

FORM	INSCRIPTION NUMBERS	CLASSICAL LATIN	REFERENCE OR EXPLANATION
[Corneli]o	5	Cornelius	Sommer 304
cornuculo	15	corniculo	altern. spell., cf. *OLD* 446, *s.v.* corni-
cosmis	3	cōmis?	Pfister 100, 1
cosoleretur	8 (3x)	consuleretur	Pfister 183 *med.*, 84 *fin.*
coventionid	8, 22	conventione	Pfister index 235 *s.v.* cov-
Cristi	100	Christi	ignorance, cf. *ILCV* 3.195 f.
culpabere	65 (1, 26)	culpabis	see note *ad loc.*
cumcumvixit	79	convixit	note *ad loc.*, cf. *ILCV* 3.502 *s.v.* convivo
curulis	34 (4¹)	curules (acc.)	alternative form
[curum]?	48	currum	see *adesent*
[Dalm]ateis	34 (29¹)	Dalmatis	see *Atheneis*
Dan[u]i	34 (30¹)	Danuvi	*ILS* 3: 2, 835 (V *simplex pro* V *gem.*)
datai	8, 29	datae	Sommer 329 *med.*
dece	79	decem	see *adfectione*
decesit	85	decessit	see *adesent*
decesus	31, 21	decessus	ditto
decreivit	7	decrevit	Pf. 64 f., §62; Somm. 561 *med.*
dedicarunt	19, 1	dedicaverunt	Leumann 336, 1st par., *fin.*
dedicatione	68, 17	dedicationem	see *adfectione*
dedise	8, 14	dedisse	see *adesent*
deicerent	8, 4	dicerent	Pfister 41 §24, 64 f., §62
deivi	22	divi	Pfister 64 §62
deivinam	19, 16	divinam	Leum. 77 last par., Pf. loc. cit.
delegast[i]	28 (2, 54)	delega(vi)sti	Sommer 562 f.
Demaratho	42 (1, 12)	Demarato	overcorrection? cf. Pf. 29 Anm. 3
denarium	34 (App. 1)	denariorum	Sommer 349, 1
deo	81	deos	carelessness
derunt	28 (2, 58)	deerunt	contracted form, cf. *OLD* 524 *s.v.* desum
descindentes	75	?	see note *ad loc.*
de[si]derat	81	desiderant?	carelessness? 2 other cops. read -*nt*
detinetur	66, 17	detinentur	carelessness
deum	34 (19², 20⁴, App. 2)	deorum	see *denarium*
devicteis	31, 10	devictis	see *Atheneis*
dibitum	81	debitis	carelessness
dictatored	48	dictatore	see note *ad loc.*
dicundo	31: 19, 32	dicendo	Sommer 617 line 3

FORM	INSCRIPTION NUMBERS	CLASSICAL LATIN	REFERENCE OR EXPLANATION
die[is]	22	diis (deis)	Pf. 65 *med.* (ref. to Lomm.), cf. Somm. 351 *init.*
Diospoleos meg[ales]	22		gen. of Διόσπολις μεγάλη
dis	34 (4²)	deis, diis	Sommer loc. cit.
dismota	8, 30	dimota	Pf. 193 *med.*, Somm. 444 *med.*
divertia	28 (2, 41)	divortia	var. form (*OLD* 565 *s.v.* divortium)
divertio	28 (1, 27)	divortio	ditto
divideretur	66, 17	dividerentur	carelessness
dividiatur	68, 13	dividantur? -atur?	ditto
divom	42 (2, 33)	divum (-vorum)	Pf. 116 *med.*, Somm. 346 §195
domni	94	domini	Pf. 109 *fin.*; note *ad loc.*
domnorum	94	dominorum	ibid.
[donavet]	48	donavit	see *cepet*
dquoltod	8, 15	occulto (abl.)	carelessness; Somm. 344 §197
Duelonae	8, 2	Bellonae	Pfister 170 Anm. 4
Duenoi?	3	Bono (or bono, dat.)	Somm. 341 §194; note *ad loc.*
Duenos	3	Bonus (or bonus)	Sommer 114, 335 §192
e	36, 52	eo	carelessness—space left but O never cut
e?	75 (2/3x)	?	affirm. part.? Norden 118–120, 287
e (or et in lig.?)	85	et	carelessness?
ead	8, 24	ea (abl.)	Sommer 418 ε
eeis	8, 4	ei (nom. pl.)	Sommer 419 *med.*
eeis	8: 5, 25	eis (abl., dat. pl.)	ibid.
ei	36, 18; 92	et	carelessness
eidem	19 (south)	idem (n. sing.)	Sommer 421 §274 α
eidem	17	idem (n. pl.)	Pfister 64 f., §62 (*ei* for *ī*)
e(ilio)	51	filio	carelessness
eire	14	ire	Pfister 64 f., §62
emancupata	28 (1, 16)	emancipata	Sturtevant 119–122 §126
emeriteis	34 (16²)	emeritis	see *Atheneis*
en	48	in	Pfister 84 Anm. 7
endo?	3	in?	*OLD* 866 *s.vv.* indu, indu-
enos?	75 (3x)	nos?	Norden loc. cit. on "e?"; *OLD* 1189 *s.v.* nos
ese	8, 4	esse	see *adesent*
es/ed	4	erit?	Pf. 146 *fin.*, Somm. 530, 6
esent	8, 3–5 (3x)	essent	see *adesent*
eset	8, 10 (2x)	esset	ditto

FORM	INSCRIPTION NUMBERS	CLASSICAL LATIN	REFERENCE OR EXPLANATION
esetis	8, 23	essetis	ditto
Eugramus	52	Eugrammus?	misspelling?
Eutyfron	71	Euthyfro (Εὐθύφρων)	Pf. 29 Anm. 3
exdeicatis	8, 22	edicatis	Pf. 86 *fin.*, 193 *med.*
exdeicendum	8, 3	edicendum	ibid.
exequi	28 (1, 51)	exsequi	altern. spell.; *OLD* 655 *s.v.* ex(s)equor
exercitum	34 (29²)	exercituum	Sommer 393 §231
exfogiont (not exfoci-)	48	effugiunt	Leum. 63 §29 b, cf. Somm. 510 §323
exibeant	78	exhibeant	Sturtevant 155–160 §180–184
eximplum	76	exemplum	*ILS* 3: 2, 821 (I *pro* E); St. 112 §117 a
Exosco	55	?	dialectical?
expectast[i]	28 (1, 12)	expecta(vi)sti	see *delegasti*
exstrad	8: 16, 28	extra	Pfister 109 *fin.*, 185 *med.*
extinctori	86	exstinctori	altern. spell. (*OLD* 657 *s.v.* ex(s)t-)
extruat	76	exstruat	ditto (*OLD* 658 *s.v.* ex(s)truo)
exuperant	65 (1, 5)	exsuperant	ditto (ibid. *s.v.* ex(s)upero)
facilumed	8, 27	facillime	Pf. 88 *med.*, Somm. 345 Anm.
faciundis	64	faciendis	Sommer 615–618 §381
faciundum	18	faciendum	ibid.
famaa	14	fama (abl.)	Pfister 32, 7
fanei	19, 17	fani	Pf. 64 f., §62; Somm. 338
feced	3	fecit?	Pfister 31 Anm. 5
fecei	12 (3x)	feci	Sommer 574 §363
fecerun	85	fecerunt	Pfister 219 Anm. 1
fecise	8: 12, 15 f., 20	fecisse	see *adesent*
fecisent	8, 24	fecissent	ditto
Felixs	71	Felix	Pfister 185 *med.*
femine	78	feminae	see *annone*
ferale	60	feralem	see *adfectione*
fidissuma	28 (2, 43)	fidissima	see *caputalem*
fifeltares	19, 15	?	*ILLRP* 2.508 p. 7 fn. 16 (dialectical?)
figier	8, 27	figi	Pf. 145 *init.*, Somm. 594 *fin.*
filis	74	filiis	see *auspicis*
flusare	19, 2	florali (abl.)	Pf. 147 Anm. 1 (dialectical)
foideratei	8, 2	foederati	Pf. 66 §63, Somm. 346 §199
foras	65 (1, 9)	foris	see note *ad loc.*, cf. *OLD* 721 *s.v.* foras, 2, a

FORM	INSCRIPTION NUMBERS	CLASSICAL LATIN	REFERENCE OR EXPLANATION
fratrum	**49**, 19	fratrem (or -tres)	carelessness
freques	**78**, 3	frequens	see note *ad loc.*
fu	**75** (3x)	esto?	Somm. 531 §345 *fin.*
fugiteivos	**12**	fugitivos	Pfister 64 f., §62
funem	**64**	funerum?	see note *ad loc.*
generis	**60**, 20	generi? generes?	ditto
gentrum	**81**	gentium	carelessness
g[eset]	**48**	gessit	see *adesent* and *cepet*
gestum	**66**, 23	gestus	carelessness? ignorance?
ginio	**76**	genio	careless? cf. Sturt. 112 §117 a
Gnaivod	**5**	Gnaeo	Pfister 63 §61, 125 *fin.*
gnoscier	**8**, 27	nosci	Pf. 177 *init.*, Somm. 594 *fin.*
habitus	**76**	habitura?	ignorance?
habuise	**8**, 3	habuisse	see *adesent*
Hadrasto	**69**, 29	Adrasto	see *abentibus*
haice	**8**, 22	haec (neut. acc.)	Pfister 63 §61 *init.*
[Hanibaled]	**48**	Hannibale	see *adesent*; for -ed, see note *ad loc.*
heic	**12**; **19**, 14	hic (adv.)	Pfister 64 f., §62
Hercolei	**6**; **13**	Herculi	Pf. 112 *init.*; see *Atheneis*
hierofantae	**92**	hierophantae	St. 84 §92 a, Pf. 29 Anm. 3
hince	**12**	hinc	Sommer 449 *fin.*
hoce	**8**, 26	hoc (neut. acc.)	ibid.
hoiusque	**19**, 4	huius	Sommer 450
honorificientia	**78**, 16	honorificentia	carelessness? ignorance?
honorificientiae	**78**, 21	honorificentiae	ditto
honos	**34** (12¹); **36**, 5	honor	Sommer index 641 *s.v.* honos
huc	**19**, 16	hoc (acc.)	Sommer 425 *fin.*
humarum	**46**, 18	humanarum	carelessness
ibei	**8**, 25	ibi	*OLD* 817 *s.v.* ibi, cf. Pf. 120 *init.*
idem	**68**, 3	eidem (dat.)	carelessness
Ienua/rivium	**78**, 29 f.	Ianuarium	ditto (*ILS* 3: 1, 204 *s.v.* Ianua-)
iusticiae (or iiu-? or i space u-?)	**81**, 6	iustitiae	carelessness? for -ci- for ti-, K/H 1.35 f., St. 168 fn. 75
illae	**65** (1, 18)	illi (fem. dat. s.)	Sommer 430 *med.*, 445 *med.*
illeis	**19**, 3	illis	see *Atheneis*
in / in	**49**, 26 f.	in	*in* repeated by dittography
inceideretis	**8**, 26	incideretis	Pfister 86 iii, 1, a
incendis	**83**	incendiis	see *auspicis*
inclyto	**88**	incluto	Pfister index 241 *s.v.* inclytus
[indi]casse	**28** (1, 41)	indica(vi)sse	Leumann 335 f., §244 b

FORM	INSCRIPTION NUMBERS	CLASSICAL LATIN	REFERENCE OR EXPLANATION
indoles	**78**, 9	indolis? inlustris?	carelessness (cf. *ILS* 7220 fn. 6)
inferentis	**34** (2)	inferentes (acc.)	alternative form
iniusiris	**36**, 2	illustris	carelessness
innocus	**95**	innocuus	see note *ad loc.*
inpeirator	**7**	imperator	Pf. 55 line 1, 179 c; Somm. 561
insequenies	**36**, 7	insequentes	carelessness
inter ibei	**8**, 20	interibi	see *ibei*
ioubeatis	**8**, 27	iubeatis	Sommer 557 *fin.*
iousisent	**8**: 9, 18	iussissent	ibid.
iousit	**7**	iussit	ibid.
iouxmen/ta	**4**	iumenta?	Pf. 70 §66, 188 §141 *fin.*
Iove?	**3**	?	see note *ad loc.* and *CIL* 1²: 2: 4, annotation
iovestod?	**4**	iusto?	Pf. 109 *fin.*, 128 *med.*
Irus	**85**	Idus	carelessness
is	**36**: 7, 44	eis, iis	*OLD* 969 *s.v.* is
it	**78**, 5	et	carelessness? cf. St. 112 §117 a
itero	**60**, 3	iterum	see note *ad loc.*
Itaiiam	**84**	Italiam	carelessness
itsis	**51**	ipsis	ditto
Iulis	**78**, 2	Iuliis	see *auspicis*
iure	**31**: 19, 32; **55**, 3	iuri (dat.)	Sommer 373 lines 4–6
kalatorem	**4**	calatorem	Pfister 31 Anm. 5
kandidato	**96**	candidato	Pf. 31 6th par.
k(apite?)	**72** (15/16x)	capite?	ibid.
karae	**66**, 13	carae	ibid.
Karth(agine)	**72**: 14, 16, 20	Carthagine	ibid. and 152 §117
kasibus	**29**, c	casibus	see *kalatorem*
lachrimans	**65** (2, 10)	lacrimans	Pf. 89 Anm. 1, 153 4th par.
lachrimas	**65** (1, 7)	lacrimas	ibid.
Laci	**16**	Lacus (gen.)	Sommer 404 line 3
laguna	**61**	lagona	Pfister 66 Anm.; *OLD* 997 *s.v.* lagona
Lases	**75** (3x)	Lares	Pfister 146 *fin.*
legitumae	**28** (1, 21)	legitimae	see *caputalem*
legitume	**31**, 41	legitime	ditto
leiberei	**7**	liberi	Pf. 64 f., §62; Somm. 346 §199
linteari	**70**	lintearii	Sommer 347
locar(unt)	**77**	loca(ve)runt	Somm. 562 f., Leum. 335 f., §244 b
locupletasti	**28** (2, 5a)	locupleta(vi)sti	ibid.
Loucanam	**5**	Lucanam	Pfister 70 §66

FORM	INSCRIPTION NUMBERS	CLASSICAL LATIN	REFERENCE OR EXPLANATION
luae	75	luem	poor writing
lue	75 (2x)	luem	see *adfectione*
Macel[am]	48	Macellam	see *adesent*
magistr[a]tos	48	magistratus (nom. s.)	see note *ad loc.* and Quintil. 1.4.16
mag[istratud]	48	magistratu	Sommer 391 §228
magistratum	36, 9	magistratuum	Sommer 393 §231
magistratuo	8, 12	magistratu	Sommer 391 §228
[m]agistratuus	31, 6	magistratus (n. pl.)	Sommer 392 §230
magistreis	13	magistri (nom. pl.)	Sommer 346 *fin.* (Greek infl. here?)
magna	49, 14	magnam	apparently carelessness
magna[a]	14	magna (abl.)	see *famaa*
Maicius	13	Maecius	Pf. 63 §61 (Greek infl. here?)
Mamor	75	Marmor	careless writing for *Marmor, q.v.*
mamoriae	78, 9	memoriae	carelessness
mandare	19, 6	mundare? emendare?	text corrupt
Marcelus	10	Marcellus	Pfister 32, 8
marid	48 (2x)	mari (abl.)	Sommer 375
maritum	100	marito (abl.)	ignorance
Marma	75	Mars	careless writing for *Marmar*
Marmar	75 (2x)	Mars	E/M 388 *s.v.* Mars, 1st par.
Marmor	75 (2x)	Mars	see *Marmar*
Marta/lem	78, 28 f.	Martialem	carelessness
Martis	68, 11; 72, 6	Martiis	see *auspicis*
Matucci	70	Matuccii	Sommer 347 *med.*
[ma]ximos	48	maximus	Sommer 325 §192
maxsimis	31, 11	maximis	K/H 41, 10 e
maxsimo	31, 46	maximo	ibid.
maxsumi	31, 8	maximi	ibid. and see *caputalem*
[ma/x]umas	48	maximas	see *caputalem*
med	3	me (acc.)	Pf. 202 *med.*, Somm. 411 §261
meilia	12 (2x)	milia	Sommer 73, 471 §298
menses	79	mensibus	careless, after *annis* (abl.)
[merset]	48	mersit	see *cepet*
meses	95	menses	Pfister 183, b
millia	34 (15x)	milia	Pfister 159 *fin.*
milliarium	66, 4	miliarium	ibid.
millibus	34 (15², 18)	milibus	ibid.
milliens	34 (7x)	miliens	ibid.
Mirquri	13	Mercuri	Pf. 54, c (Greek infl. here?)

FORM	INSCRIPTION NUMBERS	CLASSICAL LATIN	REFERENCE OR EXPLANATION
mitat	3	mitt-?	for one *t*, see *adesent*
monu/tum	62	monumentum	carelessness
moriente	60, 18	morientem	see *adfectione*
multiplicasset	31, 16	multiplica(vi)sset	see *locupletasti*
[m]unibat	28 (2, 7a)	muniebat	Sommer 522, last par.
municipis	34 (16¹)	municipiis	see *auspicis*
munis	97	muniis	ditto
Mysias	84	Moesias	var. spell., cf. *ILS* 3: 2, 630, *s.v.* Moesia
navaled	48	navali (abl.)	see note *ad loc.*
navebos	48 (2x)	navibus	Sommer 385 *init.*
naveis	48 (1/2x)	navis (acc.)	op. cit. 385 §219
necessa	78, 22	necesse	carelessness
necessest	28 (2, 40)	necesse est	unusual reproduction of (no doubt) actual speech
necesus	8, 4	necesse	Leumann 50 *med.*, *OLD* 1165 *s.v.*
neiquis	8, 3	nequis	*OLD* 1162 *s.v.* ne¹, Pf. 64 f., §62
nisei	8: 8, 16, 21	nisi	*OLD* 1179 *s.v.* nisi
nive	31: 28, 30 (3x)	neve	*OLD* 1182 *s.v.* nive, 1
nominus	8, 7	nominis	Sommer 372 *med.*
nosse	65 (2, 1)	no(vi)sse	Leumann 336 line 4
Nouceriam	12	Nuceriam	Pfister 70 §66
noundinum	8, 23	nundinum	Pfister 110 *med.*, 126 *fin.*
numei	48 (2x)	nummi	Pf. 32, 8; 64 f., §62; Somm. 346 §199
nuncquam	65 (1, 14; 2, 11)	numquam	Pfister 156 Anm. 3
nunquam	34 (10², 15¹, 30¹)	numquam	*OLD* 1204 *s.v.* numquam
nus	81	nos	carelessness (inscr. done in Greece)
obit	31, 25	obiit	see *adit*
obligarunt	53	obliga(ve)runt	see *dedicarunt*
obsirvare	76	observare	see *eximplum*
oeti	19: 6, 8	uti (fr. *utor*)	see *coeraverunt*; Leum. 78 *med.*
offeri	78, 24	offerri	carelessness
oinvorsei	8, 19	universi	Pfister 61 *init.*, 130 Anm. 2
olitoriorum	76	holitoriorum	see *abentibus*
olleis	19, 3	illis	Sommer 429 line 5
ol[or]om	48	illorum	ibid. line 4
omne	5	omnem	see *adfectione*
omneis	12	omnis (acc.)	see *naveis*
omnis	34 (27³)	omnes (acc.)	alternative form
[Op]hieu	22		Greek gen. sing., 'Οφιήου

FORM	INSCRIPTION NUMBERS	CLASSICAL LATIN	REFERENCE OR EXPLANATION
[opidom]	48	oppidum	Pfister 32, 8; 116, 4
[opsidione]d	48	obsidione	for the -d, see note *ad loc.*
ornavet	48	ornavit	see *cepet*
-oue	78	-que	carelessness
ovod	66, 8	quod	ditto
paastores	12	pastores	see *famaa*
pace	95	pacem?	see *adfectione* (or *pace* is abl.)
palereis	15	phaleris	Pf. 29 Anm. 3, Somm. 331 §188
pane	66, 12 f. (2x)	panem	see *adfectione*
pane	66, 15 f. (3x)	panis (nom.)	carelessness
Papeirio	13	Papirio	see *ceives*
pararis	28 (2, 7)	para(ve)ris	Sommer 562 f.
parasses	28 (2, 1)	para(vi)sses	ibid.
parastis	28 (1, 26)	para(vi)stis	ibid.
pa[ravet]	48	paravit	see *cepet*
parisuma	5	parissima	Pfister 32, 8; 88 *med.*
parte	49, 14	partem	apparently carelessness
patrieis	22	patriis	Sommer 331 §188
pauc[ei]s	14	paucis	ibid.
pelleis	19, 16	pelles (n. pl.)	Sommer 382 §216
pequnia	19 (5x)	pecunia	Pfister 31 *med.*
periclo	34 (5^2)	periculo	Pfister 113, 3rd par.
[perscr]iptumvest	36, 14	perscriptumve est	see *necessest*
[perp]etum	34 (10^1)	perpetuum	carelessness
perpetuom	31, 56	perpetuum	Sommer 345 §198
Persiphone	65 (1, 4)	Persephone	see *eximplum*
pertinen/tes	69, 4 f.	pertinentium	carelessness or ignorance
[p]etierit	45	peti(v)erit	Sommer 567 *fin.*
Phrates	34 (32^1, 32^2)	Phraates	altern. spell., cf. *OLD* 1375 *s.v.* Phr(a)ates
Phratis	34 (32^1, 33)	Phraatis	ibid.
Pilo	13	Philo	Pfister 29 Anm. 3
pleores	75	plures?	Sommer 455, 3
pleoris	75 (2x)	plures?	ibid.
plous	8, 19f. (3x)	plus	ibid.
Pob(lilia)	26	Publilia	altern. sp. (archaic? dialectical?)
Podlouquei	2	Polluci	see note *ad loc.*; Pf. 178 *med.*
Poenicas	48	Punicas	Pfister 67, 3, b
ponteis	12	pontis (acc.)	see *naveis*
[p(opli)]	48	populi	Pfister 113 Anm. 1
poplicas	12	publicas	Pfister 151 *init.*

FORM	INSCRIPTION NUMBERS	CLASSICAL LATIN	REFERENCE OR EXPLANATION
poplico	12	publico	ibid.
poplicod	8, 15	publico (abl.)	Sommer 273, 322 §197
poplom	48	populum	Pf. 113 Anm. 1, Somm. 342 §195
poplus	7	populus	Pfister loc. cit.
posedisent	7	possedissent	see *adesent*
poseivei	12	posivi (posui)	Sommer 573 f.
potisit	8, 27	possit	Sommer 532 *med.*
praedad	48	praeda (abl.)	Sommer 325 f., §185
praedis	34 (16¹)	praediis	see *auspicis*
praeeecto	92	praefecto	carelessness
praee(ecto)	92	praefecto	ditto
pr[aemis]	34 (3³)	praemiis	see *auspicis*
praerant	34 (17¹)	praeerant	var. spell., cf. *OLD* 1444 *s.v.* praesum
praerat	31, 19	praeerat	ditto
praerint	36, 34	praeerunt	alt. sp.; for *-erint*, Somm. 531 *init.*
praerunt	31, 32	praeerunt	alternative spelling
praesente[d]	48	praesente	see note *ad loc.*
preivatod	8, 16	privato (abl.)	*OLD* 1461 *s.v.* privatus¹, Pf. 64 f., §62
prestat	91	praestat	Pf. 63 *fin.*, Sturt. 128 f.
prestaturus	69	praestaturus	ibid.
Primitius	72	Primitivus	*ILS* 3: 2, 835 (V *simplex pro* V *gemina*)
primos	48 (2x)	primus	Sommer 335 f., §192
private	84	privatae	see *annone*
prob(arunt)	17	proba(ve)runt	see *dedicarunt*
probaveit	18 (south)	probavit	Sommer 576 *fin.*
proorsus	78, 11	prorsus	carelessness?
proprius	36, 58	propius	carelessness
provicias	34 (26²)	provincias	ditto (inscr. done in Greece)
provincis	34 (12², 16¹)	provinciis	see *auspicis*
puaellae	53	puellae	Pfister 63 f.
pug[nad]	48	pugna (abl.)	Sommer 328 f., §185
[p]ugnandod	48	pugnando (abl.)	Sommer 334 f., §197
pulcra	91	pulchra	var. sp., but cf. St. 158 §182 with fn. 50
qoi	3	qui (nom. s.? pl.?)	Sommer 27, 434
qua	8, 28	quae (indef., neut.)	Sommer 439 ε
qua	66, 16	quae (rel., fem., n. s.)	carelessness

FORM	INSCRIPTION NUMBERS	CLASSICAL LATIN	REFERENCE OR EXPLANATION
qua	**68**, 17	quae?	carelessness? see note *ad loc.*
quadrigeis	**34** (24²)	quadrigis	see *Atheneis*
quaecunque	**46**, 17	quaecumque	carelessness
quaesisse	**42** (1, 39)	quaesi(vi)sse	Leumann 335 f., §244, 1
quandiucumque	**65** (2, 18)	quamdiucumque	Pf. 178 §133, 1, a; 193 *init.*
quarto	**96**	quater	see note *ad loc.*
quasei	**19**, 14	quasi	K/H 99 line 2; 941, 11
quator	**95** (2x)	quattuor	Sommer 466 ("vulgär")
que	**100** (2x)	quae (fem., n.s.)	see *annone*
quei	**5**; **7**; **8**: 2, 4, 24	qui (n.s. or pl.)	Sommer 434 *fin.*
quei	**19**, 16	quis (indef.)	dialectical? careless? see *qui*
quemquomque	**19**, 9	quemcumque	Pfister 126 Anm. 1
ques	**8**: 3, 24	qui (indef., pl.)	Sommer 438
qui	**19**, 14	quis (indef.)	see *quei* (**19**, 16)
quiquam	**8**, 12	quisquam	K/H 620, 2, line 2
qui / qui	**78**, 26 f.	qui	careless dittography
Quinctileis	**19**, 2	Quinctilis (acc.)	Sommer 385 §219
quindecemviro	**89**, 6 f.; **92**	quindecimviro	var. spell., cf. *ILS* 3: 1, 564
[quinde-cimvir]um	**34** (7³)	quindecim-virorum	Sommer 349 §200, 1
quing[en]ties	**34** (17¹)	quingentiens	careless here, the others ending in *-iens* (cf. Somm. 474 *fin.*)
quinquens	**34** (22¹)	quinquiens	carelessness
[quin/queresmo]s	**48**	quinqueremos	see *triresmos*
quisquanst	**14**	quisquam est	*AJA* ser. 2, 32 (1928) 14, with fn. 7
quit	**46**	quid (indef.)	Pfister 203 §159
quod	**66**, 23	qui	carelessness? ignorance?
quod	**66**, 8	quid? quem?	ditto
quod	**42** (1, 6)	quot	see *aliquod*
quod annis	**31**, 31; **55**, 10	quotannis	ditto
quodannis	**68**, 11	quotannis	ditto
quoi	**4** (2x)	qui? (s.? pl.?)	Pf. 31 Anm. 5, 248 *s.v.* quoi ("N. sg.")
quoius	**5**; **28** (1, 21; 2, 9a)	cuius	Pf. 67, 2; 124 2nd par.; Sommer 436 β
quom	**8**: 9, 18; **28** (2: 12[?], 23)	cum (conj.)	Pfister 126 Anm. 1
[qu]om ?	**14**	cum (prep.)	ibid.
quosquae	**78**	quosque	Pf. 63 f., Sturt. 128 §133
qurois	**2**	(κούροις)	see note *ad loc.*
quot	**68**, 14	quod	Pfister 203 *init.*
reccidisse	**28** (1, 15)	recidisse	altern. form, cf. Pf. 158 *med.*

FORM	INSCRIPTION NUMBERS	CLASSICAL LATIN	REFERENCE OR EXPLANATION
recei (i.e. regei?)	**4**	regi? (dat. of *rex?*)	Pf. 31 Anm. 5, Somm. 373 §211
[redi]	**34** (12²)	redii	Sommer 588 §368
redidei	**12**	reddidi	Pf. 32 Anm. 8, Somm. 574 §363
redieit	**11**	rediit	Sommer 576 *fin.*
Regio	**12**; **72**: 22, 24	Rhegio	Leumann 117 §100
Regium	**12** (2x)	Rhegium	ibid.
reliquorum	**68**, 9	reliqua (acc.)	carelessness
renovasset	**31**, 16	renova(vi)sset	Sommer 562 f.
rere	**75**	fere	carelessness
rivom	**29**, b	rivum	Sommer 342 §195
rocationem	**36**, 14	rogatione	carelessness
Romam	**36**, 58	Roma	ditto
rue	**75** (3x)	ruinam?	*ILLRP* 1.8 no. 4 fn. 2
rusus	**42** (1, 33)	rursus	Pf. 191 *med.*
Sacanal	**8**, 3	Bacchanal	S for B, careless; for the rest, see *Bacanal*
sacrom	**6**	sacrum	see *argentom*
[s]aeclares	**34** (22²)	saeculares	Pf. 112, 1, a; 113 3rd par.; 173 *med.*
saeculum	**85**	saeculo	probably ignorance
sakros	**4**	sacer	Pf. 31 *init.*; 120, 2; 222 2nd par.; Somm. 336 *init.*
[sa]le, sall, sni?	**75**	sali	poor writing
Sali	**36**, 4	Salii	Sommer 347 *med.*
Samnio	**5**	Samnium?	see note *ad loc.*
Saturtino	**53**	Saturnino	carelessness
scholam	**66**, 11	schola (abl.)	ditto
scola	**78**, 3	schola	ditto, or altern. spelling
scribundo	**54**	scribendo	see *dicundo*
seculo	**79**	saeculo	Sturtevant 128 §133
sed	**8**, 13 f. (2x)	se (acc.)	Pf. 202, -d, 2nd par.; Somm. 411 §261
sei	**8** (4x); **19** (5x)	si	see *quasei*
seit	**19**, 11	sit	Pfister 104, 3, b
Semunis, Si-	**75** (3x)	Semones	Norden 204–208
senaiores	**36**, 9	senatores	carelessness
senator bus	**8**, 6	senatoribus	ditto (the I never cut, but space left)
senatuos	**8** (4x)	senatus (gen.)	Sommer 389
sententiad	**8**: 8, 17, 21	sententia (abl.)	Pf. 202 *med.*, Somm. 328 *fin.*
sepentium	**36**, 22	sedentium	carelessness
septe	**79**	septem	see *adfectione*
[septemvirum]	**34** (7³)	septemvirorum	Sommer 349, 1 f.

FORM	INSCRIPTION NUMBERS	CLASSICAL LATIN	REFERENCE OR EXPLANATION
septer[esmom]	48	septiremum	see *triresmos*
septuagensu[mum]	34 (35[2])	septuagensimum	see *caputalem*
sers?	75	sinas? siveris?	poor writing for *sins*? see *sins*
servei	7	servi	see *Atheneis*
sestertium	34 (16[1,2], 17[1,2], 21[2])	sestertiorum	see *septemvirum*
sexsiens	34 (16[1])	sexiens	K/H 1.41, 10 e; *ILS* 3: 2, 837 f. (XS *pro* X [not S])
Sexteilius	13	Sextilius	Pfister 64 f., §62
sibei	8, 4	sibi	Pfister 117, 120
sient	8, 30	sint	Sommer 529 *fin.*
signu	11	signum	see *adfectione*
simillumum	31, 13	simillimum	see *caputalem*
simitu	60, 7	simul	arch. doubl., cf. E/M 627 *s.v.*; here no doubt *metri causa*
sinc	66, 12	sing(ulis)	carelessness
sins	75 (2x)	sinas?	poor writing, cf. Norden 128–133
sng	63	sing(ularium)	carelessness
socieis	48	sociis	see *Atheneis*
socium	8, 7	sociorum	Sommer 349 line 2
Soli	92	Solis	carelessness
sollicitarunt	28 (1, 25)	sollicita(ve)runt	see *dedicarunt*
spectaclum	34 (23)	spectaculum	see *periclo*
Statiil(io)	37	Statilio	carelessness
statue	68, 13	statuae	see *annone*
stipendis	34 (3[3]?, 16[2])	stipendiis	see *auspicis*
s(tlitibus)	56	litibus	Pf. 186 §140, *OLD* 1035 *s.v.* lis ("fossilized formula")
strenuas	66, 13	strenas	carelessness? ignorance?
subsellis	36, 22	subselliis	see *auspicis*
succeptum	28 (1, 26)	susceptum	K/H 934, 27; Wistrand 35, on I 26
suffragis	36: 34, 35, 39	suffragiis	see *auspicis*
suma	12	summa	see *adesent*
suprad	8: 21, 24, 29	supra	Leumann 274 *med.*
supstituta	28 (2, 53)	substituta	see *succeptum*, ref. to K/H
surupuerit	19, 14	surripuerit	Pfister 85, γ
sustodum	36, 16	custodum	carelessness
suum	100	suo (abl.)	ignorance
tabelai	8, 29	tabellae (nom.)	Pf. 32, 8; Somm. 329 *med.*
tabelarios	12	tabellarios	see *adesent*
tabolam	8, 26	tabulam	Leumann 84 *fin.*, 97 *med.*

FORM	INSCRIPTION NUMBERS	CLASSICAL LATIN	REFERENCE OR EXPLANATION
tabula	**78**, 18	tabulam	carelessness
Taurasia	**5**	Taurasiam	see *adfectione*
ted?	**3** (2x?)	te (acc.) ?	Pf. 202, -d; Somm. 411 §261
Tig[ra]ne	**34** (27²)	Tigranem	carelessness
traductast	**14**	traducta est	see *necessest*
Tr[iacontas]-choenundi	**22**	Triacontaschoeni	ignorance? (done in Egypt)
tribuniciae / po[test]	**31**, 46 f.	tribunicia potestate	the gen. is uncommon, cf. *ILS* 3: 1, 258 f.
tribuniciae potestatis	**34** (15²)	tribunicia potes-tate (as in 15¹)	ditto
tricinta	**79**	triginta	carelessness
triresmos	**48**	triremos	see note *ad loc.*
triumfatores	**89**; **97**	triumphatores	Pfister 29, 2, Anm. 3
triumfatori	**86**; **88**	triumphatori	ibid.
triumpe	**75** (5x)	triumphe (voc.?)	see note *ad loc.* and *triumpo*
[triump]o	**48**	triumpho	Pfister 152 f. §117
[tri]umv[i]rum	**34** (7¹)	triumvirorum	see *denarium*
Trophime	**62**, 17	Trophimes (or -ae)	carelessness (cf. *ILS* 3: 2, 853, gen. sing.)
Tryferus	**71**	Trypherus	see *hierofantae*
ubei	**8**: 5, 27; **19**, 8	ubi	Pfister 120 *init.*
ultumum	**28** (2, 67)	ultimum	see *caputalem*
universisquae	**78**	universique	carelessness
usquaeque	**78**	usquequaque	ignorance? carelessness?
usqui	**31**, 21	usque	carelessness, cf. Sturt. 112 §117 a
ut	**69**	et?	carelessness? see note *ad loc.*
utei	**7**; **8** (10x); **19** (4x)	ut, uti	Pfister 121 *fin.*
utr a	**8**, 5	verba	carelessness
Veceto	**51**	Vegeto	ditto
veicus	**19**: 9, 15	vicus	see *ceives*
velent	**8**, 21	vellent	see *adesent*
velet	**8** (9x)	vellet	ditto
veniant	**66**, 6	veneant	Sturt. 112 §117 a (*periat*)
verna	**64**	vernae (dat.)	carelessness
[vicet]	**48**	vicit	see *cepet*
vinu	**66**: 15, 16 (2x)	vinum	carelessness
VIRCO	**3**	virgo?	Pfister 31 *fin.*
virei	**8**, 19	viri (nom.)	Sommer 346 §199
virei	**14**	viri (gen.)	Sommer 338 §193
virtutei	**5**	virtuti	Sommer 373 §211

FORM	INSCRIPTION NUMBERS	CLASSICAL LATIN	REFERENCE OR EXPLANATION
vivos	**65**	vivus	Pf. 116, 4; Somm. 335 §192
vobeis	**8, 29**	vobis	Sommer 413 §265
vocuam	**28** (2, 33)	vacuam	Leumann 56 *fin.*
volgo	**65** (2, 14)	vulgo	Pfister 60, h, NB
volneribus	**28** (2, 17); **31**, 11	vulneribus	ibid.
Yacintho	**64**; **76**	Hyacintho	see *abentibus*
Yllyrici	**92**	Illyrici	carelessness? ignorance?
Ypatio	**87**	Hypatio	see *abentibus*
Zmaragdus	**70**	Smaragdus	variant spell.? ignorance?
H̶S	**62**, 9–11 (3x)	H̶S (sesterces)	carelessness

APPENDIX II

ABBREVIATIONS FOUND IN THESE INSCRIPTIONS

Latin inscriptions show a very large number of abbreviations (see Intro., p. 15; as was noted above, Intro., n. 41, one inscription of 613 words (**66**, A.D. 153) has 142 of them abbreviated. Perhaps no other language shows so many abbreviations in inscrs. intended for public view. Many of the Latin ones are regular, common, and ubiquitous, such as F(*ilius, -ia*), the masculine praenomina (always abbreviated when followed by nomen or cognomen or both), the "tribal" abbrs. of three letters (e.g., ARN(*iensi tribu*)), COS and the other official titles. Other abbrs. are apparently required by lack of space (esp. at line ends, where there seems to have been, as with us, a tendency not to break words), caused in turn by poor planning; some are seldom used and may be local or regional. In case of need any word may be shortened, sometimes by as little as a single letter (e.g., CAESAR for *Caesare* in **37**, three times). One example, PARENTV̄ for *parentum* in an inscr. (**91**) of A.D. 383 (undoubtedly cut by Pope Damasus's own engraver, Philocalus) is interesting because of its rather fancy supralineate abbreviation-mark at the end of line 2 (for ca. 15 other examples of such an abbr., cf. *Supralin. Abbrs.* Table 1, pp. 67–100, passim). This parallels, or perhaps foreshadows, the use of such a mark over abbrs. in Latin MSS (cf. E. M. Thompson, *An Introduction to Greek and Latin Palaeography* [Oxford 1912] 84–90, esp. 88; for a few actual examples, cf. F. Ehrle and P. Liebaert, *Specimina cod. Latinorum Vaticanorum* [Bonn 1912] pl. 7, lines 4 f., 7 f.,

11, 16, 19, 28, 30, all but the first two *fin.* ["before A.D. 509/510"]).

Another latish, and interesting, development is the doubling, tripling, or even quadrupling of the first or last letter of an abbreviation in order to indicate two, three, or four of the persons named (cf. Gordon, *Supralin. Abbrs.* 110). In this selection the only examples are AVGG, BB VV, CONSS, COSS, DD NN FFLL, IMPP, NN, and PRAEFF, to indicate two Augusti, two *boni viri*, etc. C̄C̄ and C̄C̄C̄, for *ducenario* and *trecenario* (following C̄ for *centenario*), are special examples. So also B̵ for *beneficiario* and S̵S̵ (a rare deviant of the usual H̵S̵ for *sestertium*, gen. pl.), each with a distinctive horizontal line through the center, and QQ and QQ PP (with or without a bar above), in which these letters reproduce the Q—Q and P—P of *quinquennalis* (var. forms) and *perpetuo*. The supralineate bar over an abbr., first used to distinguish certain uses of numerals (e.g., I̅I̅I̅ VIRI, "triumvirs") and ordinals from cardinals (e.g., I̅I̅I̅, "third" or "for the third time"), became used also to mark abbrs., though sporadically and inconsistently; it eventually became a distinctive feature of some inscriptions, such as our **99** and **100**, where all eighteen abbreviations are thus marked (once with a curly mark to the right). (Cf. Gordon, op. cit., esp. 62–64, 101 f., and *Contrib.* 166–170.)

The question arises how a reader can know what word is represented by a particular abbreviation. Obviously, the longer the abbr., in proportion to the length of the word represented, the easier it is to solve; e.g., BEN(*e*) or BEATISSI-MOR(*um*). It is the single letters that are the hardest; in this selection the letter P represents twenty-six different words or forms of words. Only the context gives the solution, and sometimes this fails; see LIBR I D and N(*umerat?*) below. At times even Mommsen was forced to conjecture, not always with assurance. Fortunately, abbrs. sometimes (or often) appear filled out in other contexts, so that there is no question of their meaning (e.g., **64**, 11 f., *hoc monumentum heredem non sequitur*). There are also recurring formulas (generally legal in nature), such as B(*ene*) M(*erenti*) F(*ecit*), H(*uic*) M(*onumento*) D(*olus*) M(*alus*) A(*besto*), or the formidable Q(*uid*) D(*e*) E(*a*) R(*e*) P(*laceret*), D(*e*) E(*a*) R(*e*) I(*ta*) C(*ensuere*). (Cf. Mommsen, ed., *Notarum Laterculi*, in Keil *Gramm. Lat.* 4 [1864, repr. Hildesheim 1961] 265–352, for lists of abbrs., largely legal.)

Noteworthy are the variety of forms that an abbreviation may assume; e.g., AN/ANN, AVG/AVGVS (the month; the title seems regularly to be AVG), CAES/CAESAR, ID/IDIB, OCT/OCTOB, TRIB POT/TRIBVN POTEST (this phrase has especially many variations).

In the following list, as in Appendix I, "**66**, 12" means inscription **66**, line 12; "**31**: 3, 54, 57" means inscr. **31**, lines 3, 54, 57; "[**32**]" or "[ANI]" means an abbr. restored, therefore more or less uncertain; "**100** (2x)" means two examples in inscr. **100**; a comma separates line numbers, a semicolon separates inscr. numbers, and a

colon separates inscr. numbers from line numbers (in the same inscr.) whenever more than one line-number appears. So "**30**; **91**" means that the abbr. occurs in inscrs. **30** and **91**. References to **34** (*Res Gestae* of Augustus) include in parenthesis the chapter and, generally, by suprascript number, the section (as indicated in Gagé's ed. 3); those to **42** and **65** include in parenthesis col. 1 (or 2) and line number. Some abbreviations are so common that only the earliest and latest examples are here noted, with "passim"; e.g., F for *filius* or *filia*.

For other lists of Latin abbreviations, see *ILS* 3: 2, 752–797, the *CIL* volumes that have full indices, or any of the manuals (these give no references).

Our own abbreviations here include sing(ular), pl(ural), the names of the cases (nom., gen., etc.), as well as abbr(s)., acclam(ation), *ad loc(um)*, adv(erb), app(arently), arch(aic), conj(ecture), er(ased), esp(ecially), exc(ept), incl(uding), inscr(s)., Intro(duction), M(ommsen), prob(ably), *sc(ilicet)*, var(ious); "dat./abl." means dative and/or ablative.

Note: for the forms *adfectione*, *aede*, etc. (15 in all), which lack only the final *m* and, unlike *parentu*, are not indicated as abbreviations by a horizontal mark over the final vowel, see Appendix I, where they are listed among Unusual Forms in the belief that they are not abbrs. but serve to show that "final *m* was merely a mark of nasalization of the preceding vowel" (cf. Sturt. 151–153 §§173–175).

A	abesto	see H M D M A
A	accepit	see F P A D, etc.
A	accepto	see H A I R
A	aere	see A A A F F
A	ante	see A D
A	argento	see A A A F F
A	assium	**66**, 12
A	Auli	**31**: 3, 54, 57; **54**, 26; **55**, 1; **59**; **65**, 1; **72**, 12

A	Aulo	**19**, 2; [**34** (1²)]; **55**, 1; **59**; **66**, 24
A	Aulus	**31**, 3; **54**, 26; **72**, 12
A	auro	see A A A F F
A A A F F	aere argento auro flando feriundo	[**32**]; **49**, 4
ACT	actum	7
A D	ante diem	**7**; **15**; **19**, 2; **31**: [7], 25, 29, 51; 51
ADF	adfine/adfinibus	**53** passim
ADFECTIB	adfectibus	**52**
[AD]FU[E]R	adfuere	**31**, 1
ADIUT	adiutor	**72**, 22
AED	aedilicia	see AED POTEST
AED POTEST	aedilicia potestate	**55**, 3
AEL	Aelius	**64**
AER	aerario	**36**, 34
AEST	aestimati	**53** passim (sc. *fundi*, gen.)
AGOR	Agorianus?	**72**, 22 (see note *ad loc.*)
AMPL	amplius	**55**, 15
AN	annis (or -os)	**85**
[ANI]	Aniensi (sc. *tribu*)	**49**, 1
ANN	annis (or -os)	**52**; **61**; **98** (2x); **99**; **100** (2x)
ANN	annos	**30**; **91**
[AP]?	Appius	**12**
APR	Apriles	**66**, 15
AQUAR	aquarum	**74**
ARBITR	arbitratu	**55**, 16
ARF	arfuerunt, i.e. adf-	**8**, 2
ARIMIN	Ariminensis	**77**
ARMOR	armorum	**63** (side)
ARN	Arniensi (sc. *tribu*)	**72**: 16, 20
ATQ	atque	**36**: 47, [49]; **88**; **89**, 11
AUG	auguri	**30**
AUG	Augustali	**49**, 3
AUG	Augustalibus	**55**, 14
AUG	Augustae	**41** (erased); **72**: 2, 3 (er.); **74**
AUG	Augustas	**69**, 25; **72** (6x); **76**
AUG	Augusti	**36–84** passim
AUG	Augusto	**34–88** passim
AUG	Augustum	**46** (3x)
AUG	Augustus	**29**, c; **43**; **46** (3x); **49**, 37
AUGG	Augustis (duobus)	**72**, 1
AUGG	Augustorum (duorum)	**69**, 6; **72**, 2
AUGUS	Augustas	**61**
AUGUST	Augustalis (or Augusti)	**31**, 48
AUGUSTAL	Augustali	**68**, 3

AUGUSTAL	Augustalium	**68**, 14
AUR	Aurelio	**88**; **89**, 2
AVIT	avitum	**55**, 10
B	bene?	see B M M C
B̶	beneficiario	see B̶ PR
BB	bonorum (duorum)	see BB VV
BB VV	bonorum virorum (duorum)	**78**, 20
BEATISSIMOR	beatissimorum	**83**
BEN	bene	see BEN MER
BEN MER	bene merenti	**61**
B M M C	bene merenti memoriae causa?	**64**
B̶ PR	beneficiario praefecti	**72**, 27
BRIT	Britanniae	**74**
BRIT	Britannicus	**29**, c
C	causa?	see B M M C
C	censuere (-runt)	see Q D E R, etc., & Q F P, etc.
C	centesimo?	see F P A D, etc.
C	centum	**8**: 6, 9, 18; **68**, 14
C	clarissima	see C F
C	clarissimi	see V C and V̄C̄
C	clarissimo	see C V
C	clarissimus	see V C
C	conscripti	see P C
C	consulto	see S C
C	consuluerunt	see S C
C̄	cuncti	see Q F P, etc.
C̄	centenario	**74**
C̄C̄	ducenario	**74**
C̄C̄C̄	trecenario	**74**
CAES	Caesar	**29**, c
CAES	Caesare	[53]; **63**
CAES	Caesari	**73** (2x); **77**; **82**
CAE[S]	Caesaris	**36**, 39
CAES	Caesaris	[**36**, 57]; **77**
CAESAR	Caesare	**37** (3x)
CAESAR	Caesaris	**36**, 45
CAESAR	Caesarum	**36** (5–9x)
CAESARIB	Caesaribus	**36**, 5
CAPT	capta (est)	**11**
CASTROR	castrorum	**72**, 2
CENS	censor	**29**, b
CENTUR	centuria	**36**, 43
[CENTUR]	centuriae	**36**, 39

CENTUR	centuriarum	**36**, **41**
CENTUR	centurias	**36**: 6, [13], 15, [24], [38]
CENTURIAR	centuriarum	**36**: [46], 47
CEPONIAN	Ceponianum	**55**, 8
C F	clarissima femina	**74**
CILIC	Cilicia (abl.)	**72**, 13
CL	Claudius	**69**: 12, 27
CLA	Claudia (sc. *tribu*)	**26** (east); **52**
CLAUD	Claudii (gen.)	**49**, 6
CLAUDI	Claudius	**8**, 2
COG	cognitionum	**84**
COLL	collegi	**66**, 12; **78**, 3
COLLEG	collegi	**66**, 11
COM	comiti	see next entry
COM SACRAR LARG	comiti sacrarum largitionum	**96**
COMMENT	commentariis	**61**
CONES (*sic*)	consulibus	**79**
CONIUGIB	coniugibus	**47**; **49**, 11
CONS	consulatum	**98**
CONS	consule	**99**; **100**
CONS	consulibus	**79**
CONSS	consulibus (duobus)	**85**; **91**
CONST	constabit?	**76**
COPTIT	Coptitae	**51**
COR	Cornelia (sc. *tribu*)	**41**
COS	consul (sing./pl. any case)	**8**–[**89**], passim
COSS	consulibus (duobus)	**87**
CRUST	crustulum	**55**: 13, 14
CRUSTUL	crustuli	**55**, 12
CUIUS[CUMQ]	cuiuscumque	**36**, 27
[CUIUSQ]	cuiusque	**36**, 42
CUR	curator	**18**
CUR	curatoribus	**66**: 11, 12 (2x)
CURANTIB	curantibus	**63** (side)
CURAT	curatori	**59**
CURATORIB	curatoribus	**66**, 24
CUR VIAR	curator viarum	**18**
CUST	custos	**63** (side)
C V	clarissimo viro	**72**, 4; **74**
D	de	see Q D E R, etc., & Q F P, etc.
D	Decimo	**34** (16^2); **37**
D	Decimus	**13**
D	decreto	**40**; **59**

D	decurionum	**40**; **59**
D	dedicavit? dedicaverunt?	see D D
D	dedit?	see D D
D	depositorum?	see LIBR I D
D	Deum (i.e., Deorum)	see M D M [I]
D	devotus	see D N MQUE
D	dicundo	**54**, 5
D	die	see F P A D, etc.
D	diebus (or dies)	**52**; **85**; **99**
D	diem	see A D
D	dolo	see D M
D	dolus	see H M D M A
D	domina	see D N
D	domini	see D N
D	domino	see D N
D	dono (or -um), or dedit?	see D D
DAT	datae (or -tum? -ta?)	**76**, 13 (see *Album* 3.58, note *ad loc.*)
DAT	datus (or -tum? -ta?)	**76**, 8 (ditto)
D D	decreto decurionum	**40**; **59**
D D	dono (or -um) dedit, or dedit dedicavit	**22**; **47**
D D	dono (or -um) dederunt (or dederunt, dedicaverunt)	**47**
DD NN FFLL	domini nostri Flavii (duo)	**97**
DEC	Decembres	**15**; **72**: 19, 20, 21
DEC	decurionum	**17**
DECR	decreto	**17**
DECURIONIB	decurionibus	**55**, 13
DEDIC	dedicat-	**71**
DEDIC (or DEDICAT?)	dedicata	**68** (side) (see *Album* 2.141 f., *ad loc.*)
DEOR	deorum	**36**: 55, 58
DEP	deposita (est)	**91**
DEP	depositus (est)	**99**
DESIG	designato	**30**
DESIG	designatus	**29**, b
DIC	dicundo	**55**, 4
DIS MANIB	Dis Manibus	**65**, 1
D M	Dis Manibus	**62**, 1; **64**
D M	dolo malo	**19**, 12
D N	domina nostra	**83**
D N	domini nostri	**84**
D N	domino nostro	**86**; **88**; [**89**]
D N MQUE	devotus numini maiestatique	**86**
DP	deposita	**100**

DUCT	ductu	**11**
DUOVIR	duoviri	**17**
E	ea	see Q D E R, etc, & Q F P, etc.
[E]	est	see Q S S E
E	est?	see U V E
EMINISTRATION	eministrationem	**55**, 19
EOR	eorum	**36**, 56
EQ	eques	**36**, 33
EQ	equites	**36**: 10, 17, 24, 31
EQ	equitum	**56; 63**
EQ	Equitius?	**85** (see note *ad loc.*)
ESQ	Esquilina (sc. *tribu*)	**36**: 23, 33
F	faciundis	see S F
[F]	facta	**31**, 5
F	factus	see M F
F	fecerunt	**54**, 8
F	felici	see P F
F	femina	see C F
F	feriundo	see A A A F F
F	fidelis	see P F
F	fieri	see Q D E R, etc., & Q F P, etc.
F	filius or filia (sing., var. cases)	**5** (cover)–**72**, passim
F	filius ("junior")	**54**, 27
F	flando	see A A A F F
F	frumentum	see F P A D, etc.
FAB	Fabia (sc. *tribu*)	**72** (6x)
FABR	fabrum (gen. pl.)	**35** (earlier inscr.); **55**, 5; **78**, 3
FA[C]	faciundis	**32**
FAC	faciendum (or -iundum)	**17**
FACT	facti	**72**, 7
FACTION	factionis	**37**
FAVORABIL	favorabile	**55**, 17
FEB	Februarias	**85**
FEB	Februariis	**72**: 24, 25
FEBR	Februarias	**7; 61**
FEC	fecerunt	**52**
FECERUN	fecerunt	**85** (but prob. not an abbr.)
FFLL	Flavii (duo)	see DD NN FFLL
FIL	filio	**73** (2x)
FIL	filius	**72** (11x)
FL	Flavi (gen.)	**66**, 2; [**93**]; **97**, 1
FL	Flavio (dat./abl.)	**82; 86; 88; 91** (2x); **93; 97; 100**
FL	Flavius	**84**

FLORENTISSIMOR	florentissimorum	**83**
F P A D X T CXLIV K C	frumentum publicum accepit die decima (or -o), tabula CXLIV, kapite centesimo (partly uncertain)	**72**
FRATR	fratribus	**36**, 5
FREQUENTIB	frequentibus	**89**, 16
FRUMENT	frumento	**72**, 6
FRUMENTAR	frumentarius	**20**
FUND	Fundani (gen.)	**16**
FUND	fundi (app. gen.)	**53** passim
FURF	Furfensis	**19**, 15
FURFENS	Furfensis	**19**, 9
G	Gaius (all cases exc. voc.)	**6–84** passim
GERM	Germanico	**57**
GERMAN	Germaniae	**59**
GERMANIC	Germanicus	**27**
GN	Gnaei	**5** (cover); **13**; **22**
GN	Gnaeo (abl.)	**13**; **20**; **34** (6¹, 16¹·²)
GN	Gnaeus	**13**; **15** (2x); **34** (18); **36**: 10, 17, 41
H	hac	**36**: 17, [44], 46, 49
H	hoc (abl.)	see H M D M A
H	homines	**55**, 15
H	honore	see H A I R
H	hora (abl.)	**25**, 153
HADR	Hadrumetina	**72**, 18
H A I R	honore accepto impensam remisit	**55**, 8
HAST	hastiliarius	**63** (side)
HEMIN	hemina	**55**, 12
HEREDIB	heredibus	**62**, 4
H M D M A	hoc monumento dolus malus abesto	**64**
HOMINIB	hominibus	**66**, 8
[I]	Idaeae	see M D M [I]
I	impensam	see H A I R
I	infra	see Q I S S
I	ita	see Q D E R, etc., & Q F P, etc.
I	instrumentorum?	see LIBR I D
I	iudicandis	**56**
I	iure (arch. dat.)	**54**, 5
IAN	Ianuarias	**66**, 12; **72**, 22; **91**
IANUAR	Ianuarias	**63**

ID	Idibus	**72**: 18, 25
ID	Idus	**55**, 11; **66**: 9, 14, 15, 23; **72** (4x); **95**
I D	iure dicundo	**54**, 5
IDIB	Idibus	**68**, 11; **71**
IMAG	imaginis (or -num?)	**55**, 16
IMM	immunibus	**66**: 10, 12 (2x)
IMP	Imperator (title) or imperator (acclam.) (sing., var. cases)	**25**, 150–88 passim
IMP	imperatoris (nostri) ("emperor")	**63**
IMPEND	impendat	**55**, 16
IMPP	Imperatoribus (duobus)	**72**, 1
INCOL	incolis	**55**, 12
INCREMENT	incrementis (so Mommsen)	**55**, 14
INFELICISSIM	infelicissimi	**52**
INFERIOR	Inferioris	**59**
INL	inlustri	**96**; **97**, 2
ITAQ	itaque	**36**, 48
IUDICIOR	iudiciorum	**36**, 8
IUL	Iulia	**72**: 12, 14, 24
IUL	Iulio	**86**
IUN	Iunias	**72**, 9
IUN	Iunius	**87**
K	Kalendas	**7–72** passim
K	Kalendis	**72**, 24
K	kapite?	see F P A D, etc.
KAL	Kalendarum	**98**
KAL	Kalendas	**68** (side); **69**, 38; **76**; **87**; **89** (side); **91**; **100**
KAL	Kalendis	**72**, 6; **78**, 2
KARTH	Karthagine	**72**: 14, 16, 20
L	lege	**36**, 37
L	liberta	**37**
L	libertae	**65**, 2
L	liberti	**26** (east); **66**, 3
L	libertus	**13**, 7–12 (6x); **20**
L	Lucius (var. cases)	[**5**, cover]–**88** passim
LARG	largitionum	see COM SACRAR LARG
LEG	legato	**49**: 6, 8; **56** (2x); **59** (3x); **74**
LEG	legatus	**32**
LEG	legionis	**49**, 5; **56** (2x); **59**; **74**
LEGAT	legato	**49**: 5, 6, 8; **59**
LEGION	legionis	**59**
LIB	liberti	**66**, 18

LIB	libertis	**64**
LIB	liberto	**61**; **66**, 24; **69**, 29
LIB	libertum	**69**, 6
LIB	libertus	**61**; **64**; **66**: 17, 20; **69**, 49; **71** (18x); **72** (5x) (see also VER LIB)
LIBER	liberis	**64**
LIBR I D	librario instrumentorum(?) depositorum(?)	**72**, 27 (M.'s conj.)
LOCAR	locarunt (i.e., locaverunt)	**17**
M	Magnae	see M D M [I]
M	maior?	**19**, 15 (see *CIL* 1²: 2.756, note)
M	malo	**19**, 12
M	malus	see H M D M A
M	Marcus (var. cases)	**6–73** passim
M	Matri	see M D M [I]
M	memoriae?	see B M M C
M	menses	**91**
M	mensibus (or -ses)	**52**; **85**; **98**; **99**; **100**
M	merenti?	see B M M C
M	miles	see M F
M	milia	**66**: 5, 18, 22
M̄	milia	**68**: 7, 8, 10, 15
M	milibus	**55**, 10 (2x)
M	minus	see PL M
M	monumento	see H M D M A
Ɯ	Mani	[**32**]
Ɯ	Manius	**54**, 14
MACED	Macedonia	**72**, 19
MACED	Macedoniae	**59**
MAEC	Maecia (sc. *tribu*)	**72**, 11
MAG	magistri	**47**
MAI	Maias	**55**, 11; **66**, 15
MAMIAN	Mamianum	**55**, 9
MANIB	Manibus	see DIS MANIB
MART	Martias	**31**, 29; **51**; **66**: 9, 13, 14, 23
MAX	maximi	**41**
MAX	maximo	**40**; **88**
MAX	maximus	**29**, b; **43**
MAXIM	maximus	**29**, c; **44**
MAXIMOR	maximorum	**88**
M D M [I]	Matri Deum Magnae Idaeae	**80**
MEAR	mearum	**55**, 16
MEN	mensibus	**87**
MER	merenti	see BEN MER

M F	miles factus	**72** (16x)
MI?	minutis?	**68**, 11 (see note *ad loc.*)
MIL	militum	**59**
[MILIT]	militum	**32**
MILL	millia	**49**, 9
MINUCI	Minucius	**6**; **8**, 2
M N	milia nummum	(see each abbr.)
MOD	modiorum	**55**, 18
[MONUMENT?]	monumentum	**93**
MQUE	maiestatique	see D N MQUE
MULIERIB	mulieribus	**55**, 12
MUMMI	Mummius	**11**
MUNIC	municipes	**55**, 6
MUNICIPIB	municipibus	**55**, 12
MUNIFICENT	munificentiam	**55**, 6
$\overline{\text{N}}$	natali	**66**: 9, 11
[N]	nepos	**32**
N	nepoti	**30**
N	Nonas	**99**
N	Nonis	**8**, 1
N	Nostra	see D N
$\overline{\text{N}}$	nostrae	**66**: 6, 22
$\overline{\text{N}}$	nostram	**66**, 11
N	nostri	**66**: 9, 20; **69**, 50; **83**; **84**
$\overline{\text{N}}$	nostri	**63**; **78**, 20
$\overline{\text{N}}$	nostro	**66**, 23
$\overline{\text{N}}$	nostrum	**78**: 6, 12
N	numerat?	**53**: 16, 71 (M.'s conj.)
N	Numeri	**13**
N	Numerius	**13** (2x)
$\overline{\text{N}}$	numero	**66**: 5, 8
$\overline{\text{N}}$	numerum	see $\overline{\text{N}}$ $\overline{\text{N}}$
N	numini	see D N MQUE
N	nummi	**55**: 13, 15 (3x in all)
$\overline{\text{N}}$	nummi	**68**, 14
N	nummos	**55**, 16; **68**, 14
N	nummum (gen. pl.)	**55**, 10; **62**: 9, 10, 11
$\overline{\text{N}}$	nummum (gen. pl.)	**66**: 5, 18, 22; **68**: 7, 8, 10, 15
N[A]T	natus	**30**
NATAL	natali	**55**, 11
NEAP	Neapoli	**72**, 11
NN	nostri (duo)	see DD NN FFLL
$\overline{\text{N}}\overline{\text{N}}$	nostrorum (duorum)	**69**: 3, 6
$\overline{\text{N}}$ $\overline{\text{N}}$	numerum nostrum	**78**, 6

NON	Nonas	**20**; **63**; **66**: 11, 12, 14
NONGENTOR	nongentorum	**36**: 13, [15]
NOT	notario	**96**
NOV	Novembres	**54**, 3; **66**: 11, 14; **68** (side); **72**, 16 f. (2x)
NOV	Novembribus	**72**, 18
O	optimus	**76**
OCT	Octobres	**66**: 9, 13
OCT	Octobribus	**71**
OCTOB	Octobribus	**8**, 1
OMNIB	omnibus	**66**, 14
OPT	optione	**72**, 31
OPT	optioni	**72**, 28
ORN	ornatum	**55**, 15
OST	Ostiensi (or -ium)	**68**, 16
P	pace	**85**
P	pater	see P P
P	patre	see P P
P	patres	see P C
P	patri	see P P
P	patriae	**29**, b; **41**; **43**; **51**; **57**; **63**; **66**, 9; **72**, 2(?); **73**
P	patribus?	see P P
P	patris	see P P
P	pedes	**64** (2x)
P	piae	see P F
P	pio	see P F
P	placeret	see Q D E R, etc., & Q F P, etc.
P	pondo	**41**; **55**, 12
P	popli (i.e., populi)	see [P R]
P	populi	see P R
P	populo	see P R
P	populus	see S P Q R
P	posteris	see P S
P	Publi	**8**, 2; **13** (2x); **26**; **56**
P	publica (nom.)	**42** (1, 7); **55**, 16
P	publica (abl.)	see R P (1) & $\overline{\text{REP}}$
P	publicae	**42** (1: 24, 27); **68**, 16
P	publicum	see F P A D, etc.
P	Publio (dat.)	**72**, 27 (2x); **78**
P	Publio (abl.)	**34** (6¹, 10², 12²); **56**; **66**, 24; **68**, 1; **72**, 4; **78**, 1
P	Publius	**13** (3x); **31**, 1; **34** (18); **47**; **63** (sides) (16x); **64**; **66**: 17, 20

PAL	Palatina (sc. *tribu*)	**55**, 2
PARENT	parentes	**52** (2x)
PARENTŪ	parentum	**91**
PARTH	Parthicus	**29**, c
PATERN	Paterno	**79**
PATR	patre	**66**, 12
P C	patres conscripti	**42** (2, 30)
PECUN	pecunia	**47**
PED	pedes	**76**
PERMIS	permisit	**76**
PERPET	perpetuo (or -um, adv.)	**55**: 11, 16
P F	piae fidelis	**56** (3x); **59**
P F	pio felici	**82**; **88**
PIISSIM	piissimo	**52**
PL	placuit	**66**, 11
PL	plebis	**26**; **36**, 18
PL	plus	see PL M
PLEB	plebis	**56**; **59**
PL M	plus minus	**100**
POB	Poblilia (sc. *tribu*)	**26**
PONEND	ponendam	**55**, 7
PONT	pontifex	**43**
PONT	pontificis	**41**
PONTIF	pontifex	**29**, b; **31**: 43, 49; **44**
PONTIF	pontifici	**31**: 46, 50; **40**; **49**, 3; **55**, 5; **57**
[PO]NTIF	pontificis	**31**, 8
PONTIFIC	pontifici	**73**
PONTIFIC	pontificum	**61**
POP	populo	**53** passim
POSUER	posuerunt	**63**
POT	potestate	**41**; **43**; **57**
POTEST	potestate	**31**, 50; **40**; **55**, 3; **73** (2x)
PO[TEST]	potestatis	**31**, 47
POTESTAT	potestate	**29**, a; **51**
POTESTAT	potestatis	**29**, b
P P	pater patriae	**29**, b; **43**; **51**
P P	patre patriae	**63**
P P	patri patriae	**57**
P P	patribus patriae?	**72**, 2 (see note *ad loc.*)
P P	patris patriae	**41**; **66**, 9
PP	perpetuo	**66**, 10
[P R]	popli Romani	**48**
P R	populi Romani	**31**: 43, 49; **49**, 26
P R	populo Romano	**49**, 16

PR	praefecti	see B̶ PR
P̅R̅	praefecto	see P̅R̅ P̅R̅
P̅R̅	praefecto	72: 4, 9–25 (17x in all)
P̅R̅	praefecto	see S̶ PR
PR	praetor	26
PR	praetor	see PR URB
PR	praetore	see PRO PR
PR	praetorem	8: 4, 8, 17
PR	praetori	see PR URB
PR	praetoribus	36: 6, 18, 34
PR	praetorio	74 (see also P̅R̅ P̅R̅)
PR	praetoris	8, 21
PR	praetorum	36: [39], 48
PR	pridie	63; 66 (4x); 72, 9
PRAEE (for PRAEF)	praefecto	92
PRAEF	praefecto	55, 5; 56; 74; 94; 96
PRAEF	praefectus	35 (earlier inscr.); 41
PRAEFECTUR	praefecturam	49, 27
PRAEFF	praefectorum (duorum)	74; 84
PRAESENT	praesentibus	55, 11
PRAESENTIB	praesentibus	66, 15
PRAET	praetore	49, 8; 59
PRAET	praetori	59; 96
PRAET	praetorio (or -ii, as in 96)	92
PRI	pridie	61
PRID	pridie	20
PRIMIGEN	primigeniae	59
PRINCIP	principum	88
PRIVAT	privatae	74
PROB	probarunt (i.e., -averunt)	17
PROC	procuratori	74 (3x)
PROC	procuratoris	66, 2
[PRO COS?]	proconsul	32
PRO·COS	proconsuli (or pro consule?)	49, 8
PROCOS	proconsuli	73 (2x)
PRO·PR	pro praetore	56; 59 (2x)
PRO·PRAET	pro praetore	49, 8; 59
PROV	provinciae	74
PROVINC	provinciae	[32]; 59 (4x); 74
P̅R̅ P̅R̅	praefecto praetorio	72, 3
PR URB	praetor urbanus	32
PR URB	praetori urbano	49, 6
P S	posteris suis	52
PUB	publicum	36, 57
PUBL	publico	72, 6

PUBLICOR	publicorum	**36**, 8
PUER	pueris	**55**: 14, 17
Q	quae	see Q I S S & Q S S S
Q	quaestor	**32**
Q	quaestori	**49**, 4
Q	quaestoribus	**76**
—Q	-que	**17–94** passim (see also S P Q R)
Q	qui	see Q S S S (2)
Q	quid	see Q D E R, etc., & Q F P, etc.
Q	Quinti	**13** (2x); **23**; **31** (3x); [**45**]; **52**; **72** (3x)
Q	Quinto	**34** (1–5x); **52**; [**53**]; **77**
Q	Quintus	**8**: [1], 2–**72** (3x) passim
[Q]	quod	see Q S S E
Q D E R F P D E R I C	quid de ea re fieri placeret, de ea re ita censuere	**54**, 16
Q F P D E R I C C	quid fieri placeret, de ea re ita cuncti censuerunt	**78**, 19
Q I S S	quae infra scripta sunt	**49**, 31
Q̄Q̄	quinquennali	**66**: 11, 12, 24
QQ	quinquennalibus	**78**, 5
QQ (or Q̄Q̄)	quinquennalis	**66**: 14, 21, 22; **76**
QQ	quinquennalium	**78**, 20
Q̄Q̄ PP	quinquennali perpetuo	**66**, 10
[Q S S E]	quod supra scriptum est	**36**, 53
Q S S S	quae supra scripta sunt	**66**, 21
Q S S S	qui supra scripti sunt	**36**, 53
-QU	-que (at line end)	**7**
QUADR	quadriga (or -is)	**37** (2x) (see note *ad loc.*)
[QUAECUMQ]	quaecumque	**36**, 40
QUAEST	quaestori	**59**; **96**
QUAMQ	quamque	**36**, 24
QUANTUMCUMQ	quantumcumque	**65** (2, 17)
QUIB	quibus	**36**, 20; **97**
QUIBUSQ	quibusque	**55**, 14
QUINCT	Quinctiles	**20**
QUINQ	quinquennali	**55**, 4; **68**, 4
QUIQ CUMQ	quiquecumque (the first -que = "and")	**36**: 9, 53
QUISQ	quisque	**65** (2, 6)
QUOQ	quoque ("also")	**36**: 3, 5, [46]; **76** (2x)
QUOQ	quōque ("each")	**36**, 60
QUOQ	quoquoversus	**64**
QUOR	quorum	**55**, 10

R	re	see Q D E R, etc., Q F P, etc., & R P
R	regionis	**85**
R	rei	see R P
R	remisit	see H A I R
R	revocatus	**37** (4x)
R	rogatione	**36**: 17, [44], 46, 49
R	Romani	**31**: 43, 49; [48]
R	Romano	see P R
R	Romanorum	**56**
R	Romanus	see S P Q R
REDDID	reddidit	**55**, 10
REDEM	redemit	**55**, 9
REFERENTIB	referentibus	**78**, 5
R̄E̅P̅	republica	**96**
RESTITUER	restituerunt	**27**
REVOC	revocatus	**37**
ROM	Roma	**72**: 9, 10
ROM	Romani	**34** (heading)
R P	re publica	**55**, 9
R P	rei publicae	**55**, 10
R SEC	regionis secundae	**85**
S	sacris	see S F
S	scripta	see Q I S S, Q S S S, & S S
S	scriptae	see S S S
S	scriptam	see S S
S	scripti	see Q S S S, S S, & S S S
S	scriptis	see S S
S	scripto	see S S
S	scriptum	see Q S S E & S S
S	scriptus	see S S
S	secundas	**37** (4x)
S	semis (var. cases)	passim (in symbol for sestertii)
S	senatum	see S C
S	senatus (nom.)	see S P Q R
S	senatus (gen.)	see S C
S̵	sextariorum	**66**: 12 (5x)
S	Spurius	**8**, 1
S	stlitibus	**56**
S	suis	see P S
S	summae	**68**, 11
S	sunt	see Q I S S, Q S S S, & S S S
S	supra	see Q S S E, Q S S S, S S, & S S S

SAC	sacris	**32**
SACRAR	sacrarum	see COM SACRAR LARG
SALUT	salutem	**62**, 4
SARMATAR	Sarmatarum	**49**, 13
SATURNIN	Saturnino	**91**
SC	scribendo	**8**, 2
S C	senatum consuluerunt	**54**, 5
S C	senatus consulto	**27**; **34** ([22²], 35¹); **46**, 36; **55**: 4, 8; **68**, 5
[SCRIB]	scribendo	**31**, 1
SCRIB	scribis	**76**, 10
SEC	secundae	**85**
SEC	secundas	**37** (9x)
SENAT	senatus (nom.)	**55**, 7
SEP	Septembres	**99**
SEPT	Septembres	**69** (3x); **87**
SEPTE	septem	**97** (prob. not an abbr.)
SER	Servio	**37**
SERG	Sergia (sc. *tribu*)	**56**; **59**
SEX	Sexti	**15** (2x); **19**, 1; **20**; **31**, 4; **41**; **68**, 9
SEX	Sexto	**34** (8⁴, 2x); **37** (2x); **51**; **74**
[SEX]	Sexto	**31**, 52
SEX	Sextus	**20**; **31**, 4
SEXAG	sexagenario	**84**
S F	sacris faciundis	**25** (3–5x); **89**, 7
SIB	sibi	**52**
SIG	signifer	**63**, side (2x)
SIGN	signifer	**63**, side
SIGNU	signum	**11** (abbr.? at line end)
SILVAN	Silvano	**63**
SING (written SNG)	singularium	**63**
SING (once SINC)	singulis	**66**: 11, 12 (8x in all)
SING	singulos	**55**, 15
SPARSION	sparsionem	**55**, 18
SPORTUL	sportula	**55**, 13
S P Q R	Senatus Populusque Romanus	**73**; **82**; **88**; **94**
S̅ PR	sub praefecto (dat.)	**72**, 4
S̶S̶	sestertium (gen. pl.)	**76**
S S	supra scripta (and other forms)	**66** (14x); **68**, 17
S S S	summae supra scriptae	**68**, 11
S S S	supra scripti sunt	**66**, 20
STATIL (written STATIIL)	Statilio	**37**
SUC	Succusana (sc. *tribu*)	**36**: 23, [32]
SUM	summa	**37**

SUM	summarum	37
SUPERNAT	Supernatis	77
T	tabula?	see F P A D, etc.
T	tertias	37 (2x)
T	Titi	31: 54, 57; 72: 9, 11, 19
T	Tito	31, 54; 63; 70
T	Titum	54: 8, 18
T	Titus	27; 31: 42, [48], [57]; 54, 7; 63 (side); 72: 9, 11, 19
TER	tertias	37 (12x)
TERT	tertium (or -io)	20 (see note *ad loc.*)
TESS	tesserario	72, 29
THARS	Tharso	72, 13
THRAC	Thraciae	59
TI	Tiberius (var. cases)	13–49, 4, passim
TI	Tiberi (voc.)	42 (2, 20)
TIB	Tiberio	34 (8⁴)
TITUL	titulum	64
TR	tribunis	36, 18
T̄R̄	tribuno	72, 5
TR	tribunus	26
TRANSDANUVIANOR	Transdanuvianorum	49, 10
TRIB	tribunicia	40; 41; 43; 57
TRIB	tribuno	56 (2x); 59 (2x); 96
[TRIB]	tribunus	32
TRIB	tribu	36, 28
TRIB	tribus (acc. pl.)	36: [25], 27 (2x)
TRIB	tribuum	36, 23
TRIB POT (or POTEST)	tribunicia potestate	40; 41; 43; 57
TRIBUN	tribunicia (potest.)	31, 50
TRIBUNIC	tribunicia (potest. or potestat.)	29, a; 51; 73 (2x)
TRICLIN	triclinia	55, 13
TRICLIN	triclinio	55, 15
TRICLINIARCH	tricliniarchae	61
TUBICE	tubicen	63 (side)
TULER	tulerunt	36: 36, 41, 50
U	unā?	see U V E
ULP	Ulpia	72, 18
[UNUMQUEMQ]	unumquemque	36: 43, 45
URB	urbano	see PR URB
URB	urbanus	see PR URB
UTIN	Ut(h)ina	72, 12
U V E	unā(?) vescendum(?) est(?)	55, 14 (see note *ad loc.*)
V	verba	[31, 5]; 54, 8

V	vescendum?	see U V E
V	vir	see C V, V C, V O
VALERI	Valerius	**8**, 2
VALG	Valgus	**17**
VATIC	Vaticano	**62**, 7
V C	vir clarissimus	**80**; **84**; **86**; **87**
V C	viri clarissimi	**93**
V̄C̄	viri clarissimi	**96**
VC	viro clarissimo	**84**; **88**; **89**, 2; **90**; **92**; **93**; **94**; **97**, 2; **100**
VER	verna	**71** (see also next entry)
VER LIB	verna libertus	**71** (5x)
VETURI	Veturium	**78**, 32
VEX	vexillario	**72**, 28
VEXIL	vexillario	**72**, 30
VIAR	viarum	**18**
VIC	vicit	**37** (6x)
VIDENT	videntur	**52**
VIR	viri, -is, -o, -um (gen. pl.)	see Ī̄I VIR, ĪII VIR, etc., at end
VIRGAR	virgarum	**64**
VIX	vixit	**52**
V O	vir optimus	**76**
VV	virorum (duorum)	see BB VV
Ɔ	Gaiae	**37**
ĪI·VIR	duoviri (or duum-)	**31**: 18, 55
ĪII·VIR	triumviro	**49**, 4; **59**
ĪIII·VIR	quattuorviri (nom.)	**54**, 5
ĪIII·VIR	quattuorviro	**55**: 3, 4 (3x in all)
ĪIII·VIR	quattuorvirum (gen. pl.)	**55**, 16
VI·VIR	se(x)viris	**55**, 14
V̄II·VIR	septemvir	**26**
XV·VIR	quindecimviri	**25**, 150
⟩	centuriae	**72**: 6, 28–31 (4x in all)
⟩	centurione	**72**, 5
⟩	centurionis	**72**: 28, 31
H̶S̶	sestertii (var. cases)	**34** (15¹, 17², 21²: 5x); **55** (6x); **68**: 7, 8, 10, 14, 15
I̶S̶	sestertii (var. cases)	**62**: 9, 10, 11 (see also S̶S̶)

APPENDIX III

ROMAN DATING AND THE ROMAN CALENDAR

Bibliography: E. J. Bickerman, *Chronology of the Ancient World*, ed. 2 (London/Ithaca 1980); W. G. Hale and C. D. Buck, *A Latin Grammar* (1903), repr. 1966 University, Alabama); Agnes Kirsopp Michels, *The Calendar of the Roman Republic* (Princeton 1967); *The Oxford Dictionary of the Christian Church*[2], ed. F. L. Cross and E. A. Livingstone (London, etc., 1974); Alan E. Samuel, *Greek and Roman Chronology . . .* (Munich 1972 *Handb. der Altertumsw.* 1: 7); W. Warde Fowler, *The Roman Festivals of the Period of the Republic . . .* (London 1908). For the rest, see Abbreviations.

1. For their own history the Romans had two chief systems of dating. One was by year of the city of Rome (*anno urbis con-* ditae or *ab urbe condita*, both abbreviated A.U.C.—Cicero uses *post Romam conditam*, *De re publ.* 1.16.25), the other by the yearly consuls (or others with consular power). The Capitoline *Fasti Consulares* and *Fasti Triumphales*, which were inscribed[1] on the Arch of Augustus in the Roman Forum[2] and are now, in very fragmentary form, in the Palazzo dei Conservatori, Rome,[3] date the yearly consuls and the *triumphatores* by year of the city. The earliest extant A.U.C. designation of the consuls in the *Fasti Cons.* begins with the numeral CCXC in the left margin (Degrassi, *FTC* 24 f.), which, according to conventional ("Varronian") dating,[4] corresponds to 463 B.C. The earliest similar designation in the tri-

1. In 30 B.C. (except for later additions to A.D. 13), Degrassi thought; in 18/17 B.C., L. R. Taylor; for bibl. see Nash 1.92 *s.v.* Arcus Augusti, plus *AJA* 55 (1951) 279 f., *Album* 1.24 and 27, on the dating of nos. 9 and 11. Degrassi's main article is now in *Scritti vari* 1.239–281.

2. Either first on the Actium Arch, then transferred by moving the inscribed blocks to the triple Parthian Arch, which replaced the earlier arch, as Degrassi thought, or directly on the later arch, as Taylor thought.

3. Photos in Degrassi, op. cit., between pp. 232 f. (esp. figs. 1, 8) and between 241 f. (esp. figs. 10 f.), and in Nash 1.100 f., nos. 102 f.

4. Among various Greek and Roman opinions on when the city was "founded," traditionally on April 21 (Cic. *Brut.* 18.72: *Est enim inter scriptores de numero annorum* [of Rome] *controversia*; for Apr. 21, the Parilia, Censorinus, loc. cit. below), the one credited to Cicero's friend Atticus and to Varro, i.e., Olympiad 6.3 (= 754/3 B.C., probably 753: H. J. Rose, loc. cit below n. 6), is the one generally adopted by modern convention. The evidence for Atticus is certain, for Varro practically certain. For Atticus, see Solinus 1.27 (ed. Mommsen, ed. 2, p. 7, lines 5–10): Atticus and Cicero placed the foundation of Rome "in the third year of the 6th Olympiad" (cf. Cic. *Orator* 34.120, *Ad Att.* 12.23.2; Nepos

23.13.1, 25.18.1 f.). For Varro (whose name is generally used for the 753 date) the evidence is in Censorinus, *De die natali* 21.6. Here, after crediting Varro with clearing the "fog" surrounding the length of time from the 1st Olympiad "to us," he says: *Secundum quam rationem, nisi fallor, hic annus, cuius velut index et titulus quidam est u(rbis) c(onditae) Pii et Pontiani consulatus, ab olympiade prima millensimus est et quartus decimus, ex diebus dumtaxat aestivis, quibus agon Olympicus celebratur; a Roma autem condita nongentensimus nonagensimus primus, et quidem ex Parilibus, unde urbis anni numerantur. . . .* I.e., "according to this (Varro's) figuring," the year of the consulship of (Fulvius) Pius and (Pontius Proculus) Pontianus "is the 1014th from the 1st Olympiad," and "from the founding of Rome the 991st." Subtracting 776 (1st yr. of the 1st Olympiad) from 1014 gives 238 (the date, A.D., of P. and P.'s consulship), while adding 753 (traditional date of the founding of Rome) to 238 gives 991. The date 753 B.C., therefore, is confirmed as undoubtedly Varro's. There is no need to emend the Solinus passage to substitute *M. Terentio* (i.e., Varro) for *M. Tullio* (i.e., Cicero) in the sentence *Romam . . . placet conditam . . . Pomponio Attico et M. Tullio Olympiadis sextae anno tertio.* For an earlier view of Cicero's, which had favored Olympiad 7.2 (= 751/0 B.C.), see *De Re Publ.* 2.10.18.

umphal list ends the first line of the entry for 588 B.C. with the numeral CLXV (ibid., 64 f.). *ILS* 3: 1, 347 f., lists over thirty inscriptions in which the year of the city of Rome is indicated, including one *millesimus urbis annus* (*ILS* 4095 = *CIL* 6.488).[5] Other cities and larger units in the Roman Empire also kept records of their own traditional ages (*ILS* 3: 1, 348 f.; for the Greek world, Woodhead 57 f.). Sometimes a date is given by naming a particular year of some emperor, such as *anno xi Neronis imp(eratoris) n(ostri)* (A.D. 64/5), *ILS* 8759 a (= *CIL* 3.30). Or dates may be given by indiction numbers, which, beginning under Diocletian, indicate a year within a fiscal period (*indictio*) of fifteen years, in connection with the compulsory delivery of food supplies to the government; for dating, the indiction number is generally used along with some other dating system, as *s(u)b Idus Maias, sex(to anno) p(ost) c(onsulatum) Basilii iun(ioris), v.c., ind(ictione) decima* (A.D. 547—*ILS* 2806 = *CIL* 11.1693), i.e, the tenth year of some fiscal period. Cf. Bickerman 78 f., A. H. M. Jones in *OCD* 544 *s.v.* indictio.

2. But far commoner than dating by "eras"[6] is the naming of the consuls (or others having consular authority) of the year. Their names are listed in the Capitoline Fasti (undoubtedly of Augustan origin—see n. 1) down to A.D. 13; thereafter there seems to have been no official city-of-Rome compilation or publication like that engraved on the Arch of Augustus; but there are remains of local lists (e.g., from Ostia), much other inscriptional testimony, besides the evidence of the historians (e.g., Tacitus) and other writers, including the Chronographer of A.D. 354 (*Oxf. Dict. Christ. Church* 284 *s.v.*) and the compiler of the Fasti Hydatiani (and its later Greek version, the Chronicon Paschale), also of the 4th cent. (Degrassi, *FCT* p. 346), who list the consuls down to their own times. From all this, Degrassi in 1952[7] followed his earlier 2-vol. *Fasti Cons.* (509 B.C.–A.D. 13) *et Triumph.* (753–19 B.C.) with *I fasti consolari dell'Impero romano* (Rome) for 30 B.C. to A.D. 613; this has received some additions and corrections as new inscriptions or new views appear. This list of consuls, going from 753 B.C. to A.D. 613—a period of 1,366 years—must be one of the longest continuous lists of yearly public officials that we have in the West, despite some gaps and

---

5. "After the Olympiads, the era most frequently met with in ancient history is that of the foundation of Rome. . . . There are various opinions respecting the year" of this. Five such, ranging from Fabius Pictor to Varro, are then listed in the article "Chronology" in *Encycl. Brit.*[11] 6 (New York 1910) 313 col. 1.

6. The introduction of the Christian era, indicated by our "B.C." ("before Christ") and "A.D." (*anno Domini*, "in the year of the Lord," i.e. Christ), is credited to Dionysius Exiguus, a friend of Cassiodorus (5th/6th cent. Roman politician, writer, and monk, who writes warmly of him in his *Institutiones*, 23.2–4). D. E. dates his *Epistola Prima de ratione Paschae* (about figuring the Easter cycle) as *scripta anno Christi 525, Probo consule, indictione 3*, and says, . . . *noluimus circulis nostris memoriam impii et persecutoris innectere* ("to connect with our cycle the memory of a wicked persecutor," i.e., Diocletian); *sed magis elegimus ab Incarnatione Domini nostri Jesu Christi annorum tempora praenotare* ("to note the succession of years") . . . (J. P. Migne, ed., *Patrologia Latina*, 67 [Paris 1865] cols. 19 *init.*, 20 *init.*). (Flavius) Probus (Iun.) in fact was consul in the

West in 525. This shows that Dionysius must have accepted A.U.C. 753 as the birth year of Christ, wrongly. This date is in error by several years; the birth occurred not later than 4 B.C. (before the death of Herod the Great that year [Matthew 2.1]—he had been appointed King of the Jews by the Romans and ruled from 37 B.C.) and seems generally dated by historians between 8 and 4 B.C. Cf. *Oxf. Dict. Christ. Church* 220 f., 407, *s.vv.* Calendar, Dion. Exiguus. But see now John Thorley, "When Was Jesus Born?" *Greece & Rome*, 2nd ser., vol. 28: 1 (April 1981), 81–89, who argues persuasively that Jesus was born in 2 B.C. H. J Rose, *OCD* 1076, *s.v.* Time-Reckoning, notes that "the practice of reckoning early dates backwards from" the Christian era "is quite recent and a little complicated by the fact that astronomers do and historians generally do not insert a year 0 between 1 B.C. and A.D. 1."

7. Following similar compilations by W. Liebenam, *Fasti cons. imperii Romani von 30 v. Chr. bis 565 n. Chr.* . . . (Bonn 1909), and D. Vaglieri, in *Diz. epigr.* 2: 2 (1910) 869–1181 *s.v.* Consules (from 509 B.C. to A.D. 613).

questions in the list of consuls suffect (see Degrassi, *I fasti cons.* [1952] passim to A.D. 307, the items below the line).

Degrassi stopped at A.D. 613 probably because D. Vaglieri had done so in his 1910 article Consules in De Rugg. 2: 2; Vaglieri had done so because Heraclius novus Constantinus (613–641) was the last emperor to hold the consulship. But, though named co-emperor with his father, Heraclius, in 613, when he was only a baby, he was not consul till 632. Vaglieri apparently mixed up these two dates (an error of 20 years is evident on p. 1181 of his art., cf. p. 1114). Or, alternatively, Degrassi followed the traditional view that becoming emperor or co-emperor carried with it automatically the title of consul, in which case the junior Heraclius would have become consul in 613. (Franco Sartori of Padua, assisted by Maria Capozza and M. Silvia Bassignano, by letter of Nov. 15, 1980, to Werner Eck of Cologne, by whose courtesy a copy is at hand.)

3. Our word "calendar" and our names for the months and their sequence are of Roman origin. We have also inherited from the Romans our week and its named days and their sequence, though these are agreed to be of Eastern origin (the historian Dio says Egyptian—see below). But the Romans had also, apparently from the earliest times, an eight-day "week," called *nundinus* as marking every ninth day as market day, *nundinae*. There is evidence even of a seven-day week, attested in several of the extant Roman calendars as early as Augustus and later named *hebdomas* by the 2nd-cent. Gellius. (It may be referred to, already, by Cato the Elder, less clearly by Varro. Gellius's *hebdomas* may of course refer to either the Romans' own seven-day week or the borrowed Eastern one.) We also find in the Christian inscrip-

tions the Latin equivalent of our "first of August," *die prima mensis Augusti* (see below).

"Calendar" is from Latin *kal-/calendarium*, this in turn from *Kal-/Calendae*, the name of the first day of every month, one of three fixed points in the Roman month. *Kalendarium* (the earlier and commoner spelling, going back to the early use of K, rather than C or Q, before A: Pfister 30–32, on the gutturals) in ancient Latin meant "a book in which monthly interest on loans was recorded [interest payments were due on the first of the month], an account-book, ledger" (*OLD* 989, *s.v.*), but it acquired the modern meaning of "calendar" in medieval church-Latin, attested by the 10th cent.;[8] this meaning, passed on to English, is attested ca. 1205 (the Julian calendar) and ca. 1340 (in modern tabular form).[9]

4. Our names of the months are obviously of Latin origin (in Latin the names are adjectives modifying *mensis*, written or, often, understood), but it is less obvious that the first month of the year was originally March, not January. Varro, *L.L.* 6.33, has the "ancients" begin the year with March, Ovid, *Fasti* 1.39, says, *Martis erat primus mensis*, and Festus in his epitome of the Augustan Verrius Flaccus's *De verborum significatu* (p. 136, 6–10, L.) says, "Martius mensis initium anni fuit et in Latio, et post Romam conditam, quod ea gens erat bellicosissima; cuius rei testimonium est, quod posteriores menses, qui annum finiunt, a numero appellati, ultimum habent Decembrem."[10] Caesar and Augustus were honored by having the names *Quin(c)tilis* and *Sextilis* (i.e., the 5th and 6th months) changed to *Iulius* and *Augustus*, the former by a law proposed by Mark Antony in 44 B.C., apparently before Caesar's death (Macrob. *Sat.* 1.12.34,

---

8. O. Bloch and W. von Wartburg, *Dict. étymol. de la langue française*[5] (Paris 1968) 100 *s.v.* calendrier (formerly spelled "calendier").

9. *The Oxford Engl. Dict.* 2 (Oxford 1933 and repr.), 29 *s.v.* Calendar, 1–2.

10. The ten-month year is referred to also by Plutarch, Gellius, Solinus, Censorinus, Servius, Macrobius, and Lydus; for the details, see Michels 121 f.

quod hoc mense . . . Iulius procreatus sit; for other reff., see Degrassi, *FANI* 321), the latter by Augustus himself in 8 B.C. (Suet. *Aug.* 31.2; for other reff., Degrassi, op. cit. 321 f.) in connection with his restoration of the Julian calendar (see below) to its "pristine" system, following confusion and disorder caused by neglect (presumably on the part of the pontiffs); the month is August, not his birth-month, September, because in August he had won his "first consulship" and his "outstanding victories," notably the capture of Alexandria, 30 B.C.

5. The month names from January to June—*Ianuarius, Februarius, Martius, Aprilis, Maius, Iunius* (*sc. mensis*)—seem related to the character of each month, but the rest (including the older *Quin(c)tilis* and *Sextilis*) are obviously derivatives of the ordinal adjectives for fifth and sixth, then of the cardinals 7–10. It seems controversial whether the months of January and February were originally a part of the Roman calendar or were added later. Ovid says (*Fast.* 1.27–44) that the *conditor urbis*, Romulus, arranged a year of only ten months because he "knew more about war than about the heavenly bodies," and that it was Numa who later added the two months at the head of the list (43 f.). H. J. Rose (*OCD* 193, *s.v.* calendars, 6) accepts this original ten-month calendar and believes the Republican calendar to have been introduced from Etruria by Tarquinius Priscus, on the strength of a quotation in Censorinus (20.4) and the not pure-Latin month-name *Iunius*, "clearly connected with the Etruscan form of Juno's name, *Uni*." This seems sensible, but the matter remains hypothetical.[11] In any event, it was not until 153 B.C. that the Roman consuls entered office on January 1;[12] Warde Fowler believed that the change came about "not so much for religious reasons as because it was convenient, when the business of administration was increasing, to have the consuls in Rome for some time before they left for their provinces at the opening of the war season in March" (*Rom. Fest.* 5).

6. Before the change of the Roman calendar instituted by Julius Caesar, the twelve-month year consisted of four months of 31 days (March, May, July, October), seven of 29 (Jan., April, June, Aug., Sept., Nov., Dec.) and one of 28 (Feb.), 355 days in all, July being still named "Quin(c)tilis" and August "Sextilis." The only documentary evidence consists of the fragmentary remains of a painted (black and red) pre-Julian calendar found at Anzio (anc. Antium) in 1915 and now in the Mus. Naz. Rom., Rome.[13] Intercalation of 22 or 23 days, alternately, was supposedly added in February every other year, so as to bring the year to 377 or 378 days and every cycle of four years to 1,465 days, or an average of 366¼ days per year.[14] This was about one day too much for a solar year, with the result that by the time Caesar reformed the calendar (or, as Bickerman prefers, p. 47, "abandoned it" for a new "solar calendar of 365¼ days") "the civic year was about 3 months ahead of the solar" (H. J. Rose, *OCD* 193, *s.v.*

---

11. Warde Fowler, *Rom. Fest.* 6, had argued that Jan. and Feb. "were not mere appendages to a year of ten months." Cf. Michels 122.

12. Cassiodorus, *Chron.* 408 f., A.U.C. 601 (ed. Mommsen, *Mon. Germ. Hist., Auct. Ant.* 11 [Berlin 1894] p. 130): "Q. Fulvius et T. Annius. Hi primi conss. kal. Ianuariis magistratum inierunt . . .", whence the addition of *kal. Ian.* in editions of Livy, *Periochae* 47, where this event is dated to A.U.C. 598. (Livy here is obviously not using Varro's dating.)

13. Degrassi, *ILLRP* 1.23–41, no. 9, cf. p. 316; *Imag.* 4 f., 7, nos. 2 a–c; Michels, Illustration no. 1 (at end of vol.); a reconstruction in black and red, Ill. no.

4. This calendar Degrassi believed to be composed between 84 and 46 B.C.: *ILLRP* 1.40, n. 23.

14. For a detailed discussion of the intercalation of the Roman Republican calendar, see Michels 16, 145–172; cf. Bickerman 43–47, Samuel 156, 159–164. "The evidence about intercalation is uncertain and scanty," hence "exact dates before 46 B.C." are very questionable: T. R. S. Broughton, quoting Mrs. Michels by letter of Dec. 13, 1978. *CIL* 1²: 2: 2, p. 775, gives several examples of *interkalaris* modifying *mensis* or *eidus* (*Idus*); Degrassi, *ILLRP* 2, index, 483, has two (nos. 877, 1059).

calendars, 7). Caesar, therefore, as Pontifex Maximus (and Dictator), with the expert assistance of the astronomer Sosigenes,[15] extended the year 46 B.C. to 445 days (Censorinus, 20.8) and began afresh on Jan. 1, 45 B.C., with a cycle of four years of 365 days each, in the last of which years one day was added after the *Terminalia* in February (whence our Feb. 29 every four years). The year was now of 365 days, and the months took their present length (Apr., June, Sept., Nov. 30 days, the rest 31, but Feb. only 28, in leap years 29).

7. The Julian calendar, after a few corrections of blunders on the part of the pontiffs, lasted without change until A.D. 1582, when Pope Gregory XIII corrected an accumulated error of ten days by ordering (by Bull of Feb. 24) the day after October 4 of that year to be reckoned as October 15 and the century years to be leap years only when divisible by 400 (e.g. 1600, 2000). This Julio-Gregorian calendar is now in general use, and the year is said to exceed the true solar year by only 26 seconds.[16]

8. In the present selection of a hundred inscriptions, there are many datings given besides the dates, exact or approximate, provided by the careers set forth or the imperial titles. The datings consist of a day and a month, with or without a year indicated by consular names. Typical examples: *a(nte) d(iem) XII K(alendas) Febr(uarias)* (**7**), *Gn. Papeirio, G. Caecilio cos.* (**13**), *prid(ie) Non(as) Quinct(iles) Gn. Pompeio cos. tert.* (**20**), *Idib(us) Oct(obribus) Saturnino et Gallo cos.* (**71**). Unusual is the addition in **19** of a local, dialectical, name of the month: *a. d. III Idus Quinctileis, L. Pisone A. Gabinio cos., mense flusare,* i.e., *florali* ("month of flowers"); unusual also

such a form as *quarto Idus Quintilis* (*CIL* 1².1273 = 6.14574 = *ILLRP* 2.944), which presumably means the same as *a.d. IV Id. Quint.* (This date precedes the change of name of the month of July in 44 B.C.) In the present selection of inscrs. the latest example of the phrase *a(nte) d(iem)* is in **51** (A.D. 86); from **54** (A.D. 101 or 102) on, only such forms as *XIIII K(alendas) Nov(embres)* occur (the other examples are in **55, 61, 66, 68 f., 72, 76, 85, 87, 89, 91, 95, 98–100**). The use of *conss.* or *coss.* for *cos.* is late: here in **85, 91,** and **87** resp. (A.D. 338–383). Noteworthy is the amateurish awkwardness in versifying the consuls' names in *consulibus tunc natus eram iteroque Severo / et Fulvo pariter* (**60**), for the simple *Severo II et Fulvo cos.* Incidentally interesting is the variety in naming the consuls: three names, only praenomen (always abbreviated) plus nomen, praenomen plus cognomen, nomen plus cognomen, or only cognomen.

9. All these are varieties of one sort of dating—by day and month, with or without consular names for years. This is the common manner of dating found in Latin inscriptions down into the early-Christian period, when we find strange forms, apparently due to ignorance,[17] as well as new forms appearing. Familiar enough is the Romans' naming of the months with names which, except for the old names of July and August, are obviously the same as our own. Rather strange is the indication of the day within the month by means of three fixed dates. The first of the month, as was noted above, is named *Kalendae* because, as Varro says, *L. L.* 6.27, "on these days the Nones of the month are announced (*calantur*)[18] by the pontiffs" . . . as to "whether they will be on the 5th or the 7th. . . ." The Nones (*Nonae,*

15. Pliny, *N.H.* 18.57.211, . . . *Caesar dictator annos ad solis cursum redigens singulos, Sosigene perito scientiae eius adhibito.* . . .

16. Cf. Warde Fowler, *Rom. Fest.* 4; *Encycl. Brit.*[11] 4 (New York 1910) 990, col. 2, *s.v.* calendar; Bickerman 43–51; *OCD* 193, *s.v.* calendars; *Oxf. Dict. Christ. Church* 593, *s.v.* Gregorian Calendar; Samuel, index 281 *s.v.* julian calendar.

17. "Christianity came up from below; it was a popular movement . . . ," W. H. C. Frend, *New York Review of Books,* 25: 17 (Nov. 9, 1978) p. 28, col. 4.

18. *Kalendae* usually retains its K, as noted above, despite the C of *calare*.

"ninths," so called from being the 9th day before the Ides, as the Romans counted, inclusively) were on the 7th in March, May, July, October, otherwise on the 5th, the Ides (*Idus*, also fem. plu., of dubious etymology)[19] on the 15th of the same four months, otherwise on the 13th. These three words in the ablative denote a date ("Time When or Within Which"); *Kal. Ian.* means "on Jan. 1." The day before one of these days in *pridie* plus the accusative of the following fixed day; *pr. Kal. Ian.* is Dec. 31. The second day before is *a(nte) d(iem) III (tertium)* plus the accus. of the same fixed day; *a. d. III Kal. Ian.* is Dec. 30, and so on back to the previous fixed day: *a. d. IIII* (or *IV*) (up to a maximum of *XVIIII* or *XIX*) *Kal. Ian.* is Dec. 29 back to Dec. 14.[20] Then, still going backward, we come to Dec. 13 (*Idus*, abl. *Idibus, Dec.*), then *pr. Id. Dec.* (Dec. 12), then *a. d. III Id. Dec.* (Dec. 11) back to *a. d. VIII Id. Dec.* (Dec. 6); then the Nones (Dec. 5), then again *pr. Non. Dec.* (Dec. 4), *a. d. III Non. Dec.* and *a. d. IIII* (or *IV*) *Non. Dec.* for Dec. 3 and 2, back to the Kalends (*Kal. Dec.*). (Hale/Buck p. 354, §667 a, venture a guess at the origin of the *a. d.* phrase). These remarkable phrases, from the simple *Kal. Ian.* to *a. d. XIX Kal. Ian.*, can be treated as one word and used with prepositions, as *ex ante diem III Kal. Ian. (usque) ad* (or *in*) *Kal. Ian.*, "from Dec. 30 to Jan. 1."

10. The Romans had also a sort of eight-day week, perhaps better called, in view of the etymology, a nine-day system, *nundinum*, "the period from one market-day to the next," related to *nundinae* (sc. *feriae*),

"a market-day (occurring at regular intervals of eight days, i.e., every 9th day by Roman reckoning)," *OLD* 1206 *s.v.*[21] This may be an "artificial time-unit,"[22] or it may originally have come from observing the phases of the moon, which seem to vary in length from six to eight days.[23] To an epigraphist the two nundinal words are of interest. One reason is that all but three of the forty-four extant Roman calendars, from the pre-Julian calendar from Anzio on,[24] show in the first column to the left the letters A through H, one under the other and repeated in one series after another, from month to month; e.g., the Anzio calendar for January ends with E for the 29th day (not extant, but Jan. 27 is marked C), and February begins with the next letter, F, and so on, through the year; each new year begins with A (Degrassi, *FANI* 1–262). In a few calendars the A–H letters are preceded on the left by a seven-day series, like our week, marked A through G (ibid. 326, Litterae Hebd., and see below, on the week). The A–H letters are traditionally called "nundinal," but there is apparently "no direct reference in the whole of Latin literature" to them, though Ovid "must have had them in mind when, apropos of the types of days given in the calendar, he says *est quoque (dies) qui nono semper ab orbe redit* (*Fasti*, 1.54)" (Michels 27). "There is also the day which always recurs after the 9th day." ("*Orbe* here seems to mean 'revolution of the earth,' i.e., 'day'," G. H. Hallam, ed., *The Fasti of Ovid* [London 1881 and repr.] 187, on line 54.)

---

19. Michels, *TAPA* 80 (1949) 324 f., with n. 15, for anc. and mod. theories, and *Calendar Rom. Rep.* 19 n. 25, with ref. to Degrassi, *FANI* 327–330.

20. For the Julian calendar in graphic form, see Hale/Buck p. 355, or Bickerman 125. For an ancient example, month by month, see the manuscript *Fasti* of Polemius Silvius, of A.D. 449, in Degrassi, *FANI* 263–276.

21. *Nundinus* (adj.), whence the substantized derivatives -*dinum* and -*dinae*, is composed of *novem* ("nine") plus *din*- ("day," cf. Sanskrit -*dinam*): E/M 447, col. 1, *s.v.* nouem; *OLD* loc. cit.

22. So Bickerman 59.

23. The 1979 calendar showed four 6-day phases, twenty-four 7-day phases, twenty-one 8-day phases.

24. All forty-four are fragmentary and incomplete except the two latest, of A.D. 354 and 449, which are in manuscript form, not cut in marble; they are all from the Italian mainland except one, which is in Sicily (Degrassi, *FANI*, pp. XXI *med.*, 547); all the datable ones except the two latest date from ca. 36 B.C. to A.D. 37, none of the later annotations being datable after A.D. 49 (ibid., p. XXII *fin.*). They are all listed by Michels 187–190, with *CIL* 1²: 1 or later references.

The other point of interest is that in the *Senatus Consultum de Bacchanalibus* of 186 B.C. (**8**), lines 22 f., and in two other Republican legal inscriptions, as well as in about a dozen literary passages from Cicero to Priscian, the phrase *trinum nundinum* occurs, in three spellings (*noun-, non-, nun-*), to mean a period of time; Mrs. Michels argues cogently that it is a period of twenty-five days and that this form is never genitive plural (the short *-um* form, as in *nummum*), but either nomin. or accus.[25]

11. As was noted above, there are signs also of measuring time by a seven-day period, like our week,[26] which it is agreed is of Eastern origin and undoubtedly came West with immigration. This period is marked A to G in four calendars (Degrassi, *FANI* nos. 5, 21, 37, 42), three of which are of Augustan date. None is from Rome itself, but Augustan Roman literature shows knowledge of such a seven-day period, and of Saturday in particular; the other days, by early-Christian times, became named for the other four major planets then known (Mars, Mercury, Jupiter, Venus—Saturday being named for the fifth, Saturn) plus the sun and the moon. Tibullus 1.3.18 seems to have the earliest extant mention of Saturday as "Saturn's holy day" (*Saturni sacram . . . diem*).[27] Horace (*Sat.* 1.9.69 f.) and Ovid (*Ars amat.* 1.76, 415 f., *Rem. Am.* 219 f.) refer to *sabbata* as Jewish, or simply foreign, or to the *septima sacra* or *sept. festa*.[28] (Hebrew *shab-*

bath, "cessation," our "sabbath," is the name of the 7th day.) Next in time is a calendar (*tabula in poste defixa*) described by Petronius, *Sat.* 30, as having "the course of the moon and painted likenesses of seven stars" (perhaps *pictas* is intended to modify *cursum* as well as *imagines*: Heseltine/Warmington, Loeb transl., 1975, have "painted with the moon in her course, and the likenesses of seven stars"). Dio, early-3rd cent., says (37.18.1 f.) that "the custom of referring the days to the seven stars called planets" is now universal, and fashionable even among the Romans; he credits this system to the Egyptians.[29] It is not Jewish, the days of the Hebrew week being counted, not named, the day after the Sabbath being the first day (Bickermann 61).

12. The inscriptions, besides showing the A–G letters in a few calendars, include at least nine that name the days of the week. The earliest seems to be a Pompeian inscr. (*CIL* 1[2]: 1, p. 342, ad p. 218 = 4.4182) with the name Sunday (*dies Solis*) (cf. W. F. Snyder, *JRS* 26 [1936] 1–18, esp. 16 *fin.*–18). *ILS* 3: 2, 920, under *Dies hebdomadis planetariae*,[30] lists eight inscrs. that name six days (Friday seems not to occur in *ILS*) as *dies Solis* (Sunday), *d. Lunae* (Monday), *d. Martis* (Tuesday), *d. Mercuri* (Wednesday), *d. Iovis* (Thursday), *d. Saturni* (Saturday),[31] which, together with *d. Veneris* (Friday), remind one of the Romance-language names (but not Portuguese, which counts Mon.–Fri. as

25. Michels 191–206, esp. 197 ff.; this is a long discussion of *nundinae* and *trinum nundinum*.

26. For the week, see C. D. Buck, *A Dict. of Sel. Synonyms in the Principal I.-E. Langs. . . .* (Chicago/London 1949, 2nd impr. 1965) 1004–1009, 14.61; Bickerman 58–61; Michels 89, 167, 192; Samuel 17 f.

27. See Kirby Flower Smith's ample note in his ed. of Tibullus (New York, etc., 1913) 238–240.

28. Cato, *De Agri Cult.* 37.4, and Varro, *Res Rust.* 1.37.3, may already be pertinent, more probably Cato, advising taking out timber "within 7 days of the full moon."

29. See Foster/Cary's explanation in the Loeb Dio, pp. 3, 131, 133, n. 1.

30. Hebdomas, "week," from Greek ἑβδομάς;

this appears first to mean "the number seven," then "a number of seven," then (in Hippocrates and the Septuagint) a "period of 7 days, a week" (Liddell/Scott[9] *s.v.*). Latin *hebdomas* seems to mean "week" ("the terminal point of a 7-day period," "each 7th day in the moon's cycle," *OLD* 788 *s.v.*) as early as Gellius (3.10.7, of the 4th and 7th weeks of a woman's pregnancy).

31. Our English names for these days are part of the Germanic system, which puts the planetary names into Germanic form, keeping "Sunday," "Monday," and to some extent "Saturday" from the Latin and, for the other four names, identifying Roman and Germanic gods (Buck, op. cit. [n. 26] 1009 col. 2).

segunda feira, etc.).[32] These inscrs. all seem to be Imperial in date and to refer to pagans except perhaps one of Constantine (*ILS* 704 = *CIL* 3.4121, cf. p. 2328[114]). The most interesting is an epitaph at Lyon (*ILS* 7531 = *CIL* 13.1906),[33] which says of a man who had been a *negotiator Lugdunensis artis cretariae* (a dealer in chalk or pipe-clay at Lyon) that he *natus est d[ie] Martis, die Martis prob[a]tus (est), die Martis missione[m] percepit, die Martis def[u]nctus est* (on a Tuesday he was born, was accepted as a recruit,[34] received his discharge, and died), truly Tuesday's child. But Diehl's indices are much richer. He lists over 100 Christian inscrs. (3.311 f., sect. 10) that name the day of the week (always in the abl.); Saturday and Sunday get two names each: Sunday *die Solis* and *d. dominica* ("the Lord's"), Saturday *die Saturni* and *d. Sabbato*.[35] He has also a fair number of inscrs. (3.310, sect. 8) that name the day of the month with an ordinal number, like our "11th (day) of June"—e.g., *die xviii Ianuari, die xviii m(ensis) Iunii*.

13. Finally, a few rules for converting Roman dates to English. For the year: to obtain the year B.C., subtract the given Roman date from 754 (753 B.C. being assumed to be the date of the founding of Rome); to obtain the year A.D., subtract 753; e.g., 648 A.U.C. (Cicero's birth year) = 754, less 648 = 106 B.C.; 767 A.U.C. (the year of Augustus's death) = 767, less 753

= A.D. 14. For the day: for a Roman date given as so many days before the Kalends, if it is *pridie Kal. Ian.*, for example, our equivalent will be the last day of December (Dec. 29 in the pre-Julian calendar, Dec. 31 in the Julian and ours); if it is *ante diem III–XVII Kal. Ian.*, pre-Julian (*III–XIX* Julian), add two to the number of days of December (29, or 31, resp.) and subtract the given number; e.g., *a. d. XIV Kal. Ian.* = 29 (or 31) plus 2 = 31 (or 33), less 14 = Dec. 17 (or 19). If the Roman date is expressed as so many days before the Nones or Ides, *pridie Non.* or *Id.* is of course the day before (the 4th or 12th, resp., but the 6th or 14th in March, May, July, or October); if it is *a. d. III–IV* (or *–VI*) *Non.* or *a. d. III–VIII Id.*, add one to the date of these fixed days (the 5th and the 13th of the month, but the 7th and 15th, resp., in those same four months) and subtract the given number; e.g., *a. d. VIII Id. Dec.* = 13 plus 1 = 14, less 8 = Dec. 6; *a. d. IV Non. Oct.* = 7 plus 1 = 8, less 4 = Oct. 4.[36] In a leap year (every 4th) in the Julian calendar *a. d. VI Kal. Mart.* = Feb. 24, *a. d. bissextum Kal. Mart.* = Feb. 25, *a. d. V* = Feb. 26, *a. d. IV* = *Feb. 27, a. d. III* = Feb. 28, *pridie* = Feb. 29, the extra day ("the 6th day over again") being inserted after Feb. 24. For the intercalary months of the complicated pre-Julian calendar, see Michels, 16 and App. 1, Roman Intercalation, pp. 145–172; Samuel 160–164.

---

32. The Romance languages substitute the church name for Saturday and Sunday (Buck, op. cit. 1009 col. 1 and the table, 1006 f.). Diehl already has several examples of numbering the days of the week, as in Portuguese; e.g., *die secunda feria*, 7th cent. (*ILCV* 3.312 *init.*).

33. Dated A.D. 240/310 by A. Audin and Y. Burnand, *REA* 61 (1959) Tabl. VI, p. 1, with p. 327, 6e époque.

34. For *probatus*, see *OLD* 1465 *s.v.* probo, 6 c.

35. *Dominica* is once masc. (*-o*), sometimes abbreviated or partly missing; *Sabbato* is twice *Sabbati*, once

Sabbatorum, sometimes abbreviated, once partly missing.

36. Hale/Buck 354, §665, 1 f., with n. 1, explain why in figuring a date before the Kalends (except *pridie Kal.*) one adds *two* to the number of days in the month before subtracting the given number, whereas before the Nones or the Ides one adds only *one* before subtracting. It is because one has to figure both the last day of the month and the first of the next. In both cases the Romans used their usual inclusive dating, counting both ends.

APPENDIX IV

CONVENTIONS IN PRINTING EPIGRAPHICAL TEXTS

The largest treatment of this subject (in English, at least) seems to be that of Sterling Dow, *Conventions in Editing: A Suggested Reformulation of the Leiden System*, pp. 37 (1969—see Abbreviations). The Leiden system, which had been preceded by earlier systems with considerable variety (see Dow 14), came about as a result of a meeting of the Papyrological Section of the 18th International Congress of Orientalists at Leiden, 1931. An account of the conventions adopted was the chief feature of two publications of the Union Académique Internationale, entitled *Emploi des signes critiques, disposition de l'apparat dans les éditions savantes de textes grecs et latins, conseils et recommandations*, the first written by J. Bidez and A. B. Drachmann (Paris 1932, pp. 46), the second (édition nouvelle) by A. Delatte and A. Severyns (Brussels/Paris 1938, pp. 50).

Papyrologists had taken the lead in formulating the Leiden system, but it proved applicable to both papyri and inscriptions. Most scholars in these fields seem to have accepted it, with some individual modifications in the interest of simplicity (or, alternatively, greater exactness); hence it is always wise to see if the system used in any particular edition is explained at the beginning. The Leiden system is described by Woodhead 6–11, Dow 1 f., 14–17, and Meyer 108 f.

Woodhead's signs and symbols may be summarized as follows (pp. 7–10):

[ABC]: square brackets, for letters lost or illegible, restored by conjecture

(abc): parentheses, to fill out abbreviations

⟨ABC⟩: angled brackets, for letters accidentally omitted by the cutter, or for correct letters inserted by the editor to replace wrong ones (in this case the editor will usually give the actual reading in a note)

{ABC}: hooked brackets, for too many letters or repeated letters or words

[[ABC]]: double square brackets, for letters intentionally erased—e.g., because of *damnatio memoriae* (perhaps erroneously, as in **72**, line 4—see note); sometimes the erased text can be read, wholly or in part, even when replaced by a later text (see again **72**, lines 2 f.)

A̤B̤C̤: underdotting, for imperfect letters (but some editors use this only for letters so damaged, or so badly written in the first place, as not to be identifiable with certainty though conjecturable in the context)

[. . .]: dots on the line within square brackets, for letters presumably lost and not restorable, each dot representing one missing letter

[– – –]: dashes or hyphens within square brackets when it is uncertain how many letters are missing; but, as with dots, an approximate number may be printed above the dashes as a guide, as ‒‒‒$\underset{\rule{1.2em}{0.4pt}}{\text{c. 15}}$‒

v: one or more italic *v*'s, for letter spaces left blank, each *v* representing one letter; or *vac.* or *vacat* may be used to show that the rest of an inscribed line, or a whole line, is blank space where one might expect writing.

Ideally, the text will be presented in capital letters, followed by one in minuscule, in which the abbreviations, if not already filled out in the capital text, will be so treated here and modern punctuation added. (This, obviously, requires understanding the meaning of the inscription.) The capital text should be printed line for line, and lines 5, 10, 15, etc., indicated at the left (if the lines of the inscription are too long for the printed page, or column, and runovers are needed, then it may be well to number every line, to avoid confusion); the minuscule text should have the line divisions indicated by a vertical (or slanted) line separating the lines of text and a small suprascript 5, 10, 15, etc., placed before the lines so numbered. It may be desirable to print the capital text so as to approximate the arrangement of the inscription itself, as in the *Album*; if this is not possible for reasons of expense, then the original arrangement may be described, by such words as "paragraphing" or "centered," or a combination of these, or "straight left margin"; sometimes the editor may be in doubt. The publication that has gone much the farthest to print the capital text as it appears in the inscriptions, even to the extent of using larger and smaller type, is undoubtedly *CIL*; but it often fails to follow this with a minuscule text (with the all-important punctuation and abbreviations expanded); this lack is often remedied, more or less, by use of the indices at the end of the volume.

It should be added that all this elaborate presentation is needed only when publishing an inscription for the first time. (At this time, in fact, a full description of the inscr., and an account of where it was found, where it is now, and all the circumstances will be additionally needed, as well as photographs, notes, and at least a summary of the contents, if not a complete translation, slow and difficult as this may be.) Once an inscription has been published, only a reference to it and, where desirable, a copy of it, or of part of it, in minuscule should be needed. Of course, if one has reason to believe an inscription to be inadequately published, one may have to resort to writing to the editor (or to someone else knowledgeable) to ask questions. Directors of museums, or persons in charge of the inscriptions there, are usually helpful in these matters.

For the new rules for editing, in minuscule, inscriptions to be published in future volumes of *CIL*, see Hans Krummrey and Silvio Panciera, "Criteri di edizione e segni diacritici," *Tituli*, 2 (Rome 1980) 205–215.

CONCORDANCES

CONCORDANCE OF OTHER COLLECTIONS AND THIS VOLUME

Only *CIL*, *ILS*, and *ILCV* are listed if an inscription appears in any of these collections; if not, some other standard reference is given; but not all the references are listed here, only those to *CIL*, *ILS*, and *ILCV*. Most of the inscriptions cited from *CIL* 1^2 appear also in other volumes of *CIL*. References to this volume are to inscription number.

	THIS VOL.
CIL 1^1:25	75
1^2:1 p. 73	37
1^2:2.1	4
2	75
3	1
4	3
6–7	5
25	48
581	8
607	6
614	7
622	9
623	10
626	11
638	12
709	15
721	16
751	18
756	19
797	21
1633	17
2504	13
2662	14
2883	2
2965	20
2.5041	7

	THIS VOL.
CIL 3.550	56
14203^{22}	9
14147^5	22
pp. 769–799	34
pp. 856 XIII (cf. 1064 XIII, 1964 XVIII)	51
Suppl. 1:3 pp. 802 f., 1910, 1913	81
5.877	59
3326	40
6.220	72
284	6
331	11
506	80
872 (add.)	21
882 (add.)	35
886 (add.)	39
889	33
896	58
918	41
930	46
945 (add.)	50
946	50
960	57
1004 + 31223	67
1033	73
1052	71
1101	77
1136	83
1139 (add.)	82
1158	86
1244–1246	29
1256	44
1274	23
1284 f. (add.)	5

	THIS VOL.		THIS VOL.
CIL 6.1297	16	CIL 11.1421	31
1300	48	5748	78
1305 (add.)	18	13.1668	42
1374 (add.)	26	14.367	68
1492	54	3608	49
1585, b	69	4123	1
1698	89	16.32	51
1704	84	AE 1914, 142	98
1725	97	1915, 100	47
1751	90	1926, 124	93
1778	92	1928, 80	96
1884	61	88	24
2104, a	75	1945, 136	62
7578	60	1949, 215	36
10051	37	1952, 164	36
10234	66	1953, 251 (cf. 1954, 4)	45
10235	64	1964, 255 (cf. 1968, 531)	35
31152	63	1971, 477	38
31223	67	AJA ser. 1: 5 (1889) 428–439	81
31245	82	54 (1950) 223–226	28
31402	88	AJP 75 (1954) 225–248	36
31987	94	Esplor. 1.43–53	70
32004	87	ILCV 1.90	87
32323	25	645	79
33840	76	1266	85
33976	52	1469	100
36840	4	2.2650	99
36908	30	2921	95
37045	15	3058A	98
37053	28	3446	91
37063	27	ILS 1	5
37075	32	11	6
37965	65	15	7
39416	47	18	8
9.1455	53	20	11
3513	19	23	12
10.104	8	65	48
844	17	73	21
3513	19	98	29
5853	55	115	35
6569	74	129	58
6950	12	140	31
11.1339	10	180	39

	THIS VOL.			THIS VOL.
ILS 181	33	*ILS* 2163		72
204	40	2183		63
210	41	4144		80
212	42	4906		19
218	44	4913		4
244	46	5039		75
265	50	5050		25
294	57	5177		52
308	56	5283		37
347	67	5636		17
425	73	5892		18
478	74	5920		69
519	77	6106		54
642	81	6164		68
694	82	6271		55
731	86	6509		53
769	88	7213		66
799	94	7220		78
872	16	8364		64
881	23	8393		28
917	26	8561		1
986	49	8743		3
1052	59	8884		9
1214	84	8888		15
1257	89	8964		32
1265	90	8995		22
1284	97	9417		13
1286	87	*NS* 1913, 68		43
1792	61			

CONCORDANCE OF THE OTHER INSCRIPTIONS CITED

	Page		Page
AE 1953, 195	27	CIL 4.4874	17
1953, 73	44 (n.117)	5.5262	44 (n.117)
1971, 534	22 (n.70)	6.13	7
Ber. d. Röm.-German.		154	123
Kommiss. 3.40	43 (n.116)	164	123
CIL 1¹.195	125	230	14
551	88	266	22 (n.70)
1²:1, p. 193,		428	47 (n.128)
no. XI	16,124	488	227
p. 342, ad		505	166
p. 218	232	616* ("falsa")	8 (n.20)
1².8-9	81	701-702	110
9	49, 96	904	29 (92)
19	125	921	118
31	6	946	129
64-357	24	1055	156
583	14 (n.40), 19 (n.57)	1287	49
590	45 (n.123)	1375	102
592	47	1585, a	154
593	19 (n.57), 45 (n.123)	1745	173
613	6	1777	178, 179
617	7	1779	178
632	7 (n.16)	2288, a	112
719	38	3692	6
761	40	3732 + 31057	103
798	97	3768 + 31322	42
804	103	3824 + 31603	45 (n.120)
996	26	7303	41
1211	34	8420	42
1263	26	8983	155
1342	26	9181 a-c	162
1358	25	9182	162
1547	93	10050	113
1632	93	10230	10
1911	48	15346	34
2046	26	21414	112
2.1963	11	29896	10
3.30	227	31611	16
1933	95	32457	112
4121	14, 233	32471, a	112
9315	143	36917-18	157
4.4182	232	37834	47

	Page			Page
CIL 8.27	30		ILCV 2807A	46
6948	47		3446	39
9.1558	129		ILLRP 2-7, 504,	
2860	131		1271, 1271a	38
5136	97		5	8 (n.23)
10.3851	47		180	17
3969	62		877, 1059	229 (n.14)
4896	48		ILS 2-3	81
6835	8 (n.19)		3	49
6839	8 (n.19)		14	6
6849	7 (n.19)		26	38
11.1147	132		50-60, cf. 61-64	36, 125
1420	105		55	16, 124
1693	227		73[a]	97
3801	47		91	110
5749	164		73[a]	97
6331	38		91	110
6642	7		107	8 (n.25)
12.1357	47		112	95
1824	106		139	105
2610	43 (n.116)		222	118
4333	95		296	129
13.1906	233		704	14, 233
14.2112	11		787	30
2458	47		800	179
2464	41		880	41
2935	6		917[a]	102
3609	19		981	107
4254	32		1013	24
4710	48		1104	19
15: 2: 2.8017-			1245	173
8622	55		1258	178, 179
CIS (Corpus Inscr.			1259	178
Semiticarum)			1832	155
1.164, pp.			2216	14
214 ff.	13 (n.38)		2219	47 (n.128)
CLE 52	34		2592	47
801	165		2709	47
1175	10		2806	227
IG 2²: 3: 1.92,			2927	44 (n.117)
no. 3277	21 (n.68)		3475	47
ILCV 1230	181		3794	6
2487-91	165		3888-89	123
2501 ff.	184		4019	103

	Page		Page
ILS 4095	227	ILS 6675	132
4143	166	6858	47
4405	26	7212	11
4907	95	7221	164
5178	131	7531	233
5191	32	7763	62
5285	113	7822	25
5395	48	7823	26
5757	45 (n.120)	7863	41
5799	45 (n.120)	8358	143
5803	7	8394	10
5890	47	8403	34
6085	19 (n.57), 45 (n.123)	8759a	227
6086	45 (n.123)	OGIS 2.521	14 (n.40)
6088	11		

ADDENDA/CORRIGENDA

Preface. To the list of the many to whom I owe thanks should be added the names of E. J. Jory and Jeannot Nyles.

Page 20, col. 2, *med*. The two Quintas would undoubtedly have been distinguished by the use of nicknames. The Latin for "nickname" is *signum*.

Page 54, footnote 135. Add "meiner" in line 6 from the bottom, so as to have it read "trotz meiner äusseren Erfolge..."

Page 58, Sect. V. After the R. G. Kent entry, add this item: Anton Szantyr, "itum aditum ambitum," *Museum Helveticum* 22 (1966) 208–212 (repr. in *Beiträge aus der Thesaurusarbeit XIV*, hrsg. vom Thesaurus Linguae Latinae [Leiden 1979] 201–205).

Page 60, Sect. X. After the second Giacchero item, add these two: Michael H. Crawford/Joyce M. Reynolds, "The Aezani Copy of the Prices Edict," *ZPE* 34 (1979) 163–210, Taf. XI, and Joyce Reynolds, "Diocletian's Edict on Maximum Prices: The Chapter on Wool," *ZPE* 42 (1981) 283 f.

Page 61, Sect. XIV. After the last (Gagé) entry, add two items: T. V. Buttrey, *Documentary Evidence for the Chronology of the Flavian Titulature* (Meisenheim 1980 Beiträge zur klass. Philologie, 112), and P. Sage, "La Table claudienne et le style de l'empereur Claude: essai de réhabilitation," *REL* 58 (1980) 274–312.

Page 65. Additional Categories, 3. Miscellaneous. After the Flamm entry, add Beryl Rawson, "Family Life Among the Lower Classes at Rome in the First Two Centuries of the Empire," *CP* 61 (1966) 71–83, and after the Avi-Yonah item, add Beryl Rawson, "Roman Concubinage and Other *De Facto* Marriages," *TAPA* 104 (1974) 274–305.

Page 76, inscr. **1** (Fibula Praen.) At the end of the N.B., add A. E. Gordon's review of Guarducci, *CJ* 78 (1982–83) 64–70.

Page 113, inscr. **37**. J. S. Gordon suggests that *revocatus*, "called back (to repeat a race)," was not caused by any infraction of racing rules, but by a tie, which necessitated a re-run. That is why in the list of his races (see the full text in the photo or in *ILS* 5283) *revocatus* always precedes the listing of second place. Clearly the re-run is for first place. Cf. *OLD* 1648, *s.v.* revoco, 2 a.

Page 117, inscr. **42**. In the third paragraph, bibliography, after Momigliano, add P. Sage, the item listed in the fourth paragraph above here.

Page 126, inscr. **48**. For line 13, Ð (with medial bar, not apparent in the photo), see *Contrib.* 224, note 1, with ref. to Huelsen's testimony, *CIL* 1².25, p. 384, col. 2, on line 13: "it seemed to have been D with medial bar."

Page 136, inscr. **55**. Second paragraph after the translation. Read: Priscus's last title, *praef. fabrum*, is of uncertain meaning. Were this inscr. of Republican date, it might well mean "aide-de-camp" of some general (cf. G. R. Watson, *OCD* 428 *s.v.* Fabri), but in the Empire such a person, "generally speaking, was a purely civil official" (Kornemann, *RE* 6.1923, 36 ff., but cf. 1922, 51 ff., where this inscr. is listed, no. 5853, s.v. Fabri).

Page 143, inscr. **62**, last paragraph, commentary on lines 18–20, *fin*. Change the period after ambitus to a comma and add: and A. Szantyr, *Museum Helveticum* 23 (1966) 208–212.

SELECT INDEX

(Numbers refer to pages unless otherwise indicated.)

SUBJECTS AND ANCIENT AUTHORS

(See also the list of Abbreviations, the Addenda to the Degrassi/Calabi Limentani bibliography arranged chronologically within topics [pp. 55–56], and the chronological list of Roman Emperors, pp. 49 f.; also below, "Modern Scholars and Writers," pp. 259–264.

a potione, item a laguna et tricliniarch., lictor proximus et a comment. beneficiorum, of Trajan, 142
a veste (Imp. freedman), 142
ab epistulis Graecis, 19 (n. 56)
abbreviations in Latin (and Greek) inscriptions, 15 (with notes 41, 44), 19, 44 f., 131, 150, 207–225
abbreviations of nomina derived from emperors' names (e.g., *Ael.*), 145
abbreviations used in these inscrs., 207–225
abesto, 145
abl. absolute with participle omitted but understood?, 169
ablatives of Duration of Time, 120
ablatives, unclear meaning of, 165
abscessit ("he died"), 142
accountants, Imperial, 152 f.
acephalous inscriptions, 16, 40
Achaia, 87, 178
Acta Senatus, Rome, 117
ad Apollinis (templum), 112
ad assem, usque ("to the last cent"), 151 f.
additions made to inscrs., 37, 89, 92
additive vs. subtractive forms of Roman numerals, 46, 47, 116
adoraturos ("to pay homage to"), 127 f.
adque written for *atque,* 167, 172, 176
Adrastus, *Aug. lib.,* 27, 152 f.
-ae written *-e,* 151, 153, 163, 165, 171 (2), 177, 185
aedem omitted in such phrases as *ad Martis,* 112
aedes, fanum, templum differentiated, 95
aedes Duelonai, 83
aedes of Fons, 123
(aedes) Martis, 149
aedes(sacrae), eight, plus a *templum,* built by Augustus in Rome, 109 f.
aedilis, 81, 136
aedium sacrarum et operum locorumque [publicorum cura?], 120
Aegyptus, 130
Ael., Aurel., Fl., Ulp. as abbreviations attested as early as A.D. 102, 145, 174

Aelius P. f. Serg. Hadrianus, P. (later emp.), 137
Aemilius Sex. l(ibertus) Baro, Sex., *frumentarius,* 96
Aemilius (Paulus), Imperator, L., 82 f., 85
aeternitati Italiae suae prospexit (of Trajan), 134
aeterna, urbs (Rome), 174
Aeternus (*deus*), 141
aeternus princeps domnus noster Honorius, 180
Africa (Rom. prov.), 176
agitator factionis albae, Rome, 113
agnomina, Roman, 18, 21 (n. 66), 92, 175
Agorius. *See* Vettius
Agrippa, M., 19 (with n. 61), 43, 49, 101, 106, 139
Agrippina the Elder, 25
Aienus, L. (Vestinian), 94, 95
Aix-en-Provence, 166
Alexandrea et Aegyptus, 98, 99
Alexandria, Egypt, 99, 100, 111
[alime]nta urbi ("food supplies for the city," Rome), 179
[ali]moniae, 119
aliquis, 127, 128
allectus petitu senatus inter consulares, 170
Allia A. l. Potestas, 15, 34, 37, 145–148
alpha/omega, letters, suspended from crossbar of the monogrammatic cross, 180
altars, 102, 143 f., 165 f.
amicabilis, fidelis in omnibus, bona, prudens (of a Christian), 185
Ammianus Marcellinus, 114, 173, 174
Ancilla Christi, 184 f.
"and" omitted between names of members of groups, 124
Ankara, Turkey, 32, 108, 109
annona populi Romani, 127, *annona urbis Romae,* 175
Anonymous Einsidlensis, 8, 138
a(nte) d(iem) dropped from the early-Christian inscrs., 184; latest example here, 230
Antoninus Pius (emp.), 20, 144, 150 f.
Antonius, Marcus (cos. 99 B.C.), 90 f.
Antony, Mark, 19, 21, 24, 228
Anzio (anc. Antium), 229, 231
apices, 14, 39 f., 41, 103, 110, 114, 117, 123, 146

Appian, 92, 104
apud Constantinopolim, 175
aqueducts, Roman, 104, 118 f.
Aquileia, 140
Ara Romae et Augusti, near Lugdunum, 117
Aramaic, 13 (with n. 37)
aratores vs. *paastores*, 88
Arcadius, Honorius, Theodosius (A.D. 402–406), 30, 179 f.
Arch of Augustus in Forum, Rome, 226
Arch of Constantine, Rome, 43, 168, 170
Arch of Septimius Severus, Rome, 19 (n. 58), 37, 158
Arch of Titus, Rome, 128 f.
Arch of Trajan, Beneventum, 129
archaic/later forms mixed in one inscr., 34
archaic or notable forms, 189–206
argentarii et exceptores, Rome, 162
arka, Kalendae, kara (*k* for *c*), 161 f., 175, 228, 230
Armenia, 127
arrangement of inscrs. noted, 14, 37, 42, 88, 93, 97, 99, 107, 116, 117, 122, 126, 132, 134 f., 136, 141, 154, 162, 164, 176, 178
Arruntius Stella, L. (cos. A.D. 101 or 102), 134
Articuleius Paetus, Q. (cos. A.D. 101), 132
Arval Hymn, 8 (n. 23), 16, 35, 37, 43, 160
Arvals, 15 (n. 44), 22, 36, 37, 38, 160
Asculum (mod. Ascoli Piceno), 91 f.
Asia (Rom. prov.), 107, 127, 128
Aśoka (Indian king), 13 (with n. 37)
Assouan, Aswan (anc. Syene), Egypt, 7 (n. 18), 97
Atalanta, 146
Athens, 90, 123, 137, 166
Atticius Speratus, G., *centurio vigilum*, 156
Atticus (Cicero's friend), 22 (n. 69), 230 (n. 4)
Attis, 165 f.
A.U.C. dating, 226
augur, 105, 140, 166, 178
Augustales, seviri Augustales in same inscr., 151
Augusta as a title, 28
Augustus, 3, 15, 21, 28 (with n. 87), 30, 32, 33, 35, 36, 38, 43 f., 48, 73, 83, 87 f., 96, 97, 98, 99, 104, 105, 106 f, 108–110, 112, 113, 121 f., 124, 228 f.
Augustus, honorary cognomen, 21 f.
Augustus, the month—origin of the name, 228 f.
Augustus princeps (Nero), 120
Aurelius, Marcus (emp.), 22 (n. 71), 25, 28, 29, 33 (n. 107), 49 (with n. 130), 144, 150, 155
Aurelius Fulvius, T. (cos. A.D. 120, later emp. Antoninus Pius), 141
Aurelius Sabutius, a Christian, 165
[Aurelius Victor], *Epit. de Caes.*, 138
Aurellius (spelling), 28 (with n. 88), 33, 104
[*aureum?*], *m*[*onument(um)?*], 179
aurum, 116, 126
aurum margaritaque (a lady's), 103
avia beatissimorum et florentissimorum Caesarum nostrorum, 169
avorum honores supergressus, 181

B with medial bar (= *beneficiarius*), 156, 157
b written for *v*, 175, 181
Bacchanalia, 83–85
balnea publica (Pisa), 106

baptism, Christian, 173
bar over numerals multiplies by 1000, 44, 47, 143, 150, 151, 161
Baro, pejorative cognomen, 96
Bastarnae, 127
b.b.v.v. (= *bonorum virorum duorum*), 163
bellum Dacicum, 137
bellum Gothicum, 180
b(eneficiarius) pr(aefecti) (of a cohort of Vigiles), 156, 158
bene merenti, 142, 145 (?), 172
Bernardini Tomb, Palestrina, 13 (n. 38), 75
bilingual/trilingual inscrs., 13 (n. 37), 33, 43, 89, 97, 159
bis ("twice," i.e., for 2 yrs.), 107; ("for the second time"), 165
Bonus, Bona, as a cognomen, 18 (with n. 53)
Borustenes (Dnieper river), 127
boustrophedon. *See* run-over lines
bowdlerized version, Greek, of Latin, 98
Britain, 119, 120, 127, 128, 140, 159, 168
Britannicus or *Britt-*, 104, 156
Britannicus Maximus, 28, 33, 104
bronze, inscrs. in, 4, 5 (with n. 10), 14 (n. 40), 22 (n. 70), 32, 35, 45 (n. 123), 76, 82, 83, 90, 91, 108, 109, 111, 117, 121, 129, 131, 133, 156, 162
bronze letters, 21 (n. 68), 111, 128, 129, 139, 151, 158, 168
bureaucratese, Roman, 4 (n. 3)

C the early form of G, 15, 21 (n. 65), 73; cut for both C and G, 126
C (= 100), its origin, 44, 46 (n. 126)
C̲ reversed (Ɔ), 27, 112
C̄ (*centenarius*), C̄C̄ (*ducenarius*), C̄C̄C̄ (*trecenarius*), 159. See also *ducenarius, sexagenarius*
C, K, Q confused, 35
C/CN here transcribed as G./Gn., 73
Caecilia Metella, 24, 39, 99
caelibes, 130
Caelius Saturninus, G., 22, 170 f.
Caesar, Gaius (eldest son of Agrippa and Augustus' daughter, Julia), 105, 112
Caesar, Gaius (son of Germanicus Caesar), 107
Caesar (cognomen), 19, 21 f. (in Augustus' new name); 29, 337 f. (heir-apparent)
Caesar divi f(ilius) (Octavian), 42, 98
Caesar, Lucius (second son of Agrippa and Augustus' daughter, Julia), 105, 112
Caesarea, Israel, 13 (with n. 39), 113 f.
Cairo, Egypt, 97
Caisar (*sic*, of the emp. Claudius), 118, 119
calendars, Roman, 15 (n. 44), 105, 226–233
Caligula (Gaius, emp.), 107, 110, 114, 115, 119
Calumniosus (a Christian boy), 184
Camposanto, Pisa, 106
candidatus divi Traiani, 140
cannaba ("hut, shack"), 153
Capitoline *Fasti Consulares/Triumphales*, 15 (n. 43), 18 (with n. 54), 21 (n. 68), 82, 107, 110, 226
Capitoline Museum, Rome, 5, 91, 102, 121, 155, 156, 162, 165, 176
Caput Africae (apparently a school for training Imperial pages, Rome), 155
Caracalla (emp.), 28 (with n. 90), 29, 30 (n. 98), 33

(n. 107), 49 f. (n. 130), 104, 139, 155, 156, 158, 174

caritas, licentia pretiorum ("high prices/inflation"), 167

Carmen (Saeculare), 101

carmina (of the Salii), 112

Carthage, 157

Carthaginians, 125 f.

Cassiodorus, 227 (n. 6), 229 (n. 12)

Cassius Dio. *See* Dio

Castor and Pollux, 13, 76

Castra ("Imperial Household"), 29 (with n. 95)

catacombs, Christian, 164, 171, 180, 184

Catiline (L. Sergius Catilina), 91

Cato the Elder, 49, 228, 232 (n. 28)

caudicarii seu piscatores corporati urbis Romae, 179

causa/caussa (abl.) preceded by genitive, 91

cemetery, pagan, under St. Peter's (in Vaticano), Rome, 142, 154

censor, 81, 104, 116, 118

censor perpetuus, 130

Censorinus, 130, 226 (n. 4), 229, 230

centuria, a group of 100-plus men, in a cohort of Vigiles, 156, 157, 158

centurio vigilum, 156

certamen (musicum), Rome, 130

Chalcidicum, Roman Forum, 109

change of style in similar texts on same monument, 33

change of text over erasure, 159

changes of style and syntax in same inscr., 137

charioteer, 43, 48, 112

Cherronensis (Tauric Chersonese), 127

chiastic order of attributes, 29 (n. 91), 115, 169, 170

child-welfare: Imperial, 43, 132; private 44 (n. 117)

children in these inscrs., 119 f., 130 f., 132 f., 136, 141, 180 f., 184

Christian, or Christians, 37, 39, 43, 164 f., 171, 173, 176, 177, 180 f., 183 f., 184, 185, 227 (n. 6)

Christian formulas, 165, 172, 177, 181, 183, 184, 185

Christian symbolism, 172, 180, 183, 185

Chronographer of A.D. 354, 227

Cicero, 16, 20, 23, 28 (n. 87), 44 (n. 120), 80, 81, 83, 91, 92, 96, 112, 123, 159, 160, 226 (with n. 4)

CIL (*Corpus Inscriptionum Latinarum*), 8 f. (with n. 27), 50–54 (with nn. 135 f.); cited *passim*; headquarters, Berlin, 98

Circus of Caligula (*Gai et Neronis* or *Vaticanus Circus*), 42, 110, 142 f.

citizens, how listed by the censor, Roman, 19 (n. 57)

citizenship, Roman, given to: Spanish-cavalry troop, 91; mariners/sailors, 130; "soldiers" of a cohort of Vigiles, 156

civil-service career after Diocletian, 170 f.

civitas et conubium, 130

c(larissima) f(emina), 159

clarissimus vir, 134, 156, 159. See also *vir clar.*

clarissimus et inlustris vir (after *v.c.*), 181

classici (mariners/sailors), 130

classis, 90, 130

Claudian, *Epithalamium*, 182

Claudian letters (i.e., invented by the emp. Claudius), 43, 116, 117, 118

Claudius (I, emp.), xvi, 25, 43, 115, 116, 117, 118, 119, 120, 121, 124

Claudius (II, emp.), 165

Claudius Drusus Germanicus, Nero ("Drusus the Elder"), 102 f.

Claudius Marcellus, M. (cos. 166, 155, 152 B.C.), 36, 86; husband of Octavia *minor*, 24

[Claudius Pulcher, Appius, G.f., cos. (143 B.C.)?], 88

clientela ("patronage"), 134

Clotho (one of the Fates), 141

codicilli, 143

cognomina, Roman, 20 (with n. 62), 21 (n. 65), 23, 24, 27 (with n. 85), 83; multiple, 19 (with n. 56)

coheres, 143

cohort of *vigiles*, 4th, Rome, 156

collections of Latin inscrs., the earliest, 53

collegia principalia, Sentinum, 164

collegium (private club or association), 89, 149

collegium Aesculapi et Hygiae, 149

Collegium Fabrum (Fire Dept., and/or Building Workers' Club), 163, 164

(collegium) Larum Augusti, 151

Collegium Magnum Arkarum Divarum Faustinarum Matris et Piae, 161

collegium pontificum, Rome, 142

coloni (colonists of a Roman colony), 106

colonus ("farmer") *hortorum holitoriorum*, 161

Column of Antoninus Pius, Rome, 150 f.

Column of Marcus Aurelius, Rome, 27, 152 f.

Column of Trajan, Rome, 39, 43, 86, 99, 138

columna rostrata, 124

comes d. n. Constantini Victoris Aug., 170

comes (Imp. Traiani) expeditionis Dacicae, 137

comes et [magister utriusque militiae?], 180

comes ordinis primi, 183

comes sacrarum largitionum, 181

comes sacri consistorii, 183

commemorative or honorary inscrs., 85, 86, 104, 105 f., 118, 124, 128 f., 135, 137, 140, 151, 170 f., 174 f., 179 f.

Congress of Greek and Latin Epigraphy, International, 9 (n. 27), 53 (with n. 134)

connectives (*et*, etc.), notable use of, 126

conscripti (local senators), 134

Consilium, a general's, 91

consonants not yet doubled in writing, 81, 82, 83 f., 88, 125 f.

conss. or *coss.* for *cos.*, in later use, 230

Constantine the Great (emp.), 168 f., 169 f.

Constantinian (chi-rho) monogram, 172, 180

Constantinople, 175

Constantius, father of Constantine the Great, 168

Constantius II (emp.), 30, 172

consul designatus, 104, 105, 115, 120, 178

consul ordinarius, 176, 179, 181

consularis, 170; *c. Lusitaniae*, 178

consuls, 81–185 passim, 227, 230; in West/East, 184

conversational syntax and style of a speech reported, 117

converting Roman dates to English, 233

copies vs. originals (inscrs.), 35 f., 40 (with n. 111), 83, 91, 124, 125

Coptites, 130

Corinth, 87, 90
Corinthus, gender of, 87
Cornelii Scipiones, 20, 22, 80
Cornelius Gallus, G., xvi, 9, 31, 42, 97–99, 111, 114
Cornelius Gn.f. Scipio Barbatus, L., 80–82
Cornelius Scipio Orfitus, L. (senator and augur), 166
corporati urbis Romae, caudicarii seu piscatores, 179
corpses, transfer of, 142
Corpus Inscr. Semiticarum 1.164, 13 (n. 38)
corrections of inscrs. by original cutter, 35, 77 f., 88, 150, 177, 185
corrector Tusciae et Umbriae, 178
corrosion of the surface of marble monuments in Rome, 168
cos., "monogrammatic," 37, 87, 142, 144
Crassus, M. (or P.?) Licinius, 100
criobolium, 166
cross, the Latin, 183, 185
cross, monogrammatic, with alpha/omega, 180
culpabere, deponent ("you will blame"), 148
cum ("whereas") preceding main clause of sentence, 106, 163 f.
cum circeis (means what?), 133
cum honore discessit (of a young poet in a contest), 130 f.
cura (the office of a *curator*), 134, 151 f.
curator aquarum, 119
curator rei alimentariae, 134
curator viarum, 93, 140
curatores (of a *collegium*), 149
Curia, in the Roman Forum, 109
curia aedis Mercuri (Ferentinum), 134
curialis, 178
"Curialsprache" (which avoids *et*), 126
Cybele and Attis, 165

d, forms ending in, 124, 125
D and R with strokes through them (as marks of abbreviation?), 172
Daci, 127
Dacicus, 129, 137
Damasus, Pope (366–384), 39, 176 f.
damnatio memoriae, 28, 37, 90, 123, 156
Danube river, 128
dating and the calendar, Roman, 226–233
dating Latin inscrs., 36, 40–42 (with n. 115), 77
dative singular ending in *-ē* in names from Greek, 143
dd. nn. FFll. (= *domini nostri Flavii duo*), 183
debeto, 122
decemvir stlitibus iudicandis, 137
decennalia, vicennalia, 168
decessit plus a date, 172
Decius (emp.), 29, 162
Decius, *nobilissimus Caesar*, 162
decrees, 82, 83 f., 91, 93, 106, 115, 120, 134, 140, 149, 151, 175
decurions (municipal council), 93, 106, 115, 136, 140, 151
dedications, 76, 82, 88, 96, 97, 110, 113, 115, 116, 123, 128, 143 f., 150, 155, 156, 158, 162, 165, 168, 172, 173 f., 176, 178, 179, 181
deification of Roman emperors, 28, 128, 129
Delos, 89

Delphi, 85
denarius, symbol for, 47, 150
depilatory, use of, 146 (col. 1, line 23), 147
depositus, -ta, plus a date, 183, 184, 185
descindentes (meaning?), 160
desultores ("circus riders"), 101
deterioration in the surface of the exterior of ancient buildings and the bacterial infections involved, 5 (n. 7), 168
deus, dominus (of the Flavians), 29 (n. 92)
devotissimi milites domni nostri Arcadius, Honorius, et Theodosius, perennes Augusti, 180
devotus, -ti numini maiestatique eius, 162, 172
dictator, 82, 92
die Kal(endarum) Iuniarum, 183
die xviii (mensis) Ianuari, 233
dies kar(a)e cognationis, 150
dies violaris, dies rosae, 150
dies Solis—dies Saturni, 232
Digest of Justinian, the, 156
dimissi honesta missione, 130. See also *missi h. m.*
Dio Cassius, 7 (n. 19), 21 (n. 68), 29 (n. 95), 93, 98, 100, 105, 114, 115, 123, 138 f., 228, 232
Diocletian, 29, 45 (n. 123), 227 (with n. 6)
Diocletian's Edict on Prices, xvi, 12, 29, 43, 45 (n. 123), 73, 108, 166 f.
Diodorus, 89
Dionysius Exiguus (introduced the Christian era), 227 (n. 6)
Dionysius of Halicarnassus, 78
diploma, military, 129
D. M., Dis Manibus, 40 f., 103, 106, 143, 144, 146
Divae Faustina mater et Pia, 161
divi principes, 175
division of the Roman Empire, Western/Eastern, 46 (n. 129)
Divus Caesar divi f. Augustus, 111
Divus Titus divi Vespasiani f. Vespasianus Augustus, 129
divus Traianus, 140
Dogmatius, 22 (with n. 71), 170
d(olo) m(alo), 94
domi forisque, 158
Domina Nostra Helena venerabilis, 169
domine Salvi (voc.), 161
domini Augustique nostri, 175
domini n(ostri), 169
domini n̄n̄. (= *nostri duo*), 153
domini n(ostri) Constantini Aug. mater, 169
dominus, 29
dominus indulgentissimus (of Caracalla), 29, 155; *d. noster*, 29, 30, 153 (line 50), 169; *d. et deus noster* (of Domitian), 29
Domitian (emp.), 129, 130
domnus, domna, 29, 30 (with n. 97), 180
domus: ("family"), 163, ("house"), 181
donis militaribus donatus bis, 137
dots over *d(omini) n(ostri)* apparently to mark them as abbreviations, 170, 171
doubling/tripling/quadrupling of consonants in abbreviating titles and names, 30, 176
doubling of vowels, 14, 88, 90 f.
Drusus the Elder (second son of Ti. Claudius Nero and Livia), 37; Drusus, 115; Drusus Germanicus, 112

ducenarius a consiliis sacris, 171. *See also* $\overline{CC}$
Duelona, 83
Duenos → Bonus, 18 (with n. 53)
Duenos Vase inscr., Berlin, xvi, 8 (n. 23), 18, 77 f.
Duilius, G. (cos. 260 B.C.), 16, 35 f., 40 (with
    n. 111), 86, 124–126
dulcissimae memoriae (dat.) *eius*, 142
dum clauses, 82, 83 f. (several), 146 (col. 2, line 3)
dumtaxat ut inferat, 149
duoviri (not written with numerical prefix), 93
duplicate inscrs., 110, 111, 118, 158, 168

e an interjection, "Oh"?, 161
Eastern Roman Empire, 50 (n. 132)
editing epigraphical texts, conventions in, 234–235
Egypt, Egyptian, 7 (n. 18), 33, 97 ff., 101, 110, 111,
    116, 130, 166, 232
Egyptian Museum, Cairo, 97
Elagabalus (Heliogabalus, emp.), 159
elogia, 33, 36, 42, 80, 88, 103, 124, 146, 176 f.
eministratio potionum, 136
emperors: chronol. list of Roman, 49 f.; their
    names, 21 f., 27–30
engravers (of inscrs.), 43 (n. 116). *See also*
    Stonecutters
engravings, inscrs. embellished with, 165
Ennius, 49, 81, 159
enos (= *nos*?), 161
Entimus, Matuccius, *lintearius*, 154
eo — ne videantur, 131
Epigraphical Museum, Athens, 166
epigraphy, history of Latin, 54 (n. 136)
epitaphs, 37, 40 f., 43, 95, 99 f., 100, 101, 106 f.,
    107 f., 112, 114, 119, 127, 130, 141, 144, 145,
    154, 159, 164, 171, 173, 177, 180, 183, 184
"Epulo" true, or pseudo, cognomen?, 102
eques Romanus, 98
[equester o]rdo et populus Romanus consentiente senatu,
    120
equestrian aristocracy, municipal, 137
equestrian official, 98
equestrian, then senatorial, *cursus honorum* of same
    man, 159
Equites Singulares, 144
Eq(uitius?) Heraclius, Christian *lector*, 171 f.
erasure of Latin inscrs., or of parts of them, 102,
    110, 116, 144, 150, 171, 179 f.
erasure of names from Latin inscrs., 28, 30, 39,
    116, 123, 156 f., 158 f.
ergo (preposition), 122
esto, 94 (6 ×), 122 (2 ×)
Etruria, Etruscan/Etruscans, 4 (n. 4), 13, 15, 20, 26
    (n. 81), 46 (n. 124), 75, 77, 100, 102, 229
Eutropius, 138
ex (+ abl.) to indicate a former official, 174
ex indulgentia (of an emp.), 132
ex permissu, 142
ex senatus consulto, 151 f.
ex utilitate urbis aeternae (Rome), 174
ex voto, 166
ex voto suscepto, 116
ex votos, 82, 87, 116, 144, 165 f.
examinator per Italiam, 171
exemplar ("copy"): of an inscr., 109; of letters, 153
exemplum ("copy") *libelli*, 161

expeditio Dacica, 137
extinctor pestiferae tyrannidis, 30, 172

f for *ph*, the letter, 17, 30
Fabricius Bridge, Rome, 93
Fabricius, L. (*curator viarum*, Rome, 62 B.C.), 93
facere + subjunctive, 84, 88
factio (of Maxentius), 169
factio alba ("the Whites," Rome), 113
familia ("body of servants"), 151; ("family"), 183
Fasti Antiates Maiores, 19
Fasti Consulares/Triumphales. See Capitoline *Fasti*
Fasti Hydatiani, 227
Fasti Magistrorum Vici, 107
Fasti Ostienses, 111, 138
Fata ("the Fates"), 141
Faustina the Elder, 28, 161
Faustina the Younger, 22 (n. 71), 25, 28, 29 (n. 95),
    161
favorabile est si, etc., 136 (line 17)
fecit ("lived") *cum maritum suum* (sic), 185
felicitas of an emp., 180
Felix (as an assumed or acquired cognomen), 20,
    28, 29, 33, 92
Ferentinum (mod. Ferentino), 7 (with n. 19), 43,
    134, 135
Feriae Imp. Caesar(is), 105; *Latinae*, 137
Feriale Duranum, 33 (n. 107)
Festus, 26 (n. 80), 78, 228
FFll. (= *Flavii duo*), *FFFFllll.* (= *Flavii quattuor*), 30
Fibula Praenestina (Praenestine fibula), xv, 8 (with
    n. 23), 11 (n. 30), 16 (with n. 46), 75 f.
Fides virtusque ... Arcadi, Honori, et Theodosi, 180
Fifeltares, 95
f(ilia) omitted in a woman's filiation?, 115
fil. or *filius* written instead of *f(ilius)*, 19 (n. 58),
    155, 158 f., 162 f.
f(ilius) in a name ("junior"), 134
Filocalus, Furius Dionysius, 39 (with n. 110), 40,
    43, 177
filter paper, 31
financial matters, 125, 132, 135 f., 143, 149, 151,
    153, 161
fisci advocatus per Italiam, 171
Fl(avius) Olbius Auxentius Draucus, *v. c. et inl.*,
    183
Flavius Stilicho, *v. c. See* Stilicho
fleet, a Roman, 90, 129
Florence, Italy, 86, 111, 133 f.
Florus (engraver), 43 (n. 116)
flusaris, mensis ("month of flowers"), 94, 95, 230
Fons, 123
food and wine at a yearly party, 136
forgeries of Latin inscrs., 8, 16 (with n. 46), 76
forma (a man's), 81
formulas in Latin inscrs., linguistic, 40 f., 163. *See
    also* Christian formulas
fortis vir sapiensque, 81
forum ("market place"), 88
Forum: of Augustus, Rome, 36; *Iulium* (Alexan-
    dria), 111; *Romanum*, Rome, 8 (n. 23), 37, 77,
    78, 105, 124, 128, 172; Popilii, 87
freedmen/freedwomen, Roman, 18, 23, 27, 123,
    131, 141 (Imperial), 143, 144 (Imp./non-Imp.),
    148 f. (Imp.), 151, 152 f., 155 (Imp.), 158

Frontinus, 119
Fronto, 113
fructūs ("provisions"), 103
frumentarius, 96
frumento publico incisi ("enrolled for free grain"),
     156
fugiteivi ("run-away slaves"), 88
fuerat in apodosis of Unreal Condition, 141
Fulvia Plautilla Aug. (wife of Caracalla), 28, 156 f.
Fulvius Plautianus, G., *praefectus praetorio*, 156
fundus ("farm"), 133, 135
Furfo (Vestinian *vicus*), 94

C̦ (= 6), 46
Gaius (emp.). *See* Caligula
Galatia (Roman province), 108
Gallic capture of Rome, 78
Gellius, 48 f., 95, 96, 110, 113, 228, 232 (n. 30)
Geminius Eutychetes, vegetable farmer, 161
Genius of a *centuria* of the 4th Cohort of Vigiles,
     Rome, 156; *Iovis* 94, 95
German king, 50 (n. 132), 108
Germania, 127
"Germanicus," 37, 102 f., 115
Germanicus/Agrippina the Elder, daughter of, 25
Germanicus Caesar (elder son of Drusus the El-
     der), 42 f., 107, 111 f.
germanus ("brother"), 181 f.
gerunds, gerundives, 83, 84, 85, 93 (2 ×), 104, 106,
     107, 119, 125, 134, 135, 137, 138, 143, 145, 151,
     174
Geta (brother of Caracalla), 28, 37, 49 (n. 130), 156,
     159
gilding of Latin inscrs. in bronze, 117
Gildo, *hostis publicus*, 179
gold objects, coins, 4 (n. 4), 75, 103, 116, 126
grain merchant, 95 f.
granite, 7 (n. 18), 97, 110
Greco-Aramaic bilingual inscr., 13 (n. 37)
Greek, Greeks, 8–232 (n. 30) passim
guidelines, 39 f., 42, 117 (none visible), 123, 162

H—wrongly added to "Adrastus," 153
H—omitted initially, 161, 163, 173
Hadrian (emp.), 20, 43, 49, 137, 139, 140, 142, 144
Hadrumetum, on African coast, 157
Hannibal (son of Gisco), 126
hebdomas ("week"), 228, 232 (n. 30)
heirs, instructions to, 142 f.
Helena, mother of Constantine the Great, 169 f.
Heraclius novus Constantinus (emp. 613–641), 228
Hercules, 82, 86, 87, 89
heres, heredes, 102, 143, 145, 153
Herennius Etruscus Messius Decius, Q., *no-*
     bilissimus Caesar, 162
Herod the Great, 227 (n. 6)
hierofanta (or *-tes*), 178
hieroglyphic, Egyptian, 97
Hindu names, 21 (n. 67)
Hirrus, G. Lucilius (?) *(legatus) pro praetore)*, 19,
     90 f.
Historia Augusta, 29 (n. 95), 30 (n. 98), 139, 140, 142
hoc monumentum heredem non sequitur, 145
honestum publicum ("public rectitude"? "the public
     sense of right"? "the national honor"? "the

law-abiding public"? "public opinion"?), 167 f.
Horace (Q. Horatius Flaccus), 78, 101, 113, 124, 232
Horatius Chryseros, P., 151
Horatius Chryserotianus, Sex., 151
hospitium, 135
hospitium, aedificium, habitatio—all of the same
     building, 153 f.
Hostilius, Hostus, 78
h(uic) m(onumento) d(olus) m(alus) a(besto), 145
Hyacinthus, *verna suus*, 144 f.
Hydatius' continuation of Jerome's *Chronicle*, 168
Hygīa, Hygeia, 150

I, tall, noted, 14, 41, 42, 104, 107, 111, 126, 136,
     137, 138, 146; apexed, 14, 103
iambic senarii, 34
Idus (the Ides of the month), 231
-ii written *-i* (at end of words), 154 f., 162
-iis written *-is* (in dat./abl. endings), 121, 151, 156,
     159, 163, 183
iit ad deum plus a date, 173
illae (fem. dat. sing.), 146, 148
imagines virorum inlustris ingeni, 112
immunis, "dues-exempt member" (of a *collegium*),
     150, 151
imperatives, future, 121, 122
Imperator: general's title ("Commander") sub-
     stituted for his own cognomen, 19, 82 f., 86,
     91 f.; "as Imperator," 87; as a new praenomen
     for the emperors, created by Augustus, 21 f.
     (with n. 68), 28, 104, 130, 138, but not used by
     Claudius, 115 f.; as an Imperial acclamation,
     104, 115, 116, 118, 119, 130, 138; as Imp. accl.?
     or "emperor"?, 115; overtaken by *d. n.* as first
     element in Imp. title, 30
*Imp. Caesar d. n. Fl(avius) Valens, Max(imus), P(ius),
     F(elix), Victor ac Triumfator, semper Aug.* (co-
     emp. Valens), 174
*Imp. Caes. Fl(avius) Constantinus Maximus Pius Felix
     Augustus*, 169
*Imp. Caes. G. Messius Quintus Traianus Decius Pius
     Felix Invictus Aug.* (emp. Decius), 162
*Imperator Caesar M. Aurelius Antoninus Aug., L.
     Septimi Severi Pii Pertinacis Aug. filius, dominus
     indulgentissimus* (Caracalla), 155
Imp. Caes(ar) M. Aurellius (sic) *Antoninus Pius Felix
     Aug(ustus)* (Caracalla), 104
Imp. Caesar Nerva Traianus Augustus Germanicus
     (emp. Trajan), 132, 134
Imp. Probus Aug. (A.D. 279), 165
*Imp(erator) Titus Caesar divi f(ilius) Vespasianus Au-
     gustus* (emp. Titus), 104
imperium populi Romani propagatum, 158
Impp. (= *Imperatoribus duobus*), 156
Impp. Severus et Antoninus Augg. Brittanici (sic),
     156
in + numeral to indicate the amount of a mort-
     gage, 132 f.
in avitum ("in perpetuity"), 136
in diebus X quibus, etc. (Time Within Which), 84
in hodiernum ("to date"), 161
in ignem inferri ("to be cremated"), 96
in pace, 184
in pace decessit, 172
in saeculum (sic) ("in the world"), 171

Incertus Auctor (*Liber de praenominibus*), 17 (n. 49), 19 (n. 56), 23
incision vs. casting of bronze lettering, 5 (n. 10), 91, 111, 117, 121, 129, 156, 163
inclusive counting, at both ends, the Romans', 168
inclytus frater (of an emp.), 174
indiction numbers, 227
indulgentissimus (of an emp.), 134, 155
inflation of prices/wages, 167
inlustris vir (Stilicho), 180
innocus (sic) *puer*, 181
inpensa ("building material"), 153
Inscriptiones Regni Neapolitani Latinae, 53, 54 (n. 135)
Inscriptiones Confoederationis Helveticae, 53
instinctu divinitatis, mentis magnitudine (of Constantine the Great), 169
intercalation in the pre-Julian calendar, 229 (with n. 14), 233
interest (money), 48, 133, 151 f.
interibi ("among [them] there"), 85
interpunctuation noted, 13 f., 33 (2 ×), 36 f., 41, 42, 43 (n. 116), 77, 82, 83, 89, 93, 95, 96, 99, 103, 105, 112, 117, 120, 127, 128, 136, 137, 145, 148, 166, 169, 182, 183
Israel Museum, Jerusalem, 113
Isthmus of Corinth, 90
Italici, who are they?, 88 f.
itero, rare variant of *iterum*, 141
itus, actus, aditus, ambitus (of a tomb), 145
itus, aditus, ambitus, 143
itus, ambitus, 161
iudex sacrarum cognitionum, 171
Iulia Aug., mater Augg. et castrorum (Julia Domna), 156
Iulius, the month—origin of its name, 228 f.
Iulius Lupus, P. (cos. suff. A.D. 97 or 98), 8 (n. 20)
Iulius Marinus, L. (cos. A.D. 101 or 102), 134
Iulius Postumus, G. (prefect of Egypt, A.D. 45–47), 116
Iul(ius) Silvester, *lapidar(ius)*, 43 (n. 116)
Iunius Balbus, G., *sub praefecto (vigilum)*, 156
Iunius Bassus, *v.c.*, 173
Iunius Quartus Palladius, *v.c.*, 181
Iunius Rufinus, G., *praefectus vigilum*, 156
ius: of a monument, 145, 153; of *horti holitorii*, 161
ius habuit ("considered it proper"?), 181 f.
ius potestasque sit, 121
iustitiale (in chariot racing), 113

Jerome, St., 39 (n. 110), 177
Jerusalem, 113, 128 f.
Jesus Christ, 114, 227 (n. 6)
Joannes Antiochenus, 123
Josephus, *Ant. Jud.*, 14 (n. 40)
Judaea, 43, 113 f.
Julia (daughter of Augustus), 106
Julia Domna, 29 (with n. 95), 30 (n. 97), 156, 159
Julia Soaemias Bassiana (niece of Julia Domna), 159
Julian and pre-Julian calendars, 229 f., 231 (n. 20)
Julius Caesar, 21 (n. 68), 28, 34, 96 f., 113, 228 f.
Jupiter Liber at Furfo, 94
Juvenal, 18, 29 (n. 95)

Kalendae, 228, 230
kandidatus, 181

Karthago, 157
kasibus, 104
Kunsthistorisches Museum, Antikenabteilung, Vienna, 83

Lachesis (one of the Fates), 141
Lactantius, 167
"Lapis Niger," 78
L'Aquila, Italy, 94
Lares, 160
Lateran, the (St. John in Lateran, Rome), 5, 43, 121, 170, 171, 182
latex (liquid rubber), 31 f. (with n. 101), 35
Laudatio Murdiae, 10
"Laudatio Turiae," 10, 34, 103 f., 110
lawsuit caused by a Latin inscr., 146
lector ("Reader," Christian), 172
legal inscrs., 14 (n. 40), 83 f., 111 f., 121 f., 135 f., 145, 148–150, 151 f., 163
legal phrases, 128, 134, 137, 163
"legalese," 83, 112, 150
legatus, 98 (envoy), 107 (Imperial), 134 (envoy), 140 (Imp.), 163 (envoys), 181 (envoy)
legatus Aug. pro praetore provinc. Britanniae, 140
legatus et comes Claudii Caesaris in Brittannia, 127
legatus legionis I Adiutricis, 140
legatus legionis I Minerviae P. F. bello Dacico, 137
legatus legionis III Augustae, 159
legatus legionis V in Germania, 127
legatus pro pr. Imp. Nervae Traiani Caesaris Aug. Germanici Dacici Pannoniae Inferioris, 137
legatus pro praetore Moesiae, 127
legatus pro praetore provinc. Germaniae Inferioris, 140
legatus pro praetore provinc. Thrac(iae), 140
legatus senatus amplissimi quarto (= *quater*), 181
legio I Adiutrix, 140
legio I Minervia P. F. bello Dacico, 137
legio II Adiutrix P. F., 137
legio V in Germania, 127
legio V Macedonica, 137
legio XXII Primigenia P. F., 137, 140
lettering of inscrs. noted, 109, 110, 123, 124, 136, 139, 150, 164, 165, 166, 168, 172
letters (epistles), 152 f.
leucitite, 6, 102
Lex Acilia (?) *Repetundarum*, 19 (n. 57)
Lex Agraria (111 B.C.), 30 (n. 97)
Lex collegi Aesculapi et Hygiae, 148
Lex de Gallia Cisalpina, 47
"Lex de Imperio Vespasiani," 4 (n. 5), 43, 121 f.
Lex Iulia de civitate Latinis et sociis danda (90 B.C.), 91 f.
Lex Iulia Municipalis, 19 (n. 57), 45 (n. 123)
Lex Municipii Tarentini, 45 (n. 123)
lex publica, 145
lex rogata, 121
Lex, Rogatio Iunia Petronia, 111
Lex Rufrena, 97
Lex Sempronia Agraria (133 B.C.), 89
libellus ("petition"), 161
Liber de praenominibus. See *Incertus Auctor*
liberator urbis, fundator quietis (of Constantine the Great), 169
libr(arius) i(nstrumentorum ?) *d(epositorum* ?) (of a cohort of Vigiles), 156

liceto, 94 (2 ×)
ligatures, 33, 37, 92, 95, 99, 136, 160, 163, 165, 172 (?), 178, 184, 185
Ligures Baebiani, 132
limestone, Italian, 6, 7 (with nn. 16–18), 87, 93, 94, 113, 135
line ends, treatment of, noted, 37, 39, 135
Livius Andronicus, 81 f.
Livy, 16, 18, 80, 81, 83, 85, 92, 95 (2 ×), 110, 229 (n. 12)
local dignitaries, 135, 151
locat, a contracted perfect, 34
Louvre, Paris, 82
Lowie Museum of Anthropology, Univ. of Calif., Berkeley, 32 (with n. 104)
Lucana (sc. *terra*), 81
Lucian, 131
Lucilius (satirist), 91
"Lucio" written in full, 19 (n. 58), 158 f.
Lucretius Vespillo, Q. (cos. 19 B.C.), 103 f.
Ludi Saeculares (Secular Games), Rome, 100 f., 110
ludi scaenici ("theatrical performances"), 101
Lugdunum (Gallia Lugdunensis), 117
Luni (anc. Luna), 86
Lupercal, Rome, 109
Lusitania, 178
lustrum: primum, 123; *tertium*, 131
Lyon, France, 117

m omitted at end of words, 81, 87, 127, 141, 151, 156, 163, 164, 165, 181 (?)
M (numeral), 44, 46 (n. 126)
M̄ (= a million, not ancient), 44 (n. 120), 126 f.
Macedonia or Macedonians, 86, 140
Macrobius, 86, 228 f.
magister censuum, m. libellorum, m. studiorum, 171
magister utriusque militiae, 179
magistri II quinquennales lustri primi, 123
magistri/ministri of *Fons/Fons Scaurianus*, 123
Magnentius ("usurper"), 30
Magnus (as an acquired cognomen), 20, 92
Manes (a dead person's), 106
"Manius," generally printed "M'." in abbreviation, 21 (n. 65)
manumission of slaves, 143
marble, 5 f., 7 (with n. 16), 16, 86, 89, 90, 96 (2 ×), 99–184 passim
Marcellus, M. Claudius (nephew, and son-in-law, of Augustus), 100
March originally the first Roman month, 228
Marcianus, a boy, 140 f.
Marcius, Q. (cos. 186 B.C.), 83
maritus et pater amantissimus, 159
Marius, G. (cos. 7 times 107–86 B.C.), 19
Mars (or Marmar), 160
"Masters of Mercury, Apollo, Neptune," 89
Mater Castrorum, 28, 29 (with n. 95)
Mater Deum Magna [*Idaea*?] (Cybele), 166
matronae (of Pisa), 106
Matuccius Pallas, T., Entimus, and Zmaragdus, 154
Mausoleum of Augustus, Rome, 99, 100, 107, 114
Maxentius (rival of Constantine the Great), 168
Maxima, "Handmaid of Christ," 184 f.
Maximus (of an emp.), 33 (n. 107), 164, 174
Maximus, Pius, Felix in an emperor's title, 174

medially barred symbols, 150
Memmia Victoria, *mater numeri nostri*, 163
memoriola, memoria ("funeral monument, tomb"), 161
mensis flusaris (at Furfo), 94
Messallina (wife of emp. Claudius), 116
metrical considerations in verse, noted, 81, 130, 141
milestones, 33, 87 f.
militant, 130
military matters, 81, 82 f., 86, 87, 90, 91 f., 98 f., 106, 120, 125 f., 127, 130, 144, 156
milites of a *centuria* of a cohort of Vigiles, Rome, 156
minium, ancient, 6 (with n. 11), 31, 97
Minturno (anc. Minturnae), 97
Minucius, Marcus, dictator (217 B.C.), 82
missi honesta missione, 144. See also *dimissi h. m.*
mixture of grammatical persons in same inscr., 146, 148
module defined, 40, 42
Moesia (variously spelled), 127, 171
(*mons*) *Vaticanus*, Rome, 142 f.
monumentum ("tomb"), 143, 145
Monumentum Ancyranum, 33, 38, 73, 108–110
Monumentum Antiochenum, 108 f., 109
Monumentum Apolloniense, 108 f., 110
m[*onument(um) aureum*?], 179
mortgages (*obligationes*), 132 f.
motum oriens Sarmartarum, 127
mulieres nuptae, 136
Mummius, L. (cos 146 B.C.), 87
municipes vs. *incolae*, 136 f.
municipes et incolae et mulieres nuptae, 136
municipium, 134
munificentia in municipes suos, 135
Musée de la Civilisation Gallo-Romaine, Lyon, 117
Musae, 141
Museo Archeologico, Florence, 111, 134
Museo Archeologico Nazionale, Aquileia, 140
Museo Maffeiano, Verona, 115
Museo Nazionale, L'Aquila, 94
Museo Nazionale, Naples, 92
Museo Nazionale Preistorico "Luigi Pigorini," Rome, 75
Museo Nazionale Romano, Rome, 5, 76, 100, 103, 106, 118, 119, 123, 132, 143, 146, 161, 174, 178, 183, 184, 229
Museo Profano, Vatican Library, 129
Museo Torlonia, Rome, 5
museums. *See* Camposanto, Pisa; Capitoline Mus., Rome; Corinth; Delphi; Egyptian Mus., Cairo; Epigraphical Mus., Athens; Israel Mus., Jerusalem; Kunsthistorisches Mus., Vienna; Louvre, Paris; Musée; Museo; Palazzo dei Conservatori, Rome; Staatliche Museen, Berlin; Vatican; Victoria and Albert Museum, London; Villa Albani, Rome; Villa Giulia Museum, Rome
Mysiae (= *Moesiae*), 171

n, barred above, as an abbreviation, 150, 163, 164
names:
 "also-known-as" type, 22 f. (n. 71)

Christian, 17 (with n. 50), 22, 165, 171, 173, 177, 181, 183, 185
emperors', 27–29
family, as "Christian" names, modern, 21 (n. 66)
gentilicia, Roman, 17 (with n. 48), 18, 21 (with n. 65), 22, 145 (abbrev.)
Greek, 9 (n. 27), 17 (n. 48), 18 (n. 52)
Hernican, 135
Hindu, 21 (n. 67)
-illa, *-itta* types, 25 (n. 74)
Indo-European, 19 (n. 56), 21 (n. 65)
Italic, 17 (n. 48)
Jewish, 17 (with n. 50)
medieval/modern latinized, 23
patronymics, Scandinavian, 21 (n. 67)
Roman, 17–30, 35, 131, 157
Roman men's in chronological order, 22 (n. 71)
Roman slaves', 17 (n. 48), 25–27
Sikhs', 21 (n. 67)
Spanish, 91
women's, free-born, 21 (n. 65), 22 (n. 71), 23–25 (with n. 75)
See also agnomina; cognomina; praenomina
Naples, 5, 45 (n. 123), 50 (n. 132), 92
naval matters, 125 f., 129 f.
neocorus, 178
negotiator Lugdunensis artis cretariae, 233
neofitus ("new convert, neophyte" to Christianity), 173
Nepos, 22 (with n. 69), 226 (n. 4)
Nepos (Roman emp. in the West), 50 (n. 131)
Neratius Cerealis, *v. c.*, 172
Nerva (emp.), 43, 119, 129, 132
Nile, the, 97, 98, 99
nobil(issimus) Caes(ar), 30, 162
nomine + genitive, 181
Nonae ("Nones" of the month), 230 f.
Nonius Paternus, consul *bis* (A.D. 279), 165
Norbanus (*nomen gentilicium*), 113
n̄(oster) (barred, esp. in Imperial titles), 144, 149
notarius et tribunus, 181
note-takers/stenographers, 118
numerabit, 143
numerals, Roman, 44–49 (with nn. 118–128), 82–185 passim
n(umerat?), 132 f.
numerical prefixes, generally barred (as in *IIviri*), 47, 101, 102, 106, 107, 127, 128, 134, 135 f., 137, 140
numerus (= a *collegium*), 163
nummi ("money"), 238
nundinae, nundinus, 228, 231 (with n. 21), 232 (with n. 25)

ob memoriam + genitive, 149
obelisks, in Rome, 42, 110, 111
obligare ("to mortgage"), 132
Octavia, *maior/minor* (sisters of Augustus), 23 f., *minor*, 100
Octavia, Claudia (daughter of emp. Claudius), 25
Octavian (later Augustus), 21 (n. 68), 22 (n. 69), 98 (*Caesar deivi f[ilius]*), 100, 111
Odoacer, 50 (n. 132)

office-heads, Imperial freedmen, 154
Olympia, Greece, 5 (n. 10)
onomastics, international conference on (Paris 1975), 17 (n. 48)
optimi fortissimique principes (over an erasure), 158 f.
optimus, patronus, 154
Optimus (Imperial cognomen), 29
optimus vs. *indulgentissimus, praestantissimus*, 42
Optimus Maximus (Imperial), 33 (n. 107)
[optimus maxi]musque princeps (Trajan), 132
optio of a centurion (of a cohort of Vigiles), 157
opus caementicium, brick-faced, 101
oratio, 117 (*tua*), 127 (Vespasian's), 175
orbis terrarum, 109
order of listing titles in career inscrs., 138, 140
ordinal adjectives, 119, 137, 149, 150
ordinal adverbs (regularly barred), 47, 104, 113, 115, 116, 118, 119, 123, 128, 144, 156, 158, 163
ordo, populus, homines (the membership of a *collegium*), 150
Orestes (father of the emp. Romulus Augustulus), 50 (nn. 131 f.)
orthography, transitional, reflecting changes of pronunciation, 171
ossa / *cineres Agrippinae*, 115
Ostia, 5, 41, 151 f., 227
Otricoli (Umbria), 96
Ovid, 33, 49, 96, 113, 146, 228, 231, 232

paedagogi puerorum a Capite Africae, 155
pagan opponents of Christianity, saec. IV, 174, 178
paint added in museums, red, 35, 152, 155, 177
palaeography of Latin inscrs., 38–40, 41, 77, 93, 123 f., 125
paragraphing, 122; sign, 148; by indentation, 162
Palatina tribus, 136
Palazzo dei Conservatori, Rome, 5 (n. 7), 82, 102, 114, 116, 124, 130, 164, 179, 181, 226
Palestrina (anc. Praeneste), 6, 13 (n. 38), 24, 75 f.
Palladius. See Iunius Quartus P.
Pandateria island (mod. Ventotene), 114
Pannonia Inferior, 137
Pantheon, Rome, 43, 49, 139
papal inscrs., 129, 176
parentes ("parents"), 131, 172 (?)
pariator ("one who pays his bills properly"), 161 f.
Parthicus: Adiabenicus, 158; *Arabicus* 158; *Maximus*, 28, 33 (with n. 107), 104
Parthians, 158 f.
pater, mater (of a *collegium*), 150
pater naturalis, 112
pater patriae, 28 (n. 87), 104, 116, 118, 119, 130, 138, 158
pater sacrorum, 178
Paternus (cos. A.D. 269), 165
patres conscripti, 117
p(atres?) p(atriae?), 156
patriciae familiae vir, 183
patronage, a town's request for, 133 f.
patronus, 134, 140, 154, 163, 176
patronymics, 21 (n. 67)
pearls, a lady's, 103
peculiares eius ("his own people"), 176
pedatura ("footage in front of a tomb"), 144 f.
perennes Augusti, 180

perfect subjunctive in Result Clause after *ita praefuit*, 127
periodic-style sentences, Latin, 74, 83 f., 98, 121 f., 123, 134 f., 150, 162
Persephone, 141
Persiphone (*sic*), 146
Perseus (last Macedonian king), 85
Perusina ("a woman of Perugia"), 146
Pescennius Niger (claimant to Imp. power), 158
petitu senatus amplissimi, 183
petitus in pace (of a Christian child), 181
Petronius Arbiter, 232
Petronius Fronto, L. (of Ferentinum), 134
Petronius Probus (Sex. Claudius), *v. c.*, 176
P(ia) F(idelis) (of a legion), 137, 140
ph to *f* (sound change from aspirate to spirant), 172 f.
Philae (island in the Nile), 97, 98
philanthropy, private benefactions, 135 f., 148 f.
Phoenician, 4 (n. 4), 13 (n. 38)
"Phosphorius," 22 (n. 71), 175
piaculum factum, 142
Pisa (*Colonia Obsequens Iulia Pisana*), 105 f.
piscatores, 179
Pisidius Romulus, *v. c.*, 180
Pius, Piissimus (Imp. cognomina), 28, 29, 33
Pius, Felix in an emp.'s title, 174
placere plus accus. with infin. or *ut/ne* with subjunct., 135
planetary names of the days of the week, 232 f. (with n. 31)
Plataea, 166
Platorius Nepos Aponius Italicus Manilianus G. Licinius Pollio, A. (cos. suff. A.D. 119), 19 f., 140
Plautius Silvanus Aelianus, Ti., 127
Plautus, 8
plebis (and *plebei*) *scita*, 121
Pliny the Elder, 5 (n. 10), 6 (n. 11), 25 f. (with n. 77), 28 (n. 87), 45 (n. 120), 46, 92, 110, 119, 124, 125, 162, 230 (n. 15)
Pliny the Younger, 20 (n. 63), 29 (with n. 92), 44 (n. 117), 164
plus minus ann(is), plus a numeral, 185
Plutarch, 17 (n. 48), 18, 19, 83, 85, 87, 92
Poland, Latin inscrs. in, 41 (n. 113)
Polemius Silvius, *Fasti* (A.D. 449), 231 (n. 20)
Polla (in Lucania), 87
Polybius, 4 (with n. 4), 85, 125
pomerium, 118, 121
Pompeii, 3 (n. 2), 17, 46, 92 f., 173, 232
Pompeius (Strabo) Imperator, Gn. (cos. 89 B.C.), 91
Pompeius ... Sosius Priscus, Q. (38 names in all) (cos. A.D. 169), 19
Pompey, 19, 20, 49, 91, 92, 93
Pomponius Bassus, T. (*clarissimus vir*), 134
pons, Valentinianus (Rome), 174
pontifex, 127, 135, 142
pontifex maior, 175
pontifex maximus (of the Roman emps.), 104, 115, 116, 118, 119, 130, 138
pontifex Solis, Vestae, 178
Pontius Pilate, xvi, 13 (with n. 39), 42, 113 f.
Popilius Heracla, G. (to his heirs), 143
populus Romanus, 109, 118, 125, 127

populus senatusque Romanus, 82. See also *Senatus Populusque Romanus*
Porta Maggiore (anc. P. Praenestina), Rome, 118
Porta Tiburtina, Rome, 104
Portico of Gaius and Lucius, Rome, 105
Porticus Octavia, Rome, 109
portrait statue with inscr., 170
post consulatum plus genitive, 183
post-Silver Age Latin, 135
Postumius, S(purius) (cos. 186 B.C.), 83
potesto, 94
"Potitus" as a praenomen, 21 (n. 66)
pottery (as a help in dating), 41, 77
praedia ("properties"), 132 f.
praefectura urbis (Rome), 127
praefectura urbi (Rome), 173
praefectus aerari militaris, 159
praefectus annonae urbis (Rome), 171
praefectus annonae urbis Romae, 175
praefectus classis, 130
praefectus fabrum, 111, 135
praefectus feriarum Latinarum, 137
praefectus praet(orio) Italiae et Yllyrici (sic), 178
praefectus praetorii per annos sex Illyrici, Italiae, et Africae, 181
praefectus praetorio per Illyricum, Italiam, et Africam, 176
praefectus urbi or *urbis* (Rome), 127, 173, 175, 178
praefectus urbi (Rome) *vice sacra iudicans*, 172
praefectus urbi (Rome) *vice sacra iterum iudicans*, 180
praefectus urbis Romae, 183
praenomen omitted in name of Titus (future emp.), 124
praenomina, 15, 21 (with nn. 66, 68), 23, 113 (fancy), 164 (beginning to be used less), 175 (written in full)
[*praesentalis* ("in immediate attendance on the emp.")]?, 180
praeses provinc. Numidiae, 159
praetor, 88, 137, 140
praetor et quaestor kandidatus, 181
praetor urbanus, 83 f., 107, 178
Pratica di Mare (or Lavinio, anc. Lavinium), 76
pratum Exosco, 136
Primigen(ia) P(ia) F(idelis) (of a legion), 140
Primus, Flavius Rhodinus (procos. of Africa ca. 392), or his son (legatus of Numidia ca. 392), 177
Princeps Iuventutis ("Prince of the Youth"), 105, 162 f.
principales (= junior officers) of a cohort of Vigiles, 156
principes (foreign), 127
principes maximi (2 co-emps.), 174
Priscian, 26 (with n. 80), 44 f. (with nn. 119, 120)
pro consule, 90
proconsul Achaiae, 178
proconsul Africae, 176
procos., 158
[*procos.* or *pro consule*?] *Asiae bis*, 107
procos. (or *pro cos.*?) *Asiae*, 127
pro praefectis praetorio in urbe Roma finitimisque provinciis, 175
pro praetore, 90
pro salute dedication, 116

pro virtutum veneratione ("out of high regard for great deeds"?), 179
probatus ("accepted as a recruit"), 233 (with n. 34)
Probus (of Berytus, scholar), 26 (n. 80)
procurator Aug. qui fuit a pinacothecis, 149
procurator Columnae Centenariae (divi Marci), 153
procurator Columnae divi Marci, 153
procurator: not *Iudaeae*, 114; *aquar(um)*, 159; *prov. Britanniae*, 159; *rationis privatae*, 159
profligata in the *Monumentum Ancyranum*, 110
Proiecta (a Christian), 177
Propertius, 100
providentia of an emp., 174
provinces and the provincial system saec. I A.D., 127 f.
provincia Britanniae, 120, 140, 159
provincia Germaniae Inferioris, 140
provincia Macedoniae, 140
Prudentius, 173
puer ("[young] slave"), 25 f. (with n. 81); (young Christian), 181
pueri (probably slaves) *a Capite Africae*, 155
pueri, curiae incrementa, 136
pueri plebei sine distinctione libertatis, 136
pueri puaellaeque (sic), 132
Pulvinar ad circum maximum, 109
punctuation. *See* interpunctuation
punctuation mark, major, 101
Punic (or Phoenician), 4 (n. 4)
Pylades/Orestes, 146
Pyramid of Cestius, Rome, 101 f.
"pyramids" of Dio 53.23.5 perhaps rather "obelisks," 98

Q (= 500,000), 44 f. (with n. 120), 46
Q Q for any form of *quinquennalis*, 150
quadrigae, 101, 113
quaestor, 107, 127 (*Ti. Caesaris*), 137 (*Imp. Traiani*)
quaestor candidatus, 178, 181
quaestor provinc. Macedoniae, 140
q(uaestores) et scrib(ae) of a *collegium*, 161
quamvis + subjunctive, 127
quando ("since"), 106
quator ("vulgar" for *quattuor*), 181
quarto = quater ("four times"), 181
quattuorvir (IIIIvir) aed. potest., 135
quattuorvir (IIIIvir) iure dic., 134, 135
quattuorvir (IIIIvir) quinq., 135
quattuorviri (IIIIvir.), 136
questions in inscrs.: direct, 165, 177; indirect, 117, 138, 163
Quinctius Crispinus, T. (cos. 9 B.C.), 102 f.
Quinctius Flamininus, T. (cos. 192 B.C.), 6
Quinctius Valg(us), G. (Pompeii), 93
quincunx (= 5%), 132
quindecimviri (later -*cem*-) *sacris faciundis*, 101 (no *s.f.*), 107, 175,178 (no *s.f.*)
quinquennalis (of a *collegium*), 149, 163; *p(er)p(etuus)*, 150; *et immunis*, 151; *Faustinae matris*, 161
Quintilian, 14 (2 ×), 26 (with n. 80), 95, 116 f., 118, 124
quo = ubi ("when"), 141
quod ("whereas"), 134 (see also *cum*, "whereas"); ("because, on the ground that"), 151
quod sciam vs. *quantum scio*, 95

quoniam + subjunctive, 163
qurois (=κούροις), 76 f.

rationales (of the emps.), 153
rationalis (rei) privatae, 171
rationalis vicarius per Gallias, 171
records, public, of Roman citizens, Rome, 95 (Tabularium), 158
recutting of inscrs. over erasures, 102, 159
reditus ("income"), 149
regio secunda (of Christian Rome), 172
reliquiae of a person, 142, 143
rent, annual, paid by a farmer, 161
request for permission to build, 152 f., 161
requiescit in pace, 185
res publica, 136, 169, 183
res publica written as one word, 123, 181
res publica nostra, 167
res publica restituta, 158 f.
restitutor urbis Romae adque (sic) *orbis*, 172
restorations of Latin inscrs., 35, 37, 103, 132
retrograde writing, 76
re-use of inscribed stones, 37, 170, 171, 179 (1 or 2 ×), 184 (?)
reverse index of Latin words, 12 (n. 35)
revocatus (in chariot-racing), 113, 243
rex, reges, 78 f., 86, 98, 127
Rhegium (Strait of Messina), 88, 157
Rhoxolani, 127
rivi aquarum, rivus aquae Marciae, 104
road-making, 88
rogatio, 111, 121
Roman Forum. See *Forum Romanum*, Rome
Romana dignitas maiestasque, 167
Rome (anc. or mod.), 4–184 passim
Romulus Augustulus, 50 (with nn. 131, 132)
rub, rubbing, 30–32
run-over lines (boustrophedon), 76, 79, 87 f., 150, 164

s, final, omitted in pronunciation of verse, 91
s with medial bar (= *sub*), 156, 157
sacer ("Imperial"), 104 f., 171, 183
Sacra Via, Rome, 105, 141
sacrae largitiones, 181
sacram urbem suam (Caracalla's), 104
sacrificium, 101, 143, 145
sacrum consistorium, 183
sacrum with dative case, 111
s(a)eculum, "this wicked world" (a Christian notion), 165, 171
Salii, 112
salutem: (to heirs), 143; (to a servant), 153
Salvidienus Rufus, Q. (associate of Octavian), 95
Samnium, 81, 131 f.
Sanctio (of a *lex*), 121
sarcophagi, 80, 81 f., 159, 171, 173
Sarmatae, 127
saturnian verse, 81 f., 87, 160
Saturnina, her sons Valentinus and Eusebius (Christians), 183
scientes esetis (= *sciretis*), 84
Scipio Africanus the Elder, 81
Scipio Africanus Aemilianus, 87

Scipionic epitaphs, 8 (n. 22), 16, 36, 39, 40, 42, 49, 80, 96, 98, 126
Scirtus (freedman of M. Livius —?), charioteer, 112
scola (= *schola*) of a *collegium*, 163
scribae ("clerks") of a *collegium*, 161
sculptured: altar, 144; arch, 128, 158, 169; busts in relief above inscr., 156; column, 150; figure on gravestone, 130, 141; framework of an inscr., 135; sarcophagus, 173
Scythae, 127
secundas, tertias (sc. *partes tulit*) ("took 2nd, 3rd, place" in chariot racing), 113
Segestani (in Sicily), 125
Segiarnus Maecianus, Q. (of Ferentinum), 134, 135
seiuges ("six-horse chariot"), 113
self-addressed part of a speech, 118
self-adoption into a more respectable family, 155, 159
Selinus (in Cilicia), 142
Semones, 160
semper Aug. (in Imperial titles), 30, 172
senate, local (*conscripti*), 106, 134, 135
senate, the Roman, 83, 105, 112, 115, 121, 123, 127, 151, 152, 170, 175, 181, 183
senatorial careers, 127, 137, 140
senatum consulere, 134
senatus amplissimus (Rome), 175, 183
senatus consultum, 102, 121, 135, 151
Senatus Consultum de Bacchanalibus, xvi, 14 (n. 40), 16, 32, 83, 232
Senatus Populusque Romanus, 129, 138, 158, 169, 174, 180
Seneca the Elder, 19 (n. 61)
Seneca the Younger, 100
sentences, unusually long, in these inscrs.: nos. **8, 15, 22, 31, 36, 46, 49, 54, 66, 72, 78, 84**
Sentinum (in anc. Umbria), 163
septemvir epulonum, 102, 137
Septimius Bassianus ("Caracalla"), 104
Septimius Severus (emp.), 19 (nn. 56, 58), 27, 29 (n. 95), 104, 139, 155, 156, 158
Septimius Vegetus, G. (prefect of Egypt), 130
serifs, 39 (explained), 42, 82, 89
Servius (4th-cent. grammarian/commentator), 124
sevir turmae equitum Romanorum, 137
seviri Augustales, 135, 151
sesterces, *sestertius*, 44, 47, 48, 136, 143, 149, 151 f., 161
seu ("and"?), 179. See also *sive*
Severa Seleuciane (a Christian), 165
sexagenarius a consiliis sacris, 171
sexagenarius studiorum adiutor, 171
sextarius, symbol for, 48, 150
shading, 39 (defined), 42, 82
si quid ei humanitus acciderit ("if she dies"), 143
Sicily, 88, 125 f.
Siddus (or Siddius) (a Christian), 180 f.
Side, Pamphylia, 90
signa, supernomina, 22 f. (n. 71), 175 f.
signa (military standards) *Romana*, 127
signum ("sculptured figure"), 87, 149
Silius A. Caecina Largus, G. (cos. A.D. 13), 22 (n. 71)
Silius Italicus, 124
Silvanus, 143 f.

silver: bowl, inscribed, 13 (n. 38); coins, 126
simulacrum Apollinis, 112
sinito, 122
sive, seu (= *et*?), 166, 179
slaves, Roman, 17 f. (with n. 48), 23, 25–27, 82 f.
sling-bolts of lead, inscribed, 53
"Social" War, 90–89 B.C., 42, 53, 91
sodalis Augustalis, 127, 137
solarium ("ground rent"), 153
Solinus, 226 (n. 4)
Sosigenes (Egyptian astronomer), 230
space left within an inscr. for unknown reason, 150
spaces left in inscrs. for paragraph—and sentence—breaks, 103
Spain, Spanish, 82 f., 91
speeches, or parts of speeches, recorded verbatim in inscrs., 117, 127
splendidissimus n(umerus) n(oster) (a *collegium*), 163
S.P.Q.R. See *Senatus Populusque Romanus*
squeeze (epigraphical), 30–32 (with nn. 100, 103), 35
St. Peter's (in Vaticano, Rome), 142, 154, 160, 162, 173
Staatliche Museen, Antikenabteilung, Berlin, 77
statua, eius, 181
statua et imago (or *imagines*) *meae*, 136
statua, altera, pari splendore, 175
statua auro fulgens, 183
statua, auro inlustris, 175
statua publice ponenda in foro, 135
statue bases, statues, 82, 86, 88, 92, 96, 124, 135 f., 137, 140, 151 f., 155 (?), 170, 172, 175, 176, 178, 179, 181
statuette, gold, 116
stele, marble, Greek, 166
Stilicho, 30, 37, 178 f., 180
stonecutters or -engravers, 32 f., 39, 43 (n. 116), 82
Strait of Messina, 88
style of some inscrs. noted, 33, 73 f., 125, 135, 167, 169, 176, 183. *See also* bureaucratese; legalese; verbose style
subjunctives, 82 (4 ×), 83 f. (many), 135 f. (3 ×), 141 (4 or 5 ×), 143 (2 ×), 146 f. (7 ×), 149 (6 ×), 151 (2 ×), 152, 153 (6 ×), 161 (3 ×), 163 (11 ×), 175 (3 ×), 183 (2 ×)
sudore largo laboratum est, 167
Suetonius, 21 (with n. 68), 44 (n. 117), 87 f., 91, 99, 100, 105 (2 ×), 107, 108, 114, 115, 117, 119, 123, 124, 128, 229
suffragatio, 121
Sulla, L. Cornelius (dictator), 20, 29, 40, 91, 92
Sulpicius Eugramus, Q., 131
Sulpicius Q(uinti) f(ilius) Cla(udia tribu) Maximus domo Roma, Q., 131
sum(ma) sum(marum), 113
sunto, 94
supernomen (or signum), 22 f. (with n. 71)
supralineate abbreviations, 42, 144, 150, 151, 153, 156, 177, 183, 184, 185
supralineate numerals, 44, 45 (n. 123), 47–48, 151. *See also* numerical prefixes
Switzerland, 33, 43 (n. 116), 53
symbol for *centuria* or centurion, 157
symbolism, Christian. *See* Christian symbolism

Symmachus (father of the orator/letter-writer), 22, 174 f.
syntax, noteworthy, 87, 144, 148, 152, 153 f.

tertio, quarto, etc., used adverbially, the case of, 96
tesserarius of a *centuria* of a cohort of Vigiles, 156
testamentum ("last will and testament"), 102, 143
Testaments, Old and New, 43, 173
Tharsus, Cilicia, 157
theaters, 92 f., 114, 115, 137
theatrum tectum (Pompeii), 93
thermae incendio destructae (Rome), 169
Tiber river, Rome, 93, 174, 179
Tiberieum, 113, 114
Tiberius (emp.), 29 (n. 92), 110, 112, 114, 121 f.
Ti(berius) Caesar divi Augusti f. Augustus, 111
Tibullus, 232
tignorum vehes ("wagon loads of lumber"), 153
Tiro (Cicero's learned freedman), 49
tituli loquentes, 34, 75, 141
titulus ("inscription" or "inscribed monument"), 144, 147
Titus (emp.), 28, 104, 123 f., 125, 128 f.
Tivoli (anc. Tibur), 6 (n. 14), 8 (n. 23), 127
tombs, family, 106, 120, 127, 161 f.
tomb formulas, 145
Tracheotae, 120
trachite, 7 (with n. 18)
Trajan (emp.), 29, 33 (n. 107), 43, 119, 128 f., 132, 134, 137, 138 f., 140, 141 f., 164
Transdanuviani, 127
translating the inscrs., difficulties in, noted, 164, 180, 183
travertine, 6 f., 34 (n. 108), 82, 86, 92, 93 [2 ×], 101, 104, 107, 118 [2 ×], 128
tria nomina (of the free-born Roman), 18, 22
"tribal" names, pseudo-, 157
tribunicia potestate (usually abbreviated), 104, 115, 116, 118, 119, 130, 138
tribuniciae potestatis, 104
tribunus (numeri equitum singularium), 144
tribunus legionis II̲ Adiutricis P. F., 137
tribunus legionis V̲ Macedonicae, 137
tribunus legionis XXII Primigeniae P. F., 137
tribunus militum leg. XXII Primigeniae P. F., 140
tribunus plebis, 102, 137, 140
tribunus (vigilum), 156
tributa, 127
triclinium, 136 (2 ×)
triresmos (masc.) *naveis* (fem.), 126 (2 ×)
triticum (magno tritici modo), 127
triumfator (an emp.), 172
triumfatores principes nostri, 175
triumpe, 160
triumphal: arch, 168; honors, 127
[*trump*]*o navaled*, 125
triumvir a. a. f. f., 127; *capitalis*, 140
Troy, 100, 146
tufas, Roman and other, 6–7, 78, 80, 82, 87, 93 (peperino), 124
Tullia (Cicero's daughter), 20, 23
Tullius Cicero, Q. (Cicero's brother), 20
Turia, 103 f.
Turkey, 108, 109
Turks, Ottoman, 50 (n. 132)

turma equitum Romanorum, 137
Turris Lascutana (in Farther Spain), 82
Tuscia et Umbria, 178
twenty-six thousand sesterces *et quod excurrit* ("plus"), 161
tyrannis, pestifera (of Magnentius), 172
tyrannus (Maxentius), 168 f.

u, consonantal, written *b*, 175
Ulpius Aug. lib. Capito, M., 149
Ulpius Constantinus, M., *tribunus* (vigilum), 156
Ulpius Narcissus—his *monumentum* ("tomb"), 143
Ulpius Phaedimus, M. (freedman of Trajan), 142
-ū(m), 177
uncial H's, 181
upside-down inscr., 159
urbs Roma, 171, 172, 175 (2 ×), 179 (2 ×), 183 (2 ×)
ut omitted at beginning of subjunctive clause, 134 (line 19), 151, 161, 163 (line 24)
Uthina, Africa, 157
uxor, 24, 99 f. (omitted), 103

Valens (co-emperor), 173 f., 176
Valens Aug. lib. Phaedimianus, 142
Valentinian I (co-emp.), 174, 176
Valentinian Bridge, Rome, 174
Valeria Messallina Augusta, 116
Valerius Maximus, 104
Valerius Messalla, Potitus (earlier, Manius), 101, 106 f
Valerius Messalla Rufus, M. (cos. 53 B.C.), 107
variance in spelling within the same inscr., 94, 152, 153, 163, 171, 177
Varius Marcellus, Sex. (father of Elagabalus, emp.), 159
Varro, 17 (n. 49), 19 (n. 56), 23, 49, 78, 95, 96, 160, 226 (n. 4), 228, 230, 232 (n. 28)
Vatican, the, 5, 86, 96, 100, 107, 141, 144, 148, 151 (2 ×), 152, 154, 159 (2 ×), 162, 169, 170, 171, 173, 175, 176, 180, 182, 184
Veleia, 132, 133
Velius Longus, 14
Velleius Paterculus, 92, 105
Velletri (anc. Velitrae), 159
Veneti and Histri (of northern Italy), 176
Veranius, Q. (cos. A.D. 49), 119
verba fecerunt (of local senators), 134
verbose style at its worst, 167
Vergil, 33, 98, 100
Verminus, 103
verna, 25 (with n. 76), 145, 155
Verona, 39, 115, 176
Verrius Flaccus, 228
verse inscriptions, Latin (or Greek), 33, 37, 80 f., 87, 90, 130 f., 141, 145–148, 160, 173, 176 f.
versus extemporales subiecti ("subjoined"), 131
Verus, Lucius (co-emp.), 33 (n. 107), 49 (with n. 130), 151
Vespasian (emp.), 28, 43, 121 f., 123, 127
veterani ex numero equitum singularium, 144
Vettius Agorius Praetextatus, *v. c.*, 178, 179
vexillarius of a *centuria* (of a cohort of Vigiles), 156
Via Appia (the Appian Way), 7 (n. 19), 99, 141, 149, 165
Viae Cassia, Clodia, Ciminia, Nova Traiana, 140

Via Ostiensis, outside Rome, 161
vicarius ("deputy"): 173; *a consiliis sacris*, 171; *praefecturae urbis*, 171; *praeff. praetorio bis, in urbe et per Mysias*, 171; *summae rei rationum*, 171
vicarius ("vicar") *urbis Romae*, 183
vice in late titles, syntax of, 173
vice praefectorum praetorio et urbi functus, 159
vice sacra iudicans, 172 f.
victor ac triumfator semper Augustus, 30, 172, 174
Victoria and Albert Museum, London, 39
victory titles, 33 (n. 107)
Veicus Furfensis, 94
Vicus Laci (sic) *Fund(ani)*, Rome, 92
Vienna, 83
vigiles, Rome, 156
Villa Albani, Rome, 103
Villa Giulia Museum, Roma, 13 (n. 38), 75
Vindolanda (mod. Chesterholme), 5 (n. 8)
vinum, 136; *Supernas et Ariminense*, 162
Vipsania Agrippina (granddaughter of Atticus), 22 (n. 69)
Vipsanius Agrippa, 19 (n. 61)
vir clarissimus, 166, 170, 172, 173, 174, 175, 176, 178, 179, 181, 185. See also *clarissimus vir*
vir clarissimus et inlustris, 179
v(ir) o(ptimus), 161
vir splendidus, 163
virtus, virtutes, 81, 91 f., 134, 179, 180, 183

virtutes, insignes, domi forisque (of emps.), 158
virtutis caussa, 91 f.
volo with perfect infinitive, 85
votis X (solutis) votis XX (susceptis); sic X; six XX, 168 f.
votis XX (and *XXX*) *annalibus, feliciter*, 47 (n. 128)
Vulgate, the, 39 (n. 110), 177, 180, 185

warning against damage to tombstone, 146, 147, 148
wax tablets, inscribed, 3 (n. 2)
weavers?, 165
week, the Roman, 231 (9 days), 232 f. (with n. 26) (7 days)
white coloring added to letters of inscrs., 135
wine trade, 163
wood, writing on, 5 (n. 8)
word division at line ends noted, 39, 154, 175, 182

⌐X⌐ (= a million, Roman usage), 45 (n. 120)
XP, Christian monogram, 172

York, Britain, 168
Yuba City, California, 21 (n. 67)

Zeno (Roman emp. in the East), 50 (with n. 131)
Zeus—Helios—Phaëthon, 131
Zmaragdus, Matuccius, a *lintearius*, 154

MODERN SCHOLARS AND WRITERS

(See also the names listed alphabetically in the Preface, the list of Abbreviations, and the names listed in the addenda to the Degrassi/Calabi bibliography, pp. 55–65.)

Abbott, Frank Frost, 137
Akurgal, Ekrem, 109
Albertini, Eugène, 119
Alföldy, Géza, 12
Amyx, D. A., 156
Anderson, J. G. C., 98
Anderson, R. D., 99
Andreae, Bernard, 96
Arangio-Ruiz, Vincenzo, 103
Ashby, Thomas, 104, 119
Atkinson, Donald, 119
Audin, Amable, 233 (n. 33)

Babcock, Charles L., 3 (n. 1), 61
Badian, Ernst, 12, 16 (n. 45), 34, 36, 59, 60 (2 ×), 83, 86, 90
Bailey, Cyril, 34
Baillie Reynolds, P. K., 156, 158
Balsdon, J.P.V.D. (or J.P.B.), 92, 113, 116, 117
Bang, Martin, 78, 105, 159
Banti, Luisa, 7, 86
Barbarino, Joseph Louis, 59, 191
Barbieri, Guido, 9 (n. 27), 19 (n. 57), 47 (n. 127), 97, 121
Barnes, Timothy D., 11 (n. 32)
Bartoli, Alfonso, 134
Bastianini, G., 98, 116
Baumgart, Julius, 17 (n. 48)
Baynes, N. H., 168
Beck, C. W., 31 (n. 101)
Becker, Ferdinand, 41 (n. 112)
Bennett, Charles E., 119
Benseler, G.E. See Pape/Benseler
Béranger, Jean, 111
Beringer, W., 163
Besnier, M., 10
Betz, Artur, 32 (n. 104), 140
Bickerman, E. J., 168, 226, 227, 229 (with n. 14), 231 (n. 22), 232 (with n. 26)
Bidez, J., 234
Birley, Anthony R., 119 f., 140, 158
Birley, Eric, 119
Bloch, Raymond, 11 f., 76
Block, Herbert, 52, 53, 63, 160, 178
Blümner, H., 167
Boeckh, August, 54 (n. 136)
Boëthius, A., 100, 139
Boni, Giacomo, 78 f.

Borghesi, Bartolomeo, 54 (with n. 135)
Bormann, Eugen, 149, 159, 163
Boucher, J. P., 97
Bovini, Giuseppe, 164 f.
Bracco, Vittorio, 87
Bradley, K. R., 120
Brilliant, Richard, 158 f.
Broughton, T. Robert S., 15 (n. 43), 18 (nn. 54 f.), 40, 80, 82, 83, 86, 87, 88, 90 f., 93, 96 f., 100, 107, 229 (n. 14)
Brown, Frank E., 79, 139
Brown, P.R.L., 176, 178
Bruns, C. G., 22 (n. 70), 78, 82, 83, 94, 103, 117, 121, 132, 144, 149, 151, 153, 161
Brunt, P. A., 97 f., 108, 121
Brusa Gerra, Carla, 114
Brusin, Giuseppe, 31, 140
Buck, Carl Darling, 232 f. (nn. 26, 31, 32)
Buecheler, Franz, 33, 34 (CLE), 87, 125, 126, 141, 160, 177
Bunsen, G., 101
Buonamici, Giulio, 46 (n. 124)
Burnand, Y., 233 (n. 33)
Bury, J. B., 180

Cadoux, T. J., 17 (n. 48)
Cagnat, René, 11, 21 (nn. 65 f.), 28 (nn. 86, 90), 29 (n. 92), 37, 46, 48, 49 (n. 129), 54 (n. 136), 87, 95, 116, 129
Calabi (now Calabi Limentani), Ida, 8 (n. 25), 11 (with n. 30), 28 (n. 86), 41 (n. 112), 42 (n. 115), 49 (n. 129), 50 f. (n. 133), 53, 54 (n. 136), 75, 86 f., 90, 92, 99 f., 101, 111, 116, 125, 138, 139, 176
Calderini, Aristide, 10, 140
Caldwell, Wallace E., 10 f.
Caley, E. R., 31 (n. 100)
Cameron, Alan, 113
Campana, Augusto, 5, 54 (n. 135)
Campbell, S. G. See Sandys/Campbell
Canina, Luigi, 99
Cantarelli, Luigi, 181 f.
Capozza, Maria, 228
Cappelli, Adriano, 45 (n. 122)
Caprino, Catia, 5
Carroll, Kevin K., 21 f. (n. 68), 123
Casson, Lionel, 126
Castagnoli, Ferdinando, 76 f., 79, 110

Castrén, Paavo, 93
Catich, Edward M., 5 f. (n. 10), 138
Cencetti, Giorgio, 77
Cesano, L., 166
Chacon, P., 125
Champollion, Jean François, 31 (n. 100)
Chantraine, Heinrich, 9 (n. 27)
Chase, George D., 19 (n. 56), 21 (n. 65), 23, 25 (n. 75)
Chastagnol, André, 10, 12, 167
Christ/Schmid/Stählin, 131
Coarelli, Filippo, 6 (with n. 12), 80, 100, 129, 138, 154, 168 f.
Cole, Thomas, 81, 160
Coli, Ugo, 111
Colin, Gaston, 85 f.
Colini, Antonio M., 80, 86, 169
Collinge, N. E., 76
Collingwood, R. G., 9
Colonna, Giovanni, 4 (nn. 4, 5), 75 f.
Combès, Robert, 22 (n. 68), 83
Comparetti, D., 78, 79
Condurachi, Emil, 127
Cracco Ruggini, Lellia, 62, 64
Craddock, P. T., 5 f. (n. 10)
Crawford, Michael H., 45 f. (n. 123), 167
Cremona, J., 15 (n. 42)
Criniti, Nicola, 91
Cristofani, Mauro, 76
Crook, John, 170
Cross, F. L., 226
Cumont, Franz, 100, 141, 166
Cuq, Édouard, 171
Curtis, C. Densmore, 8 (n. 21), 13 (n. 38), 75

Daremberg/Saglio, 55
Daube, David, 85
Dawson, Lawrence E., 32
De Angelis d'Ossat, Gioacchino, 80, 86 f., 102
Degrassi, Attilio, 3–232 passim
Delatte, A., 234
Della Corte, Francesco, 103
Deman, Alb., 83
Dennison, Walter, 154, 182
De Rosalia, Antonino, 80, 82 f., 87, 125
De Rossi, G. B., 10, 53, 156, 165, 168, 171, 173, 177, 181, 184
De Ruggiero, Ettore, 55, 95, 111, 163
De Sanctis, Gaetano, 103
Dessau, Hermann (or ILS), 4–227 passim
Develin, Robert, 83, 87
De Visscher, Fernand, 142 f.
Diehl, Ernst (or ILCV), xv–233 passim
Dihle, Albrecht, 83
Dirichs, J. F. K., 78
Di Stefano Manzella, Ivan, 64
Doer, Bruno, 17 (n. 48), 18 (n. 55), 22 f. (n. 71)
Doering, Oscar, 172
Dohrn, Tobias, 13 (n. 38)
Domaszewski, Alfred von, 144
Donati, Angela, 10
Donnelly, Gertrude Joseph, 138
d'Ors, Alvaro, 82 f., 135
Douglas, A. E., 20 (n. 62)

Dow, Sterling, 3 (n. 1), 21 f. (n. 68), 33 (n. 105), 37, 90
Doyle, E. J., 167
Drachmann, A. B., 234
Dressel, Enrico (Heinrich), 77
Drexel, Friedrich, 113
Ducroux, Serge, 56, 61
Duncan-Jones, R. P., 93, 132, 133
Durrbach, Félix, 89
Durry, Marcel, 103 f.

Eck, Werner, 9 (n. 27), 228
Egbert, James C., 11
Ehrenberg/Jones (or E/J), 101, 108, 111, 112
Ehrhardt, C. T. H. R., 170
Ehrle, Franz, 207
Elcock, W. D., 25 (n. 74)
Elder, J. P., 3 (n. 1)
Ensslin, W., 162, 167, 171, 178
Erim, Kenan T., 167
Erkell, H., 92
Ernout, Alfred, 34, 75, 77, 78, 80, 82, 83, 87, 90, 125, 160
Ernout/Meillet (or E/M), 26 (n. 81), 49, 143, 191, 198, 204, 231 (n. 21)
Ewald, Jürg, 33, 43 (n. 116)

Fabia, Philippe, 5 f. (n. 10), 117
Fabretti, Raffaele, 155
Facal, Javier L., xxi
Fay, Edwin W., 125
Felch, Patricia A., xvi
Feliciano, Felice (Veronese), 39
Ferrua, Antonio, xxiii, 10, 39, 57, 177
Fine Licht, Kjeld de, 139
Fishwick, Duncan, 57
Fitzmyer, Joseph A., 4 (n. 4)
Flobert, Pierre, 146, 148
Forcellini, Egidio, 133
Forni, Giovanni, 157
Fraccaro, P., 89
Fraenkel, Eduard, 83
Fraenkel, Ernst, 17 (n. 48), 26 (n. 81)
Frank, Tenney, 6 (with n. 14), 7 (n. 17), 17 f., 34 (n. 108), 79, 80, 82, 83, 89, 99 f., 125, 126, 167
Fraser, P. M., 111
Frend, W. H. C., 230 (n. 17)
Friedlaender, Ludwig, 113, 131
Frova, Antonio, 13 (n. 39), 114
Frugé, August, xvi

Gabba, Emilio, 142
Gagé, Jean, 108 f., 111, 189, 208
Gantz, Timothy Nolan, 78
Garnsey, Peter, 132
Garrucci, Raffaele, 133, 170
Gatti, Giuseppe, 10, 91, 144, 155, 165, 171, 185 (only one person?)
Geffcken, J., 54 f.
Georges, K. E., 49
Giacchero, Marta, 45 f. (n. 123), 167
Gildersleeve/Lodge (or G/L), 112, 141, 171, 173
Goell, Kermit, 32 (n. 102)
Goidanich, P. G., 79

Gordon, Joyce S., 6, 32 (n. 103), 121, 125, 143, 146, 154, 168
Gordon, Mary L., 17 f.
Gradenwitz, Otto, 12 (with n. 35), 82, 83, 121, 153
Graindor, Paul, 137
Grant, Frederick C., 83
Graser, Elsa R., 167 f.
Gray, Nicolette, 177
Greifenhagen, Adolf, 75
Grenade, P., 109
Grimal, Pierre, 94, 95
Groag, Edmund, 47, 101 f., 166
Gruendel, R., 53
Guarducci, Margherita, 5 (n. 10), 6 (n. 11), 15, 32 (n. 103), 39, 45 f., 54 (n. 136), 57, 63, 76, 85, 109, 142 f.
Gundel, H., 93
Gurlitt, Ludwig, 43, 146

Häusle, H., 34, 146
Hainzmann, M., 9 (n. 27)
Hale/Buck, 226, 231 (n. 20), 233 (n. 36)
Halkin, Léon, 127
Hallam, G. H., 231
Hallbauer, Fr., 44 (n. 119), 49
Hamp, Eric P., 75
Hanfmann, George M. A., 173
Hansen, James, 168
Hardy, E. G., 117
Hardy, Thomas, 102
Harley, T. R.,. 10
Harmand, L., 140
Hartmann, Axel, 75
Hartmann, L. M., 53
Haslam, M. W., 59
Hassall, M. W. C., 9 (n. 27)
Hatzfeld, J., 89
Hayes, James, 3 (n. 1)
Hebald, Milton, 5 f. (n. 10)
Heintze, Helga von, 170
Helbig, Wolfgang, 76
Helbig/Speier (or H/S), 13 (n. 38), 80, 81, 82, 87, 91, 96, 102, 108, 115, 120, 121, 125
Henzen, G. (i.e. W.), 7, 8 (with n. 25), 54 (with n. 135), 76, 86, 96, 110, 125, 131, 132, 133, 159, 163, 168, 180
Heseltine, Michael, 232
Heurgon, Jacques, 4 (n. 4), 75, 77
Higgins, C. G., 33 (n. 105)
Highet, Gilbert, 12 (n. 35)
Hillinger, Charles, 21 (n. 67)
Hirschfeld, Otto, 13, 47, 108, 114
Hofmann, J. B. See Hofmann/Szantyr; Walde/Hofmann
Hofmann/Szantyr, 141, 173, 182
Hofmann, M., 127
Holloway, R. Ross, 99 f.
Holzweissig, Fr. See Kühner/Holzweissig (K/H)
Homolle, Théophile, 85 f.
Hosius, Carl, 17 (n. 49), 131, 146
Hübner, Emil, 12, 32 (with n. 103), 34 f., 44 (n. 119), 45 (n. 121), 53, 99, 110, 151, 166, 168
Hülsen, Christian, 45 (n. 120), 80, 139, 155
Hultsch, F., 44 (n. 119), 48

Ihm, Max., 177
Ilari, Virgilio, 88 f.
Iversen, Erik, 110 f.

Jacoby, F., 137
Janzén, A., 21 (n. 67)
Jeffery, L. H., 5 f. (n. 10), 75, 76, 79 f.
Johnson, A. C., 137
Jones, A. H. M., 114, 171, 173, 174, 176, 178, 179, 182, 183, 227
Jordan, H., 94 f.
Jory, E. J., 9, 12 (n. 36), 45 (n. 120), 241
Judge, Edwin A., 98

Kaibel, Georg, 131
Kajanto, Iiro, 20 (n. 62), 26 (n. 82), 27 (n. 85), 96, 131, 176, 184
Keil, Heinrich, 44 (n. 119), 208
Kent, Roland G., 167, 168
Keyes, Clinton W., 12 (n. 34)
Klebs, E., 101 f.
Kneissl, P., 33 (n. 107)
Koenen, Ludwig, 59
König, I, 9 (n. 27)
Kolbe, H. G., 9 (n. 27)
Kolbe, W., 137
Kornemann, Ernst, 136, 164
Krencker, D., 108
Krüger, Gustav, 146
Krummrey, Hans, 9 (with n. 27), 12 (n. 36), 45 (n. 120), 65, 75, 87, 88, 98, 235
Kühner/Holzweissig (or K/H), 26 (n. 81), 49, 178, 196, 198, 202, 204
Kühner/Stegmann (or K/S), 85, 95, 112
Künzle, Paolo, 110

Laffi, Umberto, 94
Lanciani, Rodolfo, 116, 174
La Regina, Adriano, 80
Larfeld, Wilhelm, 5 (n. 10), 8 (n. 25), 31 (n. 100), 46 (n. 125), 54 (n. 136), 89 f.
Larson, James L., 21 (n. 67)
Last, Hugh, 88, 121
Latte, Kurt, 160, 166
Lattimore, Richmond, 10, 34, 41 (n. 112), 143, 146
Lauffer, Siegfried, 45 f. (n. 123), 167
Le Bas, Philippe, 31
Leclercq, Henri, 172
Le Gall, Joël, 179
Leglay, Marcel, 10, 12
Lenchantin de Gubernatis, M., 146
Leon, Harry J., 57
Leumann, Manu, 26 (n. 81), 126, 191, 193, 195, 196, 197, 199, 202, 203, 204, 206
Levi Della Vida, Giorgio, 13 (n. 37)
Lewis, Martha W. Hoffman, 101
Lewis/Reinhold (or L/R), 10, 82, 83, 87, 88, 91, 98, 101, 106, 109, 117, 121, 125, 129 f., 132, 167, 168
Lewis/Short, 49, 98
Licht, Kjeld de Fine, 139
Liddell/Scott, xxi, 150, 154, 232 (n. 30)
Liebaert, Paul, 207
Liebenam, Willy, 164, 227 (n. 7)

Liebeschuetz, J. H. W. G., 169
Lier, Bruno, 141
Lifshitz, B., 114
Liljeholm, A. Filip, 146
Livingstone, E. A., 226
Lodge, Gonzalez. See Gildersleeve/Lodge
Lommatzsch, Ernst, 14, 33, 44 (n. 119), 78, 91, 96, 124 f., 126, 160, 194
Lübker, Friedrich, 54 f.
Lugli, Giuseppe, 6, 34 (n. 108), 78, 80, 86, 100, 102, 105, 108, 125, 129, 138 f., 139, 153, 155, 168, 174

MacKendrick, Paul, 78
MacMullen, Ramsay, 4 (n. 3), 167
Macpherson, I. W., 45 f. (n. 123)
Magi, Filippo, 98, 110 f., 128 f.
Magie, David, 29 (n. 95)
Mahaffy, J. P., 98
Maiuri, Amedeo, 93
Malkiel, Yakov, 55
Mallon, Jean, 5 (n. 10), 45 (n. 122), 46
Mancini, Gioacchino, 105, 123, 127, 146, 179, 183
Mansuelli, Guido A., 138 f.
Marcham, F. G., 54 (n. 135)
Marcillet-Jaubert, Jean, 109
Mardersteig, Giovanni, xxvi, 39
Marichal, Robert, 45 (n. 122), 168
Marini, Gaetano, 87
Marquardt, Joachim, 26 (with nn. 79, 81), 95, 160
Marrou, H. I., 10, 131
Martindale, J. R., xxii, 55
Martinetti, Francesco, 76
Marucchi, Orazio, 165
Mason, H. J., 47, 59, 62
Mathews, V. J., 20 (n. 64)
Mattingly, H., 168
Mattingly, Harold B., 91
McCrum/Woodhead, 121, 127
McDermott, Wm. C., 10 f., 44 (n. 117)
McHugh, M. P., 12 (n. 33)
McLean, John H., 12 (n. 34)
McLellan, J., 142
Mehta, Ved, 21 (n. 67)
Meier, P. Gabriel, 8 (n. 25)
Meiggs, Russell, 151, 179
Meillet, Antoine. See Ernout/Meillet
Meinhardt, Ekkehard, 80, 82, 86, 91, 96, 108, 115, 121, 124, 125, 153, 154, 155, 156, 159, 160, 170, 182
Meyer, Ernst, 7 f. (n. 19), 11, 14, 42 (n. 115), 44 (n. 119), 50 (n. 133), 53, 54 (n. 136), 234
Meyer, P. M., 182
Meyer-Lübke, W., 133
Meritt, Benjamin D., 31 (n. 100)
Merlin, Alfred, 96
Michels, Agnes Kirsopp, 226, 229 (nn. 11, 13, 14), 231 (nn. 19, 24), 232 (with nn. 25, 26), 233
Migne, J. P., 227 (n. 6)
Minto, A., 111
Momigliano, Arnaldo, 83, 116, 117
Mommsen, Theodor, 3–229 (n. 12) passim
Mommsen, Theodor Ernst, 54 (n. 135)
Moore, D. W., 9, 12 (n. 36)
Moore, J. M., 109

Moreau, Jacques, 54 (n. 135)
Morford, Mark P. O., xv
Morris, John, 60
Münzer, Friedrich, 96
Munro, D. C., 10
Murphy, J. P., 54
Mustilli, Domenico, 102, 125, 131, 179

Nash, Ernest, 4 (n. 6), 35 (n. 109), 78–180 passim, 226 (n. 3)
Naumann, R. and F., 45 (n. 123), 167
Neppi Modona, Aldo, 106
Nesselhauf, H., 9 (n. 27)
Neuerburg, Norman, 102
Nibby, Antonio, 159
Niccolini, Giovanni, 96
Niedermann, Max, 124, 125, 126
Nilsson, Martin P., 83
Nisbet, R. G. M., 99
Noll, Rudolf, 83
Norden, Eduard, 94, 95, 160, 190, 194, 203, 204
North, J. A., 96

Oates, John F., 28 (n. 88)
Ogilvie, R. M., 119
Olcott, George N., 12 (n. 134), 55, 99, 143, 145, 155, 175
Oliver, James H., 28 (n. 90), 64, 111 f., 120 f., 145, 165
Oliver, Revilo P., 14, 116
Oost, Stewart I., 109
Oppermann, H., 166
Orelli, J. C., 54 (n. 135), 145
Oxé, A., 26 (n. 81)

Paci, Gianfranco, 26 (n. 78)
Pais, Ettore, 53
Pallottino, Massimo, 15 (n. 42), 20
Palmer, Leonard R., 8 (n. 24), 75, 77, 78, 80, 82, 83, 87, 125
Palmer, Robert E. A., 8 (n. 23), 77, 78, 79, 80, 111 f.
Panciera, Silvio, 9 (n. 27), 22 (n. 71), 56, 59, 65, 105, 235
Pani, M., 111
Pape/Benseler, 90, 154
Paribeni, Roberto, 98, 142
Parsons, P. J., 99
Pascal, Carlo, 146
Pasquali, Giorgio, 54 (n. 135)
Pasqui, A., 185
Passerini, Alfredo, 159
Perrat, Charles, 45 (n. 122)
Peter, R., 144
Pfister, Raimund, xxii, 14, 16 (n. 47), 17, 19 (n. 60), 93, 104, 162, 175, 180, 181, 182, 190–206, 228
Pflaum, H. G., 10, 12, 18 (n. 52), 56, 60, 61, 107, 153, 154, 159
Pharr, Clyde, xvii, 85
Pietrangeli, Carlo, 56, 96
Pinza, Giovanni, 76
Piranesi, Giovanni Battista, 100, 101
Pisani, Vittore, 75, 76, 77, 78, 80, 82, 83, 125, 160
Platner/Ashby (or P/A), 78–174 passim
Plommer, H., 167
Prichard, A. M., 10 (n. 29)

Pritchett, W. K., 31 (n. 101), 32, 33 (n. 105)
Pugliese Carratelli, Giovanni, 13 (n. 37)
Pulgram, Ernst, 15 (n. 42), 75

Rackham, Harris, 25 (with n. 77)
Radice, Betty, 29 (n. 92)
Radke, Gerhard, 76, 95
Raveggi, P., 111
Rawson, Elizabeth, 96
Reichmuth, Johann, 17 (n. 48)
Reinhold, Meyer. See Lewis/Reinhold
Reynolds, Joyce M., 3 (n. 1), 12 (n. 33), 45 f.
    (n. 123), 56, 57, 60, 61, 120, 167
Richmond, Ian, 119
Richter, Franz, 94
Ridgway, David, 15 (n. 42), 75 f.
Ritschl, Friedrich, 8, 32, 34 f., 44 (n. 119), 45 f.
    (nn. 123, 126), 53 f., 81, 124, 125, 126
Robert, Jeanne and Louis, 31 (with nn. 99–101),
    107
Robert, Louis, 6 (n. 11), 107
Rocchetti, L., 138
Rogers, H. L., 10
Rolfe, John C., 87 f., 167, 168
Rose, H. J., 226 (n. 4), 227 (n. 6), 229, 229 f.
Rossi, Anna Maria, 167
Roullet, Anne, 102, 110
Roussel, P., 89
Rushforth, G. McN., 121, 127

Sachers, E., 182
Saladino, Vincenzo, 80
Salmon, E. T., 88, 132, 135
Samuel, Alan E., 226, 229 (n. 14), 232 (n. 26), 233
Sandys/Campbell (or S/C), xv, 11, 17 (n. 48), 37, 44
    (n. 119), 46 (with n. 126), 50 (n. 133), 52 f., 53,
    54 (n. 136), 87, 93, 106, 121, 127, 129, 138, 168,
    169
Sartori, Franco, 228
Scamuzzi, Ugo, 80
Schanz/Hosius, 17 (n. 49), 131
Schanz/Hosius/Krüger, 146
Schede, M., 108
Scherer, Margaret R., 101 f., 139
Schmalz/Hofmann, 141
Schulten, Adolf, 82
Schulze, Wilhelm, 15 (n. 42), 17 (n. 49), 26 (n. 81)
Scialoja, Vittorio, 162
Scott, Kenneth, 29 (n. 92)
Scott, Robert. See Liddell/Scott
Scullard, Howard Hayes, 121
Seeck, Otto, 171, 182
Severyns, A., 234
Shelley, Percy Bysshe, 102
Sherk, Robert K., 60, 106, 134
Sherwin-White, A. N., 13 (n. 39), 20 (n. 63), 44
    (n. 117), 114, 115
Shipley, Frederick W., 109
Shoe (Meritt), Lucy T., 7, 80, 86, 102
Silvagni, Angelo, 10, 171, 173, 177, 183, 184, 185
Silvia Bassignano, M., 228
Simon, Erika, 80, 131, 151
Sinnigen, William G., 171
Smallwood, Edith Mary, 117, 119, 120, 132, 134,
    138

Smith, Kirby Flower, 232 (n. 27)
Smith, Leslie F., 12 (n. 34)
Smutny, Robert J., 56
Snell, Bruno, 23 (n. 72)
Snyder, Walter F., 232
Solin, Heikki, 9 (n. 27), 18 (n. 52)
Solmsen, Felix, 26 (n. 81)
Sommer, Ferdinand, 14–206, passim
Speier, Hermine. See Helbig/Speier
Starr, Chester G., 25 (n. 76)
Staveley, E. S., 111
Steffens, Franz, 3 (n. 2)
Stegmann, Carl. See Kühner/Stegmann
Stein, Arthur, 11, 28 (n. 90), 29 (n. 95), 98, 100,
    116, 127, 144
Strong, Eugénie, 101, 131, 138
Stroud, Ronald S., 32
Stuart Jones, H., 166
Sturtevant, Edgar H., 19 (n. 60)–205 passim
Sumner, G. V., 30 (n. 96), 100
Susini, Giancarlo, 7 (n. 18), 10, 12, 17 (n. 48), 19,
    32, 44 (n. 117), 56, 58, 60, 62, 64
Swanson, Donald C., 12 (with n. 35), 25 (n. 74)
Syme, (Sir) Ronald, 8 (n. 20), 19 (n. 61), 21 f.
    (n. 68), 22 f. (n. 71), 42, 44 (n. 117), 60, 64, 83,
    107, 111, 117, 127
Szantyr, Anton. See Hofmann/Szantyr

Tarbell, F. B., 167, 168
Tarn, W. W., 90
Taylor, Bayard, 101
Taylor, Lily Ross, 19, 90, 91, 96, 101, 127, 136 f.,
    226 (nn. 1 f.)
Terzaghi, N., 146
Thomasson, B. E., 9 (n. 27), 44 (n. 119)
Thompson, Edward Maunde, 207
Thorley, John, 227 (n. 6)
Thylander, Hilding, 17 (n. 48), 27 (n. 84), 41 (with
    n. 114), 42
Tibiletti, Gianfranco, 5 f. (n. 10), 92, 111, 121,
    142
Tiffou, Étienne, 77
Till, Rudolf, 80
Tolkiehn, Johannes, 146
Torelli, Mario, 9 (n. 27), 59, 64
Torp, Hjalmar, 154
Townend, G., 142
Toynbee, J. M. C., 101 f., 143, 154
Tracy, Stephen V., 33 (n. 105)
Traube, Ludwig, 144
Travlos, John, 137
Treggiari, Susan, 17 f.
Treu, Max, 97
Turner, Eric G., xv, 5 (n. 8), 63

Vaglieri, Dante, 227 (n. 7), 228
Valadier, G., 128
Vardaman, Jerry, 114
Verbrugghe, Gerald P., 87, 88
Vetter, Emil, 75, 95
Veyne, Paul, 132, 133, 168 f.
Vighi, R., 139
Vitucci, G., 152
Volkmann, Hans, 21 f. (n. 68), 88 (the same man?),
    108, 110, 114

Walde-Hofmann (or W/H), 26 (n. 81)
Walser, G., 9 (n. 27), 87
Waltzing, J. P., 149, 150, 162, 163, 164
Ward Perkins (or Ward-Perkins), J. B., 100, 139, 142, 154
Warde Fowler, W., 103 f., 226, 229 (with n. 11), 230 (n. 16)
Warmington, E. H., 10, 34, 75, 77, 78, 80, 82, 83, 85, 86, 87, 89, 90, 91, 92, 93, 125, 160, 232
Weaver, P. R. C., 17 f. (with n. 48), 20 (n. 62), 27, 29 (n. 95), 62, 142, 155
Weber, Ekkehard, 12, 56, 57, 89, 114
Weber, Wilhelm, 142
Weinstock, Stefan, 96
Weiss, J., 138
Wellesley, Kenneth, 117
West, Allen B., 90 f.
Wickert, Lothar, 54 (n. 135)
Wilamowitz-Moellendorff, Ulrich von, 109
Wilhelm, Adolf, 89 f.

Wilson, Harry Langford, 29 (n. 95)
Wingo, E. Otha, 13, 83, 101, 109, 111
Wiseman, T. P., 93, 100
Wissowa, Georg, 95, 113, 123, 141, 150, 152, 160, 166, 178
Wistrand, Erik, 103, 189, 204
Wölfflin, Eduard, 81 f., 124, 126
Wörrle, M., 120
Woodhead, A. G., 32 (n. 103), 37, 39, 54 (n. 136), 57, 121, 127, 227, 234
Wosnik, Bernhard, 92
Wright, R. P., 9, 11 (n. 31)

Zangemeister, Karl, 53
Zevi, Fausto, 5, 80
Ziebarth, E., 53, 54 f.
Ziegler, Konrat, 139
Zoega, G., 110
Zosel, Hans, 120

PLATES

PLATE 1

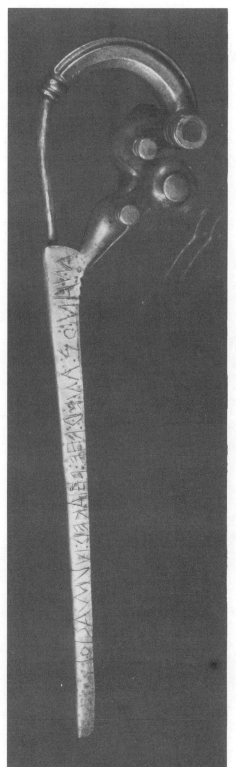

1 Gold Fibula. Rome, Mus. Naz. Preistorico. CIL 1².3

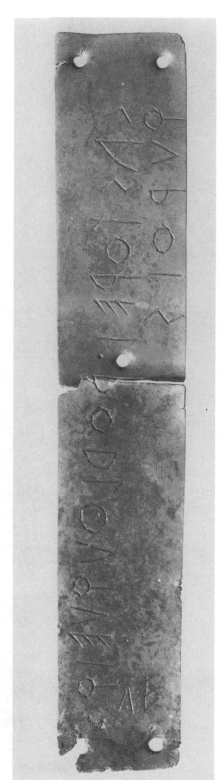

2 Castor/Pollux Dedication. Rome, Mus. Naz. Rom. CIL 1²:4.2883

PLATE 2

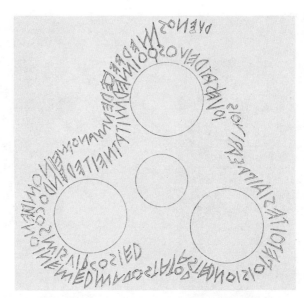

3 (a) Duenos Vase. Berlin, Staatl. Mus., Antikenabt. *CIL* 1².4

3 (b) and (c) 2 views of the vase, from top (b) and one side (c)

PLATE 3

4 (a) Forum Romanum Cippus. Rome, *in situ*. *CIL* 1².1 (line 1, at extreme right, read up; line 2 read down, etc.)

15   14   13   12   11   10   9   8   7   6   5   4   3   2   1   16

4 (b) Composite Photo of Plaster Cast of the Four Sides   (see page 79 above)

PLATE 4

5 Scipionic Sarcophagus With Epitaph. Rome, Vatican. CIL 1².6–7

PLATE 5

6 Dedication to Hercules by M. Minucius. Rome, Pal. dei Cons. *CIL* 1².607

7 Decree of L. Aemilius (Paulus). Paris, the Louvre. *CIL* 1².614

PLATE 6

8 *Sen. Cons. de Bacch.* Vienna, Kunsthist. Mus., Antikenabt. *CIL* 1².581

9 Commemorative Tablet of L. Aemilius (Paulus). Delphi, museum. *CIL* 1².622

PLATE 7

10 Honorary Inscription to M. Claudius Marcellus. Luni. *CIL* 1².623

11 Dedication to Hercules by L. Mummius. Rome, Vatican. *CIL* 1².626

PLATE 8

12 Milestone With Acephalous *Elogium*. Polla. *CIL* 1².638

13 Bilingual Dedication to Hercules. Delos. *CIL* 1².2504

PLATE 9

14 Elegiac Epigram. Corinth, museum. *CIL* 1².2662

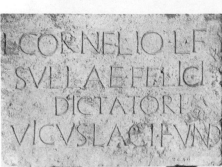

16 Slab from Statue Base of Sulla. Naples, Mus. Naz. *CIL* 1².721

17 Record of Theater Building. Pompeii. *CIL* 1².1633

PLATE 10

15 Two Decrees of Gn. Pompeius (Strabo). Rome, Capitoline Mus. *CIL* 1².709

PLATE 11

18 Main Inscription on the Fabricius Bridge, Rome. *CIL* 1².751

19 Temple Regulations from Furfo. L'Aquila, Mus. Naz. *CIL* 1².756

PLATE 12

20 Epitaph of a Grain Merchant. Rome, Palazzo Senatorio. *CIL* 1²:4.2965

21 Statue (?) Base Dedicated to Julius Caesar. Rome, Vatican. *CIL* 1².797

PLATE 13

22 Trilingual Dedication by Cornelius Gallus. Cairo, Egyptian Mus. *CIL* 3.14147⁵

PLATE 14

23 (a) Tomb of Caecilia Metella, Via Appia, outside Rome (as seen in the 1920's)

23 (b) Her Epitaph, *CIL* 6.1274

PLATE 15

24 Epitaphs of Octavia and Her Son Marcellus. Rome, Maus. of Augustus. *AE* 1928, 88

25 Part of Record of Secular Games, 17 B.C. Rome, Mus. Naz. Rom. *CIL* 6.32323

PLATE 16

26 Epitaph on the Pyramid of Cestius. Rome, *in situ*. *CIL* 6.1374

27 Record of Restoration of an Altar. Rome, Pal. dei Cons. *CIL* 6.37063

PLATE 17

28 Two Fragments of the "Laudatio Turiae." Rome, Mus. Naz. Rom. *AJA* 1950, 223

PLATE 18

29 Record of Repairs of Three Aqueducts. Rome, *in situ. CIL* 6.1244–1246

30 Senatorial Inscr. in Honor of L. Caesar. Rome, Forum Romanum. *CIL* 6.36908

PLATE 19

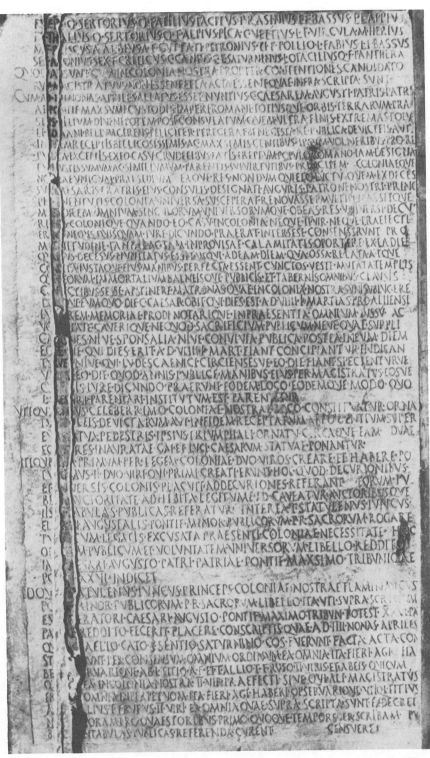

31 Record of Posthumous Honors for Gaius Caesar. Pisa, Camposanto. *CIL* 11.1421

PLATE 20

32 Epitaph of Potitus Valerius Messalla.
Rome, Mus. Naz. Rom. *CIL* 6.37075

33 Epitaph of Gaius Caesar (son of Germanicus). Rome, Vatican. *CIL* 6.889

35 (a) Duplex Dedication on Obelisk. Rome, Piazza S. Pietro. This inscription, *CIL* 6.882

35 (b) Superimposed on this, an earlier duplex inscr. as reconstructed. *AE* 1964, 255

PLATE 21

36 The *Tabula Hebana*. Florence, Museo Archeologico. *AJP* 75 (1954) 225

PLATE 22

34 (a) Monumentum Ancyranum, Ankara, Turkey. *CIL* 3:2, pp. 769ff. Right Side, with the Greek Version.

34 (b) Entrance to the Temple

PLATE 23

34 (c) Heading and Tops of First Three Columns of the Inscr.

34 (d) Close-up of Text of Col. IV, Ch. 19

PLATE 24

37 Epitaphs of a Charioteer and His Wife. Rome, Vatican. *CIL* 6.10051

38 Dedication (?) of a *Tiberieum* by Pontius Pilate. Jerusalem, Israel Mus. *AE* 1971, 477

PLATE 25

39 Epitaph of Agrippina the Elder. Rome, Pal. dei Cons. *CIL* 6.886

40 Dedication to the Emperor Claudius. Verona, Mus. Maffeiano. *CIL* 5.3326

PLATE 26

42 Part of Speech of the Emp. Claudius. Lyon, Mus. de la Civ. Gallo-Romaine. *CIL* 13.1668

PLATE 27

41 Ex-voto Dedication to the Emp. Claudius and His Family. Rome, Pal. dei Cons. *CIL* 6.918

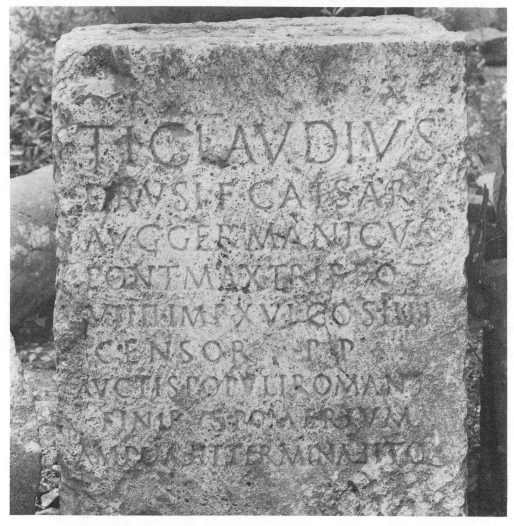

43 Pomerium Boundary-Stone. Rome, Mus. Naz. Rom. *NS* 1913, 68

PLATE 28

44 The Porta Maggiore Aqueducts, Rome. Exterior above, interior below. *CIL* 6.1256

45 Epitaph of Q. Veranius and Child. Rome, Mus. Naz. Rom. *AE* 1953, 251

PLATE 29

46 Fragment of the "Lex de Imperio Vespasiani." Rome, Capitoline Mus. *CIL* 6.930

PLATE 30

47 Dedication of a Shrine to *Fons*. Rome, Mus. Naz. Rom. *AE* 1915, 100 (*CIL* 6.39416)

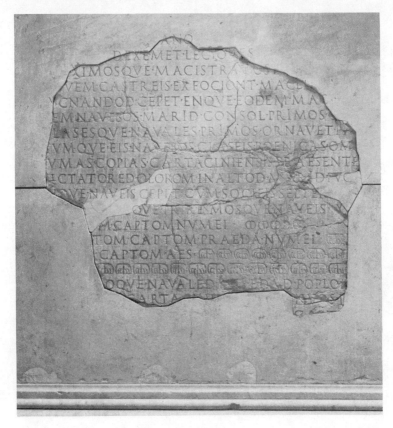

48 Elogium of Gaius Duilius. Rome, Pal. dei Cons. *CIL* 1².25, 6.1300

PLATE 31

49 Epitaph of a Soldier/Public Official. *In situ* on Rome-Tivoli road. *CIL* 14.3608

PLATE 32

50 Dedication of Arch to the Deified Titus. *In situ*, Forum Romanum, Rome. *CIL* 6.945

51 A Military Diploma. Rome, Vatican Library. *CIL* 16.32

PLATE 33

52 Latin Epitaph, with Greek Verses, of Young Poet. Rome, Pal. dei Cons. *CIL* 6.33976

PLATE 34

53 *Tabula Alimentaria*. Rome, Mus. Naz. Rom. *CIL* 9.1455

PLATE 35

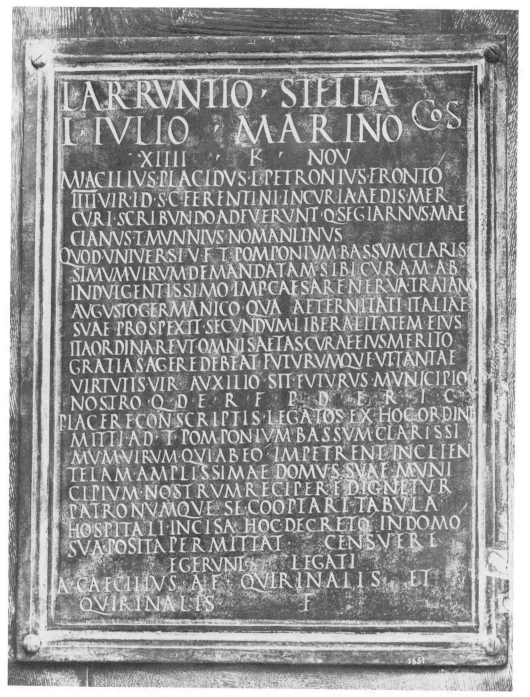

54 Record of a Town's Request for Patronage. Florence, Mus. Archeologico. *CIL* 6.1492

PLATE 36

55 Commemoration of a Local Dignitary. Ferentino, *in situ*. *CIL* 10.5853

PLATE 37

56 Statue-Base Inscr. in Honor of Hadrian. Athens, *in situ*. CIL 3.550

57 Column-of-Trajan Inscription. Rome, *in situ*. CIL 6.960

PLATE 38

58 Record of Building the Original Pantheon. Rome, *in situ*. *CIL* 6.896

60 Verse Epitaph of a Young Boy. Rome, Vatican. *CIL* 6.7578

PLATE 39

59 Commemoration of Roman Public Official. Aquileia, Mus. Arch. Naz. *CIL* 5.877

PLATE 40

61 Epitaph of a Freedman of the Emperor Trajan. Rome, Vatican. *CIL* 6.1884

62 Funerary Monument with Instructions to Heirs. Rome, *in situ*. *AE* 1945, 136

PLATE 41

63 Veterans' Dedication of Altar to Silvanus. Rome, Mus. Naz. Rom. *CIL* 6.31152

64 Funerary Monument of an Imperial Freedman. Rome, Vatican. *CIL* 6.10235

PLATE 42

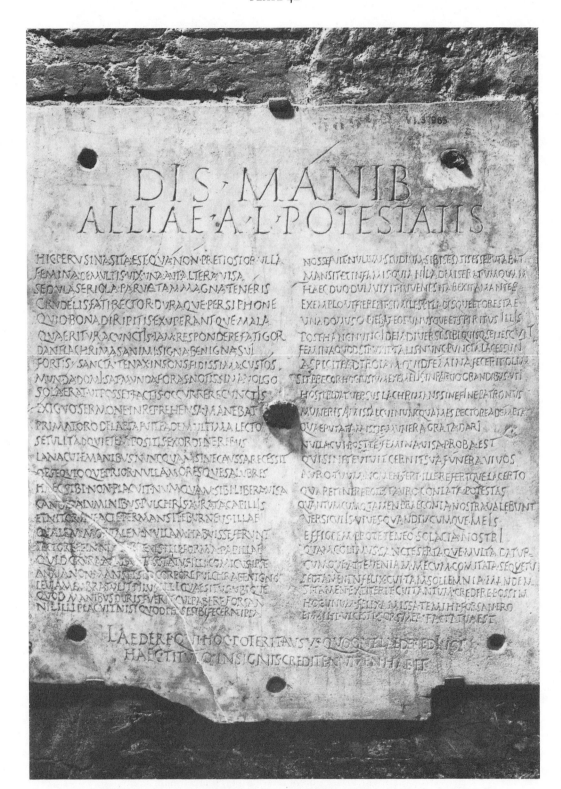

65 Verse Epitaph of Allia Potestas. Rome, Mus. Naz. Rom. *CIL* 6.37965

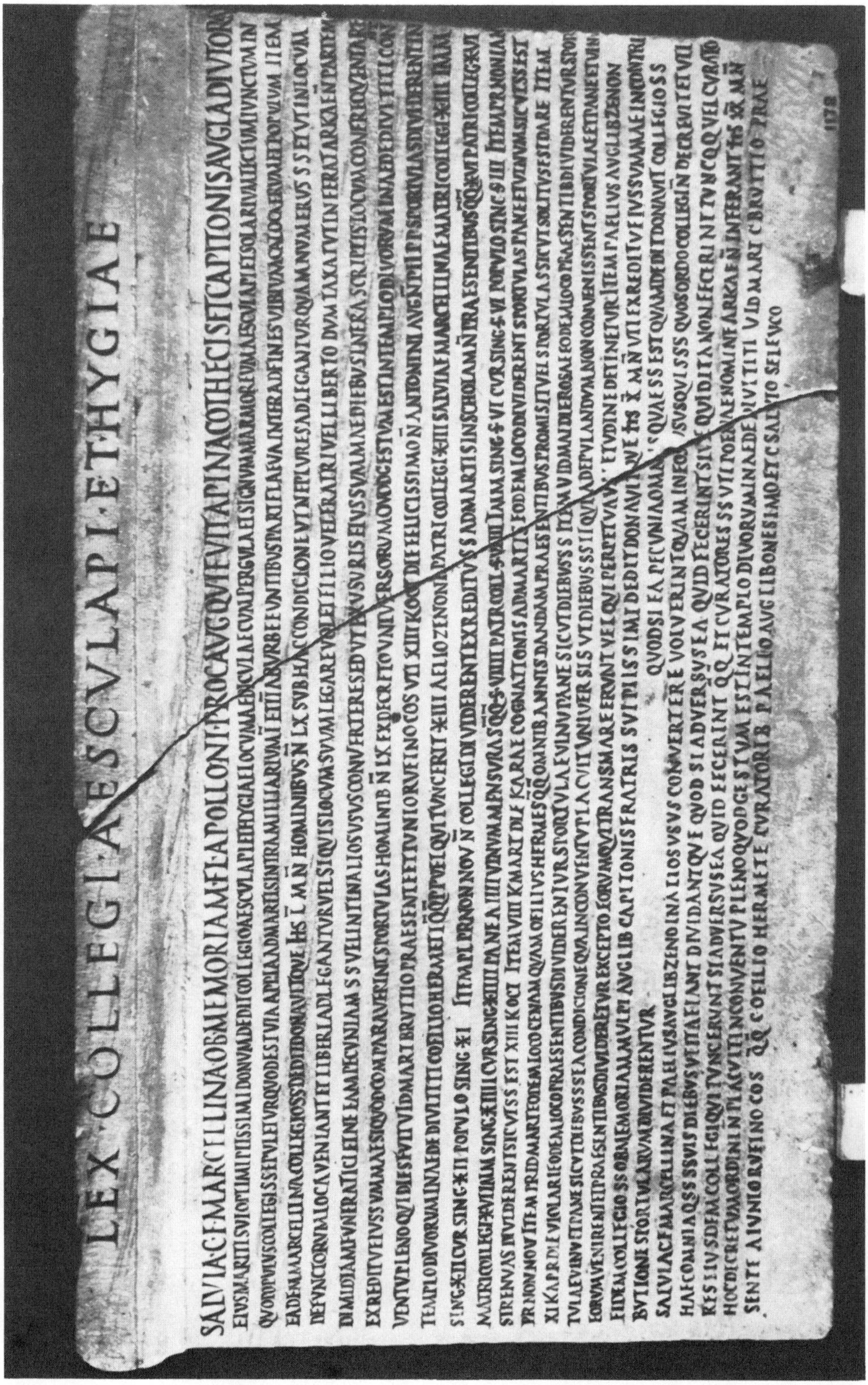

PLATE 43

66 *Lex Collegi Aesculapi et Hygiae.* Rome, Vatican. CIL 6.10234

PLATE 44

67 Dedication of Sculptured Column to Antoninus Pius. Rome, Vatican. *CIL* 6.1004, 31223

68 Commemoration of Local Dignitary at Ostia. Rome, Vatican. *CIL* 14.367

PLATE 45

69 Three Letters (with summary) from Imperial Accountants. Rome, Vatican. *CIL* 6.1585, *b*

PLATE 46

70 Pagan Epitaph from the Vatican Excavations. Rome, *in situ*. *Esplor.* 1.43, vol. 2 pl. ix *b*

71 Dedication to Caracalla by *Paedagogi*. Rome,
Capitoline Mus. *CIL* 6.1052

PLATE 47

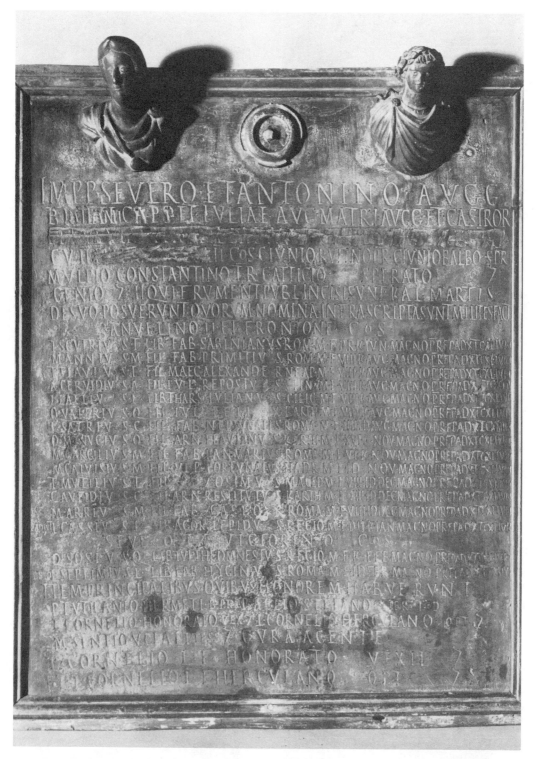

72 Dedication by Members of a Cohort of Vigiles. Rome, Capitoline Mus. *CIL* 6.220

PLATE 48

73 Dedication of Arch to Septimius Severus. Rome, *in situ. CIL* 6.1033

74 Epitaph of the Father of Elagabalus. Rome, Vatican. *CIL* 10.6569

PLATE 49

75 The Arval Hymn. Rome, Vatican. *CIL* 6.2104, *a*   (The Hymn begins near the end of the seventh line from the bottom)

PLATE 50

76 Request for Permission to Build a Tomb. Rome, Mus. Naz. Rom. *CIL* 6.33840

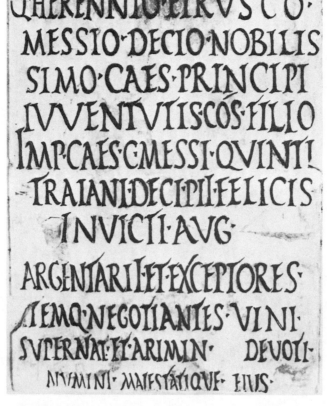

77 Dedication to Decius, *Nobilissimus Caesar*. Rome, Vatican. *CIL* 6.1101

PLATE 51

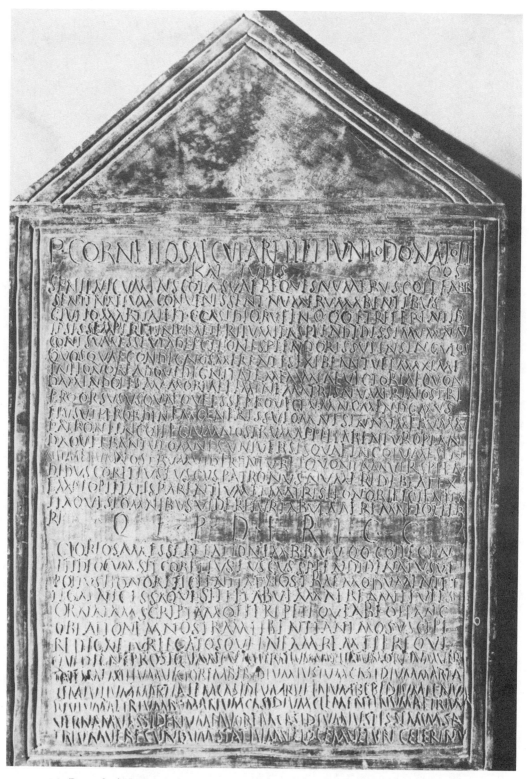

78 Record of Meeting of a *Collegium Fabrum*. Rome, Capitoline Mus. *CIL* 11.5748

PLATE 52

79 Epitaph of a Christian Woman. Rome, Pal. dei Cons. *ILCV* 645

80 Ex-voto Dedication to Cybele and Attis. Rome, Capitoline Mus. *CIL* 6.506

PLATE 53

81 Preamble to Diocletian's Edict on Prices. (a) Fragment in Athens. *CIL* 3 p. 1913

PLATE 54

81 Preamble to Diocletian's Edict on Prices. (b) Fragment in Aix-en-Provence. *CIL* 3 pp. 802f., 1910

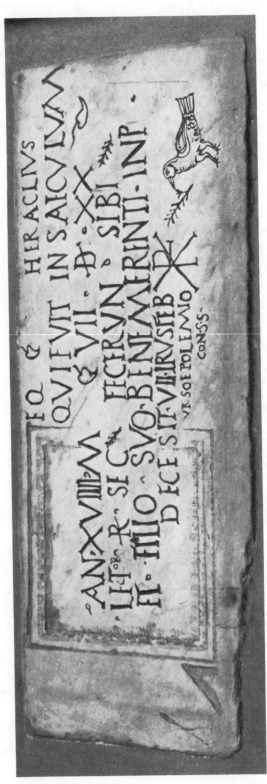

85 Epitaph of a Christian *Lector*. Rome, Vatican. *ILCV* 1266

PLATE 55

82 Dedication of Triumphal Arch to Constantine. Rome, *in situ*. CIL 6.1139, 31425

83 Record of Restoration of Public Baths. Rome, Vatican. CIL 6.1136

PLATE 56

84 Commemoration of G. Caelius Saturninus. Rome, Vatican. *CIL* 6.1704

PLATE 57

86 Dedication to Constantius II. Rome, Forum Romanum. *CIL* 6.1158

88 Dedication to Co-Emperor Valens. Rome, Mus. Naz. Rom. *CIL* 6.31402

PLATE 58

87 Epitaph of Iunius Bassus. Rome, under St. Peter's. *CIL* 6.32004

PLATE 59

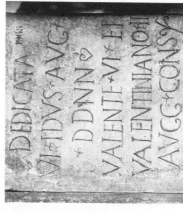

90 Dedication in Honor of Petronius Probus. Rome, Capitoline Mus. *CIL* 6.1751 (frontal inscr. above, left-side inscr. below)

89 Commemoration of Symmachus Senior. Rome, Vatican. *CIL* 6.1698

PLATE 60

QVIDLOQVARAVTSILEAMPROHIBETDOLORIPSEFATERI.
HICTVMVLVSLACRIMASRETINETCOGNOSCEPARENTV
PROIECTAEFVERATPRIMOQVAEIVNCTAMARITO
PVLCRADECORESVOSOLOCONTENTAPVDORE
HEVDILECTASATISMISERAEGENETRICISAMORE
ACCIPEQVIDMVLTISTHALAMIPOSTFOEDERAPRIMA
EREPTAEXOCVLISFLORIGENITORISABIIT
AETHERIAMCVPIENSCAELICONSCENDERELVCEM
HAECDAMASVSPRESTATCVNCTISSOLACIAFLETVS
VIXITANNXVIMNDIES XXV DEPIII KALIANFLMEROBAVDEETFLSATVRNINCONSS

91 Elogium in Verse Composed by Pope Damasus. Rome, Vatican. *ILCV* 3446

92 Dedication of (Statue) Base to Distinguished Pagan. Rome, Mus. Naz. Rom. *CIL* 6.1778

93 Dedication of (Statue) Base to Stilicho. Rome, Mus. Naz. Rom. *AE* 1926, 124

PLATE 61

94 Commemoration of Three Emperors. Rome, Forum Romanum. *CIL* 6.31987

95 Epitaph of a Christian Child. Rome, Vatican. *ILCV* 2921

PLATE 62

96 Dedication of Statue Base to a High Official. Rome, Pal. dei Cons. *AE* 1928, 80

PLATE 63

FL·OLBIOAVXENTIODRAVCOVC·ETIN·L·PATRICIAE·FAMILIAE
VIROSENATVSMVNIS·PROMPTADEVOTIONEPERFVNCTO
COMITIORDINISPRIMIETVICARIOVRBISROMAECOMITI
SACRICONSISTORIIPRAEFECTOVRBISROMAEOBEGRECIAE
EIVSADMINISTRATIONVM·MERITAQVAEINTEGRITATE
CENSVRAETMODERATIONEITAVICVERVNTVTSVBLIMISSI
MAEPOTESTATISREVERENTIAMHONORIFICAEIVSAVCTO
RITASCVSTODIRETETHVMANITATEMAMABILISCENSVRA
SERVARETPETITVSENATVSAMPLISSIMIQVIESTIVSTVS
ARBITERDIGNITATVMEXCELLENTIBVSETMAGNIFICIS
VIRISLEGATIONEMANDATAVTINPETRATORVMDIGNI
TASCRESCERETQVAEPARIBVSSTVDIISAMOREIVSTITIAE
ETPROVIDENTIAEDESIDERABANTVR·DDNN·FFLE
THEODOSIVSETPLACIDVSVALENTINIANVSINVICTI
ACTRIVMFATORESPRINCIPESSEMPERAVGVSTI·
ADREMVNERATIONEMTITVLOSQVEVIRTVTVMQVIB·
CIRCAREMPVBLICAMEXIMIASEMPERPROBITAS
INVITATVRSTATVAMAVROFVLGENTEMERIGI
CONLOCARIQVEIVSSERVNT

97 Record of Erection of Statue of Distinguished Administrator. Rome, Vatican. *CIL* 6.1725

PLATE 64

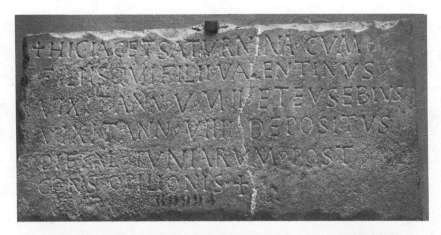

98 Epitaph of Three Christians. Rome, Mus. Naz. Rom. *ILCV* 3058A

99 Epitaph of a Christian Boy. Rome, Vatican. *ILCV* 2650

100 Epitaph of Maxima, "Handmaid of Christ."
Rome, Mus. Naz. Rom. *ILCV* 1469